CRIME
Readings Third Edition

Dedicated to Clarence C. Schrag, colleague and friend
In memory of Marvin E. Wolfgang

CRIME
Readings Third Edition

Editors

Robert D. Crutchfield
University of Washington

Charis E. Kubrin
George Washington University

George S. Bridges
Whitman College

Joseph G. Weis
University of Washington

SAGE Publications
Los Angeles • London • New Delhi • Singapore

For information:

Sage Publications, Inc.
2455 Teller Road
Thousand Oaks, California 91320
E-mail: order@sagepub.com

Sage Publications India Pvt. Ltd.
B 1/I 1 Mohan Cooperative Industrial Area
Mathura Road, New Delhi 110 044
India

Sage Publications Ltd.
1 Oliver's Yard
55 City Road
London EC1Y 1SP
United Kingdom

Sage Publications Asia-Pacific Pte. Ltd.
33 Pekin Street #02–01
Far East Square
Singapore 048763

Printed in the United States of America

Library of Congress Cataloging-in-Publication Data

Crime: Readings/Robert D. Crutchfield . . . [et al.].—3rd ed.
    p. cm.
Includes index.
ISBN 978-1-4129-4967-5 (pbk.)
    1. Crime—United States. 2. Criminology—United States. I. Crutchfield, Robert D.

HV6789.C682 2008
364.973—dc22   2007014602

Printed on acid-free paper

07   08   09   10   11   10 9 8 7 6 5 4 3 2 1

Acquiring Editor:	Jerry Westby
Associate Editor:	Deya Saoud
Editorial Assistant:	Melissa Spor
Production Editor:	Sarah K. Quesenberry
Copy Editor:	Diana Breti
Proofreader:	Gail Fay
Indexer:	Maria Sosnowski
Typesetter:	C&M Digitals (P) Ltd.
Cover Designer:	Edgar Abarca
Marketing Manager:	Jennifer Reed

BRIEF CONTENTS

DETAILED CONTENTS

FOREWORD

About a decade ago, I adopted *Crime* as required reading for my criminology course. At that point, I had been teaching criminology with great success for over 10 years at five different universities. Despite this record of success, my course improved substantially, my students were learning more, and my teaching evaluations improved. Why? In no small part it was due to the quality of this volume, which is without question the best collection of readings on crime today.

Crime has managed to optimize seemingly disparate pedagogical goals: appealing to the interests of the student without compromising the scholarly presentation. The articles selected are written in clear and lively prose, address provocative and timely issues, and represent the cutting edge of theory and research in criminology. They tend to make difficult theoretical and methodological issues comprehensible even to the novice. Collectively, they cover the field in a creative and comprehensive way, providing a historical sense of what we know about crime and showing the relationships between explanatory theory, empirical research, and public policy. Classic theoretical and empirical statements that continue to dominate the field are included, while outdated and less influential pieces are discarded. The result is a snapshot of the current state of research in crime and delinquency, as well as a window to the future.

The success of this volume at both scholarly and pedagogical levels reflects the unique abilities of the editors, Professors Crutchfield, Kubrin, Weis, and Bridges, whose careers have bridged scholarship and teaching. Each is not only a national leader in criminological research and scholarship, but has also been recognized with university teaching awards for outstanding undergraduate teaching. Their selections of readings are based on their own experience in the field *and* in the classroom.

The field of criminology is in an exciting and dynamic state, with important new advances cropping up every year. The third edition of *Crime* has been updated to reflect these changes. In particular, exciting new chapters appear on timely topics such as terrorism, genocide, cybercrime, crack cocaine, and vigilantism. Articles representing important recent developments have been added, replacing those that are no longer at the cutting edge. As a result, the new volume provides a superb overview of the most exciting and influential scholarly writing on crime. Anyone who reads this volume cover to cover will be exposed to the most advanced scholarly research, the relationship between classical and contemporary theory, and the links between criminological theory and practice. They will not only be better scholars, but better citizens as well.

—Ross L. Matsueda

FOREWORD

When I was a graduate student studying the best works in criminology, my equally striving graduate student colleagues and I knew every work worth reading in the field. I mean *every work*. I could quote volumes, numbers, pages of *Journal of Criminal Law and Criminology*. I could cite chapters from Barnes and Teeters, Kinsey, and Gillin. Nothing escaped us.

As we have shown in *Evaluating Criminology* (with Robert M. Figlio and Terence P. Thornberry, 1979), there was an explosion of criminological literature in the 28 years from 1945 to 1972. Since then, there has been an even greater increase in publication of books and articles in this field. Not even the most ardent reader can keep abreast of everything. Selections have to be made.

Having made selections for publications in the past, I know the difficulties of making choices, of screening among the enormous numbers of publications for inclusion in a series. I have carefully read the Table of Contents and many of the articles in this volume and am prepared to defend them as the best in the field.

These four editors have shown that age of publication is less important than substance. Some pieces are from 1938, 1958, and the early 1960s. Why? Because they are nearly timeless in the significance of their observations, theory, or empirical research. There are also very recent articles of excellence.

Within this volume is the essence of the best we know in causation, theory, delinquency, and criminal justice. Anyone who reads and absorbs the readings of this volume will have a full degree of knowledge to match anyone in the field of criminology.

We cannot read everything, but we can read the cream of the crop. This volume cuts across time and ideologies.

—Marvin E. Wolfgang

PREFACE

Until the 2005 crime statistics came in, the leading criminology story for more than a decade was declining American crime rates. Each year the Federal Bureau of Investigation releases its Uniform Crime Reports, which leads to a flurry of phone calls to and interviews with criminologists by those seeking to understand the decline. In 2006 the callers wanted to know what the 2005 upsurge meant. Most criminologists have been cautious to interpret the rather small increase, preferring to wait to see whether it is a one-year aberration or the beginning of a meaningful trend. Whichever of these two alternatives turns out to be most correct, it is likely that politicians will continue to "run against crime" at election time, and the popular media will remain fascinated with "true crime" shows and news of criminal events. In the academe, students and teachers alike will spend much time and energy thinking about crime and criminals, too.

Although crime rates, even with the recent up-tick, are lower than they have been in decades, no one contends that crime is no longer a major problem. In the second edition of *Crime and Justice*, Sir Leon Radzinowicz and Marvin E. Wolfgang wrote,

> There can be no doubt that optimism has gone, platitudes have proven empty. We are living through a time when, more than ever before, there can be no consensus on how to tackle crime. We do not feel it our business to try to resolve the current conflicts, but we feel it our duty . . . to try to reflect it.

That now classic three-volume set was first published in 1971, but those words still accurately describe the lack of consensus in our thinking about crime and criminal justice. Criminologists, politicians, and the general public are no closer to consensus on how to confront the problem of crime than we were 35 years ago. Perhaps we are even more divided. We see this lack of consensus in the answers given by criminologists and criminal justice practitioners when queried about those recent increases in some crime rates. Some argue that it is because the federal government cut back on the number of police officers that they supported (through local police departments) on the streets. Some believe that it is because of the large number of former prisoners being released (after the unprecedented four-fold increases in incarceration rates in the 1980s and 1990s) at the ends of their sentences. Others argue that drug markets are resurging (cocaine and methamphetamine) and gang activity has increased. There are those who point to an economy that has been stagnant and uneven, with some segments of the population doing very well while others struggle. And of course, there are those who suggest that all or many of these explanations are needed for a complete understanding of changes in crime rates. Likely, the majority of criminologists think it is important that we wait to see whether a real trend develops in the coming years before we know whether crime is really beginning to increase in a meaningful way and, if so, why.

In this, the third edition of *Crime*, we, like Radzinowicz and Wolfgang, do not try to resolve the important conflicts in criminology, but we do try to fairly represent the range of debates about the causes of crime and delinquency and the approaches to addressing these problems. The organizing principle of this and the earlier editions of *Crime* is that the scholarly literature, both the old and the new, provides an important basis for thinking about crime for professionals, students, and the general public. As a result, we have included some of the classic works of criminology along with contemporary empirical research. We again have included theoretical statements and pieces that reflect where those theories have gone since. We believe that students will be better educated if they have the opportunity to study the diversity of the criminological literature.

Although some "theory-based" collections of readings about crime have been published in recent years, most criminology readers focus on "types of crimes." Such an approach is curious because we know that most criminals do not specialize. Much crime occurs because people are presented with opportunities to act violently, selfishly, or acquisitively. As opportunities vary, so to do the types of crimes individuals commit. If opportunities for different types of crime appear, the same person may well seize—with equal likelihood—the chance to victimize people, property, or institutions. Accordingly, our message in this book is simple. We obtain a much clearer picture of crime and its causes if we focus not on the specific acts that people commit, but rather on the patterns of violation, on the social and other human conditions that lead to violation, and on how groups within society control those who are defined as criminals and outlaws. As teachers, we believe that students gain the greatest understanding of crime and social control from a selection of readings that focuses on theoretical explanations and research evidence advanced by criminologists. Publications that take the other approach, depicting the study of crime and criminals simply in terms of different types of illegal and bizarre acts, offer students little more than a criminological version of what Alexander Liazos described as the study of "nuts, sluts, and perverts." Atheoretically studying nuts, sluts, and perverts may be fun for some, but it will leave students with an incomplete understanding of modern criminology.

The collection of readings in *Crime* began in our conversations about teaching our classes at the University of Washington. We believe that students should read the actual work of scholars who study criminology. Reading the original literature is an important part of a liberal education. Public debates about crime and what to do about it will be better informed if the public is exposed to what we know and how we have come to know it, as well as to what we do not know.

Although some articles from scholarly journals may at first seem inaccessible or of limited appeal to students, we have found that when students are asked to reach a bit beyond their grasp, more often than not, they respond positively. Our experiences, as well as those of our colleagues who used the first two editions of *Crime* in their classes, confirm that students from private liberal arts colleges to research universities to community colleges can read and understand scholarly papers. We recognize that certain characteristics of some academic articles may overwhelm some students—most notably, the analytic procedures and statistics. As we did in earlier editions, we have edited out much of this material, as well as footnotes and references, leaving the presentation of theoretical ideas, results, discussions, and conclusions.

Many of the selections in *Crime* have been used in one or more of our courses. We have emphasized theories because they form the basis of scholarship in criminology, and also because most commonsense explanations of the causes of crime and delinquency have actually been captured in those theories. When we explain this to students, we help them to see why theory is important to criminologists and also why it can be of interest to them. The empirical pieces in this volume frequently reflect modifications and refinements in the major theories.

The third edition maintains the format that was successful in the first and second editions—sections on history and definitions, images of crime, measurement, correlates of crime, specific topics in contemporary criminology, theories, and social control. The section on specific topics has been moved forward in this edition and is now Part III, and the theory sections are organized somewhat differently (more on that follows). As we did in the past, we try throughout to pay attention to both historical and contemporary efforts to understand crime.

What Is New in the Third Edition?

Organization: Several small changes in the organization of *Crime* have been made. First, we moved the section titled "Enduring and Changing Patterns of Crime" from Part IX (in the first and second editions) to Part III because we felt that it fit well after students read "Images of Crime" and before they think about measurement and correlates. Second, the first two theory sections, Parts VI and VII, are now called "Foundational Theories of Modern Criminology" because these perspectives governed the study of crime from the 1920s through the end of the 20th century, and continue to be important. These theories are presented chronologically. Parts VIII and IX include newer, contemporary theoretical approaches (most of which have roots in those foundational theories).

New articles: We have added new articles (35 new pieces) in the third edition of *Crime* for two reasons. First, much research and writing has been published since the second edition was put together. We have focused particularly on keeping the contemporary research selections as current as possible. Second, we made changes when our colleagues, our students, or our own experience with earlier editions suggested that a different piece might work better.

Substantive changes: We have brought in several approaches that are new to this edition. First, in response to requests from our colleagues, we have added sections on critical criminology, psychology, and biology. Second, because criminology is, like most of social science, increasingly comparative, throughout this edition we have used some comparative articles reporting studies in societies outside the United States.

Data analysis and tables in articles: At the suggestion of several colleagues, we have left some more of the analytic descriptions, tables, and figures in some of the new empirical pieces for this edition. Those colleagues convinced us that this will give teachers opportunities to teach students how to read tables and figures and to begin to interpret statistical results. Some of the tables will be challenging to most undergraduate students, and we will not ask our students in entry- and mid-level classes to confront these. Colleagues who use this volume for more advanced classes, though, may elect to work more with these tables. In the editing, we have attempted to make these articles "undergraduate friendly" so that they can, with the permission of their instructor, simply skip sections of articles with advanced methodological approaches without sacrificing substantive understanding of the piece.

New data analysis exercises: These exercises, introduced in the second edition, are designed to give students hands-on experience in analyzing real data. Since many computers no longer have a floppy disk port, we have placed the data and exercises online at www.sagepub.com/crimereadings3study.

The exercises allow students to see how the theories explain crime and the world around them. They have been updated and expanded for the third edition. Each exercise explores the tenets of a theory and tests whether the ideas in the theory "work" to explain increases or reductions in crime. While completing the exercises, students will learn about the basic methods and statistics, two skill areas that will benefit them whether they enter graduate study or the workplace. Novice computer users and those new to statistical analyses should be able to work through the exercises with ease.

The exercises can also be used flexibly in the classroom and in assigned work. They are again divided into three sections:

1. General questions are based on the guided exercises completed by the students. These fill-in-the-blank and circle-the-answer questions accommodate the needs of instructors who want to introduce students to data analysis but require assignments that are quick to score.

2. "Further exploration" questions are closely related to the general questions but allow the students to replicate and extend ideas and conceptualizations on their own. The answers to these questions are fill-in, circle, and essay.

3. "On your own" questions allow students to explore criminological ideas independently, with minimal guidance. The answers are essay and may be used to generate course discussion.

Although exercises use only frequencies and cross-tabulations, some instructors may choose to introduce their students to multivariate analysis as well, using the exercises as a starting point. The exercises provided a flexible way for teachers to include data handling and interpretation skill in their course.

We have retained the introduction to the first edition of *Crime* that was prepared by James F. Short, Jr., as well as the foreword by the late Marvin E. Wolfgang. Our colleague, Ross L. Matsueda, has updated the foreword that he prepared for the second edition. These three essays set the stage for the very best ideas from theory and research on crime and its control produced by criminologists over the past decades. The readings represent different academic disciplines, with different theoretical and ideological orientations, and the diverse ideas on the best ways to prevent and control crime in our society.

ACKNOWLEDGMENTS

Many persons have contributed to this volume, beyond those whose work is included in the book itself. We are indebted to these individuals and to those whose work we have been able to republish here. Without their dedicated work and assistance, this edition would not have been completed. The editorial staff at Sage, especially Deya Saoud, tried to keep us on task, and she and others at Sage ensured that the production process went smoothly. We greatly appreciate their commitment to our project and their uncompromising pursuit of excellence. We want to especially thank Jerry Westby, whose patience we taxed far beyond what is reasonable. We also want to acknowledge Steve Rutter, formerly of Pine Forge Press, under whose guidance the original project and editions one and two were conceived and brought to press. We are deeply appreciative of all of the work by the staff of Sage and, before them, of those at Pine Forge Press.

We are extremely grateful to Jon'a Meyer for her excellent contributions to the third edition (as well as the second), the data analysis exercises and the questions at the end of each reading. These have improved the book immeasurably.

We are also indebted to colleagues, our former graduate students, who contributed to the conceptualization and work of earlier editions of *Crime*: Kristin Bates, Rod Engen, Randy Gainey, Eddie Pate, and Sara Steen. Kevin Drakulich did substantial heavy lifting for the production of this edition, and we are grateful.

We are also deeply appreciative of the helpful comments and suggestions supplied by reviewers and users of earlier editions, including the following:

Q. Akin Adesun, Pennsylvania State University

Lawrence L. Bench, University of Utah

Donna Bishop, Northeastern University

Eugene Bouley, Georgia College and State University

Susan Brinkley, University of Tampa

James W. Burfeind, University of Montana

Barbara Costello, University of Rhode Island

James Creechan, University of Toronto

Lauren Dundes, Western Maryland College

Joshua Freilich, John Jay College of Criminal Justice

Randy Gainey, Old Dominion University

Sarah Goodrum, Centre College, Kentucky

Helen Taylor Greene, Old Dominion University

Denise Herz, University of Nebraska, Omaha

James W. Kanan, Western Kentucky University

Joanne Kaufman, Emory University

Christopher Krebs, Florida State University

Celia Lo, University of Akron

Daniel Mears, University of Texas at Austin

Robert F. Meier, University of Nebraska, Omaha

Jon'a F. Meyer, Rutgers University, Camden

Frank Mungel, State University of New York, Buffalo

Mahesh K. Nalla, Michigan State University

Amie L. Nielsen, Bowling Green State University

Randi Rosenblum, Hunter College

Gene T. Straughan, Lewis-Clark State College

Pamela Tontodonato, Kent State University

Tim Wadsworth, University of New Mexico

Charles Walton, Radford University

Kevin Wehr, California State University, Sacramento

Despite the important comments these colleagues provided, we alone are responsible for the editing of the manuscript and for any errors or omissions in the editing process and in the drafting of introductory comments.

Finally, we want to acknowledge the contributions that our undergraduate students at the University of Washington and George Washington University have made to this effort. They have toiled through many earlier versions of this book, commenting on the books and our teaching over the years. We have benefited immensely from their reactions, both positive and negative. Without their insightful comments and suggestions, we would be much less effective as teachers and learners.

On Crime, Criminals, and Criminologists

Crime is a controversial concern in all modern societies. It is controversial, as well, among those who study crime and criminals. Politicians must not be seen to be "soft on crime," lest they incur the displeasure of a fearful electorate. Criminologists trained in scientific disciplines often skirt difficult issues, such as the racial and ethnic distribution of crime, for a variety of reasons, among them fear of being branded "racist" or otherwise prejudiced against minorities or concern that their analyses may be translated by politicians into ideologically or politically motivated counterproductive crime control policies.

These fears feed on one another. Even "enlightened" (by acquaintance with scientific analyses of the crime problem) politicians feel obligated to support control measures that are "tough on crime," as well as measures designed ostensibly (on the basis of scientific analyses) to prevent crime. Criminologists struggle with their scientific consciences to support crime prevention measures that are unproven because they fear harsh political responses to crime that are devoid of the input of scientific knowledge and carefully evaluated experience.

Among criminologists, priority is given to issues that are fundamental to understanding the nature of crime and criminals, rather than to issues of "toughness" or "softness" in the control of crime. The latter are derivative, distorted versions of the former, though crime control policies and their implementation are important to the etiology of *crimes and their control,* for crime is far from homogenous, in law, in behavior, or in effects on victims (and offenders), as individuals, families, communities, or nations.

The selections reprinted in this collection shed much light on these controversies, beginning with John Hagan's searching examination of the relationship between crime and morality. Criminology arguably begins with the sociology of law, though restriction of the concerns of criminology to behavior defined in the criminal law has been objected to on several grounds, as Hagan's article makes clear. Beyond the concerns reviewed in Hagan's fine article (and beyond the concerns of criminology, per se), the task of developing "a theory of the distinctively legal" remains elusive.

This volume organizes criminology's concerns and controversies in 10 sections, beginning with the history and definitions of crime and criminology and with scholarly attempts to understand public views and fears of crime. These are followed by selections concerned with the enduring and changing patterns of crime, the measurement of crime, and with the distribution of crime among social categories. Explanations of crime occupy the next four sections, again beginning historically with theories that were first advanced a half century or more ago, and that continue to influence scholarly and public concerns with crime problems. More recent theories and research are then examined, including relatively new theoretical developments. The final section examines the vexing problems of the social control of crime. Review questions conclude each section.

The selections reprinted here are heavily weighted toward traditional *sociological* concerns with crime, criminals, and their control. Sociologists, more than adherents of other social and behavioral sciences, focus on fundamental questions of measurement, sampling, and on *contextualizing* forces and processes of etiology. We tend to focus, that is, on the *macrosocial* level of explanation, seeking to understand what it is about social systems (such as economic and political systems, communities, and families) that produce different *rates* of behaviors of interest. The most immediate of these contexts is human activity—ongoing interaction among persons—that often exerts critical influences on behavioral outcomes, as studies at the *microsocial* level of explanation demonstrate. As will be seen in the selections that follow, sociologists also focus on the *individual* level of explanation, seeking to explain what it is about individuals that lead them to behave in sundry ways.

In the course of the inquiries, criminologists address profound questions regarding human behavior: the relationship between broad social forces and individual experience, the relationship between hard objective realities and how they are subjectively experienced, and the problem of deriving general behavioral principles from individual (and in some respects, inevitably unique) perceptions and experience. Criminology can be viewed through many social and behavioral science lenses: psychology and social psychology, for example, and through principles of organizational and group behavior. Similarly, these social and behavioral science specialties can be viewed with profit through the lenses provided by criminological inquiry.

Criminologists have not been immune to ideological concerns, though in most cases these, also, have been perused within broad scientific principles. When they are not, disciplined inquiry suffers, as does criminology as a discipline. The selections in this volume reflect both the diversity of approaches to the study of crime and criminals and some of the best examples of research and theory within these approaches.

Few serious scholars claim to be "experts" concerning crime and criminals, yet we are often viewed as authorities, based on our inquiries and our experience. As such, we face many challenges, not least of which is building and maintaining the credibility of criminology and the trust of those who rely upon our knowledge, insights, and proposals for the control of crime. The selections in this volume are an excellent sampling of the best that criminology has to offer. I am happy to commend it to those who wish to know what it is that we are all about.

—James F. Short, Jr.

PART I

WHAT IS CRIMINOLOGY?

The History and Definitions of Crime and Criminology

Though many people are content to accept a definition of crime as behavior that violates the criminal law, modern criminologists believe that defining crime is a more complex enterprise. Criminologists are acutely aware that what is considered a crime is a product of moral, political, and social processes. At times, those processes work smoothly and easily; at other times, there is substantial controversy and disagreement. How those processes actually work has become an important area of scholarship.

Some of the most interesting questions in criminology focus on the central issue of defining crime. For example, no one will disagree that murder is a vile and contemptible act, rightfully considered criminal, but we do not always agree on which instances of taking human life should be considered murder. When toxic dumping results in death, is that murder? When the state practices capital punishment, is that murder? There are those who would say yes, others no, to both questions; still others would argue that only one of these acts constitutes murder. Other acts, such as abortion and drug possession, have provoked more heated public debate and illustrate the lack of consensus in our society about which behaviors should be considered criminal.

Additionally, definitions of crime vary across societies, and it is important to understand how and why societies differ in what they choose to criminalize. Every society develops rules, and complex modern societies have more intricate and comprehensive systems of law. The fact that these laws, and the behaviors they define as criminal, are not uniform in all societies underscores the point that definitions of crime are not inevitable or universal, but depend heavily on the social contexts in which they evolve. For criminologists, it is essential to understand both those contexts and the definitions of crime that emerge in them as critical components in the scientific study of crime.

How criminologists define crime also affects their conceptions of the criminal. Both are important factors in explaining why people break the law and how society responds to these offenders. If, for example, we define crime as illegal behavior in which people choose to engage, explanations will focus on why some choose to commit crime and others choose to obey the law. With that definition of crime, the society would respond to crime by trying to change the individual's crime calculus, making it more costly to engage in crime by increasing punishment. Alternatively, if crime is conceptualized as a product of forces outside the individual's control (such as biological, psychological, or social forces), crime control would attempt to address those root causes of criminality.

In the first selection, Hagan addresses some of the complexities involved in defining crime. We have led with this piece to emphasize the notion that defining crime is not a simple exercise. Anyone who wants to understand crime, whether he or she is a professional criminologist, student of criminology, president of the United States, parent, or criminal, must be aware of the many ways in which crime is defined. We do not offer one definition of crime that we believe the student should accept. However, students should, as they move through this text, consider critically how authors define crime and what implications the definitions have for theory and empirical research.

In "Historical Explanations of Crime: From Demons to Politics," Huff provides an overview of the history of modern criminology. Many people believe that criminologists make their living by solving crimes. Members of the American Society of Criminology, the field's leading organization, do not solve crimes and rarely commit them. Instead, criminologists try to explain why people commit crimes and how societies respond to control crime. In this piece, the student will get a sense of the distance we have covered, and have yet to go, in our quest to understand crime. In reading Huff's article, look for the implied definitions of crime that theorists have used and assess how those definitions helped to shape their explanations of crime.

Together, Hagan and Huff set the stage for considering the modern state of criminology. Although neither answers the great questions of criminology, they both raise some of them. And in the asking, we have an important place to begin.

 For a data analysis exercise that accompanies the material in this section, go to www.sagepub.com/crimereadings3study.

DEFINING CRIME

An Issue of Morality

JOHN HAGAN

THE ISSUE: WHAT SHOULD BE CALLED "CRIMINAL"?

The act of defining crime is often, but not always, a step toward controlling it; that is, the ostensible purpose of defining some behaviors as criminal is to make them liable to public prosecution and punishment. However, being *liable* to prosecution and punishment is clearly not the same as actually *being* prosecuted and punished. During the twilight of the prohibition era in America, there was little attempt to enforce temperance legislation and, when arrests and convictions did occur, the sentences imposed were light. Eventually, the production and distribution of alcohol was decriminalized. Attempts to prosecute and punish Selective Service violators produced similar problems during the last stages of the Vietnam war. This law was never repealed, and it undoubtedly will be used again in the future. Meanwhile, there are many statutes that define white-collar crimes, but they are only infrequently enforced. This is not to say that such laws have no use; their mere existence at least serves the purpose of condemning certain unethical business practices. Thus, each of the above laws serves (or served) the purpose of making a moral statement, a statement about how citizens *should* behave. Yet each of these laws has proved problematic, making explicit the issue of how the criminal law can and should be used to legislate morality. In one sense, this issue is moot because the criminal law is always and everywhere used to legislate morality. However, in another sense, the issue is very much alive because the *way* in which the criminal law is used to legislate morality is constantly changing. And in the process of changing, the criminal law expands and contracts, forcing us regularly and concretely to answer the question: What should be called a crime? Should the criminal law contract and make homosexuality and some kinds of drug use legal? Should the criminal law expand and make acts of racism and sexism crimes? These are the kinds of questions this [article] is about.

THE LINK BETWEEN LAW AND MORALITY

The lengths to which the law should go in officially defining and enforcing morality has been the subject of philosophical debate for centuries. In the nineteenth century, the noted participants in this debate were John Stuart Mill and Sir James Fitzjames Stephen. In the twentieth century, the principals have been H. L. A. Hart and Lord Patrick Devlin. It is important that we begin by grounding ourselves in the opposing premises of this debate.

On one side, Mill argued in his famous essay *On Liberty* that the primary function of criminal law is to prevent individuals from doing harm *to others*.

> The only purpose for which power can be rightfully exercised over any member of a civilized community against his will, is to prevent harm to others. His own good, either physical, or moral, is not sufficient warrant, he cannot rightfully be compelled to do or forbear because it would be better, for him to do so, because it will make him happier, because, in the opinion of others, to do so would be wise or even right.

In other words, Mill regarded the criminal law as an improper instrument for regulating the private moral conduct of individuals that caused no direct harm to others. In contrast, Stephen saw the criminal law as serving a much broader function in the cultivation of personal responsibility, arguing that "the meaning of responsibility is liability to punishment." Thus, Stephen regarded the criminal law as a fundamental means for developing a sense of individual responsibility, and he considered the use of criminal law as essential for this purpose.

The debate has been focused most clearly in this century in Britain around the work of the British Governmental Committee on Homosexual Offenses and Prostitution. This body, known for its chairman as the Wolfenden Committee, issued a report in 1957 that renewed the classic debate by recommending that private and consensual homosexual behavior on the part of adults no longer be considered a criminal offense. Behind this recommendation lay a broader assumption, explicitly acknowledged by the committee, that the criminal law should not intrude on the private lives of individual citizens beyond what is absolutely necessary—to maintain public order and decency, to protect individuals from offensive and injurious behavior, and to prevent exploitation and corruption, particularly of those unable to protect themselves. The committee put the matter succinctly when it concluded that "there must remain a realm of private morality and immorality which is, in brief and crude terms, not the law's business." The committee was quick to emphasize that it did not condone these forms of behavior, but neither did it see it as the proper role of the law to condemn them. These were simply not matters for legal control.

Lord Devlin, a prominent British jurist, objected to the committee's position. Devlin argued that "the criminal law as we know it is based upon moral principle" and furthermore that "in a number of crimes its function is simply to enforce a moral principle and nothing else." Thus, Devlin's position was that "the suppression of vice is as much the law's business as the suppression of subversive activities." In other words, Devlin, like Stephen, believed that it was a proper and necessary function of the law to regulate private morality.

Another prominent British philosopher of law, H. L. A. Hart, defended the committee's work against Devlin's critique. Like Mill before him, Hart based his defense on principles of individual liberty, arguing that a right to be protected from the distress which is inseparable from the bare knowledge that others are acting in ways you think wrong cannot be acknowledged by anyone who recognizes individual liberty as a value. The extension of the utilitarian principle that coercion may be used to protect men from harm, so as to include their protection from this form of distress, cannot stop here. If distress incident to the belief that others are doing wrong is harm, so also is the distress incident to the belief that others are doing what you do not want them to do. To punish people for causing this form of distress would be tantamount to punishing them simply because others object to what they do, and the only liberty that could coexist with this extension of the utilitarian principle is liberty to do those things to which no one seriously objects.

To read the debate as it has been presented thus far, one might think the issue involved is one of simple and absolute principle: whether the criminal law should be used to control private morality. However, things are seldom so simple in law, and this debate is no exception. First, each side of the debate we have presented involves rather different assumptions about the sources and purposes of law. That is, rather different assumptions are made about where law comes from, about how law evolves and develops in primitive and modern societies, and about the purposes to which law is put. Second, the line between private morality and the concerns of the surrounding society is not clear. For example, it can be argued that while drug use imposes its most direct consequences on drug-taking individuals, there are consequences (e.g., lost productivity) for society as well. Third, part of what is at issue is not only the *propriety* of using the criminal law to control individual morality, but also the *efficacy* of trying to do so. In other words, can the criminal law be used *effectively* to control individual morality? Fourth, there is a concern with the costs and harms involved for those who are subject to control. One concern here is that such laws may have the effect of creating a permanent class of criminals, that is, a class of persons whose options for leaving a lifestyle defined as criminal are few. To fully understand the Hart-Devlin debate and the link between law and morality, it is necessary to address these several dimensions of the problem. We turn next, then, to a discussion of the sources of law, followed by a discussion of each of the additional concerns raised above.

THE ORIGINS OF LAWS

Anthropologists, philosophers, and political scientists, as well as sociologists, have pondered the question of where laws come from. Although this question is raised and addressed in a variety of ways, two discernible kinds of answers can be considered briefly here. The first kind of answer sees the law largely as a source of social order that resolves and prevents disputes, thereby allowing individuals to live more harmoniously together. The law is seen here as a product of consensus, evolving as a means of maintaining this consensus. The second kind of answer sees the law primarily as an instrument of social conflict that is used to maintain the power and privileges of one group over another. The law is seen here as having evolved out of a conflict between interest groups. These two different kinds of answers can be understood best as they have been offered by their various proponents.

Law as a Product of Consensus

According to the consensus point of view, law is a natural product of the informal rules of interaction of a society. For example, William Seagle, a lawyer, argues that the law is simply a product of custom. Indeed, for Seagle, "custom is king," and "while there is no automatic *submission* to custom, there is an automatic *sway* of custom." Similarly, Frederick von Savigny asserts "that all law . . . is first developed by custom and popular faith," and Julius Stone concludes that laws are "generalized statements of the tendencies actually operating, of

the presuppositions on which a particular civilization is based." From this viewpoint, then, there is no easy division between morality and law: Customary morality is the very source of law.

With Devlin, it is assumed that to deny this would be to deny the very foundations of law. "The folkways are the 'right' ways," wrote William Sumner, and these customs or folkways are seen as giving law both its force and its purpose. From this perspective, any separation of the law from this foundation would be both artificial and perilous.

Law as a Product of Conflict

In contrast, there is another point of view that sees the emergence of law as a very selective process. This view argues that there are many moralities representing a variety of group interests in a society. The issue, then, is whose morality will get expressed in law and with what consequences? The answer given from this perspective is that the law is a "weapon" and that it will be used as such by any group that can do so to its advantage. Chambliss and Seidman argue that this is particularly the case in complex, highly stratified societies like our own. They note that as societies become more complex in their economic division of labor, it becomes necessary to have rules, and ultimately laws, that regulate the encounters of individuals who occupy different roles. At the same time, as societies become more stratified, it is argued that it becomes necessary for those who are economically advantaged to use the law as a means of maintaining and protecting their position. In Chambliss and Seidman's terms, "The more economically stratified a society becomes, the more it becomes necessary for the dominant groups in the society to enforce through coercion the norms of conduct which guarantee their supremacy." From this viewpoint, the connection between law and morality is partial, both in the sense that the enforcement of morality is selective and in the sense that the morality enforced will be to the advantage of one group over another. In particular, this viewpoint notes that it is the alleged immorality of the poor that is much more likely to be called "criminal" than the presumed immorality of the rich. "What this means in modern times," writes Richard Quinney, "is that there is a moral basis to capitalism, a morality that supports the interests of the ruling class and, at the same time, underlies the legal system that maintains the prevailing social and economic order." Like Mill, then, those who see law as a product of conflict are usually wary of the attempt to link conventional morality closely to the law. When the closeness of this tie is preserved, they note, it is usually to the disadvantage of the less advantaged. We will have much more to say about this perspective in later parts of this [article]. Our purpose here is simply to present these viewpoints, not to arbitrate between them.

Private Morality
and the Public Interest

A second dimension of the debated link between law and morality involves the thin line that may divide considerations of private morality and the societal interest. The problem is that while many matters that could be considered only issues of private morality, including some kinds of drug use, prostitution, and pornography, may have their most direct and immediate effects on the individuals who pursue them, there may nonetheless be less direct but no less significant effects on surrounding communities and their members. A particularly poignant illustration of this point is provided by Donald Clairmont in his description of the development of a "deviance service center"—a whole community adjacent to Halifax, Nova Scotia that was given the "functional autonomy" to provide a whole range of illicit services to the adjoining city.

Clairmont notes that this community, called "Africville" by its residents, was founded around 1850 by the descendants of refugee blacks who fled slavery in the United States during the War of 1812. Initially, Africville was a viable community with a few fine houses, some small-scale businesses, plenty of space, and a strong community spirit based on a stable kinship system. However, Africville soon began to experience the problems of a sluggish surrounding economy, and this, combined with two other factors, led to its development as a deviance service center. The first of these factors was that Africville was located close to the adjoining city's dockyards and port activity. The second factor was that the city's ruling circles gave the community the functional autonomy to develop an alternative economy: "that is, not sharing fairly in society's wealth, they . . . [were] allowed by the authorities

a range of behavior that would not be countenanced elsewhere." These two factors came together during World War I when visiting seamen added to the clientele of an expanding bootlegging trade. Fearing growing crime problems and the ultimate demise of their community, residents of Africville petitioned the city council of Halifax in 1919, requesting police surveillance and protection. However, no police assistance was provided, and in the period that followed World War I, Africville continued to grow as a deviance service center. Gradually, bootlegging gave way to more hazardous forms of deviance, and, as the younger and better educated members of the community began to leave, the fears of the petitioners of 1919 eventually were confirmed. The entire community was finally designated for harbor development and urban renewal nearly a half century later. This meant that the problems of the community finally were "solved," literally, through demolition, and the few remaining residents were "relocated."

It can be argued that the problems that residents of Africville experienced would not have existed if the deviant services provided were not illegal elsewhere and therefore concentrated in that particular community. There is no clear way of evaluating how valid this argument may be. Nonetheless, this example makes it clear that the pursuit of "disreputable pleasures" can have consequences beyond the individuals who are immediately involved.

The (In)Effectiveness of
Law as an Instrument of Morality

Aside from the issue of whether the law *should* try to control private morality, there is additionally the question of whether the law *can* do so. Social scientists and students of the law have long been skeptical about what the law itself can do. Sumner asserts that the mores of a society always take precedence over the law and that it is impossible to change the mores "by any artifice or device, to a great extent, or suddenly, or in any essential element." Similarly, Sutherland and Cressey argue that "when the mores are adequate, laws are unnecessary; when the mores are inadequate, the laws are ineffective." In other words, laws that are unsupported by widely shared moral beliefs are unlikely to accomplish what their legal architects would wish. This is particularly true of crimes of private morality. In addition, it is difficult to get the information and evidence necessary to control such behaviors, not only because the behaviors are not widely and/or harshly enough condemned to generate public cooperation, but also because they customarily take place with some measure of privacy and because they are often only known to the persons whose behavior is involved. These problems are most notable at the level of police enforcement.

Skolnick makes this point in his study of a police department on the west coast of the United States. Skolnick notes that the narcotics officers of a police force often play a very central, although often corrupting, role in departmental operations. This is because the character of their work makes narcotics officers an important source of information and influence. To begin, narcotics offenses, like other crimes of private morality, rarely involve victim-complainants. As a result, information and evidence must be obtained in other ways, including the use of informers, entrapment techniques, and undercover work. Each of these techniques is potentially corrupting: The use of informers involves questionable use of cash and drugs as inducements; entrapment techniques can encourage crimes that might otherwise never occur; and undercover work provokes tempting possibilities for bribery and collusion. Nonetheless, in the course of these types of activities, narcotics officers develop sources of information that are important not only to the prosecution of narcotics cases but for other kinds of cases as well. Thus, narcotics officers become central actors in police departments, valuable to prosecutors and to other officers. Among the results of this type of law enforcement are ineffective efforts to control drug use and the corruption of narcotics and related areas of policing. In sum, crimes without complainants are difficult, if not impossible, to control. Worse still, however, efforts to control such crimes often corrupt the controllers.

LAW, MORALITY, AND THE CREATION OF CRIME

A final concern about using the law to control private morality involves the implications for persons whose behaviors are controlled. There are some alarming indications that attempts to legally control private morality have the unfortunate tendency of creating permanent classes of deviants, who must organize their lives around criminal roles. The best example of this involves the problems of drug addicts. Well into the second decade of this century, addicts in America were able to buy most opiates across the drug counter. One result was that "our grandmothers used many home remedies and patent medicines whose ingredients would shock us today." Coincidentally, early surveys of opiate drug addicts in America reveal that the majority of addicts were white women. The watershed event that changed this pattern was the passage of the Harrison Act in 1914. While it was originally only a tax measure, the effect of this law and its enforcement by the Federal Bureau of Narcotics was gradually to make opiate addiction a crime. The result was the emergence of a black market in drugs and the development of a whole new sector of the criminal underworld. Opiate addiction, therefore, shifted from being acceptable and respectable to being criminal and disreputable in a rather brief period of time, and the involvement of individuals in this world shifted as well. Cuskey et al. note that "in many ways the period from pre-Civil War to immediate post-World War I was like a film negative of the present." White American women substituted the use of various legal painkillers, barbiturates, and amphetamines for the newly illegal opium. At the same time, black American men, gradually, and in increasing numbers, were pulled into this criminal underworld, a world that proved extremely difficult to leave. Access to the drug required increasing amounts of money, which usually could only be obtained through crime, and access to medical treatment became very difficult to obtain. Drug addiction became stereotyped as a black American problem that was to be the subject of policing more than treatment. The persistence of this crime problem and the scale of the other kinds of criminal activities associated with it are ominous indications that making a form of behavior criminal can create as many, and sometimes more, problems than it can solve.

VICTIMLESS CRIME AND THE LIMITS OF LAW

Because of the above kinds of concerns, social scientists and students of law have spent considerable time and effort trying to draw an effective line between the aspects of private morality that should and should not be made a part of the criminal law. One of the best known of these efforts involves Edwin Schur's discussion of "victimless crimes." "Crimes without victims," Schur writes, "may be limited to those situations in which one person obtains from another, in a fairly direct exchange, a commodity or personal service which is socially disapproved and legally proscribed." After considering several victimless crimes (e.g., abortion, homosexuality, and drug addiction) in detail, and after weighing a number of the dimensions of the link between law and morality, Schur argues that public education about the problems of enforcing these laws, and the possibility of reforming them, is needed. Schur does not argue that all criminal laws relating to these crimes should immediately be abolished. In fact, he concludes that "legalization is not automatically or invariably to be preferred to criminalization."

A more provocative position is taken by Morris and Hawkins in their book, *The Honest Politician's Guide to Crime Control*. Morris and Hawkins argue that there is an "overreach of the criminal law" that contributes to the larger "crime problem" in the following ways that echo and extend our earlier discussion:

1. Where the supply of goods or services is concerned, such as narcotics, gambling, and prostitution, the criminal law operates as a "crime tariff," which makes the supply of such goods and services profitable for the criminal by driving up prices and, at the same time, discourages competition by those who might enter the market were it legal.

2. This leads to the development of large-scale, organized criminal groups, which, as in the field of legitimate business, tend to extend and diversify their operations, thus financing and promoting other criminal activities.

3. The high prices, which criminal prohibition and law enforcement help to maintain, have a secondary criminogenic effect in cases where demand is inelastic, as for narcotics, by causing persons to resort to crime to obtain the money to pay the prices.

4. The proscription of a particular form of behavior (e.g., homosexuality, prostitution, drug

addiction) by the criminal law drives those who engage or participate in it into association with those engaged in other criminal activities and leads to the growth of an extensive criminal subculture, which is subversive of social order generally. It also leads, in the case of drug addiction, to endowing a pathological condition with the romantic glamour of a rebellion against authority or some sort of elitist enterprise.

5. The expenditure of police and criminal justice resources involved in attempting to enforce statutes in relation to sexual behavior, drug taking, gambling, and other matters of private morality seriously depletes the time, energy, and number of personnel available for dealing with the types of crime involving violence and stealing, which are the primary concern of the criminal justice system. This diversion and overextension of resources results both in failure to deal adequately with current serious crime and, because of the increased chances of impunity, in encouraging further crime.

6. These crimes lack victims, in the sense of complainants asking for the protection of the criminal law. Where such complainants are absent, it is particularly difficult for the police to enforce the law. Bribery tends to flourish; political corruption of the police is invited. It is peculiarly with reference to the victimless crimes that the police are led to employ illegal means of law enforcement.

Based on these arguments, Morris and Hawkins conclude that a range of behaviors should be decriminalized. They suggest that public drunkenness should cease to be a crime; that neither the acquisition, purchase, possession, nor use of any drug should be a criminal offense; that no form of gambling should be prohibited by criminal law; that vaguely stated disorderly conduct and vagrancy laws should be replaced; that private sexual activities between consenting adults should not be subject to criminal law; and that juvenile courts should only retain jurisdiction over adolescents for conduct that would be criminal if committed by adults. This is obviously a sweeping set of changes. We offer these proposals here not because we believe they should all necessarily be adopted, but because they illustrate the point that what is to be called "criminal" is open to review and reform.

Thus, the significance of the debates and proposals we have been considering is the possibility they represent for contraction and expansion in conceptions of the proper content of criminal law. It is precisely this potential for variable content that poses problems for social scientists who wish to define crime for the purposes of identifying the subject matter of their work. On the one hand, it might seem desirable to simply confine our attention, and therefore our definition of crime, to what is called "criminal" in any particular jurisdiction. On the other hand, it is desirable that we remain sensitive within and between jurisdictions to the shifting divisions between what is called "criminal" and what is not, and why. This may be more apparent when it is noted that thus far in this [article] we have only considered this problem as it relates to our own culture, conveniently even ignoring the fact that each American state has its own criminal code, with significant variation between states in what is called "criminal." Our view is that the only effective way of responding to the problem of variability is to conceptualize crime as a specific instance of a broader range of deviant behavior.

QUESTIONS FOR DISCUSSION AND WRITING

1. What two answers are given to the question regarding the origin of law?

2. What do sociologists like Sumner, Sutherland, and Cressey believe about the effectiveness of criminal law to regulate morality?

3. How can law "create" crime?

HISTORICAL EXPLANATIONS OF CRIME

From Demons to Politics

C. RONALD HUFF

Man's historical concern with the existence of crime has been reflected in his diverse attempts to explain how and why crime occurs. Long before there was a scientific approach to the crime problem, there were speculative "explanations" of criminal behavior. Some of these earlier views concerning the nature of crime may seem absurd according to contemporary standards, but they must be viewed as symbolic expressions of the prevailing ideas and concerns of their own era. Similarly, it would be surprising if our currently fashionable theories of crime are not viewed as naive and unsophisticated in the next century.

Before discussing the major historical explanations of crime, it seems appropriate to ask what, if any, relevance such a discussion can have for students of criminology and criminal justice. While intellectual inquiry is justifiable for its own sake, the current discussion has contemporary relevance in at least two ways: (1) it presents an overview of the development of criminological theory, which should permit a greater understanding of contemporary explanations and their place in the continuity of thought on the subject of crime; and (2) since society's responses to crime depend, to a large extent, on its theories and its assumptions about the nature of crime, an understanding of those

views is useful in attempting to analyze the numerous attempts to "prevent . . . control," "deter," "cure," or otherwise contain criminal behavior. The operations of the various components of the criminal justice system (such as the police, the courts, and the prisons) can perhaps best be viewed by understanding the various assumptions which underlie their policies and procedures. Every major theory, explanation, or assumption about the nature and causes of crime may be viewed as having important implications for the strategies of social control which society elects to implement. The following discussion examines the existence of such connections between theory and practice.

SUPERNATURAL EXPLANATIONS

Primitive man's basic explanation of "criminal" behavior was that of diabolical possession. Criminal behavior was viewed as evidence that the culprit was under the control of evil spirits, or demons. This view of deviant behavior was simply an extension of the prevailing view of nature—that is, that every object or being was controlled by spiritual forces. Obviously, such an explanation requires *belief* or *faith*, since it does not lend itself to scientific verification.

Nevertheless, demonology had important implications for man's responses to crime.

Given such an explanation of crime, the only sensible solution was to try to exorcise the demons which were responsible for the behavior or, failing that, to do away with the criminal, either by exile or by execution. In a society where the gods were perceived as omnipotent and omnipresent, it was clearly a matter of the highest priority to appease them, no matter what the costs. Thus, the fate of the criminal was less related to the protection of society than to compliance with the will of the gods. The failure of the group to punish the wrongdoer was believed to leave the tribe open to the wrath and vengeance of the gods. As the noted historian and criminologist Harry Elmer Barnes noted,

> Not only does this transgression of the
> customary code expose the offending individual
> to untold woes, but it also renders his whole
> social group liable to the vengeance of the gods,
> for in early days, responsibility is collective from
> the standpoint of both the natural and
> supernatural world. In primitive society a crime
> and a sin are practically identical. Hence, to
> supplement the individual fear of violating the
> prescribed modes of conduct on account of
> danger from unseen powers, there is the certain
> knowledge on the part of the offender that his
> group will summarily avenge themselves upon
> him for rendering it open to destruction from
> the intervention of both human and spiritual
> forces . . . [T]he most generally accepted way of
> wiping out a crime and sin in primitive society
> is "to wipe out the sinner."

One who violated the norms dealing with endogamy, witchcraft, or treason was likely to receive the harshest punishment in primitive society. The offender might be hacked to pieces, exiled, or even eaten. All three of these sanctions accomplished the same goal—the removal of the offender from the group. Offenses of a private, rather than public, nature were generally dealt with by the victim's clan through the process known as "blood feud." Essentially, it was the duty of each member of a clan to avenge a fellow clan member. The principle which guided this pursuit of retaliation was the well-known *lex talionis* ("an eye for an eye and a tooth for a tooth"). The idea of *lex talionis*, roughly, was that the punishment

should fit the crime. Primitive obsession with making the retaliation exact was, in some cases, so fanatical that inanimate objects which had been instrumental in accidental deaths were actually "punished."

There was very little use of any form of incarceration in primitive society, except for periods of detention while awaiting disposition and the incarceration related to cannibalistic practices. The only other major type of punishment did not appear until the late stages of primitive society. It was a form of compensation or restitution. This practice developed in response to the failure of blood feud as a method of criminal justice. Blood feuds all too often resulted in prolonged vendettas which exacted heavy tolls on both sides. The practice of paying a fixed monetary penalty therefore evolved as an alternative to the potentially genocidal blood feuds. Later, in the feudal period, the extended families or clans established a system of *wergeld* (man-money) by which the victim's status determined the amount assessed against the offender. This concept was gradually broadened to include differences in degree of responsibility, the individualization of responsibility, and even a distinction between "intent" and "accident." Eventually, a specified value was set for each *type* of offense, and the system of restitutive fines paid by the offender to the victim came to be preferred over the blood feud. With the subsequent development of an appeal procedure whereby either party could protest an injustice, the roots of the modern-day court system emerged in embryonic form. Finally, through the absolute authority which accompanied kingships, especially in early *historic* society and during feudalism, all crimes became "crimes against the king's peace"; in other words, crimes came to be regarded as offenses against the *public* welfare. At that point, man had, in a sense, come "full circle" in his efforts to rationalize law and punishment:

> The heavy fines imposed on places and
> people became an important source of
> revenue to the crown and to the barons and
> the lords of manors.

The state was growing strong enough to take vengeance; the common man was no longer feared as had been the well-armed Saxon citizen of old, and to the "common" criminal was extended the ruthless severity once reserved for the slaves . . . and the idea of compensation began to wane before the revenge instinct, now backed by power.

RATIONALISM AND FREE WILL

Just as demonological explanations dominated the thinking of early man, the so-called classical period of criminology (roughly, 1700–1800) was characterized by its own conceptions of the nature of man. Man was seen as being rational, having free will, and seeking that which would be most productive of pleasure or happiness. Such views, of course, represented a significant departure from the idea that man was under the control of supernatural forces and that criminal behavior was a function of demons. For an understanding of the magnitude of this shift in thinking during the 18th century, it is best to examine the ideas of the two most influential contributors to classical criminology—Cesare Beccaria and Jeremy Bentham.

Beccaria, who was influenced by French rationalism and humanitarianism, strongly attacked the arbitrary and inconsistent "criminal justice" practices of the mid-eighteenth century. In his major work, Beccaria reacted against the secret accusations, inhumane punishments, and lack of concern for the defendant's rights that characterized criminal justice. He articulated the framework of what came to be known as the classical school of criminology, that is, (1) that the motivation underlying all social action must be the utilitarian value of that action (the greatest happiness for the greatest number); (2) that crime is an injury to *society* and can only be measured by assessing the extent of that injury (focus on the act and the extent of damage, not intent); (3) that the prevention of crime is more important than its punishment; (4) that secret accusations and torture should be eliminated and the trial process ought to be speedy and the accused treated fairly and humanely throughout the process; (5) that the only valid purpose of punishment is deterrence, not social revenge; and (6) that incarceration should be used more widely, but at the same time, conditions for those confined must be vastly upgraded and systems of classification developed to prevent haphazardly mixing all types of inmates.

Beccaria had enormous influence on the reformation of criminal justice. For example, he proposed that the courts should mete out punishments to the offender in direct proportion to the harm caused by the crime. To accomplish this, it was necessary that all crimes be classified according to some assessment of their social harm and, further, that the penal codes must prescribe for each crime exact penalties that would be useful deterrents to crime:

> A scale of crimes may be formed of which the first degree should consist of those which immediately tend to the dissolution of society; and the last, of the smallest possible injustice done to a private member of society. Between those extremes will be comprehended all actions contrary to the public good, which are called criminal. . . . Any action which is not comprehended in the above mentioned scale, will not be called a crime, or punished as such.

One need only observe the deliberations of state legislatures today during the process of revising a state's criminal code to understand and appreciate the lasting effect which Beccaria has had on our criminal laws. The arguments and considerations of lawmakers today are, for the most part, still influenced by this concept of the criminal as a rational person who acts as a result of free will on a pleasure-seeking basis. Contemporary punishments prescribed by the law are generally well defined, even though they are administered in a very inexact manner. And the widespread belief that the enactment of laws is the best method of social control clearly has at least some of its intellectual roots in the work of Beccaria.

Several of Beccaria's other ideas have contemporary significance. Perhaps the most notable of these is his assertion that the speed and certainty of punishment, rather than its severity, are the most critical factors in deterrence. The modern criminal justice system, characterized by broad discretion on the part of the police, prosecutors, judges, guards, and parole boards; discrimination against the poor and minorities; court delays and months of pretrial detainment; and the use of plea bargaining, offers neither swiftness nor certainty. Furthermore, Beccaria's advocacy of the humane treatment of incarcerated offenders has certainly never been fully realized. Indeed, many contemporary reformers claim that we have largely replaced corporal punishment with psychological and social persecution.

Jeremy Bentham, a contemporary of Beccaria, was also a major figure in utilitarian social philosophy, and he proposed that all acts must be evaluated so that "the greatest happiness for the greatest number" results. To make such assessments, one would obviously need some method of calculation; Bentham happened to have just such a method. His "felicity calculus" was a superficial, quasi-mathematical attempt to quantify the utility of all conceivable acts. Humorous in retrospect, his attempt to catalogue the almost infinite varieties of behavior was nevertheless understandable, given the uncertainties of the criminal justice system he was attempting to reform.

Bentham's theory of human motivation—that man pursues pleasure and tries to avoid pain—led him to argue that criminal penalties should prescribe a degree of punishment (pain) just sufficient to offset the potential gains (pleasure) of criminal behavior, so that the net result (negative utility) would be deterrence. Bentham further believed that the punishment should "fit the crime," and he generally seemed to favor restitution over physical punishment. Given Bentham's concept of deterrence, punishment in general was regarded as a necessary evil intended to prevent greater harm or evil.

The social control philosophy that characterized classical criminology, then, was based on the assumption that the would-be criminal could be deterred by the threat of punishment if that punishment was swift, certain, appropriate for the offense, and sufficiently unpleasant to offset any potential gains to be realized by committing the act. These principles were advocated by classicists across the entire range of available punishments, whether they involved the loss of money, the loss of freedom, or the loss of life. The impact of classical criminology on the penal codes remains clear, even though in actual practice much of the vagueness and arbitrary abuse of discretion remains problematic.

Despite the anticipated ability to administer the principles of the classical school, the fact was that enforcement and implementation were quite problematic. Especially controversial was the classical position that individual differences and particular situations were irrelevant in assigning responsibility. The focus on the act committed, rather than on any characteristics or qualities of the person, came to be regarded as imprudent as did the practice of treating persons who clearly were incompetent, for various reasons, as competent solely because of commission of a given act. These principles were criticized strongly because

they did not promote justice anywhere except on paper, in an abstract sort of way.

The idealized concept of justice held by the classicists, perhaps best symbolized by the familiar image of a blindfolded Lady Justice holding scales in her hand, was regarded by neoclassical revisionists (1800–1876) as too impersonal and rigid. The classical theorists, in their indignation over the inconsistencies and other inadequacies of the criminal justice system, had overreacted. They had designed a system which was so dispassionate and "objective" that it could not deliver justice to a society of human beings not identical to one another.

The neoclassicists were successful in introducing some modifications of the free will doctrine. Criminological thought was revised to readmit some determinism—not the magical, supernatural determinism of demonology, but rather an awareness that certain factors could operate to impair one's reason and thereby mitigate personal responsibility to an extent. While retaining the essential positions articulated by the classicists, considerations involving individual differences began to appear during the neoclassical period. Age, mental status, physical condition, and other factors which could alter one's ability to discern right from wrong were acknowledged grounds for a decision of partial responsibility.

Far from regarding their views as a general theory of human behavior, the neoclassicists were actually focusing on what they viewed as a small minority of the population. There was no attempt to assert that all persons (not even all criminals) are partially shaped and controlled by deterministic forces. On the contrary, neoclassicists continued to view man as a rational, pleasure-seeking being who was personally responsible for his behavior except in abnormal circumstances or in the case of children who were not old enough to know right from wrong.

The neoclassical revisions outlined above meant that criminology had developed a dominant theoretical perspective that viewed man as essentially rational and behavior as volitional, but allowed for some mitigation of responsibility under certain circumstances. This theoretical framework provided the foundation for many legal systems, including that of the United States. The implications for sentencing and for the criminal justice system included the recognition that a particular sentence could have different effects on different offenders and an awareness that the prison environment could affect the future criminality of the offender. This allowed for much more flexibility than did the classical school in determining the appropriate punishment. Many recent "reforms" in penology, such as probation, parole, suspended sentences, and many programs designed for certain "types" of offenders, would be inconsistent with the classical emphasis on uniformity and certainty of punishment.

DETERMINISM

A book written in 1876 by an Italian psychiatrist was to provide the impetus necessary to shift the focus of criminology from the crime to the criminal. The book was called *The Criminal Man,* and its author was Cesare Lombroso; the result was the development of the "positive school" in criminology. Lacking the moralistic tones of the earliest positivist, Auguste Comte, Lombroso's approach was clearly Darwinian, focusing on biological determinism.

As the title of his classic book implies, Lombroso believed that there was indeed a criminal type, or "born criminal," who was discernibly different from noncriminals in physical ways. In short, he was convinced that criminals bore bodily stigmata which marked them as a separate class of people. Following Darwin's monumental work by less than two decades, Lombrosian theory postulated that criminals had not fully evolved but were, instead, inferior organisms reminiscent of apelike, preprimitive man, incapable of adapting to modern civilization. Specifically, Lombroso described the criminal as "atavistic" (a concept used earlier by Darwin) in that the criminal was physically characteristic of a lower phylogenetic level. From his extensive physical measurements, autopsy findings, and other observations, Lombroso concluded that criminals disproportionately possessed an asymmetrical cranium, prognathism (excessive jaw), eye defects, oversized ears, prominent cheekbones, abnormal palate, receding forehead, sparse beard, woolly hair, long arms, abnormal dentition, twisted nose, fleshy and swollen lips, and inverted sex organs. He also noted such nonphysical anomalies as a lack of morality, excessive vanity, cruelty, and tattooing.

It would be misleading to imply that Lombroso held firmly to the idea that his was the sole explanation for crime. While continuing to believe that his theory explained part of the

difference between criminals and noncriminals, Lombroso ultimately accepted environmental and other factors as equally valid contributing causes of crime.

While positivism, since Lombroso's day, has taken in a lot of intellectual territory, there remains a unifying framework that is visible in the work of his successors. That general framework consists of the following:

1. A general rejection of metaphysical and speculative approaches;

2. Denial of the "free will" conception of man and substitution of a "deterministic" model;

3. A clear distinction between science and law, on one hand, and morals, on the other;

4. The application, as far as practicable, of the scientific method.

These principles of positivism have been applied to the study of the criminal from various and diverse theoretical perspectives. Although these perspectives differ in significant ways, they retain the essence of positivism as described above. The theories to be discussed range from purely individualistic approaches to more macrolevel, sociological theories.

The "Italian School"

The origins of positivism in criminology have a decidedly Italian character. Besides Lombroso, the other Italian pioneers in this school of thought were Enrico Ferri and Raffaele Garofalo. Although emphasizing different points as critical in the study of the criminal, both Ferri and Garofalo were adamant in their espousal of, and adherence to, the positivist approach.

Enrico Ferri, a pupil of Lombroso, is perhaps best known for his classification of criminals as insane, born, occasional, habitual, and drawn to criminality as a result of passion. This topology of offenders represented an attempt by Ferri to conceptualize in anthropological categories the continuum of criminality. He believed that the differences between categories were differences of degree and of the danger represented for society.

The third member of the "Italian school," Raffaele Garofalo, attempted to construct a universal definition of crime—one that would be based on the concept of "natural crime," or acts that offend the basic moral sentiments of pity (a revulsion against the voluntary infliction of suffering on others) and probity (respect for the property rights of others). Garofalo's approach to the crime problem was primarily psychological and legal. He perceived some criminals as psychological degenerates who were morally unfit. His background as a jurist led him to advocate reforms in the criminal justice system so that the criminal could be dealt with in a manner more in line with his theory. Garofalo believed that the criminal must be eliminated, citing Darwin's observations on the functions of biological adaptation as a rationale for this "remedy." Since, according to this bio-organismic analogy, the criminal was one who had not adapted to civilized life, Garofalo saw only three alternatives—all of which involved some type of elimination: (1) death, where there is a permanent psychological defect; (2) partial elimination for those suitable to live only in a more primitive environment, including long-term or life imprisonment, transportation, and relatively mild isolation; and (3) enforced reparation, for those whose crimes were committed as a result of the press of circumstances.

Physical-Biological Theories

The prototype for all physical-biological theories of crime was the early (and nonpositivist) craniologists-phrenologists, who believed that the "faculties of the mind" were revealed by the external shape of the skull. This vastly oversimplified and pseudoscientific approach nevertheless predates all other theories of a physical-biological nature.

Such theories have grown increasingly sophisticated and scientific since those earliest attempts to explain man's function by analyzing his cranial structure. In addition to the Italian school, there have been a number of other intellectual contributions to this physical-biological tradition.

Charles Goring has been widely credited with refuting Lombroso's contention that there is a criminal "physical type." However, Goring's critique was aimed at Lombroso's methodology, not necessarily his theory or his conclusions, for which Goring had a certain affinity. In Goring's famous book, *The English Convict,* he presented an analysis of 3,000 English convicts, and as a matter of fact, he did find what he regarded as a positive association between certain physical differences and the offender's crime and social class. As Mannheim noted,

> In the controversy "heredity or environment," . . . he was on Lombroso's side, and perhaps even more than the latter he was inclined to underrate environmental influences: "Crime is only to a trifling extent (if to any) the product of social inequalities, of adverse environment or of other manifestations of . . . the force of circumstances."

Goring's general interpretation of the height and weight deficiencies of the criminal population he studied was that the criminal suffered from hereditary inferiority. He also believed that criminals were most different from noncriminals with respect to their intelligence, which he found to be defective. Finally, Goring added a third category—that of moral defectiveness—to account for those whose criminality could not be explained by either of the first two factors. But the main thrust of Goring's theoretical position was a physiological one, thus placing him within this tradition of thought.

Not everyone agreed that Goring's criticisms of Lombroso's methodology were valid. The leading skeptic was Earnest Hooton, an anthropologist at Harvard University. In *The American Criminal,* Hooton presented data and interpretations based on a 12-year study of 13,873 criminals and 3,203 noncriminals. After analyzing 107 physical characteristics, Hooton concluded that criminals, when compared with the control group, were "organically inferior." Describing their distinctive characteristics, he included low foreheads, high pinched nasal roots, compressed faces, and narrow jaws. These he cited as evidence for his assertion of organic inferiority, and he attributed crime to "the impact of environment upon low grade human organisms."

Hooton also constructed a topology of criminals based on physical constitution. He argued that murderers and robbers tended to be tall and thin; tall, heavy men were most likely to be killers and to commit forgery and fraud as well; undersized men were disposed to commit assault, rape, and other sex crimes; and men lacking any notable physical characteristics had no criminal specialty. The primary problem with all of this is that Hooton had considered only the offender's *current* crime, whereas in fact, half or more of Hooton's prisoners had previously been imprisoned for an offense *other than* that noted by Hooton.

Studies by Ernst Kretschmer and William Sheldon are typical of the work of more recent proponents of the constitutional inferiority-body type theorists. Although differing in the details of their approaches, both men advocated the idea that body type and temperament are closely related. Both developed topologies relating body types to certain forms of behavior, including crime.

Some investigators have focused specifically on the effects of heredity, especially genetic deficiencies, in producing criminality. In this regard, the studies of "criminal families" were quite interesting. Perhaps the most well-known efforts along these genealogical lines were those of Richard Dugdale and Henry Goddard, both of whom attempted to analyze the apparently excessive criminality of entire families by relating it to feeblemindedness. The term *mental testers* has often been applied to this method of inquiry.

More recently, another line of inquiry has focused on the criminality of twins. Lange, Rosanoff, Christiansen, and others have studied twins in an attempt to determine the effect of heredity in producing criminality. The basic idea has been that if a greater percentage of monozygotic ("identical") twins than of dizygotic ("fraternal") twins are concordant in being criminal, that is, if they are both criminal, then the effect of heredity would, theoretically at least, have to be given greater weight than other factors. Although the methodological criticisms aimed at Rosanoff have been less damaging than those directed at Lange, the fact remains that neither study can be regarded as conclusive in finding that identical twins are far more likely to be concordant in terms of criminality.

Finally, some of the most sophisticated research employing a physical-biological model has been focused on the neuroendocrine system. The essential proposition of these theories has been that criminal behavior is often due to emotional disturbances produced by glandular imbalance. Often using the electroencephalogram (EEG) as a diagnostic aid, this biochemical approach to crime thus far offers more promise than clear-cut and unequivocal findings.

Psychopathology

A number of positivist theories of crime have used the paradigm based on individual psychopathology. The father of this approach was, of course, Sigmund Freud. His work, along with that of his intellectual successors, has focused on man's unconscious. The explanation for criminal behavior which grew out of this approach was that such behavior is largely the result of drives which are uncontrolled because of a defective personality structure. There are a seemingly endless number of applications of psychoanalytic theory to crime. Conditions such as psychosis and neurosis have been related to criminal behavior by psychoanalysts, as have most forms of deviant behavior. The essential contention of the psychoanalytic approach is that all behavior is purposive and meaningful. Such behavior is viewed as the symbolic release of repressed mental conflict. From this perspective, the criminal is one who acts not out of free will, as the classicists believed, but as an expression of deterministic forces of a subconscious nature. Such a view, of course, leads to a theory of social control based on a clinical model of therapeutic rehabilitation.

A derivation of the psychoanalytic approach and the "mental testers" has been the emphasis on personality deviation as an explanation for crime. Relying on theoretical constructs of the "healthy" personality and the "abnormal" personality, the personality deviation approach has become increasingly popular, though not well validated. Using psychological tests such as the Rorschach, the Wechsler Adult Intelligence Scale, the Minnesota Multiphasic Personality Inventory, the Thematic Apperception Test, and many others, psychologists have led in this attempt to construct causal theory. Advocates of this approach generally attempt to diagnose the psychopathological features of one's personality and then focus on these "target areas" using a variety of interventions.

Economic Factors

The effects of economic inequality are undeniably instrumental in producing great variability in one's "life chances." The pervasive day-to-day realities of poverty limit the chances of millions of people in securing adequate health care, housing, education, jobs, and opportunities. The crippling effects of poverty can hardly be comprehended by those not confronted with them on a daily basis. For these and related reasons, some theorists have attempted to relate at least some crimes to economic inequality. Such a theoretical position has had a special attraction for Marxists.

Historically, the most extensive application of Marxist theory to criminology was provided by Willem Bonger. The central argument Bonger made is that capitalism, more than any other system of economic exchange, is characterized by the control of the means of production by relatively few people, with the vast majority of the population totally deprived of these means. The economic subjugation of the masses, he argues, stifles men's "social instincts" and leads to unlimited egoism, insensitivity, and a spirit of domination on the part of the powerful, and the poor are subjected to all sorts of pathogenic conditions: bad housing, constant association with "undesirables," uncertain physical security, terrible poverty, frequent sickness, and unemployment. Bonger maintained that the historical condition of this class of people was severely damaged by these conditions of economic subjugation. He attempted to demonstrate connections between certain types of crime (e.g., prostitution, alcoholism, and theft) and economic inequality. This explanation of crime suggests that the socioeconomic system is causally related to crime and would have to be restructured to reduce crime.

Although Bonger did not deny the influence of hereditary traits, he attributed no causal power to them in the absence of criminogenic environmental conditions. Throughout most of his writings, he stressed a socioeconomic view of crime and attacked the views of Lombroso and others of a physical-biological persuasion. His deterministic approach, along with his application of quantitative methods and his rejection of metaphysical, speculative "explanations" for crime, places Bonger in the positivist school, even though his primary focus was on the social structure, rather than the individual. Bonger's theory, which illustrates the economic approach to criminal etiology, is quite near the sociological approach in many ways, especially in its macro level focus on the structure of society.

Sociological Explanations

The economic depression of the 1930s and the social problems which accompanied it helped further an interest in socioeconomic factors related to crime. Not only the economic condition of the nation but also the seemingly disorganized condition of many areas of major American cities were causes for great concern on the part of those seeking explanations for crime. The so-called Chicago school dominated criminological thought for a number of years, focusing on a social disorganization model. Specifically, this school of thought held that the interstitial areas of our major cities (heavily populated at the time by immigrants) reflected a high degree of sociocultural heterogeneity. This, they believed, resulted in a breakdown in social organization and norms, which made deviant behavior much more commonplace. Using analogies based on plant ecology, the Chicago school believed that rapid social change in "natural areas" of the city was undermining the basic social controls of a stable cultural heritage.

The theoretical successor to the Chicago school and its social disorganization approach was the culture conflict perspective, best articulated by Thorsten Sellin. The essential contention of culture conflict theory is that crime results from the absence of one clear-cut, consensual model of normative behavior. The increasing conflict in norms that came with immigration and the rapid pluralization of our society provided the most fertile ground for culture conflict theory. Although still applicable in nations with significant levels of immigration (such as Israel), it has largely been replaced in the United States by other perspectives.

There have been several sociological theories of cultural transmission, each of which has stressed different dynamics. One, known generally as "subcultural theory," had its general intellectual origins in the work of Emile Durkheim, but was initially applied in the United States by Robert Merton. For Merton, the explanation for crime rested in the disjunction existing for many between culturally defined success goals and the institutionalized means available to meet those goals. For some, this discrepancy results in criminal behavior, according to Merton.

Elaborations of this same general statement were made later by Albert Cohen, who saw the subculture which developed from this disjunction as a negative one that attempted to invert society's success goals and create its own, more realistic goals; and by Richard Cloward and Lloyd Ohlin, who added the idea that illegitimate, as well as legitimate, opportunity structures were differentially accessible to individuals and that one could become either a criminal or a respected citizen, depending on which means were available.

Walter Miller offered an alternative view of the lower-class subculture. He saw it as essentially characterized by its own value system and goals, not perpetually seeking to emulate the higher strata to gain status. Crime, for Miller, was a function of the normal socialization occurring in the subculture.

Another type of cultural transmission theory is that of Edwin Sutherland. Known as differential association theory, it is essentially a learning theory suggestive of the earlier work of Gabriel Tarde, a French social psychologist.

Sutherland's theory was later modified by Daniel Glaser to take into account the perceived effect of the mass media and other methods of transmitting culture. Glaser's differential identification theory substituted for Sutherland's required personal interaction the following definition of the dynamics:

> A person pursues criminal behavior to the extent that he identifies himself with real or imaginary persons from whose perspective his criminal behavior seems acceptable.

The foregoing presentation of positivism has been intended to provide an overview of the various types of theories comprising this school. No attempt has been made to be exhaustive, but merely illustrative. Numerous other theoretical and empirical contributions could have been discussed; however, the above provide a representative sampling of positivist thought. Unlike either the demonologists of the preclassical period or the classical advocates of a free will, rational view of man, the positivists' concepts of causation were deterministic and antimetaphysical. Therefore, their theories of social control have also been vastly different. They have advocated change—change of the personality, of the economic system, of the social system. Each of the positivist perspectives on crime developed its own ideas of how to deal with the crime problem, and these "solutions" were, of course, of a physical-biological, psychiatric-psychological, or social-economic nature. Their effect on penal policy is perhaps best symbolized in the name changes of our prisons—from "penitentiaries" to "correctional institutions."

But positivism is not the final chapter of this story. More recent theoretical developments have tended to concentrate on crime as a phenomenon which is determined by factors such as societal reaction (labeling), a system of laws which disproportionately reflects the interests of the wealthy and the powerful, and/or a corrupt and corrupting political system which is itself viewed as producing crime and criminals.

THE NEW EMPHASIS: "THE SYSTEM"

If positivism shifted society's focus from the crime to the criminal, then clearly that focus has shifted again with the development of the labeling and conflict perspectives, and especially with the emergence of a "radical" criminology perspective in the United States. While these theories differ substantially in their interpretations of crime, one central feature which they have in common is their emphasis on the social and political systems as factors which help to generate the crime problem. Frequently, "the system" is identified as the "cause" of crime because of its unequal distribution of social and political power. Increasingly, the criminal is viewed as a victim—a victim of class struggle, racial discrimination, and other manifestations of inequality.

While there is, to be certain, some continuity between these relatively recent theories and some earlier sociological and economic perspectives, the general thrust of these new explanations is quite different. Most important, there is a much more pervasive political emphasis in current theoretical perspectives.

Labeling, Conflict, and Radical Perspectives

The labeling or "social reaction" approach to crime is reflected in the works of Becker, Lemert, Erikson, Kitsuse, and Schur. This approach represents a significant departure from the absolute determinism of the positivists. The essence of labeling theory is its assertion that crime is relative and is defined (and thus *created*) socially. The often-quoted statement of Howard Becker perhaps best sums up the approach:

> *Social groups create deviance by making the rules whose infraction constitutes deviance,* and by applying those rules to particular people and labeling them as outsiders. From this point of view, deviance is *not* a quality of the act the person commits, but rather a consequence of the application by others of rules and sanctions to an "offender." The deviant is one to whom that label has successfully been applied; deviant behavior is behavior that people so label.

The labeling approach clearly shifts the focus of inquiry from the individual being labeled and processed to the group and the system doing the labeling and processing.

Finally, recent contributions to what has been called "radical" or "critical" or "Marxist" criminology include Richard Quinney, Ian Taylor, Paul Walton, Jock Young, Anthony Platt, Barry Krisberg, and Herman and Julia Schwendinger. While there are some theoretical differences among these writers, they occupy common intellectual ground within this overview of the development of criminological theory. Their analysis of crime and social control, essentially Marxist in nature, is to be distinguished from the applications of conflict theory to criminology made by Austin Turk and other non-Marxian conflict theorists, as well as the positivist approach taken by the formal Marxist Willem Bonger.

The "radical Marxist" criminologists focus their analysis on the state as a political system controlled by the interests of the "ruling capitalist class," especially through the use of law as a tool to preserve existing inequalities. Much of the work of these theorists deals with the historical conditions of classes, which they link, theoretically, with the development and differential enforcement of criminal law. They reject the traditional (functionalist) view that law reflects society's consensus on the norms and values which should control behavior; instead, they argue that law emerges from a conflict of competing interests and serves the interests of the elite "ruling class."

Turk, on the other hand, essentially continues the intellectual tradition of Ralf Dahrendoff and other non-Marxist conflict theorists who have analyzed crime as a result of conflict concerning the distribution of power and authority within society. Rather than isolating the economic system and the class structure related to it, this perspective takes a broader view of the structural factors which produce conflict.

The implications of these perspectives for a philosophy of social control and for the criminal justice system are dramatically different from those suggested by earlier theorists. Again, the centrality of the political dimension is inescapable, whether one is discussing labeling theory, conflict theory, or "radical Marxist" theory. The labeling perspective, which emphasizes the discrepancy between actual criminal behavior and officially detected crime, is a societal reaction theory. It is not the deviance itself that is so important, but the way in which society reacts.

This perspective generally is interpreted as advocating less intervention and less labeling of people as "criminal." The criminal justice system is viewed as one which exacerbates the problem of crime; therefore, that system should be reduced and made less powerful.

Conflict and radical Marxist theory also would suggest that there is a need for societal restructuring. However, from these perspectives, the criminal justice system merely reflects broader structural arrangements (i.e., the economy, the class system, and/or the distribution of power and authority). Radical Marxists advocate the abolition of capitalism and the development of a socialist society. They tend to view anything less than that as piecemeal "liberal tinkering" with a fatally flawed system. The alternative conflict view would argue that the particular economic system (e.g., capitalism) is not the basic problem and that crime exists in noncapitalist states as well. Crime is viewed as a structural problem resulting from the distribution of power and authority and as a reflection of unstable relationships between legal authorities and subjects.

In conclusion, it should be apparent that while man's attempts to explain crime have covered a tremendous range of ideas, there are parallels among these ideas. The idea that crime is a result of demonic possession is perhaps not a great deal different than the "mental illness" explanation advanced at a much later point in history. Both are largely deterministic, even though one is "magical" and the other "scientific."

Similarly, the rationales cited by the state for the use of imprisonment have varied from "moral reform" to "deterrence" to "rehabilitation," "public protection," and "punishment." Meanwhile, the perceptions of those imprisoned by the state have also changed, from passive acceptance of society's reaction to the increasing tendency to view themselves as "political prisoners" of an unjust legal and political system. It is apparent, therefore, that the linkage between theories of crime and social control philosophies must be evaluated on two levels: (1) the connections between theoretical explanations and formal policies, and (2) the changing rationales for employing essentially similar social control practices (e.g., "punitive" imprisonment vs. "therapeutic" correctional rehabilitation).

SOURCE: From *Crime and the Criminal Justice Process* (pp. 208–220) by C. R. Huff, 1978, Dubuque, Iowa: Kendall Hunt Publishing Company. Edited by J. Inciardi and K. Haas. Copyright © 1978 by Kendall Hunt Publishing Company. Reprinted by permission of James A. Inciardi.

QUESTIONS FOR DISCUSSION AND WRITING

1. Why were offenders often executed in "primitive" societies?

2. What are six tenets advocated by Beccaria?

3. What assumption underlies classical criminology?

PART II

HOW DO WE VIEW CRIME?

Images of Crime, Criminality, and Criminal Justice

It is always interesting for the student of criminology to listen to news broadcasts, to read the newspapers and magazines, or to listen to friends, family, or others when the topic is crime. The interest lies in the sometimes considerable distance between widely held perceptions about crime and the reality of crime revealed in criminological research. For instance, everyone knows that for several years, crime has been spiraling upward, a perception that has caused much hand-wringing among both the media and the public. But the available evidence portrays a different reality. Crime rates fluctuated between the mid-1970s and the 1990s, and in fact, the general crime trend has been fairly flat or downward until only very recently. Now, in the middle of the first decade of the twenty-first century, some data suggest that crime may again be increasing. While most criminologists are cautious about interpreting these small increases as meaningful, others are convinced that they are real and are not hesitating to offer the media their pet explanation for these perceived increases.

Another widely held view of crime is expressed as "crime is everywhere and anyone can become a victim." Technically, this statement is true; it is hard to imagine anyone who is completely free of possible victimization. The statement is also misleading. It is used to argue that the nature of crime and victimization has changed dramatically, so that people, neighborhoods, and communities that used to be safe (generally those of higher socioeconomic status) are now in danger. Again, this assertion is inconsistent with what we know about crime: Research, both old and new, indicates that the nature of crime has not really changed much. Those most likely to be the victims of crime tend to be like those who commit crimes, and they tend to live in the neighborhoods that have higher rates of crime and victimization.

"We have crime problems in America because we are soft on crime." Every reader has heard this statement from a politician in a recent election campaign. However, we cannot tell you that most criminologists would disagree with this assertion, or that the gulf between perception and reality is wide and clearly visible. This statement has provoked interesting and sometimes heated conversations among criminologists. Combatants on both sides of the debate agree, however, that the "soft on crime" argument is overly simplistic and hides important complexities that need to receive more attention in our public discourse about crime and punishment.

The point is that perceptions about crime and criminals do not always fit the facts. Even incorrect or inaccurate perceptions are important because they affect how people behave in daily life, in making important choices such as where to live or go to school, or for whom to vote. In this section, there are four articles that bear on perceptions of crime and criminal justice. The first two articles in this section, by Zimring and Humphries, challenge strongly held assumptions about crime and criminals. The third article, by Weitzer and Kubrin, considers how the media shape our perceptions of crime. In the final piece in this section, Beckett and Sasson show how politics have shaped criminal justice policy.

Zimring's piece is in response to assertions by some criminologists and some in government that the U.S. is experiencing an epidemic of youth violence. This belief, no doubt, has fueled some "get tough on kid criminals" policies and "reforms" of the juvenile courts (frequently to extend punishments and have more juveniles face adult courts and punishments). The public has clamored for holding "predatory juveniles" and gang members more responsible for their criminal conduct. In most cities, news reports have carried disturbing stories of drive-by shootings and random acts of juvenile violence. Nationally, the killing of their parents by two California boys held the public's attention, and the death of a little girl in Florida at the hands of a teenager who was practicing "wrestling moves" convinces many that children today are different and that something drastic needs to be done. What Zimring reports, though, is that while arrests for violent crimes by juveniles have increased, the best evidence indicates that most of those arrests have been for less serious crimes. Students should ask, What do these empirical patterns mean for juvenile justice policy and our concerns about violence epidemics? They should also ask whether increased arrest rates are due more to actual violations or are a result of police and criminal justice policy changes.

Societies frequently fear that the latest scourge, whether medical (the plague or HIV/AIDS) or social (crime or drug use), is certainly more dangerous that those that have come before. The invention of crack cocaine as a method of delivering an intense yet relatively inexpensive cocaine high to users created a number of new social problems; an important one was crack-addicted babies who, we were told, suffered a number of problems beyond their addictions. Humphries' piece, "Realities and Images of Crack Mothers," was taken from her book *Crack Mothers: Pregnancy, Drugs, and the Media*. She carefully examines media portrayals of this problem and the empirical realities for women and their children. Again, the popular belief frequently runs counter to reality. The crack cocaine scourge certainly has presented major crime and other social problems for people and communities, but students should consider how much more effective our efforts at helping the cocaine addicted, their families, and communities might be if we could react to the realities rather than just the images of problems.

The next piece in this section is by one of the editors of this volume and her colleague Ron Weitzer. They examine the role that the media play in creating public fear of crime. Fear is not just, or even primarily, about our actual risk of criminal victimization, but rather it is a consequence of our perceptions about crime and criminals. Weitzer and Kubrin examine how the national media, including national and local television news, newspapers, and the Internet, influence public fear of crime. Students should pay close and critical attention to how crime and criminal justice policies are discussed in both local and national media. How might these presentations help or hurt our ability to have realistic views about crime, victimization, and about our communities?

In "The Politics of Crime," Beckett and Sasson focus on how political discourse has led to changes in criminal law and criminal justice policy. They document how changes in political climate and carefully selected election strategies have been more influential than actual crime rates in determining criminal justice policy and practices. Beckett and Sasson remind us that we should be critical consumers of political discourse, and not just at election time. Who argues for policy changes, and what are their motivations? These questions should be asked regularly by the general public, but especially by students of criminology.

Criminologists may not have conclusive answers to the questions raised by these articles. But the studies, the results they report, and the questions they leave us with make a convincing case for the importance of studying both the realities and perceptions of the crime problem.

 For a data analysis exercise that accompanies the material in this section, go to www.sagepub.com/crimereadings3study.

A YOUTH VIOLENCE EPIDEMIC

Myth or Reality?

FRANKLIN E. ZIMRING

Current concerns about youth violence policy have been driven by interpretations of official statistics on youth arrests. Arrest statistics have been quoted as proof of substantial increases in the violence attributable to young offenders. These statistics have then been used as evidence that a new and more vicious breed of juvenile offender is the reason for the increase in arrests. Finally, predictions about future rates of youth violence have been based on projecting recent trends many years in the future.

This [article] is an analysis of recent trends in arrest statistics. The first section examines trends in the four Part I or Index offenses of violence over the period 1980–1996. The second section focuses on youth arrests for homicide, concluding that the increase noted in this category is attributable to increases in gun violence. The third section shows that arrests for aggravated assault—the largest growth category since 1980—may be the result of changes in police practices and reporting standards. A concluding section addresses the implications of the statistical patterns revealed in this [article] in projecting rates of youth crime.

A GENERAL TREND?

The only official statistics that provide age-specific patterns are police data on arrests. These are the statistics that have been the basis for predictions of a coming wave of youth violence. Figure 1 combines national-level data on arrests under age of 18 with census-based data on age to present trends on arrest rates per 100,000 youths aged 13 to 17 for homicide, rape, aggravated assault, and robbery. For each offense, the arrest rate per 100,000 in 1980 is expressed as a baseline level of 100, and each succeeding year's arrest rate is expressed as a percentage of that figure. This graph shows trends in all four offense categories most directly.

The estimates generated in Figure 1 express the number of arrests over the entire population of 13- to 17-year-olds despite the fact that the percentage of the U.S. population in reporting agencies varies and is never 100 percent. Thus the rates derived are an index of trends rather than a precise rate.

Two of the four offenses show pronounced trends over time—homicide and aggravated assault. The largest movements over time are noted for homicide, for which the arrest rate first dropped by just under 40 percent in the early 1980s and then began a sustained climb after 1984. The peak rate in 1993 was more than double the 1980 level. Then homicide arrests dropped sharply; the 1996 rate was 34 percent above that in 1980. The arrest level for aggravated assault did not drop much in the early 1980s and then increased slowly from 1985 to 1988. Large one-year

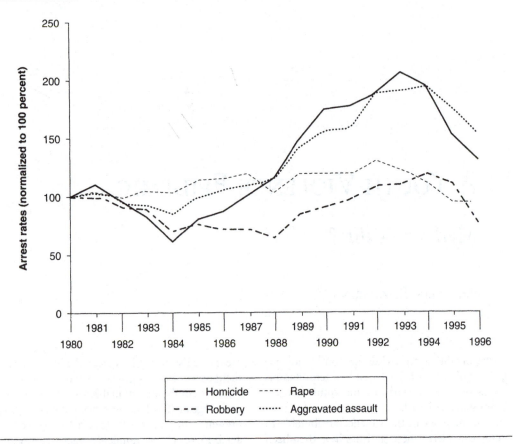

FIGURE 1   Arrest Rates for Offenders, Ages 13–17, for Four Violent Offenses, 1980–1996

SOURCE: U.S. Department of Justice, Federal Bureau of Investigation (1980–1993, 1994a, 1995–1996).

jumps in 1989 and again in 1992 raised the level to nearly double the 1980 rate. The rate declined by 20 percent over the two years after its 1994 peak, but arrests for aggravated assault stayed 56 percent above the 1980 level, by far the largest increase in the four violent crimes.

Trends in rape and robbery arrests over the 1980s and early 1990s were much less pronounced. Rape arrests never dropped lower than their 1980 baseline during the early 1980s, when homicide and assault declined. Rape arrest rates increased after 1988, reaching a high 32 percent above the 1980 level in 1992, but dropped back by 1996 to the lowest rate recorded at any time since 1977.

Robbery arrest trends differ from the others in two respects. While arrest rates for other violent crimes went up after 1984, robbery arrests declined in six of the first eight years of the 1980s and reached their lowest level of the 1980s in 1988. From 1988 to 1994, the arrest rates

increased but were never more than 20 percent above the 1980 baseline. The 1995 rate dropped to 13 percent above the 1980 rate, and the 1996 arrest rate fell another 34 percent. By 1996, the robbery arrest rate was reported at 21 percent below the 1980 level.

There are three notable elements in the aggregate pattern reported Figure 1. First, there is no common pattern for youth arrests for violent crime during the 1980–1996 period. The rate change over the 16-year period ranges from –21 percent for robbery to +56 percent for aggravated assault. Homicide, which had the highest increase as recently as 1993, recorded a 34 percent gain by the end of 1996. The four different offenses are thus four different statistical stories.

The second major conclusion is that youth violence arrest rates usually do not run up or down in long cycles. In a period that was supposed to be noteworthy because of its sustained upward trends, only three times did the arrest rate go in the same direction for an offense for more than three consecutive years. Two of the four offenses of violence were essentially trendless over the 16 years in the aggregate.

The third important characteristic is that the arrest rate often changes substantially in a short time. Over the 16 year-to-year transitions in Figure 1, homicide rates increased or decreased by over 20 percent in four years and over 15 percent a total of seven times. Aggravated assault rates recorded one-year increases of 34 percent, 19 percent, and 17 percent in the 16 year-to-year changes. The volatility of trends in arrests means that rates of offenses—which cannot be predicted—are much more important elements of future youth crime volume than population levels—which can be predicted. With large differences in rates, changes in the youth population can be expected to play a relatively minor independent role in determining the volume of youth violence.

All of the statistical features just discussed warn us that long-range predictions about the volume of youth violence are error-prone. Offense rates are far less predictable than the size of the youth population but also much more important in determining the volume of serious violence. Assuming that any trend will continue for long is foolhardy, given the cyclical nature of youth violence. There is at least as much difference between trends in the different violent offenses as there is similarity, so that projections of trends in a single aggregation of youth violence are demonstrably erroneous.

What Figure 1 shows is that rape and robbery arrests have varied substantially over the period since 1980, but there is no evidence of an underlying trend—either up or down—in the incidence of arrests over the 16 years. This removes these two offenses from further consideration in exploring the central concern of this [article]— the assessment and explanation of trends over time. Since there is no trend, there is no reason to project any trend forward.

Homicide rates in 1996 are one-third higher than in 1980. Despite the cyclical fluctuations throughout the period, this seems sufficient ground to investigate whether a change in rate has occurred and, if so, its likely explanation. This is the task of the next section. Aggravated assault levels, which increased by more than half over the period 1980–1996, are the subject of the third section. As the following two sections

show, the trends in homicide and assault are quite different in origin and policy significance.

PATTERNS OF YOUTH HOMICIDE

Figure 2 shows trends in homicide arrest rates for offenders 13 to 17 and over 18 over the two decades from 1976 to 1995. The two arrest rates move together, first up and then down, in the first decade, but then the under-18 rate takes off from 1985–1993 in a pattern that diverges from the homicide arrests in the stable, older age group.

The most important reason for the sharp escalation in homicide was an escalating volume of fatal attacks with firearms, as shown in Figure 3. The top line is the rate of homicides by all means tied to the arrest of at least one offender under 18. The bottom line is the number of arrests for homicides committed with all weapons other than guns, including knives, blunt objects, and personal force. The most important characteristic of the bottom line is flatness. There are minor fluctuations and no trend over time.

The middle line shows trends in arrests for homicides committed with guns, with each death that resulted in one or more arrests counted only once. Almost all of the variance during the years of the increase in total homicides was in gun cases, as was the decrease in total homicides in the early 1980s. The origins of this pattern are a puzzle. The proportion of homicides committed with guns did not increase among adults, so no general increase in handgun availability seems to explain the sharp increase in youth shootings.

That homicide increases are only gun cases has two important implications. First, it would require only a small number of attacks to change the death statistics during the 1985–1992 period. Because gunshot wounds are deadly, a relatively small number of woundings can produce a relatively large number of killings. My early studies in Chicago found a ratio of nonfatal gunshot wounds to fatalities of about 7 to 1, in contrast to a knife ratio of about 35 to 1. Both numbers are undercounts because many more nonfatal woundings also go undetected. But an extra 1,700 gun killings should produce only 10,000 to 15,000 extra gun-wound cases in the aggravated assault statistics, a small percentage of the total under-18 volume.

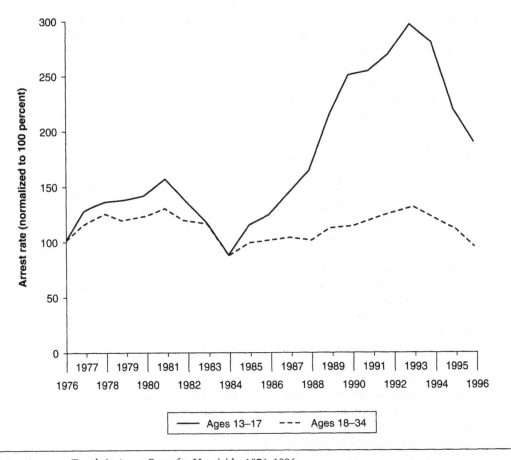

FIGURE 2   Trends in Arrest Rates for Homicide, 1976–1996

SOURCE: U.S. Department of Justice, Federal Bureau of Investigation (1976–1993, 1994a, 1995–1996).

Because the homicide patterns suggest that only gun assaults increased after 1985 (there were no additional nongun killings), the number of additional assault cases one would expect would be minimal, less than a 10 percent increase in all aggravated assaults, and all of these would be gun cases. But that is not what happened. The number of aggravated assault cases grew faster even than homicides after 1985. The fact that only gun homicides increased transforms the large increase in under-18 aggravated assaults into a mystery. If the increase in homicides had been distributed across all weapons, we would have expected an increase in assaults as large as the increase in homicides.

The second implication of the guns-only pattern is that the hardware used in many attacks seems to be the major explanation for the expanding rate rather than any basic change in the youth population involved in the assaults.

Every time there is an increase in youth violence, there is worry that a new, more vicious type of juvenile offender is the cause. The guns-only pattern of Figure 3 is quite strong circumstantial evidence against the proposition that a violent new breed is a general phenomenon, for three reasons. First, the sharp increase in gun use provides a clear alternative explanation for the higher number of killings by youths. It has long been thought that greater use of firearms in attacks can increase the death rate from violence independent of variations in intent because guns are more dangerous. This so-called instrumentality effect would explain a substantial increase in homicides without resorting to changes in the motivations or scruples of young offenders if they are willing to use guns in attacks. The second reason the gun-only pattern does not support a theory of a violent new breed of offender is that so few young attackers are involved in the switch

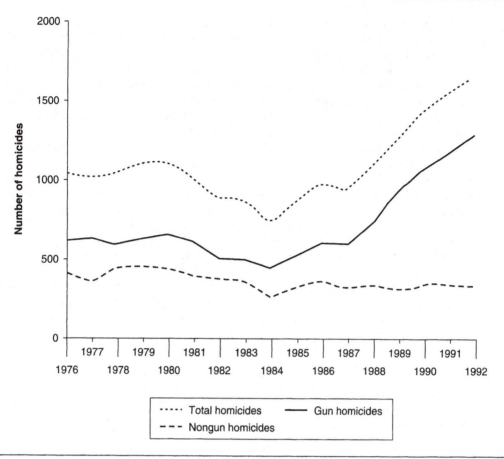

FIGURE 3   Number of Gun, Nongun, and Total Homicides by Offenders, Ages 10–17, 1976–1992

SOURCE: U.S. Department of Justice, Federal Bureau of Investigation (1994b).

to guns. At most, the shooters are 20,000 or so of the under-18 population arrested for violence. If there is a "new breed" of offender, it would have to be found only among that narrow band of firearms wounders. Third, the great majority of assaults has stayed the same over the past two decades. Knives are universally available, and are the next most deadly weapon to firearms. Yet the rate of killings with knives remained stable over the eight-year expansion in total homicides. If more destructive intentions were the major cause of rate changes in homicide, some of the increase in the death rate should be found in the category of knives and other cutting instruments.

THE GROWTH OF ASSAULT ARRESTS

The task here is to restate and explore the mystery in the previous discussion. Because the growth of homicides was restricted to gun cases, there is no reason to expect a large increase in the volume of aggravated assault cases over the years when homicides increased. If all forms of homicide double, one expects all forms of aggravated assault to double as well. If only gun homicides double, only aggravated assaults with guns should double, and the total serious assault rate should increase by less than 20 percent. Instead, the aggravated assault rate nearly doubled at its peak rate in 1991 and then declined at a slower pace than homicide. Is this evidence that a broad cross-section of adolescents was engaging in many types of serious assaults, not limited to the gun cases? If so, why was there no increase in homicides by other means?

From a policy and planning perspective, sorting out the meaning of the expansion in aggravated assault arrests is quite important. If only homicides have increased, the number of cases is quite small. A 20 percent increase in aggravated assaults for gun assault cases is still less than a quarter of the total case increase that occurs if the true rate of youth assault doubled to a peak and fell back only 22 percent from that peak. So if the growth in aggravated assault arrests reflects the magnitude of the true growth in the volume of serious adolescent violence, the problem is much broader than an analysis of the homicide statistics would suggest.

There have been indications for some time that observers should be cautious in taking evidence about trends in youth violence from fluctuations in aggravated assault arrest levels. Twenty years ago, I was tempted to label a section on trends in police arrests for this offense "the aggravations of aggravated assault" because increases in arrest rates for this offense did not always occur when homicide rates were increasing. How assaults are counted and classified is essentially a matter of police discretion.

Changing police standards can have a huge impact on statistical trends. For the period since 1980, there is significant circumstantial evidence from many sources that changing police thresholds for when assault should be recorded and when the report should be for aggravated assault are the reason for most of the growth in arrest rates.

The first evidence that reclassification is a major factor comes from arrest rates for adults. It turns out that trends over time in assault arrests for older offenders have been strikingly similar to those noted for younger offenders. But the older group experienced declines in homicide arrests over the period, so it does not seem likely that this age group is increasing in its true rate of life-threatening violence.

Figure 4 shows rates of aggravated assault arrests by year from 1980 to 1995 for 13- to 17-year-olds and for those 25 to 34. The 25-to-34 age group is the youngest population group

FIGURE 4   Trends in Arrest Rates for Aggravated Assault, 1980–1995

SOURCE: U.S. Department of Justice, Federal Bureau of Investigation (1980–1993, 1994a, 1995).

that did not have any increase in homicides. The trends in aggravated assault arrests for the two groups are quite similar over the whole period. There are 15 year-to-year transitions over the period, and the two groups increased together or decreased together in 13. Thus, an upward or downward movement in the rate for one age group predicts a move in the same direction for the other age group about 85 percent of the time. The two groups behaved over time like two peas in the same statistical pod. The similar magnitude of the year-to-year changes visible in Figure 4 is consistent with changing policy standards.

But is this evidence that trends in true rates of violence were quite similar for the two age groups, or is this evidence instead that changing police practices had the same impact on the two age groups at the same time? Homicide trends for the two age groups point toward the latter

interpretation. The parallel trends for the two age groups does not hold for homicide arrests over time. Homicide arrests were sharply up for the younger group but down for the 25- to 34-year-olds, as shown in Figure 5.

Homicide arrests for the 25-to-34 age group dropped substantially after 1981 and continued a sustained decline throughout the period. There is thus no evidence that the increasing rate of serious assaults for this age group spilled over to create more deaths from assault. This suggests that the fluctuations in the older age group could not affect the volume of life-threatening assaults. The similarity of patterns over time of younger and older offenders, then, would suggest that the major reason for movements in the 13-to-17 age group should be the same as for the older group. If so, the major reason for increasing arrest rates in the younger age bracket for assault was not a change in the

FIGURE 5   Trends in Arrest Rates for Murder and Nonnegligent Manslaughter, 1980–1995

SOURCE: U.S. Department of Justice, Federal Bureau of Investigation (1980–1993, 1994a, 1995).

behavior of young offenders but a change in the classification of attacks that are close to the line that separates simple from aggravated assaults.

One way to estimate the degree to which police reclassification, rather than increasing violent assault, drove up aggravated assault rates is to use the trends for the older group as a proxy for reclassification. Since the homicides for this group dropped, we can assume that all of the increases that occurred in both groups were due to reclassification but that increases above and beyond those of the older group were the result of real changes. By this measure, more than 85 percent of the juvenile increase would be presumptive reclassification. The adult rate increased 67 percent from 1980 to 1995, while the juvenile rate increased 78 percent. The adult increase was 86 percent of the juvenile increase, leaving 14 percent of that increase not accounted for by presumed reclassification.

The trends in arrests for simple assault lend strong support to the theory that police standards are shifting toward recording and upgrading assaults.

The chances are substantial that a greater police willingness to report and upwardly classify assault crimes and a greater willingness to arrest those who commit assaults are contributing to the increase in arrests for both younger and older offenders. The four largest one-year increases in aggravated assault arrests amount to more than 100 percent of the total increase for aggravated assault (the four one-year jumps were 166.3 per 100,000, whereas the total increase was 160) and 83 percent of the total increase for simple assault up to 1995 (the four one-year increases were 332.4 per 100,000 of a total increase of 399.6). When all or most of the increase is concentrated in a few jumps, the likelihood that reporting thresholds are changing is higher.

Perspectives on Prediction

Long-range predictions about youth violence are difficult in the best of times because rates of serious offenses tend to be cyclical in unpredictable ways. But projections forward from recent trends are also problematic because there are no clear indications for the future of any violent offense to be gleaned from a careful review of current data. There are, however, important lessons about both trends and projections that should inform any discussion of what to expect in the future.

The first important finding from this analysis of recent experience is that there is no unitary trend in the recent history of youth arrests for violent crime. Homicide and assault arrests have increased, but for different reasons. Robbery and rape have fluctuated, without any discernible long-range trend. This lack of pattern has both procedural and substantive implications. The procedural lesson to be learned from the recent past is that patterns of arrest should be carefully examined one at a time rather than aggregated into a single arrest index. The substantive conclusion is that no generalization about the behavior of the current cohort of youths can be factually supported. The absence of any discernible growth trend in nonfirearms homicide, in robbery, and in rape arrest rates just does not fit generalizations about a more violent cohort, about superpredators, and the like.

Furthermore, when the two categories of growing rates are scrutinized, it turns out that youth arrests for homicides and assault have increased for different reasons. A sharp increase in gun homicide cases was the only reason the total homicide rate increased after the mid-1980s. By 1993, the rate of arrests for gun homicides had tripled from its low point, while nongun homicide was flat. Then a sharp downward trend in these arrests eliminated about half of the previous eight years of increases.

What can be applied from current information to homicide predictions is one part cliché and one part question mark. The dynamic force in the coming decade is likely to be trends in gun cases, just as it has been. But the future trend in youth gun homicide is anybody's guess. The most recent decline in gun cases has been steep, but will it be sustained? Although there is suspicion that market changes for drugs in the 1980s produced the initial increase in adolescent gun use, speculations about why gun homicides decreased have not produced a consensus. It is difficult to predict the future course of a trend one cannot explain.

One thing is clear: There will be very little tendency for trends in homicides with guns to reflect big changes in overall rates in assault or aggravated assault. Doubling the total number of aggravated assaults with handguns would produce less than a 20 percent increase in aggravated assaults; cutting gun assaults in half would lead to a 10 percent decrease in aggravated assaults.

The largest statistical mystery of the last decade is the sharp expansion in assault and aggravated assault arrests. The same large increase occurred for the 25-to-34 age group, a group with a decline in homicide. Any reduction in the threshold between simple and aggravated assault and any shift in the minimum standard for recording an offense would have the kind of statistical impact on assault arrests that has occurred since the late 1980s. Although the matter is not beyond doubt, it appears that the willingness of police authorities to give greater priority to assaults has altered the classification of attacks across the board.

Two aspects of this possible reclassification deserve special mention. First, when this sort of reclassification occurs, there is no telling whether the old or the new threshold is the correct one. The verbal description of aggravated assault is not precise, and the large number of attacks near the border between aggravated and simple assaults creates ample opportunity to justify different behavioral standards of what constitutes an aggravated assault. Second, the change in priority that motivates reclassification by the police can be very good news from a policy standpoint. More attention to particular problems often leads to reclassification of cases. Domestic violence incidents are counted as assaults more often when the problem becomes a priority. As police rejection of rape complaints (known as "unfounding") decreases, the number of rape complaints that become officially recorded incidents increases. If similar sentiments have created a higher probability that acts of violence become official statistics about violence, this is good news.

But it is good news that can be badly misinterpreted. A lower threshold for aggravating and reporting assault can produce a totally artificial crime wave in the sense that the statistics increase while the actual behavior is stable. More than half of the growth in aggravated assault by youths may be a product of this pattern during 1980–1996.

If reclassification is the principal reason for the growth in assault statistics, what further developments can be anticipated in the next decade or so? First, it is not likely that standards for arrests and for considering attacks to be aggravated assaults will revert to previous levels. There is no recurrent, cyclic pattern in crime classification over time to serve as a precedent. The larger social concern with violence that supports the efforts of the police seems to be a long-term development. Thus, standards for assault arrest and for aggravated assault arrest will stay at their present levels or perhaps drop further over the coming years.

The result of these developments might well be more arrests of young persons for assault and aggravated assault. The heterogeneity of the offense category will tend to increase, and the overwhelming majority of offenses that produce arrests will be at the low end of the seriousness scale. More than ever, it will be necessary to sort out the more serious from the less serious assaults in fashioning sanctions and policy responses.

The statistical portrait of the last 16 years is not without irony. Between 1980 and 1996, the increasing arrest rate for youth violence was concentrated in the assault category. The aggravated assault arrest rate was 41 percent of the youth violence arrest rate in 1980, yet increases in aggravated assault arrests dominated the growth over time. In 1996, the total rate of juvenile arrests for Index crimes of violence other than aggravated assault was lower than in 1980. With most of those extra aggravated assault arrests clustering at the low end of the seriousness scale, it is very likely that the average Part I arrest for an offender under 18 was for a less serious violent offense in 1996 than in 1980. It is possible that this trend will continue, so that a larger number of violence arrests will be counterbalanced by a smaller proportion at the serious end of the scale. But this kind of expansion at the shallow end of the violent crime pool is far from the growth in crime that is projected in current policy debates.

SOURCE: From *American Youth Violence* (pp. 31–47) by Franklin E. Zimring, 1998, New York: Oxford University Press. Copyright © 1998 Oxford University Press, Inc. Reprinted by permission of Oxford University Press, Inc.

QUESTIONS FOR DISCUSSION AND WRITING

1. Which two violent offenses examined by the author showed pronounced trends over time? What was true about robbery arrests during the 1980s and early 1990s?

2. What evidence does the author present regarding the notion of a new, more vicious type of juvenile offender?

3. What three pieces of evidence does the author cite in support of his argument that much of the change in assault statistics stems from changing police standards?

REALITIES AND
IMAGES OF CRACK MOTHERS

DREW HUMPHRIES

A t the height of the crusade against crack mothers, network news defined crack mothers as criminals and focused on the harmful effects of prenatal cocaine exposure. In the crusade's concluding phases, the networks tempered their portrait of crack mothers and scaled back on their estimates of cocaine-related harm. That the news assessments changed suggests that the problem rested on less firm ground than the American public had been led to believe. This chapter tests that basic insight by comparing news images and documentary evidence. The documentary evidence consists of drug surveys, research on the prevalence of maternal drug use, and medical findings on the effects of prenatal exposure to cocaine or crack.

According to the best national surveys available, had drug use actually reached epidemic levels in the late 1980s? To what extent did survey evidence support news claims about women's crack or cocaine use? Could maternal drug use be measured accurately? What was the nature of harm that crack mothers inflicted on their babies? The answers to these questions fit into the broader inquiry concerning moral panic.

COCAINE AND CRACK "EPIDEMICS"

The National Institute on Drug Abuse's (NIDA) *National Household Survey* and its *National High*

School Senior Survey, conducted annually since 1972 and 1975, respectively, provide the most reliable and widely used estimates of drug use and trends in the United States. Based on probability and representative samples, the results can be generalized to the larger population.

Since 1979, the downward direction in drug use, including cocaine, is one of the most widely accepted general findings in drug studies (see Figure 1). The surveys do have shortcomings: The absolute numbers are open to question because drug use is measured by self-reports—that is, asking respondents to recall past drug use—and unknown differences in recall may skew results. Moreover, the omission of groups believed to use drugs heavily means that NIDA and other surveys underestimate drug use.

Still, for cocaine users, the profile was remarkably consistent throughout the 1980s: Cocaine use was common among males, whites, young adults (ages 18–25), and adults (26–34). With respect to lifetime cocaine use in the 1980s, the difference between males and females had narrowed, especially among teenagers (12–17) and young adults (18–25). White females were "significantly more likely than black females to have ever used cocaine." As the 1993 NIDA report explained, higher lifetime rates for white than for black and Hispanic females might reflect youthful "experimental" use. On the other hand, increasingly similar rates of cocaine use among

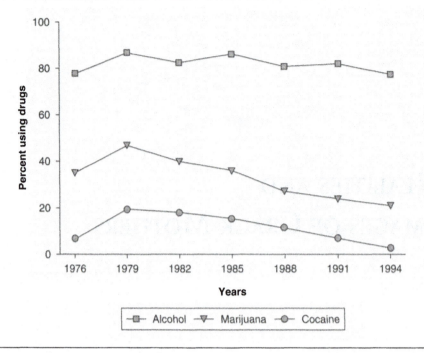

FIGURE 1   Trends in Past-Year Drug Use in the U.S., 18–25 Year Olds

SOURCE: SAMHSA, 1993a, 1995b.

whites, blacks, and Hispanics might also reflect underreporting by blacks.

Regular crack use was apparently stable between 1988, the year NIDA first distinguished it from cocaine, and 1994. Contemporaneous sources reported otherwise, however. The U.S. General Accounting Office had issued findings showing that while cocaine use had declined, the prevalence for frequent crack cocaine use had increased. Short-term changes like this are difficult to interpret because the sample sizes for weekly and daily drug use are too small to yield reliable estimates. Critics questioned the increase, wondering about the so-called epidemic, but crack had already attracted the attention of the media and policy makers. It took some time before Substance Abuse and Mental Health Services Administration set the record straight: While weekly estimates for cocaine (and crack) were too unreliable between 1988 and 1993 to report, the important point was that there were no significant differences in the rates over the survey years.

The media either neglected to report the decline in drug use, or only mentioned the trend as preliminary to the real news: the frighteningly high, and misleading, estimates of drug use. In a segment aired in 1984, NBC reported that from 4 to 5 million people regularly used cocaine (August 9). The 5 million figure was true to NIDA's *National Household Survey*, but the network distorted the problem in another way: Its filmed interviews with recovering cocaine addicts seemed to equate "regular use" with severe drug addiction. "Regular use" refers to past-month drug use, so the impression conveyed by the report that hopelessly addicted persons numbered in the millions was completely wrong.

The networks at first covered cocaine use among women by turning their attention to a group they viewed as vulnerable, white affluent women. Using traditional gender stereotypes, NBC and CBS developed news stories about the "myth of recreational drug use." Women had been taken in, believing that cocaine was a drug without addictive potential (CBS, 1983, February 7; NBC, 1984, August 10). And once addicted, the desire for cocaine impelled women to sell their jewelry, exhaust their funds, and finally exchange sex for the drug. The news stories also raised questions about the ability of drug-addicted women to mother: This aspect of coverage is discussed below.

In contrast with what they did with cocaine, the networks turned a small but enigmatic increase in weekly crack use into a clear epidemic. Technically, an epidemic refers to a cluster of cases that is greater than the background noise level; thus, if the background is zero, the appearance of any cases at all would equal an epidemic. If the background is declining drug use, then even a questionable increase in frequent crack use fits the metaphor. To the lay public, however, the term "epidemic" conveys something much more serious than the small countertendencies in drug use and, as detailed below, the equivocal estimates of maternal drug use found by NIDA. "Epidemic" describes the rapid, perhaps deadly, spread of disease. It implies a multiplying risk of infection. Any increase in the rates of morbidity or mortality is ominous proof that things are getting worse.

The networks applied the metaphor as they covered the new drug. On the ABC evening news, Robert Stutman, a spokesperson for the Drug Enforcement Administration, offered personal testimony on crack's rapid spread in New York City: "I've been a federal agent for 21 years, and I've never seen a drug phenomenon like this. Three months ago you could only buy crack in two or three areas. Ninety days later, you can buy it in almost any area of the city" (1986, May 27). Crack had already spread to vulnerable groups, from New York City to the suburbs, where "25 to 30 percent of the students in some high schools used it" (ABC, 1986, May 27). And the epidemic had national implications. The ABC report said that 15 major cities had reported "dramatic increases" in crack use. As in an epidemic, new cases of the disease added to the potential of infection throughout the population. The ABC segment quoted unnamed sources as saying, "Fifteen hundred Americans will try crack today" (1986, May 27). Finally, the infection was serious enough to require medical attention. Back in New York City, ABC reported 50 percent of emergency room admissions in some hospitals were for crack.

The networks interviewed young black and Hispanic men, linking crack to minorities against an urban landscape. Cities were portrayed as war zones where police teams rounded up drug dealers, drug dealers battled for turf, and customers came and went. Into the war zone came middle-class consumers searching out drugs. But by 1987, NBC announced a racial shift: The Drug Enforcement Administration's Robert Stutman reported that in the suburbs crack use had leveled off but that he did not believe the same held true for the inner city (1987, February 27). Stutman's impression was based on reports from the National Institute of Justice's Drug Use Forecasting showing that crack had spread from 7 to 40 cities in the previous 18 months. What the networks did not explain, however, was that the Drug Use Forecasting surveys were based on arrestees who had voluntarily submitted to drug tests and that the results did not apply to the larger population.

The *National Household Survey* showed that by 1988, women were less likely to use crack than men, a pattern that would continue. Network news, however, featured women in their coverage of crack without differentiating them from the men who peopled the scenes of urban chaos: Blacks and Hispanics of both sexes were filmed on the street, in crack houses, in court, and in drug treatment centers. For network news teams they described their drug: Crack created the most intense high, and by implication the most intense depression, including unrelenting cravings that propelled periodic binge behavior and sabotaged recovery. Under its influence people would commit every conceivable act of violence or theft. Weight loss, suicidal thoughts, and death were what awaited crack users. From these images of urban disorder, spreading drug use among minorities, and the specter of mindless addiction emerged the group known as crack mothers.

MATERNAL DRUG USE

Unfortunately, there are no satisfactory estimates of drug use by pregnant women available. Fifteen separate studies attempted to establish such estimates between 1982 and 1994, but their results were inconsistent and ambiguous. The first national, and perhaps the most widely cited, study was conducted by Dr. Ira Chasnoff, director of the National Association for Perinatal Addiction Research and Education. Based on discharge records from 40 hospitals, the Chasnoff study projected a national estimate of 375,000 drug-exposed babies, or 11 percent of the live births in 1988. Surveys of this type were important in identifying high-risk patients and designing appropriate interventions, but for reasons discussed below, their results should not have been generalized.

Another authoritative number was introduced by the National Drug Control Strategy Report: 100,000 crack/cocaine babies a year were delivered. The original survey, designed to judge the impact of crack/cocaine use on the child welfare system, was based on the number of drug-exposed babies referred to child welfare in eight cities in 1989. Even the studies designed specifically to estimate maternal drug use failed to provide clear results. They offered numbers, however, far, far below the Office of the Inspector General's 1990 estimate of 100,000 crack/cocaine babies.

A wide array of other circumstances affected estimates of maternal drug use. More than one study found that hospitals that had formal protocols produced higher estimates than those hospitals lacking protocols. Even with formal protocols, the choice of drug tested for was discretionary. When attention focused on cocaine, health workers may have screened more frequently for cocaine, producing higher estimates. Moreover, discretion extended to the choice of which patients to test. Even among patients in a single clinic, stereotypes about who used drugs influenced that decision, producing higher estimates for groups perceived as drug users. Public hospitals screened more frequently, producing higher rates of maternal cocaine use.

In covering maternal drug use, the networks quoted figures, but not once did they question the numbers on cocaine-exposed babies. Instead, the networks made authoritative assertions about prevalence, giving far more validity to the suspect estimates than they deserved. Reporters did not question local figures on the numbers of cocaine-exposed babies supplied by hospitals. ABC reported in 1988, for example, that in Florida, recent increases in the number of cocaine-exposed babies justified a statewide projection that 10,000 such infants would be born in the coming year (October 13). Despite error and bias, that projection was low, amounting to 0.25 percent of the approximately 4 million live births in 1988.

The scientific studies placed estimates even higher. A study in Dallas placed the percentage of cocaine-exposed infants at 9.8 percent. NBC's claim that 1 in 10 women who had given birth in a Miami hospital were crack users came closer to the Dallas figure (1988, October 25). Yet in 1988,

NBC would have found support for an even higher estimate: A Boston study found that 17 percent of the babies in a hospital sample had been prenatally exposed to cocaine.

Once national estimates were available, the networks seized on them—375,000 drug-exposed babies and 100,000 cocaine-exposed babies. They did not, however, always report these figures correctly. The networks asserted or implied that the 375,000 figure referred to infants who had been exposed to cocaine or crack (see, e.g., CBS, 1989, January 9; NBC, 1989, July 7). And this sort of error was not confined to the networks. Most news organizations confused drug exposure and cocaine exposure, and for a while it was difficult to associate the numbers with the appropriate problem. CBS showed the most erratic pattern. It apparently rounded off the 375,000 figure to report 370,000 cocaine babies in January, 1989, then the network used 100,000 in April, 1990 and 375,000 in June, 1990. It cited 100,000 again in December, 1990 and repeated the 375,000 figure in June, 1991. The obvious puzzlement of network news writers matched researchers' frustration with ambiguous or inconsistent findings.

COCAINE AND CRACK MOTHERS

The sociodemographic profile of maternal drug use raised difficult questions. Virtually every source consulted repeated the following description: Women who used crack or cocaine during pregnancy were black, in their mid-20s or older, came from large cities, were admitted to public hospitals, and paid for the delivery of their babies through Medicaid.

On the one hand, the profile may reflect the involvement of black women of childbearing age in using cocaine and crack. The consistency of findings on this question is persuasive. NIDA's *National Pregnancy and Health Survey*, for instance, showed that during pregnancy black women used cocaine at significantly higher rates than did white or Hispanic women: 4.5 percent of the black women (30,000), 0.4 percent of the white women (9,200), and 0.7 percent of the Hispanic women (4,400). In addition, the study showed that black women preferred crack: 4.1 percent or 27,700 had used crack at least once during pregnancy. Other studies confirmed the tie between black women, pregnancy, and crack or cocaine. An important Florida study found that among women entering prenatal care, 3.4 percent had used cocaine. Black women used it at significantly higher rates than did whites: 7.5 percent of the black women and 1.8 percent of the white women had used cocaine before visiting the clinic, hospital, or doctor for prenatal care.

On the other hand, racial and ethnic discrimination cannot be ruled out in the interpretation of this sociodemographic profile. While the Florida study found that black women were more likely to have used cocaine, results also showed racial bias in drug testing: Black women were significantly more likely than white women to be tested for drugs at the time of delivery. If black women were overselected for drug testing, then there was every reason to believe that white women were underselected. Whites did not fit the prevailing stereotypes about who used drugs. Moreover, private physicians would have hesitated to alienate their patients—who were disproportionately white—by reporting their drug use to health authorities. With so much bias in the measurements, it was difficult to know who among pregnant women actually used crack or cocaine.

The networks constructed a portrait of crack mothers based on race, by showing film footage of black women, without ever addressing troubling questions about racism. A racial breakdown of the women who appeared on camera in the news segments shows the shift from white to black. White women were associated with cocaine use during the first two stages of coverage (though only a few of these women were cocaine mothers). Black women came to be identified with maternal drug use in the last two stages: 55 percent and 84 percent of the women in stages 3 and 4, respectively, were black. The construction was consistent with other news: network news teams had interviewed minorities; crack, according to a Drug Enforcement Administration spokesperson, had not leveled off in the inner cities; crack, according to one correspondent, could be found wherever poverty, despair, and drugs coincided. And it was consistent with NIDA reports showing that crack was common among blacks and Hispanics.

Not only were their racial constructions an issue, the networks' construction of crack mothers revealed a deeply embedded moralism about women and drugs. But to understand this requires a second look at cocaine mothers. The networks

had shown an unusual degree of tolerance toward white middle-class women, filming them in conventional maternal poses, bathing and caring for their babies. As former addicts, these cocaine mothers expressed an appropriate level of remorse, appearing on television to warn other women about the dangers of cocaine use during pregnancy. In the war against cocaine, their conformity to recovery—the final stages in the moral career of an addict—was more important than were their infractions as bad mothers. Similar to that used in the 19th century to describe the moral career of drunks, this tale of addiction traced the same path: from drugs, to the loss of control, recognition of a disease state, to cure—abstinence and the burden of redemption.

Recounted by recovering cocaine and crack addicts, the moral tale began with an expression of relief. The patient was glad to be alive and restored to a normal life. The tale went on to describe addiction. The addiction had taken hold rapidly, and once it did, finding and using the drug became all-consuming. The addict was willing to sacrifice anything to get money to maintain use, squandering the family's paycheck, selling personal items, exchanging sex, and stealing. Hitting bottom generated insight. Realizing that he or she had to change or face death, the patient entered a drug rehabilitation program and headed toward recovery. The patient expressed regret and made efforts to recover the good opinion of family and friends. The moral tale, however, concluded on a cautionary note: Sobriety was a difficult and lifelong struggle.

Cocaine mothers who told this tale—expressing appropriate emotion—had greater worth in the public's eyes. Crack mothers who violated its dictates were designated as renegades. Tracy Watson, Erocelia Fandino, and Stephanie, the crack mothers introduced earlier and shown in the active stage of addiction, were renegades (NBC, 1988, October 24). Instead of showing shame, Tracy was defiant in the face of obvious censure. Instead of revealing remorse, Stephanie was indifferent to the baby she had left in the hospital. If anything, Erocelia registered surprise that smoking crack had brought on premature labor and delivery. And networks' coverage framed crack mothers as violating the standards of motherhood. In a world of surrogate mothers, successful mothering depended on a woman's capacity to provide a healthy environment, a nontoxic womb, for the developing fetus. "Capacity" encompassed self-sacrifice—putting fetal needs first. Crack mothers lacked this capacity. For them, drug use came first. And on this basis the networks castigated them.

PRENATAL COCAINE EXPOSURE

The prognosis for cocaine babies was far from good. Cocaine had been associated with premature labor and other complications of pregnancy. While the majority of babies had no symptoms, some did. Low-birthweight babies, their size attributed to cocaine, were at higher risk for mortality and morbidity. Kidney damage and malformation of other parts of the urinary tract were tied to prenatal cocaine exposure. Cocaine babies were also at risk for cardiovascular accidents—of stroke, aneurism, and infarction—and although the record indicated that these were rare events, the consequences would have been lethal. In babies without obvious defects, developmental delay remained a question, albeit an unresolved one.

Although the foregoing results are based on studies that withstood criticism, not all of the medical claims about prenatal cocaine exposure did withstand critique. Generally speaking, methodological and other criticisms were an increasing concern in medical reviews published after 1990, casting doubt on earlier studies that had shown the significant adverse effects so interesting to news organizations.

INFANT MORTALITY

Infant mortality showed promise as a reliable index of just how serious maternal cocaine use was. The collection of these data was independent: The war on drugs had not affected collection procedures, and the data series provided a basis for evaluating trends, although maternal drug use was not listed among the causes of death. Nonetheless, if the problem of maternal drug use had been as bad as the media suggested, its effects would have shown up in infant mortality rates. This was not the case on the national level: Infant mortality rates for the U.S. declined in the 1980s and 1990s. U.S. infant mortality rates were higher for babies born to

black mothers, but from 1983 to 1992 the rates for these babies declined from 20 to 17 per 1,000 live births. In 1989, NBC reported that infant mortality rates had doubled over the past six months in Washington, D.C. (1989, September 30). The report failed to mention well-documented declines, seizing on short-term dramatic jumps in the District of Columbia, the city with the highest infant mortality rates in the nation.

CONGENITAL DEFECTS

Case reports that cocaine caused birth defects sparked a contentious debate about whether cocaine was a teratogenic drug, one that produced physical defects in the fetus. Teratogenesis can occur when a drug interferes with the growth process, resulting in arrested or distorted development of an organ or of tissue or skeletal structure. The vulnerability of the fetus to teratogenesis depends on its stage of development. The first trimester of pregnancy is the time of greatest vulnerability. Some drugs are established teratogens. Thalidomide, a tranquilizer once thought safe enough for pregnant women, interrupted the development of limbs, so that hands, for example, grew attached directly to the trunk of the body. Alcohol is another teratogenic drug, producing in exposed infants mental retardation and characteristic facial features.

Animal research provided the strongest evidence that cocaine was a teratogen, but researchers recognized that the most convincing evidence would have to come from human studies. And results from human studies were far from conclusive, even though a high number examined an array of defects—some down to the molecular level. The literature reviews tended to concentrate on four malformations: those affecting the genitourinary tract, the heart, the gastrointestinal tract, and skeletal development.

Early reviews (1989–1990) concluded that organ malformation was a rare event, although it remained a risk for babies whose mothers had continued to use cocaine during pregnancy. Genitourinary tract abnormalities were confirmed, although abnormalities were confined to the urinary tract. Reviewers agreed that urinary tract malformation was the most likely teratogenic effect; other literature reviews, however, continued to include defects in the central nervous system and heart and gastrointestinal tract malformations.

After 1991, reviewers began to apply stricter standards for identifying teratogenic effects and to treat findings as more equivocal. The finding for urinary tract abnormality stood up to the higher standard, but for other abnormalities there was no agreement. Two major reviews concluded that for most effects the evidence was too equivocal to sustain any conclusions at all.

NEUROBEHAVIORAL CONSEQUENCES

Withdrawal and impairments in motor skills, emotional stability, and orientation were among the problems identified as neurobehavioral consequences of prenatal exposure to cocaine. Within medical circles, disparate views on the severity and duration of symptoms drove much of this research. A central question was whether symptoms disappeared or whether they signaled lifelong impairment.

Withdrawal in newborns was marked by tremors, irritability, and jitteriness, among other symptoms, and was a serious consequence of cocaine exposure, according to the medical literature surveyed. During the crack mother episode, the degree of seriousness of withdrawal's effects was a matter of controversy, but as panic wound down, the weight of medical opinion tended toward moderation. Cocaine withdrawal in infants, according to a 1990 review, was less severe than withdrawal from heroin, which was life-threatening and required special treatment.

Subsequent reviews acknowledged widespread reports of withdrawal in cocaine-exposed babies, but after surveying a broad spectrum of studies, one review found "no aberrant behavior" associated with cocaine withdrawal. Another concluded that symptoms attributed to cocaine deprivation were not unique to that drug. Researchers were also divided over whether the symptoms were temporary or permanent. One review asked whether symptoms were due to withdrawal or to cocaine's direct toxic effects on the central nervous system, citing evidence that symptoms persisted for at least six months. Another posed the same question about central nervous system effects,

citing evidence that the symptoms dissipated over time and concluding that the withdrawal symptoms were transitory.

SECOND THOUGHTS

The conclusion that cocaine-exposed babies exhibited serious neurobehavioral deficits, discernible from infancy through the toddler stage, was subjected to serious criticism. The samples in clinical studies were too small to rule out confounding variables; as a result, researchers had no way to eliminate alternative explanations for observed differences. For example, differences attributed to cocaine could have reflected differences in infant age or health status at the time of testing, differences in the drugs or drug combinations used by the mothers, or differences in the methods used for ascertaining the mother's drug status. Without a design powerful enough to rule out confounding factors, the results would be ambiguous.

Even as new studies remedied some design flaws, however, the results remained cloudy. One study found that cocaine-exposed babies had difficulty in adapting or shutting out aversive or redundant stimulation in the first week of life. But according to a review, the sample size was too small to test habituation, as the adaptation is called. Two other studies failed to confirm similar deficits during the first week. But according to another review, they failed to rule out alternative explanations for null findings. In one case, the infants were tested at three days. The absence of findings might have been due to the lingering effects of analgesic and anesthesia on babies in all groups. In the other case, the comparison group of mothers was not screened for drugs, raising the possibility that not all were drug free.

Even at the height of the panic over crack/cocaine mothers, Gideon Koren and his colleagues at the University of Toronto posed basic questions about the research cited. In an influential article, "Bias Against the Null Hypothesis," they documented a publication bias against research that failed to show detrimental effects for prenatal cocaine exposure. The project reviewed all the abstracts on prenatal cocaine exposure submitted to the Society of Pediatric Research for presentation at its meetings between 1980 and 1989. While 57 percent of the abstracts reporting adverse effects were accepted, only 11 percent not showing adverse effects were accepted. The studies that found no adverse effects had actually verified cocaine use more often and used control cases more frequently.

Controlled studies were essential for accurate findings, but they were difficult to conduct because, as Koren noted, women dependent on cocaine also had a "cluster of risk factors, including the use of other illicit drugs, heavy alcohol and cigarette consumption, and poor medical follow-up." Uncontrolled studies, especially those using high-risk populations, not only increased the perceived risk of cocaine use but generated inappropriate warnings. As for medical warnings against a single dose of cocaine, Koren wrote, "Counseling women exposed to cocaine in early pregnancy in Greater Toronto led us to suspect that there is a substantial distortion of medical information, which has led many women to terminations even when they were exposed briefly and mildly in early pregnancy."

NETWORK NEWS

The network news called crack/cocaine babies the newest, most innocent victims in the crack epidemic, and for most Americans the phrase appropriately described irreparable harm visited upon babies by their mothers. What the news reports failed to tell the American public, however, was that the medical research was too limited or poorly conducted to yield any reliable results. When the networks covered the story, they simplified, overstated, and mystified harm, creating the distortions that escalated concerns about maternal cocaine use to the level of legal threat.

Shocking news reports about congenital defects, such as deformities at birth, lent credence to claims that cocaine was a potent teratogenic drug. But by blending questionable claims, fragmentary evidence, and misstatements, the networks made it difficult for viewers to know what cocaine actually caused. Organ abnormalities, including kidney deformity and facial defects, were reported by CBS (1985, December 30). While the former had been accepted by the scientific community as teratogenic effects, facial defects, such as those that characterize

fetal alcohol syndrome, had not. Other defects recalled thalidomide. An ABC report announced that a study had linked cocaine to malformed arms (1989, November 14).

The babies were said to suffer heart attacks and strokes, cerebral palsy, and mental retardation (ABC, 1986, July 11). Prenatal exposure to cocaine did increase blood pressure and the risk of cardiac problems, but cerebral palsy had not been linked directly to cocaine, and although medical attention was focused on developmental delay, the claim of mental retardation overstated the concerns. While CBS said the babies were at risk for sudden infant death syndrome and unspecified defects, their link with cocaine was highly questionable (1985, September 11).

NBC reported a study conducted by the Centers for Disease Control showing that cocaine babies were five times more likely than other babies to suffer serious birth defects (1989, August 10). ABC reported that cocaine babies were three times more likely to suffer other defects (1989, November 14), but despite every effort, I was unable to identify the specific defects. CBS reported that brain tissue damaged by cocaine accounted for behavior problems observed in cocaine-exposed babies (1990, April 5). In ignoring how cocaine might bring about this result, CBS missed the debate over whether teratogenesis occurred by cocaine's direct effects on the central nervous system, as its report seemed to suggest, or whether it occurred indirectly by way of cocaine's vasoconstrictive effects, as an NBC report suggested (1984, August 9).

As evidence mounted that cocaine was not a potent teratogen, network news shifted ground: Perhaps defects were uncommon, but there were still problems. Normal-looking babies suffered from the delayed effects of cocaine (NBC, 1984, August 9). Experts confirmed that withdrawal was serious, and because the condition was visible, film crews were able to exploit it. A tiny trembling newborn, incubated and attached to monitors, was one of the most enduring images of the crack mother episode. Irrespective of its accuracy—many crack babies had no symptoms—the image was shown until the jittery, withdrawing newborn became the icon for the crusade against crack mothers.

As such, withdrawal eclipsed developmental problems. The neurobehavioral research conducted by Chasnoff and others had pointed to subtle deficiencies; motor skills, arousal states, imaginative play were all areas in which clinical studies had shown problems. Irritable babies tested parents' patience, but aside from caregivers in the act of soothing and swaddling, there was nothing to film (CBS, 1985, September 11).

Dr. Lorraine Hale of the Hale House in Harlem, a center for drug-exposed children, said in an interview that the children in her care were slow, but the toddlers-engaged-in-play scenes revealed nothing troubling (NBC, 1988, October 25). Children attending a Los Angeles school were also drug-impaired, but nothing in the scenes of children at play conveyed that they were forgetful or unable to perform tasks they had learned the day before (NBC, 1988, October 25). The older children were said to present disciplinary problems, to have difficulty with concentration, and to have mood swings that made their behavior unpredictable, but hyperactive, aggressive, or violent conduct was not to be captured on film (CBS, 1990, April 5).

In sum, despite widely accepted findings that drug use was on the decline, the networks in the mid-1980s declared an epidemic of middle-class cocaine use. It did this by ignoring trends and sensationalizing raw numbers (for example, that 20 million people had tried cocaine in *1983*), linking them to images of severe addiction. According to the *National Household Survey,* cocaine use was common among whites, males, and young adults, but the networks developed a handful of news stories about white women, a vulnerable middle-class group, ensnared by cocaine.

While this was not the major trend in cocaine use, the stories employed traditional stereotypes of sexuality and motherhood. The desire for cocaine had led young women to trade sex for the drug. Still, while cocaine mothers raised concerns about their unborn children, the networks took a tolerant attitude: The women appeared remorseful, they warned others to stay away from drugs, and thus their transgressions as mothers were less important than their role in educating others about the dangers of drugs.

With respect to crack, the networks declared an epidemic of underclass drug use. They did this by amplifying crack's reputation as a dangerous drug and by exploiting a questionable if not fabricated increase in frequent crack use. The networks illustrated their stories with images of urban chaos and poverty. This was an epidemic, they implied, that affected the poor, black, and Hispanic sections of big cities, into which went network news teams to cover the desperation of the crack houses, the madness of street arrests, and their mindlessly addicted residents.

The networks' stories employed a broad range of stereotypes to frame crack mothers as a threatening presence. Building on images of urban chaos, the networks linked prenatal crack use with poor, minority women and questioned the capacity of black women to mother. As addicts, crack mothers openly defied the prohibitionist stance taken by policy makers, in a climate of zero toleration. As crack mothers, the women violated emerging expectations about self-sacrifice and motherhood. They had given no thought to who would shoulder the long-term costs of caring for defective children.

The networks distorted the record on crack babies, representing the worst possible outcomes as the norm. Infant mortality rates in Washington, D.C. hardly generalized to the rest of country, but news about these rates dramatized the deadly effects of prenatal cocaine exposure. In addition, the networks' coverage was decidedly partial. It stressed congenital defects even as researchers argued over cocaine's role as a teratogenic drug. It stressed neurobehavioral effects of crack, omitting reference to the limitations of the studies on which the findings were based. The networks ignored entirely the gathering voices of dissent, beginning in 1989 with publication of Koren's article on publication bias against research that tended to disprove the dire news about crack. The prevailing wisdom, then, held that prenatal cocaine exposure risked the life or health of the newborn, that crack-addicted women who used drugs during pregnancy should be prevented from inflicting avoidable harm to the fetus and newborn, and that someone should take action.

QUESTIONS FOR DISCUSSION AND WRITING

1. What have studies of cocaine and crack use during pregnancy found? How might those findings reflect discrimination?

2. What did network news call crack/cocaine babies, and how was news regarding them reported?

3. Despite widely accepted findings that drug use was on the decline, how did networks in the mid-1980s treat cocaine use? How did they treat crack use?

BREAKING NEWS

How Local TV News and Real-World Conditions Affect Fear of Crime

RONALD WEITZER

CHARIS E. KUBRIN

Fear of crime is a major problem in the United States. In 2000, for instance, 40% of Whites and 47% of Blacks reported that they were afraid to walk alone near their homes at night. At the same time, there has been growing public concern about the role of the mass media—especially television—in promoting violence in American society. While public beliefs about crime and fear of victimization come from various sources, the media appear to play a substantial role in shaping these beliefs and fears. Most Americans identify the media as their primary source of information about crime—95% in one study—and the media may also be a major predictor of fear of personal victimization. This study examines the effect of several types of news consumption on citizens' fear of crime. The findings address four theoretical perspectives on the relationship between media and audience perceptions.

THEORETICAL BACKGROUND

One major approach—the real-world thesis—portrays fear of crime as largely or entirely shaped by objective conditions, such as criminal victimization, neighborhood characteristics, or city-level crime rates. According to this perspective, the media play little or no role because media reports are typically far removed from the audience's everyday lives and often cover atypical, serious, or spectacular crimes, whereas personal victimization and crime conditions are more immediate and salient. Regarding victimization, some studies find that prior victimization is positively associated with fear. Paradoxically, however, most find that persons who have the lowest victimization rates (such as women and the elderly) express the greatest fear of crime, whereas those with higher rates (e.g., young black males) express less fear. Regarding type of neighborhood, it appears that racial composition of a neighborhood influences residents' fear, with residents of minority communities more likely to fear crime. Another neighborhood factor thought to influence fear is the amount of crime or disorder in the community. Disorder includes both signs of physical disorder (e.g., graffiti, abandoned cars) and low-level street deviance (rowdy youth, panhandlers, public drinking)—conditions that may cause residents to fear for their safety.

The role of the media is the focus of the second major perspective—the cultivation thesis.

This approach portrays the media world as very different from the real world, with the implication that heavy consumption of media messages distorts audience beliefs about the world and influences cognitive and emotional states. In this view, the greater one's exposure to the media, the more likely it is that one's perceptions of the real world will match what is most frequently depicted in the media. With regard to crime, the media disproportionately report on violent crime (especially murder), largely neglect crime patterns, give little attention to the causes of crime, and leave the impression that crime is often random and inexplicable. This media world, especially television, differs greatly from the real world of crime and may cultivate a perception that the world is a scary place.

While some empirical support exists for cultivation, critics regard it as somewhat limited because it assumes that media messages have a uniform effect on audiences. Audience characteristics (race, gender, age, etc.) and experiences (e.g., victimization) may play an important role in how media content is received. The field of communication studies has increasingly regarded the reception of media messages as a dynamic process in which viewers actively interpret and perhaps reconstruct those messages in light of their personal backgrounds and experiences.

Audience differences are central in two other approaches, which specify the conditions under which media messages may contribute to fear of crime. One approach—the substitution thesis—is a variant of the cultivation perspective that is sensitive to audience and contextual differences. The substitution thesis predicts that heavy exposure to media portrayals of crime has particularly strong effects on those with no direct experience of crime; for these individuals, media images of crime become a surrogate for real-world experience. Persons who are well insulated from crime (e.g., the affluent, the elderly, women, residents of low-crime communities) should therefore be more susceptible to crime messages in the media. Few empirical studies have tested the substitution thesis. One found that crime victims were not influenced by crime-related television viewing (television dramas and documentary programs), whereas nonvictims were, and developed greater fear of crime.

A fourth perspective—the resonance thesis—predicts the opposite of the substitution thesis.

The resonance thesis holds that when media images are consistent with lived experience (e.g., criminal victimization, residing in a high-crime community), media and experience mutually reinforce citizens' fear. Because many high-crime communities are predominantly African American and because African Americans are disproportionately victimized by crime, the resonance thesis would predict a stronger media-fear relationship among Blacks than among Whites.

The resonance perspective is supported in a few studies. One found that fear increased with greater television watching, but only in high-crime neighborhoods. Television exposure had no effect on fear in low-crime neighborhoods, leading to the conclusion that television only becomes salient when it interacts with neighborhood crime conditions. A study that examined the effect of city-level crime rates in 242 Florida cities found that local television news consumption had the strongest effect on fear in cities with high crime rates, lending further support to the resonance hypothesis.

If the media do influence fear of crime, there are reasons to expect that media effects will be strongest for those who are exposed to local television news, compared to other news sources.

Why should this be the case? First, the style and content of reporting differs across the various media. Stylistically, television is a highly visual format, and seeing something on television may have a much stronger emotive impact than hearing about it on the radio or reading about it in the newspaper. Second, the resources available to different media vary considerably, which has implications for depth of investigation and for how news stories are packaged. Pressure for ratings and advertising revenue is greater for television news than for newspapers, which leads to a greater stress on marketable, shocking news in television. Third, some media sectors experience greater internal competition than others (e.g., several local television stations vs. one major newspaper in a city), which can lead to more crime coverage and more sensationalized coverage on television news. Fourth, the audience is able to take a more active role in relation to some media than others. Newspaper and Internet readers exercise considerable selectivity in what they read, whereas television and radio news audiences are more passive and less selective in their reception of newscasts.

With respect to crime news reporting, there are sound substantive reasons to expect local television news to have a stronger effect on perceptions than other types of news media. Local television news coverage is literally "close to home" for viewers, whereas national television news stories tend to be far removed from viewers' everyday lives. Local television news also operates by the maxim, "If it bleeds, it leads." A 1997 study of 100 local television stations found that 72 began their evening newscasts with a crime story. Approximately one-fourth of all local television news stories deal with crime, and, compared to newspapers and radio, local television news broadcasts are often televised live from crime scenes and presented in a graphic, sensational, or disturbing manner. The public sees this local television news reporting as believable. When asked in a 1996 Harris poll (N = 3,004) what percentage of local television evening news they "believed," the mean for a sample of Americans was 74%; the mean for national network television evening news was 69%. It is understandable, therefore, why local television news has been thought to have the most pronounced and ongoing effects on audience perceptions of crime, victimization, and criminal justice.

In sum, the literature offers mixed support for the hypothesis that exposure to the media increases fear of crime. Findings vary by type of medium, by audience characteristics, and by the control variables examined. Yet, there are also a number of deficiencies and unanswered questions in the media-fear literature.

The present study builds on, and fills some gaps in, the literature by (1) examining several types of media genres (local television, national television, newspapers, radio, the Internet), (2) assessing whether demographic factors (e.g., race, gender) and real-world conditions (e.g., neighborhood crime, personal victimization) interact with media exposure to influence fear of crime, and (3) using two measures of media exposure—both frequency of consumption and salience (i.e., the "most important source of news" to respondents).

METHODS

Data for the study come from a telephone survey of 480 residents of Washington, D.C. The survey was conducted in March–April, 2001 by the Center for Survey Research at George Washington University. The demographic characteristics of the sample, with comparable Washington, D.C.

population data from the 2000 census in parentheses, are as follows: 57.7% Black (60%); 62.5% female (53%); median age 43 (35).

Our dependent variable—fear of crime—has been operationalized in several ways in previous studies, including respondent's concern about crime or proxies for crime (e.g., safety concerns), perceived risk of victimization, and anxiety about being outside during the day or at night. Although some measures do not explicitly mention crime, crime is often implicit in the wording of the question, as it is in the present study. Our respondents were asked, "How comfortable are you walking alone at night within two or three blocks of your home? Are you very comfortable, somewhat comfortable, somewhat uncomfortable, or very uncomfortable?" Being "very uncomfortable" or "somewhat uncomfortable" are rough measures, in the present study, of concern about crime. People who feel uncomfortable are likely to be concerned with becoming a victim of crime.

In our sample, 36.5% (N = 175) stated they were very comfortable while walking alone at night near their homes, 30% (N = 144) were somewhat comfortable, 16% (N = 77) were somewhat uncomfortable, and 14.8% (N = 71) were very uncomfortable.

The present study incorporates several media (national and local television, newspapers, radio, and the Internet). Our design specifically captures exposure to the news content of the media.

Respondents were first asked how frequently, if ever, they (1) "watch national evening news programs such as *World News Tonight* with Peter Jennings or cable news programs like CNN"; (2) "watch local television news for information other than weather and sports"; (3) "read the news or editorial sections of a daily newspaper"; (4) "listen to radio shows that invite listeners to call in to discuss current events, public issues, and politics"; and (5) "go online to get information on current events, public issues, and politics."[1] Respondents were then asked, "What would you say is the most important source of news for you? Would you say it is national television news, local television news, daily newspapers, radio, or the Internet?" Not surprisingly, there was substantial variation in which medium was the most important news source for respondents, with 19.2% of the sample answering national television, 30.2% local television, 26.7% daily newspapers, 7.1% radio,

12.3% Internet, and 3.1% "other medium." The question regarding respondents' most important source of news is the independent variable of primary interest in this study.

Because some studies find that certain demographic attributes (such as gender and race) influence fear of crime, we include the following independent variables in our models: respondents' age (measured continuously), age (because the slope for age is nonlinear), gender, race (Black; White; other race, with White as the omitted category), education (college graduate or not), family income (seven categories), and victimization by violent crime (ever) or property crime (in the past year).

Another variable of interest is perceived risk of criminal victimization. Respondents were asked, "Now I am going to read you a list of items relating to safety risks to you and your family. Would you say that you and your family are at almost no risk, slight risk, moderate risk, or high risk from [violent crime/property crime/street drugs]?"

Finally, we control for the respondents' local crime conditions: violent crime rate (murder, rape, robbery, and assault) and property crime rate (burglary, larceny, auto theft, and arson). These rates are measured at the police district level.

FINDINGS AND DISCUSSION

Our findings suggest that the media play a substantial role in shaping beliefs and fear of crime. We found that those who identify local television as their most important news source are more fearful compared to those who selected national television, daily newspapers, and "other medium." This is consistent with a body of literature described earlier in the article, which predicts that local television news should have a particularly strong impact, compared to other media, on audience perceptions and fears. The results speak to the importance of disaggregating the media when studying its effect on audience perceptions. Similarly, the findings confirm the need to disaggregate audiences; media messages are not received in the same way by different people. Our analysis shows that media and real-world conditions have different effects on White and Black respondents and on respondents from communities with different levels of violent crime.

For the total sample, the results show strong support for neither the cultivation nor real-world thesis because both media and real-world conditions influence fear. Furthermore, the interaction analyses suggest a more complex and conditional relationship among the media, real-world factors, and fear of crime. When the sample is broken down by race, the findings lend support to both the resonance and the real-world theses, depending on the racial group. Whites' fear of crime is influenced not by the media but instead by their perceived risk of violent criminal victimization. The real-world thesis is partially supported for Whites, though other real-world factors such as personal victimization and risk of other types of crime are not significant.

Blacks are influenced both by local television news and by real-world conditions—namely, property crime victimization and perceived risk of street drugs to themselves and family members. That Blacks are concerned about street drugs is understandable in a city like Washington, D.C., where street-level drug markets are concentrated in poor Black neighborhoods. For Blacks, the combined effect of local television news and the above crime factors provides support for the resonance thesis.

When the sample is disaggregated by neighborhood violent crime level, residents of communities with high violent crime rates are especially likely to be affected, in their fear of crime, by local television newscasts. By contrast, local television news exposure does not increase fear for residents of low violent crime communities. The finding that local news effects are stronger for residents of high violent crime areas is consistent with findings from some previous studies and lends further support to the resonance thesis.

No support is found for the substitution thesis, which predicts that groups that have a low victimization risk—women, the elderly, and the affluent—will be especially susceptible to media influences. In the interaction analyses disaggregated by each of these characteristics, local television news was not a significant predictor of fear.

The finding that local television news is the medium with the greatest effect on fear, coupled with what we know about the selective and distorted presentation of crime on local television newscasts, raises some policy implications. Critics frequently argue for less sensationalized and more contextualized reporting, as well as for less coverage of atypical and predatory crimes and more coverage of corporate crime. An important policy question has to do with the role of media crime reporting on the public's preferences regarding crime control. The limited existing literature indicates that people who are "heavy viewers of television crime shows . . . are disposed to support the law enforcement system . . . and favor crime control over due process policies." The same may also be the case for heavy viewers of local television newscasts, but research is needed to determine whether exposure to television news has this same effect on crime policy preferences.

NOTE

1. Coding of this variable ranges from 1 to 5, with 1 = "never," 2 = "several times a month," 3 = "once or twice a week," 4 = "most days," and 5 = "every day."

QUESTIONS FOR DISCUSSION AND WRITING

1. What four theses form the theoretical background to the authors' study?

2. What do the findings suggest? With what body of literature is this finding consistent? What finding led the authors to recommending disaggregating audiences?

3. Which of the four theses were supported and under what circumstances or for which subpopulations?

THE POLITICS OF CRIME

KATHERINE BECKETT

THEODORE SASSON

Over the past several decades, the United States has declared and waged vigorous wars against crime and drugs. Popular wisdom holds that the policy choices associated with these wars are a consequence of worsening crime and drug problems. However, the best available evidence suggests that crime has not increased significantly over the past several decades. Furthermore, although drug abuse is a serious problem for many individuals and communities, levels of illegal drug use have declined sharply since their peak in the late 1970s. The incidence of crime and drug use thus cannot account for the massive expansion of the criminal justice system. Instead, the growth of U.S. penal institutions is the result of policies aimed at "getting tough" with law breakers, especially drug offenders. In what follows, we suggest that these policy choices reflect a reframing of the crime problem in U.S. political discourse and culture.

Social problems like crime may be defined or framed in a number of different ways, and these different frames have quite distinct policy implications. For example, crime may be depicted as evidence of the breakdown of law and order, of the demise of the traditional two-parent family, or of social and economic inequality. Crime-related issues are thus socially and politically constructed: They acquire their meaning through struggles over their interpretation and representation. Social actors—sometimes called "claims makers"—compete for the public's attention

and attempt to gain acceptance for the frames they prefer.

The frames that come to dominate political and media discourse have a significant impact on policy. For example, to the extent that crime is seen as a consequence of lenience within the criminal justice system, policies that "get tough" with criminal offenders seem most appropriate. Conversely, frames that depict crime as a consequence of poverty, unemployment, or inequality suggest the need for policies that address these social and economic conditions. Debates over penal policy are less influenced by criminological research than by the way crime-related problems are framed in political discourse and popular receptivity to these frames.

In this [article], we suggest that today's "tough-on-crime" policies reflect the success of conservative efforts to frame crime as a consequence of excessive lenience or "permissiveness" in government policy and in society more generally. Conservative politicians have worked for decades to alter popular perceptions of problems such as crime, delinquency, addiction, and poverty and to promote policies that involve "getting tough" and "cracking down." Their claims-making activities have been part of a larger effort both to realign the electorate and to define social control rather than social welfare as the primary responsibility of the state.

Our analysis begins in the tumultuous decade of the 1960s, when Southern officials first mobilized the discourse of law and order in an effort to discredit the civil rights movement. As the decade progressed, conservative opponents of the welfare state also used this rhetoric to attack President Lyndon Johnson's Great Society programs and the structural explanations of poverty with which these programs were associated. Conservatives offered two theories of the newly politicized crime problem:

- an individualistic theory, according to which both poverty and crime are freely chosen by dangerous and undeserving individuals who refuse to work for a living, and
- a cultural theory, according to which the "culture of welfare" is an important cause of a variety of social ills, including poverty, crime, delinquency, and drug addiction.

Although distinct in some ways, these individualistic and cultural theories both identify "permissiveness" as the underlying cause of crime and imply the need to strengthen the state's control apparatus. In the 1980s and 1990s, the ascendance of this frame has helped to legitimate the assault on the welfare state and the dramatic expansion of the penal system. As a rallying cry for Republicans, the permissiveness frame has also helped forge the party's new political majority. In short, the construction of the crime issue as a consequence of excessive permissiveness has been extraordinarily useful to conservative opponents of civil rights and the welfare state.

THE ORIGINS OF THE LAW AND ORDER DISCOURSE

In the years following the Supreme Court's 1954 *Brown v. Board of Education* decision, civil rights activists across the South used "direct action" tactics and civil disobedience to force reluctant Southern states to desegregate public facilities. In an effort to sway public opinion against the civil rights movement, Southern governors and law enforcement officials characterized its tactics as "criminal" and indicative of the breakdown of "law and order." Calling for a crackdown on the "hoodlums," "agitators," "street mobs," and "lawbreakers" who challenged segregation and Black disenfranchisement, these officials made rhetoric

about crime a key component of political discourse on race relations.

As the debate over civil rights moved to Washington, depictions of civil rights protest as criminal rather than political in nature reached the national stage. For example, after a reluctant President Kennedy finally expressed his willingness to press for the passage of civil rights legislation in 1963, Republicans and Southern Democrats assailed him for "rewarding lawbreakers." Later, retired Supreme Court Justice Charles Whittaker made the link between crime and protest more explicit when he attributed the spread of lawlessness and violence to

> the fact that some self-appointed Negro leaders who, while professing a philosophy of nonviolence, actually tell large groups of poor and uneducated Negroes . . . whom they have harangued, aroused and inflamed to a high pitch of tensions, that they should go forth and force the whites to grant them their rights.

Former Vice President Nixon also blamed civil rights leaders for the problem of crime and violence, arguing that "the deterioration of respect for the rule of law can be traced directly to the spread of the corrosive doctrine that every citizen possesses an inherent right to decide for himself which laws to obey and when to disobey them."

The rhetoric of "law and order" became even more salient in 1964, when Republican presidential candidate Barry Goldwater announced that "[t]he abuse of law and order in this country is going to be an issue [in this election]—at least I'm going to make it one because I think the responsibility has to start some place." Despite the fact that crime did not even appear on the list of issues identified by the public as the nation's most important, Goldwater, a prominent civil rights opponent, made "law and order" the centerpiece of his campaign.

Striking the now familiar theme, Goldwater promised that, unlike President Johnson, he "would not support or invite any American to seek redress . . . through lawlessness, violence, and hurt of his fellow man or damage of his property."

Initially, Goldwater's plea for a federal war on crime was controversial among conservatives and liberals alike. The United States Constitution allocates most crime control duties to local and state law enforcement. Some conservatives worried that a federally led anticrime initiative would impinge on state and local government authority. Furthermore, given that most Southern conservatives opposed federal civil rights legislation on the basis of their "commitment to states' rights," calls for a federal war on crime struck many as highly inconsistent. Liberals also expressed concern, arguing that the proposed federal anticrime effort would compete for funds with the Great Society programs and therefore impede efforts to implement social and racial reform.

In sum, the introduction and construction of the crime issue in national political discourse in the 1960s reflects the claims-making activities of Southern officials, presidential candidate Goldwater, and the other conservative politicians who followed his lead. Phrases like "crime in the streets" and "law and order" equated political dissent with crime and were used in an attempt to heighten opposition to the civil rights movement. Conservatives also identified the civil rights movement—and in particular, the philosophy of civil disobedience—as a leading cause of crime. Countering the trend toward lawlessness, they argued, would require holding criminals (including civil rights protesters) accountable for their actions through swift, certain, and severe punishment.

The racial subtext of these arguments was not lost on the public: Those most opposed to social and racial reform were also most receptive to calls for law and order. Ironically, it was the success of the civil rights movement in discrediting more explicit expressions of racist sentiment that led politicians to attempt to appeal to the public with such "subliminally" racist messages. In subsequent years, conservative politicians also found the crime issue—with its racial subtext now firmly in place—useful in their attempt to redefine poverty as the consequence of individual failure and to discredit welfare programs and their recipients.

From the War on Poverty to the War on Crime

Throughout the 1960s, civil and welfare rights activists drew national attention to the issue of poverty. According to these activists, inequality of opportunity and racial discrimination ensured that poverty would remain widespread. To remedy this, they sought, among other things, to expand President Johnson's Great Society welfare programs. Largely as a result of their activism, the welfare rolls grew dramatically. In 1960, fewer than 600,000 families applied for Aid to Families with Dependent Children (AFDC) benefits; by 1972, more than three million Americans were receiving them. Continued migration to northern cities from southern and rural areas meant that increasing numbers of those who received AFDC were African American women and their children.

During this period, liberals also argued that crime, like poverty, was a product of blocked opportunities. For example, early in his administration, President Johnson argued that programs that attacked social inequality were, in effect, anticrime programs: "There is something mighty wrong when a candidate for the highest office bemoans violence in the streets but votes against the war on poverty, votes against the Civil Rights Act, and votes against major educational bills that come before him as a legislator." Initially, then, the Johnson administration stressed the need to address crime's "root causes" through initiatives of the welfare state.

The Conservative Attack on the Great Society

By contrast, conservative opponents of Johnson's social welfare initiatives argued that both poverty and crime were caused by a combination of bad people and excessive permissiveness. According to this argument, crime and related social problems originate in individual choice rather than in social conditions. "How long are we going to abdicate law and order—the backbone of any civilization—in favor of a soft social theory that the man who heaves a brick through your window is simply the misunderstood and underprivileged product of a broken home?" demanded House Leader Gerald Ford. Later, independent presidential candidate George Wallace also ridiculed "soft social theories" that stress the social causes of crime.

Discussions of crime and poverty were linked in other ways as well. Those who attributed poverty to the immorality of the impoverished often identified crime and delinquency as evidence of dysfunctional lifestyles. For example, Daniel Patrick Moynihan's much-discussed report on the Black family attributed Black poverty to the "subculture . . . of the American Negro":

> A community that allows large numbers of young men to grow up in broken families, dominated by women, never acquiring any stable relationships to male authority, never acquiring any set of rational expectations about the future—that community asks for and gets chaos. Crime, violence, unrest, disorder, are not only to be expected, but they are very near to inevitable. And they are richly deserved.

Although Moynihan (sometimes) identified unemployment as the cause of family disorganization, subsequent newspaper accounts and conservative reinterpretations of the report did not.

Highlighting the behavioral pathologies and, especially, the criminality of the poor was an important means of transforming their image from needy to undeserving. By emphasizing street crime and by framing that problem as the consequence of bad people making bad choices, conservatives made it much less likely that members of the public would empathize with the plight of the poor and support measures to assist them. As historian Michael Katz suggests, "When the poor seemed menacing they became the underclass."

In a further attempt to marshal opposition to welfare programs, conservatives made the cultural argument that programs such as AFDC actually encouraged non-work-oriented lifestyles, thereby worsening the problems of poverty and crime. According to this argument, people will avoid work when possible and welfare programs reward this tendency. Furthermore, the mere existence of welfare encouraged people to think that they are entitled to that which they have not earned.

In this twist on the venerable "culture of poverty" thesis, conservatives argued that the "culture of welfare" undermines self-discipline and promotes "parasitism"—both legal (welfare dependency) and illegal (crime).

In the mid-1960s, then, liberals and conservatives offered very different interpretations of poverty and crime-related problems. According to conservatives, social pressures such as racism, inadequate employment, lack of housing, low wages, and poor education do not cause crime. If they did, all poor people would be criminals. Instead, people are poor, criminal, or addicted to drugs because they made irresponsible or bad choices. Ironically, social programs aimed at helping the poor only encourage them to make these choices by fostering a culture of dependency and predation. By contrast, liberals argued that social conditions—especially racial inequality and limited opportunities for youth—were the "root causes" of crime, poverty, and addiction. It is only by addressing these social conditions, they argued, that we may begin to ameliorate the problems they cause.

Defection of the Liberals

By 1965, however, the liberal emphasis on the "root causes" of crime began to weaken. Only four months after his election, for example, President Johnson declared in an unprecedented special message to Congress his new determination to fight crime: "I hope that 1965 will be regarded as the year when this country began in earnest a thorough and effective war against crime." Johnson presented his newly moderated analysis of the crime problem:

> The problem runs deep and will not yield easy and quick answers. We must identify and eliminate the causes of criminal activity whether they lie in the environment around us or in the nature of individual men. . . . Crime will not wait until we pull it up by the roots. We must arrest and reverse the trend toward lawlessness.

Toward that end, Johnson established the Law Enforcement Assistance Administration (LEAA), an agency with a mission to support local law enforcement. To coordinate law enforcement activities aimed at fighting drugs, he also created the Bureau of Narcotics and Dangerous Drugs (now called the Drug Enforcement Agency [DEA]). These initiatives represented a shift away from the view that the most important crime-fighting weapons were civil rights legislation, War on Poverty programs, and other policies aimed at promoting inclusion and social reform. Although Johnson sometimes reiterated his earlier view that social and racial reform efforts would reduce crime, administration officials and other liberal politicians now tempered this argument with the claim that these "long-term" solutions must be balanced by the "short-term" need for increased law enforcement and more efficient administration of justice. Over time, the liberal commitment to assisting the poor also attenuated.

It is not entirely clear why the liberal emphasis on the "root causes" of crime weakened. According to public opinion polls taken at the time, there was no evidence that much of the public had abandoned the view that crime has environmental causes. Indeed, most members of the public continue to favor crime measures that address the social conditions that give rise to crime. Perhaps leaders in the Democratic Party were worried about the views and sentiments of a particular segment of the public—those people who came to be known as "swing voters." As we shall see, analyses of voting patterns in the 1964 election revealed that these socially conservative White voters were shifting their loyalties to the Republicans. The liberal back-pedaling on crime was probably, at least in part, an attempt to woo these voters back to the Democratic Party.

The shift in liberal political discourse also occurred in the context of a growing chorus of criticism, from scholars and activists across the political spectrum, of "rehabilitation" as a primary justification for punishment. Conservatives opposed rehabilitation on the grounds that punishment must be harsh and painful if it is to deter crime. Liberals also criticized policies associated with rehabilitation, arguing that the open-ended ("indeterminate") sentences designed to facilitate "correction" created the potential for the intrusive, discriminatory, and arbitrary exercise of power. Under the weight of these twin (if quite distinctive) critiques, the rehabilitative project was called into question. This development undoubtedly made it more difficult for liberal politicians to offer a clear alternative to the conservative calls to crack down on criminals and may therefore have facilitated the Democratic leap on to the law and order bandwagon.

The Republican Southern Strategy

In the 1968 presidential campaign, Republican candidate Richard Nixon rejected social explanations of crime, arguing that the lenience of the criminal justice system was in fact to blame. As he put it, the real cause of crime is not poverty or unemployment but "insufficient curbs on the appetites or impulses that naturally impel individuals towards criminal activities." Nixon therefore concluded that the "solution to the crime problem is not the quadrupling of funds for any governmental war on poverty but

more convictions." The 1968 Republican Party platform concurred with Nixon's critique of liberal "permissiveness": "We must re-establish the principle that men are accountable for what they do, that criminals are responsible for their crime."

Nixon's rhetorical emphasis on crime and other social issues was part of a political strategy aimed at weakening the electoral base of the Democratic Party—the New Deal coalition. This alliance of urban ethnic groups and the White South had dominated electoral politics from 1932 through the early 1960s. As a result of Black migration to the North, this alliance also included growing numbers of Blacks, a trend that created quite a dilemma for those interested in maintaining White Southern allegiance to the party. In 1948, when President Harry Truman responded to the growing number of Black voters by pressing for a relatively strong civil rights platform, the first serious signs of strain in the Democratic partnership appeared. White Southerners organized a states' rights party, and in the subsequent election, four Deep South states (Louisiana, South Carolina, Alabama, and Mississippi) delivered their electoral votes to this insurgent political force. In the 1952 and 1956 elections, Democrats attempted to placate these Southern "Dixiecrat" delegates and pull in disaffected White Southerners. The appeasement of Southern racism was not without political costs, however, and the Republican share of the Black vote increased from 21% in 1952 to 39% in 1956.

In 1957 and 1960, partisan competition for the Black vote led the Democratic Congress to pass the first civil rights measures of the twentieth century. Convinced he could not resurrect White Southern loyalty to the Democratic Party, John F. Kennedy campaigned on a civil rights platform in 1960. Once in office, however, President Kennedy sought to minimize White Southern resistance within the Democratic coalition. This ambivalence about the Democratic Party's loss of the White South appears to account for Kennedy's weak and delayed support for civil rights legislation. Indeed, only under the extreme pressure generated by civil rights activists did Kennedy finally declare his allegiance to the civil rights cause.

By drawing significant public attention to the plight of Blacks in the South, civil rights activists forced the national Democratic Party to choose between its Southern White and Northern Black constituencies. The high degree of support among non-Southern Whites for the civil rights cause prior to 1965 and the increasing numbers of African American voters eventually led the Democratic Party to cast its lot with Blacks and their sympathizers. This decision, however, alienated many of those traditionally loyal to the Democratic Party, particularly White Southerners. "Millions of voters, pried loose from their habitual loyalty to the Democratic Party, were now a volatile force, surging through the electoral system without the channeling restraints of party attachment." These voters were "available for courting," and the Republicans moved swiftly to seize the opportunity. Initially, the GOP targeted White Southerners—voters who had formerly composed the Democrat's "solid South"—as potential swing voters. Although the 1964 presidential election was a landslide for Johnson, careful scrutiny of the returns indicated that the socioeconomic structure of the New Deal alliance could in fact be fractured by the issue of race. In the poorest White neighborhoods of Birmingham, for example, the Republican vote increased from 49% to 76%, and a similar trend was identified in other Southern cities.

Republican analysts began to argue that they might also find a responsive audience among White suburbanites, ethnic Catholics in the Northeast and Midwest, and White blue-collar workers and union members. Some conservative political strategists frankly admitted that appealing to racial fears and antagonisms was central to this strategy. For example, Kevin Phillips argued that a Republican victory and long-term realignment was possible primarily on the basis of racial issues and therefore suggested the use of coded anti-Black campaign rhetoric. Similarly, John Ehrlichmann, Special Counsel to the President, described the Nixon administration's campaign strategy of 1968 in this way: "We'll go after the racists. That subliminal appeal to the anti-black voter was always present in Nixon's statements and speeches."

New sets of Republican constituencies were thus courted through the use of racially charged "code words"—phrases and symbols that "refer indirectly to racial themes but do not directly challenge popular democratic or egalitarian ideals." The "law and order" discourse is an excellent example of such coded language, and it allowed for the indirect expression of racially charged fears and antagonisms. In the context of urban riots and reports that the crime rate was increasing, the capacity of conservatives to mobilize, shape, and express these racial fears and tensions became a particularly important political resource.

The "Southern strategy," as this tactic came to be known, enabled the Republican Party to replace the New Deal cleavage between the "haves" and the "have-nots" with a new division between some (overwhelmingly White) working- and middle-class voters and the traditional Republican elite, on the one hand, and "liberal elites" and the (disproportionately African American and Latino) poor on the other. As the traditional working-class coalition that buttressed the Democratic Party was ruptured along racial lines, race eclipsed class as the organizing principle of American politics. By 1972, attitudes on racial issues, rather than socioeconomic status, were the primary determinant of voters' political self-identification.

Nixon's Federalist Dilemma

After assuming office, the Nixon administration was forced to contend with the fact that, campaign pledges to the contrary notwithstanding, the federal government had little authority to deal directly with "street crime" outside of Washington, D.C. Dismayed Attorney General John Mitchell pointed out that "even if the federal government found an indirect way of intervening in the problem, the local government would get the credit for diminishing those classes of crime." Administration insiders concluded that the only thing they could do was "exercise vigorous symbolic leadership." They therefore waged war on crime by adopting "tough-sounding rhetoric" and pressing for largely ineffectual but highly symbolic legislation.

The Assault on Defendants' Rights

The Nixon administration's argument that crime is a consequence of "permissiveness" had important implications for criminal and constitutional law. Indeed, many of the legal rights and protections previously extended to criminal defendants were undermined or abandoned altogether during the Nixon era.

Under the leadership of Justice Earl Warren, the Supreme Court strengthened the protections offered to criminal defendants throughout the

1960s. For example, in *Mapp v. Ohio* (1961), the Court ruled that state police officers, like federal law enforcement agents, were under most circumstances obliged to obtain a search warrant before conducting a search or seizing evidence. In *Gideon v. Wainwright* (1963), the Court ruled that all persons accused of a crime were guaranteed the right to counsel. In *Escobedo v. Illinois* (1964), coerced confessions were deemed inadmissible. And in *Miranda v. Arizona* (1966), the Court ordered that suspects must be informed of their legal rights upon arrest and that any illegally obtained evidence would be inadmissible in the courts. Finally, under the Warren Court, defendants were permitted to argue that they had been entrapped when the idea of the crime in question originated with the police or when police conduct "fell below standards for the proper use of governmental power."

Some of the legislation sponsored by the Nixon administration directly undermined these legal protections. Title II of the 1968 Omnibus Crime Bill, for example, allowed for the use of confessions obtained "voluntarily" but without the use of Miranda warnings. And the Racketeer Influenced and Corrupt Organization Act (RICO) of 1970 allowed prosecutors, with a judge's permission, to seize an organization's assets before trial. This legislation also allowed federal law enforcement agents to seek and obtain "no-knock" search warrants permitting them to enter and search private homes without giving notice of the "authority and purpose" of these searches.

By appointing several conservatives (including Warren Burger and William Rehnquist) to the Supreme Court, Nixon ensured that defendants' rights were further weakened. For example, in 1973, the Burger Court undermined the Warren Court's interpretation of the Fourth Amendment's prohibition against unwarranted searches and seizures by ruling that if an arrest is lawful, "a search incident to the arrest requires no additional justification." Similarly, the Burger Court nearly eliminated the entrapment defense when it ruled that if a defendant is "predisposed" to committing a crime, he or she could not plead entrapment. All of these efforts to undermine criminal defendants' rights were rooted in the notion that the excessive leniency of the criminal justice system was an important cause of crime. These changes in criminal and constitutional law did diminish defendants'

rights, but they did not have a demonstrable effect on the rates of arrest, conviction, or incarceration.

The Reagan Years

Despite the centrality of the law and order discourse to the GOP's electoral strategy, the salience of the crime and drug issues declined dramatically following President Nixon's departure from office. Neither (Republican) President Ford nor (Democratic) President Carter mentioned crime-related issues in their State of the Union addresses or took much legislative action on those issues. For Ford, whose ascent into office was the consequence of criminal wrongdoing by his predecessor, emphasizing the Republican commitment to fighting crime would have been rather awkward. The Carter administration also seems to have had little interest in the crime issue, although it did initially advocate decriminalization of marijuana. As a result of this inattention, both the crime and drug issues largely disappeared from national political discourse in the latter part of the 1970s.

During and after the 1980 election campaign, however, the crime issue once again assumed a central place on the national political agenda. Candidate and President Ronald Reagan, following the trail first blazed by his conservative predecessors, lavished attention on the problem of "crime in the streets" and promised to enhance the federal government's role in combating it. Once in office, Reagan instructed the new Attorney General, William French Smith, to establish a task force to recommend "ways in which the federal government can do more to combat violent crime." Because state and local governments are largely responsible for identifying and prosecuting conventional street crime, however, the administration's desire to involve the federal government in combating violent crime was problematic. Nevertheless, the Reagan administration began to pressure federal law enforcement agencies to set aside their focus on white-collar offenses and shift their attention to street crime instead. By October 1981, less than one year into the new administration, the Justice Department announced its intention to cut the number of specialists assigned to identify and prosecute white-collar criminals in half. The Reagan administration's crackdown on crime also explicitly excluded domestic violence on the grounds that it was "not the kind of street violence about which the Task Force was organized."

In the ensuing years, President Reagan frequently returned to the topic of crime, striking all the now-familiar conservative themes. Time and again, he rejected the notion that crime and related social ills have socioeconomic causes.

According to Reagan, "The American people have lost patience with liberal leniency and pseudointellectual apologies for crime." Instead, Reagan argued, the new "political consensus" emphasized free will.

Furthermore, he asserted, the reality of human nature is such that only the threat of punishment will deter criminal behavior:

> The crime epidemic threat has spread throughout our country, and it's no uncontrollable disease, much less an irreversible tide. Nor is it some inevitable sociological phenomenon. . . . It is, instead, and in large measure, a cumulative result of too much emphasis on the protection of the rights of the accused and too little concern for our government's responsibility to protect the lives, homes, and rights of our law-abiding citizens. . . . The criminal element now calculates that crime really does pay.

Reagan also echoed his conservative predecessors on the putative relationship between crime and welfare. The naive view that "blocked opportunities" cause crime, Reagan suggested, led liberals to believe that the "war on poverty" would solve the problem. In fact, it is the government's attempt to ameliorate poverty—not poverty itself—that causes crime:

> By nearly every measure, the position of poor Americans worsened under the leadership of our opponents. Teenage drug use, out-of-wedlock births, and crime increased dramatically. Urban neighborhoods and schools deteriorated. Those whom the government intended to help discovered a cycle of dependency that could not be broken. Government became a drug, providing temporary relief, but addiction as well.

President Reagan thus argued that welfare programs such as AFDC not only "keep the poor poor" but also accounted, along with lenient

crime policies, for the rising crime rate. In fact, studies investigating the relationship of welfare and crime find that greater welfare spending is associated with lower—not higher—levels of crime. Despite this, the argument that welfare causes crime was used, as it had been by welfare opponents in the 1960s, in an effort to legitimate reductions in welfare spending and the adoption of increasingly punitive crime and drug policies.

Finally, President Reagan argued that the government's functions had been distorted by his liberal predecessors. The state would be on more legitimate constitutional grounds and would more effectively "help the poor," he suggested, by scaling back public assistance programs and expanding the criminal justice system and law enforcement.

Reagan thus articulated the central premise of the conservative project of state reconstruction: Public assistance is an "illegitimate" state function; policing and social control constitute its real "constitutional" obligation. The conservative mobilization of crime-related issues was thus a key component of the effort to legitimate the shift from the "welfare state" to the "security state," a shift that is illustrated in Figure 1.

Political rhetoric notwithstanding, the view that crime had its origins in welfare dependence and humankind's propensity for evil was not widely supported. Instead, throughout the late 1970s and early 1980s, most Americans continued to attribute crime to socioeconomic conditions. In 1981, for example, a national poll found that most Americans believed that unemployment was the main cause of crime. Similarly, a 1982 ABC News Poll found that 58% of Americans saw unemployment and poverty as the most important causes of crime; only 12% identified "lenient courts" as the main source of this problem. However, members of the public have become more likely to embrace the view that criminal justice lenience is an important cause of crime.

FROM THE WAR ON CRIME TO THE WAR ON DRUGS

When it came time to translate its harsh rhetoric into policy initiatives, the Reagan administration faced the same dilemma as the Nixon administration: In the United States, fighting conventional street crime is primarily the responsibility of state and local government.

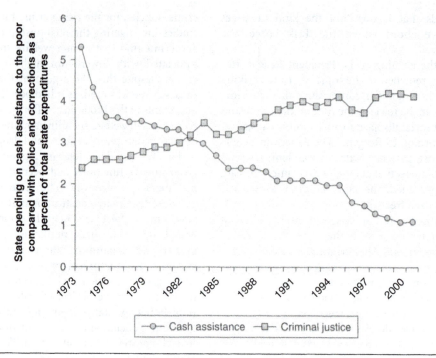

FIGURE 1   State Welfare and Criminal Justice Spending

SOURCE: U.S. Department of Commerce, 1974–2001.

Once again, the identification of drugs as a crucial cause of crime partially resolved this dilemma. In 1981, FBI Director William Webster announced that "the drug problem has become so widespread that the FBI must assume a larger role in attacking the problem." In explaining his willingness to shift the agency's attention from white-collar crime to drugs, Webster argued that "when we attack the drug problem head on, it seems to me that we are going to make a major dent in attacking violent street crime.

In sum, the Reagan administration's emphasis on the need for a tough approach to crime facilitated the emergence of the "war on drugs" and shaped the nature of that campaign. In particular, its analysis of the causes of the drug problem reflected the conservative emphasis on bad people rather than dangerous social conditions. "Narco-traffickers" and "drug pushers" were evil individuals motivated solely by greed. Drug users were also individually culpable:

If this problem is to be solved, drug users can
no longer excuse themselves by blaming society.
As individuals, they're responsible. The rest of

us must be clear that . . . we will no longer
tolerate the illegal use of drugs by anyone.

This belief in the importance of individual "accountability" also guided the recommendations made by the Department of Education under the leadership of (future drug czar) William Bennett. Students caught with drugs, Bennett argued, should be kicked out of school. Counseling these kids not only smacked of moral relativism but implied that drug abuse has "root causes" that are worth exploring.

Although public opinion has not been irrelevant to the development of federal drug policy, the "get tough" approach to drugs was not primarily a response to public attitudes. As of 1981, only 3% of the American public believed that cutting the drug supply was the most important thing that could be done to reduce crime; 22% felt that reducing unemployment would be most effective. Furthermore, the percentage of poll respondents identifying drug abuse as the nation's most important problem had dropped from 20% in 1973 to 2% in 1974 and hovered between 0% and 2% until 1982. Thus, public opinion polls do not indicate an upsurge in concern about drugs prior to Reagan's declaration of war, nor is there evidence of widespread support for the idea that fighting crime and drugs through tough law enforcement was the best solution to these problems.

The Escalation of the War on Drugs

Political and media attention to "the drug issue" intensified significantly in the summer of 1986. In part, this surge in attention to the drug issue was a response to the cocaine-related deaths of athletes Len Bias and Don Rogers and the increasing visibility of crack cocaine. The claims-making activities of federal officials also played a key role.

In October, 1985, the DEA sent Robert Stutman to serve as Director of its New York City office. Stutman made a concerted effort to draw journalists' attention to the spread of crack. "The agents would hear me give hundreds of presentations to the media as I attempted to call attention to the drug scourge," Stutman wrote later. "I wasted no time in pointing out [the DEA's] new accomplishments against the drug traffickers and using those cases to illustrate the full scope of the drug abuse problem. Stutman explains his strategy as follows:

> In order to convince Washington, I needed to make it [drugs] a national issue and quickly. I began a lobbying effort and I used the media. The media were only too willing to cooperate, because as far as the New York media was concerned, crack was the hottest combat reporting story to come along since the end of the Vietnam war.

This campaign appears to have been quite effective. The number of drug-related stories appearing in the *New York Times* increased from 43 in the latter half of 1985 to 220 in the second half of 1986. Other media outlets soon followed suit.

In an attempt to ensure that their party was perceived as taking action on the drug issue, Democrats in the House began putting together legislation calling for increased antidrug spending. Congressional Republicans warned Reagan that unless he came up with more specific antidrug proposals—and quickly—they would be compelled to endorse the $2 to $3 billion bill promoted by the Democratic leadership. And so

they were. In September, 1986, the House passed legislation that allocated $2 billion to the antidrug crusade for 1987, required the participation of the military in narcotics control efforts, imposed severe penalties for possession of small amounts of crack cocaine, and allowed the death penalty for some drug-related crimes and the admission of some illegally obtained evidence in drug trials. Later that month, the Senate proposed even tougher antidrug legislation, and in October, President Reagan signed the Anti-Drug Abuse Act of 1986 into law. In addition to the House proposals described above, this legislation prescribed harsh mandatory minimum sentences for some drug offenses. These penalties were based on the type and volume of drugs seized and prohibited judges from considering other factors, such as the offender's role in the offense.

The crime issue also enjoyed a high profile in the 1988 presidential campaign, in part as a result of George Bush's successful manipulation of what came to be known as the "Willie Horton" incident. Horton, a convicted murderer who had served most of his prison sentence, absconded from a Massachusetts furlough program while Michael Dukakis, Bush's Democratic rival, was governor. While on the loose, Horton kidnapped a couple in Maryland, tied up the husband, and raped the wife. During the 1988 campaign, Bush and his supporters used the incident in stump speeches and television commercials to mobilize outrage about crime and blame it on "liberal Democrats" like Dukakis. As one of Bush's political operatives explained, the incident was "a wonderful mix of liberalism and a big black rapist."

The Triumph of Law and Order

The outbreak of the Persian Gulf war in early 1991 eclipsed all domestic issues, and President Bush largely ignored crime and drugs during the 1992 campaign season. This shift probably reflects the failure of the war on drugs (as indicated by increases in drug-related emergency room visits and in the overall supply of cocaine and heroin within the United States), as well as candidate Clinton's relative invulnerability on these issues.

Like many "new" Democrats, 1992 presidential hopeful Bill Clinton was determined not to suffer the fate of the previous Democratic presidential candidate, Michael Dukakis, who was portrayed by the Bush administration as hope-lessly "soft on crime." As both governor and presidential candidate, Clinton expressed strong support for expanded police efforts, more aggressive border interdiction programs, and tougher penalties for drug offenders. As a result, "there was little about Clinton's crime control record in Arkansas that Bush could taunt him about the way he mocked Dukakis as a patsy for every dark-skinned murderer in Massachusetts." The 1992 Democratic platform also embraced the idea that levels of crime and drug use are a direct function of crime control efforts: "The simplest and most direct way to restore order in our cities is to put more police on the streets."

Despite his record as governor and his rela-tively tough talk during the election campaign, some speculated that on ascension to office, Bill Clinton would create space for alternatives to the "get tough" approach. His record and cam-paign rhetoric were somewhat ambiguous in this regard. On the one hand, Clinton empha-sized the need for greater law enforcement efforts and boot camps for juvenile offenders and touted his record on capital punishment. (Perhaps to make the point, Clinton returned to Arkansas in the midst of the 1992 campaign to oversee the execution of a convicted killer with an IQ in the 70s.) On the other hand, both before and after the election, Clinton occasion-ally evinced glimmers of a more sociological analysis of the crime problem. For example, in a speech to the Democratic Leadership Council shortly after the Los Angeles riots, Clinton char-acterized looters as people whose "lives and bond to the larger community had been shred-ded by the hard knife of experience." He also criticized the Reagan-Bush administrations for blaming crime problems on "them"—poor, non-White Americans. And he also spoke elo-quently of the need to reverse the trend toward racial isolation and of the government's respon-sibility to reduce social inequalities.

Clinton also offered some criticism of the Reagan-Bush war on drugs. In 1992, for example, he argued that "Bush confuses being tough with being smart, especially on drugs. He thinks locking up addicts instead of treating them before they commit crimes . . . is clever politics. That may be, but it certainly isn't sound policy, and the consequences of his craveness could ruin us." Janet Reno, Attorney General under Clinton, was also known to have derided

boasts of drug seizures and arrests as evidence of a misguided "body count mentality." In short, Clinton and his deputies sometimes espoused the notion that crime and drug abuse are related to social conditions, giving some observers hope that the new administration would advocate alternative approaches to these problems.

This potential was not realized. In August, 1993, Republicans announced an anticrime leg-islative package calling for increased federal aid for local law enforcement, enhanced federal sup-port for prison construction for states willing to adopt "truth-in-sentencing" provisions, more mandatory minimum penalties, and new restric-tions on the federal appeals process for death row inmates. One week later, Clinton and several key congressional Democrats proposed their own anticrime legislation, calling for federal support for local community policing efforts, enhanced federal support for prison construction, a ban on assault weapons, other gun control measures, and limits on appeals in capital cases. The most significant differences between the two parties' proposals were their positions on gun control, crime prevention, and the requirement that fed-eral aid to local law enforcement be used to bol-ster community policing efforts (all of which the Democrats favored and the Republicans opposed). These differences are not insignificant, but the legislation proposed by the mainstream of the two parties was fairly similar: Both emphasized the need to spend more on police and prisons. Only the Congressional Black Caucus developed anticrime proposals oriented toward a radically different goal: to "prevent crime [by making social investments, particularly in urban areas] and reform the criminal justice system to make it more fair."

The publicity associated with these legislative proposals appears to have had an impact on public concern about crime. The percentage of those polled who felt that crime was the nation's most important problem increased from 9% in June, 1993, to 22% in October, and to 32% by January, 1994. Attention to the crime issue increased still further when President Clinton used his 1994 State of the Union address to urge more Congressional action, including the adop-tion of a federal equivalent of California's "three strikes" law (which made life imprisonment mandatory for three-time convicts). Later that year, a national poll found that 72% of the voters endorsed these "three strikes" provisions;

28% opposed them. Most Democrats—pleased with new poll results indicating that Republicans no longer enjoyed an advantage on the crime issue—continued to support the expansion of the criminal justice system while offering only tepid criticism of some mandatory sentencing provisions and mild support for some preventive measures.

With Republicans demanding still "tougher" solutions to the crime problem, House and Senate campaigns in the fall of 1994 focused more on crime than on any other issue. In Florida, gubernatorial candidate (and son of the former president) Jeb Bush called for corporal punishment of the sort practiced in Singapore. On the television program *Meet the Press*, Texas Senator Phil Graham promised a "real crime bill" that "grabs violent criminals by the throat, puts them in prison, and that stops building prisons like Holiday Inns." In North Carolina, congressional candidate Fredrick Kenneth Heineman urged that provisions of the North American Free Trade Agreement be used to export U.S. criminals to Mexico, "where they can be warehoused more cheaply."

Under the leadership of then House Minority Leader Newt Gingrich, the Republican Party enthusiastically announced their "Contract With America"—including new anticrime proposals. This legislative package proposed further strengthening truth-in-sentencing, mandatory minimum sentencing, and death penalty provisions and weakening restrictions on the admission of illegally obtained evidence. In addition, despite the fact that less than one-fourth of the funds appropriated by the 1994 legislation were earmarked for preventive measures, the Republicans now proposed eliminating all such measures. Privately, Republicans argued not only that they doubted the efficacy of crime prevention programs but that their main beneficiaries were the urban poor—a group famous for its loyalty to the Democratic Party.

Despite President Clinton's embrace of virtually all of the components of conservative law and order rhetoric and policy, the election proved to be the ultimate vindication of the GOP's Southern strategy. With Gingrich leading the charge, Republicans won congressional victories in state after state, finally achieving the long-sought status of majority party in both the Senate and the House of Representatives. The goals advanced in the Contract With America were subsequently embodied in a series of bills passed easily in the House in February, 1995.

CONCLUSION

In this [article], we have argued that contemporary wars on crime and drugs reflect the ascendance of a particular way of framing the crime problem. Over the past three decades, conservatives have promoted the view that a variety of social ills, including crime, addiction, and poverty, stem not from blocked opportunities linked to class inequality and racial discrimination but rather from "permissiveness" in the forms of criminal justice leniency, tolerance of drug use, and welfare dependency. Undoubtedly, violence and drug abuse (especially in the age of crack) pose very real and significant problems, and the seriousness of these problems has increased popular receptivity to conservative claims. However, the conservative effort to frame these issues as a consequence of excessive "permissiveness" and "leniency" was not rooted in public opinion, nor is it consistent with the findings of most sociological research.

Instead, these claims-making activities were part of a larger effort to realign the electorate along racial (rather than class) lines and thus forge a new Republican electoral majority. They were simultaneously aimed at shifting the government's role and responsibilities from the provision of social welfare to the protection of personal security.

The fact that liberal politicians largely accepted this reframing of crime, drug use, and other social problems has meant that challenges to the law and order discourse have been few and far between. The liberal about-face on crime-related problems has many causes, including conservatives' ability to disseminate law and order rhetoric through the mass media and its resonance with much of the American public.

QUESTIONS FOR DISCUSSION AND WRITING

1. What do the authors suggest is the source of today's "tough-on-crime" policies?

2. The authors note that liberals and conservatives in the mid-1960s offered "very different" interpretations of poverty and crime-related problems. To what did conservatives attribute crime? Where did liberals lay the blame for crime?

3. What has the fact that liberal politicians largely accepted this refraining of crime, drug use, and other social problems meant?

PART III

ENDURING AND CHANGING PATTERNS OF CRIME

The idea that criminals specialize, that is, some are burglars, others robbers, and still others car thieves, is not quite accurate. A more correct image is one of offenders who, for whatever reason, violate norms and laws. Most are not particular about which ones they choose to violate, but while it is frequently erroneous to think about criminals as specialists, some types of crimes are clearly different from run of the mill, or "common," crimes. "Common crimes" is a label that we use to denote violations such as murder, rape, robbery, burglary, and so on. There are those who believe that some less common crimes are fundamentally different from these. Of growing concern to the general public, to law enforcement, and to criminologists are a number of types of violations that appear to be substantially different from many common crimes. In this section, we have selected articles on four types of crime that have been of concern in recent years: gang activity, sex offenses, cybercrime, and terrorism.

The first article in this section, by Esbensen and Weerman, is a comparative study of youth gangs in the United States and the Netherlands. The novice criminologist might wonder why the authors compared gangs in these two nations or even why the editors of this volume selected this type of piece. Concerning the latter question, there is growing recognition among social scientists that our understanding of human behavior and social life is enhanced if we study them comparatively. When we restrict our consideration to just the American setting, we miss opportunities to observe similarities and differences that help us to understand the phenomena in question. In the comparison of U.S. and Dutch youth gangs, we learn that they are, in some respects, very similar. This means that the existence of gangs is not a consequence of something unique to either society. The editors of this reader felt that students should have the opportunity to see the learning value in comparative analyses. Our other question, why study these two nations, requires a two-part answer. No doubt one reason that we included a comparison between the U.S. and the Netherlands is that one of the authors teaches at an American university while the other works in a Dutch research institute. Like many criminologists whose work you will read about in later chapters, Esbensen and Weerman have taken advantage of their geographic locations to teach us something important about crime. The second part of the answer to the question is that they have much in common but are very different in important respects. As they read this article, students should ask themselves about the similar causes of youth gangs in Dutch and American societies and the differences between the two nations that cause some observable differences between gangs.

The article by Miethe, Olson, and Mitchell reports on a study of one of the most feared and widely discussed categories of crime: sex offenses. Many states and the U.S. federal government have passed new laws in recent years specifically to control sex offenders. Much of that policy, and public opinion about these crimes and those who commit them, is predicated on the belief that these crimes are substantially different. Policy makers and the general public are convinced that sex offenders, unlike other common criminals, do specialize. Miethe and his colleagues examine this perception and find that it is in error. Students should question why the public is so convinced of this perception and how it leads to criminal justice policies that are likely to be less successful than promised. Students should also ask whether social policy about sex offenses is a result of knowledge obtained from good research or a product of what sociologists call "moral panics."

Explanations of cybercrime, a product of late 20th-century technological innovations, could obviously not have been on the minds of early criminological theorists. Yar reports, however, that some have suggested that theories developed to explain what can be called "terrestrial crimes" can be used to explain crimes in the "virtual" world as well. This argument is based on a belief that cybercrime is fundamentally like other crime. Students should know that most scientists believe that until a phenomenon, in this case cybercrime, has been demonstrated to be different from the broader class to which it belongs, in this case terrestrial/common crimes, we should assume that the former is not different. Yar uses Routine Activities Theory, which you will read more about in Part VII, to test the thesis that good criminological theory developed to explain terrestrial crime can effectively be used to explain cybercrime. Before reading this article, students should ask themselves how cybercrime is likely to be different from common crimes, and how they may be alike. To the extent that they are different, are there other criminal types that are byproducts of technological innovation that may also be different?

The last piece in Part III focuses on terrorism. But, one might ask, why discuss terrorism in a criminology text? After all, it is a political strategy, and understanding it requires a political or social movement analysis, right? On the other hand, terrorism violates laws and criminal justice agents are charged with controlling it, so shouldn't it be within the purview of criminology? LaFree and Dugan take on these questions. They compare terrorism to common crimes and examine the extent to which the tools of criminology can help us understand this type of crime, which, while not new, has increasingly become a part of modern life. As they read this piece, students should ask which of the forces that propel people to crime may propel some to engage in terrorism.

Criminologists have known for quite a long time that most criminals do not specialize; they rarely are just burglars, or just thieves, or just child molesters. Students new to the study of criminology should consider what we know about crime, and misperceptions of crime, in the context of the lessons learned in Part II. Our perceptions of crime are products not just of empirical realities, but also of political discourses, our fears, and media representations. And crime and criminal justice policies are frequently based more on erroneous perceptions than on solid evidence. What are the negative consequences of this for our capacity to control criminal activity?

 For a data analysis exercise that accompanies the material in this section, go to www.sagepub.com/crimereadings3study.

YOUTH GANGS AND TROUBLESOME YOUTH GROUPS IN THE UNITED STATES AND THE NETHERLANDS

A Cross-National Comparison

FINN-AAGE ESBENSEN

FRANK M. WEERMAN

INTRODUCTION

Gang research in the United States of America has a long history, one that experienced a resurgence of interest in the 1990s. No comparable history of gang research exists elsewhere, although assessments of youth gangs outside the USA have appeared periodically. In 1998, a group of European and American researchers convened the first meeting of what has become known as the Eurogang Program of Research, a multinational collaborative effort that seeks to understand gangs and troublesome youth groups. Between 2001 and 2003, this group of researchers developed instruments for use in the comparative study of youth groups. The research reported here informed some of the decisions of that group and represents a small part of this larger effort.

Gang research has been quite parochial, focusing on one gang (sometimes case studies of only a few gang members), gangs in one city, or, at best, gangs in several cities. Thus, much of what is known about youth gangs is piecemeal and relies primarily upon information gleaned from almost 100 years of gang research in the USA. As the world becomes increasingly "one world," cultures, languages, economies, religions, as well as criminal activities transcend national boundaries. Although youth gangs have traditionally been viewed as an American phenomenon, the past decade has witnessed the emergence of considerable "gang-like" behaviour in Europe, Australia, South and Central America, Africa, and Asia. To what extent are these "emerging" youth gangs around the world similar to those found in the USA? This is a simple question, but it is nonetheless an interesting and intriguing one. Oddly enough, though, it is also a question that is virtually impossible to address. There is simply a paucity of data with which to answer the question. There is even an absence of data within the USA to address adequately the issue of the nature and extent of youth gangs within the USA. The annual surveys of law enforcement agencies by the National Youth Gang Center (NYGC) provide the closest thing to a national assessment of youth gangs in the USA.

Our goal in this article is to continue the work of Huizinga and Schumann in assessing the extent to which youth gangs in the USA are similar to troublesome youth groups found in other nations. We draw upon data from two school-based surveys of young adolescents—one in the USA and the other in the Netherlands. This research was not conceived as a collaborative effort, and therefore we do not have identical measures for a number of our core concepts, but the two studies do share similar measures and procedures that allow for cross-national comparisons. Our objectives are modest yet groundbreaking. We add to the growing knowledge of youth gangs by addressing the following five questions using two school surveys of youth—one in the United States and the other in the Netherlands:

1. How prevalent is membership in gangs and troublesome youth groups?

2. What are the demographic characteristics of members?

3. What risk factors are associated with membership?

4. Are the illegal activities of Dutch and American gang-involved youth similar?

5. To what extent are Dutch and American gangs and troublesome youth groups similar?

Prior to discussion of the research and results, however, we will provide a cursory overview of the key issues that we will explore.

Definitional Issues

The term "gang" evokes considerable reaction regardless of locale or audience. Movies, music (especially rap), and other forms of the mass media have exported gang culture and concern about gangs throughout much of the industrialized world. "Drive-by," "wannabe," and "colours" are but some of the terms that have been part of this diffusion of gang culture. With the diffusion has come a moral panic in some areas and concern about formally acknowledging a gang presence in others.

In spite of the apparent spread of gangs during the past 15 years, there is still considerable debate about what constitutes a gang, with different agencies and different researchers utilizing different criteria. A common understanding of the meaning of what constitutes a gang is even more complicated within a cross-national perspective. One reason for this is that wordings and terms used for gangs have different meanings and emotional loadings in different languages. Another reason is that many non-Americans compare their youth groups with stereotypes or ideal types of a highly organized Chicago-style gang or the Bloods and Crips of Los Angeles. Within this framework, they usually conclude that no such gangs exist in their country. Interestingly, research by Maxson and Klein, among others, has documented that the majority of American youth gangs do not match this stereotypical picture. Klein has referred to this false impression as the "Eurogang paradox." To resolve this paradox, members of the Eurogang Program of Research engaged in numerous discussions and ultimately developed a definition that allows for classification of youth groups as youth gangs. A gang, or troublesome youth group, is "any durable, street-oriented youth group whose involvement in illegal activity is part of their group identity." In some languages and/or national contexts, the word "gang" either cannot be translated or carries with it such emotionally charged meaning that it cannot be meaningfully used; consensus was reached to describe such groups as "troublesome youth groups." In this article, we generally use the word "gang," but it can be replaced by the term "troublesome youth group."

Sources of Information and
Gang Member Characteristics

Varying definitions of youth gangs are not the only reason for divergent estimates of the magnitude of the "gang problem" or for the different descriptions of gang youth that permeate the gang literature. Different sources of information (i.e., police reports, field studies, general surveys of youth) provide different pictures of gang member characteristics. A clear example of this type of "methods effect" is drawn from the American study included in this research. An official with a gang task force reported in an interview that, in his jurisdiction, there were no girls in gangs. Survey results from the school sample in that same city, however, indicated that almost half of the gang members in the city were female and that they were involved in a variety of violent crimes. Not only do the law enforcement official and the survey researcher have a different picture of the extent and nature of the gang problem, they would also have different suggestions for a community response.

Within the American experience, it is well known that varying definitions and sources of information produce different pictures of gangs and gang members. In general, law enforcement data paint a picture of inner-city, minority males, generally from single-parent households. Ethnographic studies of older and more homogeneous samples tend to confirm this picture. Surveys involving younger samples, however, call into question the extent to which these stereotypes accurately depict youth gang members. A similar picture of gang members appears to be evolving in Europe, based largely on police accounts and on relatively recent ethnographic studies. To what extent, however, are these findings based upon stereotyping or on limited information? In the USA, as survey findings have raised questions about the validity of the stereotypical gang member image, findings based on law enforcement data have begun to reveal a slightly different picture of gangs in America. Results from the National Youth Gang Survey have revealed the emergence of youth gangs in small towns and rural areas. The recent NYGC surveys also reveal that the race or ethnicity of gang members is closely tied to the size of the community. Whereas white youths comprised only 11 percent of gang members in large cities (where most gang research has taken place), they accounted for approximately 30 percent of gang members in small cities and rural counties. Most ethnographic studies of gangs have been conducted in socially disorganized communities in Los Angeles and New York—in other words, in urban areas characterized by high concentrations of minority residents. The general surveys of youth conducted in the 1990s examined youth gangs in cities lacking a long tradition of gangs; nonetheless, several of these studies were concentrated in high-risk neighbourhoods that (by definition) included disproportionate representations of racial and ethnic minorities. The same appears to be the case with European ethnographers; their studies are based on gangs in Frankfurt, Oslo, Amsterdam, Manchester, and other major cities. To date, studies of gang-involved youth in small American and European cities and towns are lacking. Thus, it is difficult to ascertain not only the prevalence but also the characteristics of gang youth.

Family characteristics of gang members, such as family structure, parental education, and income, also have been revised because the traditional stereotype is too restrictive—gang youth are found in two-parent, single-parent, and recombined families. In addition, gang youth are not limited to homes in which parents have low educational achievement or low incomes. Klein summarizes gang characteristics as follows:

> In regard to who joins street gangs, then, first, it is not sufficient to say that gang members come from lower-income areas, from minority populations, or from homes more often characterized by absent parents or reconstituted families. It is not sufficient because most youths from such areas, such groups, and such families do not join gangs.

Risk Factors Associated With Gang Membership

The use of youth surveys to study gangs is a relatively new phenomenon. It is only since the beginning of the 1990s that general youth surveys became a significant source of information on gangs and gang members. In Europe, there is still no established use of surveys to study gangs or troublesome youth groups, although a few recent survey studies have included items about gangs or youth groups. Although ethnographic studies offer rich and descriptive accounts of gang members or of particular gangs, youth surveys provide information about the proportion of a population involved in youth gangs and they enable comparisons and generalizations. They inform us about the organizational characteristics of gangs at different sites, about risk factors for gang membership, and about the longitudinal development of gang members and non-gang members. They also provide information about the unique contribution of gang membership to delinquent behaviour, apart from the influence of delinquent friends. The following discussion of "risk factors" associated with gang membership draws upon this emerging field of knowledge based on more general youth surveys.

It is important to keep several methodological distinctions in mind as we review the risk factors associated with gang membership. These surveys are usually based on samples of middle and high school students. This implies that the results are primarily valid for the population of youth. Ethnographies and law enforcement statistics generally include older gang members. Moreover, ethnographic studies often rely on key informants who are core members of gangs, and law enforcement statistics are likely to be based on the most delinquent of gang members. School surveys include more respondents from the periphery of gangs, including "wannabes." Surveys cover the less serious but also more common part of youth involvement in gangs and troublesome youth groups.

Some researchers claim that, compared with non-gang youth, gang members are more socially inept, have lower self-esteem, and in general have sociopathic characteristics. Moffitt has stated that youth gang members are likely to be "life-course persistent offenders." To what extent are such depictions accurate? Are gang youth substantively different from non-gang youth? Comparisons between gang and non-gang youth have been reported from Denver, Rochester, Seattle, San Diego, and an 11-city study.

The authors of these different studies used different questions and different sampling methods, which resulted in slightly different findings. In the Seattle study, Hill and colleagues found that gang youth held more antisocial beliefs, whereas Maxson et al. found that gang members had more delinquent self-concepts, had greater tendencies to resolve conflicts by threats, and had experienced more critical stressful events. On a more generic level, both the Seattle and San Diego studies found significant differences between gang and non-gang youth within multiple contexts, that is, individual, school, peer, family, and community characteristics.

In an attempt to examine the unique relationship of gang membership to attitudinal and behavioural characteristics, Esbensen et al. examined gang youth, serious youthful offenders who were not gang members, and non-delinquent youth. They found that the non-delinquent youth were different from the delinquent and gang youth: Non-delinquent youth reported lower levels of commitment to delinquent peers, lower levels of social isolation, lower tolerance for deviance, and higher levels of commitment to positive peers.

Using a somewhat different approach, in another study Esbensen et al. examined differences among gang members. They classified gang members on a continuum, beginning with a broad definition of gang members and steadily restricting the definition until only those youth who claimed to be core members of a delinquent gang that had a certain level of organizational structure were classified as gang members. They found significant attitudinal and behavioural differences between core gang members and those classified as gang members using the broad definition. They did not find any demographic differences among the different gang definitions.

In another report from the Seattle study, Battin-Pearson and colleagues compared non-gang youth, transient gang youth (members for one year or less), and stable gang youth (members for two or more years). Both the transient and stable gang members differed significantly from the non-gang youth on a variety of attitudinal and behavioural measures. However, few distinctions between the transient and stable gang members were found. The measures on which differences occurred tended to represent individual and peer-level measures (for example, personal attitudes and delinquency of friends).

One consistent finding from research on gangs, as is the case for research on delinquency in general, is the importance of peers during adolescence. In their comparison of stable and transient gang youth, Battin-Pearson and colleagues reported that the strongest predictors of sustained gang affiliation were a high level of interaction with antisocial peers and a low level of interaction with prosocial peers. Researchers have examined the influence of peers through a variety of measures, including exposure to delinquent peers, attachment to delinquent peers, and commitment to delinquent peers. Regardless of how this peer affiliation is measured, the results are the same: Association with delinquent peers is one of the strongest predictors (that is, risk factors) of gang membership.

Gang researchers examine school factors less frequently than other factors; however, they have found that these issues are consistently associated with the risk of joining gangs. Research indicates that gang youth are less committed to school than are non-gang youth. Some gender differences have been reported in regard to this issue. In the Rochester study, expectations for educational attainment were predictive of gang membership for girls but not for boys. In a similar vein, Esbensen and Deschenes found that commitment to school was lower among gang girls than among non-gang girls. No such differences were found for boys. Studies that examine juveniles' cultures and ethnic backgrounds also attest to the role of school factors in explaining gang membership.

The community is the domain examined most frequently in regard to both the emergence of gangs and the factors associated with joining gangs. Numerous studies indicate that poverty, unemployment, the absence of meaningful jobs, and social disorganization contribute to the presence of gangs. There is little disagreement that gangs are more prominent in urban areas and that they are more likely to emerge in economically distressed neighbourhoods. Among the few studies to explore rural and suburban youth gangs, Winfree et al. studied youth gang members in Las Cruces, New Mexico, and Esbensen and Lynskey reported on gang youth in rural areas and small cities included in an 11-site study.

The traditional image of American youth gangs, however, is characterized by urban social disorganization and economic marginalization; the housing projects or "barrios" of Los Angeles, Chicago, and New York are viewed as the stereotypical homes of youth gang members. The publication of Wilson's account of the underclass—those members of society who are truly disadvantaged and affected by changes in social and economic conditions—has renewed interest in the social disorganization perspective advanced by Thrasher (1927) and Shaw and McKay (1942). Los Angeles barrio gangs, according to Vigil and Moore, are a product of economic restructuring and street socialization. In addition to the pressures of marginal economics, these gang members experience the added burden of having marginal ethnic and personal identities. These juveniles look for identity and stability in the gang and gang subculture. Social structural conditions alone, however, cannot account for the presence of gangs. Fagan comments that "inner-city youths in this study live in areas where social controls have weakened and opportunities for success in legitimate activities are limited. Nevertheless, participation in gangs is selective, and most youths avoid gang life."

In the research reported here, we utilize school-based surveys of youth to examine the similarities and differences between gang and non-gang youth in the United States and the Netherlands. Our research seeks to address the five questions posed at the outset of this article. Conceived somewhat differently, our interests are examination of individual-level issues (i.e., the demographic characteristics of gang and non-gang youth, the risk factors associated with gang membership, and the levels of involvement in illegal activity) and group-level factors (i.e., the prevalence of gang membership in a general youth sample and the characteristics of youth gangs in two different national and cultural settings) associated with membership in youth gangs.

RESEARCH DESIGN

The USA Sample

During the Spring of 1995, eighth-grade (median age 14) students in 11 cities—Las Cruces (NM), Omaha (NE), Phoenix (AZ), Philadelphia (PA), Kansas City (MO), Milwaukee (WI), Orlando (FL), Will County (IL), Providence (RI), Pocatello (ID), and Torrance (CA)—completed self-administered questionnaires as part of the National Evaluation of the Gang Resistance Education and Training (G.R.E.A.T.) programme. The final sample consisted of 5,935 eighth-grade public school students, representing 42 schools and 315 classrooms. Passive parental consent, in which excluded students were those whose parents did not want their children participating, was used at all sites except one. Participation rates, or the percentage of children providing answers to the questionnaires, varied between 98 percent and 100 percent at the passive consent sites. At the four active consent schools, the participation rates varied from a low of 53 percent to a high of 75 percent. Comparison of school district data indicates that the study sample is representative of eighth-grade students enrolled in public schools in these 11 communities.

This sample has the standard limitations associated with school-based surveys: the exclusion of private school students, the exclusion of truants and sick and/or tardy students, and the potential underrepresentation of "high-risk" youth. With this caveat in mind, the current sample comprises nearly all eighth-grade students in attendance on the days that questionnaires were administered in these 11 jurisdictions. The sample includes primarily 13- to 15-year-old students attending public schools in a broad cross-section of communities across the continental United States. This is not a random sample and strong generalizations cannot be made about the adolescent population as a whole. However, students from these 11 jurisdictions do represent the following types of communities: large urban areas with a majority of students belonging to a racial or ethnic minority (Philadelphia, Phoenix, Milwaukee, and Kansas City); medium-sized cities (population ranges between 100,000 and 500,000) with considerable racial and/or ethnic heterogeneity (Providence and Orlando); medium-sized cities with a majority of white students but a substantial minority enrolment (Omaha and Torrance); a small city (fewer than 100,000 inhabitants) with an ethnically diverse student population (Las Cruces); a small, racially homogeneous (i.e., white) city (Pocatello); and a rural community in which more than 80 percent of the student population is white (Will County).

Students completed questionnaires (paper and pencil) in their classrooms (approximately 25 students per classroom). At least two researchers administered the surveys. One person read the questionnaire out loud as students followed along and wrote their answers in the questionnaires. A second, and sometimes third, researcher monitored the classroom, enhancing respondent confidentiality and helping students requiring assistance.

The Dutch Sample

The Dutch data were collected within the framework of the School Project of the Netherlands Institute for the Study of Crime and Law Enforcement (NSCR) "School project," a larger longitudinal study focused on the roles of peer network formation, personal development, and school interventions in the development of problem behaviour. Data from the first wave (2002) of the longitudinal study are used in the analyses reported in this article. Two objectives guided the selection of respondents for the sample: obtaining a relatively "high-risk" sample (i.e., with a substantial proportion of youth involved in illegal activities) while also maintaining adequate inclusion of "lower-risk" students to allow for variation in school contexts and student populations. To accomplish this, secondary schools in the city of The Hague with students following lower forms of education were asked to participate in the study, together with secondary schools from smaller cities and villages in the vicinity. The Hague is one of the

largest cities in the Netherlands and has clear inner-city problems. The participating schools from this city have ethnically mixed populations. The other participating schools had an ethnically more homogeneous (Dutch) population of students, who mostly followed lower forms of education. This sample is not a random sample, but it is fairly representative of the youth in the southwest region of the Netherlands following lower forms of education (60 percent of all Dutch youth follow education at this level). At this educational level, youths from lower socioeconomic groups are overrepresented. The participating schools in this study represent a cross-section of school types and organizations in the Netherlands. The sample represents the following types of communities: a medium to large city (about 500,000 inhabitants) with a majority of students belonging to a racial or ethnic minority (The Hague); two smaller- to medium-sized cities (about 120,000 inhabitants) with a majority of Dutch (white) students; and a smaller village (about 30,000 inhabitants) in which most of the student population is Dutch. The community composition of this sample is largely comparable to that of the U.S. sample.

The final sample consisted of 1,978 students from the first and third years of secondary education in 12 schools with a total population of 2,370 in the first and third years. (On average, young people start secondary school at the age of 12 in the Netherlands and reach the age of 13 during their first year.) As was the case in the American study, passive parental consent procedures were used (only two parents refused their child's participation). Thus, virtually all students in attendance on the day of the survey administration completed questionnaires. Owing to some scheduling problems on the part of the school and to some minor computer problems, a small number of students were unintentionally excluded from participation.

The questionnaire was group-administered in the classroom during normal school hours. Respondents received a small reward (a voucher for CDs to the value of €5) to encourage current and future participation. Two or three researchers were present during the administration of the questionnaire to monitor the situation and to answer questions. Computers were used to administer the questionnaire instead of the usual paper and pencil method.

Measures

It is important to state at the outset that this research compares survey responses from young people of similar ages attending schools in the Netherlands and the United States. Although a similar conceptual framework guided the two independent studies, the actual measures used were not identical. This lack of exact comparability is a limitation, but at the same time the use of common concepts does allow for examination of general patterns of relationships between risk factors and gang membership in the two samples.

Gang Definition

To establish gang membership in youth surveys can be difficult. Ethnographies are usually restricted to clear cases of gang situations and use rich and varied sources of information. Youth surveys are necessarily based on a limited number of questions. The identification of youth groups as gangs (or troublesome youth groups) is further complicated by definitional and operational problems with the gang concept. In many American surveys, researchers have relied on the self-nomination technique: Respondents are simply asked "do you belong to a gang?" To control for overreporting or inclusion of youth groups that do not meet the criteria of "youth gangs," researchers have used follow-up questions. For instance, some researchers have relied on a gang name, whether the gang is involved in delinquent activity, or whether the gang has group characteristics such as leadership and organization. In a 2001 article, Esbensen and colleagues examined the effect of varying definitions and found that the self-report item was, in and of itself, a robust measure. Each additional criterion led to fewer youths classified as gang members and these youths were increasingly more antisocial in attitudes and behaviour. This procedure appears to work quite well in the American situation where the concept of a gang is familiar to most respondents. In Europe, however, the use of the word "gang" or its synonyms (*jeugdbende, bande,* etc.) is less widespread and more ambiguous than in the United States. Asking directly if a respondent belongs to a gang might result in less reliable answers than in the USA.

As reported earlier, the Eurogang Program of Research developed a consensus definition of youth gangs: "A street gang is any durable, street-oriented youth group whose involvement in illegal activity is part of their group identity." To measure gang affiliation, a funnelling approach was designed. Respondents are asked a set of questions about formal and informal peer groups, characteristics of these groups, and illegal activities within the groups. At the end of these questions, respondents are asked if they would consider their group to be a gang (or its synonym in their own language). This technique offers "objective" criteria for the researcher to define a group as a gang under the Eurogang definition. At the same time, it incorporates the more "subjective" criterion of self-identification of respondents as members of a gang.

In this article, the Dutch school survey utilized an early version of the funnelling technique developed by the Eurogang Network, defining gang members as youth who belonged to a durable street-oriented youth group and who belonged to a group with a serious level of illegal activity (indicating that illegal activity was part of the group identity). Respondents who answered that they belonged to an informal group of friends that was not an organized club or organization and also not a subculture were seen as members of a "group." When the majority of the group members were between 12 and 25 years of age, the group was regarded as a "youth group"; it was also regarded as "durable" if it had been in existence for three months or more. Groups whose members did not usually meet in schools, homes, churches, or other non-public places were seen as "street-oriented." A serious level of illegal activity meant that some or most group members were substantially involved in damaging property, assaults, shoplifting, stealing things worth more than €5, burglary, or robbery; either most group members were involved in two or more of these offences, or some group members were involved in four or more offences. Recently, the funnelling procedure that was developed by the Eurogang Network was improved to capture street orientation and illegality as part of the group identity more directly. The procedure used in this article, however, is quite close to the thoughts and formulations of the definitive instrument. Further, the Dutch data represent the first study to apply survey methods to the subject of gangs and troublesome youth groups in the Netherlands.

In the American study, respondents were asked two filter questions: "Have you ever been a gang member?" and "Are you now in a gang?" This self-identification method, common in American gang research, was followed by a number of questions seeking information about the gang and its members. In this article, we restrict our gang sample to those youths who indicated that they were currently in a gang and that their gang was involved in at least one of the following illegal activities: getting in fights with other gangs, stealing things, robbing other people, stealing cars, selling marijuana, selling other illegal drugs, or damaging property. This is comparable to the way in which illegal activity is measured in the Dutch sample.

Demographic, Attitudinal, and Behavioural Measures

Both studies collected information on the age, sex, and household living arrangements of the youths. In the U.S. sample, respondents described themselves by race/ethnicity, whereas the Dutch respondents classified themselves according to ethnicity/nationality. See Table 1 for a summary of this information.

The attitudinal measures used in these analyses are representative of social control, social learning, and self-control theory. In this article, our primary goal is description, not theory testing. We will, nonetheless, structure our discussion of the measurement and analysis results according to the theoretical groupings. Indicators of self-control theory are parental monitoring, impulsivity, and risk-seeking; social learning theory is represented by peer delinquency, peer pressure, and moral attitudes/disengagement; social control theory measures are attachment to parents and school commitment. As stated earlier, it is important to remember that the measures used in the following analyses tap conceptual areas with different operationalizations; that is, the Dutch and American studies used different, though similar, questions to measure respondent attitudes and behaviours.

We also obtained measures of self-reported delinquency. Students were provided with a list of behaviours and then asked to indicate if they had ever committed the act. If the students answered "yes," they were asked to indicate how many times they had engaged in the behaviour during the previous 12 months or school year. In addition to a general delinquency measure, we created three sub-scales of behaviour: minor offences, property offences, and crimes against the person. To facilitate discussion of the findings from these two projects, we have converted all of the risk factor and behavioural analyses to ratios of non-gang to gang scores.

Results

An overview of the sample characteristics of non-gang and gang members can be found in Table 1. As can be seen, the demographic composition of the two samples is quite similar. The Dutch sample consists of 1,978 students, of whom 55 percent are boys; the American sample comprises 5,935 students, of whom 48 percent are boys. Almost all respondents in both studies are aged between 12 and 16 years, with mean ages of 14.0 and 13.8, respectively, in the Dutch and American samples. Ethnic minorities are relatively overrepresented. Respondents with a foreign background comprise more than one-third of the Dutch sample, although respondents with Dutch parents are still in the majority (62 percent); Turkish (8 percent), Surinamese (7 percent), and Moroccan (5 percent) respondents are the most common ethnic categories other than Dutch. In the American sample, whites (41 percent), African-Americans (27 percent), and Hispanics (19 percent) are the dominant groups. Most of the youths in each sample reside in a two-parent household (80 percent and 62 percent, respectively, in the Dutch and American samples).

Focusing on the breakdown by gang membership reported in Table 1, we see that the gang youths in both samples share characteristics relative to the non-gang youths. The gang youths tend to be older, male, more likely to live in a one-parent family, and, especially in the U.S. sample, more likely to be in a minority category.

Risk Factors

Prior research in the United States has found that a number of risk factors are associated with youths who belong to gangs. Much of that research is cross-sectional, which precludes testing for causality, that is, whether the presence of these risk factors leads to gang joining or whether being in a gang results in the development of these attributes. Some longitudinal

TABLE 1   Demographic Characteristics of Non-Gang and Gang Youth in the Netherlands and the USA

	The Netherlands			The USA		
	Total	Non-Gang	Gang	Total	Non-Gang	Gang
Sample size	1978	1861 (93%)	117 (6%)	5935	5393 (92%)	467 (8%)
Mean age	14.0	14.0	14.3	13.8	13.8	14.1
Age (%)						
12 or younger	11	11	4	0.2	0.2	0.4
13 years	32	32	25	29	30	14
14 years	18	17	24	60	60	60
15 years	25	25	30	10	9	25
16 or older	16	15	18	0.6	0.5	1.3
Sex (%)						
Male	55	55	60	48	47	63
Female	45	45	40	52	53	37
Family structure (%)						
Two parent	80	82	78	62	63	46
Single parent	16	16	20	31	30	41
Other	2	2	2	7	7	13
Race/ethnicity (%)						
Dutch	62	62	61			
Moroccan	5	5	3			
Turkish	8	8	3			
Surinamese	7	7	8			
Antillean	2	2	7			
Other	17	17	19			
White				41	42	25
African-American				27	26	31
Hispanic				19	18	25
Other				14	14	19

studies, however, have established that these risk factors do precede gang involvement. Thus, although we cannot address the temporal relationship of risk factors and gang membership in this study, we can examine the extent to which these established risk factors are present in two distinct samples of youths in the Netherlands and the United States.

Self-Control

Each of the studies included three scales to measure self-control theory. Low self-control is viewed as a cause of criminal and analogous behaviours. Gottfredson and Hirschi indicate

that low levels of parental monitoring contribute to low levels of self-control. Further, they suggest that individuals with low self-control tend to be more impulsive (i.e., to act on the spur of the moment) and more likely to engage in risky behaviour.

The indicators used in the two studies to measure parental monitoring are quite similar. For instance, Dutch youths responded to the statement "My parents know where I go to outside home," and the American sample to the statement "My parents know where I am when I am not at home or at school." The other Dutch statements in this scale also measure rule enforcement at home (e.g., "At home, I have to do what my parents say"). The American scale does not include this element of parenting. Contrasting gang to non-gang youths, we see from Table 2 that gang youths in both samples reported lower levels of parental monitoring than did non-gang youths. In the Dutch sample, the ratio of 0.88 indicates that Dutch gang youths experienced 12 percent less monitoring than did non-gang youths. Similarly, gang youths in the American sample reported 18 percent less monitoring than did non-gang youths.

The indicators for impulsivity and risk-seeking are more similar in content than was the case for parental monitoring. The American statements are based on the scale developed by Grasmick and his colleagues to directly test Gottfredson and Hirschi's self-control theory and the Dutch statements are a modification of those indicators. As such, both scales are quite similar, as indicated by the following two statements: "I often do things without thinking first" (Dutch); "I often act on the spur of the moment without stopping to think" (U.S.). As with parental monitoring, the findings with regard to impulsivity and risk-seeking reveal a significant difference between the gang and non-gang youth in each country. In both samples, gang youths reported

higher levels of impulsivity and risk-seeking—between 16 and 30 percent more—than did non-gang youths. For instance, the ratios of impulsivity reported by the Dutch and American samples were 1.29 and 1.16, respectively, and for risk-seeking the ratios were 1.30 and 1.25, respectively. Thus, although employing slightly different statements to measure three components of self-control theory, statistically significant differences between non-gang and gang youth were found in each sample.

Social Learning

Each of the two studies also included three scales measuring social learning theory: peer delinquency, peer pressure, and moral attitudes. As with the self-control measures, these three indicators of social learning theory differ somewhat in their actual measurement. Peer delinquency, for instance, consisted of respondents indicating how many of their friends had committed delinquent acts during the previous year. The American study listed 16 illegal acts, whereas the Dutch study included six illegal activities. The Dutch study requested respondents to indicate whether none, some, or most of

TABLE 2   Risk Factors and Gang Membership in the Netherlands and the USA: Ratio of Gang to Non-Gang Members and Raw Scores

	The Netherlands		The USA	
	Ratio[a]	Raw Scores[b]	Ratio[a]	Raw Scores[b]
Self-control theory				
Parental monitoring	0.88	8.65/9.86	0.82	3.11/3.78
Impulsivity	1.29	12.40/9.63	1.16	3.26/2.83
Risk-seeking	1.30	12.23/9.39	1.25	3.75/3.00
Social learning theory				
Peer delinquency	4.37	4.48/1.07	1.69	3.18/1.88
Peer pressure	1.16	2.93/2.52	1.55	3.56/2.29
Moral attitudes/disengagement	1.73	8.17/4.71	1.30	3.95/3.03
Social control theory				
Parental attachment (NL)	0.92	13.28/14.46		
Mother (USA)			0.86	4.21/4.91
Father (USA)			0.86	3.85/4.50
School commitment	0.80	6.64/8.34	0.80	2.91/3.63

NOTES: All comparisons between non-gang and gang youth in each sample were statistically significant at $p < .05$.
a. Ratio of gang to non-gang members.
b. Raw scores for gang/non-gang members.

their friends had committed these acts, whereas American youth could indicate whether none, a few, half, most, or all of their friends were involved in these illegal activities. In spite of these differences, the results are once again quite similar. The ratios of gang to non-gang reports of friends involved in these activities are 4.37 in the Dutch sample and 1.69 in the American sample. It is likely that the inclusion of some relatively minor illegal acts in the American study (e.g., "Skipped school without an excuse" and "Lied, disobeyed, or talked back to adults such as parents, teachers, or others") contributed to the smaller difference between gang and non-gang youth in that sample. The differences between the gang and non-gang youth appear to be quite robust.

Comparisons of the two remaining social learning measures—peer pressure (e.g., "My friends sometimes make me do things I actually don't want to do" and "If your group of friends was getting you into trouble at home, how likely is it that you would still hang out with them?") and moral attitudes/disengagement (e.g., "It's okay to steal if you need money" and "It's okay to steal something if that's the only way you could ever get it")—produced ratios indicating that the gang youth expressed more peer pressure to commit delinquent acts and held less conforming attitudes. The gang youth were more likely than the non-gang youth in both samples to indicate that stealing, lying, and hitting people were acceptable in a variety of circumstances (e.g., ratios of 1.73 and 1.30 for the Dutch and Americans, respectively).

Social Control

Two elements of social control theory were included in the two studies: school commitment and attachment to parents (in the American study, independent measures of attachment were obtained for mother and father). As with the indicators of social learning and self-control, the risk factors associated with social control theory distinguish gang from non-gang youth. The gang youth reported lower levels of both commitment to school (0.80 for both the Dutch and U.S. samples) and attachment to parents (0.92 for the Dutch sample and 0.86 for the U.S. sample for both maternal and paternal attachment). The same caveat applies here that was discussed above about the measurement of these concepts. Although the wording of the

statements is different for the two samples, the same concept is being measured.

Self-Reported Delinquency

One last area of investigation of non-gang and gang youth is the extent to which these youths were involved in illegal activities. Relying upon self-reported measures of delinquency, both studies find that, consistent with prior American research, gang youth were much more likely to report involvement in criminal behaviour. Whether we examine minor offending, property offending, crimes against persons, or a composite measure of all these sub-scales, the gang youth reported approximately four times the level of offending compared with the non-gang youth. The findings, shown in Table 3, are strikingly similar in these two samples.

Gang Characteristics

We now turn our attention to the gang as the unit of analysis. The gang-involved youth were asked a series of questions to describe their gangs. Table 4 presents these results. A cursory review of the findings reveals that, unlike the analyses focusing on individual gang youth, there were substantial differences between the Dutch and American gangs, at least in terms of what we refer to as gang descriptors. The American gang youth estimated their gangs to be larger (having approximately twice as many members as reported by the Dutch gang youth). The American gangs tended to have more characteristics associated with more formal or organized gangs: More than half of the American gang members described their gang as having colours or symbols (92 percent), some type of initiation rites (80 percent), established leaders (76 percent), specific rules or codes (75 percent), and regular meetings (58 percent). In contrast to this picture, fewer than 40 percent of the Dutch gang members indicated that their gangs had rules (38 percent), constant meeting times (37 percent), leaders (29 percent), and symbols (24 percent) or that they had to do special things to join (21 percent). Two other dimensions, which were tapped with different questions, reflected more similarity than difference: 44 percent of the Dutch and 38 percent of the American gang youth indicated that their gangs had subgroups; 56 percent of the Dutch indicated that boys and

Table 3   Self-Reported Delinquency and Gang Membership in the Netherlands and the USA: Ratio of Gang to Non-Gang Members and Raw Scores

	The Netherlands		The USA	
	Ratio[a]	Raw Scores[b]	Ratio[a]	Raw Scores[b]
Minor offending	3.56	6.76/1.90	4.054	4.29/1.06
Property offending	6.65	3.99/0.60	4.72	3.07/0.65
Crimes against persons	4.11	2.30/0.56	4.26	2.81/0.66
Total delinquency	4.38	14.15/6.40	4.83	3.72/0.77

NOTES: All comparisons between non-gang and gang youth in each sample were statistically significant at $p < 0.05$.
a. Ratio of gang to non-gang members.
b. Raw scores for gang/non-gang members.

girls did not do the same things in the gang, and 53 percent of the Americans said that there were specific roles for girls.

Although the two samples of gang youth perceived their gangs quite differently, the levels of their involvement in delinquent activity were very similar. As reflected in Table 4, these youth gangs were involved in a variety of illegal activities. Among the Dutch gang youth, almost all of them indicated that at least some of their members committed vandalism (95 percent), assault (95 percent), theft (95 percent), and shoplifting (86 percent); burglary (43 percent) and robbery (45 percent) were less common. The American gang members revealed a similar level of "cafeteria-style" involvement in illegal activity on the part of their gang: gang fights (91 percent), vandalism (80 percent), theft (70 percent), car theft (70 percent), and robbery (61 percent).

CONCLUSION

At the outset of this article, we posed the following five questions:

1. How prevalent is membership in gangs and troublesome youth groups?

2. What are the demographic characteristics of members?

3. What risk factors are associated with membership?

4. Are the illegal activities of Dutch and American gang-involved youth similar?

5. To what extent are Dutch and American gangs and troublesome youth groups similar?

Utilizing a common definition of youth gang membership—one that required the group to be involved in group-level delinquency—resulted in the classification of 6 percent of the Dutch sample and 8 percent of the American sample as gang members. A prevalence rate of 6 percent in a general sample of Dutch school children—although this sample slightly overrepresented high-risk youths—is surprisingly similar to the American rate. A denial that there are gangs in Europe (until recently, this has been the usual response to enquiries about gangs in most European cities) appears no longer valid. As defined in this research, youth gang membership (belonging to a durable, street-oriented youth group whose involvement in illegal activities is part of their group identity) in the Netherlands is not all that dissimilar from that found in the USA. Referring to these groups as troublesome youth groups rather than gangs may be preferable to some people (e.g., politicians eager to deny the existence of youth gangs), but that does not negate the finding that the risk factors and behaviours associated with membership in these groups are remarkably similar in both the Dutch and U.S. samples.

Equally interesting is the finding that the Dutch and American gang youths "look" alike, especially on risk factors that have been found to be associated with a number of adolescent problem behaviours. In both samples, the gang youths tend to be older and are slightly more likely to be males. Race and/or ethnicity and living arrangements are not significantly different for gang and non-gang youths in the Netherlands but they are for the American youth. The finding that Dutch gang youth are

TABLE 4   Gang Characteristics: The Netherlands and the USA

	The Netherlands	The USA
Gang size (no.)	34	61
Descriptors (%)		
Constant meeting times/regular meetings	37	58
Rules/codes	38	75
Have to do something special to join/initiation	21	80
Established leaders	29	76
Symbols/colours	24	92
Subgroups/age groups	44	38
Specific roles for boys/girls	56	53
Behaviours (%)		
Vandalism	95	80
Assault	95	
Shoplifting	86	
Theft	95	70
Burglary	43	
Robbery	45	61
Gang fights		91
Car theft		70

not disproportionately "non-Dutch" is of considerable importance, given the tendency in Holland and elsewhere to identify troublesome youth groups as foreigners or immigrants. This suggests that a considerable number of troublesome youths are indeed native Dutch and are either undetected or unacknowledged.

Our analysis of risk factors provided consistent and stable similarities between the Dutch and U.S. samples. In all instances, the responses by the non-gang youths were significantly different from those of the gang youths. Importantly, the differences (as represented by the ratio of non-gang to gang responses) were of approximately the same magnitude in both samples. Theoretical constructs from self-control, social learning, and social control theories distinguish gang from non-gang youths. These findings are quite robust and provide encouragement that criminological constructs measured differently are valid indicators of risk factors for gang affiliation.

The illegal activities of the Dutch and American gang-involved youths are also similar. They are four to six times more likely than non-gang youths to be involved in minor as well as

serious forms of delinquency. Interestingly, however, although the individual gang members in the two countries look and act similarly, the gangs are described quite differently. The Dutch gangs appear to be smaller and more loosely organized than the U.S. gangs. Only a minority of the Dutch gang youths indicate that their gang has features such as leadership, gang rules, and symbols, whereas these characteristics are reported by a majority of American gang youths. In short, our results suggest that U.S. and Dutch gangs are quite different in their appearance but at the same time their members are remarkably similar in terms of demographics and risk factors.

The research reported in this article, as stated earlier, was not a planned collaborative effort. Thus, the methods and measurement in the two studies were not identical, and the design differences in the two studies introduce three issues that could have affected the results. First, although the two studies incorporated questions that measured the same criminological concepts, the actual questions differed. These differences may have biased the results. Non-identical measures tend to produce slightly different results, which suggests that the results reported here may well underestimate the similarities between gang and non-gang youths in the two countries. This highlights the importance of the recommendations of the Eurogang Program of Research to incorporate a core of identical measures that all researchers will use in the study of youth gangs.

A second concern is raised by the time difference between the two studies: The Dutch study was completed in 2002, seven years after the completion of the U.S. study. Had the gang situation in the USA changed during the course of these seven years? One recent publication reports that the number of communities experiencing gang problems declined during this period and that the number of gangs and gang members also declined slightly between 1996 and 2002. This suggests that the prevalence of gangs may be even more similar than the 6 and 8 percent, respectively, reported in these two studies. Although the magnitude of the youth gang problem may vary across time, it is less likely that the characteristics of gangs and gang members would change dramatically in such a short period. Studies of American youth gangs report considerable stability in the risk factors associated not only with gang membership but also with delinquent activity. Thus, the seven-year difference between the studies may again have underestimated, rather than overstated, similarities.

A third and final concern is perhaps the most important and potentially most biasing: The two studies used different definitions of gang membership. The U.S. study utilized self-definition and group-level involvement in illegal activity, whereas the Dutch study relied on the funnelling approach developed by the Eurogang Program of Research, combined with group-level involvement in illegal activity. One potential criticism is that two different types of groups were compared. To address this concern, analyses utilizing different operationalizations of gang membership were conducted. Results from these analyses were remarkably similar to those reported by Esbensen and colleagues. Regardless of the criteria used to identify gang youth, the risk factors distinguishing gang and non-gang youths remained statistically significant in all of the analyses; only the magnitude of the differences varied. Therefore, we are quite confident that our findings are not the result of different methodologies and measurement. Nevertheless, the differences and potential biases remain, and we encourage future comparative efforts to employ not just similar but identical measures.

In addition to the methodological issues discussed above, future researchers are encouraged to explore more fully our finding that, whereas *gang members* appear to be quite similar in the two countries, the *gangs* differ considerably. These gang differences suggest that structural and cultural features of gang life are not universal and may vary across nations. Are the U.S. gangs larger and more organized owing to the historical tradition of youth gangs in the USA? Are the differences attributable to varying portrayals of gangs in the media in the USA and the Netherlands? One recent study found that American youths accept the social reality represented by the media and, as such, gang-involved youths were more likely to exaggerate the presence of and problems associated with gangs in the community. The American media rely largely upon law enforcement sources in reporting on youth gangs and consequently promote a picture of organized gangs with leadership, symbols, and other structural elements. Conversely, the Dutch media and Dutch law enforcement view youth gangs mainly as loosely organized but, at the same time, dangerous groups of delinquent youths. The question thus remains: Are the youths responding to the media presentations of their gangs or are the media accurately reporting the nature and structure of the youth gangs?

QUESTIONS FOR DISCUSSION AND WRITING

1. To what do non-Americans compare their youth groups? What did research by Maxson and Klein document? In what did the Eurogang Program of Research engage to resolve this paradox?

2. What is one consistent finding from research on gangs? What did Battin-Pearson and colleagues report? What is one of the strongest predictors of gang membership?

3. When the authors compared gang and non-gang youths, what did they find for levels of parental monitoring? What did they find for impulsivity and risk-seeking? What did they find for peer pressure and moral attitudes/disengagement? What did they find for commitment to school and attachment to parents? What did they find for self-reported delinquency?

4. What two substantial differences did the authors find between Dutch and American gangs? What three similarities did they find?

Specialization and Persistence in the Arrest Histories of Sex Offenders

A Comparative Analysis of Alternative Measures and Offense Types

Terance D. Miethe

Jodi Olson

Ojmarrh Mitchell

S ex offenders are a major focus of current crime-control policies and public concerns about crime. Various treatment modalities have long been offered to modify the behavior of sex offenders, whereas community notification laws have been more recently passed to increase public awareness of their presence in the community. Both traditional treatment practices and current public policy are predicated on the assumption that most sex offenders are specialists and persist in sex offending across their criminal careers.

Using national data on prisoners released in 1994, the current study provided an empirical evaluation of these basic assumptions about sex offenders. Following previous research, several measures of specialization were used to compare different groups of sex offenders and nonsex offenders over their criminal careers. The observed patterns of specialization and persistence are discussed in terms of their implications for future research and public policy on sex offenders.

IMAGES OF SEX OFFENDERS UNDERLYING PUBLIC POLICY

Various images of sexual offenders and their criminal behavior patterns are widely held by members of the general public, treatment professionals, and the legal profession. Many of these images reflect basic myths and misconceptions surrounding sex offending that derive from assertions by claim makers and media stereotypes of sensationalized and exceptional cases. Whatever their source or accuracy, these social constructions and images of sex offenders often form the basis of criminal law and public policy to control these offenders. In fact, these stereotypical images have been shown by several researchers to have serious negative consequences for the effective detection, treatment, and control of sex offenders.

On the basis of previous commentaries and anecdotal evidence, the dominant contemporary image of sex offenders involves attributions of uncontrolled sexual compulsion, specialization, and persistence in behavioral patterns over their criminal careers. For example, Sample and Bray contended that current sex offender policies are predicated on a notion of "once a sex offender, always a sex offender." These authors also quoted a public official who alleged that "they will never stop. That [sex offending] is just what they do." Similarly, Zimring identified four assumptions underlying current law and policies that project a comparable image of sex offenders. Elements of this image of sex offenders include (1) pathological sexual orientation, (2) sexual specialization, (3) fixed sexual proclivities, and (4) a high level of future sexual dangerousness. According to Zimring, these elements are interrelated and represent a collective portrait of the pathology-driven behavior believed to characterize serious sex offenders.

The common belief that sex offenders exhibit specialization and persistent behavioral patterns is clearly evident in treatment practices (e.g., chemical castration to reduce sexual compulsion) and public policies (e.g., community notification, sex offender registration, extended periods of civil commitment after serving criminal sentences). In fact, the major assumption underlying these programs and policies is that sex offenders will continue to repeat these offenses unless they are controlled through chemical means or greater public surveillance and monitoring of them. Within this context, Simon considered Megan's Law a "long-term strategy for managing a permanently dangerous class." Such language continues to perpetuate the belief that sexual predators are "persistent specialists."

Empirical research that determines the accuracy of these basic assumptions about specialization and persistence is important because the success of contemporary laws and policies is tied directly to this portrait of sex offenders. For example, if most sex offenders are versatile offenders who do not specialize in sexual predation, sex-based therapies and public policies that are predicated on this belief will not have any meaningful impact on sex offending. Similarly, if

most sex offenders have low recidivism rates, these same public policies that assume persistence in sexual offending over the life course would be largely unnecessary for purposes of crime control. Under these conditions, effective public policy for sex offending is only as good as the accuracy of the basic assumptions it makes about the propensity for sex offenders to be repetitive or persistent specialists.

Previous empirical studies of criminal offenders, however, are largely inconclusive about the degree of specialization and persistence among sex offenders. In fact, this research literature provides evidence of both generality and specificity in the behavioral patterns of sex offenders and extreme variability in their persistence over the criminal career. Previous research has also documented the variability of offenses and behavioral patterns that correspond to different types of sex offending.

Several large-scale studies have been conducted on the arrest histories of sex offenders in the United States and elsewhere. When compared with other serious types of criminal behavior, sex offenders in these large-scale studies are often found to exhibit lower recidivism rates and have less extensive criminal histories: These conclusions hold for both sex offenders as a group and within specific subtypes of offenses (e.g., rapists, child molesters). For example, of the nearly 10,000 sex offenders released from prison in 15 U.S. states in 1994, fewer than half (43 percent) were rearrested for any crime within three years of their release, compared with recidivism risks of greater than two-thirds for released robbers, burglars, larcenists, and drug offenders. No substantial differences in the likelihood of rearrest existed between rapists (46 percent) and other sex offenders (42 percent). Only about 2 percent of the released rapists in this study were rearrested for another rape.

The results of meta-analyses of past studies also provide some support for the general portrayal of sex offenders as primarily nonspecialists and nonpersistent offenders. Hanson and Bussiere's meta-analysis of 61 studies yielded an average recidivism rate of 13 percent for the commission of a new sex offense within a four- to five-year follow-up period, and only about one-third of sex offenders repeated any type of criminal offense in this reference period. However, the meta-analysis by Furby et al. highlighted the substantial differences in findings across

49 studies, leading them to conclude that "by selectively contemplating the various studies, one can conclude anything one wants [about the recidivism risk of sex offenders]."

The conclusion derived from available empirical evidence on sex offenders is largely contrary to the conventional wisdom and stereotypical image of them as chronic and persistent sexual predators. It is also contrary to the findings from self-reports and clinical studies that indicate long and extensive histories of sexual abuses among these offenders. However, basic differences in methodological designs of different studies are likely to contribute to these disparate conclusions. For example, nonrandom clinical samples are likely to overestimate the extensiveness of one's history of sexual predation because of their focus on the most chronic sex offenders, whereas high rates of unreported and undetected sex offenses contribute to substantial underestimation of the prevalence of recidivism when only official arrest data are used. Under these conditions, the true profile of the behavioral histories of sex offenders may fall anywhere between these two positions.

MEASURES OF
SPECIALIZATION AND PERSISTENCE

Specialization and persistence have been measured in a variety of ways within previous research on criminal careers of sex offenders and other offenders. Specialization implies some degree of repetition of the same offense behavior over time, but the time span may represent only adjacent periods (e.g., rearrest for the same offense at time 1 and time 2) or cover the entire scope of one's criminal career. Similarly, persistence also involves the commission of criminal acts over at least two distinct time periods, but these repeat offenders may be either generalists (i.e., commit different types of offenses) or specialists (i.e., repeaters of the same offense type).

Common measures of specialization in previous research that focus on the joint offense distributions in adjacent time periods include (1) transition probabilities for the diagonal elements that represent the likelihood of repeating the same type of offense at arrest k and arrest k + 1 and (2) Farrington's forward specialization coefficient (FSC), derived from adjusted comparisons of observed and expected cell frequencies. The most widely used measures of specialization based on the entire criminal career (not just the adjacent cycles) include those derived from (1) percentage rules (e.g., specialization is represented by at least one-half of an individual's offending history involving the same offense type) and (2) the "diversity index," indicating the probability that any two offenses drawn randomly from an individual's offense history belong to separate offending categories.

Regardless of the chosen measure of specialization, however, it is important to note that substantive conclusions are strongly affected by the level of specificity and generality that underlies how offenses are classified. In fact, as the number of offense categories increases, the likelihood of finding specialization decreases, in large part because finer gradations in offense categories make it less probable on chance alone that the same particular offense would occur on consecutive arrests. Under these conditions, the empirical observation of lower rates of specialization among sex offenders in general or particular subtypes of them may simply reflect differences in the scope of criminal behaviors included within different offense categories.

Previous empirical studies suggest several general observations about the criminal histories of various types of offenders. First, there is no definitive evidence that sex offenders exhibit more specialization than other offenders. Rapists are among the least likely offenders to specialize in some studies, whereas others have found that sex offenders have far greater risks than other offenders of repeating their crimes. Second, the research literature is largely divided on whether specialization is best studied by using generic or refined categories for measuring sex offending. Soothill et al., for example, found major differences within specific sex offense categories, whereas other authors have contended that the use of specific rather than global categories may result in a sizable underestimation of the amount of specialization among sex offenders. Third, most comparative studies find that sex offenders have lower rates of recidivism than other offenders, suggesting that sex offenders are one of the least persistent types of offenders. However, wide variability exists in the number of separate arrest cycles among particular sex offenders, covering the full range from one-timers to persistent and chronic offenders with multiple prior arrests.

RESEARCH QUESTIONS

Using a large national sample of prisoners released in 1994, the current study examined several interrelated questions about the criminal histories of sex offenders. First, what are the nature and magnitude of specialization and persistence among sex offenders? Second, do sex offenders exhibit lower or higher levels of specialization and persistence than other offenders? Third, are substantive conclusions about specialization and persistence consistent across different measures of these concepts, different stages of one's criminal career, and for both generic and offense-specific definitions of criminal behavior? By conducting these comparative analyses within the same study, the current research aimed to provide a strong empirical foundation for assessing the accuracy of the basic assumption underlying contemporary public policy that sex offenders are persistent specialists across their criminal careers.

DATA AND METHODS

The data for the current study involved a sample of more than 38,000 persons who were released from prison in 15 states in 1994. Originally collected through the U.S. Department of Justice and the Bureau of Justice Statistics, the complete data file is available for secondary analysis from the Interuniversity Consortium for Political and Social Research (ICPSR) at the University of Michigan under the title "Recidivism of Prisoners Released in 1994."

Using both state and Federal Bureau of Investigation (FBI) records of arrests and prosecutions, information in this data set includes demographic information (e.g., age, sex, and race) and the entire officially recorded criminal history of each released prisoner. Each offender's criminal history includes all known arrests, adjudications, and sentences before the 1994 release date and for the immediate three-year period following this date. The merging of state and FBI records provides a chronology of the different arrests for each offender in his or her state of incarceration and all other states.

Data were compiled for the three most serious charges at each arrest date. A hierarchy of offense seriousness was used by the original data collectors. Under this offense hierarchy, felonies were designed as more serious than misdemeanors, and particular offenses were classified in the following order from most to least serious: murder, rape or other sexual assault, robbery, aggravated assault, burglary, larceny or motor vehicle theft, fraud, drug trafficking, drug possession, weapons offenses, driving under the influence, other public order crimes, and other offenses. We recoded the most serious charges into generic categories (e.g., sex offenders, violent offenders, property offenders, public order offenders) and also retained the more refined offense-specific groupings (e.g., rapists, child molesters, robbers, burglars) that were derived from state statutes. Each distinct arrest date was considered a separate transition or "cycle" in the database, and a total of up to 99 separate arrest cycles were included for each person. The number and timing of these arrest cycles, as well as the most serious offense within each transition, formed the basis of our investigation of specialization and persistence.

Strengths and Limitations of Data Source

As a basis for studying the specialization and persistence of criminal careers, the data set used in the present study has several strengths and weaknesses. The choice of this data source was based on our contention that its strengths far exceed its limitations.

Compared with other available data collections for studying criminal careers, the primary advantages of the current source include its large sample size, national coverage, comprehensiveness of criminal history records, and inclusion of multiple arrest cycles throughout different stages of the criminal career. Specifically, about 10,000 male sex offenders released from state prisons in 1994 are contained in this data file, and the entire sample of 15 states represents about two-thirds of prisoners released across the entire country in that year. This unparalleled "national" coverage is augmented by the comprehensiveness of the criminal history records (including both state and FBI rap sheets), the inclusion of both juvenile and adult arrest reports, and the ability to investigate multiple offense transitions ($k = 99$ cycles) at numerous time intervals and points in one's criminal career. In terms of both sample size and national coverage, no other data source collected in the United States is even remotely comparable.

The strengths of this national data source for studying the criminal histories of sex offenders are somewhat minimized by basic problems inherent with the data. For example, our substantive conclusions about specialization were restricted because the data source includes only official arrest records and convicted offenders who had served at least some time in state prisons. The fact that undetected and unreported criminal acts are not included becomes especially problematic if sex offenses are less likely than other offenses to come to the attention of law enforcement. Similarly, the inclusion of only released prison inmates in the sampling frame restricted our inferences to sex offenders who were incarcerated at some point in their criminal careers, a group of sex offenders who may be qualitatively different (e.g., having more extensive prior arrest records or committing more serious crimes) than sex offenders who have avoided incarceration; these offenders may also differ from offenders who were incarcerated but not released. Unfortunately, although these problems with using official records and prison populations limited the generality of our conclusions, they are not unique to this study. Given comparable problems of measurement and sampling bias in other data sources, we considered the relative strengths of the current data to provide a sufficiently sound foundation for investigating patterns of specialization and persistence among an incarcerated population.

Measures of Sex Offending and Other Offenses

Both generic and offense-specific measures of sex offending are included in the original data source and were used in the current study. Accordingly, a person was classified as a sex offender if he or she was arrested for any act of forcible intercourse (i.e., rape), child molestation, forcible sexual acts not amounting to intercourse, or nonforcible sexual acts (e.g., incest, fondling). Offense-specific comparisons were derived from separate analyses of arrests for the particular acts of rape and child molestation. Following common practices in previous research, nonsex offenses were coded into the categories of violent offenses (e.g., murder, assault, robbery), property offenses (e.g., larceny, burglary, car theft), and offenses involving public order (e.g., disorderly conduct, drug and alcohol offenses). Separate analyses were conducted using these general categories and specific offenses (e.g., rapists, child molesters, robbers, burglars) to assess how basic classification decisions affected our substantive conclusions about specialization and persistence.

RESULTS

Before addressing more completely the question of offense specialization and persistence, it is instructive to examine the average arrest profiles and demographic characteristics for different types of offenders in this sample. Table 1 summarizes these basic sociodemographic profiles by types of offenders defined by their incarceration offenses.

As a group and within specific subtypes of them, sex offenders in this sample were more likely to be male, be White, be older at first arrest, and have shorter arrest histories than other offenders (see Table 1). Sex offenders, on average, had about 7 separate arrests in their criminal careers, compared with an average of about 10 arrests or more among the other general offender categories. Among specific types of offenders, the average arrest histories were somewhat comparable for child molesters and rapists. However, both types of sex offenders had fewer arrests than robbers, burglars, and all other nonsex offenders except murderers. These data provide little credible support for the conventional belief that sex offenders are especially persistent offenders.

Several factors may account for the fewer number of arrest cycles for sex offenders relative to other offenders. First, the average age of first arrest was about two years older for sex offenders than nonsex offenders. Second, sex offenders released in 1994 served longer prison sentences than most other offenders. These average prison terms were about 18 months longer for sex offenders than both property and public order offenders (see Table 1). Rapists were surpassed only by murderers as the specific type of offender with the longest average imprisonment before release. This pattern of longer incapacitation and fewer active years for the opportunity for predation may contribute to the shorter number of different arrest cycles for sex offenders, especially among rapists.

Measures of Specialization

Specialization is defined as the extent to which offenders repeat offenses of the same type over

TABLE 1   Sociodemographic Attributes of Offenders Released in 1994

Type of Offender	Sample Size	Percentage Male	Percentage White	Mean Age at First Arrest (years)	Mean Arrests in Career	Time Served for 1994 Released Offense (months)
Sex offenders	9,806	99	62	25.2	6.8	37.2
Rapists	2,291	99	44	23.0	7.7	55.0
Child molesters	3,166	99	74	27.2	5.9	25.9
Other sex offenders	4,349	99	63	25.0	7.1	36.0
Violent offenders	6,340	93	38	21.2	9.9	36.3
Murderers or manslaughterers	1,217	90	46	23.1	6.6	60.1
Robbers	2,596	94	30	20.3	10.9	37.0
Aggravated assaulters	1,808	94	40	21.0	10.1	25.5
Other violent offenders	719	94	47	21.4	11.8	20.6
Property offenders	7,419	91	51	20.6	13.6	19.4
Burglars	3,129	96	55	20.0	12.8	23.8
Larcenists	3,272	84	47	21.3	14.8	15.9
Motor vehicle thieves	474	98	51	19.9	13.5	14.6
Other property offenders	544	94	58	20.7	12.0	19.2
Public-order offenders	10,060	91	41	22.1	11.2	16.9
Drug offenders	6,734	90	32	22.0	10.7	17.6
Other public-order offenders	3,326	94	60	22.3	12.3	15.6

their criminal careers. Previous research has used various measures of offense specialization. These measures derive from the diagonal elements of adjacent transition matrices (e.g., k to k+1 arrest cycles) and the pattern of similarity and diversity in offense types over particular stages and the entire span of one's criminal career.

Specialization in Adjacent Arrest Cycle

Several measures of specialization examine the consistency in offense types across adjacent arrest cycles. These include the basic transition probabilities and the FSC. Table 2 summarizes these two measures of specialization for the diagonal elements for various adjacent arrest cycles.

When compared by their probabilities of repeating the same offense over successive arrest cycles, sex offenders exhibited substantially less specialization than other offender types. The average diagonal probability indicates that about one-fourth (26 percent) of sex offenders repeated sex offenses at their next arrest periods, whereas about one-third of violent offenders and more than half of both property offenders and those arrested for public order crimes reproduced their same offenses in the next cycle.

The use of the average diagonal probabilities to measure the magnitude of specialization is reasonable as long as there is stability in the transition matrices over arrest cycles. However, this assumption of stationarity was clearly questioned in the arrest cycles for most offense types. In fact, a significant negative correlation ($r = -.72$) existed between the arrest cycle number (k) and the diagonal probabilities for sex offenses, whereas significant positive correlations between

TABLE 2   Measures of Specialization for Adjacent Arrest Cycles (k and $k + 1$) for General Offense Types

Offense Type at Arrest Cycles k and $k + 1$	Diagonal Probabilities for k to $k + 1$ Transitions									
	$k1$	$k2$	$k3$	$k4$	$k5$	$k10$	$k15$	$k20$	$k25$	Mean $k1$ to $k25$
Sex offense	.39	.36	.33	.28	.29	.27	.24	.25	.15	.26
Violent offense	.32	.32	.33	.35	.34	.35	.35	.31	.27	.33
Property offense	.52	.54	.53	.54	.53	.54	.56	.59	.60	.56
Public-order offense	.54	.57	.57	.59	.59	.62	.63	.59	.64	.61

Offense Type at Arrest Cycles k and $k + 1$	Forward Specialization Coefficient by Arrest Cycle k									
	$k1$	$k2$	$k3$	$k4$	$k5$	$k10$	$k15$	$k20$	$k25$	Mean $k1$ to $k25$
Sex offense	.33	.31	.29	.24	.25	.24	.22	.23	.13	.23
Violent offense	.16	.19	.19	.20	.20	.21	.23	.19	.16	.20
Property offense	.26	.29	.29	.30	.29	.30	.33	.33	.37	.32
Public-order offense	.25	.27	.26	.29	.27	.30	.31	.27	.30	.29

Offense Type at Arrest Cycle (k)	Sample Size for Offense Type at Arrest Cycle k								
	$k1$	$k2$	$k3$	$k4$	$k5$	$k10$	$k15$	$k20$	$k25$
Sex offense	2,180	2,429	1,849	1,428	1,144	474	207	86	41
Violent offense	5,015	4,980	4,540	4,296	3,950	2,278	1,265	667	373
Property offense	11,677	10,257	9,262	8,395	7,531	4,580	2,720	1,556	942
Public-order offense	10,067	10,860	10,723	10,051	9,449	5,887	3,476	2,030	1,182

these variables were found for property offenses ($r = .90$) and public order crimes ($r = .81$). There was a marginally significant, negative relationship between arrest cycle and the diagonal probabilities for violent offenders ($r = -.37$, $p < .10$). Sex offenders retained substantially lower specialization across arrest cycles even when we focused on offenders with extensive criminal records of 20 or more separate arrests.

The second panel of Table 2 displays the FSC for general offense types at various arrest cycles. The average FSC values were lower among violent offenders ($M = .20$) and sex offenders ($M = .23$) than property ($M = .32$) and public order ($M = .29$) offenders, suggesting again relatively lower specialization among sex offenders.

As was true of the analysis of diagonal probabilities, the FSC values varied across arrest cycles

and offense type. Decreases in FSC values over successive arrest cycles suggested a significant reduction in specialization among sex offenders ($r = -.61$) over their criminal careers. A pattern of rising specialization was indicated by significant increases in FSC values across successive arrest cycles for property crimes ($r = .54$) and public order crimes ($r = .55$). A positive but nonsignificant correlation was found among FSC values for violent offenses and arrest cycles ($r = .23$).

When coupled with the knowledge that sex offenders typically have less extensive arrest histories than other offenders (see Table 1), the negative correlation between arrest cycle and these measures of specialization for sex offenders provides strong evidence against their stereotypical portrayal as "persistent specialists." In fact, these results suggest that sex offenders with more extensive arrest records are actually more likely to be generalists rather than specialists. For property and public order offenders, however, the likelihood of specialization increases with increases in the extensiveness of their criminal careers. It is these latter types of offenders who are best represented by the notion of persistent specialists.

Specialization Over the Entire Criminal Career

Both diagonal probabilities and the FSC measure of specialization are based on patterns derived from adjacent arrest cycles. However, it is also important to examine specialization as measured by the degree of concentration of similar offense types in both adjacent and nonadjacent cycles. Two measures of specialization derived from the concentration of similar offenses include percentage rules and the diversity index.

A basic measure of specialization involves the percentage concentration of offense types that are repeated over the criminal career. Using a minimum of two different arrest cycles to define the criminal career, this measure of specialization requires the computation of the conditional probability of rearrest for a particular offense type given at least one previous arrest for that type of offense. The percentage concentration among offense types ranges from 100 percent specialization (all arrest cycles involve the same offense type) to 0 percent specialization (i.e., one-timers for whom no arrests involve the same offense type). Table 3 summarizes the results of this percentage concentration measure under different definitional criteria for classifying specialists and generalists.

Regardless of the particular offense type, perfect specialization is rarely observed across all arrest cycles. Public order offenders had the highest level of repetition of the same offense type over all cycles, but even among this diverse class of offenses, only 6 percent of them were perfect specialists (see Table 3). Only about 1 out of every 26 offenders (5 percent) had only sex offenses in their arrest histories, whereas the lowest level of perfect specialization was observed among violent offenders (1 percent). Under a 50 percent rule for defining specialization (i.e., at least one-half of arrests involve the same offense type), the highest degree of specialization was found among public order offenses (49 percent of these general offenses qualified under this decision rule), followed by property offenses (37 percent), sex offenses (23 percent), and violent offenses (16 percent). An identical rank ordering of offense types was found when specialization was defined by a concentration of the same offense under a 75 percent decision rule (i.e., at least three-fourths of the arrest cycles involve the same offense type).

The proportion of offenders who were nonrepeaters of the same offense is reported in the last column of Table 3. As a measure of generalists, this concentration of one-timers who did not repeat the same offense in any other cycle was substantially higher among sex offenders (61 percent) than any other offense type. Given the relatively high level of specialization among public order offenders, it should not be surprising to find that these offenders also had the lowest proportion of one-timers in their criminal

TABLE 3   Measures of Specialists and Generalists Across Criminal Careers Under Different Percentage Concentration Definitional Criterion (2 to 25 arrest cycles)

Offense Type	Sample Size	Specialists			Generalists		
		Percentage of Arrest Cycles That Repeat the Same Offense Type			Percentage of Arrest Cycles That Repeat the Same Offense Type		
		100 Percent	>75 Percent	>50 Percent	<50 Percent	<25 Percent	100 Percent Nonrepeaters
Sex offense	9,071	5.2	6.6	23.4	76.6	52.7	60.6
Violent offense	19,058	1.4	2.9	16.2	83.8	51.1	36.1
Property offense	22,574	2.8	11.1	37.0	63.0	27.8	22.9
Public-order offense	26,061	6.1	17.3	49.0	51.0	18.5	18.2

careers (18 percent). Overall, these results suggest that sex offending was typically an aberrant arrest pattern for the majority of these offenders.

The diversity index is another measure of specialization over both adjacent and nonadjacent arrest transitions. This index ranges in the limits from 0 to approximately 1.0, with a value of 0 representing complete specialization. As shown in Table 4, there was very little difference in the average diversity values across offense types. The lowest values on the diversity index were found for public order offenses (M = .48) and property offenses (M = .51), indicating that these offenses had the greatest specialization. Sex offenders were represented by the lowest degree of specialization. For each offense type (except property offenses), lower levels of specialization were found with increases in the arrest cycles. After the fifth arrest cycle, the diversity index revealed that sex offenders had less specialization for each arrest cycle than other types of offenders.

Differences in Specialization for Specific Offense Types

One possible explanation for the relatively low levels of specialization among sex offenders involves the wider range of criminal behaviors

included in each of the comparison groups. Compared with the relatively restricted behavioral domain in the category of sex offending, both the general categories of public order crimes and property offenses included various types of criminal behavior under their scope. This basic difference in the homogeneity of general categories increased by chance alone the likelihood of matching both public order crimes and property offenses over successive arrest cycles, thereby generating higher levels of specialization for those offense categories.

To evaluate the impact of coding and classification decisions on the finding of specialization, we reanalyzed these data using more specific comparative offenses. This revised classification scheme includes Part I Offenses under the FBI's Uniform Crime Reports (i.e., murder or manslaughter, rape, robbery, aggravated assaults, larceny or theft, motor vehicle theft), child molestation, and drug offenses. Measures of specialization under this more restrictive definition of offense types are summarized in Table 5.

As shown in Table 5, substantial conclusions about the relatively low levels of specialization among sex offenders differed somewhat when we examined specific offense types within general categories. The conclusions were also more measure specific (i.e., they varied more widely

TABLE 4   Measures of Specialization Using Diversity Index for Offense Types at Arrest Cycle *k*

Offense Type at Arrest Cycle (k)	Diversity Index by Offense Type at Specific Arrest Cycle k									Mean k1 to k25
	k1	k2	k3	k4	k5	k10	k15	k20	k25	
Sex offense	.42	.44	.51	.55	.57	.61	.61	.59	.59	.54
Violent offense	.51	.52	.54	.55	.56	.57	.58	.58	.57	.53
Property offense	.49	.48	.48	.48	.48	.49	.49	.48	.47	.51
Public-order offense	.41	.42	.44	.44	.46	.48	.50	.50	.51	.48

Offense Type at Arrest Cycle (k)	Sample Size for Offense Type at Arrest Cycle k								
	k1	k2	k3	k4	k5	k10	k15	k20	k25
Sex offense	2,180	2,429	1,849	1,428	1,144	474	207	86	41
Violent offense	5,015	4,980	4,540	4,296	3,950	2,278	1,265	667	373
Property offense	11,677	10,257	9,262	8,395	7,531	4,580	2,720	1,556	942
Public-order offense	10,067	10,860	10,723	10,051	9,449	5,887	3,476	2,030	1,182

TABLE 5   Measures of Specialization Using More Restrictive Offense Categories

| Offense Type | Mean Diagonal Probability | Mean Forward Specialization Coefficient | Mean Diversity Index | Percentage Rule | | | Generalists: Percentage One-Timers |
				100 Percent	>75 Percent	>50 Percent	
Rape	.16	.15	.62	1.4	1.9	12.5	73.8
Child molestation	.24	.23	.60	5.0	6.4	25.8	69.2
Murder	.11	.11	.62	.8	.9	8.8	84.7
Robbery	.21	.18	.63	.5	.9	6.6	57.0
Aggravated assault	.24	.19	.61	.4	.8	8.0	54.1
Burglary	.32	.25	.60	.6	1.6	10.2	44.4
Larceny	.21	.19	.62	.1	.2	3.1	63.4
Motor vehicle theft	.18	.17	.63	.1	.3	2.9	66.4
Drug offenses	.45	.32	.57	2.7	6.6	23.6	32.9

across different measures of specialization). Among specific offense types, drug offenses exhibited the highest degree of specialization across all measures, whereas murders were the least specialized offenses.

When differences within sex offenders were examined, child molesters were found to be more specialized than rapists, but their relative rankings compared with other offenders varied across measures. For example, approximately 70 percent of both child molesters and rapists were "one-timers" (i.e., arrested only once for their particular offense type), placing them among the lowest group along with murderers on this measure of specialization. Compared with the relatively high ranking of child molesters on the FSC, rapists were relatively low specialists on the basis of this measure. In contrast, perfect specialization was rare among all specific offenses, but child molesters and rapists were ranked relatively higher than other offenders under this 100 percent rule.

As was found in the analysis of general offense types, differences in specialization were observed across arrest cycles for specific crime types. For example, significant decreases in specialization over successive arrest cycles were found among child molesters on the basis of diagonal probabilities ($r = -.44$), the FSC measure ($r = -.42$, $p < .10$), and the diversity index ($r = .77$). Although the magnitude of the correlations was generally weaker, the same directional trends were found among rapists. In contrast, a substantially stronger and positive relationship existed between arrest cycle and specialization across measures for burglars (r values ranged from .58 to .78). The level of specialization and arrest cycles were not significantly correlated for motor vehicle theft across measures, but this correlation was substantial among drug offenders, but only when the diversity index was used to measure specialization ($r = .87$).

Given these substantial context-specific effects (i.e., the results varied by measure of specialization and arrest cycle for particular offense types), the average ratings of specialization provided in Table 5 should be viewed with some caution. In general, these results indicate that specialization was rare among each of these specific offenses. Conclusions about the relative specialization between them, however, depend in many cases on how we measure specialization and the stage of the arrest cycle in the criminal career under consideration.

Specialization and Versatility in the Arrest Histories of Serial Sex Offenders

Previous research suggests that offenders may be both specialists and generalists over their criminal careers. This idea that specialization may be superimposed on a versatile criminal career can be empirically demonstrated in at least two distinct ways. First, versatile offenders may become increasingly specialized through successive arrest cycles. Second, regardless of the stage of their criminal careers, "spree" offenders may commit the same types of offenses over several successive arrest cycles, followed by a different offense pattern.

We explored this possibility of "versatile specialists" by examining the pattern of arrest cycles for serial sex offenders (i.e., sex offenders with three or more arrests for sex crimes in their careers). Serial sexual rapists and molesters were rare in this sample (representing only 7 percent of all rapists and 8 percent of all child molesters), but these sex offenders are the group that is the most visible target of community notification programs and other crime-control efforts. Patterns of persistence, escalation, and desistance among these serial sex offenders are summarized in Table 6.

Serial sex offenders exhibited wide variability in their offense patterns over arrest cycles. More than one-half of serial rapists and child molesters had arrests for these particular sex offenses within the first third of their criminal careers, whereas only about one-tenth of them began their sexual predation during the last third of their arrest histories. A slightly higher proportion of serial child molesters (37 percent) than serial rapists (27 percent) were persistent specialists, meaning that they had at least one arrest for their particular type of sexual offense during the beginning (first third), middle (second third), and last stages of their criminal careers. About 4 out of every 10 of both types of sex offenders escalated into sexual predation in the later stages of their criminal careers. More than one-half of child molesters had concentrated sprees of at least three consecutive arrests for this offense, whereas only about one-third of serial rapists had similar sprees of consecutive arrests.

When compared with other repeat offenders, serial sexual offenders were different in several respects. First, with the exception of murderers, a lower proportion of serial offenders were found among serial rapists and child molesters than other offenders. For example, compared with less than 10 percent among rapists and child molesters, nearly half (44 percent) of drug offenders had at least three different arrests for drug offenses, and nearly one-third of burglars were serial offenders of this type of property crime. About one-fifth of robbers and assaulters had at least three arrests for their respective crimes. Second, arrests for particular offense types were more persistent and exhibited less escalation over the criminal career for nonsex offenses. Serial drug offenders and serial burglars were especially likely to persist in their respective offense types. Overall, these comparative results indicate that serial sexual predators exhibited more versatility in their arrest patterns than most other types of serial offenders. Only a modicum of specialization was embedded in otherwise versatile criminal careers, even among this small group of serial sex offenders.

DISCUSSION OF RESULTS

The current study was designed to empirically examine several questions about the absolute

TABLE 6   Patterns of Persistence, Escalation, De-Escalation, and Spree Arrest Trends Among Serial Rapists and Serial Child Molesters

Offense Type	Serial Rapists (percentage)	Serial Child Molesters (percentage)
Stage of first arrest for offense type		
First third of arrest career	56.7	53.7
Second third of arrest career	34.6	36.2
Last stage of arrest career	8.7	10.1
Persistence over criminal career	27.0	37.2
Escalation of offense type	38.8	43.1
De-escalation of offense type	22.4	11.0
Spree of three or more consecutive arrests for same offense type	38.0	58.3

and relative magnitude of specialization and persistence in the criminal careers of sex offenders. Our comparative results across different groups of offenders and various measures of specialization are summarized and discussed below.

As a group and across different measures, sex offenders in this sample are not typically specialists or persistent offenders. Of offenders with at least one arrest for a sex crime, only 5 percent were exclusively sex offenders (i.e., all of their arrests were for sex offenses), whereas the majority of them (60 percent) had only one arrest for a sex offense in their criminal careers (see Table 3). Alternative measures of specialization (e.g., transition diagonal probabilities, FSC values, the diversity index) provide similar results about the relatively lower specialization among sex offenders. In fact, using these measures, specialization among sex offenders drops substantially over successive stages of their criminal careers. For persons arrested for property and public order crimes, however, the observed degree of specialization increases through subsequent arrest cycles (see Tables 2 and 4).

When comparisons are made among specific offense types, conclusions about the level of relative specialization are more complex. Child molesters tend to exhibit more specialization than rapists across measures, but their relative position as specialists compared with other offenders depends on how specialization is measured and the career stage of the arrest cycle. Contrary to their common portrayal as serial sexual predators, arrests for sex offending tend to be an aberrant pattern for both rapists and child molesters. This is especially true compared with drug offenders and burglars, who more typically repeat the same offense at other arrest cycles. On other measures (e.g., the 100 percent rule, FSC), child molesters would be considered relatively more specialized than most other offenders. However, even among serial sex offenders, specialization exists primarily within a more general context of offense versatility.

Given the importance of specialization as a key assumption underlying various treatment programs and public policy initiatives, it is important to examine our findings more closely. Several possible explanations for our findings are described below.

As mentioned previously, conclusions about specialization are dependent on the coding and classification of offenses within general crime categories. All else constant, the more diversity of behaviors included in an offense category, the greater the likelihood by chance alone of finding this offense category repeated in subsequent arrest cycles (i.e., the greater specialization). In the present study, the category "sex offending" includes a far more restrictive range of behavioral patterns than more general categories such as property crimes or public order offenses. Accordingly, the more limited opportunity to discover high levels of specialization among more restrictive offense categories may explain the relatively low levels of specialization among sex offenders in the current sample.

Although our results are somewhat similar across measures in the current study, it is extremely important to use multiple measures of specialization in future research because of the inherent limitations and shortcomings of each approach. For example, traditional measures of specialization based on adjacent transition matrices (e.g., diagonal probability, FSC) ignore the repetition of offense patterns over nonadjacent cycles. Percentage-based computations of specialization over the entire career are affected by the number of arrest cycles, with greater specialization being more probable by chance alone the fewer the number of cycles. Similarly, numerical scores on the diversity index are a function of the amount of specialization, the number of offense categories, and the number of arrest cycles. It is only through the ability to assess the robustness of our findings across multiple measures that we have some confidence in the conclusion that sex offenders in this study are not typically specialized or persistent offenders in either relative or absolute terms.

A major limitation on the generalizability of our results involves the sample design and the use of official arrest data. Most of the arrest data were based on one's adult criminal record, limiting our ability to assess differences between juvenile and adult patterns. The use of a prison sample restricts our inferences to offenders who have served at least some time in prison, offenders who may be qualitatively different in their offense patterns than those undetected or nonincarcerated offenders. Similarly, by using an incarcerated sample, both the number and timing of arrest cycles may be shorter because of their less time "at risk" for reoffending than nonincarcerated offenders. Whether they have equal levels of specialization across arrest cycles, however, should be largely unaffected by sampling only people who have at least one incarceration experience. On the other hand, if it is true that specialization increases with age and over stages of one's criminal careers, the inclusion of more serious offenders with longer criminal histories in this prison sample may actually inflate our estimates of specialization.

Concerning the use of official data to measure criminal careers, the relative virtues and limitations of official data and self-report measures of crime are well known and need not be repeated here. Self-report studies indicate that the gap between actual and officially recorded sex offending (i.e., the "dark figures") is enormous. However, the same argument can be made for the dramatic underreporting and underrecording of other offenses as well (e.g., drug offenses, public order crimes, property crimes, violent offenses [especially domestic violence]). Similarly, we recognize that those who specialize in sex offending may be especially talented in avoiding arrest (and victims may be unwilling to report these crimes to the authorities for various reasons), but the same argument is also possible for other types of offenders.

Although there is no question that our use of official arrest data underestimates the criminal careers of all types of offenders, the biases in official data should not necessarily affect our substantive conclusions about the relative levels of specialization across different offender groups. Nonetheless, future research using both self-reports and arrest data is clearly needed to replicate the observed results in the current study.

CONCLUSIONS AND IMPLICATIONS

Contemporary public policy involving sex offenders includes offender registries, community notification campaigns, civil commitment laws, chemical castration, and increased sentences for sexual offense. These crime-control policies are based on the assumption that sex offenders are persistent specialists in their patterns of criminal activities.

Collectively, our results question this specialization assumption for sex offenders in general, particular types of sex offenders (e.g., rapists, child molesters), and across general and specific categories of other types of offenders. The number of arrest cycles and recidivism rates are lower for sex offenders than other general types of offenders, only about one-quarter of these offenders with multiple arrests repeat a sex offense in their next arrest cycle, and the vast majority of sex offenders are never arrested for another sex offense in their criminal careers. Even among serial rapists and child molesters, arrest cycles exhibit a predominant pattern of offense versatility and limited evidence of specialization.

The specialization assumption is even more problematic when the results of clinical and case studies are examined. Past research indicates enormous variability in the sexual paraphilias, motivations, target preferences, and modi operandi of various types of sexual predators. This diversity exists even within more specific categories such as preferential or situational child molesters and "power-control" rapists. The strong possibility of various types of displacement by sex offenders in response to control efforts (e.g., the substitution of different crime victims, the timing of offenses, changes in the spatial location) is additional evidence against the common stereotypical image of them as a highly specialized group of offenders.

Regardless of the actual level of specialization and persistence among these offenders, sexual predator laws have been viewed as "feel-good" legislation that symbolically serve to pacify public outrage by "doing something" about brutal, heinous sex crimes. However by focusing on only the small fraction of sex offenders who are covered by sex offender laws, both community notification laws and sex offender registration have been criticized for creating a potentially false sense of security for communities. In addition, several authors have contended that the assumption of specialization underlying sexual predator laws may also hamper law enforcement's detection and investigation of most sex offenders. By narrowing initial investigations of sex crimes to registered sex offenders, police agencies may help promote the stereotypical image of specialization and thereby inadvertently increase the victimization risks from those sexual predators who have remained undetected by the criminal justice system.

The effective treatment and control of sex offenders is a fundamental concern for the general population, criminologists, and clinicians. However, the overall effectiveness of particular public policies ultimately rests on the validity of their assumptions about whether offenders are best characterized as specialists or generalists. Given our major finding that the average sex offender in the current sample does not appear to be a persistent specialist over his or her arrest career, it seems somewhat unlikely that registration and notification policies will decrease sexual victimization. We hope that these findings serve as an empirical foundation for future critical analysis of contemporary laws and public policies directed at sex offenders.

SOURCE: From *Journal of Research in Crime and Delinquency*, Vol. 43, No. 3, 204–229, 2006. Copyright © 2006 Sage Publications. Reprinted by permission of Sage Publications, Inc.

QUESTIONS FOR DISCUSSION AND WRITING

1. What is the dominant contemporary image of sex offenders? How does the common belief that sex offenders exhibit specialization and persistent behavioral patterns affect treatment of and policy regarding sex offenders?

2. What was true about sex offenders as a group and within specific subtypes of them? When compared by their probabilities of repeating the same offense over successive arrest cycles, what was true about sex offenders? What did the analysis of FSC values show? What did the analysis of the proportion of offenders who were nonrepeaters of the same offense show?

3. As a group and across different measures, what was true about the sex offenders in this sample?

THE NOVELTY OF "CYBERCRIME"

An Assessment in Light of Routine Activity Theory

MAJID YAR

It has become more or less obligatory to begin any discussion of "cybercrime" by referring to the most dramatic criminological quandary it raises, namely, does it denote the emergence of a "new" form of crime and/or criminality? Would such novelty require us to dispense with (or at least modify, supplement, or extend) the existing array of theories and explanatory concepts that criminologists have at their disposal? Unsurprisingly, answers to such questions appear in positive, negative, and indeterminate registers. Some commentators have suggested that the advent of "virtual crimes" marks the establishment of a new and distinctive social environment (often dubbed "cyberspace," in contrast to "real space") with its own ontological and epistemological structures, interactional forms, roles and rules, limits and possibilities. In this alternate social space, new and distinctive forms of criminal endeavour emerge, necessitating the development of a correspondingly innovative criminological vocabulary. Skeptics, in contrast, see cybercrime at best as a case of familiar criminal activities pursued with some new tools and techniques—in Peter Grabosky's metaphor, largely a case of "old wine in new bottles." If this were the case, then cybercrime could still be fruitfully explained, analysed, and understood in terms of established criminological classifications and aetiological schema. Grabosky nominates in particular Cohen and

Felson's "routine activity theory" (RAT) as one such criminological approach, thereby seeking to demonstrate "that 'virtual criminality' is basically the same as the terrestrial crime with which we are familiar." Others, such as Pease, have also remarked in passing upon the helpfulness of the RAT approach in discerning what might be different about cybercrime, and how any such differences (perhaps ones of degree, rather than kind) present new challenges for governance, crime control, and crime prevention. Indeed, crime prevention strategies derived in part from RAT, such as situational crime prevention, have been proposed as viable responses to Internet crime. Nevertheless, there has yet to appear any sustained *theoretical* reflection on whether, and to what extent, RAT might serve to illuminate cybercrimes in their continuity or discontinuity with those "terrestrial crimes" that occur in what Pease memorably dubs "meatspace." The present article aims to do just that, in the hope of shedding some further light on whether or not some of our received, "terrestrially grounded" criminology can in fact give us adequate service in coming to grips with an array of ostensibly "new" crimes.

The article is structured as follows. I begin by briefly addressing some of the definitional and classificatory issues raised by attempts to delimit cybercrime as a distinctive form of criminal endeavour. I then explicate the formulation of routine activity theory that is utilized in the article, and offer some general reflections on some of the pressing issues typically raised vis-à-vis the theory's explanatory ambit (in particular its relation to dispositional or motivational criminologies, and the vexed problem of the "rationality" or otherwise of offenders' choices to engage in law-breaking behaviour). In the third section, I examine cybercrime in relation to the general ecological presuppositions of RAT, focusing specifically on whether or not the theory's explanatory dependence on *spatial and temporal convergence* is transposable to crimes commissioned in online or "virtual" environments. After considering in a more detailed manner the viability of Felson et al.'s conceptualization of "target suitability" in relation to the presence of persons and property in virtual environments, I engage in a similar examination of issues related to "capable guardianship." In conclusion, I offer some comments on the extent to which cybercrimes might be deemed continuous with "terrestrial crimes." Substantively, I suggest that, although the core concepts of RAT are insignificant degree transposable (or at least adaptable) to crimes in virtual environments, there remain some qualitative differences between virtual and terrestrial worlds that make a simple, wholesale application of its analytical framework problematic.

CYBERCRIME: DEFINITIONS AND CLASSIFICATIONS

A primary problem for the analysis of cybercrime is the absence of a consistent current definition, even amongst those law enforcement agencies charged with tackling it. The term, as Wall notes, "has no specific referent in law," yet it has come to enjoy considerable currency in political, criminal justice, media, public, and academic discourse. Consequently, the term might best be seen to signify a *range* of illicit activities whose common denominator is the central role played by networks of information and communication technology (ICT) in their commission. A working definition along these lines is offered by Thomas and Loader, who conceptualize cybercrime as those "computer-mediated activities which are either illegal or considered illicit by certain parties and which can be conducted through global electronic networks." The specificity of cybercrime is therefore held to reside in the newly instituted interactional environment in which it takes place, namely the "virtual space" (often dubbed "cyberspace") generated by the interconnection of computers into a worldwide network of information exchange, primarily the Internet.

Within the above definition it is possible to further classify cybercrime along a number of different lines. One commonplace approach is to distinguish between "computer-assisted crimes" (those crimes that pre-date the Internet but take on a new life in cyberspace, e.g., fraud, theft, money laundering, sexual harassment, hate speech, pornography) and "computer-focused crimes" (those crimes that have emerged in tandem with the establishment of the Internet and could not exist apart from it, e.g., hacking, viral attacks, website defacement). On this classification, the primary dimension along which cybercrime can be subdivided is the manner in which the technology plays a role, i.e., whether it is a contingent ("computer-assisted") or necessary ("computer-focused") element in the commission of the offence.

Although the above distinction may be sociotechnically helpful, it has a limited criminological utility. Hence, one alternative is to mobilize existing categories derived from criminal law into which their cyber-counterparts can be transposed. Thus Wall subdivides cybercrime into four established legal categories:

1. Cyber-*trespass*—crossing boundaries into other people's property and/or causing damage, e.g., hacking, defacement, viruses.

2. Cyber-*deceptions* and *thefts*—stealing (money, property), e.g., credit card fraud, intellectual property violations (a.k.a. "piracy").

3. Cyber-*pornography*—activities that breach laws on obscenity and decency.

4. Cyber-*violence*—doing psychological harm to, or inciting physical harm against others, thereby breaching laws pertaining to the protection of the person, e.g., hate speech, stalking.

This classification is certainly helpful in relating cybercrime to existing conceptions of proscribed and harmful acts, but it does little in the way of isolating what might be qualitatively *different* or *new* about such offences and their commission when considered from a perspective that looks beyond a limited legalistic framework. Consequently, most criminological commentators (especially those of a sociological bent) focus their search for novelty upon the socio-structural features of the environment (cyberspace) in which such crimes occur. It is widely held that this environment has a profound impact upon the structural properties and limits that govern interactions (both licit and illicit), thereby transforming the potential scope and scale of offending, inexorably altering the relationships between offenders and victims and the potential for criminal justice systems to offer satisfactory solutions or resolutions. Particular attention is given to the ways in which the establishment of cyberspace variously "transcends," "explodes," "compresses," or "collapses" the constraints of space and time that limit interactions in the "real world." Borrowing from sociological accounts of globalization as "time-space compression," theorists of the new informational networks suggest that cyberspace makes possible near-instantaneous encounters and interactions between spatially distant actors, creating possibilities for ever-new forms of association and exchange. Criminologically, this seemingly renders us vulnerable to an array of potentially predatory others who have us within instantaneous reach, unconstrained by the normal barriers of physical distance.

Moreover, the ability of the potential offender to target individuals and property is seemingly amplified by the inherent features of the new communication medium itself—computer-mediated communication (CMC) enables a single individual to reach, interact with, and affect thousands of individuals simultaneously. Thus, the technology acts as a "force multiplier," enabling individuals with minimal resources (so-called "empowered small agents") to generate potentially huge negative effects (mass distribution of e-mail "scams" and distribution of viral codes being two examples). Further, great emphasis is placed upon the ways in which the Internet enables the manipulation and reinvention of social identity. Cyberspace interactions afford individuals the capacity to reinvent themselves, adopting new virtual personae potentially far-removed from their real world identities. From a criminological perspective, this is viewed as a powerful tool for the unscrupulous to perpetrate offences while maintaining anonymity through disguise and a formidable challenge to those seeking to track down offenders.

From the above, we can surmise that it is the supposedly novel socio-interactional features of the cyberspace environment (primarily the collapse of spatial-temporal barriers, many-to-many connectivity, and the anonymity and plasticity of online identity) that make possible new forms and patterns of illicit activity. It is in this alleged discontinuity from the socio-interactional organization of "terrestrial crimes" that the criminological challenge of cybercrime is held to reside. I will now turn to consider whether and to what extent the routine activity approach, as a purported general theory of crime causation, can embrace such novelties within its conceptual apparatus and explanatory ambit.

DELIMITING THE ROUTINE ACTIVITY APPROACH: SITUATIONAL EXPLANATION, RATIONALITY, AND THE MOTIVATED ACTOR

Birkbeck and LaFree suggest that the criminological specificity of routine activity theory (RAT) can be located via Sutherland's (1947) distinction between "dispositional" and "situational" explanations of crime and deviance. Dispositional theories aim to answer the question of "criminality," seeking some causal mechanism (variously social, economic, cultural, psychological, or biological) that might account for why *some* individuals or groups come to possess an inclination toward law- and rule-breaking behaviour. Dispositional theories comprise the standard reference points of criminological discourse—Lombroso, Durkheim, Merton, the Chicago School, Bonger, Chambliss, and so on being "textbook" examples.

In contrast, situational theories (including various "opportunity" and "social control" approaches) eschew dispositional explanations, largely on the grounds of their apparent explanatory failures—they appear recurrently unsuccessful in adequately accounting for trends and patterns of offending in terms of their nominated causes. Routine activity theorists "take criminal inclination as given," supposing that there is no shortage of motivations available to all social actors for committing law-breaking acts. They do not deny that motivations can be incited by social, economic, and other structural factors, but they insist that any such incitements do not furnish a *sufficient* condition for actually following through inclinations into law-breaking activity. Rather, the *social situations* in which actors find themselves crucially mediate decisions about whether or not they will act on their inclinations (whatever their origins). Consequently, routine activity theorists choose to "examine the manner in which the spatio-temporal organization of social activities helps people translate their criminal inclinations into action." Social situations in which offending becomes a viable option are created by the routine activities of other social actors; in other words, the routine organizational features of everyday life create the conditions in which persons and property become available as targets for successful predation at the hands of those so motivated. For routine activity theorists, the changing organization of social activities is best placed to account for patterns, distributions, levels, and trends in criminal activity. If this is the case, then the emergence of cybercrime invites us to enquire into the routine organization of *online* activities, with the aim of discerning whether and how this "helps people translate their criminal inclinations into action." More broadly, it invites us to enquire whether or not the analytical schema developed by RAT—in which are postulated key variables that make up the criminogenic social situation; what Felson calls "the chemistry for crime"—can be successfully transposed to cyber-spatial contexts, given the apparent discontinuities of such spaces vis-à-vis real world settings.

Before such questions can be addressed, however, a number of extant issues relating to RAT must be tackled. The first relates to the specific formulation of the theory that is to be mobilized for present purposes. As with many other theoretical approaches, RAT does not comprise a single, self-subsistent set of explanatory concepts. Rather, it can take a number of different forms, utilizing a variable conceptual apparatus and levels of analysis, depending upon the specific orientations of the criminologists who develop and mobilize it. Moreover, the work of a single contributor does not remain static over time, but typically undergoes revision and development. Thus, for example, Felson has elaborated and refined his original "chemistry for crime" over a 25-year period by introducing additional mediating variables into what is an ever-more complex framework. Here I discuss RAT in something like its "original" formulation. This statement of the theory hypothesizes that "criminal acts require the convergence in space and time of *likely offenders, suitable targets,* and the *absence of capable guardians."* This definition has the virtue of including the "central core of three concepts" which appear as constant features of all routine activity models.

A second issue relates to the theory's controversial attachment to presuppositions about the "rational" character of actors' choices to engage in (or desist from) illegal activity. Routine activity approaches are generally held to be consistent with the view that actors are free to choose their courses of action and do so on the basis of anticipatory calculation of the utility or rewards they can expect to flow from the chosen course. Felson, for example, has made explicit this presupposition, and his work has been marked by a clear convergence with "rational choice theory." One common objection raised in light of this commitment is the theory's potential inability to encompass crimes emanating from non-instrumental motives. Thus, for example, Miethe et al. and Bennett conclude that, although routine activity theory exhibits considerable explanatory power in relation to property offences (those oriented to material and economic gain), it is considerably weaker in respect of "expressive" crimes, such as interpersonal violence. Similar objections can be raised from outside routine activity analysis, for example, by proponents of "cultural criminology" who highlight the neglect of emotional and affective "seductions" that individuals experience when engaged in criminal and deviant activity. I would suggest, however, that the basic difficulty here arises not so much from the attribution to actors of "rationality" per se, but from taking such rationality to be necessarily of a limited, economic kind. It may be a mistake to view effective dispositions as inherently devoid of rationality; rather, as Archer argues, emotions can better be seen as responses to, and commentaries upon, situations that we encounter as part of our practical engagements with real-world situations. Particular emotional dispositions (such as fear, anger, boredom, excitement) are not simply random but "reasonable" responses to the situations in which we as actors find ourselves. My point here is that, by adopting a more capacious conception of rationality (which includes aesthetic and affective dimensions), the apparent dualism between "instrumental" and "expressive" motivations can be significantly overcome. For the remainder of this piece I shall follow routine activity theorists in taking motivations "as given," without, however, conceding that such motivations must necessarily be reducible to instrumental calculations of economic or material utility.

CONVERGENCE IN SPACE AND TIME: THE ECOLOGY AND TOPOLOGY OF CYBERSPACE

At heart, routine activity theory is an *ecological* approach to crime causation, and as such the spatial (and temporal) localization of persons, objects, and activities is a core presupposition of its explanatory schema. The ability of its aetiological formula (offender + target − guardian = crime) to explain and/or anticipate patterns of offending depends upon these elements converging in space and time. Routine activities, which create variable opportunity structures for successful predation, always occur in particular locations at particular times, and the spatio-temporal accessibility of targets for potential offenders is crucial in determining the possibility and likelihood of an offence being committed. As Felson puts it, "The organization of time and space is central. It ... helps explain how crime occurs and what to do about it." Thus, for example, Cohen and Felson suggest that the postwar increases in property crime rates in the United States are explicable in terms of changing routine activities such as growing female labour force participation, which takes people increasingly out of the home for regularized periods of the day, thereby increasing "the probability that motivated offenders will converge in space and time with suitable targets in the absence of capable guardians." Similarly, they argue that "proximity to high concentrations of potential offenders" is critical in determining the likelihood of becoming a target of predation. Thus, at a general level, the theory requires that targets, offenders, and guardians be located in particular places, that measurable relations of spatial proximity and distance pertain between those targets and potential offenders, and that social activities be temporally ordered according to rhythms such that each of these agents is either typically present or absent at particular times. Consequently, the transposability of RAT to virtual environments requires that cyberspace exhibit a *spatio-temporal ontology* congruent

with that of the "physical world," i.e., that place, proximity, distance, and temporal order be identifiable features of cyberspace. I will reflect on the spatial and temporal ontology of cyberspace in turn.

Spatiality

Discourses of cyberspace and online activity are replete with references to space and place. There are purported to exist "portals," "sites" complete with "back doors," "chat rooms," "lobbies," "classrooms," "cafes," all linked together via "superhighways," with "mail" carrying communications between one location and another. Such talk suggests that cyberspace possesses a recognizable geography more or less continuous with the familiar spatial organization of the physical world to which we are accustomed. However, it has been suggested that such ways of talking are little more than handy metaphors that provide a convenient way for us to conceptualize an environment that in reality is inherently discontinuous with the non-virtual world of physical objects, locations, and coordinates. Numerous theorists and analysts of cyberspace suggest instead that received notions of place, location, and spatial separation are obsolete in an environment that is "anti-spatial." The virtual environment is seen as one in which there is "zero distance" between its points, such that entities and events cannot be meaningfully located in terms of spatial contiguity, proximity, and separation. Everyone, everywhere, and everything are always and eternally "just a click way." Consequently, geographical rules that act as a "friction" or barrier to social action and interaction are broken. If this is true, then the viability of RAT as an aetiological model for virtual crimes begins to look decidedly shaky, given the model's aforementioned dependence on spatial convergence and separation, proximity and distance, to explain the probability of offending. To take one case in point, if all places, people, and objects are at "zero distance" from all others, then how is it possible meaningfully to operationalize a criterion such as "proximity to a pool of motivated offenders"? Despite these apparent difficulties, I would suggest that all is not lost—that we can, in fact, identify spatial properties in virtual environments *that at least in part* converge with those of the familiar physical environment.

Positions that claim there is no recognizable spatial topology in cyberspace may be seen to draw upon an absolute and untenable separation of virtual and non-virtual environments—they see these as two ontologically distinct orders or experiential universes. However, there are good reasons to believe that such a separation is overdrawn, and that the relationships between these domains are characterized by both similarity and dissimilarity, convergence and divergence. I shall elaborate two distinctive ways in which cyberspace may be seen to retain a spatial geometry that remains connected to that of the real world.

First, cyberspace may be best conceived not so much as a "virtual reality," but rather as a "real virtuality," a socio-technically generated interactional environment rooted in the real world of political, economic, social, and cultural relations. Cyberspace stands with one foot firmly planted in the real world, and as a consequence carries non-virtual spatialities over into its organization. This connection between virtual and non-virtual spatialities is apparent along a number of dimensions. For instance, the virtual environments (websites, chat rooms, portals, mail systems, etc.) that comprise the virtual environment are themselves physically rooted and produced in "real space." The distribution of capacity to generate such environments follows the geography of existing economic relations and hierarchies. Thus, for example, 50 percent of Internet domains originate in the United States, which also accounts for 83 percent of the total Web pages viewed by Internet users. Moreover, access to the virtual environment follows existing lines of social inclusion and exclusion, with Internet use being closely correlated to existing cleavages of income, education, gender, ethnicity, age, and disability. Consequently, presence and absence in the virtual world translate real world marginalities, which themselves are profoundly spatialized ("first world" and "third world," "urban" and "rural," "middle-class suburb" and "urban ghetto," "gated community" and "high-rise estate"). In short, the online density of both potential offenders and potential targets is not neutral with respect to existing social ecologies, but translates them via the differential distribution of the resources and skills needed to be present and active in cyberspace.

A second way in which cyberspace may exhibit a spatial topology refers to the purely internal organization of the information networks that it comprises. It was noted above that many commentators see the Internet and related technologically generated environments as heralding "the death of distance" and the collapse of spatial orderings, such that all points are equally accessible from any starting point. However, reflection on network organization reveals that *not* all "places" are equidistant—proximity and distance have meaning when negotiating cyberspace. This will be familiar to all students and scholars who attempt to locate information, organizations, and individuals via the Internet. Just because one knows, suspects, or is told that a particular entity has a virtual presence on the Net, finding that entity may require widely varying expenditures of time and effort. Those domains (e.g., websites) with a higher density of connections to other domains (e.g., via "hyperlinks") are more easily arrived at than those with relatively few. The algorithms that organize search engines prioritize sites having the highest number of links to others, thereby rendering them more proximate to the online actor. Arriving at a particular location may require one to traverse a large number of intermediate sites, thereby rendering that location relatively distant from one's point of departure; conversely, the destination may be "only a click away." Thus, the distribution of entities in terms of the axis "proximity-distance," and the possibility of both convergence and divergence of such entities, can be seen to have at least some purchase in cyberspace.

Despite these continuities, it should also become clear that there exist qualitative differences between the spatial organization of non-virtual and virtual worlds. Most significantly, they exhibit significantly different degrees of stability and instability in their geometries. Non-virtual spatialities are relatively stable and perdurable. Granted, they can undergo significant shifts over time: Patterns of land use can and do change (as, for example, when the former industrial cores of cities are redeveloped for residential use; the sociodemographic configuration of locales is also subject to change (as with processes of "gentrification" and "ghettoization"); the proximity of places is elastic in light of developing transport infrastructures; and so on. However, given that non-virtual spatial orderings are materialized in durable physical artifacts (buildings, roads, bridges, walls), and their social occupation and uses are patterned and institutionalized, change in their organization is likely to be incremental rather than wholesale. It is this very stability in socio-spatial orderings that permits ecological perspectives such as RAT to correlate factors such as residential propinquity with predation rates and patterns. In contrast, virtual spatialities are characterized by extreme volatility and plasticity in their configurations. It was noted above that virtual proximity and distance may be seen as the product of variable network geometries and connection densities. Yet these connections are volatile and easily transmuted—little resistance is offered by virtual architectures and topologies. Thus, the distance or separation between two sites or locales can shift instantly by virtue of the simple addition of a hyperlink that provides a direct and instant path from one to the other. Similarly, virtual places and entities appear and disappear in the cyber environment with startling regularity—the average lifespan for a Web page is just a couple of months; actors instantaneously appear and disappear from the environment as they log in or out of the network. Consequently, the socio-spatial organization of the virtual world is built on "shifting sands." This quality presents considerable difficulty for the application of routine activity analysis to cyberspace, given its presuppositions that (a) places have a relatively fixed presence and location, and (b) the presence of actors in locations is amenable to anticipation in light of regularized patterns of activity.

Temporality

The ability to locate actors and entities in particular spaces/places *at particular times* is a basic presupposition of RAT. The explanatory power of the theory depends upon routine activities exhibiting a clear temporal sequence and order (a *rhythm*, or "regular periodicity with which events occur," and a *timing*, in which different activities are coordinated "such as the coordination of an offender's rhythms with those of a victim"). It is this temporal ordering of activities that enables potential offenders to anticipate when and where a target may be converged upon; without such anticipation, the preconditions for the commission of an offence cannot be fulfilled, nor can criminogenic situations be identified by the analyst.

The temporal structures of cyberspace, I would argue, are largely devoid of the clear temporal ordering of real-world routine activities. Cyberspace, as a *global* interactional environment, is populated by actors living in different real-world time zones, and so is populated "24/7." Moreover, online activities span workplace and home, labour and leisure, and cannot be confined to particular, clearly delimited temporal windows (although there may be peaks and troughs in gross levels of network activity, as relatively more people in the most heavily connected time zones make use of the Internet). Consequently, there are no *particular* points in time at which actors can be anticipated to be *generally* present or absent from the environment. From an RAT perspective, this means that rhythm and timing as structuring properties of routine activities become problematic—for offenders, for potential targets, and for guardians. Given the "disordered" nature of virtual spatio-temporalities, identifying patterns of convergence between the criminogenic elements becomes especially difficult.

Thus far, I have largely focused on the question of cyber-spatial convergence between the entities identified as necessary for the commission of an offence. Now I turn to consider the properties of those entities themselves, in order to reflect upon the relative continuity or discontinuity between their virtual and non-virtual forms. As already mentioned, the first of these elements, the "motivated offender," is assumed rather than analysed by RAT. Therefore, I shall not consider the offender further, but take the existence of motivated offenders in cyberspace as given. Instead, I shall follow RAT in focusing upon the other two elements of the criminogenic formula, namely "suitable targets" and "capable guardians."

Targets in Cyberspace: VIVA la Difference?

For routine activity theory, the suitability of a target (human or otherwise) for predation can be estimated according to its four-fold constituent properties—value, inertia, visibility, and accessibility, usually rendered in the acronym VIVA. Below I shall reflect on cyber-spatial targets in terms of these four dimensions.

Value

The valuation of targets is a complicated matter, even when comparing "like with like," e.g., property theft. This complexity is a function of the various purposes the offender may have in mind for the target once appropriated—whether it is for personal pleasure, for sale, for use in the commission of a further offence or other non-criminal activity, and so on. Equally, the target will vary according to the shifting valuations attached socially and economically to particular goods at particular times—factors such as scarcity and fashion will play a role in setting the value placed upon the target by offenders and others. Most cybercrime targets are *informational* in nature, given that all entities that exist and move in cyberspace are forms of digital code. Prime targets of this kind include the various forms of "intellectual property," such as music, motion pictures, images, computer software, trade and state secrets, and so on. In general terms it may well be that, in the context of an "information economy," increasing value is attached to such informational goods, thereby making them increasingly valued as potential targets. The picture becomes more complex when the range of targets is extended—property may be targeted not for theft but for trespass or criminal damage (a cybercriminal case in point being "hacking," where computer systems are invaded and websites are "defaced," or "malware" distribution, where computer systems are damaged by "viruses," "Trojan horses," and "worms"); the target may be an individual who is "stalked" and "abused," or members of a group may be subjected to similar victimization because of their social, ethnic, religious, sexual, or other characteristics; the target may be an illicit product that is traded for pleasure or profit (such as child pornography). Broadly speaking, we can conclude that the targets of cybercrime, like those of terrestrial crime, vary widely and attract different valuations, and that such valuations are likely to impact on the suitability of the target when viewed from the standpoint of a potential offender.

Inertia

This term refers to the physical properties of objects or persons that might offer varying degrees of resistance to effective predation: A large and heavy object is relatively difficult to remove, and a large and heavy person is relatively difficult to assault. Therefore, there is (at least for terrestrial crimes against property and persons) an inverse relationship between inertia and suitability, such that the greater the inertial resistance the lower the suitability of the target, and vice versa. The operability of the inertial criteria in cyberspace, however, appears more problematic, since the targets of cybercrime do not possess physical of volume and mass—digitized information is "weightless" and people do not carry their physical properties into the virtual environment. This apparent "weightlessness" seemingly deprives property in cyberspace of any inherent resistance to its removal. Information can be downloaded nearly instantaneously; indeed, it can be infinitely replicated thereby multiplying the offence many-fold (the obvious example here being media "piracy"). However, further reflection shows that even informational goods retain inertial properties to some degree. First, the volume of data (e.g., file size) impacts upon the portability of the target—something that will be familiar to anyone who has experienced the frustration of downloading large documents using a telephone dial-up connection. Secondly, the technological specification of the tools (the computer system) used by the "information thief" will place limits upon the appropriation of large informational targets; successful theft will require, for example, that the computer used has sufficient storage capacity (e.g., hard drive space or other medium) to which the target can be copied. Thus, although informational targets offer *relatively* little inertial resistance, their "weightlessness" is not absolute.

Visibility

RAT postulates a positive correlation between target visibility and suitability: "The potential offender must know of the existence of the target." Property and persons that are more visible are more likely to become targets. Conceptualizing visibility in cyberspace presents a difficult issue. Given that the social raison d'etre of technologies such as the Internet is to invite and facilitate communication and interaction, visibility is a ubiquitous feature of virtually present entities. The Internet is an inherently public medium (unlike other more closed ICT networks, such as "Intranets" and "virtual private networks" that restrict access, and hence visibility, to a selected range of actors). Moreover, since the internal topology of cyberspace is largely unlimited by barriers of *physical* distance, this renders virtually present entities *globally* visible, hence advertising their existence to the largest possible "pool of motivated offenders."

Accessibility

This term denotes the "ability of an offender to get to the target and then get away from the scene of a crime." Again, the greater the target's accessibility, the greater its suitability, and vice versa. Thus Beavon et al. identify the number of physical routes through which a target is accessible as a significant variable in the distribution of property crimes—a house situated in a cul-de-sac is less accessible than one situated on a street that intersects with a number of other thoroughfares. However, given that traversal of cyberspace is "non-linear," and it is possible to jump from any one point to any other point within the space, it is difficult to conceive targets as differentiated according to the likelihood of accessibility to a potential offender in this manner. Similarly, the availability of egress from the "scene of the crime" is difficult to operationalize as a discriminating variable when applied to cyberspace. The ability to "get away" in cyberspace can entail simply severing one's network connection, thereby disappearing from the virtual environment altogether. It is, of course, possible that an offender may be noticed during the commission of the offence (e.g., by an "Intrusion Detection System") and subsequently "trailed" back to his/her "home" location via electronic tracing techniques. However, such tracing measures can be circumvented with a number of readily available tools, such as "anonymous re-mailers," encryption devices, and the use of third-party servers and systems from which to launch the commission of an offence; this brings us back to the problem of *anonymity*, noted earlier. The one dimension in which accessibility between non-virtual and virtual targets might most closely converge is that of security devices that prevent unauthorized access. Cohen and Felson note the significance of "attached or locked features of property inhibiting its illegal removal." The cyber-spatial equivalents of such features include passwords

and other authentication measures that restrict access to sites where vulnerable targets are stored (e.g., directories containing proprietary information). Such safeguards can, of course, be circumvented with tools such as "password sniffers," "crackers," and decryption tools, but these can be conceived as the virtual counterparts of lock-picks, glass-cutters, and crowbars.

In sum, it can be seen from the above that the component sub-variables comprising target suitability exhibit varying degrees of transposability to virtual settings. The greatest convergence appears in respect of target value, perhaps unsurprisingly because valuations do not emanate from the (real or virtual) ecological environment, but are brought into that environment from elsewhere—namely, the spheres of economic and symbolic relations. However, the remaining three sub-variables exhibit considerable divergence between real and virtual settings. In the case of inertia, the difference arises from the distinctive *ontological properties* of entities that exist in the two domains—they are physical in the case of the real world and non-physical (informational) in the case of the virtual. In respect of the other two sub-variables (visibility and accessibility), divergences between the real and the virtual arise from the structural features of the environments themselves; as previously discussed, features such as distance, location, and movement differ markedly between the two domains, and these configurations will affect the nature of visibility and accessibility within the respective environments.

ARE THERE "CAPABLE GUARDIANS" IN CYBERSPACE?

"Capable guardianship" furnishes the third key aetiological variable for crime causation postulated by routine activity theory. Guardianship refers to "the capability of persons and objects to prevent crime from occurring." Guardians effect such prevention "either by their physical presence alone or by some form of direct action." Although direct intervention may well occur, routine activity theorists see the simple presence of a guardian in proximity to the potential target as a crucial deterrent. Where the guardian is a person, she/he acts as someone "whose mere presence serves as a gentle reminder that someone is looking." Such guardians may be "formal" (e.g., the police), but

RAT generally places greater emphasis on the significance of "informal" agents such as homeowners, neighbours, pedestrians, and other "ordinary citizens" going about their routine activities. In addition to such "social guardians," the theory also views *physical* security measures as effecting guardianship—instances include barriers, locks, alarms, and lighting on the street and within the home. Taken together, the absence or presence of guardians at the point at which potential offenders and suitable targets converge in time and space is seen as critical in determining the likelihood of an offence taking place (although the importance of guardianship has been questioned by some researchers).

How, then, does the concept of guardianship transpose itself into the virtual environment? The efficacy of the concept as a discriminating variable between criminogenic and non-criminogenic situations rests upon the guardian's co-presence with the potential target at the time when the motivated offender converges upon it. In terms of formal social guardianship, maintaining such co-presence is well nigh impossible, given the ease of offender mobility and the temporal irregularity of cyber-spatial activities (it would require a ubiquitous, round-the-clock police presence on the Internet). However, in this respect at least, the challenge to formal guardianship presented by cyberspace is only a more intensified version of the policing problem in the terrestrial world; as Felson notes, the police "are very unlikely to be on the spot when a crime occurs." In cyberspace, as in the terrestrial world, it is often only when private and informal attempts at effective guardianship fail that the assistance of formal agencies is sought. The cyber-spatial world, like the terrestrial, is characterized by a range of such private and informal social guardians: These range from in-house network administrators and systems security staff who watch over their electronic charges, through trade organizations oriented to self-regulation, to "ordinary online citizens" who exercise a range of informal social controls over each other's behaviour (such as the practice of "flaming" those who breach social norms on offensive behaviour in chat rooms). In addition to such social guardians, cyberspace is replete with "physical" or technological guardians, automated agents that exercise perpetual vigilance. These range from "firewalls," intrusion detection systems, and virus scanning software, to state e-communication monitoring projects such as the U.S. government's "Carnivore" and "ECHELON" systems. In sum, it would appear that RAT's concept of capable guardianship is transposable to cyberspace, even if the structural properties of the environment (such as its variable spatial and temporal topology) amplify the limitations upon establishing guardianship already apparent in the terrestrial world.

CONCLUSION

The impetus for this article was provided by the dispute over whether or not cybercrime ought to be considered as a new and distinctive form of criminal activity, one demanding the development of a new criminological vocabulary and conceptual apparatus. I chose to pursue this question by examining if and to what extent existing aetiologies of crime could be transposed to virtual settings. I have focused on the routine activity approach because this perspective has been repeatedly nominated as a theory capable of adaptation to cyberspace; if such adaptability (of the theory's core concepts and analytic framework) could be established, this would support the claim of *continuity* between terrestrial and virtual crimes, thereby refuting the "novelty" thesis. If not, this would suggest *discontinuity* between crimes in virtual and non-virtual settings, thereby giving weight to claims that cybercrime is something criminologically new. I conclude that there are both significant continuities and discontinuities in the configuration of terrestrial and virtual crimes.

With respect to the "central core of three concepts," I have suggested that "motivated offenders" can be treated as largely homologous between terrestrial and virtual settings. The construction of "suitable targets" is more complex, with similarities in respect of value but significant differences in respect of inertia, visibility, and accessibility. The concept of "capable guardianship" appears to find its fit in cyberspace, albeit in a manner that exacerbates the possibilities of instituting such guardianship effectively. However, these differences can be viewed as ones of *degree* rather than *kind*, requiring that the concepts be adapted rather than rejected wholesale.

A more fundamental difference appears when we try to bring these concepts together in an aetiological schema. The central difficulty arises, I have suggested, from the distinctive *spatio-temporal ontologies* of virtual and non-virtual environments: Whereas people, objects, and activities can be clearly located within relatively fixed and ordered spatio-temporal configurations in the real world, such orderings appear to destabilize in the virtual world. In other words, the routine activity theory holds that the "organization of time and space is central" for criminological explanation, yet the cyber-spatial environment is chronically spatio-temporally *disorganized*. The inability to transpose RAT's postulation of "convergence in space and time" into cyberspace thereby renders problematic its straightforward explanatory application to the genesis of cybercrimes. Perhaps cybercrime represents a case not so much of "old wine in new bottles" as of "old wine in *no* bottles" or, alternatively, "old wine" in bottles of varying and fluid shape. Routine activity theory (and, indeed, other ecologically oriented theories of crime causation) thus appears of limited utility in an environment that defies many of our taken-for-granted assumptions about how the socio-interactional setting of routine activities is configured.

SOURCE: From *European Journal of Criminology*, Vol. 2, No. 4, 407–427, 2005. Copyright © 2005 European Society of Criminology and Sage Publications. Reprinted by permission of Sage Publications, Ltd.

QUESTIONS FOR DISCUSSION AND WRITING

1. To what is particular attention given by criminological commentators (especially those of a sociological bent)? What do theorists of the new informational networks suggest? How does computer technology act as a "force multiplier"?

2. How is cyberspace "anti-spatial"? If cyberspace were "anti-spatial," what would be true?

3. With respect to the "central core of three concepts," what does the author suggest? What more fundamental difference appears when we try to bring these concepts together in an aetiological schema?

How Does Studying Terrorism Compare to Studying Crime?

Gary LaFree

Laura Dugan

Although the research literature on terrorism has expanded dramatically since the 1970s, with few exceptions, little of this work has been done by criminologists or has appeared in criminology journals. This may at first seem surprising, given that the most widely accepted definition of criminology includes the study of "the breaking of laws and reactions to the breaking of laws," both of which would seem to fall unambiguously under the subject heading of terrorism. Speaking of how criminologists have generally neglected the study of terrorism, Richard Rosenfeld points out that much criminological theory appears to be relevant to terrorism research and argues that criminologists should take a more active interest in studying terrorism. We strongly agree with this assertion and are convinced that terrorism should be an important area of study for criminologists.

However, there are also obvious differences between terrorism and common forms of crime. If criminologists are going to make a contribution to the study of terrorism, it seems important to keep in mind both ways in which terrorism and crime are similar and different. In this [article], we explore similarities and differences between crime and terrorism with regard to conceptualization, data collection, and research methods.

Conceptual Similarities

S1: The study of terrorism, like the study of crime, has been intensively interdisciplinary.

Researchers who have studied terrorism, like those who have studied crime, come from a range of disciplines, including sociology, political science, psychology, history, economics, anthropology, and philosophy. On the positive side, this interdisciplinary focus has stimulated research and pushed the study of both terrorism and crime well beyond the bounds of a single discipline. On the negative side, the fact that both areas of research are intensively multidisciplinary likely encourages theoretical confusion and makes the adoption of a general theory more difficult.

S2: Both terrorism and crime are social constructions.

The fact that this statement is trite does not make it less important. Forty years ago, labeling theorist Howard Becker argued that deviance and crime are not objective properties of certain actions or behavior, but rather definitions constructed through social interaction. In Becker's words, "Deviance is not a quality of the act the person commits, but rather a consequence of the application by others of rules and sanctions to an 'offender.'" While specific predictions from labeling theory have been tested and rejected, this part of the argument remains hard to refute. Few criminologists would maintain that all guilty parties are arrested and convicted for their crimes or that every individual convicted of crime is in fact guilty. The conclusion that a crime occurred must always be based on evidence that may be imprecise, inexact, or incorrect. Those actually apprehended and convicted for engaging in a particular form of crime undoubtedly bear an inexact relationship to all those who have actually committed the crime in question.

Similarly, whether a case is classified as terrorism ultimately depends on a process of social construction. That is, terrorism is not simply "out there" to be counted in the same way that we might count rocks, trees, or planets. But rather, to qualify as terrorism a particular act must be recognized and defined as such. And in fact, no matter how seemingly heinous an act, there are invariably at least some individuals who will not see it as terrorism. This fundamental reality is recognized by the common truism that "one man's terrorist is another man's freedom fighter." Examples are legion. Menachem Begin, former Israeli prime minister, was well known in the late 1940s as a leader of the notorious Irgun Zvai Leumi, a terrorist group that worked to speed the departure of the British from Palestine. Similarly, while many consider Yasir Arafat a terrorist, many others see him as a legitimate leader of the Palestine Liberation Organization.

S3. For both terrorism and crime there are major differences between formal definitions and how these definitions are applied in actual practice.

Researchers in criminology have long appreciated the fact that the actual application of law bears only a faint resemblance to legal statutes. Thus, early work by Roscoe Pound distinguished "law on the books" from "law in action." Criminologists point out that while compared to other sets of rules for human conduct, criminal law is noteworthy for its uniformity and specificity. Nevertheless, these ideal characteristics of the criminal law are rarely features of the criminal law in action. For example, in analyses of how legal agents make decisions in rape cases it is common to find extralegal variables like victim or defendant race or marital status playing a major role in predicting criminal justice outcomes.

Similarly, governments do not consistently apply their own definitions of terrorism in individual cases. Thus, the U.S. State Department defines terrorism as "premeditated, politically motivated violence perpetrated against noncombatants targeted by sub national groups or clandestine agents, usually intended to influence an audience." But in certain instances, the U.S. government resists applying this definition. For example, McCauley points out that for many years the U.S. State Department did not define the Nicaraguan Contras as engaging in terrorist activity against the leftist Sandinistas, even though the Contras were arguably a "sub national group" "using politically motivated violence" "against noncombatants." Likewise, many governments were ambivalent about labeling the actions of the African National Congress in its conflict with both white and black enemies in South Africa as terrorism—in spite of the fact that some actions of the ANC seemed to clearly fit under common definitions of terrorism.

Of course, the use of unwritten rules to classify cases as terrorism is not just a problem of governments. Individuals and groups that have collected data on terrorist activities also invariably struggle to consistently apply their formal definitions to specific cases. For example, after providing a formal definition of terrorism in its report, the Pinkerton Global Intelligence Services notes that "other forms of political violence . . . are included on a selective basis."

S4. Terrorism, like common crime, is disproportionately committed by young males.

In the U.S. in 2001, males accounted for 87.5 percent of all murder, 89.9 percent of all robbery, and 86.4 percent of all burglary arrests. Age is also consistently associated with criminal behavior across different nations and over time. Similarly, terrorism is predominantly the work of young men usually in their 20s and often in their early 20s.

S5. Sustained levels of terrorism, like sustained levels of crime, undermine social trust.

In an earlier work, LaFree argues that trust between individuals in society increases predictability by allowing people to act based on their perception that others are likely to perform particular actions in expected ways. Crime represents a particularly serious form of unpredictability and thus an important threat to trust. These connections can be seen clearly in the legendary low crime rates found in post-World War II Japan. Low crime rates in Japan allow the Japanese, even in large cities, to feel comfortable being away from their homes, in public places at night. They also allow individuals to show less concern about protecting their private property. Bicycles and other easy-to-steal items that are carefully guarded in many societies are frequently left unprotected in Japan. These characteristics make even urban Japan a relatively crime-free, mostly predictable place. This in turn fosters high levels of trust, even among strangers.

By contrast, predictability and trust are seriously undermined in societies experiencing high levels of street crime. Thus, rapidly rising street crime rates in the United States during the 1960s and early 1970s had a devastating effect on relationships of trust between people, particularly in the high crime areas of inner cities. More recently, in many of the struggling democracies of Latin America, alarming increases in rates of violent crime have fractured civic life and driven frustrated citizens to seek more punitive forms of social control and weaken or suspend altogether civil liberty safeguards. Likewise, threats of crime in the transitional democracies of Eastern Europe have raised major challenges to democratization and have resulted in calls for restraints on freedom and civil liberties in the name of maintaining social order.

Crenshaw argues that terrorism upsets the social framework upon which members of a society depend and undermines predictability in social relations. Because no one can be sure of what behavior to expect of others, levels of trust are reduced and individuals turn inward, concentrating more on their own survival. Thus, as with societies experiencing high levels of crime, societies undergoing sustained terrorist attacks are likely to experience lower levels of social solidarity, reduced cooperation and interdependence, and declining levels of trust.

Conceptual Differences

D1. While terrorist activities typically constitute multiple crimes (e.g., murder, kidnapping, extortion), for many nations, a specific crime of terrorism does not exist.

One of the most basic differences between terrorism and common crimes is that terrorism in most nations is behavior that violates a number of existing criminal statutes but is not defined as a specific separate category under criminal law. For example, suspected terrorists in the United States are typically prosecuted for a variety of criminal offenses rather than terrorism. Thus, in a study of federal prosecution of terrorists in the U.S. from 1982 to 1989, Smith and Orvis show that the most common subjects of terrorist prosecutions have been racketeering (30.2 percent of the total); machine guns, destructive devices, and other firearms (16.7 percent); and conspiracy (9.3 percent). This situation began to change in the United States after the mid 1990s, and especially after the terrorist attack of September 11, 2001. Nevertheless, even today, most persons suspected of terrorism in the U.S. are being prosecuted not for terrorism *per se*, but for a range of crimes commonly associated with terrorism.

Legal prohibitions specific to terrorism are even less well defined at the international level. An early attempt at constructing an internationally acceptable definition of terrorism was made by the League of Nations in 1937, but was never ratified by member states. The United Nations has still not developed a unified legal definition of terrorism, but instead has adopted 12 related conventions and protocols.

An important research implication of this is that it is much more difficult to develop national or international counts of terrorism than it is to develop total counts for most crime types. Thus, to study the prosecution of terrorist cases in the United States, Smith and Orvis had to begin with annual reports on terrorism provided by the Federal Bureau of Investigation, then request from the FBI an unpublished list of persons omitted from their reports that were nevertheless indicted as a result of terrorism and terrorist-related activities. They then asked the Department of Justice to match the resulting list with federal court docket numbers assigned throughout the United States and Puerto Rico. Even with these procedures, the authors estimate that they missed 29 percent of the known, officially labeled, federally indicted terrorists for the period included in their study.

D2. The response to common crime rarely moves beyond local authorities whereas the response to terrorism usually does.

For most crimes committed around the world, criminal justice issues are handled by local authorities and never gather international or even national attention. By contrast, terrorist acts are frequently reported outside of the local area where they occur and typically gather national and often international attention. This means that the type of data available on common crimes and terrorist acts are likely to be quite different. In most jurisdictions, common crimes result in an overwhelming amount of local processing information generated by police, prosecutors, courts, probation offices, prisons, and other parts of the criminal justice bureaucracy. These same local agencies develop little information on terrorism. By contrast, much of the terrorist information that exists is limited to international incidents. Thus, terrorist information collected by the U.S. State Department is limited to cases of international terrorism and excludes terrorism within nations.

This means that available data for common crimes and terrorist acts occupy opposite ends of the local-international spectrum. Thus, it is often impossible to develop cross-national estimates of common crimes because local, regional, and national differences in laws make it difficult to compile international estimates. By contrast, it is difficult to obtain data on domestic terrorism.

D3. While those who commit common crimes are usually trying to avoid detection, those who commit terrorism are often seeking maximum attention and exposure.

While common criminals are usually struggling to avoid a large audience, terrorists are often seeking a large audience. Hoffman argues that all terrorist groups strive to get maximum publicity for their actions and points out that because of this fact, the modern news media plays "a vital part in the terrorist's calculus." Because a common goal of terrorism is to gain media attention, terrorist events are often carefully staged. This is much less common with other crimes—although it does happen occasionally, as in the case of hate crimes or serial homicides or rapes.

D4. Terrorism, unlike common crime, is typically a means to broader political goals.

Most street crimes do not have larger political purposes. By contrast, the overriding objective of terrorism and its ultimate justification is the furtherance of a political cause. Hoffman argues that the criminal frequently employs violence as a means to obtain some material goal, such as money or material goods, or to kill or injure a specific victim. Thus, criminals often have selfish, personal motivations and their actions are not intended to have consequences or create psychological repercussions beyond the criminal act. By contrast, the fundamental aim of terrorists is often a political motivation to overthrow or change the dominant political system.

D5. Terrorists are more likely than common criminals to see themselves as altruists.

Although common criminals vary widely in terms of how they perceive their activities, few criminals see their crimes as altruistic behavior. By contrast, many terrorists see themselves as altruists. Hoffman claims that terrorists frequently believe that they are serving a cause that will achieve a greater good for some wider constituency.

D6. Terrorists are more likely than common criminals to innovate.

Policy recommendations in criminology are generally based on the assumption that the past informs the future. Thus, best practices evaluations in criminology tell us what worked in the past and extrapolate from this to make predictions about what will work in the future. But with terrorist activities, the relationship between past and future behavior may be much less certain. Consequently, terrorism is likely to depend more than common crime on innovation.

Conceptually Mixed

M1. Terrorism, like some forms of crime, typically includes an organizational structure and advocates who show varying levels of commitment and support for terrorist activities.

Most definitions of terrorism include the requirement that it be committed not by a lone operator but by an organized group. For example, we have seen above that the U.S. State Department definition includes the requirement that terrorism involve "sub national groups." Thus, terrorist activity implies membership and at least a loosely articulated ongoing organizational structure. By contrast, such organizational structures are rare in many forms of common crime. It is hard to imagine, for example, a group of offenders organizing to support murder or robbery. But there are major exceptions. For example, organized crime activities frequently do have an ongoing organizational structure. Similarly, hate crimes and gang activities may be at least loosely connected to support groups.

M2. Terrorist acts, like some crimes, are typically part of a sustained program of violence.

As a result of the foregoing (an organizational structure and political goals), terrorism, unlike most common crime, is usually part of a sustained program of violence. Thus, most definitions of terrorism exclude single, unplanned acts of violence. For this reason, Senechal de la Roche points out that terrorism typically expresses a "chronic" grievance. By contrast, single, unplanned acts of violence are common among criminals. But again, some forms of crime, notably organized crime, gang activities, and serial crimes, can resemble terrorism in terms of representing a relatively sustained program of violence.

M3. Terrorists, like criminals, vary in terms of the extent to which they select victims in a random, indiscriminate way.

Criminologists have long noted that a high proportion of all criminal offenders target victims that are previously known to them. Nevertheless, many criminals also target strangers. Similarly, terrorists frequently target specific individuals for assassination or hostage taking. But at the same time, many other terrorist activities pay little attention to the specific identity of the victims of their actions.

DATA COLLECTION
SIMILARITIES AND DIFFERENCES

Data Sources

Traditionally, crime data come from three sources, corresponding to the major social roles connected to criminal events: "official" data collected by legal agents, especially the police; "victimization" data collected from crime victims; and "self-report" data collected from offenders.

In the United States, the most widely used form of official crime data has long been the Federal Bureau of Investigation's Uniform Crime Report. Major official sources of data on international crime include the International Criminal Police Organization (Interpol); the United Nations crime surveys; and for homicides only, the World Health Organization. Since 1973, the major source of victimization data in the United States has been the National Crime Victimization Survey. For international data, the International Crime Victimization Survey has now collected several waves of data from samples of individuals in several dozen nations around the world. Compared to the collection of victimization data in the United States, the collection of self-report survey data has been more sporadic. Nevertheless, several major large-scale national self-report surveys now exist. Similarly, several waves of an international self-reported crime study have been undertaken.

In general, terrorism data from these three sources is either entirely lacking or faces important additional limitations. Although some countries do collect official data on terrorism, these data face at least two major difficulties. First, data on terrorism collected by government entities are inevitably influenced by political considerations. Of course, to some extent, this is also a problem with official data on common crimes. However, the political pressure is likely to be especially acute with regard to terrorism. Beginning in 1961, the U.S. State Department has produced a chronology of "significant terrorist incidents" and it now provides an annual Patterns of Global Terrorism Report that reviews international terrorist events by year, date, region, and terrorist group and includes background information on terrorist organizations. However, as noted above, the State Department faces tremendous political pressure to interpret terrorism in particular ways.

Second, while huge amounts of detailed official data on common crimes are routinely produced by the various branches of the criminal justice system in most nations, this is rarely the case for terrorism. For example, most suspected terrorists in the United States are not legally processed for their acts of terrorism, but for other related offenses. It is true that this situation continues to evolve. For example, in the United States in 1995, Chapter 113B of the Federal Criminal Code and Rules added "Terrorism" as a separate offense and the Antiterrorism and Effective Death Penalty Act was signed into law by President Clinton in 1996. Among other things, the 1996 act attempts to cut fundraising by those affiliated with terrorist organizations, enhances the security measures employed by the aviation industry, and expands the reach of U.S. law enforcement over selected crimes committed abroad. Similarly, the U.S.A. PATRIOT Act, passed in 2001, strengthens criminal laws against terrorism by adding to the criminal code terrorist attacks against mass transportation systems, domestic terrorism, harboring or concealing terrorists, or providing material support to terrorists. Nevertheless, it still remains the case that most of those persons who are officially designated as terrorists in the annual reports produced by the FBI are prosecuted under traditional criminal statutes. So, there is no easy way to gather official data on those arrested, prosecuted, or convicted of terrorist activities unless you do as Smith and his colleagues have done and assemble the data on a case by case basis.

Victimization data, which have played an increasingly important role in the study of crime, are almost entirely irrelevant to the study of terrorist activities. Several features of terrorism mean that victimization surveys are unlikely to ever have widespread applicability. To begin with, for most nations and at most points in time, terrorism is much rarer than criminal acts. This means that even with extremely large sample sizes, few individuals in most countries will have been victimized by terrorists. Moreover, because one of the hallmarks of terrorism is that victims are often chosen at random, victims of terrorist events frequently have few details to report. And finally, in many cases, victims of terrorism are killed by their attackers.

Self-report data on terrorists has been more important than victimization data, but it, too, faces serious limitations. Most active terrorists are unwilling to participate in interviews. As terrorism researcher Ariel Merari has put it, "The clandestine nature of terrorist organizations and the ways and means by which intelligence can be obtained will rarely enable data collection which meets commonly accepted academic standards." Still, we can learn a good deal from direct contact with terrorists or former terrorists. A good example is the recent work by McCauley based on an examination of the notebooks and letters left behind by the 9/11 suicide bombers.

Because of the difficulties with the use of official data, victimization data, and self-report data, most research on terrorism has been based instead on secondary data sources: the media (or media-derived databases), books, journals, or other published documents. In a review by Silke, nearly 80 percent of all terrorism research reviewed was based on secondary data sources rather than on primary contact with suspected or actual terrorists, terrorist victims, or legal agents investigating terrorists. Thus, a research source that is rarely used in criminology research is a mainstay of research on terrorism. Nevertheless, over time researchers have begun to put together these secondary sources into increasingly rigorous terrorist event databases. In the next section, we briefly review these developments.

Terrorism Event Databases

There are generally eight terrorism event databases. The Pinkerton Global Intelligence Services (PGIS) data have by far the largest number of events of any of the other data sets—about seven times more events than the next three largest—ITERATE, the U. S. State Department, and Tweed. From 1970 to 1997, PGIS trained researchers to identify and code all terrorism incidents they could identify from wire services, U. S. State Department reports, other U.S. and foreign government reporting, U.S. and foreign newspapers information provided by PGIS offices throughout the world, occasional inputs from such special interests as organized political opposition groups, and data furnished by PGIS clients and other individuals in both official and private capacities. In more recent years, PGIS researchers also relied on the Internet. The same coding form was used during the entire 28 years of data collection.

Based on coding rules originally developed in 1970, the persons responsible for collecting the PGIS database sought to exclude criminal acts that appeared to be devoid of any political or ideological motivation and also acts arising from open combat between opposing armed forces, both regular and irregular. The data coders also excluded actions taken by governments in the legitimate exercise of their authority, even when such actions were denounced by domestic and/or foreign critics as acts of "state terrorism." However, they included violent acts that were not officially sanctioned by government, even in cases where many observers believed that the government was openly tolerating the violent actions. Because the goal of the data collection was to provide risk assessment to corporate customers, the database was designed to err on the side of inclusiveness. The justification was that being overly inclusive best serves the interest of clients—an employee of a corporation about to move to Colombia would be concerned about acts of violence against civilians and foreigners, even if these acts were domestic rather than international, threatened rather than completed, or carried out for religious rather than political purposes.

The ITERATE (International Terrorism: Attributes of Terrorist Events) data, originally collected by Edward Mickolus, has probably been the most widely used archival source of terrorism data in terms of empirical research. The ITERATE data contains two different types of files: quantitatively coded data on international terrorist incidents, and a qualitative description of each incident included in the quantitative files. The quantitative data are arranged into four files, containing (1) basic information on the type of terrorist attack, including location, name of group taking responsibility, and number of deaths and injuries; (2) detailed information on the fate of the terrorists or terrorist group claiming responsibility; (3) detailed information on terrorist events involving hostages; and (4) detailed information on terrorist events involving skyjackings.

In addition to PGIS, three other data sources are private risk assessment companies: Cobra, Triton, and Tweed. All of these companies have taken an increasing interest in terrorist risk in recent years. Tweed prepares an annual register that details political, economic, and social events related to terrorist activities; Triton prints a list of current global activities of specific terrorist groups; and the Cobra Institute is currently developing a chronology of world terrorism events and detailed information about known terrorist groups.

The U.S. State Department provides a chronology of "significant terrorist incidents," beginning in 1961. Each report includes a brief description of all events. The State Department also provides an annual Patterns of Global Terrorism Report, which reviews international terrorist events by year, date, region, and terrorist group. The Report also includes background information on terrorist organizations, U.S. policy on terrorism, and progress on counterterrorism.

RAND has collected a detailed set of secondary data on international terrorist events from 1968 to 1997. In addition, RAND, in collaboration with the Oklahoma City National Memorial Institute for the Prevention of Terrorism, is currently developing a very detailed secondary database on both international and national terrorism since 1998. RAND may be unique among groups collecting data on terrorism through its use of a special "vetting" committee to determine whether a particular incident qualifies as terrorism. Cases that are suspected to be terrorism are brought to this group of experts, which studies each case before adding it to the terrorism event count database.

METHODOLOGICAL SIMILARITIES AND DIFFERENCES

While we have identified some important differences between terrorism and crime with regard to conceptualization and data collection, it also seems clear that most of these differences can be resolved with research methods currently available to criminologists. In fact, we strongly believe that the experiences of criminologists in analyzing crime data might make a real contribution to the study of terrorism. We begin this section by considering two key differences between crime and terrorism and some of the methodological implications of these differences. We then summarize several areas in which methods now being used in criminology might usefully be applied to the study of terrorism.

Methodological Differences

Compared to common crimes, most terrorist events have at least two characteristics that raise special methodological issues. First, while criminals usually commit crimes without considering how policy makers will respond to their activities, terrorists often attack in order to generate a policy response from authorities. This implies that when determining causal relationships between policy and violence, compared to those studying common crimes, those studying terrorism need to more thoroughly address issues of simultaneity between violence and government action. For example, temporal ordering of attacks might suggest a drop in terrorism after a specific policy was adopted. However, the terrorist group may have intentionally heightened their violent activity to generate this policy response. Thus, the drop in violence following the policy may simply be a regression to their average level of activity.

One methodological strategy for addressing issues such as these is to employ game theory methods. For example, Bueno de Mesquita and Cohen demonstrate that noncooperative game theory can be used to predict citizens' choices between socially acceptable behavior or criminal activity depending on their beliefs about how governments will respond. With the sequential ordering of each group's terrorist attacks and the government's policy responses, game theoretical methods could be used to identify variables that influence the behavioral choices of terrorist organizations.

Second, while most violent crime is committed by individuals, most terrorist activity is committed by groups of individuals whose membership is dynamic. This means that while the unit of analysis for most criminological research is the offender, concentrating on individual offenders is more complex and may be entirely counterproductive in terrorism research. But again, it is possible to identify methodological solutions to this problem within criminology. To begin with, criminology researchers studying gangs and organized crime networks face similar problems. While most of the current gang research examines individuals, there is growing interest in studying the dynamics of group membership using network analysis. These newer analysis methods could help us better understand how relational factors, such as social ties among peers, can influence terrorist group membership and subsequent terrorist attacks. Moreover, as in criminology, terrorism researchers can easily replace studies of individual offenders with studies of incidents or activity across geographical units.

Methodological Similarities

Methodological similarities between studying terrorist violence and common crime become apparent when we step back and recognize that criminal events and terrorist attacks look much the same regardless of the motivation behind them: Both are events that can be counted and both display non-random temporal and spatial patterns that are likely associated with endogenous and exogenous characteristics of offenders, targets, and situations. There are also substantial investigatory and forensic similarities. Thus, the same basic investigatory methods are relevant whether tracing money laundering in general or money laundering that is supporting terrorism; the same forensic methods used for crime scene investigation are equally useful for investigating terrorist violence. We offer several concrete methodological applications that seem promising.

Analysis of Distributions and Trends

As in the study of crime trends, analysis of terrorism trends can be easily disaggregated across several dimensions, including modes of terrorism (e.g., bombings, hijackings, assassinations); terrorist targets (e.g., embassies, factories, military facilities, public officials); and costs of terrorism (e.g., number of casualties, ransom dollars paid). Further, because terrorist groups often strike repeatedly, terrorism distributions can also be compared across types of groups such as ethnic separatists, left wing radicals, survivalists, or religious extremists. Because much criminological research emphasizes the understanding of crime patterns across several dimensions, criminologists should be able to offer related strategies for studying patterns of terrorism over space and time.

Geographic Mapping

An important strategy used by criminologists to study spatial and temporal patterns of events employs geographic mapping techniques. Just as these scholars have imbedded crime incidents into maps of counties and cities, terrorism researchers can create regional and world-wide maps depicting numbers and rates of terrorist activities around the globe. Point maps will make obvious the location of incidents and the groups responsible for carrying out attacks, as well as how locations evolve over time.

Recently introduced exploratory spatial data analysis techniques (ESDA) provide researchers with important new tools for distinguishing between random and non-random spatial patterns of events. While most of these ESDA methods are cross-sectional, Cohen and Tita have devised methods for extending static cross-sectional views of the spatial distribution of homicides to consider dynamic features of changes over time in spatial dependencies. This methodology can be used to identify innovative forms of terrorist activity and to demonstrate patterns of adoption by other terrorist organizations.

In criminology, these methods have also been used to distinguish *contagious diffusion* of homicide between adjoining units and *hierarchical diffusion* of homicide that spreads broadly through commonly shared influences. By applying these methods to terrorism data, we should be able to distinguish between terrorist organizations or cells that grow through direct recruitment of individuals living in neighboring territories (contagious diffusion) and groups that form instead through commonly shared influences that are geographically dispersed (hierarchical diffusion).

Time-Series Analysis

Econometric time-series methods can also be used to describe important features of terrorist event trends globally and across geographic units. These techniques were originally developed by economists to study business cycles by decomposing activity into two components: a trend component (that is, a general, long-term increase or decrease in the level of a variable over time), and a cyclical component that represents short-term, yet noticeable, deviations from the general trend. Attention to trend components is especially important here because earlier research suggests that terrorist activity is cyclical in nature. As with crime trend analysis, once trend components are isolated, scholars can address questions about similarities and differences in characteristics of terrorism (e.g., hijackings, politically or religiously motivated events) and cycles across geographic units (i.e., cities, nations, or regions).

Causal Analysis

The predominant goal of studying crime is to identify variables that either cause increases or contribute to crime desistence. Research methods used to isolate potential causal influences of crime can also be used to estimate the effects of political, economic, and social variables on the likelihood and frequency of terrorist activity. Further, because terrorism data can be structured with repeated measures of geographic units over time, standard methods of longitudinal analysis can be used to estimate the impact of variables while controlling for unobservable within-state time-invariant effects that vary across geographic boundaries.

An important consideration when investigating terrorist attacks is to disentangle simultaneous relationships. In criminology, neighborhood disorder and decline can lead to crime and crime can lead to disorder and decline. Similarly, terrorist activity could both be caused by and provoke political, economic, and social instability. By disentangling these effects using methods common to criminologists, it should be possible to more clearly understand how terrorism is both influenced by and can lead to regional changes in political, social, and economic conditions.

Life-Course Analysis

An important current interest among criminologists is to examine patterns of criminal behavior over the life-course. Ideas and strategies developed by these scholars can also be applied to the study of the life-course of terrorist groups. For example, Nagin's trajectory analysis has been used to sort individuals into groups based on their offending behavior over time. With slight modification, this method can identify developmental trajectories of terrorist organizations over time from their inception.

Conclusion

This [article] strongly advocates that criminologists join with others in advancing the study of terrorism. While we readily acknowledge important differences between common crime and terrorism, the similarities in conceptualization, data collection, and research methods suggest that the existing knowledge-base of criminology can quickly expand what is known about the patterns, causes, and consequences of terrorism. In general, many of the differences between terrorism and common crime are no more challenging than differences between common crime and more specialized crimes, such as youth-gang activity, organized crime, hate crime, or domestic violence. Each has distinctive features that require an investment of time and effort to better understand the substantive dynamics. One important role of criminology has been to inform policy makers about how to best evaluate common and specialized crime intervention. A distinctive advantage of criminology in terms of terrorism research is that framing issues in criminal rather than political terms tends to downplay the legitimacy of terrorist claims. Moreover, framing terrorism as a crime reinforces the idea that terrorism is a common problem that should be considered alongside other common problems when allocating resources or considering the relevancy of civil rights issues. By focusing on the obvious connections between terrorism and crime, we may be able to not only contribute to a better understanding of terrorism, but also to help formulate more rational policies for combating it.

SOURCE: From *Terrorism and Counter-Terrorism: Criminological Perspectives* (pp. 53–75), edited by Mathieu Deflem, 2004, Amsterdam: Elsevier. Copyright © 2004 by Elsevier. Reprinted by permission of Elsevier.

QUESTIONS FOR DISCUSSION AND WRITING

1. What five conceptual similarities between the study of common crime and the study of terrorism do the authors discuss?

2. What six conceptual differences between the study of common crime and the study of terrorism do the authors discuss?

3. What three conceptually mixed issues in the study of common crime and the study of terrorism do the authors discuss?

4. What five concrete methodological applications do the authors feel "seem promising" in the study of terrorism?

PART IV

HOW IS CRIME MEASURED?

The Observation and Measurement of Crime

In the last two sections, we pointed out several inconsistencies between perceptions of crime and the empirical realities of crime. The obvious next question is, How do we know what the realities of crime are? It is easy to argue that as a consequence of credentials or professional position, criminologists know the truth about crime. It is equally easy to identify the weakness in this approach. Many people are prepared to believe some assertions about crime if they are made in print (local newspapers, national magazines, and popular books included); disseminated via electronic media; or shouted loudly by politicians, demagogues, or even professors. The fact is, however, for criminologists the only legitimate basis for concluding that an assertion about crime or criminals is more correct than others is systematic research, particularly based on empirical observation.

Here we should take care because there is often an unfortunate confusion of the words *empirical* and *quantitative research*. Although quantitative research done by professional criminologists is empirical research, so too are studies that do not count or tally. Qualitative observations, too, are empirical studies and extremely valuable in understanding certain aspects of crime.

So our earlier statement that some perceptions are inconsistent with the realities of crime is based on our interpretation of the criminological research literature. There remain several important issues to consider. First, some would argue that published research tends to leave out ideas and styles of scholarship that do not fit with the dominant traditions of academic publishing. Second, like all readers of this literature, our interpretations are colored by our training and personal histories. Finally, the data on which modern research is based are not without complications and weaknesses, and criminologists differ in their assessments of the utility of these data and the methods that produce them. The chapters in this section focus on this latter point.

The major sources of crime data are, first, official data, or data produced by the criminal justice system. The most widely used data on crime in the United States are the Uniform Crime Reports (UCR), until recently published annually by the Federal Bureau of Investigation. The UCR can now be found online at the Bureau of Justice Statistics' Web site (http://www.ojp.usdoj.gov/bjs/). Second, victimization surveys question a large representative sample of the national population about their experiences of victimization. Since 1973, the National Institute of Justice and the Bureau of the Census have collaborated on the National Crime Victimization Survey (NCVS), the most widely used example of victimization data. Third, self-report studies of crime and delinquency have gained in importance in criminological research in recent decades. Self-report surveys ask people about their own involvement in illegal acts. This approach may strike many students as silly or naive, because the confessions of criminals cannot possibly be trusted. Strange as it may seem, however, criminologists do get useful data from these studies. Fourth, secondary data sources can provide extremely useful information about crime. Examples are records from insurance companies (excellent for tallying car theft) and the reports of medical examiners, coroners, or the Centers for Disease Control (all good sources when studying homicide). And finally, observational studies of a variety of criminals have a rich tradition in criminology, and they continue to be important sources of knowledge about criminality.

Unfortunately, we cannot simply say that one of those data sources is the best. It is not even clear that one needs to choose. All of the data collection methods have strengths and weaknesses; because they can reveal different pictures of crime, they can be complementary. An important task for a criminologist contemplating a research project is to decide which data source and research method are the best for addressing the question at hand. At times, it may not be apparent which method is most appropriate.

This section includes published research using these methods and discussions of what can be learned from using different data sources and research methodologies. Readers will see how the different data sources are used. Students should think about how some of the controversies described in preceding sections of this volume might be ameliorated by using particular forms of data and how those and other controversies may be fueled when researchers use different methodologies.

In "Locating the Vanguard in Rising and Falling Homicide Rates Across U.S. Cities," Messner and his colleagues use homicide data taken from the FBI's UCR to study large American cities. Some people have argued that there was an "epidemic" of homicide at the end of the 20th century. The authors use these officially generated data to test this thesis. Their units of analysis are cities, which mean that they studied variations in the homicide rates of the cities. Here, Messner et al. are not trying to tell us anything about individual criminals or specific homicidal events, but rather their research question focuses on changes in city homicide rates during the 1980s and 1990s.

In "Reconciling Race and Class Differences in Self-Reported and Official Estimates of Delinquency," Elliott and Ageton address two of the most interesting correlates of crime—race and social class. Discussion of these correlates has the potential for being highly socially charged; that is, people frequently get upset when the relationships between race and crime and between social class and crime are brought up. Here, Elliott and Ageton focus on what appear to be substantively important differences reported in various studies of race and class. Some studies, based on official records—ordinarily arrest records—reported considerable differences between blacks and whites, as well as between lower and middle classes, in crime involvement. When early self-report studies began to be published, however, they reported either smaller differences between races and classes or no differences at all. Obviously, if we found that minorities and lower classes did not commit more crime than others, these findings would have a major effect on both our perceptions about crime and our efforts to explain crime. Elliott and Ageton describe how the particular means of collecting self-reported crime data exaggerated the differences between the findings using these data and those using official sources. These important differences, and questions about why they exist, will be explored in subsequent sections.

Miller and White use different methods than the researchers in the preceding studies. In "Gender and Adolescent Relationship Violence: A Contextual Examination" they explore how girls and boys experience violence. To do this they used surveys and in depth interviews. They focused on "at risk" adolescents in an inner city neighborhood. This kind of research gets close to the subjects, allowing Miller and White to hear first hand what the people they studied thought, felt, and how they experienced violence.

In the final reading Hagan, Raymond-Richmond, and Parker's piece takes us again outside of the U.S. to study genocide in Darfur. Criminologists do not usually study genocide, but as we saw in our entry on terrorism, acts that violate the law are an appropriate topic for criminological investigation. Hagan and his colleagues use a victimization survey to study the racially motivated killings and rapes that are a part of ethnic cleansing and genocide in East Africa. No doubt doing a victimization survey there presents logistical problems not ordinarily confronted in conducting the NCVS in the U.S. Nevertheless, here students should appreciate the rich detail and important perspective that is discovered when researchers hear directly from the victims of crime. What do we learn here that would never be uncovered by official government or police statistics?

 For a data analysis exercise that accompanies the material in this section, go to www.sagepub.com/crimereadings3study.

Locating the Vanguard in Rising and Falling Homicide Rates Across U.S. Cities

Steven F. Messner

Glenn D. Deane

Luc Anselin

Benjamin Pearson-Nelson

Levels of homicide in the United States fluctuated dramatically during the last two decades of the twentieth century. For the nation at large, rates fell during the early years of the 1980s before turning around and climbing rapidly to a new peak of 9.8 per 100,000 in 1991, then decreasing again for the remainder of the decade. By the year 2000, the national homicide rate of 5.5 per 100,000 was almost half that of 1980, similar to levels observed in the mid-1960s. Not surprisingly, these large and sometimes abrupt fluctuations have attracted considerable attention in both the popular press and the scholarly literature.

Despite widespread agreement that these trends in homicide are genuine and consequential, their explanation remains "something of a puzzle." Researchers have attempted to gain insight into the observed trends in homicide by "deconstructing" the overall figures into constituent parts. Such analyses have revealed two very striking aspects of the pattern in homicide during the 1980s and 1990s, a pattern that has been characterized as being like an epidemic. It was heavily concentrated among young males, especially minority-group members. In other words, the epidemic was "narrowly channeled demographically." Yet, at the same time, the national pattern was not driven solely by the trends in a few of the largest population centers but instead was "national in scope."

The most influential and intriguing account for the changes in U.S. rates over recent decades is Blumstein's thesis of an arms race associated with the growth of crack cocaine markets. As explained more fully below, an attractive feature of this explanation is that it offers an account for the distinctive demographics of homicide changes—its narrow channeling. In addition, and particularly relevant to this analysis, Blumstein's thesis directs attention to the space-time dynamics of homicide levels. It implies that the timing of the upturns and downturns of homicides was not random but instead patterned spatially in a manner consistent with an underlying social process and, more specifically, a diffusion process associated with the spread of crack cocaine. According to Blumstein, and Blumstein and Rosenfeld, large cities, especially large coastal cities, were in the vanguard of rising and falling homicide rates because these are precisely those first exposed to the criminogenic pressures of the crack cocaine epidemic.

The purpose of this [article] is to probe further into the space-time dynamics of U.S. homicide rates. Using Uniform Crime Report (UCR) data on homicide for a sample of cities over the 1979–2001 period, we apply polynomial spline regression techniques to locate the number and timing of knots that signify structural breaks in homicide trends. This procedure is extremely useful because it eliminates the noise in the time-series, thereby allowing us to visualize the systematic trend for individual cities. We are thus able to differentiate cities that experienced a distinct boom and bust pattern from those that did not, and for the former, to identify the timing of the upturns and downturns in homicides. With this information, we are able to identify any structure in the timing of the phases of homicide cycles. Our overarching objective is to better understand this important period in U.S. history by attempting to link systematically the when of changes in city homicide rates to the where.

DRUG MARKETS, GUNS, AND THE DIFFUSION OF HOMICIDE

Many explanations have been offered for the wild swing in levels of lethal violence in the 1980s and 1990s, but Blumstein's provocative arguments about the preeminent role of crack cocaine's markets continue to dominate the field. According to Blumstein, the demand for crack cocaine emerged in selected urban areas in the mid-1980s and spread thereafter to other parts of the nation. Within any given locale, the increased demand for crack led to the extensive recruitment of young minority males to serve as drug dealers. Violence typically surrounds drug markets, and thus these new recruits (not surprisingly) acquired firearms to fend off other drug dealers and street robbers who typically target those carrying large amounts of cash. The increased gun-toting drug dealers then diffused throughout the community, especially to other youths, as those not involved in the drug trade took up arms for self-defense. Interpersonal

disputes became more lethal, and the homicide rate rose. Subsequently, the number of crack users dropped off, beginning in the early 1990s in some cities. This let up on the pressures to recruit more drug dealers and brought some stability to drug markets. Accordingly, as the crack epidemic began to subside, homicide rates started to fall.

An attractive feature of the drug market-arms race thesis of changing homicide levels is its symmetry. It accounts for both the rise and fall of homicide levels in a logically consistent fashion. Moreover, several types of evidence about the nature of homicide trends over the period under consideration lend credibility to the drug market-arms race thesis. As noted, the argument is consistent with the documented demographics of homicide. The epidemic-like pattern of rapid increase followed by sharp reversal and decline was most pronounced among young African American males, precisely the population hypothesized to have been recruited into, and subsequently out of, crack cocaine markets. In addition, the growth in homicides among young people during the late 1980s was driven largely by the increase in homicides committed with handguns. This is consistent with the claims about the accelerating arms race spawned by the acquisition of guns by newly recruited drug dealers.

Research also suggests that measures of illegal drug activity can explain changes in homicide rates across metropolitan areas in the United States. Ousey and Lee have analyzed the homicide/drug connection with data for 122 cities during the 1984 to 1997 period. They employ two indicators of illicit drug market activity: the arrest rate for the sale or possession of cocaine-opiates, which is available for the full sample of cities, and the percentage of arrestees who tested positive for cocaine based on urinalysis, which is available for a subset of eighteen cities participating in the Drug Use Forecasting (DUF) program (now the Arrestee Drug Abuse Monitoring program, or ADAM). Analyses based on hierarchical linear modeling techniques reveal that these indicators of within-city variation in illicit drug market activity exhibit the expected positive effects on within-city variation in homicide rates. Ousey and Lee also discover that the effects of drug market activity are contingent on levels of resource deprivation—stronger effects are detected in the more disadvantaged cities.

Using a different analytic framework, Grogger and Willis find further support for the general claim that changes in homicide rates are linked with patterns of drug use. They pose their basic research question as a counterfactual, asking what the urban crime rate would have been during the peak crime years of the 1980s if crack cocaine had not appeared on the scene. To address this question, they use data on crime rates for twenty-seven cities and the surrounding metropolitan areas from 1970 to 1991. They divide this period into "before crack" and "after crack." The time of the arrival of crack is estimated from two sources: a survey administered to each city's chief of police inquiring about the date when the police first encountered crack, and hospital emergency room data on admissions attributable to cocaine smoking, as published by NIDA as part of the Drug Awareness Warning Network (DAWN). Grogger and Willis compute the difference between violent crime rates in central cities and suburbs before the arrival of crack and after the arrival, and then compute the difference between these scores. This difference-in-difference procedure yields an estimator of what changes in city crime rates would have occurred if cities had not experienced the arrival of crack, given what transpired in the surrounding metropolitan area. Grogger and Willis conclude that the arrival of crack cocaine resulted in a substantial increase in violent crime, including homicide, and that "in the absence of crack cocaine, the crime rate in 1991 would have remained below its previous peak in the early 1980s."

An additional piece of evidence that supports the drug market-arms race thesis pertains to variation in the timing of the rise and fall of homicide rates across subnational units. Blumstein and Rosenfeld use the Supplementary Homicide Reports (SHR) to examine trends in homicide levels disaggregated by weapon use (handgun vs. non-handgun) by city size over the 1980 to 1995 period. Cities are classified into four categories based on their average population during the period—greater than 1 million, 500,000 to 1 million, 250,000 to 500,000, and 100,000 to 250,000. Counts of the two types of homicides are aggregated by city size. The time series for nongun homicide rates shows very limited variation. In contrast, distinctive boom and decline phases can be discerned in the time series for homicides committed with handguns, and the timing of the phases varies by city size. The major growth for the large cities began in 1986 but not until two years later, in 1988, for

smaller cities. Similarly, there is a lag in the initiation of the decline phase. Homicide rates dropped sharply in large cities in 1993, after reaching a plateau in 1991. In smaller cities, the decline did not appear until 1995. Fox reports a similar lag effect in a comparison of the trends for gun homicide offending rates by city size, although his timing of the changes differs slightly from those cited by Blumstein and Rosenfeld. Also, in analysis based on overall homicide rates for a sample of nineteen cities, Grogger finds that homicides peaked 1.3 years earlier in the nine largest cities than in the remaining smaller cities. The observation that the phases of the homicide cycle appeared earlier in larger cities is generally consistent with the drug market-arms race thesis. As Blumstein and Rosenfeld observe, "Crack markets generally emerged first in the largest cities, and may have diffused to smaller cities at a later time [which] could possibly account for these lag effects."

Blumstein and Rosenfeld also point to a geographical aspect of the timing of the homicide cycles. They note an early homicide decline for New York, "a large *coastal* city," and suggest that this is consistent with the geographic imprint of the crack cocaine epidemic. To support this claim, they cite research by Golub and Johnson, who assess a model of the crack cocaine epidemic by examining drug use among arrestees for twenty-four cities from the Drug Use Forecasting (DUF) program of the National Institute of Justice over the 1987 to 1996 period. They conclude that the epidemic model works well in describing the patterns of arrests and that the decline phase of the epidemic is characterized by a distinct coastal pattern, with cities on the East and West Coasts generally entering this phase earlier than those in the interior of the country.

More direct evidence emerges in Cork's research, in which Cork applies a change-point diffusion model to annual counts of juvenile gun homicides and juvenile drug arrests over the 1976 to 1996 period for a sample of cities. This approach assumes that the temporal pattern of these events in any given city follows an S-shaped (exponential) curve that is commonly associated with a diffusion process. For cities that exhibit acceptable fit with the postulated diffusion model, Cork estimates the timing of the change-point, that is, the year at which an abrupt shift occurred from a decreasing or flat temporal regime to a sharply higher level of activity.

Cork's results indicate that the change-point for juvenile drug arrests preceded the change-point for juvenile gun homicides by two years on average. This is consistent with the hypothesis that the crack cocaine epidemic instigated an arms race that subsequently led to rising homicides. Cork also performs cluster analyses on the parameters of the diffusion model and geographic coordinates to identify the spatial patterning of changing drug activity and homicides for juveniles. He finds that clusters located on the East and West Coasts experienced earlier median change-points than clusters in the interior, consistent with Blumstein and Rosenfeld's speculations about the coastal gradient in the diffusion of homicide.

In sum, the crack cocaine explanation for the dramatic fluctuations in homicides over the latter decades of the twentieth century has received a fair degree of empirical support, especially for the initial upsurge. The expected demographic patterns have been documented at the national level, and indicators of illicit drug market activity have been linked with changes in homicide rates for subnational units. In addition, for selected forms of homicide, there is evidence of a connection between the timing of the phases of the cycle and two characteristics of cities: size and coastal location.

We inquire further about the temporal and spatial structuring of homicide trends but extend previous work in several respects. The comparisons of levels of gun homicides by city size reported by Blumstein and Rosenfeld and Fox are based on compilations of cities aggregated into the respective size groups. This procedure describes the pattern in the aggregate faithfully but does not capture features of the homicide cycles as reflected in the experiences of individual cities. It is possible, indeed likely, that some of the cities contributing homicides to the dataset did not exhibit cyclical patterns at all during the period under investigation. Moreover, for cities that did go through a boom and decline cycle, the differences in the timing of phases within city-size categories might be substantial, and this variation might be explainable with reference to measurable characteristics of cities. We provide a different perspective on the relationship between the homicide epidemic and city size by examining trends at the level of individual cities, which enables us to identify those cities that actually exhibited an epidemic-like cyclical pattern.

For these cities, we determine the timing of the phases of the cycles and assess the significance of any relationship between the timing of the phases and city characteristics.

Cork's analysis of city-level trends in juvenile gun homicides and juvenile drug arrests with the use of a change-point diffusion model is, in some respects, similar to our approach. However, a potential limitation of the change-point diffusion model is that it requires strong assumptions about the nature of the homicide trends. In essence, the model entails a cubic polynomial. This functional form is likely to be realized in some places but not in others. Accordingly, the method may be overly restrictive for the identification of cities with a meaningful boom and decline cycle. In addition, the model requires an abrupt break in the time series, otherwise the location of the change-point becomes ambiguous. In these cases, Cork must rely on visual inspection of the data to supplement his formal criteria. Our alternative method—polynomial spline regression with unknown knots—allows the observed data for the city panels to determine the number and location of structural breaks, as well as the shape of the fit between the structural breaks (linear, quadratic, or cubic).

Much of the attention in the study of homicide trends has focused on selected types of homicides. Blumstein and Rosenfeld and Fox examine gun homicides; Cork models juvenile killings with guns. In contrast, we examine city-level trends in total homicides rather than trends in homicides disaggregated by demographic characteristics and/or weapon use. An examination of such disaggregated homicides at the city level would also be instructive, but methodological considerations render such analyses problematic. In all but the very largest cities, the events under investigation become rare as disaggregation proceeds. As a result, the time series for individual cities are often unstable, which makes it difficult to discern systematic trends. This problem is apparent in Cork's research, where he introduces a filtering criterion such that a city must have at least five recorded incidents to be included in the analysis. While this decision helps mitigate the problem of instability, it results in the exclusion of more than half of the original cities in his sample (124 out of 237), which suggests appreciable censoring of the data.

In addition, disaggregation requires detailed information about homicide incidents, such as circumstance (for example, weapon use) or characteristics of offenders (for example, age). The primary source of such information for criminological research is the Supplementary Homicide Reports (SHR). These data suffer from two well-known problems that are particularly consequential in efforts to compare homicide trends across cities. Some cities report to the SHR sporadically. As Blumstein and Rosenfeld note, including such cities in the analysis will confound fluctuations in reporting with changes in homicides. They thus exclude certain cities from their analyses of homicide trends, including two of the largest, Chicago and Houston. Another problem associated with any attempt to model trends based on the offender's demographic characteristics is that incidents with unknown offenders cannot be classified. The relative numbers of such incidents and the differential representation of demographic groups among the unknowns cannot be assumed to be constant across space and over time.

Finally, trends in total homicides for cities are substantively important in their own right. As McDowall observes in his analysis of the national homicide trends, the primary purpose of disaggregation is typically to understand a more general pattern; the general trends are disaggregated precisely to discover the factors that may be driving them. Accordingly, though our analyses do not reveal the nature of city-level trends for subtypes of homicides, they do indicate the extent to which the variation in trends in total homicides across cities is consistent with conventional interpretations of underlying processes that allegedly contributed to such trends.

RESEARCH QUESTIONS

Our analyses fit the trends in homicide rates for individual U.S. cities during the 1980s and 1990s using the techniques of polynomial spline regression with unknown knots. These techniques have two particularly desirable features. First, they enable us to model the systematic trend in homicide after controlling for random fluctuations in the time series, and, second, they do not impose strong restrictions on the data a priori. Applying these techniques, we address the following questions.

First, to what extent do the homicide trends in individual cities in the sample conform to the national pattern of an epidemic-like cycle with a boom and decline phase? Our operational

definition of an epidemic-like cycle is that the trend exhibits the following characteristics: (1) there must be a negative or flat slope that becomes significantly positive; (2) the positive slope must "turn around" and become significantly negative; and (3) these distinct changes in phase must be observed over a relatively short period of time, that is, during the time window under examination. Thus, a cyclical pattern that encompasses a time span that is not captured during the modeling period is not considered to be epidemic-like.

Second, for the subset of cities that conform to the aggregate national pattern, what is the true timing of the phases in homicide trends, as reflected in structural breaks in the time series? Is there any structure to the timing of the phases for the cities, or are they distributed more or less randomly? If trends in homicide rates are determined solely by factors internal to cities, or if they are simply responses to random shocks, there is no reason to expect any general pattern in the temporal distribution of upturns and downturns. By contrast, an epidemic process, such as that suggested by Blumstein, implies that the pace of the phases in homicide trends are more likely not to be random. A small number of innovators should initiate the phase change followed by the adopters.

Another question is which cities emerge as leaders and followers of the homicide boom and decline. Is there symmetry in these patterns, such that the cities that were in the vanguard for the rise in homicides were also the leaders in the decline, and the latecomers of the early phase were also the latecomers of the latter phase?

Fourth, does the timing of the phases of the homicide cycle vary significantly with sociodemographic characteristics of cities? As noted, Blumstein essentially identifies crack cocaine as the contagion that sparked the homicide epidemic, and he postulates that crack cocaine markets emerged first in large cities. Although the reasons for the emergence of drug markets are not fully understood, crack can be conceptualized as a technological innovation, and cultural innovations more generally tend to emerge first in large urban centers. Moreover, classical social disorganization theory implies that drug market activity is more likely to be accompanied by criminal violence in places with weak social control, that is, in larger and denser communities. Is there, in fact, a significant relationship between the timing of homicide phases and city population size and/or population density?

In addition to population measures, the research by Ousey and Lee indicates that the effects of drug-market activity were stronger in cities with high levels of resource deprivation. By extension, perhaps cities with high levels of resource deprivation were also more susceptible to the spread of the crack cocaine epidemic and more likely to exhibit the initiation phase of the homicide epidemic earlier than other cities.

Finally, how does the timing of the phases of homicide trends vary across geographic space? In particular, is there any evidence of a gradient from coastal regions to the interior of the nation similar to the pattern for juvenile gun homicides detected by Cork? Are these geographic patterns symmetrical for the two phases of homicide trends?

Data and Methods

The units of analysis for this study are the sixty-eight cities within the continental United States with available homicide data and minimum population totals of 250,000 for 2001, as reported in the FBI's Uniform Crime Reporting (UCR) annual reports. Homicide counts and total population for these cities were recorded from the UCR for the years 1979 to 2001. Annual city-level homicide rates for this period were computed in the usual way by dividing the number of reported homicides by the annual UCR population figures and multiplying by 100,000.

Results

The first step in the analysis is to identify cities with trends that mirror the epidemic-like cycle in the national trend in homicides. As noted, both an upturn and a downturn are required to indicate a pattern with a complete cycle. If these two qualities are not observed, the years of upturn and downturn are considered to be right censored, in the sense that these necessary features of the cycle are not observed during the period under investigation, and the upturn and downturn dates for these cities are assigned censoring values equal to the end of the time series.

When the time series for each city are modeled with spline regressions and the decision rules about epidemic-like cycles are applied, the results reveal that just over half (thirty-five) of the sixty-eight cities conform to the national trend. For those cities that do not conform, four distinct

trends commonly appear: a steady incline in homicide rates, a steady decline, a fairly steady rate followed by a later decline, and a steady increase that began sometime before the first year with data and thus have a censored point of initiation to rising homicide. Each of these nonfitting patterns is illustrated in Figure 1. The case of Buffalo (the upper left panel) is particularly instructive. Simple visual examination of the time series might suggest an epidemic-like cycle, but the spline regression indicates that, given the criteria selected, the fluctuations can be regarded as random noise around a linear trend.

Table 1 lists cities according to the year of incline and decline of homicide trends in Panels A and B, respectively, which permits an assessment of the hypothesis of symmetry of the different phases. A simple comparison of the Tables fails to support the hypothesis. The cities that were in the vanguard for the initiation of the rise in homicide (for example, Albuquerque, Anaheim, Bakersfield, Fresno, Riverside, and St. Paul) are not the cities that were in the vanguard of the decline phase. The cities with the earliest point of decline in homicide rates (St. Petersburg, Atlanta, Boston, Philadelphia, and Washington, DC) are scattered throughout the period of the initiation of the rise in homicide.

We consider the geographic patterning of the timing of homicide phases. Returning to the listing of cities by year of change points in Table 1, the appearance of four cities in California among the six cities with the earliest upturn is perhaps noteworthy. Furthermore, five out of the six cities that experienced the earliest upturn are found in the western part of the United States. However, after the first year of upturn there is no clear geographic pattern. A more striking geographic clustering emerges for the year of decline. The first five cities to exhibit the drop in homicide rate are situated in the eastern part of the country: St. Petersburg, Atlanta, Boston, Philadelphia, and Washington, DC. This evidence provides some support for a coastal diffusion of homicide downturn beginning in the East.

Conclusion

The study has explored trends in homicide rates at the city level in the United States during the so-called homicide epidemic at the close of the twentieth century. Using spline regression techniques, we have attempted to model the true trends of homicide rates to identify those cities

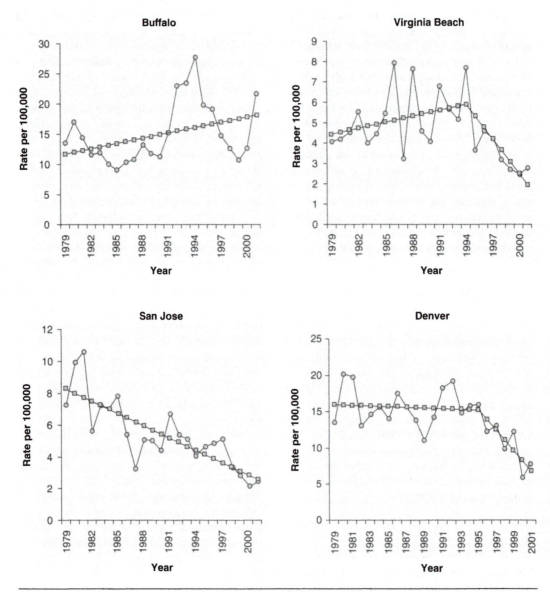

FIGURE 1   Plots Showing Four Examples of Homicide Rate Trends and Expected Homicide Rate Trends for Cities That Do Not Fit the Epidemic Pattern

that exhibited a meaningful boom and bust cycle and to estimate the timing of the phase changes of such a cycle. Our analyses have yielded several noteworthy findings.

First, the homicide epidemic of the 1980s and 1990s was reasonably widespread throughout urban America. More than half of the sixty-eight cities in our sample exhibited an appreciable rise in homicide followed by a definite reversal during the years under investigation. The pattern

in homicides thus was not driven simply by the disproportionate impact of a small number of "mega-cities." Second, the timing of the take-off and downturn was not distributed randomly throughout the period. The distribution of the dates for the respective phases of the cycle shows a relatively small number of cities in the vanguard. The bulk of cases then exhibited the upturn during a somewhat concentrated period, followed by a small number of laggards. Third,

TABLE 1 Year of Upturn and Downturn for Cities with an Epidemic Homicide Cycle

Upturn

1982	1983	1984	1985	1986	1987	1988	1989
Albuquerque	Atlanta	Kansas City	Columbus	Charlotte	El Paso	Chicago	Boston
Anaheim	Baltimore	Milwaukee	Las Vegas	Cleveland	San Francisco	San Antonio	Pittsburgh
Bakersfield	Dallas	Mobile	New Orleans	Long Beach			
Fresno	Minneapolis	Philadelphia	New York	Los Angeles			
Riverside	St. Petersburg	San Diego	Oakland	Louisville			
St. Paul			Toledo	St. Louis			
			Washington				

Downturn

1989	1990	1991	1992	1993	1994	1995	1996	1997
St. Petersburg	Atlanta	Dallas	Charlotte	Anaheim	Pittsburgh	Bakersfield	Albuquerque	Louisville
	Boston	Milwaukee	Chicago	Baltimore	Riverside	Fresno	Las Vegas	Mobile
	Philadelphia	New York	Cleveland	El Paso	Toledo	New Orleans	Minneapolis	
	Washington	San Diego	Columbus	Long Beach			St. Paul	
			Kansas City	Los Angeles				
				Oakland				
				San Antonio				
				San Francisco				
				St. Louis				

123

the timing of the phase changes was not symmetrical. Fourth, the timing of the phases was evidently related to population structure and levels of deprivation. Our analyses indicated that among cities exhibiting the pattern, homicide rates were likely to begin the rise and start the drop-off significantly earlier in larger, denser cities and in those with more extreme socioeconomic deprivation. Finally, we detect some evidence of a geographic patterning of the timing of phase changes. The first cities to experience an upturn were mostly on the West Coast, whereas the vanguard cities for declining homicide were sharply aligned along the East Coast.

The results of our analyses of city-level trends are consistent in certain important respects with the influential interpretation of the homicide epidemic advanced by Blumstein, and Blumstein and Rosenfeld. As explained, this interpretation maintains that crack cocaine markets were the impetus for the dramatic rise in homicide and that these markets were likely to take hold initially in the larger cities with extensive deprivation located on the coasts and then spread to other cities through a diffusion process. Our findings that larger cities were more likely to exhibit an epidemic-like pattern and that population size and density levels of deprivation and coastal location were related to the timing of the homicide rise and fall are in accord with this hypothesized account. Similarly, the nonrandom distribution of timing of the phases of the homicide cycle is generally compatible with some type of diffusion process. These findings are particularly striking given that they are based on the total homicide rates for cities rather than disaggregated rates. Thus, patterns in the overall city rate are interpretable, at least to some extent, with reference to processes that allegedly had greatest impact on a theoretically strategic subpopulation: young minority males.

At the same time, our findings, when considered in combination, raise several perplexing questions. Population size, population density, and resource deprivation are related to the timing of both the onset and downturn of the epidemic, and yet the cities that experienced the upturn earliest are not the same as those that experienced the downturn earliest. The timing of the phases of the epidemic thus varies for cities at comparable

levels of population and deprivation, implying that these are only some of the factors influencing features of homicide trends. An important task for future research is to enumerate more fully those factors that affect the timing of respective phases of the homicide epidemic.

The lack of symmetry in the timing across phases of the epidemic has further implications. If homicide epidemics were to unfold in a standard fashion over a fixed period, the cities experiencing the onset first would also be those that exhibit the earliest decline. Because this is not the case, the duration of the epidemic obviously varies across cities. What city characteristics influence the duration of homicide epidemics? Are these the same characteristics as those that determine the susceptibility to an epidemic? It is also evident from our graphs (not presented) that the magnitude of the rise in homicide varies across cities. Another promising topic for future research is to examine systematically how different sociodemographic characteristics of cities affect distinct dimensions of homicide epidemics, dimensions including (but not limited to) duration and magnitude.

In addition, the observation of distinct coastal patterns for the timing of the upturn (West Coast) and downtown (East Coast) of the epidemic raises intriguing possibilities. Perhaps both the initiation and recovery from homicide epidemics entail diffusion, but diffusion that differs qualitatively. To adapt a conceptual distinction introduced by Blumstein and Rosenfeld, homicide epidemics might be instigated by independent forces that are introduced from the outside and then diffuse (for example, crack cocaine), whereas recovery might be affected by "reactive forces" that entail a deliberate response to the growth in homicide. One possible reactive force is policing. A well-organized police response to combat crack markets and small arms proliferation could have emerged in certain locations along the East Coast, independently of the origins of the epidemic, and then spread to geographically proximate cities. These remarks are, of course, entirely speculative, but theorizing about and empirically examining the role of asymmetrical diffusion processes that could affect the incline and decline of homicide rates are promising avenues for further work.

SOURCE: From *Criminology,* Vol. 44, No. 3, 662–689, August 2005. Copyright © 2005 by American Society of Criminology. Reprinted by permission of the American Society of Criminology.

QUESTIONS FOR DISCUSSION AND WRITING

1. How are drug markets, guns, and homicides related?

2. What were the five "noteworthy" findings?

3. How are the results consistent in certain important respects with the influential interpretation of the homicide epidemic advanced by Blumstein, and Blumstein and Rosenfeld?

RECONCILING RACE AND CLASS DIFFERENCES IN SELF-REPORTED AND OFFICIAL ESTIMATES OF DELINQUENCY

DELBERT S. ELLIOTT

SUZANNE S. AGETON

Problems of conceptualization, definition, and measurement continue to plague researchers interested in the epidemiology and etiology of delinquency. While most would acknowledge the conceptual distinction between delinquent behavior and official responses to delinquent behavior, these distinctions are not clearly maintained in the measurement of delinquency or in the interpretation and analysis of specific delinquency data. This problem is clearly illustrated in the current controversy over the validity of self-reported (as compared with official) estimates of the incidence and distribution of delinquency in the general adolescent population. Put simply, there are those who argue that police and arrest records provide more accurate and reliable estimates of the social correlates of delinquent behavior than do self-report surveys; others hold the opposite view.

Self-report measures of delinquency provide a different picture of the incidence and distribution of delinquent behavior than do official arrest records. Both types of data indicate significant age and sex differentials, but the magnitude of these differences is much smaller with self-reported data than with official arrest data.

At the center of the controversy, however, is the fact that self-report studies generally find no differences in delinquent behavior by class or race, while studies relying upon police and court data report significant differences by both class and race.

To date, attempts to reconcile this apparent discrepancy between official and self-reported findings have taken one of two approaches. Most recently, researchers have challenged the strength of the empirical evidence for the class differential in official data. Tittle and Villemez and Tittle et al. reviewed earlier published research findings and concluded that the class differences in official data are not clearly established and that the widespread belief in an inverse relationship between class and crime is not based upon sound empirical research findings. Hindelang et al. have also concluded that police records of juvenile offenses are not strongly or even moderately related to socioeconomic status.[1] On the other hand, the race differential in official data has not been seriously challenged, to our knowledge.

The second and most frequent approach has been to challenge the methodological adequacy of the self-report technique and the adequacy of self-report research. Specifically, critics of self-report research contend,

1. There are problems inherent in the method itself which make it inaccurate and unreliable. These problems include deliberate falsification, inaccurate recall, and forward and backward telescoping.

2. There are problems with the construction of measures used in self-report research and with the procedures for administering the measures. These problems concern the lack of representativity in items, item overlapping, imprecise response sets, and the lack of anonymity of respondents.

3. There are problems with generalizing from self-report studies, due to the almost exclusive reliance upon small, unrepresentative samples.

This [article] is concerned with this second approach to reconciling official and self-reported findings with respect to class and race. We will not deal with those problems inherent in the self-report method itself, except to note that available research seems to support both the validity and reliability of the method. Instead, we will deal with the correctable problems, i.e., the construction of measures and their administration, as well as representativity and sample size. The general question we will address here is whether or not the satisfactory resolution of these methodological issues in the construction and administration of self-report measures will result in greater consistency between self-reported and official data. More specifically, will the satisfactory resolution of these problems produce race and class differentials in self-reported estimates of delinquent behavior?

The discussion that follows will focus on (1) the methodological criticisms of previous self-report delinquency (SRD) research; (2) the use of a new SRD measure in a national youth study; (3) a comparison of the race/class findings of this study with previous SRD research and with official arrest data; and (4) the epidemiological and theoretical implications of these findings.

PROBLEMS WITH SRD RESEARCH

Instrument Construction

Much of the controversy over self-report measures involves problems with instrument construction. Primarily, criticism centers on three issues: (1) the question of the representativeness of items employed in SRD measures; (2) problems of item overlap; and (3) limited or ambiguous response sets.

The major criticism concerns the unrepresentativity of the items selected. Trivial and nonserious offenses (e.g., cutting classes and disobeying parents) are often overrepresented, while serious violations of the criminal code (e.g., burglary, robbery, and sexual assault) are frequently omitted. In addition, many SRD measures tend to overrepresent certain behavioral dimensions (e.g., theft) to the exclusion of other relevant delinquent acts. As a result of such selection processes, most existing SRD measures have a restricted focus and do not represent the full range of delinquent acts; this limits the appropriateness of these scales as general measures of delinquent behavior.

Another problem is the overlapping nature of items often included in SRD measures, which results in inaccurate estimates of frequency due to duplicate counts of certain events. For example, many SRD measures include a "shoplifting" item, a "theft under $5" item, and a "theft $5–50" item. A single theft event could logically be reported on two of these items. The presence of both a "cutting school" and a "cutting class" item represents another form of measurement redundancy since cutting school necessarily involves cutting classes. This problem is not easily overcome, since a given behavioral event in fact may involve more than a single offense. Nevertheless, item overlapping creates a potential source of error in estimating the volume of delinquent behavior from SRD measures.

The type of response sets typically employed with SRD measures has been another source of criticism. One major concern has been the frequent use of normative response categories such as "often," "sometimes," and "occasionally." This type of response set is open to wide variations in interpretation by respondents and precludes any precise count of the actual number of acts committed.

Other response sets used to estimate the number of behaviors (e.g., "never," "once or twice," and "three times or more") have been challenged on the grounds that they are not precise categories for numerical estimation, and that numerical estimates based upon such categories may severely truncate the true distribution of responses. With the above set, for example, any number of behaviors in excess of two is collapsed into a single "high" category. While this procedure may allow for some discrimination between youth at the low end of the frequency distribution, it clearly precludes any discrimination at the high end. Thus, a youth involved in three shoplifting offenses during the specified period receives the same "score" as a youth involved in 50 or 100 shoplifting events during the period. This limited set of categorical responses appears particularly problematic when the reporting period involves a year or more and when such items as using marijuana; drinking beer, wine, or liquor; and carrying a concealed weapon are included in the SRD measure.

Administration Procedures

The manner in which the measures are administered is also a problematic area for self-report delinquency research. Here the issue concerns (1) anonymous vs. identified respondents, and (2) questionnaire vs. interview formats.

Many researchers have argued that anonymity has to be guaranteed or youth will not admit certain offenses—probably the more serious, stigmatizing ones. Research on this question suggests that there is slightly more reporting of offenses under conditions of anonymity, but that anonymous/identified differences are slight and statistically insignificant. These findings have led Dentler to comment that the necessity for anonymity is overemphasized, and that it may in fact lead to reduced involvement by respondents and careless or facetious answers.

On the matter of interview vs. questionnaire formats, the discussion again involves the issue of anonymity and the belief that self-administered questionnaires are more likely to produce accurate responses than personal interviews. One recent self-report delinquency research study compared results from structured interviews and self-administered check-lists,

where anonymity was guaranteed under both conditions. While seven of the eight offenses were admitted more often under check-list conditions than under interview conditions, none of the differences was significant at the .05 level. Even when education, sex, class, and IQ were controlled, no significant differences were obtained.

Some researchers, most notably Gold, have argued that the interview format has significant advantages for delinquency research in that it permits clarification of specific behaviors and, consequently, the ability to more correctly classify illegal acts. In general, however, there is still controversy over the effects of specific administration procedures when the research is directed toward illegal or socially disapproved behaviors.

Sampling Design and Generality

Another problematic area for self-report delinquency research is that of the generality of findings. Here the question focuses primarily on the adequacy of the sampling designs for (1) inferences to the adolescent population, and (2) comparisons with official data.

In most cases, SRD measures have been administered to small, select samples of youth, such as high school students in a particular local community or adolescents processed by a local juvenile court. The samples are rarely probability samples, and generalizations (about the adolescent populations sampled) cannot be made with any known degree of accuracy. Only two published studies involve national probability samples.

A further concern is that few cohort studies using normal populations have incorporated a self-report measure in their instruments. This means that the age and sex gradients of SRD measures are not known, a critical fact if this measurement approach is to become more refined and useful. Furthermore, since the studies using self-report measures have almost always been cross-sectional ones, little is known about the dynamics of self-reported behavior over time.

Finally, Empey notes that national self-report studies have not been conducted on an annual basis and, as a result, it is not possible to discern trends across time or to make direct comparisons with other standard delinquency data such as the Uniform Crime Reports (UCR) or the National Crime Panel (NCP).

The National Youth Survey

We will now report on a national youth study in which we have attempted to deal with the previously noted methodological criticisms of self-report delinquency research. Our aim will be to see if these improvements in the quality of self-report research have any impact on self-report findings relative to findings from official data.

The National Youth Survey involves a 5-year panel design with a national probability sample of 1,726 adolescents aged 11–17 in 1976. The total youth sample was selected and initially interviewed between January and March, 1977, concerning behavior during the calendar year 1976. The second survey was completed between January and March, 1978, to obtain delinquency estimates for the calendar year 1977. The third, fourth, and fifth surveys will also be conducted between each January and March of the years 1979, 1980, and 1981.

The data reported herein are taken from the first survey, completed in 1977. The estimates presented are thus for delinquent behavior during the calendar year 1976.

Construction of New SRD Measure

In constructing the SRD measure for this study, we attempted to obtain a representative set of offenses. Given our interest in comparing SRD and UCR estimates, we began by listing offenses included in the UCR. Any specific act (with the exception of traffic violations) involving more than 1% of the reported juvenile arrests for 1972–1974 is included in the SRD measure.

In addition to the list of specific offenses, the UCR contains a general category, "all other offenses," which often accounts for a high proportion of the total juvenile arrests. To cover the types of acts likely to fall within this general category, and to increase the comprehensiveness of the measure, two general selection criteria were used to choose additional items. First, items which were theoretically relevant to a delinquent lifestyle or subculture as discussed in the literature were selected for inclusion in this measure. Thus, additional items—such as gang fighting, sexual intercourse, and carrying a hidden weapon—are included. Second, a systematic review of existing SRD measures was undertaken to locate items that tapped specific dimensions of delinquent behavior not previously included.

We believe the resulting set of 47 items to be both more comprehensive and more representative of the conceptual universe of delinquent acts than found in prior SRD measures used in major, large-scale studies. The item set includes all but one of the UCR Part I offenses (homicide is excluded); 60% of Part II offenses; and a wide range of "other" offenses—such as delinquent lifestyle items, misdemeanors, and some status offenses. The vast majority of items involve a violation of criminal statutes.

Two separate response sets are being used. Respondents initially are asked to indicate how many times during the past year they committed each act. If an individual's response to this open-ended question involves a frequency of 10 or more, interviewers then ask the youth to select one of the following categorical responses: (1) once a month, (2) once every 2–3 weeks, (3) once a week, (4) 2–3 times a week, (5) once a day, or (6) 2–3 times a day.[2] A comparison of the two response sets indicates high agreement between frequency estimates given in direct response to the open-ended question and frequency estimates based upon the implied frequency associated with the midpoint of the category selected.[3]

A specific attempt was also made to eliminate as much overlap in items as possible. None of the items contains a necessary overlap as in "cutting school" and "cutting class." Although some possible overlap remains, we do not feel it constitutes a serious problem with this SRD measure.

The SRD measure asks respondents to indicate how many times, "from Christmas a year ago to the Christmas just past," they committed each offense. The recall period is thus a year, anchored by a specific reference point relevant to most youth. The use of a 1-year period which coincides almost precisely with the calendar year allows for direct comparison with UCR data, NCP victimization data, and some prior SRD data. It also avoids the need to adjust for seasonal variations, which would be necessary if a shorter time period were involved.

Administration Procedures

For the present study, the research design (a longitudinal panel design) precludes a guarantee of anonymity. Therefore, our major concern is to guarantee respondents that their answers will be confidential. This assurance is given verbally as well as being contained in the written consent form signed by all youth and their parents. In addition, a Certificate of Confidentiality from the Department of Health, Education, and Welfare guarantees all respondents that the data and the interviewers will be protected from legal subpoena.

The interview format was selected over the self-administered questionnaire format for several reasons. First, we share Gold's belief that the interview situation (if properly structured to protect confidentiality) can insure more accurate, reliable data. Second, the necessity of securing informed consents from all subjects and the complexity of the present research require, in our judgment, a personal contact with the respondents. Once this contact is made, it seems logical to use the interviewer to facilitate the data collection process and to improve the quality of the data obtained. Finally, some of our previous research suggests that the differences in responding to SRD items in a questionnaire as opposed to an interview format are not significant.

Summary of New Measure

In sum, the current SRD measure addresses many of the central criticisms of prior SRD measures. It is more representative of the full range of delinquent acts than were prior SRD measures and involves fewer overlapping items; it also employs a response set which provides better discrimination at the high end of the frequency continuum and is more suited to estimating the actual number of behaviors committed. The choice of a 1-year time frame with a panel design involving a 1-year time lag is based upon both conceptual and practical concerns. Compared with the other SRD measures, the measure involves a moderate recall period, captures seasonal variations, and permits a direct comparison with other self-report and official measures which are reported annually. And, finally, the study involves a national probability sample of youth aged 11–17.

ANALYSIS OF DATA

Race and Class Differentials

Unlike most previous self-report studies, we find significant race differences for total SRD and for predatory crimes against property. Blacks report significantly higher frequencies than do whites on each of these measures. In both cases, the differences in means are substantial. With respect to total offenses, blacks report three offenses for every two reported by whites. For crimes against property, blacks report more than two offenses for every offense reported by whites.

While there is a substantial difference in mean scores on the crimes against persons scale, it is not statistically significant. The difference in the total SRD score appears to be primarily the result of the very high level of property crimes reported by blacks.

We also observe a class differential for total SRD and for predatory crimes against persons. For total SRD scores, the difference is between lower socioeconomic status youth and others; i.e., there does not appear to be any difference between working and middle-class group means.

The differences are greater, and the trend is more linear, for the crimes against persons scale means than for total SRD. Lower-class youth report nearly four times as many offenses as do middle-class youth and one-and-one-half times as many as working-class youth. There is also a substantial class difference in the mean number of crimes against persons, but this difference is not statistically significant. There are clearly no substantial differences in means for any of the remaining subscales.

Relationship Between SRD and Official Data

In sum, it appears likely that the differences between the findings reported here and those from earlier self-report studies are, in fact, the result of differences in the specific SRD measures employed. The findings also suggest a logical connection between self-report and official measures of delinquency which, at least in part, accounts for the observed differences in the class and face distributions of these two measures.

The consistent findings of earlier self-report studies have led many sociologists and criminologists to the conclusion that race and class differences in arrests are primarily the result of processing biases and have little or no basis in behavior. The findings from the 1977 National Youth Survey suggest some behavioral basis for the observed class and race differences in official processing. In this sense, the National Youth Survey data are more consistent with official arrest data than are data from most prior self-report studies.

Further, these findings provide some insight into the mechanism whereby official actions produce exaggerated race and class (as well as age and sex) differences in delinquent behavior when compared with self-reported differences in normal adolescent populations. On both logical and empirical grounds, it seems reasonable to argue that the more frequent and serious offenders are more likely to be arrested, and that the youth population represented in official police statistics is not a representative sample of all youth.

Self-report studies are capturing a broader range of persons and levels of involvement in delinquent behavior than are official arrest statistics. Virtually all youth report some delinquent activity on self-report measures, but for the vast majority the offenses are neither very frequent nor very serious. Police contacts, on the other hand, are most likely to concern youth who are involved in either very serious or very frequent delinquent acts. Police contacts with youth thus involve a more restricted segment of the general youth population.

The findings discussed previously indicate that race and class differences are more extreme at the high end of the frequency continuum, that part of the delinquency continuum where police contacts are more likely. In fact, at this end of the frequency continuum, self-report and official correlates of delinquent behavior are relatively similar. While we do not deny the existence of official processing biases, it does appear that official correlates of delinquency also reflect real differences in the frequency and seriousness of delinquent acts.

The results of this self-report delinquency study also have implications for previous tests of theoretical propositions which used SRD data. Stated simply, earlier self-report measures may not have been sensitive enough to capture the theoretically important differences in delinquency involvement. Given the truncated frequency distributions and the restricted behavioral range of earlier self-report measures, the only distinctions possible were fine gradations between relatively nondelinquent youth.

For example, earlier distinctions were typically among (1) youth with no reported offenses; (2) those with one or two offenses; and (3) those with three or more offenses. Given the extensive frequency distribution observed in this study, there is reason to question whether or not such a trichotomy would capture meaningful distinctions among offending youth. The most significant difference may not be between the nonoffender and the one-time offender, or even between the one-time and multiple-time offender. Equal or greater significance may be found between those reporting over (or under) 25 nonserious offenses, or between those reporting over (or under) five serious offenses.

The ability to discriminate more fully among many levels and types of involvement in delinquent behavior introduces much more variance into the delinquency measure. That ability also allows for the identification of more extreme groups of offenders, and that identification may be particularly relevant for tests of theoretical propositions.

NOTES

1. Hindelang et al. have also recently studied the extent to which sex and race are differentially related to self-reported and official records of delinquency.

2. The categorical response set has led to the identification of some highly episodic events, e.g., 20 shoplifting offenses, all occurring within a 2-month period during the summer (an initial response of 20; a categorical response 2–3 times a week, and an interviewer probe revealing that the offenses all occurred during the summer).

3. The only exception involves the last two high-frequency categories. At this end of the frequency continuum, estimates based upon the midpoint of the category are substantially higher than the frequency response given directly. The open-ended frequency measure thus appears to provide a more conservative estimate of number of delinquent acts, and the estimates reported here are based upon this response.

SOURCE: From *American Sociological Review* 45:95–110. Copyright © 1980 by Delbert Elliott and Suzanne Ageton. Reprinted by permission of The American Sociological Association.

QUESTIONS FOR DISCUSSION AND WRITING

1. What are the similarities and differences with respect to age, sex, class, and race in the incidence and distribution of delinquent behavior in self-reported and official arrest data?

2. What, if any, differences did the authors find with respect to race?

3. What, if any, differences did the authors find with respect to class?

Gender and Adolescent Relationship Violence

A Contextual Examination

Jody Miller

Norman A. White

The problem of nonmarital relationship violence has been of considerable interest to scholars for the past two decades. Although most studies have focused on dating violence among college populations, a growing body of scholarship has emerged that examines the problem among adolescents. Within adolescent studies, in particular, fairly high rates of female-to-male violence have been documented. Debate continues concerning whether and how gender shapes dating and other partner violence. Some researchers suggest a gender-neutral approach is warranted, whereas feminist scholars insist that gender—and male dominance specifically—must be at the foreground for a meaningful understanding of relationship violence to emerge.

Here we weigh in on this debate by providing a contextual examination of the nature, circumstances, and meanings of partner violence in adolescent dating relationships. Drawing from a larger qualitative study of violence in the lives of African-American youths from a distressed urban community, we examine young women's and young men's accounts of male-perpetrated, female-perpetrated, and reciprocal violence in dating relationships.

The Sexual Symmetry/ Woman Abuse Debate

The case for sexual symmetry rests on two bodies of scholarship—studies that find similar rates of relationship violence perpetration across gender and, more recently, research that suggests a common psychological profile for males and females who perpetrate relationship violence. Studies that produce similar rates of relationship violence across gender typically use a version of the Conflict Tactics Scale (CTS). CTS-based research has consistently found similar or higher rates of female-perpetrated than male-perpetrated physical violence among adolescents.

As significant for feminists, the CTS provides an impoverished understanding of partner violence because "its exclusive focus on 'acts' ignores actors' interpretations, motivations, and intentions. . . . The CTS omits the contexts of violence, the events precipitating it, and the sequence of events by which it progresses." Feminists suggest that although much of women's violence "is used in response to men's violence, in self-defense or retaliation," the CTS labels these women violent and as indistinguishable from the men from whom they are defending themselves.

133

From a feminist perspective, there is concern with gender-neutral models in which gender is examined as an individual trait (more aptly, sex category), rather than conceptualized in a theoretically meaningful way as a structural and symbolic basis of inequality. For example, focusing exclusively on individual characteristics such as negative emotionality or anger ignores how these may be generated or may trigger violence within particular types of gender (and race, class) contexts. Ideologies about gender provide different normative expectations for males and females; moreover, because social conditions are structured by gender, the result is differences in the opportunities, constraints, and demands placed on women and men, again structured on the basis of race and class as well. Thus, feminists insist that it is precisely the ways in which gender structures relationship—most often to the power disadvantage of women—that the gendered nature of partner violence can be understood.

Our investigation provides one of the first attempts to compare female- and male-perpetrated dating violence from the perspective of adolescents themselves. We examine accounts across gender in order to explore both shared and discordant aspect of youths' understanding of partner violence, and to situate these in youths' accounts of the nature of adolescent dating relations and their perspectives on gender and violence. This approach lends itself to the examination of gender as an integral facet of everyday life that actively structures social life and, in turn, provides a base of meanings for interpreting social action.

GENDER AND THE SOCIAL CONTEXTS OF DATING VIOLENCE

There is some evidence that adolescent dating violence may have features distinguishing it from partner violence in adulthood. Gary and Foshee's survey of adolescents suggests that "violent adolescent dating relationships are more often mutually violent than one-sided."

One reason we would expect differences in adolescent versus adult experiences is the nature of adolescence as a developmental stage. Adolescence is associated with the onset of puberty, and it is the life stage when romantic relationships first become a significant part of peer interactions. Thus, youths are encountering new relationship experiences at the same time that status among peers heightens in significance. These changes are coupled with intense emotionality and gendered romantic scripts for behavior.

Another explanation for potential differences between adolescent and adult partner violence comes from research on the relationship characteristics that tend to be associated with violence, including the correlation between length and seriousness of relationships and partner violence. Magdol et al. found that rates of partner violence were significantly higher among young adult cohabitators than dating partners of the same age. They suggest a number of relationship characteristics help explain this finding, including the increased extent of shared time and activities, greater areas for potential conflict, and greater power imbalances that may arise when couples live together.

A second area of research that is indicative of meaningful differences across gender is the examination of motives for partner violence. Although studies of dating violence find that males and females both rank consistently high for describing anger and jealousy as motives for violence, significant gender differences emerge with regard to the issue of control. O'Keefe reports that anger was the most frequent motive mentioned by both females and males, followed by self-defense for girls and the desire to get control over their partner for boys, with jealousy the third most-cited motive for both sexes. The most conclusive evidence of a distinct control motive among men who perpetrate partner violence comes from Felson and Messner's recent examination of NCVS data.

Felson and Messner suggest that the control motive is linked not just to individuals' desire to exert influence within the relationship, but also to their relative coercive power. This is where the greatest gender difference may lie: "[A] threat delivered by the less powerful party is likely to lack credibility, and it may lead to retaliation rather than to fear and compliance." Follingstad et al. found that a control motive is most likely to be expressed by individuals whose dating violence perpetration is severe or frequent. They suggest that although initial incidents of violence may not have a control motive, control of one's partner may be an outcome of violence that eventually results in violence committed for the purpose of control. These findings bolster Felson and Messner's hypothesis that males may disproportionately have a control motive for partner violence because they can better execute a credible threat.

This is where a third body of scholarship—research on the gendered meanings of partner violence—is particularly relevant. Research consistently shows that males minimize female-perpetrated partner violence, which suggests females are less able to execute violence for the purpose of controlling their male partner. Over half of the males in Molidor and Tolman's sample reported that their response to dating violence victimization was to laugh, and a third reported ignoring it. In contrast, a larger proportion of girls reported fighting back, obeying their partner, or trying to talk to him.

Overall, the research suggests that despite gender parity in reported rates of partner violence among adolescents, it is premature to conclude that partner violence is a gender-neutral phenomenon. To assert this conclusion requires treating gender as a sex category, and it belies the importance of gender as a social structure and meaning system with significance for understanding violence in relationships. Although the studies reported provide strong evidence of this, almost without exception, they are based on survey research, which is unable to examine fully the contexts surrounding partner violence. Here we draw from qualitative interviews and base our investigation on the belief that an improved understanding of adolescent dating violence emerges when this violence is situated in an analysis of the nature of relationships, conflicts, and the gendered power dynamics within interviewees' peer culture.

METHODOLOGY AND STUDY SETTING

Data for this investigation come from a broader study of gender and violence among urban African-American adolescents, and they include survey and in-depth interviews with 70 African-American youths in north St. Louis, Missouri. The sample includes 32 young women and 38 young men. Respondents ranged in age from 12 to 19 (12 to 18 for females, 13 to 19 for males) with a mean age of approximately 16 for both genders.

We narrowed our study to urban African-American youths because our knowledge base is particularly limited with regard to both adolescent dating violence and gender-based violence in highly distressed urban African-American communities. There is evidence that structural conditions such as unemployment and unbalanced gender ratios in inner-city communities increase cultural support for violence against women, that gender inequality remains a salient feature of the urban street milieu, but also that African-American girls in impoverished urban communities may have higher rates of participation in both general and dating violence than their counterparts in other racial groups and settings. Respondents were drawn from neighborhoods characterized by intense racial segregation, social isolation, limited resources, concentrated poverty, and high rates of violent crime.

Our goal was to interview youths at risk or involved in delinquent activities, as previous research suggests these youths have a higher risk for victimization and participation in dating violence. We did not target youths known to have experience with dating violence. As noted previously, much feminist research on the meanings and nature of partner violence has relied on samples of known "battered women" or "batterers." We expected that our approach would allow us to investigate less serious forms of dating violence not likely to be reported or intervened upon. Moreover, our inclusion of both young women and young men—and our focus on both groups' experiences as perpetrators and victims of dating violence—provided an opportunity to examine the nature of dating violence and the role gender plays in shaping it without the introduction of sampling biases resulting from the use of known cases, and in keeping with sampling frames used in CTS-based research. Finally, our sampling approach allowed us to situate youths' accounts of their own experiences of dating violence in the context of youths' accounts of the nature of dating relationships and conflicts regardless of the presence of violence, and youths' interpretations of and exposure to dating violence regardless of their personal experiences. This provided us with a means of comparing youths who reported dating violence with those who had not with regard to their attitudes and the meanings they attached to the phenomenon.

Data collection began with the administration of a survey, and youths were then asked to participate in an in-depth interview.

In-depth interviewing provided us with a method for understanding the social world from the points of view of the research participants. Rigorous examination of such accounts offers a means of "arriving at meanings or culturally embedded normative explanations [for behavior, because they] represent ways in which people organize views of themselves, of others, and of their social worlds." In our analysis, we took care to ensure that the concepts developed and illustrations provided typified the most common patterns in youths' accounts. This was achieved using grounded theory methods, including the search for and explication of deviant cases. Reliability was strengthened through our triangulated data collection technique, by asking youths about their reports at multiple points across two interviews, and asking for detailed accounts during the in-depth interviews.

THE GENDERING OF ADOLESCENT RELATIONSHIP VIOLENCE

According to the survey results, young men were more likely to report being pushed or shoved, slapped, kicked, bit, or hit with a fist by a girlfriend. Young women were more likely to report having experienced verbally abusive behaviors, and they were significantly more likely to report having a dating partner cheat on them. It is notable that about a quarter of girls reported being pressured or forced into unwanted sex in the context of a dating relationship.

We begin with a discussion of hegemonic masculinity and its impact on the social organization of gender relations, including the relevance of dominant definitions of masculinity on adolescent dating relationships. Second, we move to a discussion of the primary facets of relationship conflict described by participants, focusing on jealousy, distrust, and control issues and examining how these are shaped by gender. Finally, we examine relationship violence, analyzing its normative aspects as well as incidents of female-perpetrated, male-perpetrated, and reciprocal violence, and the contexts, progression, and interpretations brought to bear on these events.

The Playa' and the Cool Pose: Hegemonic Masculinity and the Social Organization of Gender Relations

A characteristic feature of adolescence is the "shift from the relatively asexual gender systems of childhood to the overtly sexualized gender systems of adolescence and adulthood." This shift has different meanings and consequences across gender. Girls face a sexual double standard in which they receive status for their association with and attractiveness to males but are denigrated for sexual activities deemed "promiscuous," whereas boys receive status for sexual exploits. Among the youths we spoke with, being a "playa" [player]—using girls for sex and having multiple sexual conquests without emotional attachment—was described as a prominent model for male behavior that offered the potential for status and prestige within male peer groups.

A number of boys described feigning interest in a relationship in order to convince girls to have sex with them. Tyrell described girls as easy "to persuade" and said,

> You can easily talk to girls and have 'em thinking [that you like them]. . . . You tell 'em what they wanna hear, they gonna give you what you want, thinking that you really care about them for real but you really don't. You'll have 'em loving you but you ain't even care about 'em.

Likewise, Duane explained, "You gotta spend some time with 'em first. You can't just go buy her something and expect just to take her home the same day. You gotta chill out with her for a little minute. Like talk to her and stuff. . . . [But] I do it just because I wanna have sex."

Girls who gave in to boys' advances too readily, even under false pretenses, were labeled "hood rats" or "hoes," were liable to be targeted by additional boys, and were disempowered in their relationships. For example, Bobby was in a fairly new relationship, but he did not respect the girl and was ambivalent about the relationship because he felt she had sex with him too readily:

Bobby: This girl I got now, like the first day we met (pause), well I don't consider her as my girlfriend for real 'cause, you know, okay, if you had met a girl on yo' first date, you had sex with her on yo' first date, what would you think? What would you call her?

Interviewer: I guess it depends on how it evolves from there.

Bobby: Yeah, see like the first day I met this girl . . . we had went to a telly [hotel]. It was me, my brother, his girlfriend and her lil sister [Bobby's girlfriend], we was all sharin' the same room with 'em.

So I consider her as like a rat, which I don't know 'cause it just happened, how I talked to her, you know what I'm saying, and she just up and gave it to me, you know what I'm saying, just that fast so I don't know.

This sexual double standard and the playa ethos were also associated with a clear message boys received from their peers: Love equals softness. For some, this encouraged the avoidance of committed relationships, as Ronald's description exemplifies: "I'm a one-month person. I like movin' on."

Many of the young men we interviewed described not being open about their relationships with friends, and instead talking primarily about the sexual facets of their relationship, and about other girls. Several, like Tyrell, who were in long-term or serious relationships described having one trusted confidant that they could talk to openly about their relationship, but on the whole, this talk was discouraged or sanctioned through ridicule. In contrast, most of the girls we talked to described openly talking with their friends about their own and their friends' relationships, including what Rennesha called "normal stuff, like we went here and there last night," and their fights and conflicts.

Both girls and boys described positive facets of their relationships. In fact, boys were more likely to highlight positive features of their relationships—most notably, the intimacy and emotional support they received from their girlfriends. Travis explained that there was "a special bond between" him and his girlfriend because "I could talk to her about anything." Boys also spoke most positively about their girlfriends when the girl had not been sexually active with them too quickly. Girls spoke especially positively about boyfriends who did not pressure them into having sex, but generally seemed to be more ambivalent about their relationships. Yvonne noted, "We real close, we talk a lot each other. He more like a friend. He's real dependable and I enjoy being with him sometimes when he don't get ignorant." Likewise, Cleshay described her relationship as "Good. It only have rocky spots but twice, but that's because he cheated on me. . . . But other than that he's a decent guy. I like him, he cool."

Boys in particular, then, valued intimacy in their relationships, as this was less available in their friendships with other boys, where status depended on not revealing these qualities. Boys found competing expectations in their romantic relationship and their friendship groups, which were a source of potential conflict with their girlfriends. In fact, young men's concern with their appearance in front of friends led many to adopt what Majors and Billson describe as a "cool pose"—a mask to conceal vulnerabilities that is characterized by detachment, control of emotions, aloofness, and toughness.

Given its emphasis on sex without emotion (and often with manipulation), playa behavior fit well with the cool pose. Boys' minimization of their commitment in relationships, further facilitated through sexual talk about their girlfriends and other girls, helped project a detached persona.

Jealousy, Distrust, and Control: Gender and Relationship Conflict

The playa climate and the cool pose were facets of hegemonic masculinity that structured gender relations to the disadvantage of girls, but also created a cultural ethos that led to widespread jealousy, distrust, and conflict in relationships. Even youths who were genuinely trying to maintain committed relationships described the negative consequences of this ethos for building and sustaining trust. Combined with the sexual double standard, this environment served to disempower many girls in their relationships with young men. It also contributed to girls tending to have a greater emotional investment in their relationships, particularly early on, which boys sometimes fostered.

Some boys fostered a greater emotional stake from their girlfriends by purposely doing things to make the girl jealous and uncertain about his commitment to the relationship. Bobby, for example, described "playing" with his girlfriend by pretending to be on the phone with another girl. Once when she called, he "be like, 'What's up?' and then be like, 'Hold on, let me go tell this girl I'll call her right back.' You playin' with her [put the mute button on the phone], then you take it off and be like, 'Yeah, alright what's up?' [She] be like, 'How you gone have me on hold while you sittin' up there talkin' to [another girl]?" Tyrell and Travis both made comments about how attractive other girls were in the presence of their girlfriends. And Ricky said he would sometimes ignore his girlfriend or do things to make her mad because "it's easy to frustrate her and I know I can so I be doin' it to see how she gone react that day. I just mess with her."

Girls also described such situations. Shauntell got angry because her boyfriend purposely walked past her arm-in-arm with another girl and ignored her. In the most extreme form of emotional manipulation, several girls reported that their boyfriends would pressure them for sex with the threat that if she did not provide it, he would seek it elsewhere. Such behavioral techniques undermined girls' security in their relationships. Notably, youths did not describe such strategies being adopted by girls in relationships. In part, this was because to do so would function to put the girl's sexual reputation in jeopardy.

The Gendering of Jealousy in Relationships

Both young women and young men described jealousy as a key problem in their dating relationships.

Although youths described these issues affecting both males and females, their discussions also revealed gender-specific elements to both jealousy and the conflicts that ensued. Because of the playa environment, it was more likely for girls' jealousy to be based on valid concerns. Jamal explained, "Women have the tendency to always think that men are dogs and we gonna do what we want to do anyway [and] for most guys it's true." In fact, 63% of the boys said they had cheated on their girlfriends, and a number of girls described these events in the course of talking about their relationships. Jamellah, for example, had recently ended a three-year relationship with a young man six years her senior after she found out he had been cheating on her. Her description also illustrates the nature of informal policing and her application of the sexual double standard described earlier in her evaluation of her boyfriend's infidelity:

The girl was bragging about having sex with him and [my god sister] came and told me and, she not the only one who came and told me, like three other girls came and told me the same time she did. . . . And this girl she was his age too, she like 24, 23. But she got like five kids. She ain't have no high school diploma. She ain't doing nothing with herself but smokin' weed and drinkin', smokin' weed and drinkin'. Ain't got not job, on welfare. Just looked like

she wore out and then she was having sex with everybody too. Everybody out the neighborhood she done gave some to. So I was like, "You gone cheat on me with that?" I confronted him, and he denied it and denied it [though it was confirmed by one of his friends]. . . . Then it got to the point when I'll be around him and I just be like upset. Like I didn't break up with him that soon. 'Cause I couldn't after being with him for so long, it's hard to break up with somebody. But it got to the point where . . . the hurt really make me mad, and that insulted me. I'm up here trying to do something with myself, I ain't got no kids, and you are going cheat on me with that? A hood rat at that.

In most cases, boys' jealousy also did not appear to result from actual infidelity. Tami said she and her boyfriend argued occasionally when he accused her of flirting with other guys. Once this occurred after she was seen talking to another boy in the school cafeteria:

Like we was in the lunchroom and this dude was up in my face and he was asking me why my boyfriend wasn't over here talking to me. So I was like, "I don't know, I guess he down there with his homies" or whatever. And he was like, "He should be up here with you, 'cause somebody else could try to get you." I was like, "I don't know what's wrong with him." And then [my boyfriend's] partna, my play-brother, he came and was like, "Tami, who was that you was talkin' to in the lunchroom?"

Tami and her boyfriend later fought because "he was hearing things" about the incident.

In sum, although jealousy was a salient issue for both genders, girls were more likely to have experienced infidelity, and this exacerbated insecurity and distrust. Girls' concerns were heightened by the playa climate, and sometimes exacerbated by their boyfriends' behaviors. Moreover, because of the sexual double standard, accusations of girls' infidelity were also implicit challenges to their reputations—a meaning that was lacking when boys were accused of being unfaithful.

The Management of
Relationship Conflict and Control

The other area where notable gender difference emerged with regard to jealousy and distrust was in the relative efficacy of partners' responses. Both girls and boys described attempting to intervene or exert control over their partner's behavior, particularly when they were suspected of flirting or cheating. However, girls were less successful in their attempts. Both girls and boys described a pattern of male unresponsiveness during conflicts stemming from female jealousy that often functioned to escalate girls' angry reactions.

Boys usually described disengagement as a strategy to maintain control or send the girl a message. Leon explained, "I'll just walk away and I might ignore her. That'll make her think 'well he ain't talking to me so I must of did something to make him mad.' Just stay away from her. I won't say nothing to her." Describing conflicts with her ex-boyfriend, Ramara confirmed, "If we had a argument he'll just walk away, he wouldn't yell at me or nothin'. That's what made me mad 'cause I would want him to yell at me and stuff but he never did it, he'll just walk away." Walter offered the most exacting description of this strategy: "If we like get into an argument and it's like a real bad argument and I don't like what she said or something like that I won't say nothing to her for like a week. And if she call I just tell my stepmother and father to keep telling her that I ain't here. I wait for like a week and then I'll probably call her."

In contrast to young men's descriptions of their own emotional disengagement strategies, a number of them complained that girls were emotionally out of control, and they viewed girls' attempts to exert control in the relationship through this framework.

Ricky said "females have the tendency to go overboard sometimes." He explained that men are "stronger mentally and physically, so you can't really blame [females]" for the way they behave. Framing girls' actions in this way often meant boys dismissed the gender inequalities that resulted in girls' insecurity and emotional reactions, and instead located girls' behavior as rooted in naturalized gender difference.

Conflicts emerging from male jealousy were more likely to end with the young man getting his way. Britney described a recent conflict with her boyfriend of five months:

His cousin like me so if I go like to the store with his cousin he'll be like, "Why you go to the store with him? You know he like you." And I'll be like, "'Cause he asked me and I want to go anyway and you wasn't around so I couldn't

ask you and I didn't want to go by myself." And he be like, "It don't matter, you ain't supposed to go 'cause he like you." And I be like, "You can't tell me what I can and I cannot do." He be like, "I'm your boyfriend, I can do what I want."

Young women also described boyfriends who attempted to control their physical appearance. Girls were discouraged from wearing clothing that, as Katie described, "draw too much attention from other people." She said her boyfriend "always tryin' to tell me what I can wear, what I can't wear, like [he says I can't wear] short shorts and tight shorts and stuff like that. [He wants me to wear] church girl clothes, long skirts, he just like for me to be covered up." She admitted she would sometimes change clothes simply to avoid conflicts. Michelle was upset when her boyfriend was "up in my face, 'How many other boys you be talkin' to today?' And just stupid stuff like that." He often initiated these fights when "I go get my hair done [or] when I'll buy me an outfit or something. He be like, 'Who you wanna impress now?' or something like that." Lisa complained that her boyfriend "talk like he my daddy, like he be tryin' to tell me what to wear, what not to wear, sayin' I look like a hoochie. I look like a rat when I put that on, I look sleazy. He just say stupid stuff."

It is notable that male controlling behaviors appeared to manifest themselves primarily in long-term relationships, whereas girls' attempts to exert control were more likely to begin early in the relationship when they were especially unsure of where the relationship stood. Young men clearly had the upper hand early in relationships when the possibility remained that they were just "playing" the girl. They could draw from a repertoire of behaviors that functioned to sustain power imbalances in their relationships, including using the playa ethos and detachment strategies to undermine girls' security. Although these remained salient issues even in long-term relationships, it was nonetheless the case that as relationships progressed, the potential existed for power imbalances to lessen as boys themselves became emotionally invested in the relationship.

REAL MEN AND EMOTIONAL WOMEN: THE GENDERING OF DATING VIOLENCE

A sizable minority of girls and over half of the boys described at least some experience with minor forms of violence in relationships.

Four types of dating violence were routinely described by the youths: female-initiated violence against a male dating partner, male violence in response to female-initiated violence, nonreciprocal male violence, and mutual "play" violence. Girls were as likely to describe initiating violence as to describe nonreciprocal male violence. None described reciprocating when males initiated violence. Boys were twice as likely to describe female violence as to report that they had engaged in violence, and they primarily described their own violence as a response to female-initiated violence. We found two notable differences in girls' and boys' reports: First, of those girls who initiated violence, nearly three-quarters said their boyfriends responded with violence. In contrast, nearly two-thirds of boys described female-initiated violence in their relationships as nonreciprocal. Second, although seven girls (22%) described having experienced nonreciprocal male violence, only two boys (5%) admitted to having engaged in such violence.

Young Women's Dating Violence

Girls' use of violence in dating relationships was interpreted within the framework of their perceived emotionality. Jermaine explained that "girls get mad real easy so [they] can't hold it back." Likewise, Lisa said that "a girl will trip faster than a boy will." As girls did not face the constraints of the "cool pose," they had more latitude to express their emotions, including through the use of minor forms of violence. But the consequence was that they were often viewed as emotionally out of control. This meant that in some instances, girls' actions were seen as excusable (i.e., "they can't help it"), whereas in other instances, their "out-of-control" emotions were viewed as in need of (male) control.

Young men did not define girls' violence as threatening. Describing what happened when a girl called him in his girlfriend's presence, Andrew explained, "She got mad or whatever and she got to going off and she slapped me or whatever. It wasn't really nothing, really." Marvin said his girlfriend once got mad and threw a baseball at him, but "it missed [and] I laughed at her. It made her madder but you know she just got frustrated and just sat there." Likewise, Ricky said, "If we have an argument or something, she'll just like hit me, punch me in my chest or something or like slap on my back or push me in my head or something. It ain't, I mean . . . it's not too much."

Because girl's violence was not viewed as physically threatening, youths espoused the belief that under most circumstances, boys should not hit girls back. Many felt girls used violence because of this tacit understanding. Ramara explained, "If [he] think he a man, he should be man enough to take what a woman give to him. If she cussin' him out, he supposed to be able to take it. If she hit, he just supposed to walk away." Bobby noted, "You know how girls are, they'll hit you, you know what I'm saying, 'cause they know, hit a dude and a dude ain't gon' hit 'em back. So that's how they get carried away by hittin' boys." Darnell said his girlfriend "know I ain't gonna fight her, that's why she'll try to fight." However, this was a contingent belief, and there were situations in which male violence was an approved response to girls' actions.

As these accounts suggest, girls' violence was often precipitated by anger resulting from jealousy or the belief that their boyfriend had been unfaithful.

Kristy said she had been violent in her relationship only once, and the result was a two-month breakup: "I had confronted him because I heard that he had been unfaithful. So I confronted him and he got loud about it and he called me a B [bitch]. So I pushed him, then he pushed me back and he was like, 'Just leave, get out my face 'fore I hit you.' I was like, 'It's like that?' He's like, 'It's like that.'" Lisa was one of two young women who described having engaged in a serious assault on her boyfriend. At the time of her interview, she had a swollen black eye that was the result of a recent fight she had initiated:

I got this [black eye] 'cause . . . Thursday when I came to school, this girl tellin' me that my boyfriend be comin' over to they house, this, this, this and that. So me bein' stupid, knowing the girl didn't like me anyway I shouldn't have listened to her. Me bein' stupid, went home tryin' to fight him. He blockin' the punches or whatever like, "Go'n. Get off of me, go'n, stop, stop." He kept on tellin' me to stop, stop, go'n, go'n. So I'm steady hittin' him, steady hittin' him. I had on some sandals. I'm hittin' him with the sandals. I run outside, I'm hittin' him. I'm hittin' his car or whatever and so he said something to me as he was closin' his door and

I punched him in his eye and he pushed the car up in park, he got out the car and smacked me and got back in the car and left.

Young women also described initiating violence as a result of anger or frustration resulting from what they perceived as their boyfriend's emotional detachment or uncaring response. Alicia described a conflict that emerged "'cause I want him to walk me to the bus stop and he ain't feel like it so we got to arguing. I was like, 'It's all late outside and you won't walk me to the bus stop?' He like, 'It ain't that far' so I just got real mad and I hit him." Alicia said that "he ended up walking [me], he was playing but I ain't find it funny. I wasn't playing."

Finally, girls' violence sometimes resulted from the combination of perceived infidelity and a boyfriend's "cool pose." Christal, the girl who described engaging in serious violence, said her ex-boyfriend "used to treat me alright, he just a hoe, go with everybody and they momma." A jealous conflict emerged and Christal "was like, 'Well I don't wanna go with you no more.'" Expecting him to fight for her, she was angered when instead

he was like, "Oh well." That's when I got mad and threw a brick. And the first time it missed and then I got it again and threw it and it hit him right between his legs. And then when he came in my face I slapped him and then he grabbed me, pulled my hair, and then he had threw me on the ground.

Ironically, although most girls believed their boyfriends should not hit them back when they initiated violence, in some instances, girls seemed to be trying to push their boyfriends into an emotional reaction, even if that reaction was a violent one. Describing a fight she witnessed between her friend and the friend's boyfriend, Tami said,

I don't know what they was arguin' about but she was all up in his face talkin' about "do it" and "do it." I guess she was tellin' [daring] him to hit her or whatever. And he was like, "Man I ain't gon' hit you," and he was tryin' to go to class and she grabbed him back and was all up in his face. I'm like, "You crazy."

Thus, there was a tension between definitions of "real men" as capable of walking away, but also a desire to break through that detachment and elicit an engaged response.

Young Men's Dating Violence

Although girls' dating violence was attributed to their being emotionally out of control, youths' attitudes toward male dating violence revealed a more complex set of interpretations. Youths' discussions centered to a large extent on explicating the general inappropriateness but situational acceptability of male violence. An overarching theme across the interviews was that males should not hit females.

The imperative that males not hit females was primarily framed in one of two ways: First was the belief, grounded most clearly in hegemonic masculinity, that to do so was unmanly—men should fight individuals who pose a physical challenge, not individuals they know they can beat. Antwoin noted, "You a punk if you fight a girl." Rennesha said, "I feel a man has too much strength to hit a female; it is just not a man to hit a female. . . . Some girls think they tough, want to keep up. But still, you walk away. You a man." Cooper explained, "We have more strength than them. Why hit a female? When they hit you back it won't hurt for real. No competition in that." In addition to being viewed as physically unmanly, several young men also linked hitting girls with evidence of too great of an emotional investment in the relationship—a contrast to the valued cool pose.

The second framework for explaining why men should not hit women was a more chivalrous variation of the first. Here the emphasis was specifically on female vulnerability and linked with respect for their mothers. In fact, a number of young men said they were taught by their mothers not to hit girls. Ricky's explanation clearly links this norm back to the family:

When you think about it, we already got the advantage 'cause we men. . . . All of us live with women, I mean, and I think about it like I wouldn't want my ma to be in a relationship and they have an argument then he feel like he can just punch on her, black her eye, choke on her or something like that. Then I think about it too, I got a sister. I wouldn't want my sister getting in no relationship with nobody and they feel like they can beat on her because they together and they call theyself a couple.

But the conversation with Ricky also alludes to one of the key contradictions in how youths viewed male-on-female violence: Punching or beating up a woman was viewed as distinct from other forms of physical violence. He continued, "My friends don't too much hit they girlfriends. If anything, they'll just push 'em and yank 'em and grab 'em but it ain't really like a balled up fist or smack type of thing."

Male Violence as a Response to Female-Initiated Violence. Despite the belief that they should be able to "take it like men," both girls and boys posited several ideologies that justified a violent response when a girl initiated violence. These were important contingencies that coexisted with the strong overall taboo.

Some youths believed more serious male violence was called for when the girl seemed to have forgotten her place. Asked to explain why his friends sometimes hit their girlfriends, Larry responded, "Most of the time I've been there, I know why. Gal be trippin'. Like one gal, she crazy, she be swinging on him. He be like, he be trying not to hit her but I be like, 'Don't keep lettin' her hit you like that dawg, go on, swing back.'" Shontana said, "If you big enough to hit a man, you big enough to take that lick back." Walter concurred, "Certain times I feel that if a girl is man enough to hit you, she man enough to get hit back." Cleshay put this ideology in perhaps the starkest terms. Although she noted that "a man shouldn't hit no woman," a moment later she clarified, "When the women step up to her husband like she a man and try to go head up with him, I think he should let her know, 'You can't whoop me.' Because some girls be needin' it. . . . Sometimes you need to put people in they place."

Nonreciprocal Male Violence. Only two young men admitted to having initiated violence against a girlfriend, whereas 22% of the girls we spoke with described having been the victim of such violence. Two girls were in relationships that fit the profile of chronic battering. In addition, a number of young women described having friends in battering relationships, and youths reported that witnessing male violence was a fairly common occurrence, both among their peers and in their neighborhoods. Despite the normative constraint against nonreciprocal male violence *in the abstract,* youths did not uniformly condemn it when it occurred. Instead, it

was typically explained as either brought on by girls' behaviors, the result of some boys having "bad tempers," or some combination of these. Girls and boys both espoused these beliefs, although with the notable caveat that girls were more disturbed by such events than were boys.

Youths most often defined girls as deserving male violence when they "runnin' they mouth." Frank said, "Man she just getting on my nerves. I'm like, 'Shut up, just shut up.' Get all up in my face. Pow—shut up!" Likewise, Kevin described his use of violence:

> Like sometimes we'll be talking or something or arguing and she get loud and she start putting her hand in my face and stuff and I'll, she'll put her hand in my face and I slap her hand. One time I had just got, I ain't try to, I just got mad and I, I smacked her then she started looking at me crazy then she walked off or whatever. Sometimes she just, it be her fault for real. She don't know when to shut up. That's her main problem, she do not know when to shut up.

Girls sometimes espoused these beliefs as well. Sheron described nonreciprocal male violence in her relationship. She described a recent incident: "He had my jacket and I was like, 'Hey can you give me my jacket?' and he was like, 'You know my name, my name not hey.' And he got mad and he choked me and then he threw my coat at me and walked off." Sheron said she was mad and "felt embarrassed . . . because he did it in front of everybody, all my associates at school." As noted earlier, he had also pressured her into sex. She described their phone conversation the day before her interview: "He was talking about oral sex and I was like, 'No, you already know I don't do that' or whatever. And he was like, 'F [fuck] you then.' You know, he hung up the phone." She speculated that boys are violent in relationships "just to show that they are the male in the relationship and they got control."

DISCUSSION

Our goal was to examine young women's use of violence in relationships by comparing it with that of young men, and by situating both in the context of youths' accounts of the broader gender dynamics within their peer culture, the nature of relationship conflicts, and the meanings youths brought to bear in their interpretations of dating violence.

We document a series of gender inequalities in adolescent peer groups with important implications for the nature of relationship conflict and violence. These include features of hegemonic masculinity—the playa and the cool pose—and a sexual double standard that rewards male sexual exploits but sanctions unconstrained female sexuality. As our analyses show, each functions to structure the nature of adolescent relationship conflict and to diminish young women's efficacy within relationships. This is mirrored as well within relationship violence. Young women's use of violence is often rooted in their responses to the playa (concerns about infidelity) and the cool pose (frustration at emotional detachment strategies); however, girls' violence is interpreted as ineffectual and as rooted in their greater emotionality.

Young men's violence, although condemned in the abstract, is situationally explained and justified as a reaction to young women's behaviors. Despite a strong overall taboo against male violence, this taboo coexists with a number of important contingencies—which both girls and boys espouse—that function to diffuse boys' responsibility for the use of violence and hold female victims accountable. Thus, despite documenting fairly high rates of female-initiated violence, our research demonstrates that the meanings and consequences of girls' violence are strikingly different than those of young men's. Moreover, our research suggests that young men maintain greater situational control over violence itself—including whether girls' violence is permitted to occur or is met with violent sanction.

SOURCE: From *Criminology*, Vol. 41, No. 4, 1207–1247, 2003. Copyright © 2003 by the American Society of Criminology. Reprinted by permission of the American Society of Criminology.

QUESTIONS FOR DISCUSSION AND WRITING

1. Why do feminists consider the CTS as providing an impoverished understanding of partner violence?

2. Why did the authors narrow their study to urban African-American youths?

3. What gender inequalities in adolescent peer groups with important implications for the nature of relationship conflict and violence did the authors document, and what did their analyses show?

THE CRIMINOLOGY OF GENOCIDE

The Death and Rape of Darfur

John Hagan

Wenona Rymond-Richmond

Patricia Parker

As the Sudanese soldiers and Janjaweed attacked our village they said, "We will kill all men and rape the women. We want to change the color."

—31-year-old Eranga woman, Chad refugee camp, August 2004

UNANSWERED QUESTIONS

Does racially motivated, lethally destructive, state supported, and militarily unjustified violence constitute genocide? The legal and social scientific answers to this question may sometimes differ, but in the case of this research on the Darfur region of Sudan, we argue the answers should coincide. The history of American criminology, and the wider world of events beyond its disciplinary borders, has often impeded the pursuit of answers to questions about genocide, crimes against humanity, and war crimes more generally. Confronting such questions and the absence of answers to them is important in defining the boundaries modern criminology.

The United States, the United Nations, African Union, Amnesty International, and Human Rights Watch differ on whether and why the atrocities occurring in Darfur are best defined as a genocide, a crime against humanity, or ethnic cleansing. Each term implies different legal and symbolic consequences and can influence the international community's response to the events involved. For example, if the events in Darfur are designated as a crime against humanity rather than as genocide, the evidence likely needed for conviction is reduced, and this naming of the events will lack the symbolic force and probably mean less in the collective memory than would a legal determination of genocide. In fact, all genocides by definition are crimes against humanity, but not all crimes against humanity are elevated to the symbolic significance of genocide. Similarly, the term ethnic cleansing may rightfully describe the intentions of the Sudanese government, yet this does not carry the same legal meaning and recourse as a determination of genocide. In this [article], we argue that the violence in Darfur is a genocide.

According to Article II of the Genocide Convention, genocide means any of the following acts committed with intent to destroy, in whole or in part, a national, ethnical, racial, or religious group, as such:

- killing members of the group,
- causing serious bodily or mental harm to members of the group,
- deliberately inflicting on the group conditions of life calculated to bring about its physical destruction in whole or in part,
- imposing measures intended to prevent births within the group, and
- forcibly transferring children of the group to another group.

Although we report evidence below of most, if not all, of the required elements of the legal definition (even though any one may constitute genocide), and although we advocate calling the conflict a genocide, we recognize that the history of this legal category is contentious. A concern is that the traditional legal meaning of genocide is limited and ambiguous—indeed, the term genocide itself may contain elements of denial and misrecognition that should be a focus of theory and research. This may be an important reason why so few convictions have resulted from the legal drafting and ratification of genocide law.

THE POWER AND CONTROL OF DENIAL

The answers we find depend on the questions we ask, and in turn, the questions we ask are socially and politically selected. Cohen demonstrates how reluctant we are as citizens and criminologists to entertain questions, much less answers, about some of the most momentous criminal atrocities committed against humanity. Many, if not most, crimes involve forces of power and control, and most, if not all, crimes against humanity reflect these same forces, although they have seldom been studied by criminologists in this way.

Indigenous groups in weak states may be especially vulnerable to the use of power and control, particularly through the silencing of questions about the fate of these subordinate groups during periods of their criminal displacement and destruction. Thus, Scheper-Hughes and Bourgeois emphasize that "collective denial" and "misrecognition" are prerequisites for mass

violence and genocide. Misrecognition is the term meant to emphasize that collective forms of denial often are so deeply embedded in our socially induced unconsciousness that they become a matter of habit. This [article] illustrates these points by critically assessing accounts of institutionally embedded, and thus culturally powerful, voices that have denied the Darfurian genocide. Our critique of these denials is based on survey data gathered during the period of the displacement and destruction of African tribal groups in the Sudanese region of Darfur.

The power politics of Darfur are of a deeper detail and duration than this account can sufficiently provide, but several aspects of this story are essential to understanding how political and military power has been used to control the African tribal groups of Darfur. By nearly any measure, Sudan is a weak state, or in United Nations parlance, a Least Developed Country (LDV), ranking 139 on its Human Development Index. The African population of the Darfur region—the Zaghawa (their Arab-given name, but among themselves called the Beri or Bari), Massaleit, Fur, Eranga, and other groups—are tribal in history and patriarchal in family structure, with lives organized principally around subsistence farming. Meanwhile, the government of Sudan is dominated by Arab military figures and politicians who receive support from neighboring Arab states.

Although for much of its history African Darfurians shared their lands with nomadic Arab cattle herders, often intermarrying and resolving disputes in traditional legal forums, more recently circumstances have changed. A Darfurian refugee in the survey analyzed below recalled that "I don't know [why they attacked]. We are just poor people staying at one place planting. Suddenly, they come and attack us. Before that we had no problem with them." Pressed in recent years by the climatic circumstances of desertification, the Arab nomadic herders have encroached on the shrinking arable lands of the African farmers for water and grazing of their herds. It is important to emphasize that it is this access to the land and its resources as well as race, rather than religion, that separates these groups. The Arab cattle herders and their African counterparts are both Muslims, with the latter retaining traces of their tribal religion.

The Sudanese government has increasingly imposed its political power through local authorities, bringing land holdings under its control, and most notably, beginning in February of 2003, by supporting and joining Sudanese government troops with largely Arab Janjaweed militias—a term translated to mean men with guns on horses or camels and colloquially used by Africans to mean devil on horseback—for purposes of attacking African farmers and villagers. A common sequence described in interviews for the survey involves Russian-built Sudanese planes and helicopter gunships bombing and strafing villages, with Sudanese troops in vehicles and Janjaweed militia on horses and camels following in land attacks, resulting in men being killed and women being raped and killed, their villages being destroyed and their property being taken. More than two million Africans have been displaced from their farms and villages inside Darfur, and another 200,000 have taken refuge in camps in neighboring Chad.

We present survey evidence below that these deaths and displacements are the result of the genocidal "conflict moves" of the Arab-dominated Sudanese government that has used systematic killing and rape as instruments for the imposition of power and control over the tribal African men and women of Darfur. These conflict moves have involved using Sudanese military forces to empower local Janjaweed militias in racially motivated and targeted killing and rape.

In terms of the conflict perspective we are advancing, the genocidal violence is driven by the competition between patriarchal and hierarchically organized racial and ethnic groups to impose their power and control in propertied terms. The Arab-dominated Sudanese government seeks to use its military power to preserve and extend its control over the land and inhabitants of Darfur by empowering local Arab Janjaweed militias to destroy and drive the non-Arab African tribal groups from their farms and villages. One Zaghawa survivor reported in the survey analyzed below, "The soldiers said, 'Kill the men, kill the baby boys, rape the beautiful girls.'" The gendered form of these attacks that combines rape with killing is important. The use of rape is important not only materially as an instrument of terror, but also symbolically in making a point about racial displacement and replacement in propertied sexual and racial terms.

The explicit mediating role of racism is important to this analysis of genocidal power and control not only in legal terms that are spelled out

below, but also in terms of our social scientific understanding of how and when genocide occurs. We already have noted the sociopolitical background of ethnic cooperation and conflict between Arab and African groups in relation to the increasingly scarce land and water resources of Darfur. The African groups are indigenous to Darfur; the Arab groups migrated there from the north. In the case of Darfur, we will see that traditional cultural knowledge is provoked and incited through the poisonous transformation of prior race relations, as explicitly verbalized in the form of racial epithets that are part of the dialogue and choreography of the violent attacks. Nonetheless, the Sudanese government insists that its military activities are counterinsurgency efforts aimed at rebel groups in Darfur that have attacked government installations and stolen weapons for their own use. Our survey evidence speaks further to the activities of rebel groups. Known as the Sudan Liberation Movement or Army (SLM/A) and the Justice and Equality Movement (IEM), they claim the Arab-dominated government has neglected the interests of Africans. This conflict in Darfur is indirectly related to a longer-term insurgency in the south of Sudan, where discoveries of oil and its projected exploitation have fueled a 10-year armed insurrection recently addressed, if not settled, in negotiations led by the United States.

The power politics of Darfur are further complicated by large-scale investments of China in the Sudanese oil industry, by the sale of Russian military hardware to the Sudanese government, and by the often opposing efforts of American evangelical Christians to support and protect Africans with whom they are doing missionary work in southern Sudan. The JEM movement in particular has argued its case in terms of the economic and political disparities of privilege and power protected by the Arab-dominated government of Sudan and its military mobilization of the Janjaweed forces in Darfur. In the power politics of the United Nations, the oil interests of China and the arms industry interests of Russia constrain and control use of international criminal law as a response to Darfurian death and destruction.

The confluence of power and privilege we have described and the hesitance of the United States and the United Nations have nurtured a tendency long observed in human history to deny acknowledgment and protection to weak and subordinate groups from their victimization in crimes against humanity and genocide. This assertion does not discount that the U.S. Congress and its state department and secretary of state have all called the events in Darfur genocide. Yet before and after these designations of genocide, powerful voices have dissented, and the U.S. government has been slow to act on the genocide treaty obligations this designation should invoke. The dissenting voices are highly respected and therefore powerful forces to overcome for purposes of mobilizing the force of international criminal law.

THE CRIME OF CRIMES?

The two dissenting voices might be thought to come from unlikely sources: the *New York Times Magazine* and the United Nations Commission of Inquiry on Darfur. Together, these authoritative and therefore powerful voices have argued that the death and destruction in Darfur is the product of inept and incompetent self-defense, or clumsy counterinsurgency. The effect is to say that it is more random and accidental than systematic and intended. Because the crime of genocide is defined as the "intent to destroy in whole or in part a national, ethnical, racial, or religious group," evidence of systematic intention is essential, and denials based on arguments of randomness, accident, and self-defense must be taken seriously.

Scott Anderson is the author of the *New York Times Magazine* article "How Did Darfur Happen?" His claim is that "there are enough grains of truth to almost all the government's defenses to muddy the charges against it." The heart of this defense is accident and ineptitude. Anderson bases his denial of the genocide claim on interviews in Sudan with government and rebel leaders.

Anderson's thesis is basically that the government of Sudan was so preoccupied with its problems of insurrection in the southern and prospectively oil-rich part of the country that it allowed and ignored events getting out of control in Darfur. Of course, ignorance and neglect are even weaker defense claims for governments and leaders than for mere citizens, but Anderson's arguments may nonetheless speak to the issue of intent that the definition of genocide makes so emphatic, and to the issue of control that a

power-oriented conflict theory makes explicit. Counter-evidence of coordination and planning is needed to refute this denial and to support the charge of intent involved in genocide, as well as the claim of control involved in a power-control conflict theory of genocide.

Meanwhile, less than a month before Anderson's *New York Times* article appeared, the United Nations appointed an International Commission of Inquiry on Darfur to report to its secretary-general "whether or not acts of genocide have occurred." The commission was chaired by an Italian jurist and past president of the International Criminal Tribunal for the former Yugoslavia, Antonio Cassese, and concluded that evidence existed of serious crimes against humanity and other war crimes. However, on the explicit question of whether acts of genocide occurred, "The Commission concluded that the Government of the Sudan has not pursued a policy of genocide."

Although the commission had access to the survey analyzed below, it chose instead to proceed in a more anecdotal manner that appeared to substitute legal reasoning for scientific data. Its central argument addresses the issue of genocidal intent. In response to indications of racial motivation in the attacks targeted solely against African tribes, the commission chose to argue that there were other "more indicative elements" that showed lack of genocidal intent.

It maintained that in a number of villages attacked and burned by both militias and government forces, the attackers refrained from exterminating the whole population that had not fled, and instead selectively killed groups of young men. This was taken as an important indication of lack of genocidal intent.

Although the commission had access to the survey we analyze—with which it could have better assessed the extensiveness of the killing, its links to rebel activity, and competing claims of genocide and counterinsurgency as self-defense—this evidence was neither considered nor addressed. The commission instead further used its authoritative power and control to deny the meaning of the genocidal charge.

ATROCITIES DOCUMENTATION TEAM SURVEY

In the summer of 2004, then-U.S. Secretary of State Colin Powell found his department in an unexpected position. Both houses of Congress had unanimously passed resolutions concluding and condemning the occurrence of a genocide in Darfur. Yet Congress had essentially done so without evidence. The State Department and Powell urgently needed legal—and ideally scientific— evidence to set a foundation for advocating new policy moves.

Powell was persuaded to commission interview-based research in the refugee camps of Chad, where more than 200,000 displaced Darfurians were receiving UN protection and assistance. The Atrocity Documentation Team led by Stephanie Frease of the Coalition of International Justice [CIJ] was authorized by the State Department to conduct interviews in the Chad camps from July through August of 2004. She developed a semi-structured protocol for the interviews that mixed the narrative structure of legal witness statements with the closed-ended format of health and mortality surveys. In essence, the format was an elaborated crime victimization survey.

By the end of August, 2004, the team had completed interviews with 1,136 randomly sampled respondents, which formed the background for Powell's testimony before the Congressional International Relations Committee on September 9, 2004.

One of the many challenges in developing estimates of the deaths in a genocide involves accurately measuring the variable degree and duration of the events involved, recognizing that the level of violence in a genocide can fluctuate over time.

We have an estimate that 396,563 Africans may have died and disappeared in the two-year conflict in Darfur. The surveys further reveal that as measured in the late summer of 2004, the combined Crude Mortality Rate for Darfur (over 3) is six times the African average and three times the level indicating "elevated mortality." The surveys indicate that as of mid-2004, the attacks and health problems in Darfur were generating approximately 15,000 deaths per month, or about 500 per day.

About the time of the arrival of the second group of interviewers, the leadership of the survey realized that the issue of rebel activity in or near the villages the respondents had left was central to the government self-defense claim of counterinsurgency. This realization resulted in the following new questions being added to the survey: "Was the village defended from attack?" and "Was there rebel activity in or near the village?" Because this information is so salient, we restrict our analysis below to the final 501 cases in which these questions were asked.

Describing the Violence

The sample is more female (53 percent) than male (47 percent), and the men (40.1 years) are on average older than the women (31.2), which reflects that young males were more often killed than females. The patriarchal and polygamous practices of these African tribes is reflected in the larger average family size reported by males (7.1, compared to females, 6.2), who may have more than one wife; by the greater likelihood of females having no schooling (77.1 percent versus 42 percent); and by the greater employment of males outside the home (12.3 percent compared to 3 percent).

The two tribal groups most highly represented in the sample are the Zaghawa (36.9 percent) and Massaleit (46.5 percent). Male refugees are more likely to be Massaleit (53 percent compared to 40.8 percent among females), which may reflect the greater involvement of the Zaghawa in rebel activity and the tendency of Zaghawa men to stay behind in Darfur to fight. However, it is also important to emphasize how common reports are in this survey of rebel activity and village defense.

The descriptive statistics further indicate the imbalance of power in that very few of the refugees report that their villages were defended in any way (7.8 percent). Defending the village most often meant that the men used sticks and sometimes spears against attackers using airplanes, tanks, guns, and machetes.

A pattern of villagers being attacked regardless of rebel activity in the village or surrounding areas is apparent. The descriptive statistics indicate that very few refugees report that there was any rebel activity either in the village or in the surrounding area (10 percent). Because both the defense and rebel activity in this patriarchal context would have been nearly exclusively male, if this activity was targeted in attacks, it should have been (but is not) reflected by more reports of this activity from surviving women and fewer from surviving men (because most would have been killed). Meanwhile, the great majority of refugees report that their villages were attacked by combined Sudanese and Janjaweed forces (66 percent), with far fewer reporting being attacked by Sudanese forces acting alone (16.9 percent), and the smallest number reporting being attacked by the Janjaweed acting alone (13.8 percent).

The racial targeting of the attacks is indicated by the finding that more than a third (37 percent) of the refugees reported hearing the incoming forces using racial epithets, such as "this is the last day for blacks," "we will destroy the black-skinned people," "kill the slaves," "kill all the blacks," and references to "nuba, nuba" (in this context a derogatory term used for black Africans).

Meanwhile, about 1 in 10 (9.8 percent) of the refugees reported that neighboring Arab villagers were spared from any violence when the attacks occurred.

Finally, the descriptive statistics reveal the extensiveness of the killing and rape. Consistent with the expectation that the killing would be stratified in patriarchal terms that reflect racialized and gendered hierarchies of power and control, these statistics indicate that men (so that they cannot take up arms and rebel in defense) are killed more than women, and that women are both raped and killed (so that they cannot bear their own children and will be sufficiently terrorized to leave). Rapes were also further used as a means of altering the race of children in this patrilineal culture where descent is understood as being transmitted along male lines. The shame associated with rape in this culture ensures that this form of victimization is underreported in the survey: The interviewers frequently noted their suspicions of this. "The attackers sliced open the stomachs of pregnant women and ripped out their stomachs. If it was a boy, they destroyed the fetus."

The greater loss of men's lives is reflected in that two-thirds of surviving women report the death of a male family member (66.5 percent), while just over half of the men (53.8 percent) do so. Nonetheless, 18.1 percent of the women report a woman family member killed, as do 12.7 percent of the men, and 12.4 percent of the women report a family member being raped, as do 2.1 percent of the men. Nearly a fourth of the sample (23.1 percent) report a female family member killed or raped, and 60.6 percent report a male family member killed. Overall, nearly two-thirds of the sample report a family member killed or raped (65.9 percent), and 5.8

percent indicate that one or more family members were both killed and raped.

Analyzing the Violence

First, the findings show that more than two-thirds of the refugee households reported that the attack on their home or village involved combined Sudanese and Janjaweed forces. The findings further reveal that there is a step-like progression, from refugees reporting that they heard racial epithets in 16.5 percent of the cases involving Sudanese forces acting alone, in 31.9 percent of those involving Janjaweed forces acting alone, and in 44.3 percent of those involving combined forces. However, more interesting is the effect that the joining of Sudanese with Janjaweed forces had in increasing racial epithets. Our power and control conflict theory interprets this relationship as reflecting the Arab Sudanese government's motivational empowerment of local Arab Janjaweed militia by intensifying their racialized expression of hostility against African tribal groups.

We extend the analysis by linking the perpetrator forces and racial epithet relationship to killing and raping of family members in the attacks. The findings indicate that there is a statistically significant relationship between hearing racial epithets and having a family member killed or raped. When these epithets are heard, nearly three-quarters of respondents (73 percent) report a family member was killed, compared to less than two-thirds (60.2 percent) when these epithets are not heard. Interestingly, in nearly all the cases where Sudanese forces were involved and racial epithets were heard, a family member was killed or raped. However, this combination was relatively rare, involving only 2.6 percent of the sample.

The Sudanese government counterargument is that the attacks against the African farmers and villagers were counterinsurgent self-defense. To assess this claim, we divided the sample into reported rebel activity in the village and reported rebel activity in the surrounding area, and then looked at the relationship between hearing rebel epithets and having a family member killed or raped. The implication of the self-defense claim is that this relationship would appear only in settings that were attacked on the basis of rebel activity. Even here it would not have been lawful to have the attacks (or to allow the attacks to be) concentrated on civilians, but Anderson's *New York Times Magazine* claim is that this was the product of ineptitude. Yet findings indicate the relationships between epithets and killings are significant regardless of whether there was rebel activity or not.

There is the further question of where rebel activity was occurring. There are areas of Darfur where Arabs live alongside or near African tribal groups. As mentioned, in 9.8 percent of the cases, the respondents reported that Arabs were spared in the attacks. Our thesis is that the Arab-dominated government advanced its interest in its power and control of Sudan by empowering local Arabs and destroying and dislocating local African groups, using racist ideology as a divisive and destructive means to accomplish this goal. Support for this thesis is found. This finding provides a specific indication of the racial polarization involved in the Darfur conflict.

Confronting "The Crime of Crimes"

The evidence presented above from victim survey reports demonstrates that the attacks beginning in February 2003 on Africans who lived in the farms and villages of the Darfur region of Sudan have been racially motivated, lethally destructive, state supported, and militarily unjustified. Reports from the same victim surveys are a foundation for estimates that nearly 400,000 deaths may be attributable to these attacks. Both killing and rape are instruments of terror, and more than two million Africans from Darfur have been displaced from their homes and today are living and dying in refugee camps in Sudan and Chad. The dislocation of this population has made it impossible for African Darfurians to engage in the subsistence farming and related activities that are essential to the reproduction of their traditional way of life.

The evidence presented above is therefore persuasive that the state supported attacks are, in the language of criminological conflict theory, the lethally destructive exercise of power and control, so that, in the language of the Geneva Genocide Convention, the effect is to inflict on these non-Arab African tribal groups "conditions of life calculated to bring about their physical destruction in whole or in part." The great majority of attacks involve government forces and local militias acting together. In contrast,

there is little or no evidence from the victim surveys to support the claim of the government of Sudan that the attacks are aimed at rebel groups, which threaten this government. Rather, the evidence of state support for the attacks undermines the claim that they are accidental or without intent to destroy African Darfurians and their farm and village way of life "in whole or in part." The Sudanese government's claims are, by this analysis, not the basis for a credible self-defense-counterinsurgency claim, but rather of the exercise of power and control through denial.

The victim surveys are, furthermore, unique in providing evidence that this exercise of power and control is aimed and animated with explicit racial animus by the Arab-dominated government of Sudan against African Darfurians. This evidence takes three forms: in the exclusively African identities of its victims, in the sparing of neighboring Arab villagers, and in the use of racial epithets during the fatal attacks. Furthermore, the latter racial epithets are most often heard when government troops and local militias act together, and in the context of spared Arab villagers. This is further evidence of the use of the authority and resources of the Sudanese state to empower local Arab forces in the lethal subordination of African Darfurians.

Sutherland classically drew the distinction between defining behavior as criminal for the purposes of administration and science. He famously argued, "The definition of crime, from the point of the present analysis, is important only as a means of determining whether the behavior should be included within the scope of a theory of criminal behavior." He went on to assert that

> The essential characteristic of crime is that it is behavior which is prohibited by the State as an injury to the State and against which the State may react, at least as a last resort, by punishment. The two abstract criteria generally regarded by legal scholars as necessary elements in a definition of crime are legal description of an act as socially harmful and legal provision of a penalty for the act.

This argument can now be taken to the supranational level of international jurisdiction, but Sutherland's lesson is that we need not await the determinations of international commissions, tribunals, and courts to initiate the study of genocide and of other war crimes and crimes against humanity.

Modern criminology possesses the theory and methods to document, describe, analyze, and explain "the crime of crimes" and other important violations of international criminal law. The denial and neglect of these crimes in modern criminology itself needs explanation.

SOURCE: From *Criminology*, Vol. 43, No. 3, 525–560, 2005. Copyright © 2005 by the American Society of Criminology. Reprinted by permission of the American Society of Criminology.

QUESTIONS FOR DISCUSSION AND WRITING

1. According to the authors, on what do "the answers we find" depend? What did Cohen demonstrate regarding man's search for answers about atrocities committed against humanity?

2. What did Scott Anderson conclude regarding the situation in Darfur? What did the United Nations International Commission of Inquiry on Darfur conclude regarding the situation in Darfur?

3. How do the authors tie the evidence they presented to criminological theory? What evidence do the authors use to support their arguments?

PART V

WHO ARE THE CRIMINALS?

The Distribution and Correlates of Crime

Confusion over the difference between correlation and cause is a problem when we are trying to explain criminal behavior. What statisticians mean when they say that two variables are correlated is that they are associated or vary together. For example, if unemployment goes up and then crime goes up, the two variables are positively correlated. If one of them increases and the other decreases, the correlation is negative. So if we are looking at a sample of young people and find that those in families from the higher social classes have lower rates of delinquency than those in lower-class families, then social class and delinquency can be said to be negatively correlated.

In neither of those examples, however, can the simple observation of the correlation be interpreted to mean that one of the variables caused a change in the other. In the first example, all we know is that there is a pattern indicating that when unemployment goes up, crime tends to be higher. We should not conclude that the fluctuations in unemployment have caused the fluctuations in crime. Similarly, even though some studies report a negative relationship between social class and delinquency, this should not be interpreted to mean that the class positions of the young people studied causes their delinquency (in the case of the lower-class children) or inhibits their delinquency (the upper class).

There are a host of cute examples that sociologists are fond of parading past their students to make the point that a correlation is not necessarily a cause. There may be a positive correlation between the number of storks in an area and birth rates, but few college students believe that more storks cause more births (storks live in rural areas rather than in cities, and rural areas tend to have higher birth rates than do cities). Similarly, there is a positive correlation between the presence of fire trucks and fires, but most people will not confuse correlation and causality in this type of obvious case. It is when the distinction is not so obvious that confusion and controversy arise.

Criminologists make the step from observing correlations to interpreting them with the help of theory. Theories not only provide a framework to interpret the meaning of correlations (as well as other observed patterns), but they also help us determine when these correlations are meaningful and when they are not.

A number of variables have been demonstrated to be correlated with crime, but the articles in this section focus on the four big correlates of crime: social class, race, age, and sex. Although patterns associated with each of these four correlates have been central to criminology for a very long time, there continue to be major controversies surrounding each of them.

For most of criminological history, we have taken it as an article of faith that those from the lower social classes are more criminal than those from higher positions on the social ladder. In the past 40 years, however, many criminologists have raised important challenges to this assumption. First there were those who argued that lower-class people did not actually commit more crime; they were simply more likely to be arrested and punished for committing crimes than law violators from the middle or upper classes. Today, criminologists generally believe that general delinquency is widespread across social classes, but that serious violent behavior may be more concentrated among the most disadvantaged populations—the interesting question is why. Baumer and his colleagues, in "Neighborhood Disadvantage and the Nature of Violence," use NCVS (victimization) data to study whether living in very poor neighborhoods causes serious violent crime. How might the place where people live affect their likelihood of acting violently, and more to the point of this study, how might it affect the probability of being a victim of criminal violence?

McNulty and Bellair address the correlation between race/ethnicity and crime. To be more precise, they examine violent crime because that is where criminologists have most consistently observed racial differences in involvement. They use data from a national youth survey to study differences in, and the causes of, violence among Asians, blacks, Hispanics, Native Americans and whites. Their results indicate that there are differences in the level of self-reported violence between these groups, but interestingly, the causes of violence are different for each group. This study, like the one by Baumer et al., points us toward an appreciation of how social forces outside of the individual influence crime. In the first half of the 20th century, sociologists who came to be known as "The Chicago School" demonstrated that crime and delinquency were not properties of any specific ethnic group, but rather a product of particular social conditions. Students should keep this in mind as they begin to study the theories developed to explain crime later in this volume. We also suggest that students ask themselves how social conditions influence crime as they watch and read news accounts of crime and crime rates.

Age is an established correlate of crime that few, if any, criminologists would question. The observation that crime peaks between the ages of 14 and 18 and drops precipitously after the mid-20s, nearly disappearing among those past the mid-30s, is virtually universal among those who study crime. Controversy comes from attempts to relate this invariant pattern to theories and public policy. Hirschi and Gottfredson disagree with those who argue that this age/crime pattern validates some theories and that we should focus criminal justice policy on a small group of hard-core offenders who do not age out of crime.

To discuss sex differences in criminal behavior, we again turn to comparative research. It is especially critical to discuss this important crime correlate because criminological researchers have long argued that males everywhere are more likely than females to violate the laws, to violate them more often, and to commit more serious violations than females in the same societies. Junger-Tas, Ribeaud, and Cruyff are European researchers who have used survey data to examine sex differences in delinquency across a number of European nations. They find that the overall sex differences they observed also exist across ethnic groups within those countries. Students should take note of the theoretical explanations that the authors offer for delinquent involvement. This sets the stage for our forthcoming presentations of theories of crime, social control, and criminal justice.

The identification of important correlates of crime can answer many questions for criminologists. As is the case with these four correlates of crime, however, the observation of patterns is really only a first step toward understanding why they exist. As stated above, the attempts of criminologists to build and test criminological theories are the way we begin to make sense of the observed correlations.

 For a data analysis exercise that accompanies the material in this section, go to www.sagepub.com/crimereadings3study.

NEIGHBORHOOD DISADVANTAGE AND THE NATURE OF VIOLENCE

ERIC BAUMBER

JULIE HORNEY

RICHARD FELSON

JANET L. LAURITSEN

The present study evaluates several hypotheses about the relationship between neighborhood socioeconomic conditions and the quality, or nature, of violence. Drawing on Anderson's discussion of neighborhood conditions and violence, we hypothesize that victims of assaults in disadvantaged neighborhoods are more likely to resist their attackers and to be injured, whereas victims of robberies from these areas are less likely to resist and suffer injury. In addition, we hypothesize that victims of robberies and assaults from disadvantaged neighborhoods are more likely to be attacked by an offender who is armed with a gun. We also explore whether these neighborhood differences are stronger in urban areas, or among males, youth, and African Americans.

THEORETICAL BACKGROUND

Anderson integrates elements of each of the major macrolevel theories of crime (e.g., social disorganization, subcultural, anomic, and structural strain) in his discussion of how community characteristics affect both the quantity and quality of violence. Anderson refers broadly to a large number of community characteristics, but his discussion emphasizes the adverse consequences that tend to materialize in predominantly black neighborhoods that are characterized by high levels of poverty, joblessness, and welfare dependence and a large proportion of families headed by females.

Much of Anderson's discussion is devoted to the relatively high levels of violence and other social dislocations observed in disadvantaged neighborhoods, but his work also details how the code of the street affects the nature of violence. In particular, as we elaborate below, Anderson's research suggests that violence in disadvantaged neighborhoods is distinctive from violence that occurs elsewhere in the extent to which it involves victim resistance and injury and the use of weapons by offenders. Anderson's interpretation of these patterns implies a relatively large difference across neighborhoods in the nature of violence that is not merely a function of neighborhood differences in the types of victims and offenders involved in violent incidents.

Anderson suggests that the code of the street defines the appropriate ways in which individuals

155

are expected to respond when someone assaults or attempts to assault them. He argues that in disadvantaged neighborhoods, standing up to others when challenged is critical to preserving one's reputation and gaining or maintaining respect. One consequence of this is that in such environments, "people often feel constrained not only to stand up and at least attempt to resist during an assault but also to 'pay back'—to seek revenge—after a successful assault on their person . . . their very identity, their self-respect, and their honor are often intricately tied up with the way they perform on the streets during and after such encounters." In contrast, "in the wider society, particularly among the middle class, people may not feel required to retaliate physically after an attack . . . they are much more likely than street-oriented people to feel that they can walk away from a possible altercation with their self-esteem intact." Thus, Anderson's description suggests that residents of disadvantaged neighborhoods, where the code of the street is more strongly embedded, will be more likely than others to stage resistance when involved in an assault. In addition, because the code of the street discourages disputants from backing down and attaches social value to demonstrating physical prowess and toughness through fighting, we would expect assaults in disadvantaged neighborhoods to result in injuries more often than those that occur in other areas.

However, Anderson argues that robberies represent very different types of situations, and that the code of the street outlines behavioral expectations that are unique to such situations. In a robbery, the power lies almost exclusively in the hands of the perpetrator and the victim has relatively few options if he or she wants to walk away unharmed. When one ends up on the wrong end of a stickup, the code of the street prescribes an etiquette to be observed that grants the offender the respect he or she has demanded and maximizes the chances that the victim will survive. The most critical aspect of this etiquette is compliance on the part of the victim. "Nothing conveys this recognition better than the clear act of total deference. Not to defer is to question the authority, the worth, the status, even the respectability of the assailant in a way that easily suggests contempt or even arrogance . . . it may be much safer to acquire the street knowledge of the etiquette and then help the assailant carry out his job of robbery."

Anderson argues that the initial reactions of robbery victims vary across neighborhoods. Specifically, he claims that in disadvantaged neighborhoods, the code of the street dictates that people "behave or act ad lib in accordance with the demands and emergent expectations of the stickup man. In effect, such knowledge may provide the victim with the background knowledge of how to get robbed: it may even allow him or her the presence of mind to assist the assailant in his task, thus defusing a dangerous situation." In contrast, in more affluent areas, people are much less knowledgeable about the code of the street, and when an individual is robbed, he "may misread the situation and believe he is in more danger than he actually is. He may then panic, flooding the situation out and effectively bringing what began nonviolently to a violent end." Thus, Anderson suggests that residents of disadvantaged neighborhoods are less likely than others to resist when they are robbed. In particular, his discussion implies that, owing to their socialization into the ways of the street as well as personal and vicarious experiences with violence, residents of disadvantaged neighborhoods who are robbed are less likely than others to engage in the type of nonforceful resistance (e.g., yelling, panic, etc.) that can increase substantially the use of violence by robbers.

The greater composure and compliance of robbery victims in disadvantaged neighborhoods should also result in a lower probability that they will be injured.

Anderson also implies that violence in disadvantaged neighborhoods shares some common elements, regardless of the type of offense situation it represents (i.e., robbery or assault). In particular, Anderson's research suggests that violent incidents in disadvantaged neighborhoods are more likely to involve guns. Guns are symbolic of the core components of the code of the street—respect, toughness, and status—and have proliferated in many disadvantaged neighborhoods. Moreover, Anderson suggests that the ever-present threat of violence and the lack of faith in formal mechanisms of social control to offer adequate protection from violent attacks may lead individuals from disadvantaged neighborhoods to arm themselves for protection, giving rise to an "arms race" in these areas since offenders and other residents think they must be armed to counter the fact that others are armed. If guns proliferate in disadvantaged neighborhoods, then we would expect that incidents in these neighborhoods are more likely to involve an armed offender than incidents in other neighborhoods.

In summary, Anderson's ethnographic research suggests the following hypotheses about how violence in disadvantaged neighborhoods should differ from violence in more affluent neighborhoods. First, victims of assault who reside in disadvantaged neighborhoods should be more likely to resist during the assault and should be more likely to be injured. Second, victims of robbery who live in disadvantaged neighborhoods should be less likely to resist and less likely to be injured. Finally, offenders who assault or rob residents of disadvantaged neighborhoods should be more likely to use firearms. We evaluate each of these empirical predications in the present study.

Data and Methods

The data for this research come from two sources: the 1995–1997 area-identified NCVS and the 1990 decennial census. The NCVS is an annual survey of approximately 80,000 persons (in 43,000 households). All persons age 12 and older in sampled households are asked whether they have experienced a violent victimization during the previous six months. In addition, for each incident of violence reported, respondents are asked several questions about the demographic characteristics of the offender and various details about the incident.

In the present research, we use the area-identified NCVS to examine the nature of violence experienced by residents of neighborhoods that exhibit strikingly different socioeconomic conditions. We use census tracts as approximations of residential neighborhoods.

Anderson's discussion implies that the code of the street that characterizes disadvantaged neighborhood shapes how residents of these areas experience and respond to violence, especially when it occurs within their neighborhoods. The exact geographic location of violent incidents reported in the NCVS is unknown, but victims are asked whether the incident occurred "at, in, or near their home," "within one mile of their home," "within five miles of their home," "within 50 miles of their home," or "more than 50 miles from their home." For the analyses presented below, we assume that if incidents were reported to have occurred within one mile of

respondents' homes, they occurred in their neighborhoods (i.e., census tracts) of residence.

Anderson's discussion focuses largely on how residents of disadvantaged neighborhoods respond to assaults and robberies. Accordingly, our analyses are based on all assaults (N = 3,327) and robberies (N = 468) reported by NCVS respondents between 1995 and 1997 that occurred within their neighborhood and for which valid data on the dependent and independent variable were available.

Incidents that involve theft or attempted theft of something directly from the victim by force or threat of force are classified as robberies, whereas incidents that involve a physical attack, an attempted physical attack, or a verbal threat of attack (including death threats), but not theft or attempted theft, are classified as assaults.

Dependent Variables

We examine the effects of neighborhood disadvantage on three dependent variables. First, offender weapon use is a variable that distinguishes among incidents in which the victim reported that the offender was armed with a gun *(offender had gun)*; armed with a non-gun weapon, including a knife or other sharp object, or a blunt object such as a club or rock *(offender had other weapon)*; or not armed *(offender did not have weapon)*. Second, victim resistance is a variable that contrasts incidents in which victims forcefully resisted the offender *(forceful victim resistance)* and those in which victims nonforcefully resisted *(nonforceful victim resistance)* with those in which victims did not resist *(no victim resistance)*. Third, victim injury is a variable that contrasts incidents in which victims reported being injured by the offender *(victim injured)* with those in which victims were not injured *(victim not injured)*.

Independent Variables

Anderson specifies the types of neighborhoods in which the code of the street is most likely to emerge: predominantly black communities with high levels of poverty, joblessness, and welfare dependence, and a large proportion of families headed by females. Our main independent variable, which we term *neighborhood disadvantage*, is an index that encompasses 1990 census indicators of each of these structural dimensions of neighborhood context. Consistent with several recent studies of neighborhood effects on violence, we measure neighborhood disadvantage with a standardized, weighted index that combines the percentage of persons in households with incomes below the poverty line, percentage of families with children that are headed by a female, percentage of households that receive public assistance income, the adult unemployment rate, and the percentage of persons who are black.

Control Variables

The empirical literature has identified a number of individual and situational factors associated with the outcomes considered in our research. These include the age, race, and sex of victims and offenders; the number of offenders; victim-offender relationship; presence of a third party; and region.

Findings

The results show that neighborhood disadvantage exerts a significant positive effect on offender gun possession. The odds of being attacked by an offender armed with a gun increase by 19% with each unit increase in neighborhood disadvantage. Although it is important to keep in mind that the overall prevalence of weapon use in assaults reported in the NCVS is relatively low, this amounts to a 41% greater probability that assaults will involve an offender with a firearm in extremely disadvantaged neighborhoods than in communities with average socioeconomic conditions.

The results also reveal that those who offend in disadvantaged neighborhoods are not significantly more likely than those who offend in more affluent neighborhoods to be armed with knives and other weapons, after other factors are held constant.

In addition, controlling for victim, offender, and incident characteristics, neighborhood disadvantage continues to exert a significant positive effect on forceful victim resistance. Thus, consistent with Anderson's ethnographic observations, residents of disadvantaged neighborhoods are more likely to stage resistance during an assault than residents who reside in more affluent communities. However, these neighborhood differences are relatively small: The predicted probability

of forceful resistance by assault victims in extremely disadvantaged neighborhoods is only 17% higher than the probability of forceful resistance by assault victims in socioeconomically average neighborhoods.

Neighborhood disadvantage is not significantly associated with the likelihood of injury, net of other factors. Thus, although residents of disadvantaged neighborhoods have a significantly higher risk of assault, they do not have a higher risk of nonfatal injury than other persons when they are assaulted. Additional analyses revealed that the number of offenders involved in the assault is largely responsible for the attenuation of the influence of neighborhood disadvantage on victim injury. In other words, assault victims from disadvantaged neighborhoods are more likely to experience injuries primarily because they are attacked more frequently by multiple offenders.

We present a parallel analysis for robbery. The findings show that, controlling for victim, offender, and incident characteristics, incidents in disadvantaged neighborhoods are not significantly more likely to involve an armed offender than incidents in more affluent areas.

Net of the effects of the control variable, neighborhood socioeconomic disadvantage is not significantly related to forceful resistance by robbery victims. However, neighborhood disadvantage has a significant negative effect on the likelihood of nonforceful resistance, net of the control variable. Consistent with Anderson's argument, this suggests that robbery victims from disadvantaged neighborhoods are significantly less likely to resist nonforcefully (i.e., stall, argue, scream, cry for help) than victims from more affluent areas. The probability of nonforceful resistance is 27% lower among robbery victims from extremely disadvantaged neighborhoods than among victims from neighborhoods with average socioeconomic conditions.

Finally, neighborhood disadvantage is not significantly related to victim injury. Thus, similar to our findings for assault, although residents of disadvantaged neighborhoods have a significantly higher risk of being robbed, those who are robbed are not significantly more likely than other victims to experience nonfatal injuries.

Summary and Discussion

Our analyses reveal support for Anderson's ethnographic description of the nature of violence in neighborhoods with varying socioeconomic conditions, but only mixed support for his argument that those differences are due to neighborhood effects.

The results provide some support for the idea that neighborhood disadvantage affects what occurs during an assault, controlling for the characteristics of the participants. We find that victims from disadvantaged neighborhoods are significantly more likely to resist forcefully when they are assaulted. This result is consistent with Anderson's argument that the importance of maintaining reputation and defending honor in disadvantaged areas compels residents to "stand up and at least attempt to resist during an assaults." In addition, offenders who commit assaults in disadvantaged neighborhoods are more likely to be armed with guns. Either they are more likely to arm themselves before the assault, in anticipation of violent resistance by victims, or they are more likely to carry guns on their person at all times.

We did not find support for the hypothesis that assault victims in disadvantaged neighborhoods are more likely to be injured, after controlling for demographic and situational factors. The greater tendency for victims in disadvantaged neighborhoods to resist apparently does not increase the risk of a nonfatal injury during an assault in these neighborhoods. We suspect that forceful resistance sometimes increases the risk of injury and sometimes decreases it. Victims who resist sometimes put themselves in greater danger, but other times their resistance is successful and enables them to avoid injury. Moreover, we would not argue from the injury results that the proliferation of guns in disadvantaged neighborhoods does not increase the dangerousness of violent incidents. We suspect that the use of guns in disadvantaged neighborhoods is partially responsible for higher homicide rates, given that assaults involving firearms are much more likely to have lethal outcomes.

Unlike assault offenders, robbery offenders in disadvantaged neighborhoods are no more likely to use firearms than robbery offenders in other neighborhoods. This difference across crime types may be related to target substitutability in robbery and the robber's option to select vulnerable victims. If robbers do not have a gun available, or if they think a particular target might be armed, they can always settle for a weaker victim. Assault offenders, on the other hand, are usually interested in attacking a particular person who has offended them. If that person is armed or otherwise dangerous, they are likely to think they need a firearm.

Our results do provide support for Anderson's assertion about the composure and compliance of robbery victims in disadvantaged neighborhoods. Victims in these neighborhoods are significantly less likely to nonforcefully resist when they are robbed (compared to victims from relatively affluent areas). Apparently, their familiarity with the robbery script enables them to comply with the offender's threats without panicking. Alternatively, it may be that victims of robbery in disadvantaged neighborhoods do not stall, scream, or cry for help because they are less confident that third parties will come to their rescue, or because some of these behaviors imply weakness and fear, which is stigmatized by the code of the street in disadvantaged neighborhoods.

Overall, our research indicates that the neighborhood variation in violence that Anderson observed reflects the individuals' race and social class as well as neighborhood socioeconomic conditions. The effects of neighborhood and sociodemographic variables appear to be primarily additive. The influence of the code of the street does not appear to be stronger among blacks, males, or residents of central cities, as implied by Anderson's discussion. It apparently affects residents of disadvantaged neighborhoods irrespective of their own demographic characteristics. The only interaction consistent with expectations involved the age of offenders. Younger offenders (i.e., those under age 30) in disadvantaged neighborhoods were particularly likely to use firearms during assaults. This finding is consistent with discussion of the proliferation of firearms among youth in disadvantaged neighborhoods.

SOURCE: From *Criminology*, Vol. 41, No. 1, 2003: 39–63, edited. Reprinted by permission of the American Society of Criminology.

QUESTIONS FOR DISCUSSION AND WRITING

1. How does Anderson suggest the code of the street defines how victims are expected to act in assaults? What does Anderson argue about the initial reactions of robbery victims?

2. What do the results show for gun possession? What do the results reveal about those who offend in disadvantaged neighborhoods?

3. What do the results show regarding victims' likelihood of staging resistance during an assault? What were the findings for injury occurrence?

4. What did the parallel analysis for robbery find?

EXPLAINING RACIAL AND ETHNIC DIFFERENCES IN ADOLESCENT VIOLENCE

Structural Disadvantage, Family Well-Being, and Social Capital

THOMAS L. MCNULTY

PAUL E. BELLAIR

Differential rates of involvement in juvenile violence by race/ethnicity have been well documented in the United States. Data from various sources have consistently shown higher rates of violence for American Indian, black, and Latino adolescents and lower or similar rates for Asians, compared to whites. Studies of these differences have not provided a unified explanation that considers both individual and community-level causes of violence. Yet there is a growing consensus that a full explanation requires micro-macro theoretical integration and contextual models that examine causes of violence across levels of analysis.

In addition, theories about racial-ethnic differences in violence have been developed primarily in reference to comparisons between whites and blacks. One potential consequence is that conclusions about white-black differentials in violence may be generalized to differences between whites and other racial-ethnic minorities. Such a generalization may not only be unwarranted, but may lead to public policy that fails address the issues that are most pertinent to specific groups.

This article integrates theory and research in criminology and urban sociology to specify a contextual model of differences in violence between youths who are white and those from five racial-ethnic groups (Asians, American Indians, blacks, Latinos, and those of "other" origins). We test the model using a nationally representative sample of adolescents drawn from the National Education Longitudinal Survey (NELS), matched with community-level data from the U.S. census. The dependent variable is self-reported involvement in physical fights, a pertinent outcome, given research that has shown fighting by adolescents to be a significant predictor of future involvement in serious violent crime. Our model views racial-ethnic differences in fighting as a function of variation in community contexts, family socioeconomic well-being, and the social capital available to adolescents and families.

RACE-ETHNICITY, COMMUNITY CONTEXTS, AND VIOLENCE

Integrating insights from stratification and social disorganization research, Sampson and Wilson spearheaded a structural approach that emphasizes the contextual sources of the race-violence link among individuals. A central tenet of this approach is that the causes of violence are rooted in community structures and are invariant across racial-ethnic groups. From this perspective racial-ethnic differences in violence are a function of patterns of racial residential inequality in the United States, not causative factors unique to groups (e.g., a culture of violence). Place-stratification research shows that irrespective of human-capital characteristics or family circumstances, minority groups are at relative residential disadvantage compared to whites. Blacks, in particular, are differentially distributed in urban neighborhoods that are characterized by "structural social disorganization" and "cultural social isolations."

Criminological research has shown that community disadvantage and instability diminish the prevalence and interdependence of social networks that facilitate the social control of children. The lack of internal resources inhibits the maintenance of community organizations that promote overlap-networks of mutual affiliation and undermines the stability of local institutions (e.g., families and school) that play a critical role in fostering conventional values and social bonds. Studies have found that community cohesion is more problematic in contexts of high disadvantage and instability owing to fear and mistrust. As a result, residents are less likely to engage in mutual guardianship, are reluctant to intervene in local disturbances, and mechanisms of informal surveillance and collective supervision that enmesh youths within a web of ongoing monitoring fail to develop.

From the perspective of social disorganization theory, racial differences in violence reflect the relative exposure of groups to criminogenic structural conditions. Blacks and other minorities exhibit higher rates of violence than do whites because they are more likely to reside in community contexts with high levels of poverty, unemployment, family disruption, and residential instability. The argument implies that if whites were embedded in similar structural contexts, they would exhibit comparable rates of violence.

FAMILY STRUCTURE AND SOCIOECONOMIC STATUS

The social and economic well-being of families is also hypothesized to be related to racial-ethnic differences in violence, given the documented variation in family structure and socioeconomic status across groups. Children who are reared in disadvantaged community environments are more likely to grow up in single-parent families with limited socioeconomic resources and to experience disruption in the form of parental divorce or separation. In general, the demands of family life tend to be more overwhelming in single-parent families, especially when economic resources are depressed, which may make the control and socialization of children more difficult than in homes with two biological parents. Single parents have fewer resources (e.g., educational) to provide their children, have less time to monitor and supervise them, and may be less likely to form strong parent-child bonds.

Some studies have suggested that low family incomes result in economic pressure and marital conflict, which increases children's risk for violence.

Poor families also have fewer resources to draw on in supplying social control, such as access to child care and money for youth activities (e.g., recreational sports and summer camps) that foster conventional values and bonds. The daily stress of meeting financial obligations may also diminish the ability of parents to provide social and emotional support for their children. In addition, parents of low socioeconomic status and/or with limited educational backgrounds may have more tolerant attitudes toward violence (e.g., encouraging "toughness," particularly in boys), which may foster violent behavior in children.

SOCIAL CAPITAL

Social capital refers to the structure and process of relationships between adults and children that can facilitate or inhibit access to resources and action for mutual benefit. Coleman identified the family as a key mechanism through which social capital is transmitted. Prior research has shown that the social capital available to children is greater in two-biological-parent families with higher incomes and levels of parental education.

Structural differences across communities may also produce variability in the social capital available to children and families. High levels of community disadvantage and residential instability diminish the prevalence of networks of affiliation that promote social capital and the engagement of adults in the support and control of children. Greater stocks of social capital have been shown to have a positive effect on children's performance in school and the acquisition of conventional norms and bonds and to divert youths from delinquent involvement.

One key form of social capital is intergenerational closure—the extent to which the activities of children are intertwined with those of adults. High levels of adult-child closure are evident when parents know the parents of their children's friends and when youths have adults (a parent, teacher, coach, or religious leader) they can look up to and turn to for support. The social ties formed when parents know their children's friends' parents facilitate social control by providing for mutual support, the exchange of information, common ground for establishing shared expectations, and collective supervision of youths' behavior. This type of closure in local networks embeds youths in relationships of mutual trust and obligation, which further reinforce norms and practices that promote pro-social behavior. Children who are connected to adults whom they respect and admire are more likely to abide by adults' expectations and to consider the reactions of others when contemplating delinquent behavior and hence are less likely to engage in it.

These types of closure and exchange processes may vary across racial-ethnic groups—given differential exposure to family and community disadvantages—and therefore be important to the explanation of group differences in delinquent and violent behavior.

DATA AND METHODS

Our analysis draws from three waves of the NELS and U.S. zip code data on local communities. The NELS is a large, nationally representative data set, with student, parent, teacher, and principal components. The survey was designed to provide data about critical transitions through school and from school to work. During the first wave in 1988, the National

Center for Education Statistics (NCES) drew random samples of about 25 eighth graders in each of about 1,000 middle schools. Students were then traced to high school in 1990 (Wave 2) and 1992 (Wave 3), with high follow up response rates. There were 16,489 respondents with completed questionnaires in the base year and first and second follow-ups. We matched the individual-level data with zip code-level data drawn from the 1990 U.S. Census. After missing values on the dependent-variable were accounted for, the sample for the analysis included 14,358 adolescents across 2,988 locales.

The dependent variable—fighting—is a straightforward indicator of adolescent violence. Our indicator was derived from two questions in the third wave of the NELS that asked the respondents how many times they had been in a physical fight at or on the way to or from school over the previous half year and was measured as a binary response (1 = once or more). Approximately 15% of the sample reported having been in at least one fight.

Race-Ethnicity and Individual-Level Controls

Membership in a racial-ethnic group was measured with a set of dummy-coded variables that distinguished whites, Asians, American Indians, blacks, Hispanic, and respondents of "other" backgrounds. The analysis included several standard control variables to provide a baseline from which to evaluate racial-ethnic differences in fighting. Greater involvement in violence among males is well documented, and hence we controlled for the respondents' gender. To control for changes in residence and potential disruptions in adolescents' well-being that sometimes accompany moves, we included a binary measure distinguishing adolescents who had *moved* within the past two years.

As we mentioned earlier, we included controls for prior involvement in fighting and attitudes toward fighting. *Prior fighting* was coded 1 for respondents who reported being in a physical fight (in the past six months) in either the 8th or 10th grades. *OK to fight* is a binary variable distinguishing between respondents who reported that it is often/sometimes OK to fight and those who reported that it is rarely/never OK. Research has indicated that commitment to school insulates youths from involvement in delinquency.

Hence, we controlled for school achievement, measured as the average of the respondent's *school grades* in four subjects: English, math, history, and science. Finally, given prior research showing that *alcohol/drug use* is predictive of violence, we included a variable for respondents who reported that they had used alcohol, marijuana, or cocaine within the past 30 days.

Community-Level Measures

The community-level measures were derived from zip code-level data from the 1990 U.S. Census. *Concentrated disadvantage* is a composite index comprised of four dimensions: (1) the percentage of persons with 1989 incomes below the poverty threshold, (2) the percentage of households headed by women, (3) the percentage of the civilian labor force who are unemployed, and (4) the percentage of the population who are African American. This index captures the concentration of cumulative forms of disadvantage.

We also included community-level indicators of stability, age structure, and urbanism, given their associations with crime and delinquency in prior research. Since residential stability may be important to the maintenance of social capital in families, we controlled for the percentage of housing units that are owner occupied, a commonly used indicator of stability. Homeowners have a greater financial stake in the local area and hence are more likely to engage actively in efforts to maintain it. We also controlled for the percentage of the population in the crime-prone ages (15–24 years) and the percentage of residents who reside in urbanized areas.

Measures of Family Well-Being

Family structure was measured as a two-biological-parent family, with single-parent/stepparent families serving as the referent. We included three indicators of family socioeconomic status which have been documented as predictors of adolescent delinquency. *Family income* refers to reported annual income in dollars (ranging from zero to $30,000). *Welfare receipt* is a binary variable drawn from the 1990 student survey, which asked whether the respondent's family was on welfare in the past two years. *Parental education,* derived from the 1990 parent survey, refers to the highest level of education attained by either parent.

Measures of Social Capital

We measured three dimensions of social capital that tap closure and exchange processes that have been shown in recent studies to influence the well-being and the social control of children. *Parents know friends' parents* is a dummy-coded indicator distinguishing whether adolescents' parents/guardians know none, some, or many of the parents of their children's closest friends. *Parental interaction at school* is an index summing responses to three items in the parent survey, which asked the parents how often they discuss things with other parents at their children's school, including their children's education and career plans. *Adolescent's interaction with adults* measured the frequency with which adolescents spend time talking or doing things with adults: rarely/never, less than once a week, and once a week or more.

Analytic Strategy

The analysis proceeds in three steps. First, to establish group differences in adolescents' fighting, we estimate a baseline model, including racial-ethnic background and individual-level controls. Second, we examine reductions in the race-ethnicity coefficients (from the baseline model) uniquely accounted for by the indicators of community context, family well-being, and social capital by entering each block separately. Doing so permits an assessment of which particular intervening dimensions are most relevant to explaining disparities in fighting between each minority group and whites. Third, to compare the effects of the explanatory variables on fighting and their accumulative contributions to an explanation of racial-ethnic differences, we build a fully specified model by sequentially entering them in a manner consistent with the causal ordering specified in our theoretical discussion.

Multivariate Results

The results reveal that American Indian, black, and Latino adolescents have significantly higher involvement in physical fights than do whites. The differences among whites, Asians, and other ethnic groups are not significant. As would be expected, male adolescents are more likely than female adolescents to engage in fighting, but a recent residential move does not have a significant effect. The strong, positive effect of prior fighting indicates substantial stability in fighting behavior over time. In addition, adolescents with more favorable attitudes toward fighting and who consume alcohol and/or drugs face a greater risk of involvement in physical fights, while stronger commitments to school—as indicated by higher average grades—reduces involvement.

We now examine whether variation in the community contexts in which groups are embedded explains the racial-ethnic disparities in fighting just revealed. Concentrated disadvantage has the expected significant, positive effect on fighting, but the effects of the remaining community-level controls do not reach significance at conventional levels. Most important, the inclusion of concentrated disadvantage fully explains the white-black disparity in fighting. The baseline black coefficient is reduced by 38% to nonsignificance, indicative of the relatively more advantaged community environments in which white adolescents reside. Concentrated disadvantage is consequential but appears less central to explaining the differences between whites and American Indians/Latinos. The baseline American Indian and Latino coefficients are reduced by 20% and 23%, respectively, but remain statistically significant.

Another model alternatively incorporates the indicators of family socioeconomic well-being. Relative to adolescents whose parents have not completed high school, the odds of fighting decrease significantly as parental educational attainment increases from a high school degree to a professional degree. The effects of family structure, family income, and welfare receipt on fighting are not significant once parental education is controlled. Of most direct substantive interest, controlling for parental education reduces the white-Latino difference in fighting by 48% to nonsignificance, reflecting the lower socioeconomic status of Latino families. The American Indian and black coefficients are reduced by about 11% and 17%, respectively, but remain highly significant.

Another model incorporates the indicators of social capital into the baseline model. Consistent with recent theory regarding social capital, youths are less likely to fight when their parents have established links to their friends' parents. Similarly, adolescents who at least sometimes talk to or do things with adults face a lower risk

of involvement in fighting, compared to those who rarely or never interact on a regular basis with adults. The measure of parental interaction at school, however, does not have a significant effect on adolescents' fighting.

DISCUSSION AND CONCLUSION

In this article, we performed a contextual analysis of adolescents' fighting that considered both community and individual- and family-level factors. The results of this analysis are fairly straightforward. The white-black disparity in adolescents' fighting is explained by higher levels of disadvantage in the communities in which black children often live. The disadvantage index accounted for the largest reduction in the black effect on fighting, reflecting the well-documented concentration of disadvantage in black communities. Our results also indicate that the effect of concentrated disadvantage on fighting is mediated by more proximate processes that are linked to family well-being. This mediation is suggested by the reduction of the concentrated disadvantage index coefficient to nonsignificance when family well-being is controlled.

Variation in structural disadvantage appears less central to explaining the white-Latino difference in fighting, but it is still consequential. Irrespective of community context, this difference can be explained by variation in family well-being between Latino and white families and, more specifically, by parental education. Although the average Latino adolescent resides in a more disadvantaged community relative to whites, the disparity is not nearly as pronounced as that between blacks and whites. The only remaining significant difference in the likelihood of violent behavior is between American Indian and white adolescents. It is possible that American Indians may confront unique historical disadvantages that are not adequately captured by the explanatory variables used in this analysis.

Yet we are able to explain the differences between white and black and Latino adolescents, which indicates the contribution of contextual approaches to a comprehensive explanation of group differences in violent behavior.

Our findings suggest that social policy that is directed toward reducing violence among racial and ethnic minorities should be careful not to generalize from one racial or ethnic group to the next. Concentrated community disadvantage appears central to the explanation of white-black differences in violence. Social programs that are designed to encourage and facilitate the relocation of poor families into low-disadvantage neighborhoods are, therefore, likely to be successful.

White-Latino differences appear to be more a function of family disadvantage, and thus policies that are designed to assist struggling families and to encourage higher education would be the most useful. Although policy implications with respect to addressing the needs of American Indians are not easily derivable from our study, attention to the factors mentioned would help. Finally, our results suggest that programs that are designed to strengthen social capital for adolescents would reduce involvement in violence, but may not ameliorate racial and ethnic differences in violent behavior unless they simultaneously address the consequences of living in disadvantaged communities (for blacks) and/or disadvantaged families (for Latinos).

QUESTIONS FOR DISCUSSION AND WRITING

1. What is social capital? What is intergenerational closure? How are they related to delinquency?

2. What do the results reveal?

3. What happened when the authors included in their model variation in the community contexts in which groups are embedded? What did the authors find when they incorporated indicators of family socioeconomic well-being? What did the authors find when they incorporated indicators of social capital?

4. What do the authors suggest about programs that are designed to strengthen social capital for adolescents?

AGE AND THE EXPLANATION OF CRIME

TRAVIS HIRSCHI

MICHAEL GOTTFREDSON

According to a recent criminology textbook, age is the easiest fact about crime to study. In one sense, the statement is true: The age of the offender is routinely recorded, and age distributions of crime covering a variety of contexts over a long period are not hard to find. As a result, no fact about crime is more widely accepted by criminologists. Virtually all of them, of whatever theoretical persuasion, appear to operate with a common image of the age distribution. This distribution thus represents one of the brute facts of criminology. Still, the statement that age is an easy fact to study is decidedly misleading. When attention shifts to the meaning or implications of the relation between age and crime, that relation easily qualifies as the most difficult fact in the field. Efforts to discern the meaning of the large amount of research on the topic in terms supplied by those doing the research have turned out to be futile, as have efforts to explain the relation in statistical terms.

Faced with this intransigent fact, the response in criminology has been generally scientific and logical. Theorists are frequently reminded that their explanations of crime must square with the age distribution, and theories are often judged by their ability to deal with "maturational reform," "spontaneous remission," or the "aging-out" effect. Although some theories fare better than others when the age criterion is invoked, no

theory that focuses on differences between offenders and nonoffenders avoids altogether the complaint that it provides an inadequate explanation of the age distribution. Given the persuasiveness of the age criticism of traditional theories, it is not surprising to find recent explanations of crime explicitly tailored to fit the accepted variability in crime by age. In fact, there is reason to believe that age could replace social class as the master variable of sociological theories of crime.

On the research side, the age effect has been instrumental in the rise of the longitudinal study to its current status as the preferred method of criminological research. The major studies of the past decade, including several still underway, have used this design. This research emphasis gains much of its attractiveness from the association between age and such concepts as "career criminal," "recidivism," and "desistance," all of which are thought to be of considerable theoretical and practical import and all of which are thought to require, by definition, longitudinal designs for their study.

Given the increasing role of age in criminological theory and research, and the widely accepted critique of sociological theories on the basis of the age effect, it seems to us that those in the field should consider the possibility that current conceptions of the age effect and its implications for research and theory are misguided.

To that end, in this [article] we advance and attempt to defend the following thesis: The age distribution of crime is invariant across social and cultural conditions. We recognize the difficulty in establishing our thesis. Nevertheless, we find nothing in the available research literature inconsistent with our position, and we find a good deal to support it.

THE AGE EFFECT IS INVARIANT

Theoretical and textbook discussions of the age effect often presuppose or flatly assert (the former is more common) variations in this effect over time, place, demographic subgroups, or type of crime. Typically, the current age distribution of crime in the United States as revealed by the Uniform Crime Reports (UCR) is shown, and the reader is left with the impression that this distribution is only one of many such distributions revealed by research.

Time and Place

We can consider three age distributions of criminality: one from England and Wales in 1842–44 as reported by Neison in 1857, another from England in 1908 as reported by Goring in 1913, and another from the most recently available UCR for the United States. Looking at one of these distributions, Goring concluded that the age distribution of crime conformed to a "law of nature." The similarity between the three distributions is sufficient to suggest that little or nothing has happened to Goring's law of nature since he first discovered it. The shape or form of the distribution has remained virtually unchanged for about 150 years. Recent data, the basis for many assertions of variability in the age distribution, force the same conclusion: While population arrest rates have changed in absolute magnitude over time (almost doubling between 1965 and 1976), the same pattern has persisted for the relative magnitudes of the different age groups, with 15- to 17-year-olds having the highest arrest rates per population of any age group.

We do not know how England and Wales in the 1840s differed from the United States in the 1980s. Presumably, the differences are large across a variety of relevant dimensions. We do know, however, that in the 1960s, the age distribution of delinquency in Argentina was indistinguishable from the age distribution in the United States, which was in turn indistinguishable from the age distribution of delinquency in England and Wales at the same time. If the form of the age distribution differs from time to time and from place to place, we have been unable to find evidence of this fact.

Demographic Groups

Most discussions of the age distribution in a theoretical context assume important differences for demographic subgroups. Textbooks often compare rates of increase in crime for boys and girls for particular offenses, thus suggesting considerable flexibility in the age distribution by sex. "Age-of-onset" studies easily suggest that, say, black offenders "start earlier" than white offenders; such a suggestion gives the impression that the age distribution of crime varies across ethnic or racial groups. Such suggestions tend to obscure a basic and persistent fact: Available data suggest that the age-crime relation is invariant across sex and race.

Type of Crime

A consistent difference in the age distribution of person and property offenses appears to be well established, at least for official data. In such data, person crimes peak later than property crimes, and the rate declines more slowly with age. The significance of this fact for theories of criminality is, however, problematic. For one thing, self-report data do not support the distinction between person and property offenses; they show instead that both types of offense peak at the same time and decline at the same rate with age. The peak years for person and property offenses in self-report data are the mid-teens, which are also the peak years for property offenses in official data. In contrast, person offenses in official data peak in the late teens or early 20s.

If the self-report results are taken as indicative of the level of criminality, the difference in the peak years for person and property offenses in official data may be accounted for by age-related differences in the *consequences* of person and property crimes. One of these differences lies in the seriousness of offenses. Wolfgang and his colleagues report that "injury seriousness scores advance dramatically at each offense rank number," while the increase in seriousness for theft offenses is negligible. Offense rank is correlated with age (as a group, second offenders are older than first offenders). It should follow that age is positively correlated with the seriousness of injury offenses but not with the seriousness of theft offenses. By extension (and this is consistent with everyday observation), "injury" offenses by the very young are unlikely to be sufficiently serious to attract the attention of officials. Indeed, as long ago as 1835, Quetelet presented data on the correlation between physical strength and age alongside data on the age distribution of crime, the idea being that some crimes appear only when the strength necessary to inflict injury or coerce others has been attained. Apparently, the tendency to commit criminal acts, as reflected in theft offenses, however measured, and in violent offenses, as measured by self-reports, peaks before the physical ability necessary for serious violent offenses. The peak age for person offenses is thus a consequence of the confluence of the "tendency" and "ability" curves. Since strength continues to increase after the peak age of criminality has been reached, the person-crime curve declines from a later point. For a brief period, increases of the dangerousness of offenders more than offset their declining tendency to commit offenses.

The slower decline of person offenses in official data may reflect the fact that a greater proportion of such offenses involve primary group conflicts. Primary group conflicts may be assumed to be relatively constant over the age span and to produce a relatively stable number of assaultive offenses during the period of capability (i.e., among those neither very young nor very old). If these offenses were subtracted from the total number of person offenses, the form of the age curve for person offenses would approximate more closely than for property offenses. These speculations are consistent with the self-report finding of no difference between person and property crimes with respect to the long-term effects of age.

Since our thesis is that the age effect is invariant across social and cultural conditions, it may appear that our explanation of the apparent difference between person and property crimes requires modification of our thesis. Actually, in some social conditions, the effects of age may be muted. As people retreat into the primary group context with increasing age, the relatively rare criminal events that occur in this context continue to occur. Outside the primary group context, the effects of age on person offenses show themselves even more clearly. So, while we may find social conditions in which age does not have as strong an effect as usual, the isolation of such conditions does not lead to the conclusion that age effects may be accounted for by social conditions. On the contrary, it leads to the conclusion that in particular cases the age effect may be, to some extent, obscured by countervailing social processes.

Life-Course Explanations

Age is correlated with important events thought to be related to crime, such as leaving school, marriage, and gainful employment, but its effects on crime do not appear to depend on these events. Age affects crime whether or not these events occur; research indicates that marriage does not affect delinquency:

> Marriage has often been invoked as the reason for the observed decrease in convictions after age 18, and indeed as the most effective treatment for delinquency. The Cambridge study found that both official and self-reported delinquency decreased between 18 and 21. Men who married during this period were compared with those who stayed single, to see if the married group decreased more. The groups didn't differ in official or self-reported delinquency at age 21, even after attempts were made to match them up to the date of the marriage.

Although not designed as direct tests of life-course questions, studies of crime during military service are, in our view, also consistent with the argument that life-course change cannot account for the age effect. The persistence of the age effect in incarcerated populations casts doubt on the assumption that such status changes as marriage, parenthood, or employment are responsible for decreases in criminality associated with age. Perhaps more fundamentally, the stability of the age effect across societies and demographic groups would not be expected were life-course factors responsible for an "apparent" age effect.

Theories that try to explain the age effect by relying on life-course events will always sound plausible. Their plausibility stems from the fact that the age effect is confounded with the effects of its correlates (e.g., marriage and "settling down" do go together because age predicts them both). Age is correlated with beliefs and practices themselves correlated with crime—for example, respect for authority, punitiveness toward offenders, church attendance—but we believe that these correlates are not responsible for the age effect. Although crime-relevant beliefs and practices indeed vary greatly over the life cycle, the data suggest the effects of age will be found in all categories of these beliefs and practices. Once again, the plausibility of explanations of the age effect based on such correlates results from the universal tendency to assign the effects of age to its correlates. The statistical difficulties inherent in this tendency are obvious once it is realized that none of these correlates can compete with age in predicting criminality.

Implications

Age is everywhere correlated with crime. Its effects on crime do not depend on other demographic correlates of crime. Therefore, it cannot be explained by these correlates and can be explained without reference to them. Indeed, it must be explained without reference to them.

Although correlated with crime, age is not useful in predicting involvement in crime over the life cycle of offenders. For predicting subsequent involvement, to know that a child of 10 has committed a delinquent act is no more useful than to know that a child of 15 has done so. The implications of this fact for contemporary research practice are profound. It denies, for example, the suggestion (at the heart of the longitudinal survey and the career criminal notion) that "prevention and treatment efforts should be concentrated on those boys who begin their criminal careers early in life."

Our argument also implies that the traditional division of the etiological problem into juvenile and adult segments is unlikely to be useful. Because the causes of crime are likely to be the same at any age, the choice of sample should depend on the complexity of the theoretical argument and the causal analysis it presupposes. Resources should not be devoted to establishing the effects of a variable whose influence on crime is noncontroversial and theoretically uninteresting, especially when, almost by definition, examination of the effects of this variable precludes adequate examination of the effects of theoretically intriguing variables.

QUESTIONS FOR DISCUSSION AND WRITING

1. Do time and place affect the age distribution?

2. Do sex and race affect the age distribution?

3. Does type of crime affect the age distribution?

Juvenile Delinquency and Gender

Josine Junger-Tas

Denis Ribeaud

Maarten J. L. F. Cruyff

The police, juvenile justice officials and researchers alike have repeatedly found that females consistently show considerably lower delinquency rates than males. This is true for all countries and earlier times for which there are records, and continues to be true all over the world to this very day. Despite political and social upheaval in western countries in the second half of the 20th century, which brought fundamental change in the social and economic position of women and girls, and contrary to what many observers had expected, comparison of male and female delinquency continues to show lower rates among females.

In this article, we will consider some of the factors that might cause these disparities in criminal involvement between adolescent males and females. In doing so we will consider the results of two empirical studies of young people aged 12–18 and 14–21. We focus on delinquency as it appears in adolescence, the peak period of delinquent behaviour. In this respect our analysis contrasts with the longitudinal study of Moffitt and her colleagues, which considers delinquency rates of males and females over the life course.

Both studies reported here show important differences in socialization patterns between males and females, which, we argue, are related

to differences in delinquent behaviour. Both include tests of social control theory, from which we develop the thesis that continuing differential socialization of girls is an important causal factor inhibiting female criminal behaviour. However, the second study also includes some psychosocial variables and introduces some additional viewpoints. Our data further indicate that the balance in delinquent behaviour between males and females varies according to offence type, and shifts at different points in the life course. We argue that, although socialization is an important factor in explaining gender differences in delinquency during adolescence, it is not the whole explanation. Gender-related temperamental differences at birth, as well as culturally determined parental attitudes toward bringing up daughters and sons, have a great impact on parental socialization patterns and the different developmental paths of the sexes and contribute to the explanation of specific differences in delinquent behaviour during the teenage years.

The ISRD Study

The data are taken from the International Self-Report Delinquency Study (ISRD), a comparative study of 11 countries, all but one of them

European. The study was based on a common methodology. On the original plan, each survey was to be based on a national random sample of young people aged 14–21 of both genders. A common instrument was designed, covering 30 delinquent acts as well as some "problem behaviours," such as truancy, running away and alcohol and drug use. The survey covered a range of explanatory variables, including socioeconomic status, formal and informal responses to delinquent behaviour, and a number of factors relevant to social control theory such as relationship with parents, parental supervision, attachment to school and commitment to school achievement and to peers. Screening questions were used for information on lifetime prevalence ("Did you ever . . . ?"), followed by specific questions on current prevalence ("Did you do this last year . . . ?"). The execution of the study met with considerable difficulties owing to financial constraints. This meant that some of the participating countries were not able to draw a national sample and had to limit the study to one or several big cities. Five countries had a random national sample, six others a city sample. In three cases (Italy, Helsinki and Omaha) school samples were used. Participation rates varied from 57 percent in The Netherlands to 95 percent in Portugal, depending also on mode of administration. Despite a common code book, countries (or their marketing institutes) used different methods in coding, cleaning, analyzing and delivering the data, making it a difficult and lengthy task to merge the data sets into the single database that underpins the present comparative analysis.

In order to simplify these comparisons, we clustered the countries in the study. Based on supporting empirical data, comprising economic, social and cultural information, we combined the following countries: (1) an Anglo-American cluster consisting of England and Wales, Northern Ireland (Belfast) and Nebraska (Omaha); (2) a northwest European cluster consisting of Finland (Helsinki), Germany (Mannheim), Belgium (Liège), the Netherlands and Switzerland; (3) a southern European cluster consisting of Spain, Portugal and Italy (three cities).

The Ethnic Minority Study

In order to analyse the relationship between gender and delinquency among different ethnic groups, we make use of data collected from a youth cohort in Rotterdam, the Netherlands. This study was part of a programme of longitudinal research developed by the City of Rotterdam, which follows a single cohort from age 4 to 18, in order to measure psychosocial health and identify where there is need for remedial action. The data used here come from a questionnaire completed when the young persons in this cohort were aged 14–15.

The cohort of about 4,500 schoolchildren was ethnically heterogeneous, comprising Dutch, Surinamese, Antillean, Turkish, Moroccan and Cape Verdean juveniles. Ethnic group was defined by country of birth, or parents' country of birth if at least one parent was born abroad—the definition that is currently most commonly used in the Netherlands. The sample for the present data collection consisted of pupils in the third year of secondary education. It was drawn from a representative sample of Rotterdam schools. The self-completion questionnaire consisted mainly of previously existing questions and scales that had already been tested for internal consistency, face validity and factorial validity. A pilot was conducted among 300 third-year pupils in five secondary schools. In addition to social bonding variables, the questionnaire included questions measuring psychological well-being and a number of serious life events that might have an impact on the behaviour of young people. Since the questionnaire was administered in schools, the response rate was high (90 percent). Comparison of the sample with the youth population of the same age in Rotterdam revealed a similar distribution across types of school as well as a similar ethnic composition, with 60 percent belonging to an ethnic minority. The percentage of 14- to 15-year-olds attending a school for vocational training was higher in Rotterdam than for the Netherlands as a whole. Also, the proportion of young people belonging to an ethnic minority was much higher in Rotterdam than nationally (60 percent compared with 22 percent).

THEORETICAL CONSIDERATIONS

Up to the 1970s female criminality was rarely studied. Criminologists knew that girls and women were hardly represented in police and judicial statistics. In some countries, such as the

Netherlands, prisons for women did not even exist. This is probably one of the factors explaining criminologists' lack of interest in female delinquency. Since the 1970s, however, female criminality has been increasing. Indeed, there are indications from police data in both Europe and the United States that there has been a sizeable increase in arrests and convictions of girls and women. This may have led to an increasing interest in female delinquency.

Three central questions arise in connection with female crime and delinquency. First, how big is the gap between males and females in criminal involvement? Does that gap vary according to population group? To what extent is the gap between the males and females actually narrowing, as suggested in official statistics? Second, how can we explain the contrast in criminal behaviour between males and females? And, third, do the correlates of criminal behaviour differ according to gender and, if so, will it be necessary to develop different theories to explain male and female delinquency?

These are not easy questions to answer, and their complexity is enhanced by disagreements about facts that seem related to ideological assumptions. For example, some have claimed that female delinquency in the USA is slowly approaching male levels, whereas others have opposed this view. Members of this latter school have seen little change, and have stated that females continue to be considerably less delinquent than males. The former position may be partly inspired by the publications of Adler and Simon, who claimed that the increase in female delinquency, as it appears in criminal statistics, is strongly related to the feminist movement and female emancipation. These writers argued that increased independence, self-esteem and labour market participation would also lead to greater female criminal involvement and more violence. Other researchers, although admitting an increase in recorded criminality among females, have attributed this to the fact that female offenders are often victims of sexual abuse. As a consequence of abuse, girls would show more problem behaviour, such as running away from home and having premature sexual experiences. More for girls than for boys, such problem behaviour would lead to interventions by the juvenile justice system, for example increasing the numbers sent to institutional care. Others have claimed that this is meant not so much as punishment but more as

a form of protection from greater dangers, such as pimps and drugs dealers.

Biological differences are one possible explanation for the differential involvement of males and females in crime. Maccoby and Jacklin claimed that differences between males and females in aggression have a biological origin because they emerge very early in life and apply across cultures. Rowe et al. concluded from a self-report study of 418 sibling pairs that the predictors of delinquency were similar for both genders, but that the higher level of male delinquency arose because the risk factors were more often present in males than in females; for example, hyperactivity is a predictor of antisocial behaviour and it is more common in males than in females. Conduct disorders also occur twice as often in males as in females, and antisocial personality disorders in adult life are five or six times as common in males as in females, so males are clearly more vulnerable than females to this kind of disorder. However, there are difficulties with this type of explanation. For one thing, there is considerable overlap in antisocial behaviour between males and females, suggesting more similarity than difference. For another, since most of these studies are cross-sectional, they do not give us real insight into the interactions between biological factors and environmental influences. That is not to deny that biological factors influence behaviour, but longitudinal studies such as the Dunedin study are required to provide more empirical foundation for these assertions. Since there is a continuous interaction between biological and environmental influences, the latter will always be more easily demonstrated than the former in the absence of elaborate research designs that monitor or control for biological factors. All that can be said at the moment is that the universal character of gender differences in criminal involvement suggests that these differences may have at least some biological basis.

There are also indications that the behaviour of females is determined to a large extent by social and cultural expectations. Normative social expectations about female behaviour and socialization patterns may strongly affect girls and inhibit delinquent behaviour. For example, girls who accept traditional definitions of femininity tend to report fewer delinquent acts than less traditional girls. Gender definitions may also vary according to social class, race, and single-mother versus two-parent family: for example, gender roles are more rigid in working-class families, whereas they may be less traditional in specific ethnic minority groups and in mother-only families. Lanctôt and LeBlanc proposed a theory that integrates all of these dimensions into one unified framework, inspired by social control theory and including biological constructs, female victimization experiences, external and internal constraints, self-control and concepts of differential association theory. This indeed seems an attractive approach and it should probably guide future investigations.

However, although we made a small first step in that direction in the Rotterdam study, by systematically conducting separate analyses for both genders, our aim in this article is more modest. The position we want to defend is that, although there has been an undeniable increase in female delinquency since the 1970s, related essentially to greater freedom of movement and greater participation in social and economic life for girls and women, and although this has created more criminal opportunities for females, nevertheless, disparities in criminal involvement between the genders persist. These persisting disparities, we argue, should be explained essentially by equally persistent differences in socialization by parents and by society at large. In order to examine this hypothesis we draw mainly on social control theory as it has been developed by Hirschi and tested by others. Within this framework, there should be no need to develop wholly different theories to explain male and female delinquency; it would seem sufficient to recognize that "female delinquents are both similar to *and* different than male delinquents," leading to a delinquency theory that allows for and explains gender differences.

FEMALE INVOLVEMENT IN DELINQUENCY

Official Data

In 2000, American juveniles were involved in 16 percent of all violent crime index arrests and one-third of all property crime index arrests. About 2.4 million juveniles aged 12–17 were arrested. In broad terms, total juvenile crime arrests increased from 1980 to 1994 and then declined. This overall trend was similar for both genders, but there were some shifts in the gender distribution for specific offences.

As can be seen from Table 1, the proportion of boys among juveniles arrested in the USA was highest in 2000 for the more serious offences such as burglary, offences against life, robbery and car theft, whereas the proportion of girls was highest, although always considerably less than 50 percent, for theft, fraud and simple assault. Girls also represented a high proportion of those arrested for running away from home, an example of what is called a "status offence" in the USA, which would not be an offence in most European countries. Between 1980 and 2000, male property crime index arrests of juveniles declined by 46 percent, whereas comparable female arrests increased by 3 percent. Although between 1994 and 2000 property index arrests declined for both genders, the decline was greater for males (41 percent) than for females (25 percent). Violence arrests of juveniles increased between 1988 and 1994 for both genders, and then declined. Among girls, however, the violence arrest rate rose by 66 percent between 1980 and 2000, whereas among boys it declined by 16 percent. The change can be illustrated by reference to the statistics for simple assault. In 1980, the male arrest rate for simple assault was more than 3.5 times the female rate. In 2000, the male rate was only twice the female rate. In summary, looking at all juvenile arrests in the USA, including those relating to what would be called problem behaviour in Europe, male rates of arrest were 2.6 times higher than female rates in 2000. Between 1980 and 2000 there were increases in female arrest rates for less serious property and violent crimes, as well as for behaviour such as drug abuse and running away, which reduced the contrast in total arrest rates between girls and boys. Nevertheless, arrest rates remain considerably lower overall among girls than among boys.

In England and Wales, most offences committed by juveniles (aged 10–17) were either theft and handling stolen goods or those relatively minor offences (known as "summary offences") that are tried by summary process in the magistrates' courts (see Table 2). Two-thirds of boys and over three-quarters of girls who came to notice were sentenced or cautioned for these offences. In more detail, the profile of offences for which they were sentenced or cautioned varied to some extent between girls and boys. Theft and handling formed a considerably higher proportion of cautions and sentences among girls than boys, whereas burglary, drug offences and summary offences (including disorderly behaviour in public) formed a higher proportion among boys than girls.

Overall, male offending rates per 100,000 young people in England and Wales indicate a change from 7,000 in 1981 to 5,400 in 1999, a substantial decrease of 23 percent. In the case of females, however, the rate increased from 1,300 to 1,400 over the same period, a rise of 8 percent. All the same, the level of girls' involvement in juvenile offending remains low. In England and Wales in 1999, 1.4 percent of 10- to 17-year-old females were cautioned or sentenced, and for every known female offender there were four male offenders. The peak age of offending was 18 for males and 15 for females. Summarizing official statistics, Rutter et al. noted that the current overall ratio of males to females in the adolescent phase of the life cycle was around 4:1, the male preponderance being greatest for violence and sex crimes. Females tend to commit fewer and less serious crimes, and their offending career tends to be shorter.

The most reliable official crime figures in the Netherlands are from the police and refer to "known suspects." In 1999, there were 225 juveniles per 10,000 young people aged 12–17 who had been interrogated by the police, compared with 116 per 10,000 of the whole resident population. The great majority (87.5 percent) of young offenders interrogated were males. The median age of the first recorded juvenile offence was 17; about half of all recorded offences for juveniles were property offences, about 25 percent were vandalism and public order offences,

TABLE 1   Arrests of Juveniles Aged 12–17 for Selected Offences by Gender: USA, 2000

Offences	% of Juvenile Arrests		Juveniles as % of total arrests
	Males	Females	
Total	72	28	17
Burglary	88	12	33
Larceny/theft	63	37	31
Motor vehicle theft	83	17	34
Arson	88	12	53
Fraud	68	32	3
Stolen property/fencing	84	16	23
Against life	89	11	9
Robbery	91	9	25
Aggravated assault	77	23	14
Simple assault	69	31	18
Weapons carrying	90	10	24
Sex offences	93	7	19
Vandalism	88	12	41
Driving under the influence	85	15	1
Deviant behaviour (incl. status offences)			
Disorderly conduct	71	28	26
Vagrancy	77	23	–
Runaways	41	59	–
Drug abuse	85	15	13
Prostitution	45	55	2
Drunkenness	80	20	3

SOURCES: Office of Juvenile Justice and Delinquency Prevention; National Criminal Justice Reference Service; Statistical Briefing Book.

TABLE 2   Sentenced and Cautioned Young Offenders Aged 10–17 by Type of Offence and Gender: England & Wales, 1999 (Percent)

Offences	Males (N = 146,000)	Females (N = 36,000)
Theft/handling stolen goods	30	52
Burglary	9	3
Robbery	2	1
Fraud/forgery	1	2
Criminal damage	3	1
Violence against the person	8	8
Sexual offences	1	0
Drug offences	8	3
Summary offences	38	30
Total	100	100

and 19.5 percent were acts of violence against the person. First offenders formed a considerably higher proportion of young females than of young males coming to the attention of the police, whereas repeat offenders and especially persistent offenders formed a considerably higher proportion of males than of females (Table 3). Statistics for the period 1996–2001 show that, whereas the proportion of females among young first offenders marginally increased, the proportion of females among young persistent offenders declined.

It would seem from this summary review that, in the USA, England and Wales and the Netherlands, not only is there a considerable difference between boys and girls in the prevalence of known offenders, but female crime is less serious and girls tend to stop offending earlier than boys.

Self-Report Data

Passing now to gender differences in delinquency involvement found in the ISRD study,

the outcomes are in agreement with official data: females clearly commit a lower number of delinquent acts than males do and the peak age of their involvement is also slightly lower. Self-report data show considerable variation according to type of delinquent behaviour. For example, gender differences in vandalism and property offences are rather small, whereas they are much larger with respect to violent and serious offences. Violence among girls is a very rare event in all participating countries.

Table 4 summarizes these findings by showing the rates for the three sample clusters. In all three groups of countries, females have considerably lower levels of delinquency than males do, in particular with respect to violent offences, drug abuse and serious delinquent acts. Despite the "normal" character of soft drug use for most young people in Europe and the USA, the female drug-use curve flattens after an initial rise. In all participating countries, instead of rising continuously up to age 21, as is the male pattern, drug use among girls tends to stabilize after about age 17. Both lower

TABLE 3   Young Suspects Aged 12–24 Interrogated by the Police, by Repeat Offending and Gender: The Netherlands, 1999 (Percent)

Offending Patterns	Males (N = 48,193)	Females (N = 6,960)
First offenders	68.6	87.5
Repeat offenders	26.8	11.6
Persistent offenders	4.6	0.9
Total	100	100

TABLE 4   Prevalence Rates (% in Previous Year) for Different Offence Types by Country Cluster and Gender (Weighted Data): ISRD Study

	Northwestern Europe		Anglo-American Countries		Southern Europe	
	Males (N = 2596)	Females (N = 2400)	Males (N = 2596)	Females (N = 2400)	Males (N = 2596)	Females (N = 2400)
All Offences	65.1	52.2**	56.2	36.4**	64.2	49.1**
Vandalism	18.1	12.3**	16.5	9.2**	19.9	13.9**
Property	33.5	21.2**	34.7	19.2**	18.0	11.7**
Violence	24.5	7.1**	25.2	10.0**	26.2	7.8**
Drug use	13.8	8.7**	23.1	17.6**	14.5	8.2**
Serious Offences	11.7	3.4**	21.7	6.4**	11.4	3.5**

NOTES: ** Difference between males and females significant at $p < .001$.

delinquency levels and lower drug use may point to a greater reluctance to take risks among females, as compared with males. With respect to truancy and running away, differences between boys and girls are slight. This tends to confirm earlier research in showing that boys and girls participate equally in these types of problem behaviour, in contrast to the considerable gender differences in involvement in crime and delinquency.

Since the ISRD study was based on representative samples of the general population of young people in the various countries, the numbers from ethnic minorities included were generally too small for separate analysis. However, ethnic minorities constitute 60 percent of the 14- and 15-year-olds covered in the Rotterdam study, so we use this sample to examine gender differences in delinquent behaviour among six distinct ethnic groups. Differences both between the genders and between ethnic group are significant; Antillean boys score highest, followed by Cape Verdean, Moroccan and Surinamese boys (see Figure 1). Although girls' delinquency is indeed lower in all ethnic groups, it should be observed that delinquency involvement of Antillean girls, followed by Cape Verdean girls, is nearly as high as that of Dutch boys, whereas delinquency involvement of Muslim (Moroccan and Turkish) girls is low.

AGE, FAMILY BREAK-UP, AND GENDER

Age of onset of delinquent behaviour is an important variable because previous studies have shown that juveniles who start committing offences at an early age commit more frequent and more serious offences and usually go on for longer than those who start offending later. Therefore, we checked whether the age of onset of delinquent behaviour among girls was later than among boys. This appeared to be somewhat the case in northwestern Europe, and in the Anglo-American cluster only with respect to vandalism, but it did not seem to be true in southern Europe. In this respect our findings tend to support Moffit et al.'s conclusion that girls and boys start these activities at about the same age. Also, we found no gender difference in the age of onset of use of drugs. One may speculate about the reasons for this similarity. Since initiation in drug use generally takes place in the peer group, it may be related to the fact that, education in most western countries being mixed, both genders go to the same schools and may well start going out to parties and discos at about the same age. Using the Rotterdam study to compare the findings for different ethnic groups, there was little difference between boys and girls in use of alcohol or drugs within the Dutch group, thus confirming ISRD data; drug and alcohol use was considerably lower among boys from the ethnic minority groups (with the exception of the Antilleans) than among Dutch boys. Girls from ethnic minority groups, compared both with boys and with Dutch girls, had very low levels of use, with Muslim girls having the lowest rates.

Probably no variable has been studied as often as families broken by death, desertion or divorce. Most scholars have presented family break-up as having deep and lasting negative

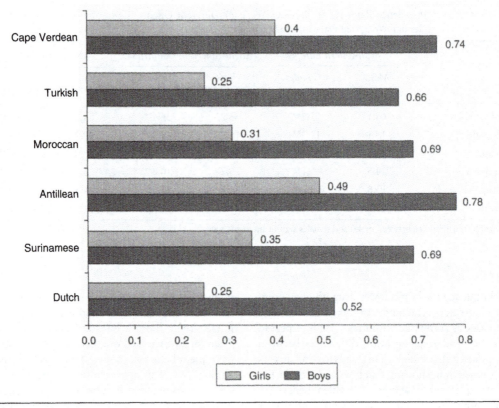

FIGURE 1   Mean Delinquency Score by Ethnic Group and Gender: Rotterdam Study

SOURCE: Junger-Tas et al. (2003:59).

NOTE: Gender: $F = 214.46$; $df = 1$; $p < .001$. Ethnicity: $F = 14.95$; $df = 5$; $p < .001$.
Interaction: $F = 2.43$; $df = 5$; $p < .05$.

effects on the behaviour of children and as a major determinant of delinquency. This is an important issue because rising divorce rates, especially in southern European countries and among ethnic minorities where change has come late, may be a major factor in delinquency. One study examined gender differences in self-reported delinquency related to family variables in a national probability sample of adolescents. As expected, young people from broken homes reported significantly more delinquent behaviour than did those from intact homes; a more unexpected finding was that a broken home had more effect on boys than on girls. A self-report study among high school students confirmed earlier findings about the effects of family structure on delinquency, but specified that the effect tends to be observed for status offences rather than for criminal acts. Moreover, family structure was related to parental supervision, which

may be the key influence on delinquency, rather than family structure itself. Johnson administered a self-report questionnaire to 734 high school students in a large American city to measure the relationship between a broken home and delinquency. He measured vandalism, theft and assault, as well as "trouble" with the authorities, such as school, police or the court. He found that family structure was not related to self-reported delinquency, but was related moderately and significantly to self-reported and official "trouble." The overall results were similar for males and females and for all racial groups. Johnson concluded that his data support the claim that family structure is moderately related to delinquency.

Wells and Rankin looked at studies differentiating between father absence and mother absence and at possible differential effects of father absence on boys and mother absence on girls. Some years later, Wells and Rankin conducted a meta-analysis, covering 50 studies completed between 1925 and 1985. Using correlation coefficients to measure effect sizes, the authors found a consistent and reliable association between a broken home and delinquency, ranging from .05 to .15. The largest correlations were found for status offences, such as truancy, running away and drug use, and the lowest were for violent offending. No consistent differences were found in the impact of a broken home on males and females or on whites and blacks.

Although the mere fact that the family was broken by death, separation or divorce has only a moderate relation with delinquency, the quality of family dynamics is much more strongly related. For example, there is ample empirical evidence that family conflict and violence, inconsistent and harsh discipline, and a lack of parental supervision are strongly related to the development of delinquent behaviour, both violent and nonviolent. Indeed, quality of family life appears to be considerably more important than family structure. To the degree that family break-up reflects the quality of relationships, it may be related to various forms of delinquent behaviour.

With few exceptions, these studies have been conducted in the United States. It is worth examining how far the results may be replicated in Europe, especially since some European countries differ considerably from the USA in terms of family, social structure and culture. The ISRD findings show that father absence is more frequent than mother absence. Father absence is lowest in southern Europe (7.5 percent), higher in northwestern Europe and highest in the Anglo-American cluster (England and Wales, 16.5 percent; Nebraska, 22.5 percent). Mother absence ranges from 2.5 percent to 3.5 percent. Table 5 shows how overall delinquency, serious offending and drug use vary according to whether the father is absent. Three findings stand out. First, the relationship between absence of a father and delinquency seems to be less strong in northwestern Europe than in the two other clusters. Second, in northwestern Europe father absence affects boys more than it does girls: it is significantly related to higher male delinquency rates, whereas differences for girls are slight. Third, the exception is drug use: in all clusters, absence of a father is associated with higher drug use. The impact of the absence of the mother is harder to analyse with the sample sizes available, since mother absence is relatively rare. However, the findings on the impact of mother's absence run roughly parallel to those on father's absence as far as males are concerned, although the associations are much weaker and reach significance only in rare cases.

TABLE 5   Prevalence Rates (% in Previous Year) by Whether Father Absent (With Mother Present), Country Cluster and Gender: ISRD Study

	Northwestern Europe[a]			Anglo-American Countries			Southern Europe[b]		
	Father absent	Father present	p[c]	Father absent	Father present	p[c]	Father absent	Father present	p[c]
Boys									
Overall delinquency	73.0	61.9	.00	66.2	53.7	.00	71.6	61.3	.06
Serious delinquency	14.2	10.6	.13	31.2	18.6	.00	23.9	13.9	.01
Drug use	23.2	12.3	.00	30.7	19.1	.00	26.1	16.0	.02
Girls									
Overall delinquency	44.7	49.6	.20	42.9	34.2	.01	59.4	44.3	.01
Serious delinquency	1.6	3.0	.29	11.2	4.5	.00	9.4	4.7	.05
Drug use	10.5	7.0	.09	20.7	15.0	.02	17.5	9.7	.02

NOTES:
a. Excluding Finland where the question was not asked.
b. Excluding Italy where the question was not asked.
c. Significance of the difference between the father absent and father present groups. Results in bold are significant at $p < .05$.

In contrast to the large differences in delinquent behaviour, we find that the frequency of problem behaviour such as truancy and running away is largely similar in males and females. A further question is whether the association of father or mother absence with problem behaviour is stronger than that with delinquency, as found by several authors. The ISRD results show that father absence is clearly related to problem behaviour in males. When there is no father present, both truancy and running away from home increase significantly among males in two of three sample clusters, whereas there is no consistent effect of this kind in the case of girls.

Findings from the Rotterdam study show that there are large differences between ethnic groups in family structure. About 90 percent of Turkish and Moroccan youths are living in complete families, compared with 80 percent of Dutch teenagers. By contrast, only half of Surinamese and Cape Verdean youths and scarcely one-third of Antilleans are living in families with both biological parents. As can be seen from Table 6, both delinquency and problem behaviour are lowest when young people are raised in a complete family, and this applies to all ethnic groups, although the difference is slight for certain groups, possibly because of small sample sizes. In the case of Antilleans and Cape Verdeans, both delinquency and problem behaviour are highest in families with a step-parent, in most cases a stepfather.

To summarize this section: females appear to have lower involvement in delinquency than males in all countries, according to both official statistics and self-reports. The age of onset of delinquency, not including drug use, is later in females than in males. In the ISRD study, absence of the father seems to have a stronger impact on behaviour in southern Europe and Anglo-American countries than it does in northwestern Europe. In addition, looking at the findings of the two studies, family structure seems to be more strongly related to problem behaviour, including alcohol and drug use, than to delinquency among both boys and girls.

INFORMAL SOCIAL CONTROL BY PARENTS

The concept of social control is essentially based on two subconcepts: *direct control* and *indirect control*. Direct external control is exercised by means of informal negative reactions to norm infractions and by formal sanctioning authorities. Indirect controls operate by giving youth a stake in conformity to society's rules, that is, by strengthening the bond with society or what some have called "a commitment to conformity." The transfer of norms from institutions such as the family, school, church and sports and youth organizations produces internal controls. To the extent that parents represent conventional culture and the young person has internalized their norms, he or she will be protected against criminal involvement. Again, this is partly achieved by direct control and supervision, but also by the relationship parents

TABLE 6   Mean Delinquency Score (Previous 12 Months) and Problem Behaviour Score (Previous 4 Weeks) by Family Composition and Ethnicity: Rotterdam Study

	Netherlands	Surinam	Antilles	Morocco	Turkey	Cape Verde
Delinquency scores						
2 parents	.36	.47	.42	.48	.45	.56
1 parent	.52	.54	.69	.56	.55	.57
1 step-parent	.51	.57	1.10	.52	.47	.75
Problem behaviour scores						
2 parents	.38	.21	.25	.12	.21	.17
1 parent	.61	.25	.33	.34	.29	.22
1 step-parent	.53	.28	.52	.03	.17	.36

NOTES: Delinquency: $F = 4.99$, df = 5, $p < .001$; no interaction.
Problem behaviour: $F = 18.39$, df = 5, $p < .001$; interaction: $F = 1.91$, df = 10, $p < .05$.

develop with their children. The closer that relationship, the more effectively the process of norm transfer will operate.

In many societies parents exercise more direct social control over their daughters than over their sons. This was true in the past and remains true today. For example, data from the International Crime Victims Survey of 1996 show that in all participating countries males go out at night more often than females do, both in cities and in rural areas. The differences are smallest in countries such as Finland and the Netherlands, and largest in Italy and Spain, where traditional family structures and attitudes have started to change more recently.

There is considerable evidence that boys and girls are socialized differently. For example, a national survey in the Netherlands of a representative sample of adults aged 18–70 included a number of questions about patterns of informal parental control at the time when respondents were aged 17; the results showed that even in the 1990s, twice as many males as females were going out at weekends. Also, girls were expected to be home earlier than boys; nearly half of the males came home after midnight compared with only 25 percent of females. Qualitative research has found that girls were less likely than boys to be allowed to hang about on the streets and to come home late, so that the girls' freedom of movement both in time and in space was considerably more restricted. Also, girls had less freedom with respect to type of activity and type of social contacts. Moreover, they had to spend much more time on household chores and caring tasks than boys did. At the same time, girls participated twice as often as boys in family outings, and boys spent more time on sports. Tighter control over girls starts very early: a study on community life in a small Dutch town showed that little girls aged less than 6 were allowed to play outside only in front of the house and were not permitted to leave the street, whereas little boys of that age were allowed to play anywhere in the neighborhood. An English study of a national sample of 751 families with children aged 14–15 also found that boys were more likely than girls to receive low parental supervision. Similar findings emerged from another study in England and Wales.

In the ISRD study we asked young people if their parents generally knew where they were and whom they were with. The findings from these questions (Table 7) imply that parents are considerably more worried about their daughters than they are about their sons. According to the young people, only one-fifth or less of parents do not know where they are going or whom they are with when they go out with a peer group, but this proportion is about twice as high for boys as for girls. This contrast between girls and boys is found in all participating countries, the differences being highly significant. The frequency of "going out with the family" was also measured because this variable was hypothesized to indicate an active and positive family life. This may of course be culture dependent: in some countries it may be more unusual for adolescents to go out with the rest of the family. The results show that girls' participation in this kind of family activity is significantly higher than boys' in two of three clusters (northwestern Europe and Anglo-America) suggesting that, except in southern Europe, girls tend to be more strongly involved in family life than are boys. This would be in line with other patterns of activity—for example, with more outdoor recreation (as opposed to activities with the family) among male than among female adolescents.

Informal controls over girls and boys varied widely between ethnic groups in the Rotterdam sample, as shown by the results of the two questions, on parents knowing where you are going and whom you are with. Turkish parents exercise tight control over both boys and girls, whereas Moroccan parents strongly control their daughters but not their sons. Among the Caribbean groups, there is considerably less control over both boys and girls, especially in single-mother families. The tight control over Muslim girls is related to (very) low delinquency involvement, but it seems to have some negative consequences. For example, psychological well-being is exceptionally low in the Turkish group, boys and girls alike, and Turkish girls, as compared with the other girls, more often reported thoughts about suicide and suicide attempts. In addition, both Moroccan and Turkish girls are less satisfied than other girls with their relationship with their parents.

SCHOOL AND GENDER

According to ISRD data, in the Anglo-American cluster and in southern Europe girls tend to have

TABLE 7   Parental Supervision by Gender and Country Cluster: ISRD Study

	Northwestern Europe			Anglo-American Countries			Southern Europe[a]		
	Males	Females	p[c]	Males	Females	p[c]	Males	Females	p[c]
Parents know where[b]	N = 2310	N = 2027		N = 1429	N = 1335		N = 924	N = 864	
Yes	82.4	91.6	.00	85.4	93.4	.00	78.9	88.4	.00
No	17.6	8.4		14.6	6.6		21.1	11.6	
Parents know with whom[b]	N = 2298	N = 2025		N = 1269	N = 1166		N = 924	N = 864	
Yes	81.5	88.9	.00	86.3	94.7	.00	83.2	91.2	.00
No	18.5	11.1		13.7	5.3		16.8	8.8	

NOTES:
a. Excluding Italy, where most of parent supervision questions were not asked.
b. Restricted to those living with at least one parent.
c. Pearson chi-square (results in bold are significant at $p < 05$).

a significantly greater commitment to school than boys do. They like school better, they repeat classes less often, they skip school less frequently and they tend to work harder for examinations. However, independently of gender, two of the variables are uniformly powerful and significant correlates of delinquent behaviour: whether the respondent likes school and whether he or she has played truant during the previous 12 months. This is the case across all countries, which seems again to indicate some general characteristics of western education systems, despite differences between individual countries. In the case of serious and violent delinquency, the data suggest an additional and strong relationship with repeating classes, and thus with school failure, but this is not the case as far as non-serious offending is concerned. These relationships are stronger among males than among females. Skipping school, and to a lesser degree disliking school, are associated with female as well as male delinquent behaviour, but in many cases the relationship is not significant. Working hard for examinations is not related to low delinquency in girls, nor is repeating classes. Taking all of the results together, they do suggest that, since school is an important socializing institution, behaviour that might eventually lead to dropping out of school may have negative outcomes for both boys and girls. However, the findings show that low school achievement is a more important factor in relation to delinquency for boys than for girls. This suggests that males, much more than females, realize the importance of school achievement, especially in terms of its social and economic consequences. It is a very general finding, as there is no difference between the clusters in this respect. It is also a somewhat surprising finding, which one would not expect at the end of the 20th century, since it seems to indicate that girls continue to consider school achievement to be of less importance to their future life than do boys.

The Rotterdam study confirms these findings. Although both males and females report more offences where their relationship with teachers is bad than where it is good, that association is stronger in the case of boys, pointing again to the greater significance of the school for males than for females. For the most part, ethnic minority youths are rarely found in the more academic schools or streams; instead, most of them attend lower schools that emphasize vocational training. Surinamese youths are an exception. They are better represented in higher-level schools and their educational level is higher than that of the other groups. One reason for the lower school involvement of minority girls, in particular those who attend lower vocational training schools, is that they tend to marry at earlier ages than Dutch girls and preparations for marriage start earlier.

PEERS AND GENDER

Much has been written about group delinquency, frequently in the framework of subculture theory and—in the USA—gangs. It should be observed, however, that group membership in adolescence is a normal phenomenon and not necessarily synonymous with delinquency. Indeed, most things young people do, whether conforming or deviant, they do in groups.

It is well known that there is a gender difference in this respect: girls report more often than boys that they have a limited number of friends. Thus about 33 percent of the boys and 21 percent of girls in northwestern Europe and the Anglo-American countries say they have six or more friends. Southern Europe is different, with only 17 percent of boys versus 11 percent of girls reporting that they have six friends or more. The number of friends is related to neither a bad relationship with father nor poor progress at school, but rather to whether the young person likes school or not. Age and attending school are related to group membership: older youths having left school are less likely to belong to a group. The main factors related to group membership are age, gender, "never" going out with the family and lack of parental supervision.

The Rotterdam study shows comparable differences between boys and girls in the number of friends they have within each ethnic group. About 70 percent of boys in most of the groups report that they have four or more friends, with the exception of the Cape Verdean boys, where the proportion is even higher (89 percent). In all of the ethnic groups, the proportion of girls with four or more friends is lower: 55 percent among Dutch girls, 58 percent among Cape Verdean girls and lower still among the Muslims (42–49 percent), probably because Muslim girls are more often kept at home and under tighter control.

Some of the gender differences in delinquency might be explained by differences in leisure-time activities. In fact, more boys than girls participate in organized sports or leisure, although differences are small in northwest Europe and in the Anglo-American cluster, whereas they are greater in southern Europe. As well as having more friends, boys report that they spend more leisure time with the peer group than girls do. In addition, some delinquent acts, such as vandalism, gang fights or even car theft, are archetypal group activities. Considering the question of with whom young people spend most of their free time, gender differences are quite large in northwestern Europe, but only moderate in Anglo-American countries and in southern Europe. We should not forget that many group activities are not intrinsically connected with offending—for example, going to discos or house parties, activities in which girls frequently participate. It is young people who have no friends at all and those who have many friends who report the highest delinquency scores, and this applies to both boys and girls, although the female level of delinquency is half that for boys. We find that 60 percent of all offences committed in the previous 12 months were committed with other peers (not necessarily the peer group, often with one or two companions), and among those who reported two or more offences the figure is 85 percent. In fact we cannot rule out the hypothesis that part of the gender difference in delinquency is due to differences in leisure activities. For example, Maccoby, as reported by Moffit et al., presented evidence of some differences between boys' peer groups and girls' groups, such as the fact that male groups are more oriented toward status and dominance and tend to take more risks in testing the limits of what is acceptable social behaviour. However, considering the fairly small differences between boys and girls in their leisure-time activities in our studies, and the increasing participation of girls in all kinds of social and public activities, we feel that leisure patterns will be only a small part of the explanation for male/female differences in delinquency.

SOCIAL CONTROL AS AN EXPLANATION FOR GENDER DIFFERENCES IN DELINQUENCY: A MULTIVARIATE ANALYSIS

From the results of the ISRD survey, we can summarize the differences in deviance between boys and girls by calculating the odds that someone has committed some deviant act in the previous 12 months, then calculating the odds ratios between boys and girls. We find that boys are four times more likely than girls to have committed a serious offence in northwestern Europe and three times more likely in the

Anglo-American countries and in southern Europe. In the case of overall offending, the odds ratios are 1.55 in northwestern Europe, 2.16 in the Anglo-American cluster and 1.89 in southern Europe. In other words, the gap between girls and boys is much greater for serious offences than for a broad measure of delinquency. For drug use, the difference is smaller again: girls are about 20 percent less likely than boys to have used drugs in northwestern and southern Europe, and 33 percent less likely in the Anglo-American cluster.

The main gender differences relate to family variables. Whereas parental supervision and control are a predictor of problem behaviour for both genders, three other variables predict girls' problem behaviour but not boys'. First, being raised by a single mother increases the risk of problem behaviour for girls. Second, life events (essentially negative family events) appear also to increase that risk. Third, a bad relationship with parents is associated with a lower risk of problem behaviour for girls. This third finding may seem paradoxical, but is probably connected with interactions with the ethnic group that have not been investigated in these models. Good relationships with parents are more common among Dutch girls whose parents are less restrictive, whereas bad relationships are more common among Muslim girls whose parents are more restrictive, and who do not get involved in problem behaviours such as using alcohol and drugs. Finally, both life events and low psychological well-being are predictors of female but not male problem behaviour. This fairly strong association for girls—and not for boys—of family life events and psychological well-being with problem behaviour indicates again the importance of family factors for girls and suggests slightly different socialization processes for girls and boys.

DISCUSSION AND CONCLUSION

With respect to female delinquency, we recall the three questions posed at the beginning of this article. The first question was whether delinquent behaviour continues to be less common and less serious among females than males. All the available evidence indicates that, according to official statistics and surveys of self-reported delinquency, female crime continues to be lower and less serious. In addition, the delinquent

"careers" of females cover a shorter period, since the great majority of young women with an official record of offending are one-time offenders in terms of their contact with the authorities (see Table 3). The ISRD study, comparing 11 countries, confirms the male preponderance in offending. The data indicate that in some cases, such as vandalism and property offences, gender differences are rather limited. On the whole, however, girls are considerably less involved than boys in delinquent behaviour of most kinds in all participating countries. The Rotterdam study shows, further, that this is also the case among various ethnic minorities, despite the fact that these groups have come from very different countries and cultures. Although, beginning in the 1970s, female delinquency has increased and does include some occasional violence, the disparity in criminal involvement between boys and girls has not disappeared. Moreover, there seems to be no reason to believe that this situation will change in the near future.

The second and third questions are closely related. How can the gap in delinquency between males and females be explained? Are the correlates of offending different in boys and girls and, if so, do we need different theories to explain male and female delinquency? Our data indicate that globally these correlates are similar for males and females and that no greatly significant gender differences appear in the correlations of delinquency with important background variables, such as family bonding, the bond with teachers, truancy and the role played by the number of friends. This is clearly the case for the three clusters of countries studied by the ISRD, and is also true in the Rotterdam study. On the basis of our findings, therefore, there seems to be no need for radically different explanations of offending in girls and boys.

Our analysis has focused for the most part on testing measures connected with social control theory. This analysis has confirmed that a range of measures of social controls connected with the family and the school are related to youth delinquency. However, it also seems clear that social control theory cannot completely explain gender variations in delinquency. Testing for gender effects on delinquency while controlling for each social control variable showed that gender differences do not all disappear. For example, bonds with parents varied considerably between boys and girls. Nevertheless, controlling for the level of parental supervision explained only a part of the gender gap, and this was also the case for most of the school variables. We would like to add, however, that the mechanism of social control seems to operate in a slightly different way in the case of females, compared with males. For example, the Rotterdam analysis shows that, as far as male delinquency is concerned, direct parental control variables have the strongest effect on behaviour, whereas female delinquency appears to be affected as well by family composition, negative life events and psychological well-being. These aspects are all part of the family bonding process, of course, but the data suggest that in females the bonding process may operate more effectively through the relationship with the father and mother, that is, through emotional controls, whereas in the case of males formal controls seem to be more important than emotional ones. In the Rotterdam study, strongly family-related and generally adverse life events predict female but not male delinquent behaviour. Similar relationships are found in the case of problem behaviour. Drug use, truancy and running away from home are all significantly related to the relationship with parents as well as to parental control, a finding that holds true for all ISRD sample clusters as well. However, having a bad relationship with parents, life events and psychological well-being are all predictors of female but not of male problem behaviour. The outcomes do suggest that we have come across an essential differential element in the socialization of girls and boys, which applies across countries and ethnic groups and appears to have a great impact on the behaviour of young people. This is not to say that differential cultural elements do not play a role. For example, very strong controls over Muslim girls greatly reduce their opportunities for delinquent behaviour, whereas the culturally determined low control and supervision of Moroccan adolescent boys and of Caribbean girls contribute toward explaining their high criminal involvement. However, although these factors explain part of the inter-ethnic differences in delinquency, the fundamental family predictors of delinquent behaviour are similar across ethnic groups. It is a question of degree in the predictors, such as differences in the quality of the emotional relationship and variation in the amount of supervision.

We would also like to emphasize that we have found evidence for other intervening elements or mechanisms that contribute to the explanation of gender differences, such as individual and biological factors, since our analysis shows a strong gender effect on delinquency after controlling for the relationship with parents. It seems clear that biological, cultural, socialization and environmental factors all play a role in the prediction of delinquent behaviour. However, more (longitudinal) research is needed to document these factors and to unravel the interaction between them. Without denying other contributing factors, the present results show that differential socialization patterns are a powerful predictor of female and male delinquent behaviour.

QUESTIONS FOR DISCUSSION AND WRITING

1. What gender differences are shown by the USA data in Table 1? What gender differences were revealed by the examination of changes between 1980 and 2000?

2. Regarding social control by parents, what is true in many societies? What is true about how boys and girls are socialized?

3. What differences were found when the authors examined the odds that someone had committed some deviant act in the previous 12 months?

4. How do the authors answer the question "Are the correlates of offending different in boys and girls and, if so, do we need different theories to explain male and female delinquency?" When the authors tested for gender effects on delinquency while controlling for each social control variable, what happened to gender differences?

PART VI

How Do We Explain Crime?

Foundational Theories of Modern Criminology I

In the first five sections of this volume, we addressed definitions of crime, traced the historical development of criminological theory, examined the variability of perceptions of criminality, considered some different types of crime, and looked at correlates of crime. In examining each of these topics, we were always led back to the importance of theory in the criminological enterprise. As we pointed out in Part I, for example, the selection of a particular definition of crime by a theorist indicates that certain assumptions have been made about crime and criminals. (Earlier we used the example of what is implied if we define crime as illegal behavior a person chooses to engage in.) As criminology teachers have been saying in lectures for decades, the beginnings of answers to the "why do they do it?" questions are in our theories.

Some students may have found it surprising that we have not more fully considered assertions by other criminologists that blacks engage in more common law personal crimes than whites. During the past 30 years, other sources of data have been used to study race and crime, and they have tended to confirm this pattern. We would argue that the interesting debate is no longer whether there are race differences in criminality, but why there are race differences. In short, criminology has moved from a debate about data and measurement to one about theory.

This section is the first of four that consider modern criminological theory. When we say modern, we are not speaking only of new theories. We have also included older theories that contemporary criminologists are still using to explain crime. The first two of the theory sections (Parts VI and VII) focus on what we are calling "foundational theories," and Parts VIII and IX present contemporary theoretical developments. All four of the theory sections present an original statement of a theoretical perspective, which is then accompanied by an example of contemporary research in that tradition. These theories, particularly the oldest of them, have changed considerably between the publication of the original theoretical statements and the contemporary research pieces. So with each combination of theory and contemporary research, the student will see the evolution of the core ideas of the theory.

Whenever criminologists try to classify theories, there is often disagreement on how to categorize them. They would agree, in general, on the major theoretical approaches, but would probably disagree more on which theories should be grouped within an approach as well as on the theory and category names. We believe that, past the point of that initial broad agreement, much of the difference in how we divide theories is simply a matter of taste. Because we cannot even agree among the four of us on the finer distinctions, we have decided to simply organize these sections chronologically.

Part VI focuses on three theories that emerged and became prominent before mid-20th century: social disorganization theory, differential association theory, and anomie theory. Social disorganization theory was formulated in the 1920s by University of Chicago sociologists Robert Park and Ernest Burgess. The selection included here is by Shaw and McKay, who are also associated with the Chicago school. They were not formally on the faculty of the University of Chicago, but were doing research in Chicago based on the ideas of their colleagues at the university. They focus on the importance of the urban setting as a factor affecting delinquency rates. They showed in their empirical research and in their version of the theory that community breakdown or social disorganization led to increases in juvenile delinquency. The contemporary research example included here is by Morenoff, Sampson, and Raudenbush. This is not only an excellent example of contemporary social disorganization research, but students will be introduced to a new concept, "collective efficacy." A focus on levels of community collective efficacy, or the willingness of residents to act on behalf of the neighborhood, is at the heart of a resurgence in social disorganization research.

Sutherland's differential association theory attempted to correct what he saw as problems with the theory of social disorganization being proposed by his colleagues at the University of Chicago. He tried to explain why only some individuals, even in high-crime-rate areas characterized by social disorganization, actually become criminals. Sutherland wrote not only about the social psychological processes of differential association but also about differential social organization, which he saw as similar to social disorganization but modified to take into account intracommunity conflicts in the degree of organization for or against crime. Hochstetler and his colleagues provide a test of differential association theory as they focus on explaining differences and similarities in solo and group offending by juveniles.

Anomie theory, or strain theory, was initially advanced by Robert Merton in the late 1930s. Based, as was social disorganization theory, on Durkheimian conceptions of normative disruption, Merton argued that crime, and deviance more broadly, is a consequence of a disjuncture between the legitimate goals of a society and conventional means for achieving those goals. Sang and Pridemore's article not only is an example of contemporary strain theory because of its focus on poverty as a cause of homicide, but it also introduces students to an evolved version of the theory: "institutional anomie theory."

These three theories (social disorganization, differential association, anomie) dominated criminological thought into the 1960s. Criminologists were largely in camps that favored one over the other—although to be sure, a number of criminologists tried to integrate aspects of these competing explanations. After many years of dominance, they fell out of favor. As the three contemporary pieces demonstrate, however, recent research has produced a resurgence of their basic ideas. Modern criminologists have taken the good ideas in those pioneering theories and, mindful of the weaknesses identified by critics, are using them to improve our understanding of crime.

 For a data analysis exercise that accompanies the material in this section, go to www.sagepub.com/crimereadings3study.

JUVENILE DELINQUENCY AND URBAN AREAS

CLIFFORD R. SHAW

HENRY MCKAY

This [article] is concerned with the geographic distribution of delinquent or alleged delinquent boys and the manner in which rates of delinquent boys vary from area to area in the city of Chicago. Questions pertaining to the total number of such boys in the city at any given time or to the trend in the total number during a given period of years are extraneous to the primary purpose of this discussion. The data presented serve as a means of indicating the pattern of distribution of delinquency in the city and the extent to which this pattern has changed or remained constant during a period of forty years. As an initial step in this study, it is important to make clear the sense in which the term "delinquency" is used.

Definitions. The term "male juvenile delinquent," as used in the studies reported in this [article], refers to a boy under 17 years of age who is brought before the juvenile court, or other courts having jurisdiction, on a delinquency petition, or whose case is disposed of by an officer of the law without a court appearance. "Alleged delinquent" is the more accurate term, since it sometimes happens that charges are not sustained. Legally, a boy is not a delinquent until he is officially known to have violated some provision of the law as currently interpreted. Only in terms of this official definition can the data here presented be considered as an enumeration of male juvenile delinquents.

Several different types of series will be analyzed in the following pages—school truants, alleged delinquents as above defined, and repeated offenders or recidivists—representing in various degrees of inclusiveness boys who have been dealt with either by the juvenile police officers or by the court. Although these are official cases only, it is assumed that their utility in differentiating areas extends beyond the limits of the legal definition. Many boys commit serious offenses yet are not apprehended. In recent years, there has been a tendency to extend the term "delinquent" to include all boys engaging in the type of activities which, if known, would warrant action by official agencies. The White House Conference of 1930 adopted as its definition of delinquency: "Any such juvenile misconduct that might be dealt with under the law." In the present [article], the term "delinquent" will be restricted to those boys dealt with officially, while those defined as delinquent according to the more inclusive use of the term will be referred to as boys engaging in "officially proscribed activity." The data presented here, therefore, may be considered as a sample or index, but not as a complete enumeration, of the total number of boys engaging in officially proscribed activity in any given area.

The total amount of officially proscribed activity in a community, recorded and unrecorded, and the number of children involved are, of course, difficult to estimate and practically impossible to measure exactly at the present time. This fact underscores the need for a workable index—data which are available and which are known, or believed, to vary in close association with the series of events inaccessible to direct measurement. Such an index may be also a sample or incomplete enumeration of the whole, as are the data of this [article]. Where two or more series of official delinquents exhibit close geographical association and covariance, even though separated in time by 10, 20, or 30 years and regardless of changes in nativity or nationality composition of the population, it seems reasonable to consider any one of them as a probable index of the more inclusive universe—the total number of boys within the area engaging in officially proscribed activity.

It is not possible to test conclusively the validity of any of the indexes of proscribed activity presented in this [article], since there is no satisfactory measure of such activity or complete enumeration of those who engage in it. Experience in various Chicago communities, however, furnishes a basis for confidence that the official cases do constitute an adequate and useful indication of the relative numbers of boys engaging in similar activity in various types of urban areas.

It is necessary, finally, to distinguish "officially proscribed activity," as above defined, from the still broader category of "problem behavior," including mischief, aggression, and personality problems of the type which often bring about a child's referral to a behavior clinic or other agency. The authors do not feel that rates of delinquents based on official cases can be used as indexes of this type of behavior. It is entirely probable that, in spite of overlapping, the distribution of these problem cases is quite different from the distribution of boys who are officially delinquent or who engage in activity similar to that engaged in by official delinquents.

The present series of data, then, are offered as fairly accurate measures of the relative numbers of delinquents living in contrasted types of areas in the cities studied, and also as probable indexes of the total number of boys engaging in officially proscribed activity within these communities.

Series Studied. Traditionally, police arrests, court appearances, and convictions have been used to indicate the amount of adult crime. In the present study of the distribution of juvenile delinquents throughout the city, it was possible to secure variations of each of these types of data, but since conviction is not a juvenile court concept, commitments were substituted. The data fall into three groups: (1) series of alleged delinquents brought before the juvenile court on a delinquency petition; (2) series of delinquents committed by the juvenile court to correctional institutions; and (3) series of alleged delinquents dealt with by police probation officers with or without court appearance.

Probably anyone of these series would serve to establish the facts of distribution and variation in rates of official delinquents because in no one of them are any apparent selective factors operating which would seriously distort this geographic distribution. Yet there are many advantages in using all three. In the first place, the three types of series will present the facts more adequately than would any one type alone, since the whole range of cases, from arrests through commitments, will be represented. Second, findings based upon the three will be more conclusive and convincing than those based upon a single index, provided, of course, that the findings are uniform and consistent. Finally, comparison of the findings of the police and commitment series with the findings of the juvenile court series will serve to check the validity of the latter as an index of the total number of boys engaging in officially proscribed activity.

In this Chicago study, the distribution of delinquents, based upon juvenile court cases and commitment, will be presented for periods roughly centered about 1900, 1920, and 1930; and series of police cases, for three different years around 1930. These studies of the distribution of delinquents at different periods of time afford a basis for comparisons and for analysis of long-time trends and processes that could not be made for a single period. Likewise, it will be possible to compare the rates of delinquents in the same areas at different periods, not only in those areas which show significant variations either in physical and economic characteristics or in the nationality and racial composition of the population but also in those where there has been comparatively little change. This comparison furnishes a basis for an evaluation of the relative importance of physical and economic conditions, as contrasted with race and nationality, in relation to delinquency.

In Chicago, all boys who are arrested or who come to the attention of the police for investigation are dealt with by juvenile police probation officers, one of whom is assigned to each police district in the city. The individuals dealt with by these officers comprise our police series and include, as would be expected, some boys guilty of serious offenses, many guilty of lesser offenses, and also those held only for investigation, for identification, or for some other reason. On the average, about 85 percent of the cases dealt with by the police probation officer are disposed of by him without court action, while the remaining 15 percent are taken before the juvenile court on petitions alleging delinquency. The fact that such a large percentage of the boys are dealt with without court action does not mean that these boys are not delinquent. It suggests, rather, that the police probation officer, who has broad discretionary power, has decided that they should not be taken into court, either because they are too young, because they are first offenders, because the offenses with which they are charged do not appear to him to be serious, or for other reasons best known to himself. The 15 percent taken to court are, presumably, either those who have committed the most serious offenses, who are recidivists, or who for any other reason are assumed by the officers to present serious problems.

The juvenile court, in turn, ultimately commits to training or correctional schools somewhere between one-quarter and one-half of the boys against whom delinquency petitions have been filed. These boys are, for the most part, guilty of serious delinquencies, and most of them are recidivists. The numerical relationship between this group, the boys who are brought before the juvenile court, and the boys dealt with by the police probation officers over a period of years is roughly expressed by the ratio 30:5:2. This means that, of every 30 boys dealt with by the police probation officers, 5 are taken to court on delinquency petition and 2 are ultimately committed by the court to correctional institutions.

Because of Chicago's size, a rather large sample of cases is needed. Just what the minimum could be is not known, but from experience it seems that series including several thousand individuals

show the facts of distribution most clearly. The number of individuals dealt with by the police probation officers in a single year approaches 10,000; therefore, a year was taken as a unit in the police series. It is evident, however, that the number of boys taken to court in a year would not furnish an adequate sample. Accordingly, the three juvenile court series were based on the boys brought to court on delinquency petition during a 7-year period. Similarly, the commitment series cover 7-year periods. Logically, the latter should extend over a longer period than the juvenile court series, since fewer boys are included. In this study, however, the same periods were used for both, with the result that the commitment series contain fewer cases than either the juvenile court or the police series.

In the calculation of rates of delinquents, the basic assumption as to population is the same in a series extending over several years as in a series for a single year. The population for any given area, although stated in the census volumes as the population for a year, is actually the population as of the census date only. Thus, the 1930 population is the population as of April 1, 1930, the only day on which the exact population of an area is known, and the only day, therefore, for which exact rates of delinquents might be calculated. Since it is impossible to calculate number of delinquents for this one day, an assumption must be made as to the average population in a given period. If the population is changing very little, it can be assumed that at any other day, month, year, or period of years it will be about the same as on the day of enumeration. For a changing population, adjustments can be made if the rate of increase or decrease is known.

Since the same assumptions as to the constancy of population are made for a month, a year, or a period of years, the period of time covered by a series of cases is not important, providing the date of the known population is near the midyear of the series. The only advantage in a short period is that there is less probability of change in the rate of population growth or decline in local areas. On the other hand, there are advantages in having rates of delinquents for series covering a longer period of time. In this study, rates are calculated for series covering from 1 to 7 years; accordingly, the reader can make his own comparisons and draw his conclusions as to the advantages and disadvantages of each time interval.

A. The Distribution of Alleged Delinquents Brought Before the Juvenile Court of Cook County

1. The 1927–33 Juvenile Court Series

Series Studied. These 8,411 different alleged male delinquents were brought before the Juvenile Court of Cook County from Chicago on petitions alleging delinquency during the 7-year period between January 1, 1927 and December 31, 1933. They are all separate individuals, as duplications from year to year, as well as within the separate years, have been eliminated from the series.

Distribution of Delinquents. Map 1 shows the distribution by place of residence of the 8,411 different male delinquents. Each dot represents the home address of one delinquent boy; only one dot was used for each individual, regardless of the number of times he appeared in court from any area.

Upon inspection, Map 1 reveals some very interesting characteristics. It will be observed immediately that there are areas of marked concentration of delinquents, as compared with other areas where the dots are widely dispersed. These concentrations are most obvious immediately north and northwest of the Loop along the North Branch of the Chicago River, in the areas some distance south of the Loop along State Street, and in the areas immediately outside and extending westward from the northern part of the Loop. In addition to these major concentrations, lesser clusters of dots will be noted in several outlying areas, in the Back of the Yards and the South Chicago steel-mill districts.

This distribution of delinquents is closely related to the location of industrial and commercial areas and to the composition of the population. In the first place, as has already been noted, the areas of heaviest concentration are, in general, not far from the central business district, within or near the areas zoned for light industry or commerce. As one moves outward, away from these areas into the residential communities, the cases are more and more scattered until, near the periphery of the city, they are, in general, widely dispersed.

The concentrations of delinquents not adjacent to the central business district are, for the most part, near outlying heavy industrial areas, especially along the two branches of the Chicago River and in the Stock Yards and South Chicago districts. The alleged delinquents are concentrated mainly in areas characterized by decreasing population and low rentals, with high percentages of families on relief. Here, too, industrial workers predominate. The population in these neighborhoods was, during 1927–33, largely foreign born, with high proportions of recent arrivals, aliens, and migrants from the rural South.

As to national heritage, the area of concentration of delinquents on the Near North Side was, during the period covered, predominantly Italian; the lower Northwest Side, mainly Polish; the Near West Side, Italian and American Negro; and the Lower West Side, chiefly Czechoslovakian. Among the more outlying areas, the Humboldt Park population included Poles, Swedes, Italians, and Russian Jews; the Back of the Yards district was Polish and Lithuanian; while the predominant nationalities in South Chicago were Polish, Italian, Hungarian, Mexican, and Yugoslavian.

This scattering of delinquents among many national groups is characteristic of each of the three periods studied, although the disproportions in each nationality vary. The groups producing the most alleged delinquents are, in every instance, those most recently segregated into the areas of lower economic status, as a result of the ongoing processes of American city life.

In order to compare the number of delinquents by areas and to relate this number in each instance to the population of the same age and sex, the city was divided into 140 areas. Most of these are square miles, bounded on all four sides by the section lines of the government survey. In some instances, where much of the territory was occupied by industry or where, for other reasons, the population was sparse, it was necessary to combine several units, regardless of size, which will be referred to as "square-mile areas."

When the distribution of the 8,411 delinquents is analyzed in terms of these 140 square-mile areas, wide differences are evident. In each of 3 areas there are more than 300 delinquents, while 8 have more than 150 each. At the other extreme, there is 1 area from which only 3 delinquents were taken to court, 15 with fewer than 10, and 25 with fewer than 15 delinquents. Moreover, the actual difference in concentration is greater than these comparisons suggest, since many areas with large numbers of delinquents have less residential space and population than

MAP 1   Distribution of Male Juvenile Delinquents, Chicago, 1927–1933

those with fewer. The theoretical significance of these facts is at least twofold. First, they reveal the wide variation in distribution; second, they indicate, quite apart from density of population, the differential probability of a boy's having contact with other delinquent boys in the same area or of observing their activities.

Rates of Delinquents. Map 2 shows the rates of delinquents in each of the 140 square-mile areas. These rates represent the number of alleged delinquents taken to the juvenile court from each area during 1927–33, per hundred of the aged 10–16 male population in that area as of 1930. It should be borne in mind that the 7-year rate here presented is less than the sum of 7 yearly rates, since all duplications have been eliminated.

The range in this series is from 0.5 to 18.9. The median is 2.5 and the rate for the city as a whole, 4.2. Three of the 140 areas have rates above 17.0, and 14 below 1.0. Similarly, there are 12 areas where the rates are more than 10.0, and 50 where they are less than 2.5. This comparison brings out two fundamental facts, namely, that there are wide differences among areas and that the number of areas with low rates far exceeds the number where they are high. The areas with the highest rates are located directly south of the central business district, and the areas with the next highest rates north and west of the Loop. At the other extreme, low rates of delinquents will be noted in many of the outlying areas.

Most of the areas characterized by high rates of delinquents, as well as by a concentration of individual delinquents, are either in or adjacent to areas zoned for industry and commerce. This is true not only for areas close to the central business district but also for outlying areas, such as those near the Stock Yards, the South Chicago steel mills, and other industrial sections. On the other hand, the areas with low rates are, for the most part, those zoned for residential purposes.

Between the center of the city and the periphery the rates, on the whole, show a regular decrease. There are, of course, deviations from this general tendency. In some outlying sections there are areas of high rates, especially in the Stock Yards and Southwest manufacturing districts and adjacent to the South Chicago steel mills. On the other hand, not all areas close to the central business district have high rates. Area 60, for example, located just north of the Loop and including the

"Gold Coast," has a rate of 2.7; and Areas 37 and 45, not far to the north, have comparatively low rates. It may be noted, however, that the physical and social characteristics of these areas differ from those of the surrounding areas.

One apparent exception to the general tendency of the rates to decrease from the center of the city outward may be noted south of the central business district, between Areas 74 and 115. Here the highest rates are in the second, third, and fourth areas (81, 87, and 93). When rates were calculated separately for the Negro and white delinquents in these areas, however, it was found that both decreased uniformly, in contrast to the combined rate. The rates for white boys, calculated necessarily on small samples, followed with some irregularities the common radial pattern, ranging from 13.4 in Area 74, the highest rate, to 2.5 in Area 115. The corresponding range for Negro delinquents was from 21.2 in the first area south of the Loop to 6.0 in the seventh area. This drop is significant because it shows that the rates of delinquents for Negro boys, although somewhat higher than those for the whites, exhibit similarly wide variations among different communities.

It was for the purpose of reducing the fluctuations resulting from chance that square-mile areas were selected for the presentation of rates of delinquents, in place of the smaller census tracts into which the city of Chicago is divided. There are, however, some advantages in considering the rates of delinquents by census tracts or even by smaller units. In an area as large as a square mile there may be many different types of neighborhoods. On the other hand, it is difficult to ascertain whether the variations in rates in the smaller areas within a square mile represent actual differences which would be sustained by subsequent studies or whether they are purely chance variations.

In order to illustrate the variations for small units within square-mile areas, rates are presented for the census tracts combined in the construction of three areas. These variations are given in Table 1. The variations in Area 2, as shown in the Table, are proportionately great, but they are not significant, since the sample of delinquents on which they were based was very small.

Square-mile Area 51 is relatively homogeneous, since rates for the tracts within it do not vary widely from the rate for the area as a whole. The critical ratio for the most widely separated rates in this area is 1.66.

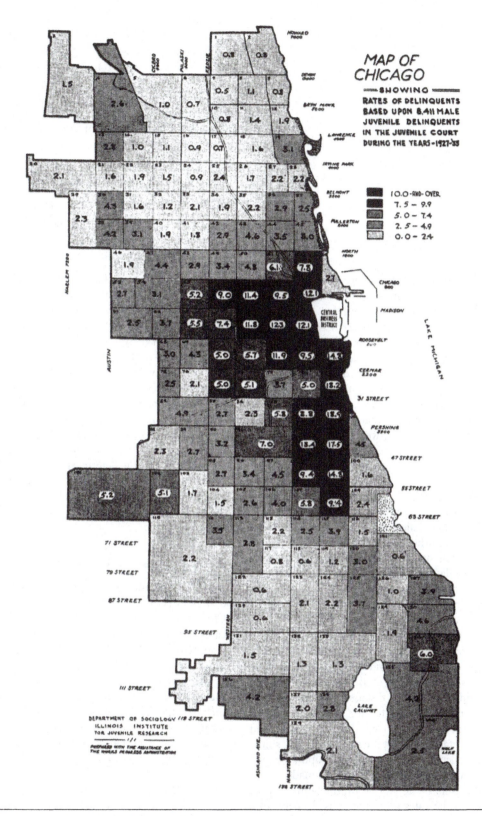

MAP 2   Rates of Male Juvenile Delinquents, Chicago, 1927–1933

TABLE 1   Rates of Delinquents for Census
Tracts Included in Areas 2, 51, and 97

Area 2	Area 51	Area 97
0.0	5.0	2.1
0.3	5.5	2.1
0.4	6.1	3.0
0.5	7.2	6.0
1.1	9.5	6.7
1.3		6.7
1.4		7.0

There is reason to believe that in Area 97, however, the rates in the north half are significantly higher than in the south half. This is supported by the fact that the critical ratio of the rate in one of the tracts in the north half and the rate in a tract in the south half is 3.42. The critical ratio of the rate of delinquents in the entire north half of this square mile (6.2) and the rate in the south half (2.6) is 4.34.

These data indicate that, in some instances at least, the differences between rates of delinquents within areas are statistically significant. For the study as a whole, the rates for small areas may be said to conform, in a general way, to those for the square-mile areas, but as indicated above, they exhibit some variation and irregularities, both because they reflect actual differences among local neighborhoods and because of the chance fluctuations due to small samples. The rates by square miles smooth out some of these variations, give a more general picture of the delinquency situation, and reveal more clearly the general trends and tendencies. Rates for successively larger areas smooth the picture more and more and present with increasing clarity the general trends. This is clearly indicated in the zone rates presented at the end of this section. It should be evident from this discussion that rates both of delinquents calculated for small areas and of those for large areas have their advantages and disadvantages and that the size of area best suited to the calculation of rates depends upon the purposes for which the calculations are made.

It should be noted that on the South Side of Chicago the rates of delinquents decrease to a low point about 7 or 8 miles from the central business district and that beyond this point, as in South Chicago and the Pullman industrial districts, they are noticeably higher. From the standpoint of city growth these South Chicago areas are independent centers, not related to the radial expansion of Chicago proper. They may be said, therefore, to confirm the radial pattern, being, in effect, secondary industrial and business centers—from each of which, in turn, the rates of delinquents tend to decrease as distance outward increases.

B. DISTRIBUTION OF MALE JUVENILE DELINQUENTS, CHICAGO, 1934–40

1. The 1934–40 Juvenile Court Series

The most recent data available comprise a series of 9,860 Chicago boys brought before the Juvenile Court of Cook County during the 7-year period 1934–40. Map 3 presents the distribution of these alleged delinquents by census tracts, each dot being placed within the tract in which the boy's home was located, but not at the exact address. Rates have not been computed, as the necessary population totals, by age groups, of the 1940 census were as yet unavailable.

Map 3 reveals a configuration quite similar to that for the 1927–33 series, except for increased concentration in the deteriorated areas south of the Loop and more dispersion into the outlying sections to the north and west, reflecting, no doubt, the movement of population away from the city's center.

2. The 1917–23 Juvenile Court Series

In the foregoing section, the distribution of delinquents and the variation in rates for Chicago were studied by analyzing a series of cases brought into the Juvenile Court of Cook County during the years 1927–33 in relation to the 1930 census data. In the present section, a similar series covering a period centered about the 1920 census will be presented. This series includes the 8,141 alleged male delinquents brought before the Juvenile Court of Cook County from Chicago on delinquency petition in the 7-year period 1917–23.

Series Studied and Types of Offenses. The 1917–23 juvenile court series was secured in the same manner and from the same sources as the 1927–33 series. With the exception of the

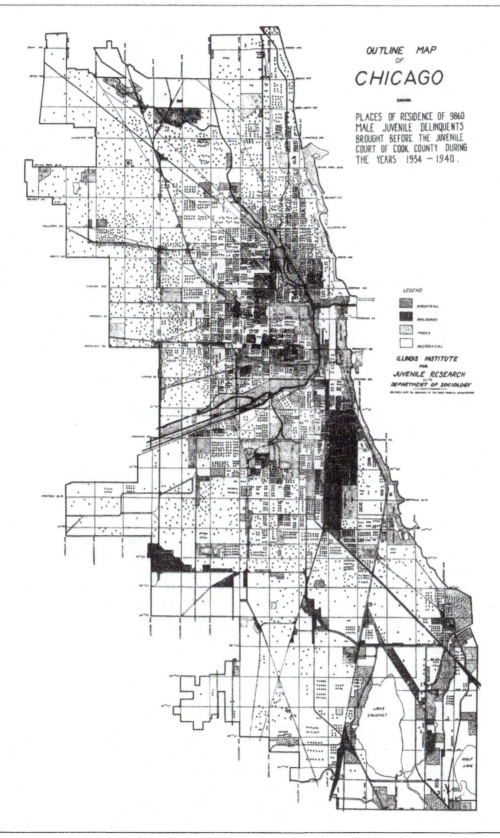

OUTLINE MAP
OF
CHICAGO

SHOWING

PLACES OF RESIDENCE OF 9860
MALE JUVENILE DELINQUENTS
BROUGHT BEFORE THE JUVENILE
COURT OF COOK COUNTY DURING
THE YEARS 1934 – 1940.

LEGEND

INDUSTRIAL
RAILROADS
PARKS
RESIDENTIAL

ILLINOIS INSTITUTE
FOR
JUVENILE RESEARCH
DEPARTMENT OF SOCIOLOGY

changes in the number of areas for which rates of delinquents were calculated, the data will be analyzed in the same way. Since no important change has taken place in the basic procedure of taking boys to the juvenile court, these boys also represent those charged by police probation officers with relatively serious offenses.

The nature of the offenses committed by these 8,141 individuals is indicated by the classification of the 12,029 petitions filed against them in the juvenile court. This classification shows that 29.4 percent of the alleged offenses were burglary, 12.2 percent larceny of automobiles, and 20.4 percent petty stealing. These offenses, together with a total of 7.5 percent for other stealing offenses, such as holdup, shoplifting, and purse-snatching, give a total of 69.5 percent classified as "all stealing." The remaining 30.5 percent included incorrigibility, 17.1 percent; disorderly conduct, 4.4 percent; and all sex offenses, 2.1 percent. There can be little doubt that these boys were, on the whole, involved in serious delinquency.

In this series, 16.7 percent of the boys were under 13 years of age, 12.7 percent were 13, and 18.3 percent were 14. The highest frequencies are in the 15- and 16-year age groups, these two comprising 51.9 percent of the total.

Distribution of Delinquents. Map 4 shows the distribution by place of residence of the 8,141 boys in this series. This map indicates that the distribution is very similar to that previously presented and that the areas of concentration coincide quite closely with similar areas on the 1927–33 map. The one distinctive difference is that the concentrations in the areas later occupied by Negroes are much less evident in the 1917–23 series. Otherwise, the areas of heavy concentration, as in the previous series, are adjacent to the central business and industrial districts and to certain outlying industrial centers, while the areas in which the dots are widely dispersed fall in the outlying sections of the city.

The distribution indicates that this series also presents very great geographical variations in the number of delinquents. One of the 113 square-mile areas contains 6 delinquents, while another contains 312. Four areas contain fewer than 10 delinquents each, while 5 contain more than 250 each. When the distribution is analyzed further, it is found that 11 areas contain fewer than 15 delinquents, and 18 fewer than 20

delinquents each. At the other extreme, a total of 7 areas contain more than 200 delinquents each, and 14 contain more than 150.

Rates of Delinquents. The area rates for the present series are given on Map 5. These represent the number of boys brought to the juvenile court from each of the 113 square-mile areas during the 7-year period, per 100 of the aged 10–16 male population in each of these areas as of 1920. The range of rates is from 0.8 to 19.4; the median for the series is 4.3, and the rate for the city, 5.4. Three areas have rates of less than 1.0, and a total of 19 areas less than 2.0. At the other extreme, 4 areas have rates of 15.0 or over, and 8 areas of 12.0 or over. In other words, 8 areas have rates of delinquents that are more than twelve times as great as those in 3 other areas, and more than six times as great as the rates in 19 other areas.

Map 5 reveals variations in the rates of delinquents quite similar to those of the previous series. The range between high- and low-rate areas is not so great, however, and the areas with high rates of delinquents extend only about 4 miles south from the Loop in the present series, as compared with 6 or 7 miles in 1927–33.

3. The 1900–06 Juvenile Court Series

Series Studied and Types of Offenses. Third in this sequence is the series of 8,056 male delinquents brought into the Juvenile Court of Cook County from Chicago during 1900–06 (the first 7 years of the juvenile court's existence). By comparing this series with that for 1927–33 it will be possible to determine the extent to which variations in the rates correspond and the extent to which changes in rates can be related to changes in the physical or social characteristics of the local areas.

The age distribution of the boys in the 1900–06 series indicates that, on the whole, they were a little younger than those in the more recent series. At that time, the upper age limit in the juvenile court was 15 instead of 16, and a somewhat larger number of boys were under 15 years of age (6.1 percent). The highest frequencies were in ages 13, 14, and 15. With regard to offenses, it seems probable that some boys were taken to court in these earlier years on charges for which no petitions would be filed by the police probation officers at the present time. This is indicated both by the fact that the

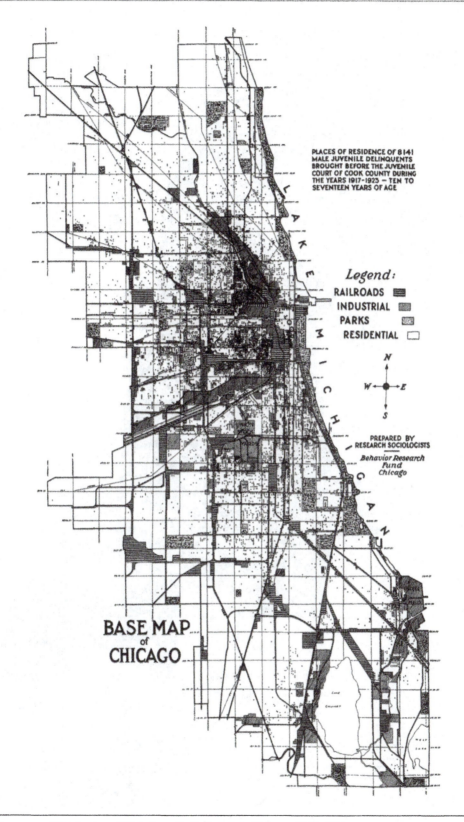

PLACES OF RESIDENCE OF 8141
MALE JUVENILE DELINQUENTS
BROUGHT BEFORE THE JUVENILE
COURT OF COOK COUNTY DURING
THE YEARS 1917-1923 — TEN TO
SEVENTEEN YEARS OF AGE

Legend:
RAILROADS
INDUSTRIAL
PARKS
RESIDENTIAL

PREPARED BY
RESEARCH SOCIOLOGISTS

Behavior Research
Fund
Chicago

BASE MAP
of
CHICAGO

Map 4   Distribution of Male Juvenile Delinquents, Chicago, 1917–1923

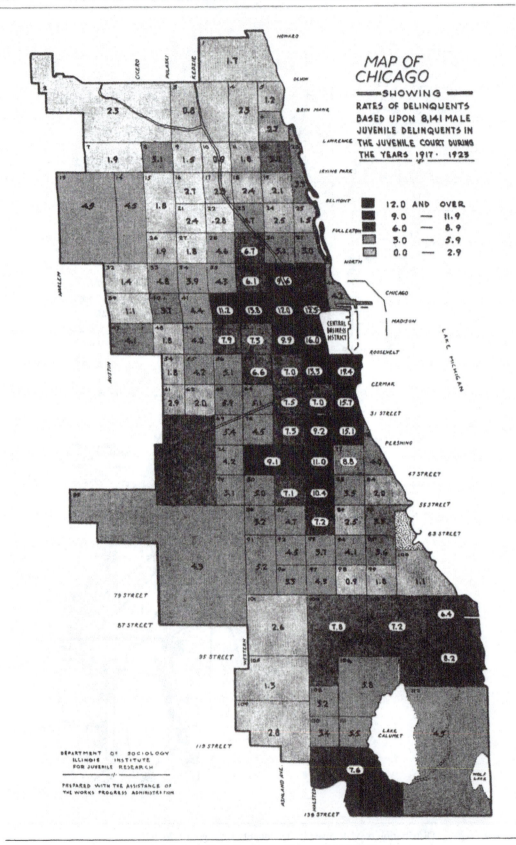

Map 5   Distribution of Male Juvenile Delinquents, Chicago, 1917–1923

number of cases in court was greater in proportion to the population than at present and by the fact that the classification of offenses indicated a somewhat higher proportion of less serious charges.

Distribution of Male Juvenile Delinquents, Chicago, 1900–06

Distribution of Delinquents. Map 6 shows the distribution by home address of the 8,056 boys brought to court in the 7-year period 1900–06. In this series, as in those previously discussed, it will be noted that a preponderance of the delinquent boys lived either in areas adjacent to the central business and industrial district or along the two forks of the Chicago River, Back of the Yards, or in South Chicago, with relatively few in other outlying areas.

While this series exhibits the same general configuration found in the others, there are two noticeable variations. First, the concentrations are somewhat more restricted and closer to the central business district and to the industrial centers than in the later series. This is to be expected, since many of the areas used for residential purposes in this early period have since been depopulated by expanding industry and commerce. Second, on this map there are relatively few delinquents in the areas east of State Street, south from the Loop. These areas, it will be remembered, contained many delinquents in the 1917–23 map and were also areas of heavy concentration in 1927–33.

Rates of Delinquents. Map 7 shows the rates of delinquents in the 106 square-mile areas used for this 1900–06 series. The population upon which these rates were calculated was secured by combining into 106 comparable areas the 1,200 enumeration districts of 1900 and the 431 census tracts of 1910 and computing the yearly increase or decrease of population in each. The population for the midyear of this series was then estimated from the aged 10–15 male population in 1910. The areas for which rates are presented are practically the same as those used in the 1917–23 juvenile court series, except that in 7 instances it was necessary to construct combinations of the 113 areas in order to secure a larger population in districts which were sparsely settled at that time.

The rates in this series range from 0.6 to 29.8. The median is 4.9 and the rate for the city as a whole 8.4. Four areas have rates of 20.0 and over; 7 have rates of 15.0 or over; and 12 have rate of 12.0 or over. At the other extreme, 3 areas have rates of less than 1.0, and 12 of less than 2.0.

Rates of Male Juvenile Delinquents, Chicago, 1900–06. Map 7 indicates that the variation in rates of delinquents is quite similar to the variations presented previously. The 4 areas with highest rates are all immediately adjacent to the Loop, and other high-rate areas are in the Stock Yards district and in South Chicago. The areas with low rates, on the other hand, are located, for the most part, near the city's periphery. As compared to rate maps for subsequent series, it can be seen that the areas with very high rates are somewhat more closely concentrated around the central business district. This is especially noticeable south from the Loop and east of State Street, where, after the first 2 miles, the rates of delinquents are below the average for the city as a whole.

4. Comparisons Among Juvenile Court Series, 1927–33, 1917–23, and 1900–06

Three methods will be employed to determine the extent to which the variations in rates of delinquents in the several time series correspond: (1) comparisons by zones, (2) area comparisons and correlations, and (3) extent of concentration.

Rates by Zones. Rates of delinquents were calculated for each of 5 zones drawn at 2-mile intervals, with a focal point in the heart of the central business district. These rates were computed on the basis of the number of delinquents and the total aged 10–16 male population in each zone.

It should be borne in mind that zone rates of delinquents are presented chiefly because of their theoretical value. They show the variations in rates more conceptually and idealistically than do the rates for smaller units. The number of zones used for this purpose is not important, as it is not assumed that there are actual zones in the city or sharp dividing lines between those presented. It is assumed, rather, that a more or less continuous variation exists between the rates of delinquents in the areas close to the center of the city and those outlying and that any arbitrary number of zones will exhibit this difference satisfactorily.

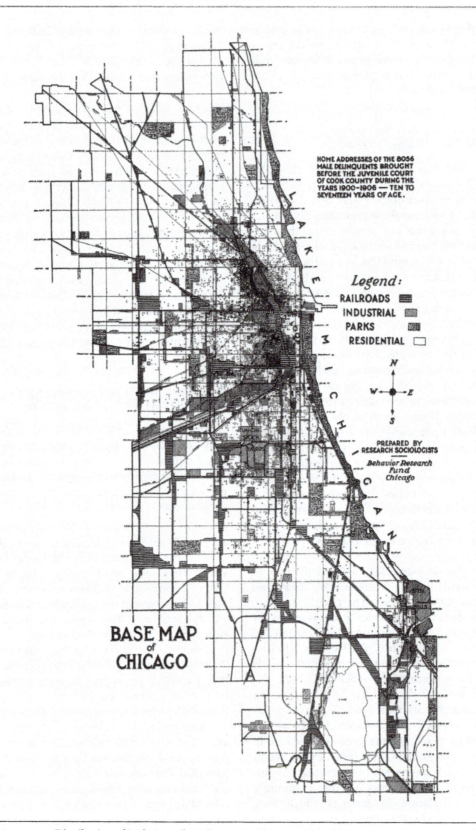

HOME ADDRESSES OF THE 8056
MALE DELINQUENTS BROUGHT
BEFORE THE JUVENILE COURT
OF COOK COUNTY DURING THE
YEARS 1900-1906 — TEN TO
SEVENTEEN YEARS OF AGE.

Legend:
RAILROADS
INDUSTRIAL
PARKS
RESIDENTIAL

N
W — *E*
S

PREPARED BY
RESEARCH SOCIOLOGISTS
*Behavior Research
Fund
Chicago*

BASE MAP
of
CHICAGO

MAP 6   Distribution of Male Juvenile Delinquents, Chicago, 1900–1906

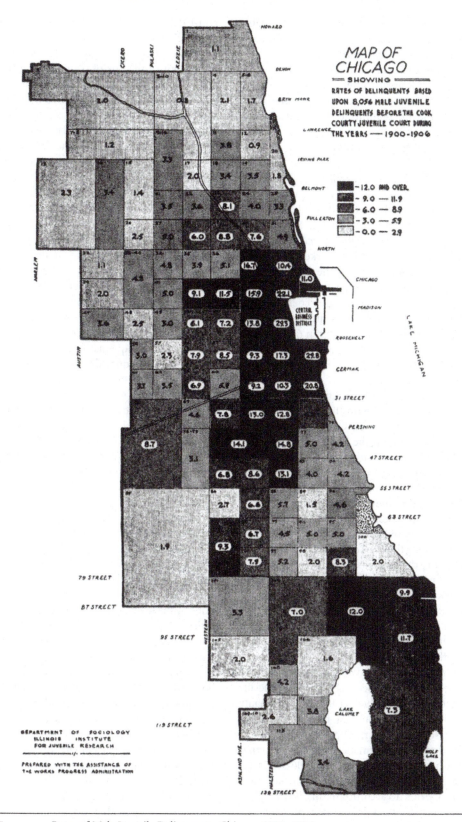

MAP OF
CHICAGO
═══ SHOWING ═══
RATES OF DELINQUENTS BASED
UPON 8,056 MALE JUVENILE
DELINQUENTS BEFORE THE COOK
COUNTY JUVENILE COURT DURING
THE YEARS —— 1900-1906

■ — 12.0 AND OVER.
▨ — 9.0 — 11.9
▦ — 6.0 — 8.9
▨ — 3.0 — 5.9
□ — 0.0 — 2.9

DEPARTMENT OF SOCIOLOGY
ILLINOIS INSTITUTE
FOR JUVENILE RESEARCH
─── // ───
PREPARED WITH THE ASSISTANCE OF
THE WORKS PROGRESS ADMINISTRATION

MAP 7   Rates of Male Juvenile Delinquents, Chicago, 1900–1906

There are wide differentials among the rates of delinquents for the square miles within each zone, just as there are among rates for census tracts within each square-mile area. These fluctuations do not greatly affect the general trend, however; in fact, it is because the zone rates eliminate the fluctuations evident for smaller areas and present the general tendencies that they are interesting and important.

Area Comparisons and Correlations. Of the 24 areas with the highest rates of delinquents in the 1927–33 series, 20 are among the 24 highest also in 1917–23. On the other hand, a few areas where significant changes took place in community characteristics show also marked changes in rates of delinquents. When the 1917–23 and 1927–33 rates are correlated by the 113 areas used for the earlier series, the coefficient is found to be .70 ± .02. This coefficient is greatly reduced by the fact that the rates in 6 areas have changed so much that the points representing them fell entirely outside the line of scatter on the correlation sheet.

Most of the areas of high rates in the 1900–06 series also correspond with those ranking highest in the two later series. Of the 12 highest in 1900–06, 9 were among the 12 highest in 1927–33. Three of the 5 highest-rate areas in the latter series, but not in the former, are the same 3 found among the high-rate areas as of 1917–23. Although some new areas appear among those with high rates in the more recent series, it is significant to note that all 12 of the areas of highest rates in the 1900–1906 series are among the areas of high rates in 1927–33. Because of these areas, the correspondence between the series is even more clearly seen when comparisons involving a larger number of areas are made. Of the 25 areas with the highest rates of delinquents in the 1900–06 series, 19 are included among the 25 highest in the 1917–23 series, and 18 among the 25 highest in 1927–33, even though these series are separated by approximately two and three decades, respectively. This is especially significant in view of the fact that the nationality composition of the population has changed completely in some of these neighborhoods.

A more general statement of the relationship is found when the rates in the 1900–06 series are correlated with those for each of the other juvenile court series. To accomplish this, it was necessary to calculate rates in the two later juvenile court series for the same 196 areas used in the early series. The coefficient secured for 1900–06

and 1917–23 was .85 ± .04, and that for 1900–06 and 1927–33 was .61 ± .04. In the latter case, the coefficient was reduced by the few values which fell far out of the line of scatter, indicating areas where considerable change had occurred.

These coefficients are remarkably high when it is recalled that the series are separated by about 20 and 30 years, respectively. They reveal that, in general, the areas of high rates of delinquents around 1900 were the high-rate areas also several decades later. This consistency reflects once more the operation of general processes of distribution and segregation in the life of the city.

Extent of Concentration. The distribution of delinquents in relation to male population 10–16 years of age for each of the three juvenile court series has been further analyzed by dividing the population into four equal parts on the basis of the magnitude of rates of delinquents, then calculating the percentage of the total number of delinquents and total city area for each population quartile, as shown in Table 2.

It is apparent that the quarter of the population living in the areas of highest rates occupied only 19.2 percent of the geographic area of the city in the 1927–33 series, 17.8 percent in 1917–23, and 13.1 percent in 1900–06. Yet in each instance this quarter of the population produced about one-half of the delinquents.

C. THE DISTRIBUTION OF COMMITTED DELINQUENTS

This section is concerned with the least inclusive enumeration of delinquent boys in Chicago, namely, those committed to correctional institutions by the Juvenile Court of Cook County. Three series will be presented: (1) the 1927–33 commitment series, (2) the 1917–23 commitment series, and (3) the 1900–06 commitment series.

As has been noted, roughly two-fifths of the boys taken to the juvenile court on delinquency petition are ultimately committed to correctional institutions. Since these series cover the same periods as the juvenile court delinquency series, it follows that they will contain only about two-fifths as many boys. On the other hand, these boys committed to institutions are the most serious delinquents known to the court. Most of them are recidivists, since few boys are committed on their first appearance, and some have served time previously in institutions for delinquents.

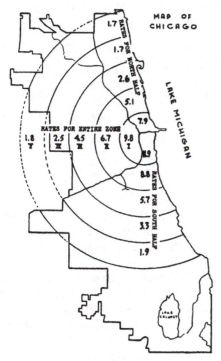

A. Zone rates of male juvenile delinquents, 1927–33 series

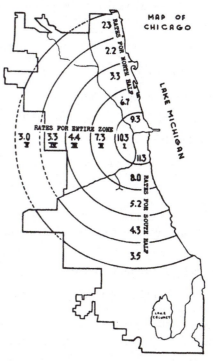

B. Zone rates of male juvenile delinquents, 1917–23 series

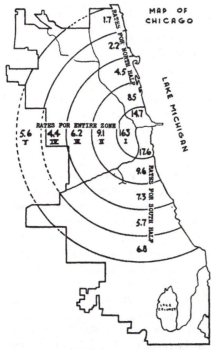

C. Zone rates of male juvenile delinquents, 1900–1906 series

CRITICAL RATIOS OF SELECTED ZONE RATES
Juvenile Court Series (Individuals)

Zones	Difference	Standard Error of the Difference	Critical Ratio
	A. 1927–33		
1 and 4.......	7.3	.301	24.2
1 and 5.......	8.0	.302	26.5
2 and 4.......	4.2	.142	29.6
2 and 5.......	4.9	.142	34.5
	B. 1917–23		
1 and 4.......	7.0	.293	23.9
1 and 5.......	7.3	.314	23.2
2 and 4.......	4.0	.162	24.7
2 and 5.......	4.3	.196	21.9
	C. 1900–1906		
1 and 4.......	11.9	.371	32.1
1 and 5.......	10.7	.467	22.9
2 and 4.......	4.7	.241	19.5
2 and 5.......	3.5	.371	9.4

FIGURE 1   Zone Maps for Three Juvenile Court Series

TABLE 2   Percentage of Delinquents and of City Area for Quartiles of Male Population Aged 10–16, When Areas Are Ranked by Rate of Delinquents: Three Juvenile Court Series

Quartiles of Population	Percentage of Delinquents			Percentage of City Areas		
	1927–33	1917–23	1900–06	1927–33	1917–23	1900–06
Upper one-fourth, in high-rate areas	54.3	46.1	47.3	19.2	17.8	13.1
Second one-fourth	23.9	27.3	26.6	19.4	24.8	12.1
Third one-fourth	14.6	17.7	17.4	32.3	27.1	21.7
Lower one-fourth, in low-rate areas	7.2	8.9	28.7	9.1	30.3	53.1

The graphic presentation of these commitment series will be limited to rate maps and zone maps.

1. The 1927–33 Commitment Series

This series includes 2,593 individuals committed by the juvenile court to correctional institutions during the 7-year period 1927–33. The majority of these boys had committed serious offenses and were recidivists. With respect to age they were, on the whole, somewhat above the average for boys appearing in the juvenile court.

Distribution. When distributed by home address, wide areal variations are found in the number of committed delinquents. There were 7 areas from which more than 60 boys were committed. At the other extreme, no delinquents were committed from 3 areas, and 1 boy only from each of 9 others, while not more than 2 boys were committed from each of 19 areas.

Rates. Map 8 shows the rate of committed delinquents in each of the 140 areas. These are 7-year rates, as were those in the corresponding juvenile court series, and calculated by the same method, on the basis of the same population. They represent in each area, therefore, the number of boys committed in a 7-year period per 100 of the aged 10–16 male population as of 1930. To distinguish them from the rates of juvenile court delinquents, these will be referred to as "rates of commitments" or "rates of committed delinquents."

Although the separate rates in this series are low because of the relatively small number of committed delinquents, the variation is even greater than in the juvenile court series: The range is from 0.0 to 9.2, the median is 0.7, and

the rate for the city as a whole is 1.3. Three areas have rates of 7.0 or over, and 6 of 5.0 or over. At the other extreme, 3 areas have rates of 0.0, and 12 of 0.1 or less.

Map 8 reveals the same general configuration that was found in the juvenile court series. The areas with highest commitment rates surround the Loop and extend directly south, with relatively high rates also in the Stock Yards areas, near the Southwest manufacturing district, and in South Chicago. Low-rate areas, on the other hand, are to be noted in the outlying districts.

2. The 1917–23 Commitment Series

The second series of committed delinquents includes the 2,639 Chicago boys committed to institutions by the Juvenile Court of Cook County during the 7-year period 1917–23. Since the boys in this series appeared in the 1917–23 juvenile court series and were committed, they include the most serious delinquents known to the court for this period.

Distribution. When these committed delinquents were tabulated on the basis of the 113 areas into which the city was divided for this series, it was found that there were 3 areas from each of which more than 50 boys had been committed, 6 with 1 commitment, and 14 with less than 5 commitments each.

Rates. When rates of committed delinquents were calculated, it was found that the range extended from 0.1 to 6.9. The median area rate for the series is 1.2 and the rate for the city 1.8. Four areas have rates of 5.0 or over, and 17 of 3.0 or more, while at the lower end of the range 14 areas have rates under 0.5, and 46 of less than 1.0.

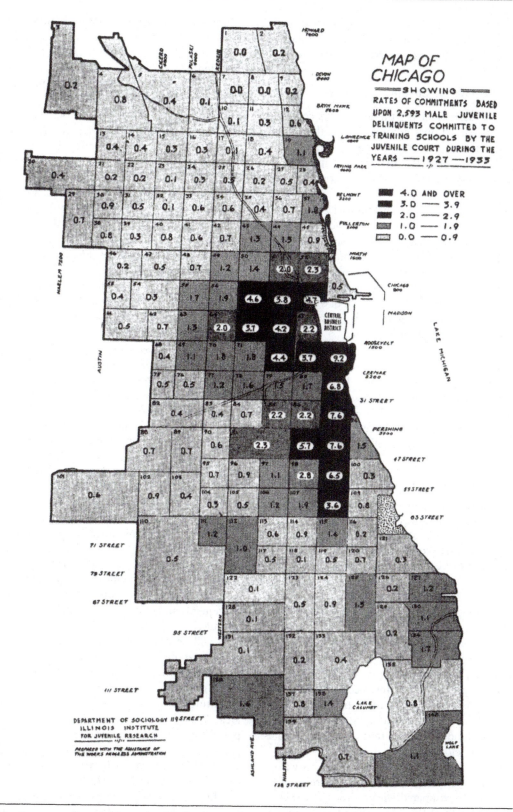

MAP 8   Rates of Committed Delinquents, Chicago, 1927–1933

Map 9 shows clearly that the geographic distribution and variation of rates in this series closely resemble the two series previously presented.

3. The 1900–06 Commitment Series

This series includes the 3,224 boys committed to correctional schools during the first 7 years of the existence of the juvenile court (1900–06), out of the total number included in the corresponding juvenile court series.

Distribution. When distributed by home address, wide variations were found among the 106 areas into which Chicago was divided for this early series. More than 150 boys were committed from each of 3 areas, and more than 1,900 from each of 8. At the other extreme, only 3 boys were committed from each of 8 areas, and 2 from each of 4; while 10 areas showed 1 commitment each, and 2 areas none.

Rates. The rates of committed delinquents range from 0.0 to 12.5, the median is 1.7, and the rate for the city as a whole 3.4. Six areas have rates under 0.5, and 26 under 1.0. Four areas, on the other hand, have rates above 9.0, and 10 above 6.0. Map 10 shows the configuration.

4. Comparisons Among Commitment Series

The extent to which the variations in rates of committed delinquents correspond for the three time series will be stated in terms of zone comparisons, area comparisons and correlations, and extent of concentration.

Rates by Zones. Since the rates in these three series of committed delinquents are based on smaller samples than were those for the juvenile court delinquency series, the variations are somewhat less regular. When zone rates are calculated, however, these irregularities are smoothed out and the general trends revealed. As Maps A, B, and C, Figure 2, show, these trends based on juvenile court commitments correspond closely to the trends based on rates of all individuals brought before the court.

In the 1927–33 series, the city rates vary from 3.4 in Zone I to 0.4 in Zone V, a decrease of 88 percent, as compared with a drop of nearly 75 percent in the 1917–23 series and of 70 percent for the 1900–06 data.

The zone rates for the north and south halves of the city also exhibit variations corresponding to those in the broader delinquency series. As indicated previously, the South Chicago industrial district constitutes a new locus from which, in turn, analysis might be made on a zonal basis.

Area Comparisons and Correlations. The same general configuration of rates is seen for 1900–06 as has been noted for the two other series. The most important difference is in the areas south from the Loop. In 1900–06, it will be seen, only the first 2 areas to the south are characterized by high rates; whereas in the 1917–23 series the rates are high in the first 4 areas, and in 1927–33 these areas of high rates extend southward 6 or 7 miles.

When the 1917–23 and 1927–33 series are compared, it is found that of the 25 areas with the highest rates in the former series, 20 are included among the 25 highest a decade later. As in the juvenile court delinquency series, 3 of the 5 areas among the highest in 1927–33, but not in the earlier series, are areas where marked changes in community characteristics have occurred.

When the rates of delinquents in the 113 areas of the 1927–23 series are correlated with the corresponding rates for 1927–33, $r = .74 \pm .03$. For 1927–33 and 1900–06, by 106 areas, the coefficient is $.66 + .04$; and for 1917–23 and 1900–06 it is $.81 \pm .02$.

Extent of Concentration. The concentration of committed delinquents in each series has been analyzed by ranking the areas by rate of committed delinquents, then dividing the aged 10–16 male population into four equal parts and computing the proportion of total committed delinquents and of city area for each population quartile.

It will be noted that more than half of the committed delinquents in each of the three series come from the quarter of the population living in areas of highest rates, although these constitute less than one-fifth of the total city area. At the other extreme, the quarter of the population in lowest-rate areas produced 7.3 percent of the committed delinquents in 1900–06, 7.2 percent in the 1917–23 series, and only 4.3 percent during 1927–33.

This concentration is again evident when the total number of committed boys in each series is divided into quartiles according to rate of

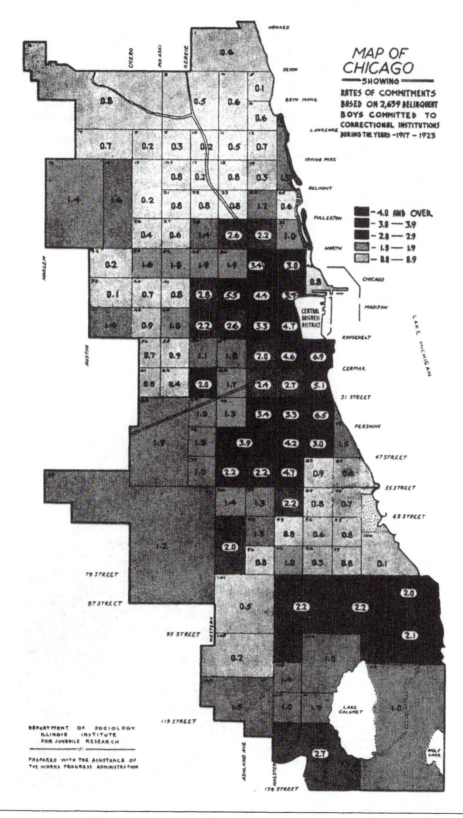

MAP OF
CHICAGO
SHOWING
RATES OF COMMITMENTS
BASED ON 2,659 DELINQUENT
BOYS COMMITTED TO
CORRECTIONAL INSTITUTIONS
DURING THE YEARS –1917 – 1923

— 4.0 AND OVER
— 3.0 — 3.9
— 2.0 — 2.9
— 1.0 — 1.9
— 0.0 — 0.9

DEPARTMENT OF SOCIOLOGY
ILLINOIS INSTITUTE
FOR JUVENILE RESEARCH

PREPARED WITH THE ASSISTANCE OF
THE WORKS PROGRESS ADMINISTRATION

MAP 9   Rates of Committed Delinquents, Chicago, 1917–1923

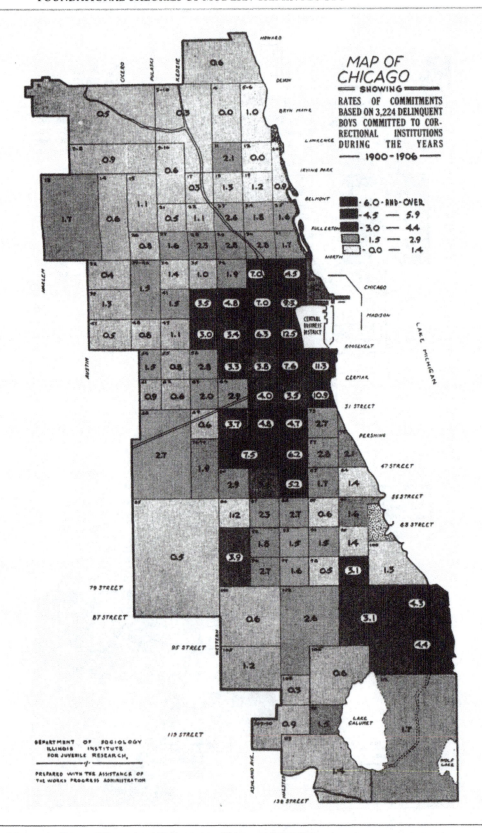

MAP 10   Rates of Committed Delinquents, Chicago, 1900–1906

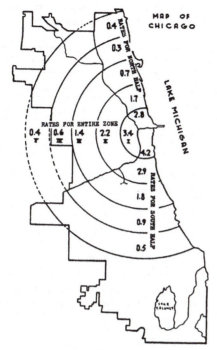

A. Zone rates of committed delinquents, 1927–33 series

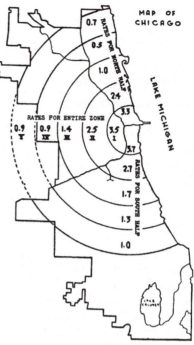

B. Zone rates of committed delinquents, 1917–23 series

C. Zone rates of committed delinquents,
1900–1906 series

CRITICAL RATIOS OF SELECTED ZONE RATES
Commitment Series

Zones	Difference	Standard Error of the Difference	Critical Ratio
A. 1927–33			
1 and 4	2.8	.182	15.4
1 and 5	3.0	.182	16.5
2 and 4	1.6	.080	20.0
2 and 5	1.8	.079	22.8
B. 1917–23			
1 and 4	2.6	.176	14.8
1 and 5	2.6	.186	14.0
2 and 4	1.6	.095	16.8
2 and 5	1.6	.113	14.2
C. 1900–1906			
1 and 4	5.4	.250	21.6
1 and 5	4.9	.306	16.0
2 and 4	2.0	.151	13.2
2 and 5	1.5	.233	6.4

FIGURE 2   Zone Maps for Three Series of Committed Delinquents

TABLE 3   Percentage of Male Population Aged 10–16 and of City Area for Quartiles of Committed Delinquents When Areas Are Ranked by Rate of Committed Delinquents: Three Commitment Series

Quartiles of Committed Delinquents	Percentage of Population			Percentage of City Area		
	1927–23	*1917–23*	*1900–06*	*1927–23*	*1917–23*	*1900–06*
Upper one-fourth, from high-rate areas	5.5	9.1	9.6	4.34	6.2	4.4
Second one-fourth	10.6	15.0	15.3	6.8	10.8	4.7
Third one-fourth	21.7	22.0	24.0	14.3	15.0	12.5
Lower one-fourth, from low-rate areas	62.2	53.9	51.1	74.6	68.0	78.4

committed delinquents and the corresponding percentages of population and of city area are computed (see Table 3).

It will be seen from Table 3 that the one-fourth of the committed boys living in high-rate areas represented less than 10 percent of the population and 7 percent of the city area, in each time series. On the other hand, the one-fourth in lowest-rate areas came from more than 51 percent of the population and 68 percent or over of the city area. Both Tables show the greatest concentration in the 1927–33 series.

D. THE DISTRIBUTION OF POLICE ARRESTS

The third, and most inclusive, basic enumeration of delinquents or alleged delinquents and index of the number of boys engaged in officially pro-scribed activity in Chicago includes all boys dealt with by the juvenile police probation officers, one of whom is assigned to each police station. Most of the boys charged with delinquencies are brought to the attention of these officers, who decide whether the boy is to be dismissed with a warning or taken into court. In considering the seriousness of the offenses charged, it should be borne in mind that in some court systems all the boys in these series would be taken to court, although in Chicago only about 15 percent have delinquency petitions filed against them.

Since no permanent official record is made of these police cases, it has not been possible to study their distribution over widely separated periods of time. The following series, however, will be presented: (1) the 1931 police series,

(2) the 1927 police series, and (3) the 1926 police series. These series will be analyzed in less detail than those preceding, as it is necessary only to determine the extent to which the findings agree.

1. The 1931 Police Series

This series includes the boys whose names and addresses appeared in the records of the police probation officers during 1931. They were, as a group, somewhat younger than the boys taken into court, about 30 percent being under 13 years. A rough classification of the offenses charged indicates that stealing; shoplift-ing; snatching pocketbooks; stealing auto-mobiles; breaking into stores, residences, or factories; and similar offenses accounted for approximately half the total. The remaining half of the boys were charged with a variety of offenses, including truancy from home, assault, malicious mischief, destruction of property, trespassing, manslaughter, and sex immorality.

Distribution. When these cases were plotted by home address, the resulting configuration was quite similar to that in the 1927–33 juvenile court series (see Map 1). Analysis on the basis of 140 square-mile areas shows that 2 areas contain over 300, and 13 areas over 200, boys each. At the other extreme, fewer than 20 boys appear in each of 18 areas.

Rates. Rates of police arrests were likewise calcu-lated by areas, on the basis of the 1930 aged 10–16 male population. These are 1-year rates and may be conveniently thought of as the percentage of all boys who were arrested during the year. The range of rates is from 0.5 to 19.4. The city rate is 5.4 and the median 4.0. The rate map for this series has been omitted because it closely resembles those previously presented.

Zone Rates. The variation in police cases from the center of the city outward is indicated by zone rates calculated for the same zones used in the other series. These are shown in Figure 3, A. Here, again, regular decreases in the rates are to be noted as distance from the Loop increases, for the two halves of the city considered separately and for both together. As in the other series, the South Side rates are considerably higher than those for corresponding zones on the North Side.

2. The 1927 Police Series

The second police series comprises the 8,951 boys who appeared in the records of the police probation officers during 1927. With respect to age and offense, these boys were not widely different from those in the 1931 series. Approximately 55 percent were charged with some form of stealing.

Distribution. The configuration resulting from the plotting of these cases on the map by home address is similar to that in the other series. Of the 113 square-mile areas, 15 contained fewer than 10 arrested boys, as compared with 12 which contained over 250 each.

Rates. A rate was calculated for each local area on the basis of the estimated aged 10–16 male population for 1927. The range of rates is from 0.0 to 21.8, the median being 3.4, and the city rate 4.9.

Zone Rates. As in the 1931 series, rates calculated by zones show a regular decrease, with one or two minor exceptions, from the central business district outward, for the two halves of the city separately and for both together.

3. The 1926 Police Series

The third police series includes the 9,243 individual Chicago boys whose names and addresses appeared in the records of the juvenile police probation officers during 1926. They correspond closely, as to age and type of offense, with the 1931 and 1927 series.

Distribution. With regard to distribution by home address, the configuration in this series is likewise similar to that of the previous series. Of the 113 local areas, 12 contain fewer than 10 arrested boys each, whereas 14 areas have more than 200 each.

Rates. Rates of police arrests were calculated by square-mile areas on the basis of the aged 10–16 population as estimated for 1926. The range of area rates is from 0.0 to 26.6, with a median of 3.4 and a city rate of 5.2. In each of 5 areas the rate is over 20.0, and in 5 additional areas it is between 15.0 and 20.0. At the other extreme, the rate is under 1.0 in 17 areas. In general, the distribution of high- and low-rate areas shows no noticeable variation from the series already presented.

Zone Rates. The decrease in rates of police arrests from the center of the city outward is indicated by Figure 3, C.

4. Recreation Survey Study

A computation of rates based on data furnished by the Chicago Recreation Survey, representing boys whose names appear in the juvenile court police records for 1935, revealed a distribution comparable both to the above police series and to the juvenile court series already analyzed. Zone rates are presented in Figure 3, D. Correlation of these data with the 1927–33 rates of delinquents yields an r of .84 ± .02. This evidence from an independent source constitutes an additional index of delinquent activity in Chicago and tends to strengthen the conclusions drawn.

5. Comparisons Among Police Series

Correlation. Nineteen of the 25 areas with highest rates in 1927 and 18 of the highest in 1926 are included among the first 25 in 1931. Correlation between the 1927 and 1931 series yields an r of .87 ± .01, and the corresponding correlation for 1926 and 1931 results in a coefficient of .83 ± .02. The correlation between the 1926 and 1927 series is much closer. The 12 areas of highest rates for these 2 years are the same, and the coefficient secured when the two series are correlated is .96 ± .005.

Extent of Concentration in Juvenile Police Arrests. The residential concentration of boys arrested

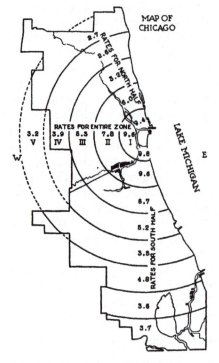

A. Zone rates of police arrests, 1931

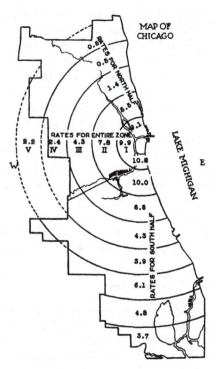

B. Zone rates of police arrests, 1927

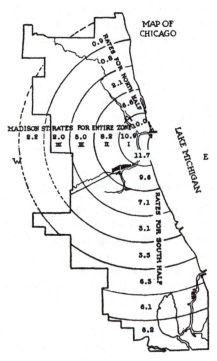

C. Zone rates of police arrests,
1926

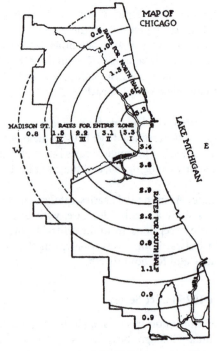

D. Zone rates of juvenile court police
records, 1935

FIGURE 3   Zone of Maps for Police Arrests Series

by the police can be readily seen when their distribution is analyzed in relation to that of the total aged 10–16 male population. As in the previous series, the square-mile areas were arranged in rank order on the basis of the rate of police arrests. The population was then divided into four equal parts and the percentage of police arrests and of total city area was calculated for each population quartile.

One-fourth of the aged 10–16 male population living in the areas of highest rates produced 49.0 percent of the delinquents in the 1931 series, 58.9 percent in 1927, and 59.8 percent in 1926; while the one-fourth living in areas of lowest rates produced only 9.1, 3.1, and 3.8 percent of the delinquents, respectively.

The absolute differences among percentages in these three series should not be taken as proof of a trend in the distribution of delinquents. Such variations might be due to changes in policy in some police districts, to the fact that the population base for the 1926 and 1927 series was estimated, or to a variety of other factors. The important point is that, in spite of minor variations, all three series present the same general features.

One-quarter of the delinquents from the highest rate areas represented only 9.6 percent of the population in the 1931 series, 7.1 percent in the 1927 series, and 7.0 percent in the 1926 series; while the one-quarter of the delinquents in the low rate areas came from 49.6, 61.6, and 63.2 percent of the population in the 1931, 1927, and 1926 series, respectively.

In each series, likewise, the upper one-fourth of the delinquents came from less than 7 percent of the total city area, while the lower one-fourth represented more than 60 percent of the city area.

On the basis of the above facts, several deductions as to the relative usefulness of the different types of series can be made. It is evident, first, that the findings in the three types are so similar that any one of them might be used as an index of the others. The juvenile court series, however, show somewhat less concentration and variation in rates than either the police or commitment series. They are less inclusive than the police series, yet not limited to the serious offenders comprising the committed group; and they presumably represent, therefore, a conservative sample of the boys engaging in officially proscribed activity throughout the city. It is the authors' conclusion that, where a single set of data must serve, juvenile court series may be used safely as an index of this broader universe.

QUESTIONS FOR DISCUSSION AND WRITING

1. What does an "inspection" of Map 1 (of the 1927–1933 series) reveal? Where are the alleged delinquents concentrated? Where are the groups "producing the most alleged delinquency" located?

2. What "characterized" the areas with high rates of delinquency? What is the "general tendency" of the rates?

3. How do the 25 areas in 1900–1906 compare with the highest rates in the other time periods?

Neighborhood Inequality, Collective Efficacy, and the Spatial Dynamics of Urban Violence

Jeffrey D. Morenoff

Robert J. Sampson

Stephen W. Raudenbush

Over the course of the past century, criminological research in the ecological tradition has continually discovered the concentration of interpersonal violence in certain neighborhoods, especially those characterized by poverty, the racial segregation of minority groups, and single-parent families. Still, fundamental questions remain about what it is that communities "supply" (or fail to supply) that may explain the link between these structural features of neighborhood environments and the rates of violent crime. The traditional or perhaps idyllic notion of local communities as "urban villages" characterized by dense networks of personal social ties continues to pervade many theoretical perspectives on neighborhood crime. Yet such ideal typical neighborhoods appear to bear little resemblance to contemporary cities where weak ties prevail over strong ties and social interaction among residents is characterized by increasing instrumentality.

Despite marshalling impressive evidence that neighborhoods matter even in the modern city, criminologists by and large continue to rely on the classic urban village metaphor to explain why. This [article] builds on recent criminological research to integrate key dimensions of neighborhood-level structure, process, and spatial embeddedness that may help to explain the puzzle of crime's ecological concentration. In particular, we incorporate local institutional processes related to voluntary associations and local organizations, along with extra-local processes related to the spatial dynamics of violent crime. We integrate these dimensions of the urban landscape with a theoretical framework highlighting the role of social control and cohesion—even if not rooted in strong personal ties—and neighborhood structural inequality.

SOCIAL DISORGANIZATION THEORY AND BEYOND

Our approach draws its motivation from an intellectual tradition that seeks to explain variation in rates of crime and violence. In their classic work, Shaw and McKay argued that low economic status, ethnic heterogeneity, and residential instability led to community disorganization, which in turn accounted for delinquent subcultures and ultimately high rates of delinquency. It was not until the 1970s and 1980s, however, that social disorganization was defined explicitly as the inability of a community structure to realize the common values of its residents and to maintain effective social controls.

More recently, the intellectual tradition of community-level research has been revitalized by the increasingly popular idea of "social capital." Social capital is typically conceptualized as embodied in the social ties among persons and positions. Putnam defines social capital as "features of social organization, such as networks, norms, and trust, that facilitate coordination and cooperation for mutual benefit." The sources of social capital stem not from the attributes of individuals but from the structure of social organization. Neighborhoods bereft of social capital (e.g., interlocking social networks) are less able to realize common values and maintain the informal social controls that foster safety.

The intuitive appeal of social capital notwithstanding, there are reasons to problematize the process by which strong social ties translate into low crime rates. First, in some neighborhood contexts, strong ties may impede efforts to establish social control. Wilson, for example, has argued that many poor neighborhoods where residents are tightly interconnected through network ties do not produce collective resources such as the social control of disorderly behavior. His research suggests that disadvantaged urban neighborhoods are places where dense webs of social ties among neighbors may impede social organization. In her study of a black middle-class community in Chicago, Patillo-McCoy also acknowledges the limits of tight-knit social bonds in facilitating social control. She argues that although dense local ties promote social integration, they also foster the growth of networks that impede efforts to rid the neighborhood of drug and gang-related crime.

A second reason that it is problematic to assume a simple connection between strong social ties and low crime rates is that in many urban communities, shared expectations for social control are maintained in the absence of thick ties among neighbors. Strong ties among neighbors

are no longer the norm in many urban communities because friends and social support networks are decreasingly organized in a parochial, local fashion. Moreover, as Granovetter argued in his seminal essay, "weak ties"—i.e., less intimate connections between people based on more infrequent social interaction—may be critical for establishing social resources, such as job referrals, because they integrate the community by bringing together otherwise disconnected subgroups. Bellair extended this logic to the study of community crime by demonstrating that weak ties among neighbors, as manifested by less frequent patterns of social interaction, are predictive of lower crime rates. Research on dense social ties thus reveals somewhat of a paradox for crime theory. Many urbanites interact with their neighbors on a limited basis and thus appear to generate very little social capital. Moreover, urbanites whose strong ties are tightly restricted geographically may actually produce an environment that discourages collective responses to local problems.

To address these changes in urban reality, Sampson et al. proposed a focus on mechanisms that facilitate social control without requiring strong ties or associations. Sampson et al. highlighted the combination of a working trust and shared willingness of residents to intervene in social control. This linkage of trust and cohesion with shared expectations for control was defined as neighborhood "collective efficacy." Just as self-efficacy is situated rather than global (one has self-efficacy relative to a particular task), a neighborhood's efficacy exists relative to specific tasks such as maintaining public order.

Viewed through this theoretical lens, collective efficacy is a task-specific construct that highlights shared expectations and mutual engagement by residents in local social control. Moving from a focus on private ties to social efficacy signifies an emphasis on shared beliefs in neighbors' conjoint capability for action to achieve an intended effect and, hence, an active sense of engagement on the part of residents.

Distinguishing between the resource potential represented by personal ties, on the one hand, and the shared expectations among neighbors for engagement in social control represented by collective efficacy, on the other, may help clarify the systemic model. In particular, social networks foster the conditions under which collective efficacy may flourish, but they are not sufficient for the exercise of control.

Thus, collective efficacy may be seen as a logical extension of systemically based social disorganization and social capital theory. The difference is mainly one of emphasis: Although we recognize the relevance of systemic networks for neighborhood social organization, we argue that collective capacity for social action, even if rooted in weak personal ties, may constitute the more proximate social mechanism for understanding between-neighborhood variation in crime rates.

RESEARCH STRATEGY AND NEW DIRECTIONS

In this [article], we strive to make both substantive and methodological contributions to neighborhood-level research on violence. We are thus interested in how neighborhoods fare as units of guardianship and collective efficacy. Applying this framework, we highlight two neglected dimensions of neighborhood context: (1) spatial dynamics arising from neighborhood interdependence, and (2) social-institutional processes.

Spatial Dynamics

We argue that neighborhoods are interdependent and characterized by a functional relationship between what happens at one point in space and what happens elsewhere. Spatial interdependence is theoretically motivated on three grounds. First, we expect it to arise as a result of the inexact correspondence between the neighborhood boundaries imposed by census geography and the ecological properties that shape social interaction. One of the biggest criticisms of neighborhood-level research to date concerns the artificiality of boundaries; for example, two families living across the street from one another may be arbitrarily assigned to live in different "neighborhoods" even though they share social ties. From the standpoint of systemic theory, it is important to account for the social and institutional ties that link residents of urban communities to other neighborhoods, particularly those that are more spatially proximate to their neighborhood.

Second, spatial dependence is implicated by the fact that homicide offenders are disproportionately involved in acts of violence near their homes. Moreover, to the extent that the risk of becoming a homicide offender is influenced by contextual factors such as concentrated poverty, concentrated affluence, and collective efficacy, spatial proximity to such conditions is also likely to influence the risk of homicide victimization in a focal neighborhood.

A third motivation for studying spatial dependence relates to the notion that interpersonal crimes such as homicide are based on social interaction and thus subject to diffusion processes. Acts of violence may instigate a sequence of events that leads to further violence in a spatially channeled way. For example, many homicides, not just gang-related, are retaliatory in nature. Thus, a homicide in one neighborhood may provide the spark that eventually leads to a retaliatory killing in a nearby neighborhood.

There is, then, reason to believe that spatial dependence arises from processes related to both diffusion and exposure, such that the characteristics of surrounding neighborhoods are, at least in theory, crucial to understanding violence in any given neighborhood. In this [article], we focus on the independent effect of spatial proximity on the likelihood of homicide, accounting for key structural and social characteristics of life within the boundaries of focal neighborhoods.

Informal and Institutional Processes

Our second major goal is to integrate the study of neighborhood mechanisms with regard to informal and institutional social processes. A growing number of studies have turned to original survey-based approaches to assess neighborhood-level social ties and associations.

Most neighborhood studies to date have focused on social ties and interaction to the exclusion of organizations. For example, Sampson et al.'s test of collective efficacy highlighted cohesion and mutual expectations among residents for control. But as noted earlier, communities can exhibit intense private ties (e.g., among friends, kin) and perhaps even shared expectations for control, yet still lack the institutional capacity to achieve social control. The institutional component of social capital is the resource stock of neighborhood and organizations and their linkages with other organizations. Similar to the idea of "bridging" social capital, Bursik and Grasmick also highlight the importance of public control, defined as the capacity of community organizations to obtain extra local resources (e.g., police protection, block grants, health services) that help sustain neighborhood stability and control. It may be that high levels of collective efficacy come about because of such controls, such as a strong institutional presence and intensity of voluntary associations. Or it may be that the presence of institutions directly accounts for lower rates of crime. In addition to incorporating the spatial dynamics of interpersonal violence, structural characteristics, and the systemic dimensions of collective efficacy and social ties, we therefore address this gap by simultaneously examining institutional density and the intensity of local voluntary associations as reported by residents.

DATA SOURCES

The data on neighborhood social processes stem from the Community Survey of the Project on Human Development in Chicago Neighborhoods (PHDCN). Chicago's 865 census tracts were combined to create 343 "Neighborhood Clusters" (NCs) composed of geographically contiguous and socially similar census tracts. Major geographic boundaries (e.g., railroad tracks, parks, freeways), knowledge of Chicago's local neighborhoods, and cluster analyses of census data were used to guide the construction of relatively homogeneous NCs with respect to distributions of racial-ethnic mix, SES, housing density, and family structure. The Community Survey (CS) of the PHDCN was conducted in 1995, when 8,782 Chicago residents representing all 343 NCs were personally interviewed in their homes.

To assess collective efficacy, we combined two related scales. The first is a five-item Likert-type scale of *shared expectations for social control*. Residents were asked about the likelihood that their neighbors could be counted on to take action if children were skipping school and hanging out on a street corner, children were spray-painting graffiti on a local building, children were showing disrespect to an adult, a fight broke out in front of their house, and the fire station closest to home was threatened with budget cuts. *Social cohesion/trust* was measured by asking respondents how strongly they agreed that "People around here are willing to help their neighbors"; "This is a close-knit neighborhood"; "People in this neighborhood can be trusted"; "People in this neighborhood generally

don't get along with each other" (reverse coded); and "People in this neighborhood do not share the same values" (reverse coded). Social cohesion and informal social control were combined into a summary measure of "collective efficacy."

In addition to the cohesion and control scales that define collective efficacy, our analysis takes into account institutional neighborhood processes and social networks. *Organizations* is an index of the number of survey-reported organizations and programs in the neighborhood—the presence of a community newspaper, block group or tenant association, crime prevention program, alcohol/drug treatment program, mental health center, or family health service. *Voluntary associations* taps the "social capital" involvement of residents in (1) local religious organizations; (2) neighborhood watch programs; (3) block group, tenant associations, or community council; (4) business or civic groups; (5) ethnic or nationality clubs; and (6) local political organizations. The measure of *social ties/networks* is based on the combined average of two measures capturing the number of friends and relatives that respondents reported living in the neighborhood.

Structural Characteristics

Based on our theoretical framework, we examine five neighborhood structural characteristics. *Concentrated disadvantage* represents economic disadvantage in racially segregated urban neighborhoods. It is defined by the percentage of families below the poverty line, percentage of families receiving public assistance, percentage of unemployed individuals in the civilian labor force, percentage of female-headed families with children, and percentage of residents who are black.

Focusing on the pernicious effects of concentrated disadvantage, while obviously important, may obscure the potential protective effects of affluent neighborhoods. The resources that affluent neighborhoods can mobilize are theoretically relevant to understanding the activation of social control, regardless of dense social ties and other elements of social capital that may be present. We thus extend our focus by introducing a measure that captures the concentration of both poverty and affluence. The index of concentration at the extremes ("ICE") is defined for a given neighborhood by the following formula: [(number of affluent families − number of poor families)/total number of families], where "affluent" is defined as families with income above $50,000 and "poor" is defined as families below the poverty line.

Other structural covariates include the relative presence of *adults per child* (ratio of adults 18+ to children under 18) and *population density* (number of persons per square kilometer). *Residential stability* is defined as the percentage of residents five years old and older who lived in the same house five years earlier, and the percentage of homes that are owner-occupied. The second scale captures areas of *concentrated Latino immigration*, defined by the percentage of Latino residents and percentage of persons foreign born.

Violence Measures

We analyze homicide as an indicator of neighborhood violence. Our principle data source comes from reports of homicide incidents to the Chicago Police Department. These data consist of aggregate homicide counts that have been geocoded to match the neighborhood cluster in which the events occurred. We use the homicide count data from two time periods, the years 1991 to 1993 and the years 1996 to 1998.

EXPLORATORY SPATIAL DATA ANALYSIS

We begin our analysis by examining the geographic distributions of homicide and collective efficacy across Chicago neighborhoods in an exploratory spatial data analysis. Consistent with much past research, homicide events are not randomly distributed with respect to geography. In fact, supplementary tabulations reveal that 70% of all homicides in Chicago between 1996 and 1998 occurred in only 32% of the neighborhood clusters. We thus examined the geographic correspondence between the distribution of neighborhood homicide rates and that of collective efficacy, a key social process from our theoretical perspective.

We draw two general conclusions. First, there is a high degree of overlap between the spatial distributions of collective efficacy and homicide. For example, 67 of the 93 neighborhoods that have spatial clustering of high levels of collective efficacy (72%) also experience statistically significant clustering of low homicide. Second, despite the strong association between the geographic distribution of collective efficacy and

homicide, there are many observations in which the two typologies are at variance with one another. For example, 14 of the 93 homicide cold spots (15%) appear in neighborhoods with low levels of collective efficacy that are surrounded by high levels. Moreover, 15 of 103 homicide hot spots (15%) are in neighborhoods that have high levels of collective efficacy but are surrounded by neighborhoods with low levels.

MULTIVARIATE ANALYSIS

We turn to a regression framework to investigate three substantive issues in the analysis of neighborhood homicide rates—the role of multiple social processes as neighborhood mechanisms, the spatial dynamics of homicide, and the endogeneity of collective efficacy.

We find a fairly robust set of results. Concentrated disadvantage, collective efficacy, and the ICE index are consistently related to homicide. These results obtain even after controlling for prior homicide rates. Strong spatial effects are also evident, which again remain after controlling for the strong stability in homicide risk over time.

Although the regression results affirm that collective efficacy in achieving social control is an important factor for understanding variation in neighborhood homicide rates, they are less sanguine about the role of social ties. The results show that there is no independent association between social ties and neighborhood homicide rates after controlling for collective efficacy. These findings offer insight on the social disorganization tradition of recent neighborhood research, much of which focuses on the role of social ties. To bring these findings into sharper relief and possible reconciliation, we constructed a social-process typology that classifies neighborhoods based on whether they fall above or below the median score on the indices of social ties and collective efficacy, yielding the following four categories: low ties—low efficacy; low ties—high efficacy; high ties—low efficacy; high ties—high efficacy.

We expect homicide rates to be lowest in neighborhoods that possess high levels of both social ties and collective efficacy. Indeed, 41 of the 93 homicide "cold" spots (44%) are located in areas that are high in both ties and efficacy. However, 31 of the cold spots (36%) are located in neighborhoods that are low in ties but high in collective efficacy. The traditional perspective on social disorganization predicts that homicide "hot" spots should be found predominantly in neighborhoods that are low in both ties and efficacy. Instead the findings show that hot spots are divided almost evenly between neighborhoods that are low in both ties and efficacy (40 out of 103) and those that are high in ties and low in efficacy (38 out of 103). Dense networks do not appear to be necessary or sufficient in explaining homicide. These findings do not necessarily contradict the systemic perspective, however. Integrating the collective efficacy and systemic model, we would suggest that social ties create the capacity for informal social control, but it is the act of exercising control that is related to crime rather than the existence of social networks per se.

Overall, these findings clarify a point that has been left ambiguous in much previous research on the systemic model: Social ties and institutional processes appear to operate indirectly on homicide rates by fostering collective efficacy.

CONCLUSION AND IMPLICATIONS

Our results suggest that spatial embeddedness, internal structural characteristics, and social organizational processes are each important for understanding neighborhood-level variations in rates of violence. In particular, spatial proximity to violence, collective efficacy, and alternative measures of neighborhood inequality—indices of concentrated disadvantage and concentrated extremes—emerged as the most consistent predictors of variations in homicide across a wide range of tests and empirical specifications. Interestingly, extreme inequality in resources—whether measured by "underclass" disadvantage or the concentration of income at both the upper and lower tails of the distribution (ICE)—exhibits unmediated effects on violence despite the control for prior homicide.

Against the backdrop of these patterns, we believe four points should be emphasized, each of which carries implications for future research. First, a great deal remains to be learned about the relationship between social ties and crime. Future research may better understand the indirect relationship between social ties and crime by investigating the conditions under which strong social ties foster trust and social control.

The second major theme of our analysis is that homicide is a spatially dependent process, and that our estimates of spatial effects are relatively large in magnitude. Indeed, the spatial effects were larger than the standard structural covariates and an array of neighborhood social processes. The tendency of past research has been to focus on internal neighborhood factors, but they are clearly not enough to understand homicide. Local actions and population composition make a difference, to be sure, but they are severely constrained by the spatial context of adjacent neighborhoods.

A third theme that emerges is the potential importance of further refining our understanding of "structural covariates" that have traditionally been linked to the poverty paradigm. Concentrated poverty is without any doubt a risk factor for the concentration of homicide. But at the other end of the distribution, the 1980s and 1990s have seen the quiet but increasing separation of educated and affluent residents from the middle class. This "upper" inequality or stratification of place has resulted in an increasing concentration of affluence, which in turn has yielded important consequences for the distribution of homicide. Our analysis introduced a new measure tapping such inequality of affluence relative to poverty, with results suggesting that it does matter for the explanation of violence.

Fourth, one of our goals was to integrate the institutional and informal aspects of social process, following recent developments in systemic social disorganization, social capital, and collective efficacy theory. Somewhat to our surprise, however, the set of institutional processes was not that strong in predicting homicide. Organizations and voluntary associations turned out to be relatively unimportant, suggesting that perhaps criminological theory has overstated the benefits to be derived from local forms of institutional organization.

SOURCE: From *Criminology*, Vol. 39, No. 3, 2001: 517–558, edited. Reprinted by permission of the American Society of Criminology.

QUESTIONS FOR DISCUSSION AND WRITING

1. What happened to the definition of social disorganization? What happened more recently?

2. What is collective efficacy? Are social networks alone sufficient for the exercise of social control?

3. What do the results suggest?

A THEORY OF CRIME

Differential Association

EDWIN H. SUTHERLAND

TWO TYPES OF EXPLANATIONS OF CRIMINAL BEHAVIOR

Scientific explanations of criminal behavior may be stated either in terms of the processes which are operating at the moment of the occurrence of crime or in terms of the processes operating in the earlier history of the criminal. In the first case, the explanation may be called "mechanistic," "situational," or "dynamic"; in the second, "historical" or "genetic." Both types of explanation are desirable. The mechanistic type of explanation has been favored by physical and biological scientists, and it probably could be the more efficient type of explanation of criminal behavior. However, criminological explanations of the mechanistic type have thus far been notably unsuccessful, perhaps largely because they have been formulated in connection with the attempt to isolate personal and social pathologies among criminals. Work from this point of view has, at least, resulted in the conclusion that the immediate determinants of criminal behavior lie in the person-situation complex.

The objective situation is important to criminality largely to the extent that it provides an opportunity for a criminal act. A thief may steal from a fruit stand when the owner is not in sight but refrain when the owner is in sight; a bank burglar may attack a bank which is poorly protected but refrain from attacking a bank protected by watchmen and burglar alarms. A corporation which manufactures automobiles seldom or never violates the Pure Food and Drug Law, but a meat-packing corporation might violate this law with great frequency. But in another sense, a psychological or sociological sense, the situation is not exclusive of the person, for the situation which is important is the situation as defined by the person who is involved. That is, some persons define a situation in which a fruit stand owner is out of sight as a "crime-committing" situation, while others do not so define it. Furthermore, the events in the person-situation complex at the time a crime occurs cannot be separated from the prior life experiences of the criminal. This means that the situation is defined by the person in terms of the inclinations and abilities which the person has acquired up to date. For example, while a person could define a situation in such a manner that criminal behavior would be the inevitable result, his past experiences would, for the most part, determine the way in which he defined the situation. An explanation of criminal behavior made in terms of these past experiences is a historical or genetic explanation.

The following paragraphs state such a genetic theory of criminal behavior on the assumption that a criminal act occurs when a situation appropriate for it, as defined by the person, is present. The theory should be regarded as tentative, and it should be tested by all other factual information and theories which are applicable.

GENETIC EXPLANATION OF CRIMINAL BEHAVIOR

The following statement refers to the process by which a particular person comes to engage in criminal behavior:

1. Criminal behavior is learned. Negatively, this means that criminal behavior is not inherited, as such; also, the person who is not already trained in crime does not invent criminal behavior, just as a person does not make mechanical inventions unless he has had training in mechanics.

2. Criminal behavior is learned in interaction with other persons in a process of communication. This communication is verbal in many respects but includes also "the communication of gestures."

3. The principal part of the learning of criminal behavior occurs within intimate personal groups. Negatively, this means that the impersonal agencies of communication, such as movies and newspapers, play a relatively unimportant part in the genesis of criminal behavior.

4. When criminal behavior is learned, the learning includes (a) techniques of committing the crime, which are sometimes very complicated, sometimes very simple; and (b) the specific direction of motives, drives, rationalizations, and attitudes.

5. The specific direction of motives and drives is learned from definitions of the legal codes as favorable or unfavorable. In some societies an individual is surrounded by persons who invariably define the legal codes as rules to be observed, while in others he is surrounded by persons whose definitions are favorable to the violation of the legal codes. In our American society, these definitions are almost always mixed, with the consequence that we have culture conflict in relation to the legal codes.

6. A person becomes delinquent because of an excess of definitions favorable to violation of law over definitions unfavorable to violation of law. This is the principle of differential association. It refers to both criminal and anticriminal associations and has to do with counteracting forces. When persons become criminal, they do so because of contacts with criminal patterns and also because of isolation from anticriminal patterns. Any person inevitably assimilates the surrounding culture unless other patterns are in conflict; a Southerner does not pronounce "r" because other Southerners do not pronounce "r." Negatively, this proposition of differential association means that associations which are neutral so far as crime is concerned have little or no effect on the genesis of criminal behavior. Much of the experience of a person is neutral in this sense, for example, learning to brush one's teeth. This behavior has no negative or positive effect on criminal behavior except as it may be related to associations which are concerned with the legal codes. This neutral behavior is important especially as an occupier of the time of a child so that he is not in contact with criminal behavior during the time he is so engaged in the neutral behavior.

7. Differential associations may vary in frequency, duration, priority, and intensity. This means that associations with criminal behavior and also associations with anticriminal behavior vary in those respects. "Frequency" and "duration" as modalities of associations are obvious and need no explanation. "Priority" is assumed to be important in the sense that lawful behavior developed in early childhood may persist throughout life, and also that delinquent behavior developed in early childhood may persist throughout life. This tendency, however, has not been adequately demonstrated, and priority seems to be important principally through its selective influence. "Intensity" is not precisely defined, but it has to do with such things as the prestige of the source of a criminal or anticriminal pattern and with emotional reactions related to the associations. In a precise description of the criminal behavior of a person, these modalities would be stated in quantitative form and a mathematical ratio would be reached. A formula in this sense has not been developed, and the development of such a formula would be extremely difficult.

8. The process of learning criminal behavior by association with criminal and anticriminal patterns involves all of the mechanisms that are involved in any other learning. Negatively, this means that the learning of criminal behavior is not restricted to the process of imitation. A person who is seduced, for instance, learns criminal behavior by association, but this process would not ordinarily be described as imitation.

9. While criminal behavior is an expression of general needs and values, it is not explained by those general needs and values since noncriminal behavior is an expression of the same needs and values. Thieves generally steal in order to secure money, but likewise honest laborers work in order to secure money. The attempts by many scholars to explain criminal behavior by general drives and values, such as the happiness principle, striving for social status, the money motive, or frustration, have been and must continue to be futile since they explain lawful behavior as completely as they explain criminal behavior. They are similar to respiration, which is necessary for any behavior but which does not differentiate criminal from noncriminal behavior.

It is not necessary, at this level of explanation, to explain why a person has the associations which he has; this certainly involves a complex of many things. In an area where the delinquency rate is high, a boy who is sociable, gregarious, active, and athletic is very likely to come in contact with the other boys in the neighborhood, learn delinquent behavior from them, and become a gangster; in the same neighborhood the psychopathic boy who is isolated, introverted, and inert may remain at home, not become acquainted with the other boys in the neighborhood, and not become delinquent. In another situation, the sociable, athletic, aggressive boy may become a member of a Scout troop and not become involved in delinquent behavior. The person's associations are determined in a general context of social organization. A child is ordinarily reared in a family; the place of residence of the family is determined largely by family income; and the delinquency rate is, in many respects, related to rental value of the houses. Many other aspects of social organization affect the kinds of associations a person has.

The preceding explanation of criminal behavior purports to explain the criminal and noncriminal behavior of individual persons. As indicated earlier, it is possible to state sociological theories of criminal behavior which explain the criminality of a community, nation, or other group. The problem, when thus stated, is to account for variations in crime rates and involves a comparison of the crime rates of various groups or the crime rates of a particular group at different times. The explanation of a crime rate must be consistent with the explanation of the criminal behavior of the person, since the crime rate is a summary statement of the number of persons in the group who commit crimes and the frequency with which they commit crimes. One of the best explanations of crime rates from this point of view is that a high crime rate is due to "social disorganization." The term "social disorganization" is not entirely satisfactory and it seems preferable to substitute for it the term "differential social organization." The postulate on which this theory is based, regardless of the name, is that crime is rooted in the social organization and is an expression of that social organization. A group may be organized for criminal behavior or organized against criminal behavior. Most communities are organized both for criminal and anticriminal behavior, and in that sense the crime rate is an expression of the differential group organization. Differential group organization as an explanation of variations in crime rates is consistent with the differential association theory of processes by which persons become criminals.

•

SOURCE: From *Principles of Criminology*, 4th Edition, Chicago: J.B. Lippincott, 1947. Copyright © 1989 Elaine Cressey. Reprinted with permission.

QUESTIONS FOR DISCUSSION AND WRITING

1. What are the nine propositions of differential association theory?

2. Provide an example (using people you know or have knowledge of from the media) that supports differential association theory.

3. Who is more likely to become delinquent in a high-delinquency area: a sociable, gregarious, active boy or one who is a psychopathic loner?

DIFFERENTIAL ASSOCIATION IN GROUP AND SOLO OFFENDING

ANDY HOCHSTETLER

HEITH COPES

MATT DeLISI

INTRODUCTION

Criminologists devote as much attention to the relationship between having delinquent friends and delinquent behavior as they do any other topic. Since Sutherland formalized the notion that definitions favorable to crime are learned by interacting with people who find lawbreaking acceptable, hundreds of articles have been published on the topic. A search of Sociological Abstracts reveals that more than eighty articles indexed since 1990 include the words "differential association" in their abstract or title. Today, it is common for researchers to incorporate the influence or presence of deviant friends as variables in causal models even when they are not testing differential association. This is especially true with most attempts at theoretical integration. As a result, the central concepts from differential association appear in criminological studies of social support, self-control, identity, the life-course, and most other areas of research that rely on individual data. Additionally, friends' attitudes and behaviors are prominent parts of criminology's most esteemed and heavily referenced individual-level data sets. In sum, differential association is a pillar of criminological thought and research.

One reason for the widespread acceptance of differential association is that investigators consistently find that individuals are more likely to offend themselves if they associate *with peers* who condone and commit crime. Indeed, the significant relationship between peer associations and lawbreaking has been produced by an array of studies employing diverse methodologies and sources of data. These range from qualitative research based on semi-structured interviews with convicted felons to longitudinal survey research from the National Youth Survey (NYS) and Cambridge Study in Delinquent Development. It is clear that peer networks and associations are especially significant for understanding juvenile delinquency since "most young offenders have co-offenders in their offending and associate in other group activities with still other offenders."

There is, however, considerable controversy about why associating with criminal or delinquent friends affects offending. More than a decade ago, Warr and Stafford noted that "although the association between delinquent friends and delinquent behavior is well established, the mechanism by which delinquency is socially transmitted remains unclear." Unfortunately, the fog surrounding the understanding of the mechanism has cleared only slightly.

Investigators often find support for the central proposition of traditional differential association theory. In survey research, friends' attitudes typically correlate with attitudes held by respondents and directly or indirectly with respondent offending. There are at least three reasons to be skeptical of differential association theory in its most simple form, however. First, it appears that individuals' perceptions of their friends' behaviors influence offending more significantly than does their perception that friends have crime-condoning attitudes. The finding that friends' behaviors significantly influence offending does not contradict differential association theory, but it does undermine the claim that attitudes are transmitted during noncriminal acts and casual interaction with peers. Therefore, it does not appear that attitudinal transmission or transformation is the most important part of learning crime, as implied in the original statement of differential association theory.

A second perplexing finding is that recent peer associations are more significant predictors of offending than longstanding relationships. Recent interaction with delinquent peer groups has a significant effect on offending despite the fact that these groups are situational, transitory, and generally disorganized. This suggests that delinquent friends' influence does not alter individuals' thinking so much as it has temporary and immediate effects on their actions. The effects of differential association may not be the result of cumulative life-long learning from interaction with friends. Instead, immediate and current relationships with delinquent peers result in criminal behavior, whatever the mechanism explaining the influence of these recent relationships.

A third and related complication is that friends' attitudes and behaviors have direct effects on offending that are not mediated by one's own attitudes. This finding suggests that associating with deviant friends influences individual offending levels in ways that have nothing to do with the offender's attitudes about crime. There are several well-known theoretical interpretations of alternative paths from friends' behavior to crime that might explain this direct effect. For example, Cloward and Ohlin contend that peers are important primarily because they provide differential "performance structures," including values, skills, and social approval, that enable crime. In his symbolic interactionist theory, Matsueda suggests that delinquency is the outcome of "reflected appraisals" in which the self is situationally produced by delinquent peer influences. McCarthy suggests that, without criminal peers, some potential offenders may never be provided the means to commit a crime; by definition, these criminally disadvantaged persons will not have reliable criminal contacts or access to co-offenders needed to accomplish some offenses. Criminal situations and opportunities are easily available to those who, by accident or management, surround themselves with offenders.

Most investigators neglect the most parsimonious explanation for friends' influences. Those who associate with offenders are obviously more likely to find themselves in a criminal event. No learning or transference of attitudes from disreputable contacts is necessary if others are present to commit or encourage crime. The current authors are aware of no studies of differential association that differentiate between crimes committed alone and with others. Moreover, adolescents are the typical subjects of differential association studies and especially likely to co-offend. This magnifies the danger of assuming that differential association operates by attitude transference or other cognitive manifestations of interaction with delinquents. If it is accepted that associations with criminal peers are important, it must also be acknowledged that the influence of peers may operate without the transference of attitudes from the model to the observer. Deviant peers potentially foster situational inducements and group processes that produce offending. Therefore, at least part of what appears to be the effects of learning by association may actually reflect the fact that most offenders are under the direct influence of peers when they offend.

RESEARCH PURPOSE

The current study examines the effects of peer behavior, peer attitudes, and respondent attitudes on criminal offending, solo, and group offending. Any significant influence from association with friends that exists in solo crimes is extra-situational and explained by cognitive effects. The presence of friends' attitudes and behaviors is significant for solo offending; this suggests that attitude transference or learning is a significant component of differential association and that differential association operates similarly even when co-offenders are not present.

Co-offenders can exude immediate pressures, set an influential example, and provide opportunities to offend, in addition to any attitude transference that persists when friends are not present. Therefore, it is expected that one's own attitudes will mediate the relationship between friends' attitudes and behaviors for solo crimes. This may not be the case for group crimes where situational encouragement and friends' choices are potentially more important than learning definitions favorable to crime. Differentiating between crimes committed by groups and an individual offender allows investigators to assess whether findings for core theoretical variables are contingent on the presence or absence of others. In so doing, this study will examine whether friends' attitudes and behaviors are only important when friends are present. This might raise serious questions about the importance of attitude transmission, and as a result would challenge findings from previous tests of differential association that did not disaggregate dependent variables into group and solo crimes. Conversely, significant effects for differential association variables in the presence and absence of co-offenders would provide strong support for the theory.

METHODS

Sample

Data from the NYS were used to examine the effects of differential association on crimes committed alone and by groups. The NYS is a panel study of a national probability sample of persons that were ages eleven to seventeen in 1976. The current analyses were based on 1,492 youths who participated in Wave 6 in 1983, with lagged independent variables drawn from Wave 5 in 1980. Most analysts of NYS data use offense counts, or some transformation of offense counts, for the year previous to the interview as their dependent variables. The current analyses required data on whether an offense was committed in a group or alone. Regrettably, group-offending data were not available for all delinquent acts recorded in the NYS. Fortunately, follow-up questions about a subset

of serious criminal offenses had respondents report if their most recent offense was committed in a group or alone. These data did not allow for the investigation of the frequency of solo and group offending, but they did provide a measure of group offending.

Independent Variables

Three independent variables were used: (a) respondent attitudes toward deviance, (b) perceptions of friends' attitudes toward deviance, and (c) perceptions of friends' offending behaviors. The respondent's own attitudes toward a variety of acts were measured using the questions, "How wrong is it for someone your age to [act]?" Responses ranged from *not wrong at all* = 1 to *very wrong* = 4. Attitudes of friends were measured by asking if friends would approve or disapprove of these same behaviors. Responses ranged from *strongly approve* = 1 to *strongly disapprove* = 5. The direction of the attitude scales was recoded so that a high score indicated approval of the act. Friends' participation in a variety of deviant acts was measured by asking respondents to estimate how many people in their immediate friendship network participated in the acts in the past year. Responses ranged from *none* = 1 to *all* = 5. These acts were combined to form additive measures of friends' attitudes and deviance. Attitudes and deviant acts of friends were general measures, but the dependent variables referred to a specific crime. For example, the current analyses did not examine whether attitudes toward theft contributed to theft, but whether attitudes condoning a variety of deviant acts contributed to theft.

Dependent Variables

Dichotomous codes measured the presence or absence of theft, assault, and vandalism. Total offending was operationalized by 0 = *no crime*, 1 = *crime*, group offending was operationalized as 0 = *no or solo crime*, 1 = *group crime*, and solo offending was operationalized as 0 = *no or group crime*, 1 = *solo crime*. Each criminal offense was examined for each respondent. The crimes were chosen because they were relatively prevalent in the NYS, encompassed property and personal offending, and were likely to be committed in a group context. Moreover, the questions about group offending were difficult to interpret for some crimes. For example, it is unclear what is meant when respondents claim that they sell drugs in a group by comparison to those who claim to sell alone. The personal and property crimes herein were among those most commonly committed with delinquent peers.

FINDINGS

Both friends' attitudes and behaviors were significant determinants of all three forms of criminal offending. Warr and Stafford found that for cheating and larceny in previous Waves of NYS data, peer attitudes did not have significant direct effects on the number of offenses committed. The current study found more robust effects for friends' attitudes on the offense variables. Own attitudes also significantly correlated with offending for all three crimes. To test whether respondent attitudes explained the effects of friends' attitudes and behaviors, friend variables and own attitudes were entered into the same equation. Both variables retained their significance as predictors of total offending for all three crimes. This suggests that both friends' attitudes and friends' behaviors affected offending by means other than their influence on respondent attitudes.

Turning to group crime, all independent variables were significant predictors of group offending. Predictably, significance levels dropped since there were fewer cases of group offending than total offending. Nevertheless, findings revealed that the effects on group crime held independent of the effects on attitude; the influence of friends' attitudes only fell to insignificant levels for assault. Friends' behaviors maintained its significance for all three crimes. The current analyses confirmed that it is a mistake to assume that own attitudes are the mechanism for transferring friends' influences into group crimes, just as it would be a mistake to make the same claim for total offending.

Just as for total and group crime, all three independent variables were significant predictors of participation in solo crime. Both friends' attitudes and behaviors maintained their significant effects on solo offending, controlling for own attitudes. This finding suggests that even when crime was accomplished alone, friends' attitudes and behaviors were relevant and the significance of these variables was not completely explained by the intervening effect of respondents' own attitudes.

DISCUSSION AND CONCLUSION

Differential association theorists assert that friends' attitudes and behaviors affect crime indirectly through the transfer of criminogenic attitudes. Previous findings of direct effects, at least for friends' behaviors, called this claim into question. In the current analysis, nearly all of the effects of attitudes and behaviors remained significant predictors of offending when controlling for respondent attitudes. This was true for group and solo crime, suggesting that the effects of friends' attitudes and behaviors did not operate solely through respondents' attitudes. In fact, adding respondent attitudes to the equations had remarkably little impact, other than alleviating the significance of friends' attitudes for assault.

Previous investigators of differential association found unexpectedly weak relationships between respondent attitudes and offending relative to the direct effects of friends' attitudes or behaviors. For example, Warr and Stafford found that peer behavior had a strong direct effect on respondent behavior. In their words, "notwithstanding their own attitudes toward delinquency, then, adolescents are strongly influenced by the behavior of their friends." Using dichotomous dependent variables, the current study also found significant direct effects for both friends' attitudes and behaviors.

The current research revisited the relationship between friends' attitudes, respondent attitudes, and friends' behaviors to vandalism, theft, and assault. Since approval of crime by friends may manifest itself in offending by learning or through more direct avenues like situational inducements to offend, offenses committed by groups and solo offenders were examined. Generally, findings support differential association theory. Like prior studies, own attitudes did not seem to be the method of transferring friends' influences into criminal decisions. No support was found for the possibility that prior researchers neglected an important element when they failed to disaggregate crimes into group and solo events.

As expected, in initial equations friends' attitudes and behaviors were significant predictors of total offending. In addition, differential association variables appeared to influence offending through psychological mechanisms. Even if one's own crime-condoning attitudes did not explain the entire effects of friends' attitudes and behaviors on offending, the findings for solo offending suggest that friends' influences are manifested by something that individual offenders bring to the situations of the offense. Significant results for friends' attitudes and behaviors for lone offenders lend support to differential association theory as originally formulated. Friends' influences can only operate on solo offending through extra-situational means. Presumably, an offender carries the influence of his or her friends even when offending alone. Again, significant effects for friends' influences controlling for own attitudes suggests that attitudes may not be the vehicle for transporting social influences into solo offenses or group offenses. Despite the support for differential association theory, the current results call into question its central notion that attitudes are the mechanism of transference between associates.

Admittedly, the current findings may be due to measurement problems, albeit ones that many differential association studies do not address. For example, respondents may know that their friends are deviant because they have repeatedly offended with them. Consequently, significant effects for friends' influences in the solo equations implied that crime is learned by transference of some sort.

Warr and Stafford suggested that convincing tests of differential association would need to ask questions about the intervening processes between friends' attitudes and behaviors and deviance. Do friends reward deviant behaviors? Does criminal profit vicariously reward friends of the offender? Do friends influence legitimate aspects of offenders' lives, say their goals or academic successes, and thereby influence deviance? Must friends' behaviors be witnessed to influence offending? How accurate are the perceptions of friends' behaviors? Why do the opinions of friends shape decisions when they are not present? Is continued offending the result of continued contact with the same friends over time? While recent research is beginning to address some of these questions, the criminological understanding of peer influence remains primitive.

The most important conclusions of this study were that neither own attitudes nor the situational influence of friends appeared to be the mechanism of transference. Within the constraints of the data, the current study has eliminated group influences as the mechanism of differential association. Hopefully, this research will inspire others to refine measures of friendship influence. It is acknowledged that friends almost certainly affect criminal decision making when they are present, but it is important to recognize that significant findings supporting differential association are not biased by failure to examine the presence or absence of co-offenders. It is unknown if the friends that influence subjects' attitudes also are their co-offenders. Furthermore, it is unclear which deviant friends matter most. Surely, the influence of delinquent friends varies by a number of variables. Females with deviant friends, for example, may be less likely to condone crime and more likely to fall into crime by happenstance since their crimes are less likely to be solitary. As offenders age, they are less likely to associate with others and probably are less susceptible to influences from casual associates.

Presently, the NYS is the most complete data set for testing differential association and the only nationally representative data set that includes questions on group offending. New panel data sets that speak to the issue are under construction, but these too will fall short of addressing many issues. Questions surrounding the potential sources of friends' influences will not be resolved until data that include both background information on subjects and detailed situational data on at least some of the offenses they commit are available.

SOURCE: Reprinted from *Journal of Criminal Justice*, Vol. 30, No. 7, 559–566. Copyright © 2002, with permission from Elsevier.

QUESTIONS FOR DISCUSSION AND WRITING

1. What three reasons do the authors provide for being skeptical of differential association theory in its most simple form?

2. What did the authors find regarding the effects of friends' attitudes and behaviors on criminal offending? How do their results differ from those found by Warr and Stafford? What happened when friend variables and own attitudes were entered into the same equation, and what does this suggest?

3. What did the authors find when they examined the effects of their independent variables on group crime, and what did those analyses confirm? What did they find when they examined significant predictors of participation in solo crime, and what do those findings suggest?

SOCIAL STRUCTURE AND ANOMIE

ROBERT K. MERTON

There persists a notable tendency in socio-logical theory to attribute the malfunc-tioning of social structure primarily to those of man's imperious biological drives which are not adequately restrained by social control. In this view, the social order is solely a device for "impulse management" and the "social process-ing" of tensions. These impulses which break through social control, be it noted, are held to be biologically derived. Nonconformity is assumed to be rooted in original nature. Conformity is by implication the result of a utilitarian calculus or unreasoned conditioning. This point of view, whatever its other deficiencies, clearly begs one question. It provides no basis for determining the nonbiological conditions which induce devi-ations from prescribed patterns of conduct. In this [article], it will be suggested that certain phases of social structure generate the circum-stances in which infringement of social codes constitutes a "normal" response.

The conceptual scheme to be outlined is designed to provide a coherent, systematic approach to the study of sociocultural sources of deviate behavior. Our primary aim lies in discov-ering how some social structures *exert a definite pressure* upon certain persons in the society to engage in nonconformist rather than conformist conduct. The many ramifications of the scheme cannot all be discussed; the problems mentioned outnumber those explicitly treated.

Among the elements of social and cultural structure, two are important for our purposes. These are analytically separable although they merge imperceptibly in concrete situations. The first consists of culturally defined goals, pur-poses, and interests. It comprises a frame of aspirational reference. These goals are more or less integrated and involve varying degrees of prestige and sentiment. They constitute a basic, but not the exclusive component of what Linton aptly has called "designs for group living." Some of these cultural aspirations are related to the original drives of man, but they are not deter-mined by them. The second phase of the social structure defines, regulates, and controls the acceptable modes of achieving these goals. Every social group invariably couples its scale of desired ends with moral or institutional regula-tion of permissible and required procedures for attaining these ends. These regulatory norms and moral imperatives do not necessarily coin-cide with technical or efficiency norms. Many procedures which from the standpoint of *partic-ular individuals* would be most efficient in securing desired values, for example, illicit oil-stock schemes, theft, fraud, are ruled out of the institutional area of permitted conduct. The choice of expedients is limited by the institu-tional norms.

To say that these two elements, culture goals and institutional norms, operate jointly is not to say that the ranges of alternative behaviors and aims bear some constant relation to one another. The emphasis upon certain goals may vary independently of the degree of emphasis upon institutional means. There may develop a disproportionate, at times, a virtually exclusive, stress upon the value of specific goals, involving relatively slight concern with the institutionally appropriate modes of attaining these goals. The limiting case in this direction is reached when the range of alternative procedures is limited only by technical rather than institutional considerations. Any and all devices which promise attainment of the all-important goal would be permitted in this hypothetical polar case. This constitutes one type of cultural malintegration. A second polar type is found in groups where activities originally conceived as instrumental are transmuted into ends in themselves. The original purposes are forgotten and ritualistic adherence to institutionally prescribed conduct becomes virtually obsessive.

Thus, in competitive athletics, when the aim of victory is shorn of its institutional trappings and success in contests becomes construed as "winning the game" rather than "winning through circumscribed modes of activity," a premium is implicitly set upon the use of illegitimate but technically efficient means. The star of the opposing football team is surreptitiously slugged; the wrestler furtively incapacitates his opponent through ingenious but illicit techniques; university alumni covertly subsidize "students" whose talents are largely confined to the athletic field. The emphasis on the goal has so attenuated the satisfactions deriving from sheer participation in the competitive activity that these satisfactions are virtually confined to a successful outcome. Through the same process, tension generated by the desire to win in a poker game is relieved by successfully dealing oneself four aces, or, when the cult of success has become completely dominant, by sagaciously shuffling the cards in a game of solitaire. The faint twinge of uneasiness in the last instance and the surreptitious nature of public delicts indicate clearly that the institutional rules of the game *are known* to those who evade them, but that the emotional supports of these rules are largely vitiated by cultural exaggeration of the success-goal. They are microcosmic images of the social macrocosm.

Of course, this process is not restricted to the realm of sport. The process whereby exaltation of the end generates a *literal demoralization,* that is, a deinstitutionalization, of the means is one which characterizes many groups in which the two phases of the social structure are not highly integrated. The extreme emphasis upon the accumulation of wealth as a symbol of success in our own society militates against the completely effective control of institutionally regulated modes of acquiring a fortune. Fraud, corruption, vice, crime, in short, the entire catalogue of proscribed behavior, becomes increasingly common when the emphasis on the culturally induced success-goal becomes divorced from a coordinated institutional emphasis. This observation is of crucial theoretical importance in examining the doctrine that antisocial behavior most frequently derives from biological drives breaking through the restraints imposed by society. The difference is one between a strictly utilitarian interpretation which conceives man's ends as random and an analysis which finds these ends deriving from the basic values of the culture.

Our analysis can scarcely stop at this juncture. We must turn to other aspects of the social structure if we are to deal with the social genesis of the varying rates and types of deviate behavior characteristic of different societies. Thus far, we have sketched three ideal types of social orders constituted by distinctive patterns of relations between culture ends and means. Turning from these types of *culture patterning,* we find five logically possible, alternative modes of adjustment or adaptation *by individuals* within the culture-bearing society or group. These are schematically presented in the following table, where (+) signifies "acceptance," (−) signifies "elimination," and (±) signifies "rejection and substitution of new goals and standards."

	Culture Goals	Institutionalized Means
I. Conformity	+	+
II. Innovation	+	−
III. Ritualism	−	−
IV. Retreatism	−	−
V. Rebellion	±	±

Our discussion of the relation between these alternative responses and other phases of the social structure must be prefaced by the observation that persons may shift from one alternative to another as they engage in different social activities. These categories refer to role adjustments in specific situations, not to personality *in toto.* To treat the development of this process in various spheres of conduct would introduce a complexity unmanageable within the confines of this [article]. For this reason, we shall be concerned primarily with economic activity in the broad sense, "the production, exchange, distribution and consumption of goods and services" in our competitive society, wherein wealth has taken on a highly symbolic cast. Our task is to search out some of the factors which exert pressure upon individuals to engage in certain of these logically possible alternative responses. This choice, as we shall see, is far from random.

In every society, Adaptation I (conformity to both culture goals and means) is the most common and widely diffused. Were this not so, the stability and continuity of the society could not be maintained. The mesh of expectancies which constitutes every social order is sustained by the modal behavior of its members falling within the first category. Conventional role behavior oriented toward the basic values of the group is the rule rather than the exception. It is this fact alone which permits us to speak of a human aggregate as comprising a group or society.

Conversely, Adaptation IV (rejection of goals and means) is the least common. Persons who "adjust" (or maladjust) in this fashion are, strictly speaking, *in* the society but not of it. Sociologically, these constitute the true "aliens." Not sharing the common frame of orientation, they can be included within the societal population merely in a fictional sense. In this category are *some* of the activities of psychotics, psychoneurotic, chronic autists, pariahs, outcasts, vagrants, vagabonds, tramps, chronic drunkards, and drug addicts. These have relinquished, in certain spheres of activity, the culturally defined goals, involving complete aim inhibition in the polar case, and their adjustments are not in accord with institutional norms. This is not to say that in some cases the source of their behavioral adjustments is not in part the very social structure which they have in effect repudiated nor that their very existence within a social area does not constitute a problem for the socialized population.

This mode of "adjustment" occurs, as far as structural sources are concerned, when both the culture goals and institutionalized procedures have been assimilated thoroughly by the individual and imbued with affect and high positive value, but where those institutionalized procedures which promise a measure of successful attainment of the goals are not available to the individual. In such instances, there results a twofold mental conflict insofar as the moral obligation for adopting institutional means conflicts with the pressure to resort to illegitimate means (which may attain the goal) and inasmuch as the individual is shut off from means which are both legitimate *and* effective. The competitive order is maintained, but the frustrated and handicapped individual who cannot cope with this order drops out. Defeatism, quietism, and resignation are manifested in escape mechanisms which ultimately lead the individual to "escape" from the requirements of the society. It is an expedient which arises from continued failure to attain the goal by legitimate measures and from an inability to adopt the illegitimate route because of internalized prohibitions and institutionalized compulsives, *during which process the supreme value of the success-goal has as yet not been renounced*. The conflict is resolved by eliminating *both* precipitating elements, the goals and means. The escape is complete, the conflict is eliminated, and the individual is socialized.

Be it noted that where frustration derives from the inaccessibility of effective institutional means for attaining economic or any other type of highly valued "success," that Adaptations II, III, and V (innovation, ritualism, and rebellion) are also possible. The result will be determined by the particular personality, and thus, the *particular* cultural background involved. Inadequate socialization will result in the innovation response whereby the conflict and frustration are eliminated by relinquishing the institutional means and retaining the success-aspiration; an extreme assimilation of institutional demands will lead to ritualism wherein the goal is dropped as beyond one's reach but conformity to the mores persists, and rebellion occurs when emancipation from the reigning standards, due to frustration or to marginalist perspectives, leads to the attempt to introduce a "new social order."

Our major concern is with the illegitimacy adjustment. This involves the use of conventionally proscribed but frequently effective means of attaining at least the simulacrum of culturally defined success—wealth, power, and the like. As we have seen, this adjustment occurs when the individual has assimilated the cultural emphasis on success without equally internalizing the morally prescribed norms governing means for its attainment. The question arises, Which phases of our social structure predispose toward this mode of adjustment? We may examine a concrete instance, effectively analyzed by Lohman, which provides a clue to the answer. Lohman has shown that specialized areas of vice in the near north side of Chicago constitute a "normal" response to a situation where the cultural emphasis upon pecuniary success has been absorbed, but where there is little access to conventional and legitimate means for attaining such success. The conventional occupational opportunities of persons in this area are almost completely limited to manual labor. Given our cultural stigmatization of manual labor, and its correlate, the prestige of white collar work, it is clear that the result is a strain toward innovative practices. The limitation of opportunity to unskilled labor and the resultant low income cannot compete in terms of conventional standards of achievement with the high income from organized vice.

For our purposes, this situation involves two important features. First, such antisocial behavior is in a sense "called forth" by certain conventional values of the culture *and* by the class structure involving differential access to the approved opportunities for legitimate, prestige-bearing pursuit of the culture goals. The lack of high integration between the means-and-end elements of the cultural pattern and the particular class structure combine to favor a heightened frequency of antisocial conduct in such groups. The second consideration is of equal significance. Recourse to the first of the alternative responses, legitimate effort, is limited by the fact that actual advance toward desired success-symbols through conventional channels is, despite our persisting open-class ideology, relatively rare and difficult for those handicapped by little formal education and few economic resources. The dominant pressure of group standards of success is, therefore, on the gradual attenuation of legitimate, but by and large ineffective, strivings, and the increasing use of illegitimate, but more or less effective, expedients of vice and crime. The cultural demands made on persons in this situation are incompatible. On the one hand, they are asked to orient their conduct toward the prospect of accumulating wealth and on the other, they are largely denied effective opportunities to do so institutionally. The consequences of such structural inconsistency are psychopathological personality, and/or antisocial conduct, and/or revolutionary activities. The equilibrium between culturally designated means and ends becomes highly unstable

with the progressive emphasis on attaining the prestige-laden ends by any means whatsoever. Within this context, Capone represents the triumph of amoral intelligence over morally prescribed "failure," when the channels of vertical mobility are closed or narrowed *in a society which places a high premium on economic affluence and social ascent for all its members.*

This last qualification is of primary importance. It suggests that other phases of the social structure besides the extreme emphasis on pecuniary success must be considered if we are to understand the social sources of antisocial behavior. A high frequency of deviate behavior is not generated simply by "lack of opportunity" or by this exaggerated pecuniary emphasis. A comparatively rigidified class structure, a feudalistic or caste order, may limit such opportunities far beyond the point which obtains in our society today. It is only when a system of cultural values extols, virtually above all else, certain *common* symbols of success *for the population at large* while its social structure rigorously restricts or completely eliminates access to approved modes of acquiring these symbols *for a considerable part of the same population* that antisocial behavior ensues on a considerable scale. In other words, our egalitarian ideology denies by implication the existence of noncompeting groups and individuals in the pursuit of pecuniary success. The same body of success-symbols is held to be desirable for all. These goals are held to *transcend class lines*, not to be bounded by them, yet the actual social organization is such that there exist class differentials in the accessibility of these *common* success-symbols. Frustration and thwarted aspiration lead to the search for avenues of escape from a culturally induced intolerable situation; or unrelieved ambition may eventuate in illicit attempts to acquire the dominant values. The American stress on pecuniary success and ambitiousness for all thus invites exaggerated anxieties, hostilities, neuroses, and antisocial behavior.

This theoretical analysis may go far toward explaining the varying correlations between crime and poverty. Poverty is not an isolated variable. It is one in a complex of interdependent social and cultural variables. When viewed in such a context, it represents quite different states of affairs. Poverty as such, and consequent limitation of opportunity, are not sufficient to induce a conspicuously high rate of criminal behavior. Even the often-mentioned "poverty in the midst of plenty" will not necessarily lead to this result. Only insofar as poverty and associated disadvantages in competition for the culture values approved for all members of the society is linked with the assimilation of a cultural emphasis on monetary accumulation as a symbol of success is antisocial conduct a "normal" outcome. Thus, poverty is less highly correlated with crime in southeastern Europe than in the United States. The possibilities of vertical mobility in these European areas would seem to be fewer than in this country, so that neither poverty *per se* nor its association with limited opportunity is sufficient to account for the varying correlations. It is only when the full configuration is considered, poverty, limited opportunity, and a commonly shared system of success symbols, that we can explain the higher association between poverty and crime in our society than in others where rigidified class structure is coupled with *differential class symbols of achievement.*

In societies such as our own, then, the pressure of prestige-bearing success tends to eliminate the effective social constraint over means employed to this end. "The-end-justifies-the-means" doctrine becomes a guiding tenet for action when the cultural structure unduly exalts the end and the social organization unduly limits possible recourse to approved means. Otherwise put, this notion and associated behavior reflect a lack of cultural coordination. In international relations, the effects of this lack of integration are notoriously apparent. An emphasis upon national power is not readily coordinated with an inept organization of legitimate, that is, internationally defined and accepted, means for attaining this goal. The result is a tendency toward the abrogation of international law, treaties become scraps of paper, "undeclared warfare" serves as a technical evasion, the bombing of civilian populations is rationalized just as the same societal situation induces the same sway of illegitimacy among individuals.

The social order we have described necessarily produces this "strain toward dissolutions." The pressure of such an order is upon outdoing one's competitors. The choice of means within the ambit of institutional control will persist as long as the sentiments supporting a competitive system, that is, deriving from the possibility of outranking competitors and hence enjoying the favorable response of others, are distributed throughout the entire system of activities and are not confined merely to the final result. A stable social structure demands a balanced distribution of affect among its various segments. When there occurs a shift of emphasis from the satisfactions deriving from competition itself to almost exclusive concern with successful competition, the resultant stress leads to the breakdown of the regulatory structures. With the resulting attenuation of the institutional imperatives, there occurs an approximation of the situation erroneously held by utilitarians to be typical of society generally wherein calculations of advantage and fear of punishment are the sole regulating agencies. In such situations, as Hobbes observed, force and fraud come to constitute the sole virtues in view of their relative efficiency in attaining goals which were for him, of course, not culturally derived.

It should be apparent that the foregoing discussion is not pitched on a moralistic plane. Whatever the sentiments of the writer or reader concerning the ethical desirability of coordinating the means-and-goals phases of the social structure, one must agree that lack of such coordination leads to anomie. Insofar as one of the most general functions of social organization is to provide a basis for calculability and regularity of behavior, it is increasingly limited in effectiveness as these elements of the structure become dissociated. At the extreme, predictability virtually disappears and what may be properly termed cultural chaos or anomie intervenes.

This statement, being brief, is also incomplete. It has not included an exhaustive treatment of the various structural elements which predispose toward one rather than another of the alternative responses open to individuals; it has neglected, but not denied the relevance of, the factors determining the specific incidence of these responses; it has not enumerated the various concrete responses which are constituted by combinations of specific values of the analytical variables; it has omitted, or included only by implication, any consideration of the social functions performed by illicit responses; it has not tested the full explanatory power of the analytical scheme by examining a large number of group variations in the frequency of deviate and conformist behavior; it has not adequately dealt with rebellious conduct which seeks to refashion the social framework radically; it has not examined the relevance of cultural conflict for an analysis of culture-goal and institutional-means malintegration. It is suggested that these and related problems may be profitably analyzed by this scheme.

SOURCE: From *American Sociological Review* 3:672-682. Copyright © 1938 by Robert K. Merton. Reprinted by permission of The American Sociological Association.

QUESTIONS FOR DISCUSSION AND WRITING

1. What two elements of social and cultural structure are important for Merton's theory?

2. How does "extreme emphasis on the accumulation of wealth" relate to crime?

3. What are Merton's five adaptations? How does SES fit into Merton's theory?

POVERTY, SOCIOECONOMIC CHANGE, INSTITUTIONAL ANOMIE, AND HOMICIDE

SANG-WEON KIM

WILLIAM ALEX PRIDEMORE

This study tested institutional anomie theory (IAT) in the context of widespread poverty and large-scale socioeconomic change in Russia. Although developed to explain crime in the capitalist culture of the United States, IAT has been tested cross-nationally and Bernburg recently argued that the theory should also apply to the effects of social change on crime. Russia has experienced tremendous social, political, and economic change during the last 15 years as totalitarianism and a command economy are being replaced by a free-market democracy. Since these changes began in the early 1990s, Russians have faced a wide array of social problems, including high levels of poverty and unemployment, increasing inequality, and a mortality crisis. It is likely that the anomic environment accompanying the rapid social change has played a role in the increase in and wide cross-sectional variation of Russian homicide rates during the1990s.

Durkheim argued that during times of rapid social change norms become unclear and society's control over individual behavior decreases. He believed that as people's aspirations become less limited and as conventional social institutions are weakened, deviance and crime should increase.

Large-scale changes have occurred since the Soviet Union collapsed, including fundamental shifts in political and economic philosophies and decreased formal social control, leading to normative uncertainty. Russians' aspirations are now less limited because of newfound individual freedoms and because a free market creates desires, whereas totalitarianism and a planned economy stifles them. Similarly, conventional Soviet institutions are gone and enduring social institutions such as the family and education are weakened by the ongoing changes and the collapse of the Soviet welfare system. The pace and outcome of these changes vary widely throughout the vast nation, however, and deprivation and anomie theories lead us to expect violence to be higher in areas facing greater poverty and change. Institutional anomie theory also leads us to expect that the strength of noneconomic social institutions such as family, education, and polity will moderate the effects of poverty and change on violence.

BACKGROUND: TRANSITIONAL RUSSIA

In the early 1990s, Russia launched a program of privatization meant to convert the command economy to a free market. Economic, legal, political, regulatory, and social institutions are a fundamental part of a properly functioning market economy, however, and these institutions were absent or underdeveloped in Russia. This vacuum played a role in the ensuing problems, including increased rates of interpersonal violence. There was severe economic instability and uncertainty throughout the decade. According to Goskomstat, in 2000 nearly 30 percent of the population was living in poverty and the unemployment rate of 10.5 percent was double what it had been in 1992. Regional levels of economic dislocation are not uniform, however, but vary widely throughout the country based on the type of local industry, access to raw materials, and the presence of the requisite legal protections for business transactions.

The transition also has had a dramatic impact on mortality, which is often an indicator of stressful, anomic, and abnormal conditions. Middle-aged males were the most vulnerable to the increased stress resulting from the rapid social and economic change toward an uncertain future, and male life expectancy declined sharply to less than 60 years. This group also has the highest homicide offending and victimization rates in Russia.

Based largely on the supposed Soviet experience, there was a belief in the past that crime rates were lower under state socialism than in democratic countries with capitalist economies. A higher degree of social justice and social integration in socialist countries were reasons often cited for this assumption. Such low crime rates might also be explained by other more ominous factors, such as "tight social control practiced through a dense network of secret police activities and the considerable power difference between members of the Communist party and nonmembers."

One of the benefits of Russia's democratic transformation is increasing transparency and thus broader availability of demographic, economic, and social data. Under the totalitarian regime, crime and other data were strictly controlled and often falsified when made public. Pridemore has used newly available historical data on homicide mortality to dispute the claim that rates of interpersonal violence were low during the Soviet era. These data showed that the Russian homicide victimization rate has been comparable to or even higher than the U.S. rate for at least the past 40 years. More important for the present study, the Russian homicide rate rose dramatically following the collapse of the Soviet Union. According to data from the Russian Ministry of Health, the 2001 homicide victimization rate of 29.8 homicides per 100,000 persons was three times what it had been a decade earlier and nearly five times the U.S. rate. As with the levels of poverty and socioeconomic change mentioned before, however, these rates vary widely throughout Russia, ranging from a low of around six per 100,000 in the Republic of Kabardino-Balkaria to over 130 per 100,000 in the Republic of Tyva.

INSTITUTIONAL ANOMIE THEORY

Institutions are patterned mutually shared ways that people develop for living together, providing socially sanctioned rules that define and regulate conduct. According to Bellah et al., institutions "are the substantial forms through which we understand our own identity and the identity of others as we seek cooperatively to achieve a decent society." If these institutions remain stable they allow social organization to persist over time despite the constant change of members of society. These institutions are critical for increasing predictability among societal members, which in turn increases trust because it allows "individuals to act based on their perception that others are likely to perform particular actions in expected ways."

According to Messner and Rosenfeld, culture and structure operate together to create higher crime rates. At the cultural level, capitalist culture "exerts pressures toward crime by encouraging an anomic cultural environment, an environment in which people are encouraged to adopt an 'anything goes' mentality in the pursuit of personal goals . . . [and] the anomic pressures inherent in the American dream are nourished and sustained by an institutional balance of power dominated by the economy." Messner and Rosenfeld argue that capitalist culture promotes intense pressures for economic success at the expense of pro-social noneconomic institutions such as family, education, polity, and religion. Social structure comes to be dominated by the economic structure, thereby weakening institutional controls. As former communist countries move toward a free market it is likely their citizens are beginning to adopt capitalist ideologies, including an emphasis on individual economic success at the expense of noneconomic social institutions, making institutional anomie theory appear applicable to the Russian situation.

While the negative socioeconomic changes in Russia are expected to create higher crime rates, this association may be conditioned by the strength of noneconomic social institutions such as family, education, and polity. First, even in the face of difficult structural conditions, strong families and the accompanying social cohesion can inhibit crime. According to institutional anomie theory, families can mitigate anomic pressures by providing emotional support and social bonds for their members. Pridemore has shown family structure to be associated with regional homicide rates in Russia and Pridemore and Shkolnikov found marriage to be an individual-level protective factor against homicide victimization in the country. Second, the educational system can reduce crime by effectively monitoring and supervising the behavior of children and by creating environments in which children are strongly committed to their education and aspirations. Since education is directly connected to socialization, the system's capacity to exercise social control may lessen the impact of social change on crime. An educated population is also more likely to possess networks and social skills that allows it to cope better with social change. Third, trust in political institutions reflects the legitimacy of these institutions among the populace, which may be closely related to social control efforts. Given the wide variation in poverty, negative socioeconomic change, and the strength of social institutions throughout the country, post-Soviet Russia provides a unique opportunity to test IAT.

Only a handful of studies have specifically tested institutional anomie theory. According to Chamlin and Cochran, Messner and Rosenfeld's model implies that economic stress will be less salient as a predictor of serious crime in the presence of strong noneconomic institutions. They hypothesize that the impact of poverty on property crime is thus moderated by the strength of religious, political, and family institutions. Results from their state-level analysis are consistent with this hypothesis, since they show that high church membership, low divorce rate, and high voter turnout significantly reduced the effect of poverty on property crime.

Piquero and Piquero tested institutional anomie theory with cross-sectional data from the United States, employing several different operationalizations of the main social-institutions variables. Their findings provided some support for the institutional anomie hypotheses, but they also concluded that the inferences drawn about IAT may depend on how the institutional variables are operationalized.

A study by Messner and Rosenfeld draws on Esping-Anderson's decommodification index as the indicator of economic dominance in the institutional balance of power. According to Esping-Anderson, decommodification is the degree to which the state's policies protect the individual standard of living of its citizens from the forces of the market. Messner and Rosenfeld argue that decommodification influences crime independently of economic stratification. Using cross-national data, the authors found support for this hypothesis since the index of decommodification had a relatively strong negative effect on national homicide rates, controlling for economic discrimination, income inequality, and the level of socioeconomic development.

Savolainen pointed out the differences between Chamlin and Cochran's and Messner and Rosenfeld's studies. The main difference was that Chamlin and Cochran emphasized that IAT implies an interaction effect between economic conditions and the strength of noneconomic institutions, while Messner and Rosenfeld were concerned with the main effect of the institutional balance of power on homicide rates. Savolainen hypothesized that the positive effect of economic inequality on lethal violence is strongest in nations where the economy dominates the institutional balance of power. This implies a negative interaction effect between economic stratification and the relative strength of noneconomic institutions, which is what he finds in his analyses. Savolainen concluded that nations that protect their citizens from market forces appear to be immune to the effects of economic inequality on homicide.

Since contemporary Russia is moving toward capitalism, it is likely that citizens of the country have begun to adopt capitalist ideologies such as an emphasis on individual economic success. Thus the "American dream" may now be the Russian dream (and that of other nations in an era of globalization), and as in other capitalist nations, Russia's institutional balance of power may be tilting toward the economy and away from social welfare. Pridemore and Pridemore and Kim have shown elsewhere that poverty and negative socioeconomic change, respectively, are positively related to the cross-sectional variation of homicide in Russia. Further, the main focus of the empirical literature on IAT has become testing for moderating effects of noneconomic social institutions, and Bernburg argues that we should expect similar conditioning effects of these institutions on any association between social change and crime. Our study is the first of its kind to test Bernburg's hypothesis and to test IAT in a single country other than the United States, and thus provides a bridge between studies of the United States and the cross-national studies that use nations as the unit of analysis.

Summary of Hypotheses

This review of literature led us to test the following hypotheses.

1. The level of poverty is positively related to the cross-sectional variation of homicide rates in Russian regions.

2. Negative socioeconomic change is positively related to the cross-sectional variation of homicide rates in Russian regions.

3. The strength of social institutions is negatively related to the cross-sectional variation of homicide rates in Russian regions.

4. The strength of social institutions conditions the effects of poverty and negative socioeconomic change on homicide rates in Russian regions.

DATA AND METHOD

This was a cross-sectional study of Russian regions. With the exception of the measures used to create the change index, all data were for 2000 unless otherwise noted. Of the 89 regions, nine are autonomous districts embedded within a larger region and their data are covered by the larger unit. Data from the neighboring Ingush and Chechen Republics are unreliable and were not used. This left 78 cases for analysis. In Russia, local data are aggregated to the regional level and only the aggregate data forwarded to Moscow and published. Thus, while a lower level

of aggregation might be preferable, the nature of data collection makes this untenable. Versions of institutional anomie theory have been tested at even higher levels of analysis, such as the nation, however, so we are confident with our use of regions.

Dependent Variable

Regional homicide estimates are available from both police (MVD) and vital statistics data, though the former are highly suspect. For example, annual estimates from the vital statistics reporting system have reported nearly 40 percent more homicides than the MVD data over the last 15 years, and there is a relatively low correlation between the two reporting systems among the regions. We thus used the regional homicide victimization rate per 100,000 persons as our dependent variable. Russia used the abridged Soviet cause of death coding system until 1999, when it began to use the International Classifications of Diseases Codes, 10th revision. Regional mortality rates, including homicide, are published annually by the Russian Ministry of Health. Table 1 provides descriptive statistics and brief descriptions of all variables.

Independent Variables: Poverty and Socioeconomic Change

Poverty was measured as the proportion of the regional population living below the poverty line. Data were unavailable for 2000, so 1999 data were used. These data are available from Goskomstat. We used the natural logarithm of these values because of the pronounced positive skew in their distribution.

We created a composite index to account for regional variation in socioeconomic change. The variables used to measure the index represent multiple dimensions of change (e.g., population, economic, and legal) and thus should not be considered different attempts to capture a single underlying concept. As described below, the measures were coded in a way that highlighted those regions that have experienced the worst effects of change relative to other regions. The measures of these different dimensions were population change, unemployment change, poverty change, privatization, and foreign capital investment. Data for these measures were

TABLE 1   Descriptive Statistics (N = 78)

Variable	Description	Mean	SD
Homicide rate	Deaths per 100,000 population due to homicide	30.14	17.44
Poverty	Proportion of population living below subsistence minimum	0.43	0.16
Socioeconomic change	Index of socioeconomic change (Δ population + Δ poverty + Δ unemployment + privatization + foreign capital investment)	1.38	1.13
Family	Proportion of households with only 1 parent and at least 1 < 18 years old (reverse coded)	–0.16	–0.02
Education	Rate per 1,000 population enrolled in college	26.96	13.81
Polity	Proportion of registered voters who voted in 2000 presidential election	0.69	0.05
Inequality	Ratio of income of the top 20% of wage earners to bottom 20% of wage earners	6.00	2.78
Unemployment	Proportion of active labor force unemployed	0.12	0.04
Alcohol	Deaths per 100,000 population due alcohol poisoning	28.73	17.52
Males	Proportion of population that is male aged 25–44	0.15	0.01

obtained from Goskomstat. Population change and the proportion of the active labor force unemployed were measured as residual change scores when 2000 values were regressed on 1992 values. The poverty variable was measured as the residual change score when 1999 poverty rates (2000 data unavailable) were regressed on poverty rates from 1994 (earlier data unavailable). For poverty, for example, the equation was Δ Poverty = Poverty 2000 – (α + β * Poverty 1992). Residual change scores are superior to raw change scores since they are independent of initial values. Since all the regions were used to estimate the regression, the residual scores also take into account changes in the entire ecological system under study.

Since the Soviet economic system was characterized by state ownership, two further important indicators of legal, political, and economic change are privatization and foreign investment. The former was measured as the percentage of the labor force employed in private companies and the latter as foreign capital investment per capita in U.S. dollars. In essence, these are change scores since both were virtually zero until the adoption in 1992 of the "Basic Provision for the Privatization of State and Municipal Enterprises in the Russian Federation." Foreign capital investment is an especially interesting measure since it is an indicator not simply of worthwhile investment potential but of political and economic

stability and of the presence of the relatively strong legal framework required for a free market.

In the context of this study, privatization and foreign investment were "positive" since they represent economic revitalization in economically depressed areas by providing jobs, income, and other advantages. An increasing population is also considered positive, since a decreasing population usually represents a concentration of poverty as people with greater resources move out and leave behind residents with fewer resources and thus a higher proportion of people who are economically dependent. Recent research has shown this to be the case for regional mobility in Russia. Therefore, in order to create our index of negative change, we coded privatization, foreign investment, and population change as 1 if they were more than 0.5 standard deviations below the mean (i.e., they were substantially worse off than other regions on these measures), 0 otherwise, and coded unemployment and poverty as 1 if they were more than 0.5 standard deviations above the mean (i.e., they had substantially higher levels of poverty and unemployment relative to other regions), 0 otherwise. These scores were summed, providing a value of 0–5 (with 5 being the worst) for each region. In one respect, this approach means we lose information since we turn interval variables into dummies and thus restrict their variance. Creating a factor or constructing an index by summing z scores, however, might not allow us to capture the different components of socioeconomic change in the manner we wish.

Institutional Anomie Variables

Our measure of family stability was the proportion of households with a single parent and at least one child under the age of 18. This was reverse coded to interpret it in terms of institutional anomie (i.e., family strength). Although new data on this variable will soon be available from the 2002 Russian census, at the moment we must use data from the 1994 Russian microcensus, which are available from several Goskomstat publications. Educational strength was measured as the number of people enrolled in college per 1,000 residents. Voter turnout or proportion voting for a specific party/candidate is often used as a measure of trust, apathy, or anomie in macro-level studies, including in studies of institutional anomie. We thus measured polity as the proportion of registered voters who voted in the 2000 Russian presidential election.

Control Variables

Two further economic measures common to macro-level studies were included as controls. Inequality was measured as the ratio of the income of the top 20 percent of wage earners to that of the bottom 20 percent of wage earners. Unemployment was measured as the proportion of the active labor force that was unemployed. Data for these measures were obtained from Goskomstat and both were logged due to heavy positive skews.

Recent research on Russia by Andrienko and Pridemore has found alcohol consumption to be positively and significantly associated with regional homicide rates after controlling for other structural factors. We thus controlled for this by using the latter's proxy for consumption (i.e., deaths per 100,000 persons due to alcohol poisoning; examples of and reasons for using this proxy in Russia are explained elsewhere: Chenet et al. and Shkolnikov, McKee, and Leon). These data are from the Russian Ministry of Health (2001).

Research has shown that the age distribution of Russian homicide offenders and victims is very different from that in the United States. The mean age of Russian homicide arrestees is 10–11

years older than in the United States and victimization is highest among males in their mid-20s to late 40s. Since factors such as the labor market and migration have led to variation in the size of this group by region, we included the proportion of the population male 25–44 as a control. Values were logged due to the heavy positive skew in the distribution.

Finally, homicide victimization rates in Russia are geographically patterned. Controlling for other factors, rates have been shown to be significantly lower in the northern Caucasus and higher east of the Ural Mountains. We thus included two regional dummy variables to control for these differences.

Missing Data

Northern Osetia and the Chukot Autonomous Okrug had missing data on foreign capital investment and the latter also on education, and the missing observations were replaced in order to retain these cases for analysis. Mean substitution can be problematic because it may produce biased estimates of variances and covariances, so we replaced the missing values by using information from other variables in the model, which can be used as instruments to predict the missing observations if we assume they are uncorrelated with the error term. We regressed the variable with the missing observation on all the other independent variables that had complete data and used the predicted value to replace these three missing observations.

Method

Homicide is a rare event and its distribution is usually positively skewed, which can lead to several methodological problems. The skew statistic for the distribution of regional homicide victimization rates in Russia is several times its standard error. Further, regional populations vary widely, which may result in violation of the OLS assumption of homogeneity of error variance since prediction errors likely vary by population size. One way to account for the skewed distribution is to logarithmically transform the homicide rate to help normalize its distribution. Recent work has shown, however, that misleading findings can result from logging the dependent variable. A more appropriate alternative is to use negative binomial regression since it does not assume homogeneity of error variance. The negative binomial model is being increasingly used in macro-level criminological studies and we employed this method with our data. Negative binomial regression is normally used for count data, so a small change was necessary since we are interested in crime rates relative to population size. This was accomplished by adding to the model the log of the population at risk and assigning this variable a fixed coefficient of 1. Common exploratory data analysis techniques and regression diagnostics were carried out and are discussed below where appropriate.

RESULTS

Table 1 shows descriptive statistics. The mean regional homicide victimization rate of 30 per 100,000 persons in 2000 was about five times higher than the rate of six per 100,000 in the United States that year. On average, over 40 percent of the regional populations were living in poverty. As for institutional strength, both the mean for single-parent households of 16 percent and mean voter turnout in the presidential election of 69 percent were very similar to comparable measures in the United States.

Table 2 shows the correlation matrix. As expected, poverty $(r = 0.30)$ and negative socioeconomic change were positively correlated with homicide rates $(r = 0.40)$, and the strength of family $(r = -0.44)$, education $(r = -0.20)$, and polity $(r = -0.37)$ were all negatively correlated with homicide rates. Other results show that alcohol consumption had the strongest correlation with homicide $(r = 0.50)$ and confirmed that homicide rates were lower in the northern Caucasus $(r = -0.26)$ and higher in the regions east of the Urals $(r = 0.56)$.

The regression results reveal the direct effects of poverty and institutional variables on homicide, as well as the interaction effects for poverty with each of the three institutional measures. The findings indicate that poverty is positively and significantly associated with homicide rates net of all other variables in the model. The results also indicate that regions with stronger family and polity have lower homicide rates. The results for the education variable are in the expected direction, but its negative association with homicide is not significantly different from zero. Homicide rates in the northern Caucasus did not remain significantly lower when controlling for the other structural factors, but rates in the east remained significantly higher. The results also suggest that none of the interaction terms conditioned the effect of poverty on homicide. The slope coefficients for the family and polity interaction terms are in the expected negative direction but are not significant.

The next set of models is similar except the negative socioeconomic change index has been

TABLE 2   Correlation Matrix

	1	2	3	4	5	6	7	8	9	10	11	12
1. Homicide rate	1.00											
2. Log poverty	0.30	1.00										
3. SE change	−0.40	0.41	1.00									
4. Family	−0.44	0.14	0.19	1.00								
5. Education	−0.20	−0.05	0.21	0.12	1.00							
6. Polity	−0.37	0.13	0.05	0.46	0.04	1.00						
7. Log inequality	−0.01	−0.07	0.04	0.14	0.39	−0.05	1.00					
8. Log unemploy	0.28	0.64	0.38	0.08	−0.12	0.05	−0.16	1.00				
9. Alcohol	0.50	−0.05	0.07	0.20	−0.30	−0.26	−0.25	−0.06	1.00			
10. Log males	0.10	0.22	0.16	0.29	−0.20	−0.33	−0.01	0.01	0.04	1.00		
11. Caucasus	−0.26	0.36	0.03	0.30	0.13	0.26	0.09	0.05	−0.41	−0.37	1.00	
12. East	0.56	0.15	0.35	−.33	−0.01	−0.38	0.06	0.30	0.06	0.43	−0.21	1.00

included (and thus the poverty and unemployment variables excluded). Again, the inferences are the same across all four models and are essentially the same for all variables. As expected, those regions that have faced more negative effects of socioeconomic change have higher homicide rates. The results for the direct effects of the institutional variables are the same as above, though the p value for family strength is around 0.06 in each model. Once again, the interaction terms indicate that the strength of institutions such as family, education, and polity do not condition the effects of negative socioeconomic change on homicide rates in Russia.

Overall, the results provide (1) support for the first hypothesis that poverty is positively associated with regional homicide rates, (2) support for the second hypothesis that negative socioeconomic change is associated with homicide rates, (3) partial support for the hypothesis that institutional strength is negatively associated with homicide rates (i.e., family and polity were negatively associated with homicide but educational strength was not), and (4) no support for the hypothesis that institutional strength conditions the effects of poverty and of negative socioeconomic change on homicide rates.

DISCUSSION

Russia has experienced widespread poverty since the collapse of the Soviet Union. The level of poverty, however, varies widely among the Russian regions as a result of many factors, including type of industry, level of development, and the quality of social services provided by the state. Our results show that poverty is positively and significantly related to regional homicide rates in Russia, which provides support for the first hypothesis and is consistent with research in the country using data from the mid-1990s and with the U.S. literature on social structure and homicide.

Aside from poverty, Russia experienced other forms of change following the collapse of communism that likely disrupted the social equilibrium and produced anomic conditions that in turn were partially responsible for the increase in and wide variation of crime and violence in the country. Our results show that regions experiencing the worst effects of socioeconomic change had higher homicide rates. This result provides support for the second hypothesis,

based on Durkheimian anomie theory, and is consistent with recent research on socioeconomic change and crime in Russia.

The third hypothesis was drawn from institutional anomie theory and concerned the direct effects of social institutions on homicide rates. Our results provide partial support for this hypothesis. First, according to institutional anomie theory, families function to mitigate anomic pressures by providing emotional support and social bonds. We found that regional family strength was negatively and significantly associated with regional homicide rates, which provides support for this hypothesis. Further, this association is consistent with Pridemore's findings using Russian homicide data from the mid-1990s and with Pridemore and Shkolnikov, who found that marriage is an individual-level protective factor against homicide victimization in Russia. Second, education appears to have no relationship to homicide rates. This is somewhat surprising given the disruption of the Russian educational system resulting from underfunding and changing curricula. Third, our results show a negative and significant association between polity and homicide rates. One interpretation of this is that faith in political institutions decreases crime rates since it represents a level of trust and social cohesion. Distrust in political institutions threatens their legitimacy, which can reduce the effectiveness of the social-control system, and our result is consistent with research in the United States that has shown that distrust in political institutions is positively associated with crime. Although these findings are largely consistent with one aspect of institutional anomie theory, they are also consistent with other structural-level theories that may claim these same variables or measures. The real heart of IAT lies in the claim that these institutions moderate the negative effects of other structural factors on crime.

Institutional Anomie

Institutional controls are expected to condition the effects of culture and structure on crime rates. Research has shown that crime rates are lower where social institutions and informal control are stronger, and studies using cross-national and U.S. data have shown support for this aspect of institutional anomie theory. Further, Bernburg argued that the strength of social institutions should also act to reduce the effects of social change on crime. We followed a strategy common to previous studies of IAT by testing the hypothesis that the effects of poverty and of negative socioeconomic change on homicide rates are dependent on the strength of social institutions such as family, education, and polity. The results show that none of the interaction terms was significant, indicating that the strength of noneconomic social institutions does not appear to condition the effects of poverty and socioeconomic change on homicide in Russia.

There are a few possible substantive reasons for these results. First, any potential conditioning effects of social institutions simply may be overwhelmed because the changes were so strong and so swift in Russia. Thus our results may represent a period effect, an artifact of the current transitional conditions. Perhaps in the context of slower-paced societal development, social institutions retain their ability to temper the effects of change on crime. Second, social institutions may be weakened by socioeconomic change, thereby reducing their ability to condition its impact. Several studies have shown, for example, that institutional characteristics are shaped by economic and social changes, and many theories of crime posit that anomie weakens social institutions and thus leads to crime and deviance.

Finally, institutional anomie theory was not developed to explain the role of rapid socioeconomic change on crime. It focuses instead on the specific cultural pressure for monetary success that gives rise to anomie because of the (1) imbalance between the economic institution and other noneconomic institutions and (2) interplay between cultural pressure for material desire and the structural imbalance of social institutions. However, Bernburg argued that institutional anomie theory links crime, anomie, and contemporary social change by bringing in the notion of the disembedded market economy, a central notion in the institutionalism of Durkheim and Polanyi. Thus, while institutional anomie theory was not developed to explain the relationship between social change and crime, it appears a logical extension to test it in this context.

SUMMARY AND CONCLUSION

Despite important gains in individual freedoms and the move toward democracy, the Russian transformation has not been smooth. The transition led to a collapse of Soviet state paternalism such as social guarantees of health, housing, and education, and price controls on many staples such as food products. Russia and Russians are also experiencing uncertainty and instability as many former social values and institutions are being replaced by a completely new political economy. These rapid structural and cultural changes have likely created anomic conditions that may contribute to various social problems in the country, including increases in and a widening variation of homicide rates.

Our findings suggest that poverty and socioeconomic change are positively and significantly related to the variation of regional homicide rates in Russia. This is consistent with our first and second hypotheses and provides support for deprivation theories and for Durkheim's anomie theory. Stronger families and polity appear to reduce regional homicide rates, providing partial support for one part of institutional anomie theory, though again these variables are also claimed by other macro-level theories. The main hypothesis tested here, a version of the key aspect of institutional anomie theory, finds no support. That is, our results show that none of the social institutions moderate the positive effects of poverty and socioeconomic change on homicide. One interpretation of these results is that change was so swift and powerful in Russia that social institutions were unable to buffer the effect of the anomic conditions. Similarly, social institutions may have been weakened by these changes, and in their weakened state do not have the power to condition the effects of change on violent crime.

In building on the present study, future research might more fully develop and extend the construct for socioeconomic and political change. It will also be useful to use alternative research designs and model specifications. For example, time-series analysis should be employed to examine whether socioeconomic change influences crime over time in Russia, and one could also test the alternative model specifications that we suggest in the discussion section of this article, such as the hypothesis that socioeconomic change negatively influences the strength of social institutions, thereby reducing or negating their ability to reduce crime rates. Further research also must test specific pathways through which socioeconomic change affects crime. For example, among the control variables included here, alcohol consumption is consistently, significantly, and positively related to homicide rates. Many researchers suggest that negative socioeconomic change, repeated crises, and continued uncertainty in Russia likely played a part in increased levels of alcohol consumption during the 1990s. This presents yet another alternative model to explore, and thus further research should test the hypothesis that socioeconomic change influences rates of crime and violence indirectly via alcohol consumption.

Other potential alternative explanations to anomie theory should also be examined in the context of transitional Russia. For example, less authoritarian law enforcement, together with the overall disarray and corruption of the police force, may have resulted in less fear of the state in general and less fear of being caught and punished for violent acts. Finally, we should note that the idea here is not simply that Russia shifted from a low-violence country to a high-violence country with the move toward capitalism. Pridemore has already shown that Russia has had homicide rates comparable to or higher than the those of the United States for several decades. The results of our study instead suggest that the poverty and anomic conditions associated with the transitional period between communism and capitalism and between totalitarianism and democracy are associated with the cross-sectional variation of homicide rates in Russia. Those regions that felt the more negative consequences of these changes are those regions with higher rates of violence.

In conclusion, our study is the first of its kind to test institutional anomie theory in a nation besides the United States and it provides a link between the single-country studies of IAT in the United States and cross-national studies of IAT that use nations as units of analysis. The study also provides the first empirical test of Bernburg's hypothesis that IAT should help explain the association between social change and crime rates. Russia offers an excellent *locus in quo* for researchers to test this hypothesis and to examine more general aspects of the impact of large-scale social change on society. Rigorous research on social change, institutions, and crime in the country should not only provide knowledge about Russia but important theoretical and empirical findings that are more broadly applicable to other societies and to *our* criminological knowledge.

SOURCE: From *Social Science Quarterly,* Supplement to Vol. 86. Copyright © 2005 by the Southwestern Social Science Association. Reprinted by permission of Blackwell Publishing Ltd.

QUESTIONS FOR DISCUSSION AND WRITING

1. According to Bellah et al., what are institutions and how do they affect social organization?

2. Regarding the third hypothesis, which was drawn from institutional anomie theory and concerned the direct effects of social institutions on homicide rates, what do the results provide?

3. What do the authors note about the main hypothesis tested in this article?

PART VII

How Do We Explain Crime?

Foundational Theories of Modern Criminology II

The major theoretical influences in criminology of the late 1950s through the 1970s have their intellectual roots in early sociology. This is not extraordinary. Sociology is one of a number of disciplines that contribute to the vibrant interdisciplinary criminology of today, and the early 20th-century criminological theorists were sociologists. Science typically advances when scholars build on discoveries and knowledge learned by their predecessors, and in Part VII students will read about four very different theories that all trace their lineage to early sociological thought.

The Chicago school theorists, represented by Shaw and McKay in the previous section, traced their intellectual lineage to early European sociologists who wrote about the effects of rapid social change on social life. Anomie theory was based on Durkheimian ideas, as well as on conceptions of social life articulated by social disorganization theorists. Merton added his own unique contribution to these earlier explanations of crime and deviance. These works show how criticism of the original theories leads to revision and fine-tuning, as each generation of scholars takes what is valuable and moves forward. This is how knowledge advances in science, the social sciences included. The articles in this section push our understanding of crime forward, too. Although the branches look rather different from the roots, the strong connection between them enables criminologists to take the original ideas in new directions.

Two very different theoretical traditions are included in this section. Subcultural explanations and control theory, like the theories in Part VI, are generally considered to be "consensus theories" because an underlying assumption is that societies are characterized by a broad-based consensus. Theories of this sort tended to build on one another, to use legal definitions of crime (crime is behavior that violates the criminal law), and to be compatible with official sources of crime statistics such as those collected by the Uniform Crime Reports. Labeling theory and conflict theory, by contrast, are examples of "conflict theories." Theorists in this tradition frequently characterize themselves as being in opposition to the theories that have dominated criminological discussion during the middle and late 20th century.

To be accurate, most modern sociologists believe that dividing ideas into those that reflect consensus images and conflict images is a false dichotomy. We agree, but at the same time, we find it useful to think in these terms when categorizing theories; it simply makes it easier to discuss them. The assumption (or image) underlying consensus theories is contained in the answer to the question, How is society possible? The answer is because there is a consensus, or broad-based agreement, among the members of the society on important norms and values. Those who reject this assumption do not assume consensus; rather, they believe that societies are characterized by conflict. That is, societies are divided into competing interest groups; there are important cleavages that separate and distinguish groups within societies. These divisions may be along the lines of class, race, gender, age, and so on. For conflict theorists, the answer to the question "How is society possible?" is that society can exist either when one group has sufficient power that it can dominate competitors, or when power is shared by multiple groups so that each has an interest in creating a truce.

In reality, neither consensus nor conflict alone characterizes societies. There are aspects of every society that are consistent with both images, and some societies are more divided than others. But in explaining crime, criminologists have found it useful to emphasize one aspect or the other.

In "The Subculture of Violence," Wolfgang and Ferracuti present an explanation of homicide and other forms of criminal violence. They argue that although there are exceptions, the typical homicide is the result of a cultural system of values and beliefs that is more favorable to the use of violence than is the dominant culture. Carriers of this subculture of violence engage in more violence because they are more likely to approve of the use of violence and to define violence as appropriate in more circumstances than do carriers of the dominant culture's values and norms. Regions, areas of cities, or other places where carriers of the subculture of violence are concentrated (some criminologists have written about a southern subculture of violence) will therefore have higher rates of homicide and other forms of violent crime. The contemporary example of research in this tradition is by Patchin and his colleagues, "Exposure to Community Violence and Childhood Delinquency."

In "Causes and Prevention of Juvenile Delinquency," Hirschi lays out an explanation of crime and delinquency that begins from a different point than others. This type of theory, control theory, begins by arguing that we have been asking the wrong question. Most criminologists have sought to answer the query, "Why do people break the laws?" Control theorists suggest that we should ask instead, "Why *don't* people break the laws?" The fact is that most people do not violate laws even when it may appear to be in their interests to do so. For example, we regularly wait for traffic lights to turn green even in the middle of the night when neither other cars nor police officers are around. Why do we do this, or more accurately, why do most of us do this? That, according to control theorists, is the behavioral pattern we should seek to understand. Obviously, if we can answer the "why don't we" question, we will gain a greater understanding of why some people are criminals or delinquents.

Hirschi was not the first control theorist; this perspective, like many others, can be traced to the work of Emile Durkheim. In the 1950s, Reckless and Nye offered their answers to the question of why most of us don't violate the rules. Reckless focused on the development of what he called "inner containment" (norms and beliefs about how we should behave, which we internalize) and "outer containment" (external sources of sanctions and disapproval, including our families, law enforcement, and other institutions). Nye focused on the controlling force of the family. Hirschi's answer to the question is "social bonds." Those with well-developed social bonds are less likely to engage in acts of delinquency. He posits that we develop bonds (attachments, commitments, involvements, and beliefs) to important institutions such as families, schools, and the conventional order. Those who are not well bonded are more likely to violate the law than those who are well bonded. The contemporary research piece is by Huebner and Betts, who not only offer a test of control theory, but they consider the theory's utility for explaining differences in the causes of boys' and girls' delinquency.

As we described earlier, subcultural theories and control theories can generally be categorized as consensus theories. We'll now shift gears and examine two conflict theories. In an earlier edition of this reader, we called these theories "the loyal opposition" because although criminologists of this tradition have been critical of the theoretical mainstream, they continue to belong to the major scholarly associations and continue to publish in the same journals. Their criticisms have been essential in the development of criminology. Not only have they offered important ideas of their own, but their critiques have also improved the quality of mainstream theorizing. For instance, many conventional criminologists now use unofficial data sources in their research, in part because critical scholars argued convincingly that official data sources may be biased by the institutionalized coercive and discriminatory practices of the criminal justice system.

Not all criminologists would categorize labeling theory as a conflict perspective, just as many would not consider differential association to be a consensus theory. Both trace their intellectual ancestry primarily to symbolic interactionists, like Cooley and Mead, at the University of Chicago. Labeling theorists argue that the societal reaction to behavior affects the identity of the person whose behavior is being judged, and subsequent behavior reflects this change in identity. Shur's "Labeling Criminals," taken from his book *Our Criminal Society*, describes how societies create deviance and criminality through their efforts to control it. When we react to individuals as "violators," we set in motion a continuing series of interactions that eventually change their identity. They come to see themselves as criminals, which then affects their behavior—leading to more criminal action. Bernburg, Krohn, and Rivera study juveniles who are officially labeled delinquents by the court and find that, consistent with the theory, the resulting new identity results in those individuals increasing their criminal involvements.

The selection by Chambliss, "Crime and Structural Contradictions," outlines the basic arguments of Marxist criminology, a variant of more general conflict theories that focus on social class cleavages. Chambliss argues that economic interests determine what behavior is defined as crime, how the law is enforced, and the sanctions levied against violators. Much of Chambliss's work makes the point that we cannot fully understand crime and enforcement unless we study it in the context of the economic and political interests and forces in society. Our recent research piece by Jacobs, Carmichael, and Kent is a historical analysis of death sentences. They confirm that important political considerations predict use of the most severe sanction, death.

The four theories presented in this section have been and continue to be important in criminological research. Their influence has ebbed at times, but we believe that they continue to be important influences in criminology. This is especially true of control theory, which although not unchallenged, is considered by many scholars to be the dominant theoretical perspective in criminology. Students will see in Part VIII two important descendents of it, life course criminology and self-control theory.

In the case of conflict theory, or radical criminology as some refer to it, students should recognize that criminologists working in this tradition are critical of the state, the criminal justice system, and mainstream criminology itself, and the development of criminology has been moved forward as a result. When reading about "critical theories" in Part IX, students should remember that this line of thinking and research has its roots in conflict theory.

 For a data analysis exercise that accompanies the material in this section, go to www.sagepub.com/crimereadings3study.

THE SUBCULTURE OF VIOLENCE

MARVIN E. WOLFGANG

FRANCO FERRACUTI

The analysis of violent aggressive behavior has been the focus of interest of many social and biological researches, and psychology has attempted to build several theories to explain its phenomenology, ranging from the death-aggression instinct of the psychoanalytic school to the frustration-aggression hypothesis. The present discussion is the result of joint explorations in theory and research in psychology and in sociology, using the concept of subculture as a learning environment. Our major area of study has been assaultive behavior, with special attention to criminal homicide. Some of the main trends in criminological thinking related to this topic must now be anticipated for the proper focus of the present discussion.

Isolated sectional studies of homicide behavior are extremely numerous, and it is not our intention to examine them here. There are basically two kinds of criminal homicide: (1) premeditated, felonious, intentional murder; and (2) slaying in the heat of passion, or killing as a result of intent to do harm but without intent to kill. A slaying committed by one recognized as psychotic or legally insane, or by a psychiatrically designated abnormal subject, involves clinical deviates who are generally not held responsible for their behavior and who, therefore, are not considered culpable. We are eliminating these cases from our present discussion, although subcultural elements are not irrelevant to the analysis of their psychopathological phenomenology.

Probably fewer than 5 percent of all known homicides are premeditated, planned intentional killings, and the individuals who commit them are most likely to be episodic offenders who have never had prior contact with the criminal law. Because they are rare crimes often planned by rationally functioning individuals, perhaps they are more likely to remain undetected. We believe that a type of analysis different from that presented here might be applicable to these cases.

Our major concern is with the bulk of homicides—the passion crimes, the violent slayings—that are not premeditated and are not psychotic manifestations. Like Cohen, who was concerned principally with most delinquency that arises from the "working-class" ethic, so we are focusing on the preponderant kind of homicide, although our analysis will include much of the available data on homicide in general.

THE CULTURAL CONTEXT

Like all human behavior, homicide and other violent assaultive crimes must be viewed in terms of the cultural context from which they spring. De Champneuf, Guerry, and Quetelet early in the nineteenth century, and Durkheim later, led the way toward emphasizing the necessity to examine the *physique sociale,* or social phenomena characterized by "eternality," if the scientist is to understand or interpret crime, suicide, prostitution, and other deviant behavior.

Without promulgating a sociological fatalism, analysis of broad macroscopic correlates in this way may obscure the dynamic elements of the phenomenon and result in the empirical hiatus and fallacious association to which Selvin refers. Yet, because of wide individual variations, the clinical, idiosyncratic approach does not necessarily aid in arriving at Weber's *Verstehen*, or meaningful adequate understanding of regularities, uniformities, or patterns of interaction. And it is this kind of understanding we seek when we examine either deviation from, or conformity to, a normative social system.

Sociological contributions have made almost commonplace, since Durkheim, the fact that deviant conduct is not evenly distributed throughout the social structure. There is much empirical evidence that class position, ethnicity, occupational status, and other social variables are effective indicators for predicting rates of different kinds of deviance. Studies in ecology perform a valuable service for examining the phenomenology and distribution of aggression, but only inferentially point to the importance of the system of norms. Anomie, whether defined as the absence of norms (which is a doubtful conceptualization) or the conflict of norms (either normative goals or means), or whether redefined by Powell as "meaninglessness," does not coincide with most empirical evidence on homicide. Acceptance of the concept of anomie would imply that marginal individuals who harbor psychic anomie that reflects (or causes) social anomie have the highest rates of homicides. Available data seem to reject this contention.

Anomie as culture conflict, or conflict of norms, suggests, as we have in the last section, that there is one segment (the prevailing middle-class value system) of a given culture whose value system is the antithesis of, or in conflict with, another, smaller, segment of the same culture. This conceptualism of anomie is a useful tool for referring to subcultures as ideal types, or mental constructs. But to transfer this norm-conflict approach from the social to the individual level, theoretically making the individual a repository of culture conflict, again does not conform to the patterns of known psychological and sociological data. This latter approach would be forced to hypothesize that socially mobile individuals and families would be most frequently involved in homicide, or that persons moving from a formerly embraced subvalue system to the predominant communal value system would commit this form of violent deviation in the greatest numbers. There are no homicide data that show high rates of homicides among persons manifesting higher social aspirations in terms of mobility. It should also be mentioned that anomie, as a concept, does not easily lend itself to psychological study.

That there is a conflict of value systems, we agree. That is, there is a conflict between a prevailing culture value and some subcultural entity. But commission of homicide by actors from the subculture at variance with the prevailing culture cannot be adequately explained in terms of frustration due to failure to attain normative-goals of the latter, in terms of inability to succeed with normative-procedures (means) for attaining those goals, nor in terms of an individual psychological condition of anomie. Homicide is most prevalent, or the highest rates of homicide occur, among a relatively homogeneous subcultural group in any large urban community. Similar prevalent rates can be found in some rural areas. The value system of this group, we are contending, constitutes a subculture of violence. From a psychological viewpoint, we might hypothesize that the greater the degree of integration of the individual into this subculture, the higher the probability that his behavior will be violent in a variety of situations. From the sociological side, there should be a direct relationship between rates of homicide and the extent to which the subculture of violence represents a cluster of values around the theme of violence.

Except for war, probably the most highly reportable, socially visible, and serious form of violence is expressed in criminal homicide. Data show that in the United States rates are highest among males, nonwhites, and the young adult ages. Rates for most serious crimes, particularly against the person, are highest in these same groups. In a Philadelphia study of 588 criminal homicides, for example, nonwhite males aged 20–24 had a rate of 92 per 100,000 compared with 3–4 for white males of the same ages. Females consistently had lower rates than males in their respective race groups (nonwhite females, 9–3; white females, 0–4, in the same study), although it should be noted, as we shall discuss later, that nonwhite females have higher rates than white males.

It is possible to multiply these specific findings in any variety of ways, and although a subcultural affinity to violence appears to be principally present in large urban communities and increasingly in the adolescent population, some typical evidence of this phenomenon can be found, for example, in rural areas and among other adult groups. For example, a particular, very structured subculture of this kind can be found in Sardinia, in the central mountain area of the island. Pigliaru has conducted a brilliant analysis of the people from this area and of their criminal behavior, commonly known as the *vendetta barbaricina*.

In Colombia, the well-known *violencia* has been raging for the past 15 years, causing deaths of a total estimated between 200,000 and 300,000. The homicide rate in several areas has been among the highest in the world, and homicide has been the leading cause of death for Colombian males aged between 15 and 45. Several causes, some political, initially associated with the rise of this phenomenon continue to exist, and among them, a subcultural transmission of violence is believed to play an important role.

We suggest that, by identifying the groups with the highest rates of homicide, we should find in the most intense degree a subculture of violence, and, having focused on these groups, we should subsequently examine the value system of their subculture, the importance of human life in the scale of values, the kinds of expected reaction to certain types of stimulus, perceptual differences in the evaluation of stimuli, and the general personality structure of the subcultural actors. In the Philadelphia study, it was pointed out,

> The significance of a jostle, a slightly derogatory remark, or the appearance of a weapon in the hands of an adversary are stimuli differentially perceived and interpreted by Negroes and whites, males and females. Social expectations of response in particular types of social interaction result in differential "definitions of the situation." A male is usually expected to defend the name and honor of his mother, the virtue of womanhood . . . and to accept no derogation about his race (even from a member of his own race), his age, or his masculinity. Quick resort to physical combat as a measure of daring, courage, or defense of status appears to be a cultural expression, especially for lower socioeconomic class males of both races. When such a culture norm response is elicited from an individual

engaged in social interplay with others who harbor the same response mechanism, physical assaults, altercations, and violent domestic quarrels that result in homicide are likely to be common. The upper-middle and upper social class value system defines subcultural mores, and considers many of the social and personal stimuli that evoke a combative reaction in the lower classes as "trivial." Thus, there exists a cultural antipathy between many folk rationalizations of the lower class, and of males of both races, on the other.

This kind of analysis, combined with other data about delinquency, the lower-class social structure, its value system, and its emphasis on aggression, suggest the thesis of a violent subculture, or, by pushing the normative aspects a little further, a *subculture of violence*. Among many juvenile gangs, as has repeatedly been pointed out, there are violent feuds, meetings, territorial fights, and the use of violence to prove "heart," to maintain or to acquire "rep."

Physical aggression is often seen as a demonstration of masculinity and toughness. We might argue that this emphasis on showing masculinity through aggression is not always supported by data. If homicide is any index at all of physical aggression, we must remember that in the Philadelphia data nonwhite females have rates often two to four times higher than the rates of white males. Violent behavior appears more dependent on cultural differences than on sex differences, traditionally considered of paramount importance in the expression of aggression. It could be argued, of course, that in a more matriarchal role than that of her white counterpart, the Negro female both enjoys and suffers more of the male role as head of the household, as parental authority and supervisor; that this imposed role makes her more aggressive, more male-like, more willing and more likely to respond violently. Because most of the victims of Negro female homicide offenders are Negro males, the Negro female may be striking out aggressively against the inadequate male protector whom she desperately wants but often cannot find or hold.

It appears valid to suggest that there are, in a heterogeneous population, differences in ideas and attitudes toward the use of violence and that these differences can be observed through variables related to social class and possibly through psychological correlates. There is evidence that modes of control of expressions of aggression in children vary among the social classes. Lower-class boys, for example, appear more likely to be oriented toward direct expression of aggression than are middle-class boys. The type of punishment meted out by parents to misbehaving children is related to this class orientation toward aggression. Lower-class mothers report that they or their husbands are likely to strike their children or threaten to strike them, whereas middle-class mothers report that their type of punishment is psychological rather than physical, and boys who are punished physically express aggression more directly than those who are punished psychologically. As Martin Gold has suggested, the middle-class child is more likely to turn his aggression inward; in the extreme and as an adult he will commit suicide. But the lower-class child is more accustomed to a parent-child relationship which during punishment is, for the moment, that of attacker and attacked. The target for aggression, then, is external; aggression is directed toward others.

The existence of a subculture of violence is partly demonstrated by examination of the social groups and individuals who experience the highest rates of manifest violence. This examination need not be confined to the study of one national or ethnic group. On the contrary, the existence of a subculture of violence could perhaps receive even cross-cultural confirmation. Criminal homicide is the most acute and highly reportable example of this type of violence, but some circularity of thought is obvious in the effort to specify the dependent variable (homicide), and also to infer the independent variable (the existence of a subculture of violence). The highest rates of rape, aggravated assaults, persistency in arrests for assaults (recidivism) among these groups with high rates of homicide are, however, empirical addenda to the postulation of a subculture of violence. Residential propinquity of these same groups reinforces the sociopsychological impact which the integration of this subculture engenders. Sutherland's thesis of "differential association," or a psychological reformulation of the same theory in terms of learning process, could effectively be employed to describe more fully as impact in its intensity, duration, repetition, and frequency. The more thoroughly integrated the individual is into this subculture, the more

intensely he embraces its prescriptions of behavior, its conduct norms, and integrates them into his personality structure. The degree of integration may be measured partly and crudely by public records of contact with the law, so high arrest rates, particularly high rates of assault crimes and high rates of recidivism for assault crimes among groups that form the subculture of violence, may indicate allegiance to the values of violence.

We have said that overt physical violence often becomes a common subculturally expected response to certain stimuli. However, it is not merely rigid conformity to the demands and expectations of other persons, as Henry and Short seem to suggest, that results in the high probability of homicide. Excessive compulsive, or apathetic, conformity of middle-class individuals to the value system of their social group is a widely recognized cultural malady. Our concern is with the value elements of violence as an integral component of the subculture which experiences high rates of homicide. It is conformity to *this* set of values, and not rigid conformity per se, that gives important meaning to the subculture of violence.

If violence is a common subcultural response to certain stimuli, penalties should exist for deviation from this norm. The comparatively nonviolent individual may be ostracized, but if social interaction must occur because of residential propinquity to others sharing in a subculture of violence, he is most likely to be treated with disdain or indifference. One who previously was considered a member of the in-group, but who has rebelled or retreated from the subculture, is now an out-group member, a possible threat, and one for the group to avoid. Alienation or avoidance takes him out of the normal reach of most homicide attacks, which are highly personal offenses occurring with greatest frequency among friends, relatives, and associates. If social interaction continues, however, the deviant from the subculture of violence who fails to respond to a potentially violent situation may find himself a victim of an adversary who continues to conform to the violence values.

It is not far-fetched to suggest that a whole culture may accept a value set dependent upon violence, demand or encourage adherence to violence, and penalize deviation. During periods of war, the whole nation accepts the principle of violence against the enemy. The nonviolent citizen drafted into military service may adopt values associated with violence as an intimately internalized reinforcement for his newly acquired rationalization to kill. War involves selective killing of an out-group enemy and in this respect may be viewed as different from most forms of homicide. Criminal homicide may be either "selective" or nondiscriminate slaying, although the literature on homicide consistently reveals its intragroup nature. However, as in wartime combat between opposing individuals when an "it-was-either-him-or-me" situation arises, similar attitudes and reactions occur among participants in homicide. It may be relevant to point out that in the Philadelphia study of criminal homicide, 65 percent of the offenders and 47 percent of the victims had previous arrest records. Homicide, it appears, is often a situation not unlike that of confrontations in wartime combat, in which two individuals committed to the value of violence came together, and in which chance, prowess, or possession of a particular weapon dictates the identity of the slayer and of the slain. The peaceful noncombatant in both sets of circumstances is penalized, because of the allelomimetic behavior of the group supporting violence, by his being ostracized as an out-group member, and he is thereby segregated (imprisoned, in wartime, as a conscientious objector) from his original group. If he is not segregated, but continues to interact with his original group in the public street or on the front line that represents the culture of violence, he may fall victim to the shot or stab from one of the group who still embraces the value of violence.

An internal need for aggression and a readiness to use violence by the individual who belongs to a subculture of violence should find their psychological foundation in personality traits and in attitudes which can, through careful studies, be assessed in such a way as to lead to a differential psychology of these subjects. Psychological tests have been repeatedly employed to study the differential characteristics of criminals, and if a theoretical frame of reference involving a subculture of violence is used, it should be possible to sharpen the discriminatory power of these tests. The fact that a subject belongs to a specific subculture (in our case, a deviant one), defined by the ready use of violence, should, among other consequences, cause the subject to adopt a differential perception of his environment and its stimuli. Variations in the surrounding world, the continuous challenges

and daily frustrations which are faced and solved by the adaptive mechanism of the individual, have a greater chance of being perceived and reacted upon, in a subculture of violence, as menacing, aggressive stimuli which call for immediate defense and counter-aggression. This hypothesis lends itself to objective study through appropriate psychological methodologies. The word of Stagner on industrial conflict exemplifies a similar approach in a different field. This perceptual approach is of great importance in view of studies on the physiology of aggression, which seem to show the need of outside stimulation in order to elicit aggressive behavior.

Confronted with many descriptive and test statistics, with some validated hypotheses and some confirmed replications of propositions regarding aggressive crime in psychological and sociological studies, interpretative analysis leading to the building of a theory is a normal functional aspect of the scientific method.

But there are two common and inherent dangers of an interpretative analysis that yields a thesis in an early stage of formulation, such as our thesis of a subculture of violence. These are (a) the danger of going beyond the confines of empirical data which have been collected in response to some stated hypothesis, and (b) the danger of interpretation that produces generalizations emerging inductively from the data and that results in tautologous reasoning. Relative to the first type of danger, the social scientist incurs the risk of "impressionistic," "speculative" thinking, or of using previous peripheral research and trying to link it to his own data by theoretical ties that often result in knotted confusion typically calling for further research, the *caveat* of both "good" and "poor" analyses. Relative to the second danger, the limitations and problems of tautologies are too well known to be elaborated here. We hope that these two approaches to interpretation are herein combined in degrees that avoid compounding the fallacies of both, but that unite the benefits of each. We have made an effort to stay within the limits imposed by known empirical facts and not to become lost in speculative reasoning that combines accumulated, but unrelated, facts for which there is no empirically supportive link.

We have said that overt use of force or violence, either in interpersonal relationships or in group interaction, is generally viewed as a reflection of basic values that stand apart from the dominant, the central, or the parent culture. Our hypothesis is that this overt (and often illicit) expression of violence (of which homicide is only the most extreme) is part of a subcultural normative system, and that this system is reflected in the psychological traits of the subculture participants. In the light of our discussion of the caution to be exercised in interpretative analysis, in order to tighten the logic of this analysis, and to support the thesis of a subculture of violence, we offer the following corollary propositions:

1. *No subculture can be totally different from or totally in conflict with the society of which it is a part.* A subculture of violence is not entirely an expression of violence, for there must be interlocking value elements shared with the dominant culture. It should not be necessary to contend that violent aggression is the predominant mode of expression in order to show that the value system is set apart as subcultural. When violence occurs in the dominant culture, it is usually legitimized, but most often is vicarious and a part of fantasy. Moreover, subcultural variations, we have earlier suggested, may be viewed as quantitative and relative. The extent of difference from the larger culture and the degree of intensity, which violence as a subcultural theme may possess, are variables that could and should be measured by known sociopsychological techniques. At present, we are required to rely almost entirely upon expressions of violence in conduct of various forms—parent-child relationships, parental discipline, domestic quarrels, street fights, delinquent conflict gangs, criminal records of assaultive behavior, criminal homicides, and so on—but the number of psychometrically oriented studies in criminology is steadily increasing in both quantity and sophistication, and from them a reliable differential psychology of homicides should emerge to match current sociological research.

2. *To establish the existence of a subculture of violence does not require that the actors sharing in these basic value elements should express violence in all situations.* The normative system designates that in some types of social interaction a violent and physically aggressive response is either expected or required of all members sharing in that system of values. That the actors' behavior expectations occur in more than one

situation is obvious. There is a variety of circumstances in which homicide occurs, and the history of past aggressive crimes in high proportions, both in the victims and in the offenders, attests to the multisituational character of the use of violence and to its interpersonal characteristics. But, obviously, persons living in a subcultural milieu designated as a subculture of violence cannot and do not engage in violence continuously, otherwise normal social functioning would be virtually impossible. We are merely suggesting, for example, that ready access to weapons in this milieu may become essential for protection against others who respond in similarly violent ways in certain situations and that the carrying of knives or other protective devices becomes a common symbol of willingness to participate in violence, to expect violence, and to be ready for its retaliation.

3. *The potential resort or willingness to resort to violence in a variety of situation emphasizes the penetrating and diffusive character of this culture theme.* The number and kinds of situations in which an individual uses violence may be viewed as an index of the extent to which he has assimilated the values associated with violence. This index should also be reflected by quantitative differences in a variety of psychological dimensions, from differential perception of violent stimuli to different value expressions in questionnaire-type instruments. The range of violence from minor assault to fatal injury, or certainly the maximum of violence expected, is rarely made explicit for all situations to which an individual may be exposed. Overt violence may even occasionally be a chance result of events. But clearly this range and variability of behavioral expressions of aggression suggest the importance of psychological dimensions in measuring adherence to a subculture of violence.

4. *The subcultural ethos of violence may be shared by all ages in a subsociety, but this ethos is most prominent in a limited age group, ranging from late adolescence to middle age.* We are not suggesting that a particular ethnic, sex, or age group all share in common the use of potential threats of violence. We are contending merely that the known empirical distribution of conduct, which expresses the sharing of this violence theme, shows greatest localization, incidence, and frequency in limited subgroups and reflects

differences in learning about violence as a problem-solving mechanism.

5. *The counter-norm is nonviolence.* Violation of expected and required violence is most likely to result in ostracism from the group. Alienation of some kind, depending on the range of violence expectations that are unmet, seems to be a form of punitive action most feasible to this subculture. The juvenile who fails to live up to the conflict gang's requirements is pushed outside the group. The adult male who does not defend his honor or his female companion will be socially emasculated. The "coward" is forced to move out of the territory, to find new friends and make new alliances. Membership is lost in the subsociety sharing the cluster of attitudes positively associated with violence. If forced withdrawal or voluntary retreat are not acceptable modes of response to engaging in the counter-norm, then execution, as is reputed to occur in organized crime, may be the extreme punitive measure.

6. *The development of favorable attitudes toward, and the use of, violence in a subculture usually involves learned behavior and a process of differential learning, association, or identification.* Not all persons exposed—even equally exposed—to the presence of a subculture of violence absorb and share in the values in equal portions. Differential personality variables must be considered in an integrated social-psychological approach to an understanding of the subcultural aspects of violence. We have taken the position that aggression is a learned response, socially facilitated and integrated, as a habit, in more or less permanent form, among the personality characteristics of the aggressor. Aggression, from a psychological standpoint, has been defined by Buss as "the delivery of noxious stimuli in an interpersonal context." Aggression seems to possess two major classes of reinforcers: the pain and injury inflicted upon the victim and its extrinsic rewards. Both are present in a subculture of violence, and their mechanism of action is facilitated by the social support that the aggressor receives in his group. The relationship between aggression, anger, and hostility is complicated by the habit characteristics of the first, the drive state of the second, and the attitudinal interpretative nature of the third. Obviously, the immediacy and the short temporal sequence of anger

with its autonomic components make it difficult to study a criminal population that is some distance removed from the anger-provoked event. Hostility, although amenable to easier assessment, does not give a clear indication or measure of physical attack because of its predominantly verbal aspects. However, it may dispose to or prepare for aggression.

Aggression, in its physical manifest form, remains the most criminologically relevant aspect in a study of violent assaultive behavior. If violent aggression is a habit and possesses permanent or quasi-permanent personality trait characteristics, it should be amenable to psychological assessment through appropriate diagnostic techniques. Among the several alternative diagnostic methodologies, those based on a perceptual approach seem to be able, according to the existing literature, to elicit signs and symptoms of behavioral aggression, demonstrating the existence of this "habit" and/or trait of the personality of the subject being tested. Obviously, the same set of techniques being used to diagnose the trait of aggression can be used to assess the presence of major psychopathology, which might, in a restricted number of cases, have caused "aggressive behavior" outside, or in spite of, any cultural or subcultural allegiance.

7. *The use of violence in a subculture is not necessarily viewed as illicit conduct and the users therefore do not have to deal with feelings of guilt about their aggression.* Violence can become a part of the lifestyle, the theme of solving difficult problems or problem situations. It should be stressed that the problems and situations to which we refer arise mostly within the subculture, for violence is used mostly between persons and groups who themselves rely upon the same supportive values and norms. A carrier and user of violence will not be burdened by conscious guilt, then, because generally he is not attacking the representatives of the nonviolent culture, and because the recipient of this violence may be described by similar class status, occupational, residential, age, and other attribute categories which characterize the subuniverse of the collectivity sharing in the subculture of violence. Even law-abiding members of the local subculture area may not view various illegal expressions of violence as menacing or immoral. Furthermore,

when the attacked see their assaulters as agents of the same kind of aggression they themselves represent, violent retaliation is readily legitimized by a situationally specific rationale, as well as by the generally normative supports for violence.

Probably no single theory will ever explain the variety of observable violent behavior. However, the subculture-of-violence approach offers, we believe, the advantage of bringing together psychological and sociological constructs to aid in the explanation of the concentration of violence in specific socioeconomic groups and ecological areas.

Some questions may arise about the genesis of an assumed subculture of violence. The theoretical formulation describes what is believed to be a condition that may exist in varying manifestations from organized crime, delinquent gangs, political subdivisions, and subsets of a lower-class culture. How these variations arise, and from what base, are issues that have not been raised and that would require research to describe. Moreover, the literature on the sociology of conflict, derived principally from Simmel; on the social psychology of conflict; and on the more specific topic of the sociology of violence would have to be carefully examined. That there may be some universal derivatives is neither asserted nor denied. One could argue (1) that there is a biological base for aggressive behavior which may, unless conditioned against it, manifest itself in physical violence; (2) that, in Hegelian terms, each culture thesis contains its contra-culture antithesis; that to develop into a central culture, nonviolence within must be a dominant theme, and that therefore a subtheme of violence in some form is an invariable consequence. We do not find either of these propositions tenable, and there is considerable evidence to contradict both.

Even without returning philosophically to a discussion of man's prepolitical or presocietal state, a more temporally localized question of genesis may be raised. The descriptions current in subcultural theorizing in general sociology or sociological criminology are limited principally to a modern urban setting, although applications of these theories could conceivably be made to the criminal machinations in such culture periods as Renaissance Florence. At present, we create no new statement of the genesis of a subculture of violence, nor do we find it necessary to adopt a single position. The beginning could be a Cohen-like negative reaction that turned into regularized, institutionalized patterns of prescription. Sufficient communication of dominant culture values, norms, goals, and means is, of course, implicitly assumed if some subset of the population is to react negatively. The existence of violent (illegitimate) means also requires that some of the goals (or symbols of goals) of the dominant culture shall have been communicated to subcultural groups in sufficient strength for them to introject and to desire them and, if thwarted in their pursuit of them, to seek them by whatever illegal means are available. The Cloward-Ohlin formulation is, in this context, an equally useful hypothesis for the genesis of a subculture of violence. Miller's idea of a "generating milieu" does not assume—or perhaps even denies—the communication of most middle-class values to the lower class. Especially relevant to our present interest would be communication of attitudes toward the use of violence. Communication should, perhaps, be distinguished from absorption or introjection of culture values. Communication seems to imply transmission cognitively, to suggest that the recipients have conscious awareness of the existence of things. Absorption, or introjection, refers to conative aspects and goes beyond communication in its power to affect personalities. A value becomes part of the individual's attitudinal set or predisposition to act, and must be more than communicated to be an integral element in a prepotent tendency to respond to stimuli. It might be said that both in Cohen's and in Cloward-Ohlin's conceptualizations, middle-class values are communicated but not absorbed as part of the personality or idioverse of those individuals who deviate. In Miller's schema, communication from middle to lower class is not required. A considerable degree of isolation of the latter class is even inferred, suggesting that the lower-class ethic had a developmental history and continuity of its own.

We are not prepared to assert how a subculture of violence arises. Perhaps there are several ways in different cultural settings. It may be that even within the same culture a collective conscience and allegiance to the use of violence develop into a subculture from the combination of more than one birth process, that is, as a negative reaction to the communication of goals from the parent culture, as a positive reaction to this communication coupled with a willingness to use negative means, and as a positive absorption of an indigenous set of subcultural values that, as a system of interlocking values, are the antithesis of the main culture themes.

SOURCE: From *The Subculture of Violence* by Marvin E. Wolfgang and Franco Ferracuti. Copyright © 1967 Routledge Publishers. Reproduced by permission of Taylor & Francis Books UK.

QUESTIONS FOR DISCUSSION AND WRITING

1. Among which groups are homicides "the most prevalent"?

2. According to the Philadelphia study, were either the offenders or their victims individuals who had little contact with the police before?

3. What are the seven propositions of the authors' theory?

Exposure to Community Violence and Childhood Delinquency

Justin W. Patchin

Beth M. Huebner

John D. McCluskey

Sean P. Varano

Timothy S. Bynum

The effect of neighborhood environment on child development has received significant scholarly attention in recent years. Research has suggested that children reared in disadvantaged neighborhoods are at an elevated risk to engage in deviant behaviors. Other research, however, has shown that the vast majority of children who grow up in disorganized environments fail to initiate serious offending. The goal of this research is to examine why some children raised in neighborhoods with similar structural and economic disadvantages engage in delinquent behaviors, whereas others abstain from crime.

Literature Review

Scholars in the Chicago School of Sociology and elsewhere have argued that "characteristics of the urban environment are critical to explaining the emergence of crime in specific communities" and empirical attention has been devoted to structural characteristics such as residential mobility, concentrated disadvantage, and population heterogeneity. Each of these elements is thought to have direct and indirect effects—through decreased informal social control capabilities—on crime.

Ecological research has consistently linked community disadvantage to between-neighborhood differences in violence and crime. More recently, researchers have begun to examine the factors within neighborhoods that are associated with delinquency, specifically, exposure to community violence.

Aggressive reaction to noxious stimuli such as exposure to community violence is consistent with broader criminological theories such as Agnew's general strain theory and Bernard's theory of angry aggression. Consistent with general strain theory, delinquent coping behaviors may result when vicarious strain (in the form of neighborhood violence) leads to anger or frustration. According to Agnew, strains that occur "in settings that are frequented by the individual," such as his or her immediate neighborhood, are particularly salient. Thus, one avenue through which exposure to community violence has been found to influence youth is through psychological functioning, in the sense that there is increased anxiety and promotion of anger in those who witness violence.

Exposure to community violence may also contribute to the generation of learned aggressive behaviors. The use of aggressive situational responses or adoption of weapons for self-defense could be viewed as "learned" responses, consistent with social learning theory and cultural perspectives. In a violent environment, willingness to express toughness is often revered. Youth who understand this "code" may be more inclined to engage in assaultive behaviors or to carry a weapon such that they gain respect from their peers.

Studies in other fields (notably public health) have also linked exposure to community violence with negative behavioral outcomes in children and adolescents, most notably aggressive behavior. For example, Colder and colleagues found that perceived neighborhood danger was associated with positive beliefs about aggression. In addition to promoting aggressiveness, exposure to violence promotes dysfunctional defensive responses such as weapon carrying and fighting behaviors. Sheley and Wright found youths' gun possession was strongly related to a self-reported need for protection. In short, exposure to violence may directly influence aggressive behavior through the changing of the mental calculus of those most often exposed.

This study serves to expand on this line of research by isolating the effect of exposure to community violence on delinquency from that of neighborhood disadvantage and individual social situation.

METHOD

Data

Data for the study were drawn from a larger research project designed to examine the efficacy of police-centered intervention programs in reducing serious, violent behavior among preadolescent and adolescent youth. Individual-level data were obtained through comprehensive interviews of youth, and community-level data were acquired from the U.S. Census Bureau. Personal interviews conducted with 187 youth between the ages of 9 and 15 living in a moderately sized midwestern city served as the foundation of the research. Youth who resided in neighborhoods within the northwest quadrant of the city were targeted for the study because the area had been identified by city officials as disproportionately disadvantaged.

Measures

Dependent Measures

The goal of this research is to examine the effect of exposure to community violence on child participation in serious personal delinquency, controlling for individual-level demographic factors and delinquency correlates. The main research question, then, is as follows: Are youth who live in disorganized neighborhoods, or who perceive their immediate environment to be violent, more likely to carry a weapon or engage in assaultive behavior?

Self-reported weapon possession and assaultive behavior serve as dependent variables; the personal assault measure is dichotomous (1 = individual reported that he or she had assaulted an adult, assaulted a peer, or thrown rocks or bottles at others during the previous 12 months; 0 = respondent did not report assaultive behavior during the past 12 months); the weapon possession measure includes individuals who reported that they had carried a weapon for any reason during the previous 12 months (1 = youth reported possessing a weapon on one or more occasions during the last 12 months; 0 = youth did not report weapon possession).

Even though the average age of the sample was quite young (mean = 12.0), the participants reported substantial involvement in serious delinquency during the prior year. More than half (58%) of sample members reported that they had committed assaultive behavior during the past year, and 18% of youth indicated that they were in possession of a weapon during the past 12 months. Specifically, of those youth who were in possession of a weapon, 54% reported carrying a knife, and 41% reported carrying a gun.

Neighborhood Influences

Two measures of neighborhood influence are included in the models. The first exposure to community violence, measured at the individual level, was designed to reflect personal experience with neighborhood violence and is operationalized using a seven-item additive scale. Respondents were asked how often in the previous 12 months they heard gun shots, saw somebody arrested, saw drug deals, saw someone being beaten up, saw someone get stabbed or shot, saw gangs in their neighborhood, and saw somebody pull a gun on another person.

The neighborhood disadvantage construct included the percentage of residents below the poverty line, households receiving public assistance, female-headed households, residents older than 16 who are unemployed, population younger than 18 years old, and population that is African American.

Individual Characteristics and Delinquency Correlates

A number of individual-level variables are included in the model as controls. Gender was dichotomized into male respondents and female respondents. Race was dichotomized into non-White and White. The age variable represents the youth's age in years. A final measure is included in the models to control for previous arrests.

In addition, four variables are included in the models as delinquency correlates, both to control for their individual effects and to determine their potential relationship to neighborhood-level factors in terms of serious childhood violence. The single-parent family construct reflects whether the child lived with only one primary caregiver or otherwise. Family supervision is measured using a five-item additive scale. Respondents were asked, "How much does your primary caregiver know about who your close friends are, what you do with your friends, who your close friends' parents are, who you are with when you are not at home, and what you are doing in school?"

A four-item additive scale was designed to measure the respondent's attachment to school. Individuals were asked to report their agreement with the following statements: "I try hard in school"; "Education is so important that it is worth it to put up with things I don't like"; and "In general, I like school."

Finally, an eight-item additive scale is included, representing peer delinquency. Respondents were asked in the past year how many of their friends drank beer, wine, or liquor; used a weapon or force to get money or things from people; attacked someone with a weapon or with the idea of seriously hurting him or her; hit someone with the idea of hurting him or her (e.g., fist-fighting); stole something worth more than $100; stole something worth more than $5 but less than $50; damaged or destroyed someone else's property on purpose; or took a car for a ride without the owner's permission.

FINDINGS

Neighborhood Influences and Correlates of Delinquency

Exposure to violence had a moderately strong and significant effect on each of the delinquency correlates, net of individual controls. Youth who indicated personal exposure to neighborhood violence reported lower levels of parental supervision and school attachment and were more likely to associate with delinquent peers. As expected, community disadvantage had little effect in the models. Because youth resided in the same general neighborhoods, there was little variation in the level of disorganization. Nevertheless, it appears that youths' perceptions of neighborhood violence are more indicative of delinquency correlates than the global indicator of neighborhood disadvantage.

Personal Assault

Males and youth with a previous arrest were more likely to report committing an act of personal assault in the previous 12 months. The strength of the relationship between arrest history, gender, and personal assault was quite strong. Both males and individuals with a previous arrest were greater than three times as likely to report a personal assault when compared with females and individuals without previous exposure to the criminal justice system.

The inclusion of neighborhood influences improved the explanatory power of the model, even though the exposure to violence construct was the only measure found to be statistically significant. The results of this model also support the study hypotheses. Individuals who reported higher levels of exposure to violence in their community were significantly more likely to report participation in personal assault behaviors over the previous year. However, the strength of association for community violence exposure was small; for every 1 unit increase in the exposure to violence construct, youth were 1.16 times more likely to report personal assault.

None of the delinquency correlates was found to be statistically significant in the final model. Moreover, the inclusion of the delinquency correlates did little to change the effect of exposure to violence on personal assault. Net of individual controls and ecological domains, individuals who reported higher exposure to violence in their neighborhoods were more likely to indicate participation in personal assault.

Weapon Possession

Individuals with previous arrest histories were significantly more likely to report possessing a weapon during the past year. In fact, youth with previous arrest histories were nearly 14 times more likely to report possessing a weapon. The exposure to community violence measure was also significantly related to weapon possession; for each unit increase in the exposure to violence measure, youth were 1.22 times more likely to report the possession of a weapon during the past year. Consistent with the results from the personal assault model, neighborhood disadvantage was not significantly associated with weapons possession.

Contrary to the assault model, peer influence was significantly related to weapon possession. The explanatory power of the delinquency correlates as a whole were also moderately strong. The effect of peer delinquency was particularly strong, with a 1-unit increase in the measure of peer delinquency associated with a 23% increase in the likelihood of weapons possession. This finding highlights the importance of peer influences in understanding certain forms of serious personal delinquency, specifically weapons possession.

DISCUSSION

The study was able to build on previous research by more fully exploring the neighborhood-level variables associated with childhood violence. The specific research question posed was as follows: What community-level factors differentiate offenders from nonoffenders who live in the same communities? Results from the analyses supported the hypothesis that individuals who are exposed to more community violence are more likely to engage in serious personal violence. Youth who reported higher levels of exposure to community violence were significantly more likely to report possessing a weapon and engaging in personal assault.

In contrast, larger social indicators of neighborhood disadvantage did not have a significant effect on delinquency. This is not to suggest that disadvantage, per se, is unimportant. But research that simply tests the relationship between structural or physical attributes of the community may miss another important variable, namely, the exposure to community violence that often occurs in these contexts.

The research also highlights the importance of considering the potential effect of delinquency correlates in understanding involvement in serious, personal delinquency. Exposure to violence was significantly related to parental supervision, school attachment, and peer delinquency. The effect was particularly strong for the peer delinquency model. It is noteworthy that the exposure to violence measure remained significantly associated with childhood violence, even after controlling for other common correlates of delinquency. Although associating with delinquent peers does appear to influence the relationship between exposure to violence and weapon possession, exposure to violence did have a significant effect on weapon possession and personal assault, net of controls for individual demographic characteristics and delinquency correlates.

Even though our results stress the virulent effects of witnessing community violence as opposed to disorder or disadvantage per se, community mobilization that enables citizens to proactively protect adolescents, particularly those most at risk for delinquency, appears to be a viable crime reduction strategy.

SOURCE: From *Crime & Delinquency*, Vol. 52, No. 2, 307–332, April 2006. Copyright © 2006 Sage Publications. Reprinted by permission of Sage Publications, Inc.

QUESTIONS FOR DISCUSSION AND WRITING

1. What have scholars in the Chicago school of sociology argued and which structural characteristics have they studied? What have researchers recently begun to examine?

2. What did the authors find with respect to exposure to violence? How much of a role did community disorganization play?

3. According to the authors, what else does this research highlight?

CAUSES AND PREVENTION OF JUVENILE DELINQUENCY

TRAVIS HIRSCHI

A RESTRAINT OR CONTROL THEORY OF DELINQUENCY

Delinquent acts are acts contrary to law. Since the law embodies the moral values of the community (and insofar as it does not, the task of explaining delinquency is even easier), it follows that (1) delinquent acts are contrary to the wishes and expectations of other people; (2) they involve the risk of punishment, both formal and informal; (3) they take (and save) time and energy; and (4) they are contrary to conventional moral belief.

If these assumptions are true, it follows further that those most likely to engage in delinquent acts are (1) least likely to be concerned about the wishes and expectations of others; (2) least likely to be concerned about the risk of punishment; (3) most likely to have the time and energy the act requires; and (4) least likely to accept moral beliefs contrary to delinquency.

This, in brief form, is an example of control theory. It asserts that the delinquent is "relatively free of the intimate attachments, the aspirations, and the moral beliefs that bind most people to a life within the law." Such theories assume that the potential for asocial conduct is present in everyone, that we would all commit delinquent acts were we not somehow prevented from doing so. Put another way, they assume that we are born amoral, that our morality has been

added by training and is maintained by ties to other people and institutions.

In control theories, the important differences between delinquents and nondelinquents are not differences in motivation; they are, rather, differences in the extent to which natural motives are controlled. Control theories thus focus on the restraints on delinquent behavior, on the circumstances and desires that prevent it. Factors traditionally viewed as causes of delinquency, such things as poverty or "learning disabilities," remain potential causes and retain whatever significance their statistical relation with delinquency allows. They are not seen, however, as producing delinquency in the same way that friction produces heat. Instead, they are interpreted as factors that weaken the conscience or reduce the effectiveness of controlling institutions. Such causes do not require that the individual become delinquent; instead, they affect the likelihood that he will be exposed and that he will give in to temptation.

While these theories do not imply that the delinquent act is produced by any single cause, they retain the assumption that it is determined by all causes present at the moment it is committed. Some of these causes are the calculations and desires of the actor himself. It is he who wants sex, money, or peace; it is he who decides they may be had by robbing a liquor store; it is he who concludes that no policeman is near the scene. If he miscalculates the risk-benefit ratio, so does everyone, once in a while. If he is "compelled" to commit the act, it is not by force peculiar to him, but by forces common to all of us. These theories thus locate the immediate causes of delinquent acts in the desires of the actor and his evaluation of the situation. While such causes provide reasons and motives, they cannot be interpreted as forcing the actor to act against his will or as freeing him from responsibility, since they originate with him.

Control theories come in a variety of forms and borrow from several social science disciplines. Since all of them agree that people require training, guidance, and at least a little supervision if they are to become and remain law abiding, no useful purpose is served by suggesting that one is superior to the others.

One important variant considers the effectiveness of child rearing or the adequacy of socialization as the key to delinquency. Learning theories of the control variety assume that the purpose of socialization is to teach law-abiding conduct, that the delinquent has been *improperly* trained or *inadequately* socialized. They assume that we must learn to be law abiding, that some lessons are more to the point than others, and that some of us are better teachers and better pupils than others. Theories that focus on learning are *not* control theories insofar as they assume that crime is a product of socialization, that the delinquent has been properly trained or adequately socialized from the point of view of those training him. Such a view makes crime social rather than a social behavior, the product of positive rather than negative causes. On the whole, psychologists have favored learning theories of the control variety, while sociologists have preferred theories based on quite different assumptions about the nature of crime and the value structure of American society. It goes without saying that the choice between these views should be a matter of evidence rather than disciplinary allegiance or policy advantage.

A second way to account for delinquency from a control perspective is to consider the effectiveness of institutions, such as the family and the school, and the extent to which they work together or at cross purposes in the control of delinquent conduct. Such an analysis may follow groups through the life cycle, noting variation *over time* in the likelihood that they will commit delinquent acts, or it can compare groups *at one point in time* with respect to their institutional affiliations and loyalties. Such explanations assume that all individuals are equally well socialized. They therefore concentrate on external rather than internal controls. Although they cannot explain all variation in delinquency among individuals, they are often effective in accounting for differences in delinquency rates across groups and over time. These were once known as *theories of social disorganization.* They assume that delinquency is evidence of institutional breakdown and failure. Their competitors are theories that deny that some institutions are more effective than others in meeting human needs and in controlling the behavior of their members.

Let us explore some of the traditional causes of delinquency from this perspective.

The Family and Attachment to Others

Sociologists use terms such as "significant others" or "reference groups" to refer to those people we consider important, to those whose good opinion we value, to those capable of influencing our behavior. These ideas correctly imply that there are still other people not very important to us. The danger with such concepts as applied to delinquency is that they suggest that each of us *has* significant others or important reference groups, which may or may not be the case. Thus sociologists sometimes say that "behavior is an attempt to maintain and enhance favorable judgments from our reference groups," which implies that delinquency, as behavior, has similar sources. Control theory reminds us that while we are all closer to some people than others, it does not follow that we are all equally close to someone. It reminds us that some of our behavior must be interpreted as reflecting lack of interest in the opinion of others.

One set of people we are expected to be close to, at least in childhood, is parents. *Parents do not want their children to be delinquent* (although they may, in some cases, want the product of the child's delinquency, such as the color television set "found" on the way home). We may therefore assume that delinquency often says something about the quality of relation between parent and child.

And, indeed, those least attached to their parents are most likely to commit delinquent acts. Evidence for this assertion comes from a variety of sources and cultures. However this dimension is measured, whether by asking the parent or child or by observing their behavior with each other, and whatever it is called, whether "cohesiveness," "respect," or "love," the results are the same. Academic opinion differs about whether the father or the mother is more important as a controlling agent. As of now, the best guess is that they are equally important, partly because the child tends to view them as a "team," a view that is often correct.

Those who do not care or think about the reactions of their parents are more likely to commit delinquent acts because they have less to lose. Risking the good opinion of some other person is easy when that person's opinion is not valued anyway. There are, to be sure, many sources of lack of concern for parental opinion. Some parents are simply less "worthy" of respect: They have fewer resources with which to coerce or buy conformity; they do not live up to the adolescent's standards of appearance and demeanor; they are easily fooled and manipulated. (Put more objectively, they have less money and education.) Still others do not care to earn the love or respect of their children, being consistently cruel to or neglectful of them.

Lack of attachment to parents easily spills over into lack of "respect" for teachers and the police, for adults in general. This spillover is both psychological and structural. A good deal of the controlling power of adults outside the family lies in the threat of reporting the child's misbehavior to his parents. When this threat is removed by parental impotence, the sanctioning power of all institutions is reduced. By the same token, when relatives, friends, neighbors, and teachers do not or cannot report the misbehavior of the child, whatever control his parents might exercise is no longer possible.

Given the centrality of the family in the system of internal and external (psychological and structural) control, its absence from most sociological theories of delinquency is something of a mystery. The mystery is deepened by recent efforts to justify the absence: "We do not accept ... that delinquency may result from differential attachment to parents, and learning processes which result in children being differentially attached to moral authority in general—especially at a time when the hold of the nuclear family is, by all accounts, being weakened." One way of reading such statements is that the family is no longer important in the control of delinquency because the family is no longer important in anything. However, when we look at adolescents whose allegiance to their families is profound (the vast majority), we see the error in assuming that because the hold of the family has weakened for some it has weakened for all. In fact, once we admit variation in the effectiveness of family control, it becomes apparent that the family may become more important as a cause of delinquency as the number of "weak" families grows.

Variations in the effectiveness of family control help account for many of the major correlates of delinquency. Girls are more closely supervised by their parents than boys and are more likely to be emotionally dependent on them, as well as on other adults. (As a consequence, there is evidence that girls are more likely than boys to "suffer" from family disruption.) Low-income and ethnic minority families are less able to control their children, for the variety of reasons mentioned earlier. In addition, such families are more likely to be disrupted and to live in neighborhoods where control is made difficult by the lack of support from the community at large.

In a much-quoted statement on the policy implications of these facts, Wilson says, "If a child is delinquent because *his family made him so* ... it is hard to conceive what society might do about *his attitudes.*" Such enlightened pessimism being the order of the day, it may be worth repeating that control theory does not suggest that the family *makes* the child delinquent in a way contrary to the implications of deterrence "theory." (Nor does it suggest that all the families that will ever be exist now—a suggestion admired by those wishing to conclude it is too late to do anything about the family anyway.) In fact, there is no reason to believe that those wishing to increase the costs and decrease the benefits of crime may not do so as well (and as cheaply) by strengthening the family as by increasing the number of policemen.

The School: Commitment to or Stake in Conformity

Perhaps the best predictor of delinquency in American society is difficulty in school. For three-quarters of a century, there has been a large grain of truth in the statement that "truancy is the kindergarten of delinquency." The school is expected to engage the attention and maintain the interest of the child for some ten to fifteen years. Yet, for many, it is quickly clear that education is not their game, that proficiency in reading, writing, and arithmetic is not going to come. Given the hours and years such "students" are expected to remain in school, we should perhaps wonder at how so many manage to avoid serious involvement in delinquency. In any event, those who do poorly in school are considerably more likely than those who do well to end up in trouble with the law. There are several ways to explain these differences from a control perspective.

One line of thought suggests that, in the school as in the family, the bond of affection or respect is crucial. The poor student simply learns to dislike school and therefore to deny the legitimacy of the school's authority. While true, such analysis is incomplete, since the school has other resources at its disposal. Institutions that prepare adolescents for the future may rely on their interest or investment in that future as a means of controlling them. The student who aspires to be a doctor or lawyer and who has worked long and hard to attain the grades required for access to these professions will presumably not want to risk his investment by engaging in delinquent acts. He is committed to, or has a stake in, conformity.

The student with low grades in the "prevocational track" does not have such an investment. His prospects for future status are not bright; there appears to be little connection between his present behavior (inside or outside the classroom) and his adult life. He will end up in a low-paying (or a high-paying) manual job, virtually regardless of what he does during the school years. He therefore has no stake in conforming to the rules; the risks from engaging in delinquent acts are slight; he is therefore more likely to engage in them.

Another consequence of the school's lack of relevance to the student is that it frees him from the shackles of childhood. Completing one's education, whether by graduation or by simply giving up, is to become, in one sense, an adult. Consistent with this premise, those who complete their education while still in school are much more likely to adopt attitudes and behavior patterns normally reserved for adults. They are more likely to smoke, drink, date, and be interested in automobiles. It is wrong to conclude that such freedom to behave in adult ways,

coupled as it is with the normal freedom of childhood magnified by lack of concern for school, is particularly painful. It is not. In fact, it is a species of happiness. It is also highly conducive to delinquency.

In sum, the poor student is less likely to be concerned about the good opinion of the adults who run the system; he is unlikely to accept the argument that education is the royal road to success; and he is more likely to behave like an adult. Adult behavior on the part of children comes close to being delinquent in its own right and is, in any event, conducive to actual delinquency.

As might be expected, school performance is also an important key to many of the other correlates of delinquency. As of now, it appears to account for the marked differences in intelligence between delinquents and non-delinquents. It accounts for much of the differences by class and race, and it helps us understand part of the effects of family disruption. If "learning disability" turns out to be important in delinquency, it stands ready to account for that relation, too. (Actual school performance explains only a little of the considerably lower delinquency rate of girls. Girls are, however, much more likely than boys to be sensitive to the opinion of teachers, so that "school" in general explains still more of this difference.)

In general, it appears that the school has become the major institution of social control in American society. Or perhaps it has become the major generator of delinquency in American society. Which of these views is more nearly correct? Or are they identical? Again, control theory suggests that the former view is appropriate, that school failure represents not a motive for auto theft, but instead a reduction in the potential cost of apprehension for this crime. The school may "fail" to win the interest and loyalty of many of its pupils, but it does not *make* them delinquent. And there is no good evidence that efforts to pretend that all students are equal in academic ability (by eliminating IQ tests, tracking, and by inflating grades) fool anyone but the pretenders.

The Peer Group or Gang

The adolescent free of such adult institutions as the school and the family is free to take up with others in a similar situation, and he clearly tends to do so. The peer group, or gang, has thus for a long time been correctly seen as a concomitant of delinquency. At one period in American theorizing, the gang came to be seen as the key link in the chain, the most important cause of delinquency. The attitudes and values that produce delinquent behavior, it was said, are a product of gang membership. This image of delinquent behavior as a product of group membership was especially appealing to sociologists, partly because it suggests that delinquency, too, is social rather than asocial behavior. If true, control theory would be in trouble: Delinquency would be a product of training rather than a consequence of lack of training; it would result directly from strong rather than weak bonds to others; it would be moral rather than amoral behavior (at least from the perspective of the group in question).

Fortunately for the theory, the image of the gang as an "intimate group" bears little resemblance to the facts. Delinquents do tend to associate with delinquents, just as kids interested in chess tend to associate with each other, but the ties among delinquents are not equal in quality to those among other peer groups. On the contrary, there is now considerable evidence that gang members tend to see each other as unpredictable and untrustworthy, that their ties to each other reflect their weakened ties to other social groups.

Consistent with this revised image, it is now clear that gangs organized around or for delinquent activity, if they exist at all, are extremely rare. The bases of gang membership are age, sex, ethnicity, and territory; the sources of cohesion in the gang are external rather than internal—all members are caught in a common situation; they are to some extent forced together rather than attracted to each other. And, indeed, gang members are only slightly more likely than non-gang members to commit delinquent acts.

Belief

Belief has played a major role in sociological theories of delinquency. In perhaps the most famous of these theories, the person becomes delinquent because of "an excess of definitions favorable to violation of law over definitions unfavorable to violation of law." The basic assumption in some theories is that we cannot act contrary to our beliefs unless forced to do so. This means that criminals and delinquents either have beliefs or values that require delinquency or that they are under considerable pressure to act contrary to beliefs that forbid delinquency. Control theory offers an alternative to these views: The

belief system of the delinquent neither requires nor forbids delinquency. Rather, it makes the choice between law-abiding and delinquent behavior a matter of expediency. This amoral or instrumental belief system asserts that "It is okay to get around the law if you can get away with it," that "Everybody does it, so you have to do it first," and that "Suckers deserve what they get."

These beliefs are consistent with (or effects of) the delinquent's alienation from conventional persons and institutions. That is, they reflect and rationalize the position of the unattached. Such beliefs are reasonably seen as "causes" of delinquency in the sense that those holding them are, as a consequence, more likely to commit delinquent acts. Now consider the following: "If causal theories explain why a criminal acts as he does, they also explain why he *must* act as he does, and therefore they make any reliance on deterrence seem futile and irrelevant." We have at least partially explained why a criminal acts as he does, but we have not implied that he *must* act as he does, nor have we suggested that deterrence is futile and irrelevant. On the contrary, the theory suggests that deterrence should be effective, that in the extreme case it is *all* that stands between the crime and the potential criminal. Wilson and others who would use deterrence *against* causal explanation have both the logic of causation and its implications for deterrence simply wrong.

Age

One of the most troublesome correlates of delinquency, both in terms of accurate measurement and explanation, is age. The tendency of delinquency, as measured by official records, to increase rapidly in early adolescence is clearly established. This increase is not readily explained by changes in the adolescent's beliefs, his attitudes toward or performance in school, or by changes in family structure. Rather, it appears to be a function of the increasing responsibility granted and required of the child at this time.

That greater responsibility is required is evident: The law allows a child of 7 to get away with things it hesitates to ignore in a youth of 14. By the same token, it is even less tolerant of the same behavior in an adult of 21. These varying attributions of criminal responsibility on the basis of age go back a long time. That they remain with us is clear in statistics on criminality and in the provision of separate legal institutions for juveniles and adults. And, whatever the trends in the juvenile court, it seems safe to assume that in one form or another they will remain with us always.

In this case, the law again presumably reflects the sentiments of the community as a whole. Thus it seems reasonable to assume that at the same time the requirement of legal responsibility is increasing, the granting of social responsibility is increasing at the same rate. In other words, as the child becomes more accountable to the law, he becomes less accountable to adults in general, especially to his parents. Delinquent behavior is thus most likely to *occur* and is most likely to be defined as *delinquent* at the point where the line of decreasing tolerance (by the law) crosses the line of increasing freedom from adult supervision. This point of maximum likelihood of "delinquency" is probably the point at which the child first appears to be physically mature.

Such a conception helps explain how delinquency in adolescence can be predicted from school performance and from family and school "misbehavior" at an early age. It is not so much that the child suddenly "becomes delinquent" in middle adolescence as that he has, in many cases, been "delinquent" all along.

Summary

Causes of delinquency are often interpreted as motives propelling the individual to crime. Such interpretations suggest that, once a cause has operated, not much can be done to prevent delinquent acts; that restriction, supervision, and the threat of punishment are unlikely to be effective. They also suggest a statistical relation between cause and effect sufficiently close that at least "most people" exposed to the cause should become delinquent.

Many social scientists, convinced that deterrence can be effective and certain that most people exposed to the causes of crime do not become criminals, have concluded that the concept of causation is inappropriate to the study of delinquency and that the search for causes should be abandoned.

Still, it remains true that causes of delinquency can be (and have been) discovered. It also remains true that adolescents exposed to the causes are amenable to restriction, supervision, and the threat of punishment. Since this is so, it must be that the *interpretation* of causes as supplying the motive force behind delinquency is the root of the problem.

An alternative interpretation is that the traditional causes of delinquency do not produce delinquency directly but rather by affecting the system of internal and external controls. In other words, causes free the potential delinquent from concern for the ordinary costs of crime. In this interpretation, the benefits of crime—such things as money, revenge, sex, and excitement—are available at the moment the crime is committed to anyone committing it. Crime is not a response to unusual psychological needs or the product of a profound sense of duty. It is, rather, the product of ordinary desires operating on people ill-equipped to resist them.

It follows that delinquent behavior may be prevented by restoring its ordinary costs (removing its causes), by providing its benefits in other ways, and by adding extraordinary or more certain penalties. The genius of most social groups is that they are able to control the behavior of their members without frequent resort to severe penalties. Those who say this cannot now be done ignore the fact that it is being done, cheaply and efficiently, in countless collections of basically amoral creatures.

SOURCE: From *Sociological Inquiry* 47(3–4):329–340. Copyright © 1977 by the University of Texas Press. Reprinted by permission of Blackwell Publishing Ltd.

QUESTIONS FOR DISCUSSION AND WRITING

1. What does control theory assert about delinquents? What do control theories assume?

2. With respect to parental attachment, which youths are most likely to commit delinquent acts?

3. How does thinking about reactions of one's parents affect delinquency? How can lack of attachment to parents lead to lack of respect for other adults?

EXPLORING THE UTILITY OF SOCIAL CONTROL THEORY FOR YOUTH DEVELOPMENT

Issues of Attachment, Involvement, and Gender

ANGELA J. HUEBNER

SHERRY C. BETTS

In most communities in America, adolescents spend about 6 or 7 hours a day in formal school settings, leaving a large amount of free time available for other activities. According to the Carnegie Corporation, the out-of-school hours make up the single largest block of time available to adolescents. Because incidents of juvenile violence peak during the after-school hours, it is not surprising that parents, educators, law enforcement officials, policy makers, and other adults have become increasingly concerned with how young people spend the time when they are not in school. Many believe that the non-school hours represent an opportunity to provide youth with positive learning, developmental, and recreational opportunities. Scores of organizations have developed programs to fill the out-of-school hours. In fact, more than 17,000 youth-serving organizations exist in this country, and it is estimated that at least 300,000 people work in a full- or part-time capacity for youth-serving organizations. Unfortunately, when it comes to understanding youth development during the non-school hours, it

seems that theory development and research have lagged behind practice. For us to understand and promote youth development in the out-of-school context in a comprehensive way, research, theory, and practice must complement each other.

From a theoretical standpoint, much of what has been written in the academic literature about youth development as it occurs in the out-of-school hours has been couched within a developmental ecological model, developmental contextualism, and/or a risk and protective factor framework. Bronfenbrenner's developmental ecological model suggests that human development should be examined as a joint function of the individual and of the environment. This examination would include, for example, factors such as the interplay between the youth and the family, the youth and school, parents and workplace, and community norms and values. Developmental contextualism expands this model by recognizing that the relationship between the individual and his or her environment is in a constant state of fluctuation across the life span. Bogenschneider's ecological risk/protective theory suggests that we must consider both risk and protective factors within each context described in the developmental ecological model and the developmental contextualism model.

Although such frameworks are helpful, they have not been used within the youth development arena to generate specific research questions or hypotheses that lend themselves to more traditional methods of scientific inquiry. Instead, they have been used to generate principles of effective practices in targeting high-risk youth for program delivery, evaluation, and policy. Such work has helped to advance the field of youth work, but it has done little to help the practice of youth development gain credibility in the academic arena. In a review of the scientific foundations of youth development, Benson and Saito make the statement that "[youth development] practice . . . is considerably ahead of the scientific foundation of this work" and "what we seem to have here is an example of the classic split between theory and application." Based on their review of the evaluation literature of youth development programs, Roth, Brooks-Gunn, Murray, and Foster conclude that "the current mismatch between the enthusiasm for these programmatic efforts and the empirical evidence calls into question the effectiveness of such efforts." Benson and Saito suggest that to gain respectability within the academic arena, we need to do a better job of articulating and testing specific models of youth development.

Rather than developing new models of youth development, this article borrows an existing model of youth behavior, reflected in the tenets of social control theory (SCT). Broadly stated, control theories focus on the relationship between the individual and his or her bonds to society. Deviant acts are thought to occur when one's bond to society is broken. Positive development has been defined by Roth et al. as "the engagement in prosocial behaviors" and avoidance of health-compromising and future-jeopardizing behaviors. Instead of suggesting that youth development is necessarily a deviant act, we suggest that youth development occurs on a continuum with negative and positive outcomes on opposite ends of the spectrum. Given this, we assume that an individual's bonds to society are the mechanisms through which positive development occurs and negative outcomes are avoided. Although SCT has been one of the most widely used theories in the examination of deviant

behavior in young people, it has not been used to examine positive developmental outcomes. The tenets of SCT are consistent with the three frameworks mentioned above and also provide guidelines for testable research questions related to youth development outcomes. This study examined the predictive utility of two SCT bonds—attachment to caring adults and involvement in out-of-school time activities—as they relate to delinquency and academic achievement.

LITERATURE REVIEW

In the following section, we will review the tenets of SCT, the literature on attachment to caring adults, the research on involvement in out-of-school time activities, and their relationship to both delinquency and academic achievement. Because SCT has traditionally been employed as an explanation of male deviance, potential gender differences in the relationship among the variables will be examined.

Theoretical Framework: SCT

As defined by Hirschi, SCT assumes that "delinquent acts occur when an individual's bond to society is weak or broken." These "bonds" include (a) attachment to parents, school, and peers; (b) commitment to conventional lines of action; (c) involvement in conventional activities; and (d) belief in a common value system. Consistent with the developmental ecological model and developmental contextualism, these bonds reflect the interplay between multiple developmental contexts (e.g., family, school, peers, and community values and norms). As Jessor, Turbin, and Costa point out, "protective factors operate by providing personal or social controls against problem behavior, by promoting activities that are alternatives to or incompatible with problem behavior, and by strengthening orientations toward and commitments to conventional institutions, such as church, school, or family, or to the larger adult society." We consider each bond of SCT a powerful protective factor for youth, consistent with Bogenschneider's risk/protective theoretical perspective.

For this study, it is important to note that we limited our focus to only the "attachment" and "involvement" bonds of SCT. These bonds are of particular interest because they are consistent with the general aim of most youth development programs, namely, providing relationships with caring adults and opportunities for involvement in prosocial competency-building activities. In Hirschi's model, *attachment* is further defined as the affections and emotions one holds for significant others and social institutions in one's life, and *involvement* refers to the amount of time one spends in conventional activities. For this study, we examined attachment as it related to parents and peers. In addition, we expanded the notion of attachment to include nonparent adults.

Significance of Gender

Many researchers and theorists have suggested that boys and girls negotiate different developmental pathways as they mature to adulthood. In his review of the literature, Cosse concludes that a feminine pathway includes a strong emphasis on relationships with others, whereas a masculine pathway focuses more on autonomy and development of skills. Other researchers have also concluded that women tend to emphasize care and concern for interpersonal relationships, empathy, and understanding of emotional needs, whereas men tend to be focused more on individuality, rationality, separation, impersonality, fairness, and rules. Some evidence suggests that during adolescence, pressure to behave in more stereotypically male or female ways actually intensifies, making the adolescent years a particularly salient time to examine gender differences. Indeed, gender differences have been documented with respect to the variables of interest in this study: academic achievement, delinquency, attachment, and involvement.

Keeping gender in mind, the remainder of the literature review is organized around the independent (IV) and dependent variables (DV) of interest. Specifically, the following sections will examine the literature on (a) the relationship among gender, academic achievement (DV), attachment (IV), and involvement (IV) and (b) the relationship among gender, delinquency (DV), attachment (IV), and involvement (IV).

Gender, Academic Achievement, Attachment, and Involvement

Several researchers have noted the discrepancies in factors related to academic achievement between boys and girls. Findings by Dweck and Licht suggest that girls have been socialized to believe that achievement is out of their control; other studies suggest that girls are more likely to attribute their successes to hard work whereas boys are more likely to attribute their success to intelligence. Several researchers suggest that girls have a higher fear of success than do boys and that girls may intentionally get lower grades than boys in school because being intelligent is not considered feminine. Finally, despite no documented differences in ability, girls are far less likely than boys to pursue and remain in advanced courses in math and science.

The important role of caring adults in the lives of young people has been clearly documented as a protective factor for youth. A relationship between caring adults and academic achievement has also been established. Most of these findings are related to mentor/mentee relationships between caring adults and youth. For example, in their evaluation of the Big Brothers/Big Sisters program, Grossman and Tierney found that youth who participated in the program reported being more confident about their performance at school. In a qualitative study of a mentoring program for at-risk youth, de Anda found that mentees reported a number of positive outcomes, including increased academic achievement. In a qualitative examination of success factors for youth attending alternative school, Little found that successful students were connected with caring staff members who helped them solve problems and generate future plans.

The positive relationship between activity participation and academic achievement has also been well documented. For example, in their study of 6th-grade to 12th-grade students, Cooper, Valentine, Nye, and Lindsay found that participation in extracurricular activities such as school sports and clubs, as well as participation in groups outside of school (e.g., non-school sports, Scouts, religious groups), were associated with higher achievement test scores. These findings remained constant even when the effects of gender were controlled. In a longitudinal study of the effects of out-of-school activities on educational outcomes, Jordan and Nettles reported that participation in structured activities and spending time interacting with adults had significantly positive effects on later educational outcomes. Gerber also reported a positive relationship between extracurricular activity participation and academic achievement.

Gender, Delinquency, Attachment, and Involvement

Historically, behaviors considered delinquent have been different for boys and girls. Boys' offenses typically included aggressive behavior, vandalism, and theft, whereas girls' offenses were usually related to status offenses such as running away or truancy. Although boys have traditionally reported higher rates of participation in delinquent activities, recent statistics suggest that during the past decade, the number of girls involved in violent activities has increased at a faster rate than boys (16.5% versus 4.5%).

With few exceptions, studies examining gender differences in attachment and delinquency are rare. The notable exceptions suggest that attachment bonds have different effects for males and females. In their study of attachment to families, Canter found that, although girls reported stronger bonds to parents than boys, the protective function of parent attachment was greater for boys. Anderson et al. found that attachment to parents reduced the severity of adolescent boys' delinquency, whereas attachment to peers and school reduced the severity of adolescent girls' delinquency.

In a comparison between boys' and girls' attitudes and behaviors in gangs and ganglike illegal activities, Esbensen, Deschenes, and Winfree reported that girls in gangs report greater social isolation from friends and family than do boys in gangs. One interpretation of this finding could be that girls join gangs at least in part to fulfill their need for relationships, whereas boys join to fulfill their need for instrumental success. Finally, in a parks and recreation study of park court usage, Thurber reported that boys were more likely to show up without invitation to participate in pick-up sports games than girls. Girls' participation rates were much higher when they were invited to use the court at a specific time.

Researchers have also examined the relationship between activity participation and delinquent or antisocial behavior. Recent research has suggested that all after-school activities are not created equal; that is, the type and context of the activity makes a difference in youth outcomes. In their recent study of the extracurricular activities of 1,259 Caucasian adolescents, Eccles and

Barber suggest that the "protective" function of participation in extracurricular activities depends in part on the type of extracurricular activities considered as well as the gender of the adolescent. For example, they found that youth involved in prosocial activities such as church and volunteer work were less likely to participate in risky behaviors than were their noninvolved peers. In addition, their study revealed that whereas participation in team sports was related to higher GPA, college attendance, and positive connections to school, it was also associated with an increased likelihood of alcohol use for boys. Based on his examination of longitudinal data, Larson concluded that although participation in sports did not lead to a decline in participation in delinquent activities, participation in other youth organization activities did. In their study of more than 700 14-year-olds and their parents, Mahoney and Stattin found that youth participation in highly structured leisure activities was inversely related to antisocial behavior. Participation in minimally structured leisure activities was related to higher levels of antisocial behavior, especially for boys.

In sum, it appears that both attachment and involvement, as defined generally by SCT, have the potential to have a positive influence on academic achievement and to be powerful protective factors against delinquency. The role of gender in determining the salience of these bonds for both deviant and positive outcomes remains less clear.

The following hypotheses were created:

Hypothesis 1: For males and females, attachment bond variables and involvement bond variables will be inversely related to delinquent behavior and positively related to academic achievement.

Hypothesis 2: The attachment bonds will account for more variance in both delinquency and academic achievement in females, and the involvement bonds will account for more variance in both delinquency and academic achievement in males.

Method

Sample

Data for this study were gathered as part of a larger study of youth attitudes, behaviors, values, worries, and hopes. Participants were students in Grades 7 through 12 in a high school in a southwestern U.S. mining community of approximately 11,000 residents. This community is located about 90 miles east of a major metropolitan area. Approximately 12% of its residents have reported incomes below the poverty level. Of the 1,060 students enrolled in the school, 911 students (86%) participated in this study. A 159-item comprehensive survey was administered during regular classes on 1 day to all students who were present, had parent permission to participate, and chose to participate. Fifty-one percent of the students responding to the survey were male and 49% were female. Forty-eight percent reported their ethnic group as Caucasian non-Hispanic, 26% as Hispanic, 19% as Native American, 1% as Asian, and 6% as Other. The mean age was 15 years. The youth in the sample reported a number of different living situations and family structures. Fifty-one percent lived with two parents (biological or adoptive), 20% lived with a single parent, 3% lived half time with each parent, 17% lived in a blended or step-family, and 9% lived in other arrangements such as foster home, alone, or with a nonparent adult.

Measures

Four measures in this study assess attachment and seven measures assess involvement in conventional activities. These measures were adapted from Small and Rodgers. The measures are not intended to be exact replications of Hirschi's instruments; however, they do reflect theoretical constructs consistent with theories of social control.

Attachment

Attachment to Parents. Perceived parental quality (PRNTQUAL) was used as a measure of attachment to parents. Parental quality was assessed using a five-item scale. Items included "my parents are good parents," "my parents trust me," "my parents are there for me," "my parents care about me," and "my parents are fair." Responses ranged from 0 (never) to 4 (always) (Cronbach's alpha = .83; female $M = 3.24$, $SD = .81$; male $M = 3.23$, $SD = .78$). Time spent with family doing fun activities (TIMEFAM) was used as a second measure of attachment to parents (and other siblings). This one-item

measure asked, "How often do you spend time doing things for fun with family members (other than watching TV)?" Responses ranged from 0 (never) to 5 (just about every day) (female $M = 2.66$, $SD = 1.54$; male $M = 2.68$, $SD = 1.62$).

Attachment to Adults. One item was used to assess attachment to nonparent adults (ADULTBND): "If I were having a serious personal problem, there is an adult who's not my parent whom I would feel okay talking to." Responses ranged from 0 (strongly agree) to 3 (strongly disagree) (female $M = 2.49$, $SD = .72$; male $M = 2.38$, $SD = .83$).

Attachment to Peers. One item was used to assess attachment to peers (FRNDBOND): "I have at least one good friend I can count on." Responses ranged from 0 (strongly agree) to 3 (strongly disagree) (female $M = 2.58$, $SD = .69$; male $M = 2.52$, $SD = .75$).

Involvement

Involvement in Conventional Activities. Involvement in conventional activities was assessed via seven items. Students were asked to report how often they spent their time in school extracurricular activities (females $M = 2.39$, $SD = 2.07$; males $M = 2.60$, $SD = 2.05$); working at a job for pay (females $M = 1.77$, $SD = 1.83$; males $M = 2.08$, $SD = 2.78$); in after-school activities, clubs, or hobbies (females $M = 2.60$, $SD = 1.80$; males $M = 1.82$, $SD = 1.72$); doing volunteer work (females $M = 1.38$, $SD = 1.46$; males $M = 1.25$, $SD = 1.45$); or being involved in religiously related activities (females $M = 1.84$, $SD = 1.71$; males $M = 1.71$, $SD = 1.64$). Responses ranged from 0 (never) to 5 (just about every day). Students were also asked to report on the number of hours they actually spent studying (females $M = 4.09$, $SD = 1.32$; males $M = 3.46$, $SD = 1.62$) or helping out at home (females $M = 3.99$, $SD = 1.30$; males $M = 3.36$, $SD = 1.57$). Responses ranged from 0 (none) to 5 (7 or more hours per day).

Delinquency

The delinquency scale was made up of nine questions tapping self-reported frequency of cheating, fighting, carrying weapons to school, damaging property, using false identification, using drugs or alcohol at school, breaking and entering, stealing, and trouble with police. Responses ranged from 0 (never) to 3 (often), with higher scores indicating more frequent delinquent behavior (Cronbach's alpha = .79; females $M = .26$, $SD = .49$; males $M = .49$, $SD = .62$).

Academic Achievement

Self-reported grades were used as a measure of academic achievement. Students were asked, "What is the average grade you usually get in your courses at school?" Responses ranged from 0 (mostly below D) to 7 (mostly A's) (females $M = 4.88$, $SD = 1.87$; males $M = 4.43$, $SD = 1.99$).

RESULTS

Table 1 presents the correlation matrices for males and females on all variables in the study (males above the diagonal).

All four of the attachment bond variables (time in family, adult bond, friend bond, and parent quality) were inversely and significantly related to reported delinquency in females. With the exception of a bond with a nonparent adult, the remaining three attachment bond variables (time in family, friend bond, and parent quality) were inversely and significantly related to delinquency for males. Examination of the involvement bond variables (time in activity, time working at a job, time in clubs or hobbies, time volunteering, time in religious group activities, hours studying, and hours doing chores) revealed that only time in school-based extracurricular activities, time in after-school clubs or hobbies, hours spent studying, and hours spent doing chores were significantly and inversely related to reports of delinquency in males. For females, only time spent in school extracurricular activities, hours spent studying, and hours spent doing chores were significantly and inversely related to self-reported delinquency.

For females, all of the attachment bond variables and five of the seven involvement bonds (time in extracurricular school activities, time working at a job, time in after-school clubs or hobbies, hours studying, and hours doing chores) were positively and significantly correlated to grades. For males, only two of the four attachment variables (parent quality and time spent with family) and five of the seven involvement

variables (time in extracurricular school activities, time in after-school clubs or hobbies, time in church-related activities, hours studying, and hours doing chores) were positively and significantly related to academic achievement.

These findings support the hypothesis of an inverse relationship between all of the attachment bond variables and delinquency, as well as the hypothesis of a positive relationship between all the attachment bond variables and academic achievement for females. With the exception of the bond with a nonparent adult, all the attachment bond variables were inversely related to delinquency in males as hypothesized; only the parent/family bonds of attachment were positively related to academic achievement. Support for the hypothesis of an inverse relationship between the involvement variables and delinquency received mix support for both males and females. For females, less than half the involvement variables (time in activity, hours studying, and hours doing chores) were inversely related to delinquency; for males, slightly more than half the involvement variables (time in activity, time spent in club or hobby, hours studying, and hours doing chores) were inversely related to delinquency.

The hypothesis of a positive relationship between the involvement bond variables and academic achievement was generally supported. For females, with the exception of time spent volunteering and time spent in church-related activities, all the involvement bond variables were related to academic achievement in the hypothesized direction. For males, with the exception of time spent working at a job and time spent volunteering, all the involvement bond variables were related to academic achievement in the hypothesized direction.

Taken together, this study's findings support the notion that the tenets of SCT can successfully be applied to models of healthy development. Our findings illustrate that both the attachment and involvement bonds are useful in examining both prosocial (academic achievement) and antisocial (delinquent) behavior. Further, the findings support our hypothesis of gender differences in the protective function of attachment and involvement bonds such that attachment bonds seem to be consistently more protective for females than for males and that the involvement bonds are protective for both. It is important to note that these findings are

TABLE 1   Product-Moment Correlations Between Dimensions of Attachment and Involvement (Males Above the Diagonal, Females Below)

	1	2	3	4	5	6	7	8	9	10	11	12	13
1. Delinquency	1.00	−.306**	−.299**	.007	−.198**	.057	.020	−.396**	−.337**	.246**	.140**	−.102	−.259**
2. Grades	−.195**	1.00	.405**	.092	.148**	.073	.099*	.269**	.159**	.204**	.032	.082	.098*
3. Time in activities	−.223**	.405**	1.00	.098	.208**	.236**	.287**	.304**	.264**	.417**	−.017	−.002	.158**
4. Time at job	.013	.101*	−.136**	1.00	.208**	.206**	.166**	.031	.077	.101*	−.024	−.010	.068
5. Time in hobbies	−.080	.128*	.249**	.109*	1.00	.292**	.288**	.329**	.236**	.329**	.062	.125*	.099
6. Time volunteering	−.030	.091	.267**	.263**	.359**	1.00	.381**	.088	.071	.189**	−.109*	−.039	−.046
7. Time in church	.013	.045	.226**	.171**	.290**	.359**	1.00	.145**	.169**	.266**	−.093	.067	.059
8. Hours studying	−.383**	.289**	.239**	−.005	.233**	.141**	.074	1.00	.480**	.369**	.151**	.136**	.168**
9. Hours doing chores	−.316**	.139*	.134**	.031	.175*	.119*	.043	.437**	1.00	.389**	.160**	.071	.168**
10. Time with family	−.244**	.218**	.306**	.164**	.310**	.304**	.246**	.320**	.250**	1.00	.077	.110*	.263**
11. Friend bond	−.246**	.149**	.160**	.049	.040	.064	.017	.181**	.134**	.142**	1.00	.393**	.186**
12. Adult bond	−.366**	.125*	.173**	.010	.138**	.071	.032	.272**	.216**	.301**	.429**	1.00	.288**
13. Parent quality	−.358**	.256**	.183**	.121*	.149**	.174**	.076	.179**	.174**	.350**	.166**	.352**	1.00

NOTES:
* $p < .05$.
** $p < .001$.

based on cross-sectional rather than longitudinal data, so exact causality cannot be determined. Longitudinal designs would be necessary to discover if attachment and involvement caused youth to get better grades and be less delinquent or if youth who are less delinquent and get better grades become more involved and attached. This question has been examined with respect to delinquency and the latter explanation holds; this question has not been examined with respect to prosocial behaviors.

DISCUSSION

The purpose of this study was to examine the utility of SCT tenets in predicting both positive and negative behaviors. Because SCT has traditionally been used to examine delinquent behavior, an extension of its application to prosocial behavior is unique. Specifically, this study examined the utility of SCT's attachment and involvement bonds to predict gender differences in reports of delinquency and academic achievement. Taken together, these findings provide support for the notion that different bonds of social control can be considered protective factors for males and females. Specifically, the present findings suggest that the involvement bonds of SCT are evident for both genders but that the attachment bonds seem to provide more protection for females than for males.

This emphasis on attachment for girls is consistent with other research suggesting that the notion of attachment or relationship is more salient for girls than for boys. Girls tend to have fewer and closer intimate relationships with friends than do boys; boys tend to have more friends but focus less on intimacy and more on activities than do girls. The importance of attachment for girls is also revealed in preferences of coping styles. Research suggests that females tend to rely more on social networks for support than do males, whereas males tend to use methods of distraction more than females. Several researchers believe that these differences are due more to socialization processes than to any innate differences in the need for relationships. Boss states that the gender role socialization that occurs in the United States deprives each gender of effective coping resources, thus interfering with successful stress management.

The findings in this study were consistent with research suggesting the positive impacts of activity involvement and academic achievement for both boys and girls and the research documenting the inverse relationship between extracurricular involvement and delinquency. In general, boys and girls who are involved in structured activities tend to perform better academically. According to SCT, participation in structured activities may enhance a young person's bond to the school or community, thus motivating him or her to behave in a prosocial way (e.g., getting good grades). This bonding may be due to the relationships formed with peers who are also participating or relationships formed with the adult coaches/mentors. Boys and girls who are involved in extracurricular activities may also be less involved in deviant activities, for similar reasons.

From a programmatic perspective, findings in this study have implications for both parents and youth development professionals. First, the study results suggest that, regardless of gender, parents should not discount the importance of their adolescents' out-of-school time activity involvement. Parents should ensure that their community provides multiple out-of-school time programming options so that their youth can participate and develop the competencies they will need to become successful adults. Parents should encourage their adolescents to become involved with other caring adults. Because young people need a variety of role models in their lives, parents should be proactive in surrounding their adolescents with other adults whom they respect.

Youth development professionals should be as intentional about the relationships they foster with adolescents as they are of the activities they offer. They should be aware that relational aspects of the program might be particularly important for females. This could mean, for example, that girls need to be invited and encouraged to participate in activities by a caring adult. With boys, youth development professionals should consider using conventional activities as a means of fostering boys' positive relationships with adults and peers. To emphasize the importance of attachment, staff development programs should include information about establishing appropriate relationships with adolescents as one core component.

The field of youth development could be strengthened if researchers would continue to explore the utility of existing theories for models of youth development. Whenever possible, more specific microtheories should be tested within broader frameworks, such as Bronfenbrenner's ecological model, Lerner's developmental contextual model, or Bogenschneider's risk/protective ecological model. In this study, we attempted to do this by using SCT in a study that examined youths' perceptions of multiple ecological contexts (parents, peers, adults) as well as both positive and negative behaviors (academic achievement and delinquent behavior). Such testing and revision of existing models of youth behavior will help to ensure the scientific foundation necessary to support the emerging field of youth development as an area of study of interest for both academics and practitioners.

SOURCE: From *Youth & Society,* Vol. 34, No. 2, 123–145, December 2002. Copyright © 2002 Sage Publications. Reprinted by permission of Sage Publications, Inc.

QUESTIONS FOR DISCUSSION AND WRITING

1. As defined by Hirschi, what does SCT (Social Control Theory) assume? What interplay is reflected in the bonds discussed in SCT? How do protective factors operate?

2. What were the findings for the four attachment and seven involvement bond variables for delinquency? What were the findings for the four attachment and seven involvement bond variables for grades?

3. How is "this emphasis on attachment" consistent with other research?

LABELING CRIMINALS

EDWIN M. SCHUR

A nother important sociological perspective, in which there has been a marked renewal of interest recently, emphasizes the role played by society's reactions to offending behavior in shaping social problem situations. Sociologist Howard S. Becker has stated this view succinctly:

> Social groups create deviance by making the rules whose infraction constitutes deviance, and by applying those rules to particular people and labeling them as outsiders. From this point of view, deviance is *not* a quality of the act the person commits, but rather a consequence of the application by others of rules and sanctions to an "offender." The deviant is one to whom that label has successfully been applied; deviant behavior is behavior that people so label.

This does not, of course, mean that the *acts* we commonly term homicide, theft, and drug use would never occur if they were not considered deviant or criminal. Rather the point is that their nature, distribution, social meaning, and implications and ramifications are significantly influenced by patterns of social reaction. Society, in other words, determines what we make of these acts socially.

"Criminal" in this view is in some measure what sociologists call an "ascribed status." An individual's designation as an offender depends crucially on what *other people* do with respect to him and his behavior; it does not result simply and directly from his own acts. This means that

research on crime problems must pay a good deal of attention to the substantive nature of these reactions (how and why we react to particular "offenses" as we do); the direct reactors and "labelers" (agencies of formal control, such as the police and the courts); and the typical processes of interaction between these control agents and the individuals they treat as criminals (with special reference to how this interaction may affect the development of criminal self-images and "careers" among the people so "labeled"). This point about interaction is important because a great value of this orientation is the stress it places on *processes* involved in the development of criminal outlooks and behavior. Crime is not simply a matter of static conditions—under which some individuals clearly "are" criminals (for all time and in all places) whereas others clearly "are not." On the contrary, both the individual's behavior and his self-conceptions are constantly undergoing change, and they are highly responsive to the reactions of others.

To a large extent, this view is little more than a recasting or amplification of a classic sociological dictum of W. I. Thomas to the effect that "when men define situations as real, they are real in their consequences"—a theme developed further by Robert Merton as the "self-fulfilling prophecy." If we treat a person like a criminal, he is likely to become one. This point was nicely described by Frank Tannenbaum in an early work on crime and delinquency:

> No more self-defeating device could be discovered than the one society has developed

in dealing with the criminal. It proclaims his career in such loud and dramatic forms that both he and the community accept the judgment as a fixed description. He becomes conscious of himself as a criminal, and the community expects him to live up to his reputation, and will not credit him if he does not live up to it.

We have already seen how the identification of young people as "troublemakers" by teachers and school officials may backfire—rather than acting as a preventive technique, such labeling may drive the child into new trouble and progressively greater alienation. Clearly the police and the courts also have substantial power to activate and reinforce criminal careers and self-concepts. I have mentioned the ease with which we often "change" a person into a "criminal" (that is, our view of him changes) during the course of his trial on criminal charges. Indeed, the criminal trial is a prototype of what one sociologist has called the "status-degradation ceremony"—a ritualized process by which a condemned individual is stripped of his old identity and given a new (degraded) one. It is very difficult for an individual to sustain a favorable image of himself under the pressure of such public definitions. And if the defining process is clearly unfair (recall the criteria for official disposition in the "police encounters with juveniles" study), then however unwilling the "offender" may be to define himself as such, and even if harsh sanctions are not invoked in his particular case, he is likely to develop a hostility toward the official "system" that may increase the likelihood of anti-social behavior on his part in the future.

Under the impact of negative social reactions the individual may, then, be propelled from isolated acts of criminality into more complete involvement in criminal ways of life (heightened "commitment" to criminal roles), and he may come increasingly to view himself as an enemy of society (since society seems so determined to consider him one). Sociologist Edwin Lemert has suggested the distinction between "primary" and "secondary" deviation, the latter occurring when an individual comes to employ his deviance "as a means of defense, attack, or adjustment to the overt and covert problems created by the consequent societal reaction to him."

Concern with the impact of social reactions on individual self-conceptions and behavior (that is, focusing not on the pressures that initially drive the person into deviating behavior, but rather on the *consequences* for him of engaging in such behavior and being publicly identified as doing so) is but one aspect of this orientation to crime. Another involves examining the general impact, *on the society*, of defining a particular form of behavior as criminal. I have already referred to a prime example of this sort of impact—seen in the consequences of treating as criminal various borderline "offenses." As we shall note in more detail, the "criminalizing" of certain types of behavior may exacerbate the social problems in question in ways that take us quite beyond the level of individual social psychology. Thus, we may find significant economic consequences flowing from "criminalization" (as when a society's reaction to some form of deviating behavior provides the groundwork for a thriving black market) and also significant effects on the behavior and outlooks of law enforcement officials—as well as the predictable proliferation of much "secondary" crime among the "offenders" themselves.

Finally, the emphasis on social reactions suggests still another broad area of research which should increase our understanding of crime problems. This has to do with the social meaning of the "creation" of crimes (by lawmaking), both generally and with respect to particular offenses. Thus we are led to ask what general functions are served by ensuring that there are *some* crimes and "criminals" in a society (do we, in other words, really need crime?). And we are also drawn to comparative and historical analysis of rule-making in particular behavior areas (for example, what led up to our present drug laws, why do they differ from those in other Western countries, etc.). Unfortunately it will not be possible in this [article] to deal with such questions at any length—important as they may be for a comprehensive analysis of crime problems.

QUESTIONS FOR DISCUSSION AND WRITING

1. To what must research on crime problems pay a good deal of attention? How can the identification of young people as "troublemakers" by teachers and school officials backfire?

2. What is the difference between primary and secondary deviance?

3. What happens in a complex modern society with respect to groups and sets of values?

OFFICIAL LABELING, CRIMINAL EMBEDDEDNESS, AND SUBSEQUENT DELINQUENCY

A Longitudinal Test of Labeling Theory

JÓN GUNNAR BERNBURG

MARVIN D. KROHN

CRAIG J. RIVERA

In recent years, there has been a revived interest in the labeling approach in the field of criminology. A prominent theme that has reemerged in revisionist work on labeling theory has been an emphasis on the social structural consequences of deviant labeling that trigger processes leading to movement into deviant groups. In light of the role that the individual's social ties to unconventional groups play in criminological theory, such processes should be of great interest to criminology. Yet existing research bearing upon this line of investigation has been both limited and inconclusive.

In the present study, we use a sample of urban adolescents to examine the effect of formal criminal labeling on subsequent delinquency, focusing on the intervening role of peer social networks. Using measures from three successive periods, we test if juvenile justice intervention positively influences subsequent involvement in serious delinquency through increased probability of involvement in deviant groups, namely, association with gangs and delinquent peers.

CRIMINAL LABELING AND CRIMINAL EMBEDDEDNESS

Official, or formal, adjudication for an offense may create or enhance the reputation of a juvenile as a criminal in his or her community, most notably among other teenagers in the school and among parents in the community. Insofar as the information about the formal sanction spreads throughout the community, others will tend to define the juvenile as a criminal deviant. Hence, stereotypical images of criminals in the mainstream culture are driven to the forefront of the person's life.

There are a few processes in which labeling may increase the probability of associating with deviant peers. Labeled teenagers may become aware of stereotypical beliefs in their communities, or they may think that these beliefs exist based on their learned perception of what people think about criminals; fearing rejection, they may withdraw from interaction with conventional peers. Goffman has pointed out that social interaction between "normal" people and the stigmatized is often characterized by uneasiness, embarrassment, ambiguity, and intense efforts at impression management, and that these experiences are felt by those who bear the stigma as well as those who do not. Nonlabeled adolescents and labeled adolescents may tend to avoid one another in order to avoid uncomfortable interaction dynamics.

Warr has underscored the importance of the principle of homophily (people associating with others who are similar to them on a number of different dimensions) in friendship formation. Official labeling highlights the similarity shared by delinquents while also differentiating them from those who are not labeled. Increased association with deviant peers should be of particular importance in translating official labeling into subsequent deviance during adolescence.

In addition to the direct impact of official labeling on associating with deviant others, there is also the probability that the official label will lead indirectly to increased participation in deviant groups through exclusion from conventional peer groups. The negative stereotypes associated with the criminal label may create feelings of fear and mistrust among peers and other members of the community toward juveniles known to have been officially treated as criminals. The perception that negative beliefs exist in the community may also lead youths to avoid publicly known deviants, "fearing that social stigma may rub off." Hence, the labeled juvenile is at increased risk of being excluded from conventional social networks in the community, resulting in movement into deviant groups.

Although we are unable to examine peer rejection in the present study, our data allow us to test directly the link between official labeling and subsequent social ties to deviant peers, thus providing a test of one central position in labeling theory, namely, that ties to deviant others mediate the influence of official labeling on subsequent deviance.

The Mediating Role of Criminal Embeddedness

The proposition that involvement in deviant networks leads to increased levels of delinquent

activity has been widely studied by criminologists. The concept of criminal embeddedness is particularly relevant here. Criminal embeddedness refers to immersion, or involvement, in ongoing criminal networks. These networks can consist of more than just peers—they can also contain deviant family members or other acquaintances. The important point is that these individuals comprise a distinct network of which an individual is an "active" member and that this particular set of relationships is oriented toward criminal values, acts, and opportunities.

It is generally hypothesized that criminal embeddedness can directly increase delinquent behavior, perhaps through the learning of definitions favorable toward deviance and through modeling and reinforcement. Delinquent peer associations constitute one component of criminal embeddedness. Another form of criminal embeddedness is membership in a delinquent gang. Thornberry et al. found that youths who are members of a gang have higher levels of delinquent activity both during and after the time period of gang membership. This relationship holds even while controlling for peer delinquency.

Although there is ample evidence supporting the causal role of deviant networks in the development of delinquency and crime, research on the potential role of deviant networks in translating official labeling into subsequent deviance and crime is both limited and inconclusive.

The present analysis focuses on the impact of juvenile justice intervention in early and middle adolescence on both association with deviant groups and subsequent deviant behavior. Our discussion implies that embeddedness in deviant groups should mediate the effects of juvenile justice intervention on subsequent involvement in delinquent behavior. We are particularly interested in early contact with the juvenile justice system because these experiences are likely to have the most significant impact on youth. Specifically, adolescents who experience juvenile justice intervention at ages 13.5 to 14 should be more delinquent at age 15 than those who do not. Moreover, this relationship should be mediated by the fact that labeled youths are more likely to be involved in deviant networks at age 14.5.

METHOD

The analysis is conducted with data from the Rochester Youth Development Study (RYDS), a multi-wave panel study of the development of drug use and delinquent behavior among adolescents and young adults. This panel is based on an initial sample of 1,000 students selected from the seventh and eighth grades of the public schools in Rochester, New York during the 1987 to 1988 academic year. Interviews were conducted at six-month intervals with each adolescent and his or her parent or primary caretaker. Data on subjects were also collected from school, police, courts, and social service agencies. Because we are particularly interested in the effect of early formal contact with the juvenile justice system, the current analysis uses data from Waves 1 to 4, when the subjects were between the ages of about 13.5 and 15.

Measures

Juvenile Justice Intervention. The RYDS contains self-reported data on involvement with the juvenile justice system for 13 offenses representing a range of delinquent behavior in terms of types and seriousness, including violent and property offenses and drug use. If the subjects indicated that they had committed any of these offenses, we asked them whether the police knew about it. If they indicated the police knowing, we asked them to think about the most serious time that this happened and to indicate whether they had further juvenile justice system involvement (put on probation, sent to a correctional center, referred to community service, put in detention, brought to court, or referred to a treatment program in Waves 1 and 2). A dummy variable, *juvenile justice intervention,* was constructed with 1 equal to some involvement with the juvenile justice system and 0 equal to no involvement.

Delinquent Behavior. We used two measures of delinquent behavior, both taken from Wave 2 and Wave 4. Interviews included a self-report inventory in which information on offending over the past six months was elicited. The first measure, *serious delinquency,* consists of seven items, including robbery, gang fights, attacks with a weapon, breaking and entering, theft of $50 to $100, theft of more than $100, and car theft. The second measure, *substance use,* consists of frequency of use of alcohol and controlled substances.

Deviant Groups. Subjects were asked if they had been members of a gang during the past six months. A dummy variable measured *gang membership* at Wave 2 and at Wave 3. The variable was coded 1 if a subject reported having been a member of a gang. We also constructed a variable, *peer delinquency,* at Wave 2 and Wave 3. Subjects were asked how many of their friends had engaged in various forms of delinquency, including robbery, violent attack, theft, and vandalism. The response categories ranged from 1 *(none of them)* to 4 *(most of them).*

Control Variables. Gender is indicated by a dummy variable coded as 1 for female. Two dichotomous variables represent the three racial or ethnic categories—African Americans, Hispanics, and Whites—with White serving as the reference category. Information about the income of parents was obtained directly in interviews with the primary caretakers of the subjects in the first wave. Parents' poverty status was measured by a dummy variable with 1 equal to families having income below the poverty level and 0 equal to parents' income being above the poverty level.

RESULTS

The results lend considerable support to the hypothesis that juvenile justice intervention is associated with increased probability of subsequent involvement in deviant networks. In support of our hypothesis, youths who experience juvenile justice intervention are significantly more likely to be members of a gang during the successive period relative to those who have no intervention experience. Our results indicate that this effect is substantial; in our data, juvenile justice intervention increases the odds of gang membership by a factor of 5.2. The effects of the control variables are in line with our expectations. Earlier gang membership significantly increases the odds of subsequent gang membership. Delinquent behavior and substance use have positive effects on subsequent gang membership, although substance use is not significant. African Americans are more likely than others to be gang members.

Other results examine the effect of juvenile justice intervention on peer delinquency. Again, the results support our hypothesis. Juvenile justice intervention has a significant, positive effect on subsequent peer delinquency, net of controls. Also, as expected, peer delinquency at Wave 2 has significant, positive effects on peer delinquency at Wave 3.

Labeling theory argues that juvenile justice intervention should be positively associated with subsequent delinquency and that this effect should be mediated by involvement in delinquent groups. We test this hypothesis by first regressing delinquency at Wave 4 on formal criminal intervention and then adding to the equation the measure of deviant networks at Wave 3.

First, we examine the effect of juvenile justice intervention on subsequent delinquency. As predicted, intervention is significantly, positively related to involvement in subsequent delinquency. The odds ratio indicates that experiencing juvenile justice intervention increases the odds of involvement in serious delinquency at Wave 4 by a factor of 5.5. The effect of gang membership at Wave 2 is positive, as expected, but slightly below the significance level. The effect of Wave 2 gang membership in Model 1 is net of Wave 2 serious delinquency; hence, we expected this effect to be weak. The effects of the control variables conform to expectation. Delinquency and substance use significantly increase the odds of subsequent delinquency. Females are significantly less likely to be involved in subsequent delinquency, net of controls.

Second, we add the mediator variable *gang membership* at Wave 3. As predicted, adding gang membership to the equation produces a drop in the effect of juvenile justice intervention on subsequent delinquency. The coefficient drops by about 22 percent but remains statistically significant. Moreover, as predicted, gang membership is strongly and significantly associated with subsequent delinquency. Youths who are gang members at Wave 3 are substantially more likely to report delinquent involvement at Wave 4 relative to those who are not gang members during this period. This finding indicates that the effect of juvenile justice intervention on subsequent delinquency is mediated by the change in gang membership.

In other models, we use peer delinquency as the mediator. The findings again show that juvenile justice intervention is strongly, positively related to subsequent delinquency; formal criminal intervention increases the probability of subsequent delinquency by a factor of about 5.4.

The findings also show that adding Wave 3 peer delinquency to the equation again produces a drop in the coefficient for intervention. The coefficient drops by about 17 percent and remains statistically significant. Wave 3 peer delinquency has a significant, positive effect on subsequent delinquency and significantly mediates part of the effect of intervention on subsequent delinquency. Again, this finding indicates that the effect of juvenile justice intervention on Wave 4 delinquency is mediated by the change in delinquent peer associations.

Gang membership and peer delinquency thus jointly account for a substantial proportion of the effects of juvenile justice intervention on subsequent involvement in serious delinquency.

SUMMARY AND DISCUSSION

The goal of this article was to examine the consequences of official deviant labeling for ties to deviant peers and subsequent deviance. We have focused on the proposition that official labeling tends to embed the individual in deviant social groups, thereby increasing the likelihood subsequently of deviance and crime. Applying this argument to juvenile delinquency, we have examined the effect of juvenile justice intervention on subsequent involvement in serious delinquency and the mediator role of deviant networks.

The results lend considerable support to our hypotheses. First, our findings lend support to the idea that official labeling triggers processes that increase involvement in deviant groups. We have shown that teenagers who experience juvenile justice intervention are substantially more likely than their peers to become members of a gang in a successive period. Also, the peer networks of these youth in a successive wave tend to become increasingly nonconventional in the sense that they are more likely to be involved in peer networks that have high levels of delinquency.

Second, our findings indicate that official labeling plays a significant role in the maintenance and stability of delinquency and crime at a crucial period in early and middle adolescence. Juvenile justice intervention is significantly associated with increased probability of serious delinquency in a subsequent period, while accounting for initial levels of serious delinquency and substance use and other controls.

Finally, the present study demonstrates how labeling theory can complement established sociological approaches to crime and deviance by providing a broader viewpoint on the causes and consequences of social marginalization. Theories of differential association and social learning assume that associating with delinquent and criminal others is an important immediate cause of delinquent behavior. Labeling theory broadens the viewpoint of this research, pointing out that deviant groups provide social shelter from stigma as well as providing collective rationalizations, definitions, peer pressure, and opportunities that encourage and facilitate deviant behavior. The exclusionary processes triggered by deviant labeling may, in many cases, explain the individual's movement into a deviant group, as well as the isolation of deviant groups from mainstream social life. Our findings lend empirical support to this notion, showing that the effect of official labeling on subsequent delinquency is substantially mediated by an increased probability of involvement in deviant networks.

SOURCE: From *Journal of Research in Crime and Delinquency,* Vol. 43, No. 1, 67–88, February 2006. Copyright © 2006 Sage Publications. Reprinted by permission of Sage Publications, Inc.

QUESTIONS FOR DISCUSSION AND WRITING

1. How may labeling increase the probability of associating with deviant peers?

2. Why is the concept of criminal embeddedness particularly relevant here?

3. What do the results show? What about for peer delinquency? What about subsequent delinquency?

CRIME AND STRUCTURAL CONTRADICTIONS

WILLIAM J. CHAMBLISS

One conclusion to be drawn from the analysis of our knowledge about crime is that the structural tradition holds the greatest promise of leading to reliable scientific knowledge. It asks questions amenable to systematic investigation and capable of leading to reliable knowledge, for it assumes that criminal behavior is a response of groups and social classes to the resources and constraints of the social structure rather than the adaptation of individuals to personal biology, psychology, or social experiences. Our theory therefore draws from the structural tradition for its starting point. We seek to answer questions about why criminal behavior exists, why it is distributed as it is, and why it varies from place to place and from one historical period to another. We do not seek to answer why Johnny steals and Bobby makes airplanes, why one politician accepts bribes and another does not, or why one manager violates health and safety regulations and another does not. We understand that paradigms trying to explain individual criminal behavior are bound to end in either tautologies or empirically false theories. Either way, they are unsatisfactory as explanations. We wish to avoid this by focusing on questions that seek to understand the relationship between crime and social structure. Such an approach holds the most promise for the development of a reliable body of scientific knowledge.

CONTRADICTIONS AND CONFLICTS

A contradiction exists in a given set of social relationships (political, social, economic, and ideological) when, in the normal course of events, existing social relations simultaneously maintain the status quo and produce the conditions necessary to transform it—that is, when conforming to one set of demands, goals, or institutionalized processes creates situations that are fundamentally antagonistic to the existing social relations.

Under these circumstances, "contradictions tend to intensify with time and cannot be resolved within the existing social framework." Every historical era, every society, and every human group in the process of constructing ways to survive invariably creates contradictory forces and tendencies that serve as an unseen force moving the group toward new social, political, and economic relations. Change is thus an inexorable part of every human group. To understand this, it is essential that we adopt an attitude toward social life that flies in the face of conventional wisdom. We must accept the fact that social life is contradictory, that opposites exist simultaneously, and that people both create their own history and are created by it. "The world is not to be comprehended as a complex of ready made *things*, but as a complex of *processes*."

The contradictions lead inexorably to conflicts between groups, classes, and strata. The conflicts reflecting contradictions are manifested as antagonistic relations that reflect the struggle of people to deal with contradictory social, political, and economic relations. The following are examples: Workers go on strike, women demonstrate against unequal pay, farmers march on Washington, small landowners take up arms against agribusiness, and Indians barricade themselves on their reservation against federal agents.

Every historical era has its own unique contradictions and conflicts. The most important conflicts existing in a particular time and place are those that derive from the way the social, economic, and political relations are organized. The following are the most basic characteristics of any human group: how people make a living, the work they do, the way they organize their labor to produce the things that are useful and necessary for survival, and how they distribute the results of their labor and organize power relations. People may create a political organization that strives for equality or one that creates vast differences in wealth between the rich and the poor. People may create a political structure that allows every member of the community a voice in every decision or they may organize their politics so that only a few people have the right to decide. There exists an apparently infinite number of possible combinations and permutations.

For an understanding of crime, it is the way people organize their economy, politics, and social relations that must be the starting point for constructing an adequate theory.

Criminal behavior is generated because of the contradictions that inevitably arise in the course of life. The type of crime, the amount of crime, and the distribution of crime in a particular historical period and society depend upon the nature of the existing contradictions, the conflicts that develop as people respond to the contradictions, and the mechanisms institutionalized for handling the conflicts and dilemmas produced by the contradictions.

The emergence of criminal law can be understood in just these terms. That is, criminal laws emerge, change, and develop as people attempt to respond to conflicts generated by contradictions in the political and economic organization of their world. It will be recalled, for example, that in capitalist economies there is a basic contradiction between the public nature of production and the private ownership of the means of production. Goods cannot be produced unless people can be forced, coerced, encouraged, cajoled, or persuaded to do the necessary work. This is the public nature of production. Under capitalism, however, the ownership of the goods produced does not reside with those who produce them but with those who own the means of production—the tools, the factories, and the necessary knowledge. This leads inexorably to conflict, which invariable changes the existing relationships. As workers struggle to increase their share of what they produce and owners struggle to maintain or increase their share, workers and owners are locked in conflict, each seeking to increase their share of the surplus.

The public production-private ownership contradiction—combined with a political organization of democratic, electoral politics—led in the formative years of industrialization in the United States and Europe to ubiquitous conflict between workers and owners. These conflicts were responded to politically by the passage of innumerable laws making it a crime for workers to organize collectively against owners, to strike, to refuse to work, and so forth. The attempted solution, it must be stressed, was *not* attending to the contradictions that generated the conflicts; it was focusing solely on the conflicts created by the contradictions. This attempted "solution" to the conflict did *not* suffice to silence worker demands. Indeed, the more oppressive the laws became, the more virulent the workers' rebellion. In the 1930s, another political tack was tried—laws giving workers the right to bargain collectively and to strike under certain circumstances were passed. Other laws restricted these rights and gave the government the right to arbitrate and, under certain circumstances, to intervene. [Also,] the behavior of women seeking the vote, the right to determine their own economic role in society, and even their right to decide whether or not to bear children were defined as criminal.

One way to resolve the conflicts generated by a class society is to define some groups or classes of people as less than human. This resolution, however, generates its own contradictions on an ideological level. To convince people that they live in a just and fair society, ideologies of equality, and freedom, and the inherent integrity of the individual may be promulgated. Yet the treatment of some people as less than human is a useful way of maintaining a compliant labor force. If some people—because of their race, gender, or age—are treated as though they are less human than others, then conflicts are inevitable. Dealing with these conflicts then becomes part of the state apparatus. Laws are passed that institutionalize differential access to the resources. Some people are legally prohibited from full participation in what are ideologically touted as the fundamental rights and privileges of all. Thus, when slaves or women are defined as less than human and denied their rights, the structure of political and economic relations is ripe for the emergence of conflicts. The criminal law will respond in an attempt to resolve these conflicts; some responses will be increasingly repressive, others will be ameliorative. In time, slaves were freed, women got the vote, and workers earned the right to strike. But, in the interim, there was conflict defined by law as criminal.

As Sutherland once pointed out, an understanding of the processes by which the criminal law is created is also an answer to the question of why there is crime. There is crime, in this sense, because there is law that defines certain acts as criminal.

We want to go beyond this, however. We want also to be able to answer why the types of crime differ between sexes, social classes, ethnic groups, and age groups in a particular society, and we want to be able to know why crime varies by type, frequency, and intensity from one society or historical period to another. . . .

CRIME IN CAPITALIST SOCIETIES

The capitalist economy depends upon the production and consumption of commodities by large numbers of people. There is, then, at the outset a twofold problem to be solved: How do we make people work to produce the commodities and how do we create a desire for the commodities on the part of large numbers of people?

Some commodities—food, clothing, and shelter—are essential for survival. If the only means available for obtaining these essentials is to work for someone who owns them, people will generally choose to work rather than starve or freeze to death. But capitalism does not depend upon the production and consumption of necessities alone. It also depends upon the production and consumption of goods and services that have little or nothing to do with survival. For capitalism to develop, people must be motivated to work in order to purchase unessential commodities.

There are many ways that people are taught to want nonessential commodities—advertising, socialization into a world in which the acquisition of nonessential commodities bestows status and a sense of personal integrity on those who can display them, and the necessity to accumulate property in order to stave off the possibility of falling below the level of consumption necessary for survival.

Creating the desire to consume, though, simultaneously creates the seeds of discontent and the possibility that people will discover ways of being able to increase consumption without working. If—instead of spending 8 hours at a boring, tedious, and sometimes dangerous occupation—a person can obtain the money necessary for purchasing commodities by theft, fraud, trickery, or bribery, then some people will choose that option. In an effort to avoid this possibility, the people who own the means of production and those who manage the state pass laws making such acts illegal. In this way, they try to reduce the attractiveness of alternative routes to consumption.

There are other forces at work that push people to discover alternative ways of accumulating capital. Not all people have an equal opportunity to consume the products they are taught to want. Different kinds of work pay different wages. Some jobs pay only enough for survival. In capitalist economies, there are vast differences in the wages people receive and in the wealth they can accumulate.

How, then, can a set of social relations be sustained that requires the vast majority of people to spend their lives working at tasks they find unsatisfactory in order to be able to have a large enough population of consumers to fuel the engines of capitalist production and consumption? There are many possible solutions to this dilemma, and most of these have been tried at one time or another in the history of capitalism. One solution to this contradiction is to create a class of people who can be forced to work but do not form an essential part of the consuming population. This was the solution tried during the period of capitalism that depended on slavery. Slaves were not a major part of the consuming population, but they did provide most of the essential labor for a minimum expense. This solution, however, created its own contradictions: "The system could justify slavery only by defining the Black as inhuman—but the system depended on mutual obligations, duties, responsibilities and even rights that implicitly recognized the slave's humanity."

Today, capitalism depends upon wage labor. People must work for wages in order to have the power to consume and must consume in order for the economy to survive. This, too, creates its own contradictions. There is only one source of profit for the capitalist: the difference between the wage that the capitalist pays the worker and the price for which the product of that worker's labor is sold. If the worker is paid the full amount for which the product is sold, then there is no profit, and the economic system comes to a grinding halt. Without an accumulation of surplus to reinvest, the economy collapses. If, on the other hand, the worker is not paid enough to survive, then the population is decimated, and there is no one to purchase the commodities produced. Thus there is a fundamental *wages, profits, and consumption contradiction* in capitalist economies. Dealing with that contradiction explains a large part of the history of modern capitalism. Workers seek to earn higher wages and owners seek to pay the minimum amount. When workers do not have high enough wages to buy cars, houses, luxury items, and products of new technologies, the economy is sluggish. When workers are paid high wages that cut into the profits of the owners, there is less money to reinvest in new technologies and improved production. Foreign competition then cuts even further into the profits. This contradiction creates different conflicts and attempted resolutions: Economists argue over whether it is better to increase profits to encourage investment in new productive capacities or to increase wages to encourage more consumption. Government policy vacillates in an attempt to accommodate these contradictory tendencies.

From the point of view of crime, the conflicts culminate in criminal behavior on the part of both workers and owners. Owners cut corners, violate health and safety regulations, illegally deal in the stock market, and violate securities and exchange regulations; workers steal from employers, supplement their wages by selling illegal drugs, illegally strike and organize, and join illegal political groups. The state sits squarely in the midst of the contradiction: Although generally influenced more by owners than workers, it cannot allow the ongoing conflict to disrupt social, political, and economic relations to the point of destroying the existing economic system (capitalism) or the existing political system (democracy). It responds by passing laws to keep workers from disrupting production or stealing property and owners from disregarding the health and safety of workers and consumers. It also passes laws prohibiting certain economic activities that undermine the state's own interests (avoiding taxes by laundering money through overseas banks) or give one group of capitalists an advantage over another (insider trading on the stock market, which disenfranchises those who are not privy to secret corporate information, or forming monopolies). State and government officials work to block efforts by extranational bodies (such as the United Nations) to establish codes of conduct for multinational corporations in developing nations. Another tactic is to maintain laws that allow the reserve labor force available in less-developed countries to enter the country for temporary jobs (such as in agriculture) where it can be employed at low wages without accruing any benefits from state-supported institutions such as welfare, education, and unemployment.

Under capitalism, there is also a fundamental *wages-labor supply contradiction*. The owners pursuing the logic of capitalist economies will strive to pay as little as possible to the workers. It is not possible, however, to pay nothing, unless there is an overabundance of labor that allows workers to be used up and discarded and then replaced with others flowing in. In advanced industrial societies, such a solution is impossible (as is slave labor) because much of the labor needed requires skills that take time to learn. However, if there is full employment under capitalism, workers have an advantage in the struggle for increased shares of profits with owners. If there is a reserve labor force—that is, a significant proportion of the labor force that is unemployed or underemployed—then, when the demands of labor threaten the profits of the owners, the owners can turn to the reserve army of labor to replace the workers. The reserve army, though, forms an underclass that cannot consume but nonetheless is socialized into a system in which consumption is the necessary condition for happiness. Criminal behavior offers a solution for the underclass:

What they cannot earn legitimately they can earn illegitimately. . . .

Public Corruption

The corruption of public officials in capitalist societies is as much a part of the landscape as the air we breathe. Politicians from local aldermen to presidents and Congress people are exposed throughout the capitalist world as having accepted bribes, payoffs, and illegal campaign contributions. In Puerto Rico in 1968, the FBI indicted a former San Juan police lieutenant colonel and three detectives (one of whom was a lawyer) for the murder of seven people and the theft of over a million dollars in jewelry and gems. In New York City during the same period, a borough president committed suicide when it was revealed that he was taking bribes from companies seeking contracts from the government. Dozens of other New York City politicians and government officials were indicted in the same probe—including a former deputy director of New York City's Parking Violations Bureau and an assistant to the mayor in charge of letting hospital and health care contracts. The companies themselves were indicted and fined $600,000. At the federal level, every administration since George Washington's has experienced a rash of resignations and criminal indictments of high-level officials, a pattern that some thought reached its peak when Vice-President Agnew was indicted and pleaded "no contest" to a charge of soliciting and accepting bribes for giving contracts and President Nixon was threatened with impeachment for criminal acts. Under the administration of Ronald Reagan, over 200 high-level appointees were forced to resign either because they were indicted or suspected of criminal acts.

The widespread corruption of public officials suggests that choosing between administrations in terms of a propensity for corruption may be as difficult as choosing the healthiest stalk in a stack of rotten hay.

Electoral politics demands that candidates for office spend huge sums of money on political campaigns—for the presidency, over $100 million; for a seat in Congress, between $500,000 and $3 million. Governor Rockefeller of West Virginia spent over $10 million in a reelection campaign in which he was unopposed in the Democratic primary and his Republican opponent was given no chance whatsoever to win. Electoral politics combined with a capitalist economy create a seed-bed for corruption. Politicians must amass huge amounts of money to compete successfully for elected office. People with the money to contribute do so in order to gain favorable treatment in dealing with the government, whether it be in legislative decisions or in obtaining contracts, licenses, and franchises. If contributions to political campaigns are allowed, the possibility and probability of corruption is omnipresent. If campaign contributions are not allowed, the electorate may not have maximum exposure to the candidates. Resolving that dilemma in the United States led to a system of campaign financing that guarantees corruption.

America is not alone in generating political corruption as a result of financing campaign contributions. Helmut Kohl, the chancellor of West Germany, admitted that, while he was chairman of the Christian Democratic Union (1974–1980), he accepted illegal political contributions from the Friedrich Flick Industrieverwaltung. To make matters worse, Chancellor Kohl apparently lied about his knowledge of the illegal campaign contributions before a parliamentary committee. The Bonn public prosecutor's office investigated the allegations that Kohl perjured himself and the possibility of pursuing criminal charges against him. Some capitalist countries limit the funds for campaigning to those that are supplied by state taxation. That system, however, produces its own contradictions and does not solve the problem, as the case of Chancellor Kohl indicates. There may be better or worse ways of encouraging or discouraging corruption in politics, but electoral politics—in which money influences success or failure—is bound to breed varying degrees of corruption.

In a similar vein, the corruption of the police is institutionalized in capitalist countries. Basically the problem is that for the police to appear to do their job most efficiently, they must (1) permit some forms of criminality (gambling, drug dealing) to take place in order (2) to manage crime better in the community and keep the citizenry from being aware of what is taking place.

The law enforcement system is placed squarely in the middle of two essentially conflicting demands. On the one hand, the job obligates police to enforce the law, albeit with discretion; at the same time, considerable dis-agreement rages over whether or not some acts should be subject to legal sanction. This conflict is heightened by the fact that some influential persons in the community insist that all laws be rigorously enforced, while others demand that some laws not be enforced, at least not against them. Faced with such a dilemma and such an ambivalent situation, the law enforcers do what any well-managed bureaucracy would do under similar circumstances. They follow the line of least resistance. Using the discretion inherent in their positions, they resolve the problem by establishing procedures that minimize organizational strains and that provide the greatest promise of rewards for the organization and the individuals involved. Typically this means that law enforcers adopt a tolerance policy toward the vices, selectively enforcing the laws when it is to their advantage to do so. [By] limiting the visibility of such activity as sexual deviance, gambling, and prostitution they appease those who demand the enforcement of applicable laws. At the same time, since controlling visibility does not eliminate access for persons sufficiently interested to ferret out the tolerated vice areas, those demanding such services are also satisfied.

The contradiction between appearance and reality leads to cooperation between some criminals and the police, which leads in turn to institutionalized corruption.

Street Crime

The forces that lead to street crime are not very different. As we have seen, capitalism produces a large class of people unable to consume the commodities they are taught to want. These people live with a constant dilemma, to accept failure by conventional standards and do without the "good things of life" or even necessities, or discover alternative ways of getting the money to buy the commodities they desire. Alternative ways are available to the lower classes as well as to the white-collar workers, corporate executives, and government officials. But lower-class people cannot engage in insider trading, embezzlement, "long firm" fraud (unless they learn the skills from someone experienced in the trade),

or bribery. They can steal from grocery stores, traffic in drugs, pick pockets, run a crap game, or burgle houses. These activities require some skill, but they are not dependent upon having a particular occupation or position. Like the factory owner who commits violence against workers by refusing to adhere to factory safety and health regulations, lower-class crime also may involve violence to avoid detection or to commit the criminal act. Street crimes are less profitable, probably more likely to lead to detection, and certainly, if the criminal is caught, more likely to culminate in criminal sanctions. To protect themselves from being caught and punished, it may be necessary for criminals to engage in violence. The specifics change, but the overall pattern of responding to contradictions in the political, economic, and social relations of our historical moment remain the cause of the criminality. This applies whether it is the criminality of middle-class women who shoplift, lower-class women who prostitute themselves or sell drugs, street-gang members who steal and fight, or bankers who launder money for organized criminals. . . .

Conclusion

In this [article], we have set forth a theory of crime and criminality that attempts to answer why crime exists and why different types of crime are distributed as they are. The theory suggests that every society contains within it ubiquitous contradictions that generate conflicts accounting for the emergence of criminal laws and the propensity of different social classes and groups to violate those laws. We do not pretend to explain why individual A commits crime and individual B does not. The history of criminology, combined with the facts we know about crime, proves the futility of asking that question. To be scientific requires that we ask questions that focus not on the individual but on the social structure and how different social structures generate different types of criminality. Crime in both socialist and capitalist societies reflects the particular contradictions of those societies.

QUESTIONS FOR DISCUSSION AND WRITING

1. What is the "starting point" for constructing an adequate theory of crime? On what do the type of crime, the amount of crime, and the distribution of crime in a "particular historical period and society depend"? What is a "basic contradiction" in capitalist economies?

2. What is "one way" to resolve the conflicts generated by a class society?

3. What is the "fundamental wages, profits, and consumption contradiction" in capitalistic economies? What "offers a solution" for the underclass?

VIGILANTISM, CURRENT RACIAL THREAT, AND DEATH SENTENCES

DAVID JACOBS

JASON T. CARMICHAEL

STEPHANIE L. KENT

In comparison to other nations, U.S. race relations have been exceptionally antagonistic and violent. After African American slaves were freed by a brutal Civil War, white citizens sought to maintain the prior racial caste system with illegal violence directed largely against ex-slaves. From 1882 to 1951, more than 4,600 persons were lynched. In the Jim Crow South, a set of social and legal codes enforced by legal coercion and vigilantism ensured the separation of the races and almost complete black subjugation. Many scholars have claimed that the current death penalty is a partial replacement for vigilantism used in the past to maintain this caste system. This claim seems plausible because the states that once had the highest lynching rates now appear to use the death sentence most often.

In this study we consider whether the vigilantism used primarily to control ex-slaves created an enduring repressive tradition that continues to produce additional death sentences where lynchings had been most common.

We analyze recent death sentences to discover whether the vigilantism directed largely against blacks in the past and current racial threats to white dominance attributable to larger black populations operate together to produce additional

death sentences. Evidence for such a combined relationship between prior vigilantism and recent minority threat would support claims that the death sentence is currently imposed partly because it is a legal and therefore more acceptable replacement for lynchings.

Minority Threat, Vigilantism, and Death Sentences

Lethal Vigilantism. A common dominant group reaction to the threat to their ascendance posed by larger minority populations involves extralegal violence. The lynching of ex-slaves that occurred after Reconstruction is an excellent example. According to many scholars, whites often used lynchings to control ex-slaves and to ensure that they did not forget their subordinate place in a racial caste system.

The aberrant nature of this repeated violence, which went so far beyond even the accepted standards of the day, shows the intensity of this mass commitment to racial domination.

After the Civil Rights era, "while whites begrudgingly accepted integration in principle, in practice they strove to maintain an unbridgeable social and symbolic gulf with their compatriots of African American descent. They abandoned public schools, shunned public space, fled to the suburbs in millions to avoid mixing, . . . [and] they extended enthusiastic support for law and order policies" that helped to enforce these racial boundaries. One implication is that where these enduring racial taboos had been most intensely enforced by illicit violence, the use of legal violence now can be expected achieve the same ends.

The fervor that evoked this fierce repression suggests that violence used to ensure black subordination would endure in one form or another. But the unacceptability of vigilantism, particularly after the violent efforts to repress the Civil Rights movement that awakened the national conscience and destroyed Jim Crow, meant that this repression would have to take a different, more acceptable form. This fierce passion for violent control in the past nevertheless enhances the plausibility of claims that the harsh methods used to maintain the dominance of whites over blacks persist in sufficient strength to influence recent legal decisions about death sentences.

Zimring shows how this local violence helped erode inhibitions about a legal death penalty. "The critical significance of a vigilante tradition . . . is that it neutralizes a powerful argument against allowing the state to kill its enemies: the fear of government power." Such a tradition that regards the punishment of criminals as a local concern removes a major claim against a state-managed death penalty. "The citizen who has positive feelings about vigilante violence will identify more closely with the punishment process, [and] will think of punishment as a community activity" rather than as an act by a distrusted government separate from the community. Vigilante customs thus reduced the public's normal distrust of the institution that administers the death penalty. Yet the main point is that the fierce mass passions based on taboos about racial impurity that had provided a foundation for this now non-acceptable vigilantism could be expressed with a legal, and therefore far more acceptable, death penalty.

Because current legal and past illicit killings may be used for the same repressive ends, we expect *the number of death sentences to be greater in states with a history of multiple lynchings because this tradition should still produce greater pressures on court officials and juries to impose the death penalty.*

Racial Threat. The threat of larger minority populations also should matter. Prejudice is greater where black presence is more substantial. With crime rates controlled, Liska, Lawrence, and Sanchirico and Quillian and Pager found that black presence leads to enhanced fear of crime. A legal death penalty is likely in states with the most black residents. Findings that public support for capital punishment is associated with black presence and racial prejudice also suggest that *the number of death sentences will be greater in states with more blacks.* In some states, Hispanics are the largest minority, so *death sentences should be more frequent where Hispanic populations are largest.*

This relationship may not be linear. Theory suggests that whites will make greater demands for punitive measures after expansions in black presence. Yet when such minority populations reach a threshold and their political influence becomes sufficient, the positive relationship between minority presence and punitive responses should become negative. Further growth in black presence past this threshold should give this minority enough political influence to reduce death sentences. Hence, *the relationship between the percentage of blacks and death sentences should be positive, but where the black population has reached a threshold, this relationship should become negative.*

An Interactive Hypothesis. The links between these events, however, may be more complex. Historical outcomes can be contingent on the joint appearance of more than one set of conditions that must be present in sufficient strength. In the absence of a black population sufficiently large to pose a current threat, a prior tradition of vigilantism may not be enough to lead to additional death sentences. And without a history of frequent lynchings and a concomitant tradition that justified this exceptional mass violence, the threat posed by the current presence of a substantial African American population may not be sufficient to produce increased death sentences.

This leads to an expectation that an interactive relationship should be present because *death sentences should be most common in states that currently have larger proportions of African Americans combined with a history of repeated lynchings.*

Alternative Explanations for Death Sentences

Because political and religious ideologies and partisanship affect death sentences, these accounts should be examined as well.

Political Ideology. Conservatives view criminals as responsible for their acts. If crime is a decision, increases in the expected costs of such acts should be effective, so conservatives often believe that deterrence is the best antidote for crime. But liberals believe that crime is caused by inequitable conditions, so they are skeptical about harsh sanctions. Capital punishment is likely to be legal in the most conservative states. Hence, *we expect more death sentences where conservative values dominate.*

Fundamentalism. Religious conservatives stress retribution for crime. Historical studies show that religious views have helped to shape criminal punishments. Attitudinal results show that fundamentalist values are associated with enhanced support for severe criminal measures. Where fundamentalism is strongest, prosecutors should be more likely to ask for the death penalty, and judges and juries should be sympathetic. Hence, *death sentence frequencies should be greater in states with the most fundamentalist church memberships.*

Judicial Selection. Death sentences should be more likely where judges must face the voters. Lenient judges who ignore the substantial public support for capital punishment and block death sentences should be particularly vulnerable in states that use partisan judge elections. Partisan elections inhibit judicial independence, so *death sentences should be more common if judges face partisan elections.*

Partisanship. Criminal punishment is inherently political. In contrast to rivals to their left, findings show that conservative parties support harsh punishments. Law and order campaign appeals have helped Republicans win elections. Capital punishment is likely to be legal where Republican strength is greatest, and more death sentences occur in such states. Hence, *death sentences should be increasingly likely in states with a Republican governor because of the sensitizing effects of Republican rhetoric and because the success of such law and order candidates indicates greater support for harsh punishments.*

Additional Controls. Research on legal punishment has focused on the neo-Marxist hypothesis that punishment is used to control the excess supply of labor in capitalist societies. We expect that high joblessness rates will increase death sentences because the prosperous may view the unemployed as a threat to the social order, or because substantial unemployment produces greater resentments against street criminals and magnifies demands for severe punishments.

Violent crime rates must be held constant because death sentences should be frequent in jurisdictions that experience more of these crimes. High property crime rates also may enhance perceptions of threat and produce successful public demands for more death sentences.

METHODS

Except for lynchings, in the primary analyses we use explanatory variables in 1970, 1980, and 1990 to explain death sentence counts in states in 1971–1972, 1981–1982, and 1991–1992.

Explanatory Variable Measurement

One type of minority presence and racial threat is gauged with both continuous and threshold measures of the percentage of blacks. Findings show that a dummy variable threshold measure of black presence has the greatest explanatory power when the legality of the death penalty is at issue. We follow this precedent and report models with a dummy variable scored 1 if the percentage of blacks in a state is greater than the state medium (6.4 percent). Yet because black presence is a component of the interaction term, we use the percentage of blacks in the primary equations designed to explain death sentence counts. Another form of minority presence is assessed with the percentage of Hispanics.

In the 48-state analyses, we compute lynching rates with the NAACP data on state lynchings from 1889 to 1931 divided by mean state populations in this period.

Berry et al. viewed public political ideologies as the mean position on a liberal-conservative continuum. They identified the ideological position of each member of Congress with interest group ratings of that representative's voting record. They estimated public ideology within each congressional district with the ideology score for the district's incumbent and an estimated score for that incumbent's challenger in the last election. Incumbent ideology scores are combined with estimated challenger ideology scores weighted by within-district election results to capture district ideologies.

We assess fundamentalism with a scale created by Morgan and Watson that is based on the percentage of residents who are members of fundamentalist churches. We capture the threat attributable to crime with Uniform Crime Rate violent and property crime rates, and we control for capital offenses by entering the number of state murders. We use the *number* of murders rather than the *rates* to capture the number of offenders at risk for the death penalty. Judge selection is measured with a dummy variable coded 1 for partisan elections and unemployment is measured with decennial Census rates. Population and its square are included to adjust for the likelihood that the number of death sentences will be greater in the most populated states, yet this relationship may not be linear. In the models that assess the determinants of black death sentences, we instead use the number of African Americans and its square. In the primary analyses, dummy variables for two of the three periods are included in the models to capture cross-state trends, and regional dummies are entered to capture otherwise unmeasured factors such as culture.

The results show that the interaction between African American presence and prior lynchings explains state propensities to use the death sentence one or more times. Expectations based on Blalock's version of threat theory are supported as well.

The findings support another threat hypothesis because they suggest that jurisdictions with higher violent crime rates are more likely to use this sentence after the number of murders has been held constant. Fundamentalist church memberships also have positive effects in this analysis of all death sentences. The results suggest that the joint effects of lynchings and black threat lead to additional death sentences, a finding that supports the primary theoretical supposition that prompted this research.

Other results focus on black death sentences. As might be expected, because the dependent variable is restricted to African American death sentences, the nonlinear relationship between the percentage of African Americans and death sentences now is stronger and has more consistent effects in these analyses. In contrast to the results when all death sentences were at issue, the unemployment rates explain black death

sentences, but there is no evidence that religious fundamentalism leads to additional death sentences for blacks.

As discussed earlier, theories suggest that in states with high lynching rates, it should take a far larger African American presence before the number of death sentences begins to fall as a consequence of increased black populations. This is so because the threat attributable to larger black populations should be more menacing to whites in these jurisdictions. Hence, white resistance to black political influence should be greater in such states. The findings suggest that this expectation is correct because the inflection point at which the relationship between the percentage of African Americans and the number of African American death sentences shifts from positive to negative materializes only after the percentage of African Americans exceeds 20 percent in the states with a high lynching rate.

Analyses of 10 Southern States

It is possible that the 48-state results are biased by measurement error in the NAACP lynching data. The only available alternative counts were enumerated by Tolnay and Beck, but these counts are restricted to lynchings in 10 Southern states. We nevertheless can check the findings with models computed on this 10-state lynching data.

It is noteworthy that the two 10-state analyses support the prior findings based on the NAACP lynching counts. As expected from threat theory, after the number of murders and the percentage of Hispanics reach modest thresholds in these Southern states, the relationships between such threats and death sentences become increasingly positive. But the main implication of these new models is that results based on different lynching counts and a different sample support the 48-date findings. The interaction between current black presence and past vigilante violence explains death sentence frequencies in both the 48-state and the 10-state analyses.

CONCLUSIONS

We find consistent support for the primary theoretical suppositions that prompted this analysis. If current death sentence frequencies are attributable in part to the combination of prior illegal violence directed largely against blacks and the current racial threat based on the size of contemporary African American populations, an interaction term that assesses the joint effects of current racial threat and past vigilantism should have a positive relationship with recent death sentences. Our repeated findings that this relationship is present support claims that a prior tradition of lethal vigilantism enhances recent attempts to use the death penalty as long as the threat posed by current black populations is sufficient to trigger this legal but lethal control mechanism.

We find inconsistent support for the alternative minority threat hypothesis. Evidence that Hispanic threat matters can be found only in the Southern state analyses. Such contrasting findings about the explanatory power of racial rather than Hispanic threat should not be surprising in light of the exceptionally divisive and violent conflicts about race throughout U.S. history, which should give racial threat greater explanatory power than its Hispanic alternative. Yet because only a few states had substantial Hispanic populations before 1991, this ethnic group may not have been sufficiently large in enough states to trigger repressive responses. Subsequent studies, therefore, may support this ethnic threat account because the Hispanic population has expanded rapidly since 1990.

Other threat findings are noteworthy. After the number of capital offenses and many additional factors have been held constant, we always find that jurisdictions with the highest violent crime rates are likely to sentence capital offenders to death. Such results are supported by findings showing that a positive relationship exists between violent crime rates and public support for the death penalty. Yet our results go further because they suggest that the menace produced by non-capital violent offenses also leads to a greater use of the death sentence. But the primary theoretical implication concerns repeated finding that states with larger black populations and a history of violent repression directed largely against this racial minority still are likely to use a deadly legal punishment against this racial minority.

SOURCE: From *American Sociological Review,* Vol. 70, No. 4, 656–677, 2005. Copyright © 2005 by David Jacobs, Jason Carmichael, and Stephanie L. Kent. Reprinted by permission of The American Sociological Association.

QUESTIONS FOR DISCUSSION AND WRITING

1. What do the authors consider in this study?

2. Due to current legal and past illicit killings, what do the authors expect? Why do the authors expect the threat of larger minority populations to matter? What is expected as the number of minorities reaches a threshold?

3. What do the findings show? What happened after the number of murders was held constant?

4. What did the 10-state analysis show?

PART VIII

How Do We Explain Crime?

Contemporary Theories and Research I

Students usually ask two questions when their criminology instructor insists on teaching theory. The first is, Which theory gives the right answer? The second question comes after several "old" theories have been presented and critiqued or thoroughly debunked: If we know a theory does not give the right answer, why study it? This last question is probably easier for most teachers to answer. Simply put, old theories are worthy of study because we can learn from how they were wrong. But also, as we have shown by including in this volume both classic and contemporary pieces from each theoretical tradition, there were many good ideas in the original articulations of the old theories that are still useful.

The answer to the first question, Which theory is correct?, is more difficult for some students to accept. It is unsettling for anyone searching for answers to be told that no single approach is the right one. In any intellectual pursuit, wise people will often disagree. When one studies something very complex, such as criminal behavior, there is additional room to disagree. And when the measurement of that behavior is made more difficult because those engaging in it seek to hide and elude detection, it is easy to understand why there continue to be disagreements among criminologists about how best to explain crime.

In this section and the one that follows, we have selected what we believe to be important contemporary criminological perspectives whose ties to the major theoretical traditions of criminology are not as tight as the current versions described in the past two sections. To be sure, not all of the new and important directions are represented here. Of course, some of our colleagues will feel that we have left out something important, whereas others will question whether all of the articles do represent significant new directions in criminological theory. We have elected to present here theories and perspectives that are important and give students a sense of the range of explanations that today's criminologists are using to advance our understanding. Some of the ideas presented here can be seen as complementary, yet it will be obvious to the reader that some of the writers included in this section are in wholehearted disagreement with one another.

Gottfredson and Hirschi published *A General Theory of Crime* in 1990. The piece that appears here, "The Nature of Criminality: Low Self-Control," is taken from that larger work. They elaborate the cornerstone of their theory: Crime, like other forms of deviance, is a product of the individual's failure to develop adequate self-control. Readers will recognize that the basic features of this theory are consistent with Hirschi's social control theory. Gottfredson and Hirschi hypothesize that children learn self-control within the family. That is, they learn the appropriate way to behave as a result of parents' teaching, rule enforcement, and positive sanctioning of good behavior. An important feature of this theory is that its creators believe that most people develop effective social control before adolescence, and that the vast majority of people who don't develop it by then will not. Such people are likely to have behavior problems throughout the life course. Mitchell and MacKenzie test the stability of self-control (and the lack thereof) in a sample of adult offenders—people with behavior problems long after (Gottfredson and Hirschi argue) self-control would have been developed, if it were going to be.

Sampson and Laub's article, "Toward an Age-Graded Theory of Informal Social Control," is taken from their book *Crime in the Making*. Here, in what is also clearly a theory derived from Hirschi's version of control theory elaborated in 1969 in *Causes of Delinquency*, Sampson and Laub argue that social bonds are important determinants of criminal involvement, and these bonds differ over the life course. This perspective is very different from the position taken by Gottfredson and Hirschi discussed in "The Nature of Criminality: Low Self-Control." An interesting aspect of Sampson and Laub's work is that they empirically test their ideas with data collected by Glueck and Glueck in the middle of the 20th century. They have used modern technology and contemporary analytic techniques to enhance the value of those important data. We elected to break with our pattern to select an example of empirical research using this theory. Rather than using the work of another criminologist as an example, we have included a recent article by Sampson, Laub, and Wimer. In "Does Marriage Reduce Crime?" they use an updated version of the Glueck and Glueck data—they have been able to find information on many of the teenagers that the earlier research team studied in the 1940s. With these data, they are able to examine the effects of marriage as an important crime-controlling social bond later in life.

Cohen and Felson's routine activities perspective, presented in "Social Change and Crime Rate Trends: A Routine Activity Approach," has proven to be very useful in research on crime trends and in the study of victimization. Some scholars have also used it in combination with a number of other criminological theories (notably control theory). It is used to explain macro-criminological patterns of violation and victimization by showing how changes in the routine behavior of segments of the population can increase or decrease crime rates. Tita and Griffiths's article, "Traveling to Violence: The Case for a Mobility-Based Spatial Typology of Homicide," is an example of a macro-level homicide analysis (a study of social aggregates) using the routine activities approach.

Robert Agnew has developed an explanation of individual criminality that he calls "general strain theory." It draws on the Durkheimian tradition on which Merton based "Social Structure and Anomie" (see Part VI). Merton sought to explain variations in crime rates. In doing so, he described adaptations that were available to people in the face of living in anomic circumstances (a disjuncture between society's legitimate goals and legitimate means). Agnew builds on developments in psychology and social psychology, addressing personal stress as a criminogenic factor. Lisa Broidy's article presents a test of Agnew's theory.

Earlier, we tried to convince students that disagreement among scholars should be expected and is a positive contribution to the dynamic process of building knowledge. Rather than defining the lack of a single right answer as a source of frustration, many criminologists see the opportunity for debate as one of the things that makes scholarly life interesting and intellectually fruitful. When reading the selections in this portion of the volume, students should imagine the disagreements and resulting intellectual jousting that some of these ideas produce among criminologists. It is from these disagreements, and the thrust-and-parry of scholarly discourse, that fresh and exciting ideas emerge.

 For a data analysis exercise that accompanies the material in this section, go to www.sagepub.com/crimereadings3study.

THE NATURE OF CRIMINALITY

Low Self-Control

MICHAEL GOTTFREDSON

TRAVIS HIRSCHI

THE ELEMENTS OF SELF CONTROL

Criminal acts provide immediate gratification of desires. A major characteristic of people with low self-control is therefore a tendency to respond to tangible stimuli in the immediate environment, to have a concrete "here and now" orientation. People with high self-control, in contrast, tend to defer gratification.

Criminal acts provide *easy or simple gratification* of desires. They provide money without work, sex without courtship, revenge without court delays. People lacking self-control also tend to lack diligence, tenacity, or persistence in a course of action.

Criminal acts are *exciting, risky, or thrilling*. They involve stealth, danger, speed, agility, deception, or power. People lacking self-control therefore tend to be adventuresome, active, and physical. Those with high levels of self-control tend to be cautious, cognitive, and verbal.

Crimes provide *few or meager long-term benefits*. They are not equivalent to a job or a career. On the contrary, crimes interfere with long-term commitments to jobs, marriages, family, or friends. People with low self-control thus tend to have unstable marriages, friendships, and job profiles. They tend to be little interested in and unprepared for long-term occupational pursuits.

Crimes require *little skill or planning*. The cognitive requirements for most crimes are minimal. It follows that people lacking self-control need not possess or value cognitive or academic skills. The manual skills required for most crimes are minimal. It follows that people lacking self-control need not possess manual skills that require training or apprenticeship.

Crimes often result in *pain or discomfort for the victim*. Property is lost, bodies are injured, privacy is violated, trust is broken. It follows that people with low self-control tend to be self-centered, indifferent, or insensitive to the suffering and needs of others. It does not follow, however, that people with low self-control are routinely unkind or antisocial. On the contrary, they may discover the immediate and easy rewards of charm and generosity.

Recall that crime involves the pursuit of immediate pleasure. It follows that people lacking self-control will also tend to pursue immediate pleasures that are *not* criminal: They will tend to smoke, drink, use drugs, gamble, have children out of wedlock, and engage in illicit sex.

Crimes require the interaction of an offender with people or their property. It does not follow that people lacking self-control will tend to be gregarious or social. However, it does follow that, other things being equal, gregarious or social people are more likely to be involved in criminal acts.

The major benefit of many crimes is not pleasure but relief from momentary irritation. The irritation caused by a crying child is often the stimulus for physical abuse. That caused by a taunting stranger in a bar is often the stimulus for aggravated assault. It follows that people with low self-control tend to have minimal tolerance for frustration and little ability to respond to conflict through verbal rather than physical means.

Crimes involve the risk of violence and physical injury, of pain and suffering on the part of the offender. It does not follow that people with low self-control will tend to be tolerant of physical pain or to be indifferent to physical discomfort. It does follow that people tolerant of physical pain or indifferent to physical discomfort will be more likely to engage in criminal acts whatever their level of self-control.

The risk of criminal penalty for any given criminal act is small, but this depends in part on the circumstances of the offense. Thus, for example, not all joyrides by teenagers are equally likely to result in arrest. A car stolen from a neighbor and returned unharmed before he notices its absence is less likely to result in official notice than is a car stolen from a shopping center parking lot and abandoned at the convenience of the offender. Drinking alcohol stolen from parents and consumed in the family garage is less likely to receive official notice than drinking in the parking lot outside a concert hall. It follows that offenses differ in their validity as measures of self-control: Those offenses with large risk of public awareness are better measures than those with little risk.

In sum, people who lack self-control will tend to be impulsive, insensitive, physical (as opposed to mental), risk taking, shortsighted, and nonverbal, and they will tend therefore to engage in criminal and analogous acts. Since these traits can be identified prior to the age of responsibility for crime, since there is considerable tendency for these traits to come together in the same people, and since the traits tend to persist through life, it seems reasonable to consider them as comprising a stable construct useful in the explanation of crime.

THE MANY MANIFESTATIONS OF LOW SELF-CONTROL

Our image of the "offender" suggests that crime is not an automatic or necessary consequence of low self-control. It suggests that many noncriminal acts analogous to crime (such as accidents, smoking, and alcohol use) are also manifestations of low self-control. Our image therefore implies that no specific act, type of crime, or form of deviance is uniquely required by the absence of self-control.

Because both crime and analogous behaviors stem from low self-control (i.e., both are manifestations of low self-control), they will all be engaged in at a relatively high rate by people with low self-control. Within the domain of crime, then, there will be much versatility among offenders in the criminal acts in which they engage.

Research on the versatility of deviant acts supports these predictions in the strongest possible way. The variety of manifestations of low self-control is immense. In spite of years of tireless research motivated by a belief in specialization, no credible evidence of specialization has been reported. In fact, the evidence of offender versatility is overwhelming.

By versatility we mean that offenders commit a wide variety of criminal acts, with no strong inclination to pursue a specific criminal act or a pattern of criminal acts to the exclusion of others. Most theories suggest that offenders tend to specialize, whereby such terms as robber, burglar, drug dealer, rapist, and murderer have predictive or descriptive import. In fact, some theories create offender specialization as part of their explanation of crime. For example, Cloward and Ohlin create distinctive subcultures of delinquency around particular forms of criminal behavior, identifying subcultures specializing in theft, violence, or drugs. In a related way, books are written about white-collar crime as though it were a clearly distinct specialty requiring a unique explanation. Research projects are undertaken for the study of drug use, or vandalism, or teen pregnancy (as though every study of delinquency were not a study of drug use and vandalism and teenage sexual behavior). Entire schools of criminology emerge to pursue patterning, sequencing, progression, escalation, onset, persistence, and desistance in the career of offenses or offenders. These efforts survive largely because their proponents fail to consider or acknowledge the clear evidence to the contrary. Other reasons for survival of such ideas may be found in the interest of politicians and members of the law enforcement community who see policy potential in criminal careers or "career criminals."

THE CAUSES OF SELF-CONTROL

We know better what deficiencies in self-control lead to than where they come from. One thing is, however, clear: Low self-control is not produced by training, tutelage, or socialization. As a matter of fact, all of the characteristics associated with low self-control tend to show themselves in the absence of nurturance, discipline, or training. Given the classical appreciation of the causes of human behavior, the implications of this fact are straightforward: The causes of low self-control are negative rather than positive; self-control is unlikely in the absence of effort, intended or unintended, to create it. (This assumption separates the present theory from most modern theories of crime, where the offender is automatically seen as a product of positive forces, a creature of learning, particular pressures, or specific defect.)

At this point, it would be easy to construct a theory of crime causation, according to which characteristics of potential offenders lead them ineluctably to the commission of criminal acts. Our task at this point would simply be to identify the likely sources of impulsiveness, intelligence, risk taking, and the like. But to do so would be to follow the path that has proven so unproductive in the past, the path according to which criminals commit crimes irrespective of the characteristics of the setting or situation.

We can avoid this pitfall by recalling the elements inherent in the decision to commit a criminal act. The object of the offense is clearly pleasurable, and universally so. Engaging in the act, however, entails some risk of social, legal, and/or natural sanctions. Whereas the pleasure attained by the act is direct, obvious, and immediate, the pains risked by it are not obvious, or direct, and are in any event more greatly removed from it. It follows that although there will be little variability among people in their ability to see the pleasures of crime, there will be considerable variability in their ability to calculate potential pains. But the problem goes further than this: Whereas the pleasures of crime are reasonably equally distributed over the population, this is not true for the pains. Everyone appreciates money; not everyone dreads parental anger or disappointment upon learning that the money was stolen.

So, the dimensions of self-control are, in our view, factors affecting calculation of the consequences of one's acts. The impulsive or short-sighted person fails to consider the negative or painful consequences of his acts; the insensitive person has fewer negative consequences to consider; the less intelligent person also has fewer negative consequences to consider (has less to lose).

No known social group, whether criminal or noncriminal, actively or purposefully attempts to reduce the self-control of its members. Social life is not enhanced by low self-control and its consequences. On the contrary, the exhibition of these tendencies undermines harmonious group relations and the ability to achieve collective ends. These facts explicitly deny that a tendency to crime is a product of socialization, culture, or positive learning of any sort.

The traits composing low self-control are also not conducive to the achievement of long-term individual goals. On the contrary, they impede educational and occupational achievement, destroy interpersonal relations, and undermine physical health and economic well-being. Such facts explicitly deny the notion that criminality is an alternative route to the goals otherwise obtainable through legitimate avenues. It follows that people who care about the interpersonal skill, educational and occupational achievement, and physical and economic well-being of those in their care will seek to rid them of these traits.

Two general sources of variation are immediately apparent in the scheme. The first is the variation among children in the degree to which they manifest such traits to begin with. The second is the variation among caretakers in the degree to which they recognize low self-control and its consequences and the degree to which they are willing and able to correct it. Obviously, therefore, even at this threshold level the sources of low self-control are complex.

There is good evidence that some of the traits predicting subsequent involvement in crime appear as early as they can be reliably measured, including low intelligence, high activity level, physical strength, and adventuresomeness. The evidence suggests that the connection between these traits and commission of criminal acts ranges from weak to moderate.

Obviously, we do not suggest that people are born criminals, inherit a gene for criminality, or anything of the sort. In fact, we explicitly deny such notions. What we do suggest is that individual differences may have an impact on the prospects for effective socialization (or adequate control). Effective socialization is, however, always possible whatever the configuration of individual traits.

Other traits affecting crime appear later and seem to be largely products of ineffective or incomplete socialization. For example, differences in impulsivity and insensitivity become noticeable later in childhood when they are no longer common to all children. The ability and willingness to delay immediate gratification for some larger purpose may therefore be assumed to be a consequence of training.

Much parental action is in fact geared toward suppression of impulsive behavior, toward making the child consider the long-range consequences of acts. Consistent sensitivity to the needs and feelings of others may also be assumed to be a consequence of training. Indeed, much parental behavior is directed toward teaching the child about the rights and feelings of others, and of how these rights and feelings ought to constrain the child's behavior. All of these points focus our attention on child rearing.

Conclusions

Theories that cannot incorporate or account for the stability of differences in offending over time are seriously at variance with good evidence. Theories that assume specialization in particular forms of crime or deviant behavior are seriously at odds with good evidence. Theories that propose to examine the parameters of criminal careers (such as onset, persistence, and desistance) or the characteristics of career criminals are at odds with the nature of crime. Theories that assume that criminal acts are means to long-term or altruistic goals are at odds with the facts.

Our theory explicitly addresses the stability and versatility findings. It accounts for them with the concept of self-control: with deferred gratification at one extreme and immediate gratification at the other, with caution at one extreme and risk taking at the other. The mechanism producing these differences has been described as differences in child-rearing practices, with close attention to the behavior of the child at one extreme and neglect of the behavior of the child at the other.

The theory incorporates individual properties insofar as they have an impact on crime or on self-control. . . . We note that the theory is a direct response to analysis of the concept of crime and to our analysis of the failings of the theories of the positivistic disciplines. It incorporates a classical view of the role of choice and a positivistic view of the role of causation in the explanation of behavior. It produces a general explanatory concept that can be measured independently of the phenomenon it is alleged to cause, and it is thus directly testable.

QUESTIONS FOR DISCUSSION AND WRITING

1. What is a major characteristic of people with low self-control, and how does this explain criminality?

2. Throughout the first seven paragraphs, the authors describe people with low self-control. What are they like?

3. Do the authors suggest that crime is an automatic or necessary consequence of low self-control? What causes low self-control?

THE STABILITY AND RESILIENCY OF SELF-CONTROL IN A SAMPLE OF INCARCERATED OFFENDERS

OJMARRH MITCHELL

DORIS LAYTON MACKENZIE

In *A General Theory of Crime,* Gottfredson and Hirschi theorize that individual differences in criminal and analogous behaviors (e.g., premarital sex, smoking, gambling) are attributable to individual differences in self-control. That is, individuals differ in the extent to which they are "attracted to acts that provide immediate and apparently certain pleasure with minimal effort, whatever their collateral consequences." Gottfredson and Hirschi's central thesis is that "people with high self-control are less likely under all circumstances throughout life to commit crime." Individuals with low self-control are distinguished by six interrelated personality dimensions that comprise the construct of self-control. Specifically, individuals with low self-control lack diligence, prudence, sensitivity to the needs of others, high-level cognitive functioning, the ability to deter gratification, and the ability to control their temper.

According to the theory, "*self-control is acquired in the early years of life* ... [primarily through] the actions of parents and other responsible adults." Parents who care for their children, monitor their behavior for deviance, recognize such behavior when it occurs, and admonish inappropriate behaviors instill in their children high levels of self-control. However, when anyone of these elements of effective socialization is missing, low self-control and continued deviance may be the result.

Although clearly emphasizing that self-control is instilled primarily by the actions of parents, Gottfredson and Hirschi also acknowledge the role of at least one other social institution: "To some degree, the school also plays a role in the development of self-control. Children attached to school develop long-term aspirations and commitments to the future inconsistent with self-serving impulses and behavior that are costly to others." Given that formal education usually begins around age 6, before individual differences in self-control are established, schooling is another key means of infusing self-control.

Many aspects of Gottfredson and Hirschi's theory are controversial; however, two of the theory's propositions appear to be particularly contentious. First, Gottfredson and Hirschi contend that after the age of 8 to 10, one's level of self-control becomes a stable trait in the relative sense. That is, Gottfredson and Hirschi argue that the absolute level of self-control within individuals increases with age, and therefore, the likelihood of involvement in criminal acts declines with age. However, relative differences between individuals of the same age will endure over time: "Differences between high- and low-rate offenders persist during the life course. Children ranked on the frequency of their delinquent acts will be ranked similarly later in life." Thus, Gottfredson and Hirschi propose that within-individuals' self-control increases monotonically with age, but the relative rankings of self-control between individuals remains stable over time.

Second, and perhaps more controversially, Gottfredson and Hirschi follow the stability proposition by predicting that once formed, an individual's level of self-control is resilient to change. Gottfredson and Hirschi are unusually bleak in their outlook on the effectiveness of criminal justice interventions in reducing recidivism. In their words, "because low self-control arises in the absence of the powerful inhibiting forces of early childhood, it is highly resistant to the less powerful inhibiting forces of later life, *especially the relatively weak forces of the criminal justice system.*"

EMPIRICAL TESTS OF GOTTFREDSON AND HIRSCHI'S THEORY OF CRIME

In a relatively short period of time, Gottfredson and Hirschi's theory has stimulated a tremendous amount of research.

In spite of this body of research, relatively few researchers have explicitly scrutinized the stability and resiliency propositions. Whereas research has consistently demonstrated the stability of individual differences in antisocial behavior during the life course, to our knowledge, only two studies have directly assessed the stability of self-control. Arneklev, Cochran, and Gainey examined the stability hypothesis in a sample of university students using a two-wave panel design. These authors assessed students' level of self-control using a self-control scale at the beginning and end of a semester (approximately 4 months apart). Arneklev and his colleagues found that the overall self-control scale was stable (e.g., the correlation between the two times was 0.82). Yet analyses of the six dimensions of self-control found somewhat less evidence of

within-individual stability. The authors conclude, "the overall self-control construct and its constituent dimensions appear to be *relatively* stable over a short time period."

Turner and Piquero extend this work by testing the stability hypothesis in a national probability sample using both behavioral and attitudinal measures of self-control during a considerably longer period. In contrast to the work of Arneklev et al., Turner and Piquero focused on examining differences in self-control between offenders and nonoffenders and assessing within-group variation in self-control. Thus, these authors began by distinguishing offenders from nonoffenders based on self-reported behavior during late adolescence.

Findings from Turner and Piquero are particularly relevant to the current discussion. First, in support of Gottfredson and Hirschi's contention that differences between offenders and nonoffenders in self-control appear after the age of 8 to 10, Turner and Piquero found that prior to approximately age 8, offenders and nonoffenders did not differ significantly on self-control; however, after this age, offenders exhibited statistically lower levels of self-control than did nonoffenders. Second, and also in support of Gottfredson and Hirschi's theory, Turner and Piquero found that self-control increases with age for both offenders and nonoffenders. Third, within groups the correlations between measures of self-control over time were all positive and statistically significant; however, these correlations were more modest than Gottfredson and Hirschi suggest. The authors interpret these modest correlations as supporting "within-group stability over time, [yet] they also indicate that change in levels of self-control is occurring." Overall, Turner and Piquero interpret their findings as providing mixed support for Gottfredson and Hirschi's stability hypothesis.

This study supplements the existing body of research by testing the stability and resiliency hypotheses in a largely urban and non-White sample of incarcerated offenders. The present research examines the continuity and change in self-control both within and between individuals. Furthermore, the present research employed a fully randomized design that permits a rigorous direct test of the resiliency hypothesis—at least to one specific criminal justice intervention.

In concordance with Gottfredson and Hirschi's theory, we hypothesize that self-control is stable over time within and between individuals. That is, we expected that an individual's *absolute* level of self-control does not vary during a short period of time, and individuals' *relative* rankings on a measure of self-control do not vary over time. We also hypothesize that self-control is resilient to criminal justice intervention. In particular, this research directly assesses the resiliency of self-control to participation in a boot-camp program for adults by taking preintervention and postintervention measurements of self-control using an attitudinal measure that assesses each of the six dimensions of self-control suggested by Gottfredson and Hirschi. We expect participation in the boot-camp program of interest to have no influence on self-control.

METHOD

The data used in this study derive from a randomized experimental evaluation of Maryland's only correctional boot camp for adult offenders, the Herman L. Toulson Correctional Boot Camp (TBC).

As in all boot-camp programs, TBC is centered on a military component. TBC integrates a military atmosphere with a strong treatment component that includes academic education, life skills training, and substance abuse education and treatment. All of these treatment components have the potential to affect self-control, yet the life skills component is particularly important as it focuses on decreasing impulsivity via teaching inmates basic decision-making skills.

Male inmates who volunteered for participation in the boot-camp program were randomly assigned to either the boot camp or the comparison facility.

DATA COLLECTION

At the beginning of each month, a new platoon of 8 to 20 inmates was drawn into the research sample. Eligible inmates were contacted by trained survey facilitators, who solicited participation in a 45-minute voluntary self-report survey. The first self-report survey (baseline survey) was typically administered 3 to 4 days before each platoon was scheduled to start the boot-camp program. After the research team

surveyed consenting inmates, those inmates randomly assigned to the control facility were diverted from the boot camp and transferred to the alternative facility.

Approximately 6 months later, the same group of trained survey facilitators administered a second voluntary, self-support survey (the exit survey). The survey facilitators gathered the outgoing group of inmates and asked each inmate to participate in the exit survey, which also took approximately 45 minutes to complete.

Both surveys contained a self-control scale. Response options were coded on a 5-point Likert-type scale, $0 =$ *strongly agree* to $4 =$ *strongly disagree*, with $2 =$ *neither agree nor disagree*. Thus higher scores indicate greater levels of self-control.

Descriptive statistics indicate that this sample of offenders was overwhelmingly comprised of young African American males convicted of drug trafficking (i.e., distribution, sales) offenses. In general, these inmates had tenuous ties to conventional society; most were unmarried, did not complete high school, and lacked full-time employment prior to incarceration. Furthermore, in spite of the fact that all of the inmates were serving their first extended term of incarceration, these offenders had considerable histories of contact with the criminal justice system. On average, members had approximately 4.5 prior arrests and 1.5 prior convictions. Note that these characteristics did not vary by experimental condition; in fact, there were no statistically significant differences between the experimental and control groups on the baseline measures, including the measure of self-control.

ANALYSES

To assess the stability of self-control over time, three analyses were performed. First, because Gottfredson and Hirschi hypothesize stability in self-control between individuals, Spearman's correlation coefficient was computed to examine the relationship between the distribution of scores at baseline and exit. Given Gottfredson and Hirschi's assertions, we expected the correlation between baseline and exit scores for the whole scale and each dimension of the scale to be large and statistically significant. Second, as an alternative method of examining the between-individual relative stability of self-control, offenders in the lowest quartile of self-control were distinguished. If self-control was stable, in the relative sense, between baseline and exit, we expected to find that individuals with the lowest levels of self-control at baseline also have the lowest levels of self-control at program exit. Finally, to assess the stability and resiliency of self-control simultaneously, the main effects of time (within subjects) and participation in the boot camp (between subjects) as well as the interaction effect between these two factors were assessed on each dimension of self-control and self-control total score. If self-control was relatively stable between assessments and resilient to the intervention of interest, we expected to find neither the main effect of time nor the interaction effect between time and boot camp participation to be statistically significant.

RESULTS

The findings show that comparing the baseline and exit means reveals that in absolute terms, self-control decreases between the two time periods. Specifically, the total score at baseline was 56.21, whereas the total score at exit dropped to 51.5. In fact, the exit scores are lower on each dimension of self-control with the exception of preference for physical tasks. Thus, self-control is not stable in absolute terms.

To further examine the rank-order stability of self-control over time, offenders in the lowest quartile on self-control (total score) at baseline and exit were distinguished. Of the 55 offenders in the lowest quartile (actually 26%) at baseline, 28 (51%) of these offenders were also in the lowest quartile at exit. Thus, both the correlation and quartile analyses indicate that measures of self-control are modestly positively related, but the rank-ordered stability of self-control does not appear to be as robust as Gottfredson and Hirschi suggest.

Finally, the resiliency and stability of self-control were assessed simultaneously. These analyses investigated the main effects of time, experimental condition, and the interaction between these two factors. An examination of these means indicated that self-control generally decreased between program entry and exit, and participants in the boot-camp program typically reported smaller decreases in self-control than non-participants. For example, comparing changes in self-control by group reveals that

participants reported a drop in self-control of −2.96 points, whereas nonparticipants reported a drop of −5.91. Thus, participation in the boot-camp program had no statistically significant effect on the self-control measures, and therefore, self-control appears to be resilient to the intervention.

DISCUSSION

This study tested two of the central propositions in Gottfredson and Hirschi's self-control theory. First, Gottfredson and Hirschi contend, once established after approximately age 10, self-control is stable in the relative sense over time; yet because socialization continues throughout the life course, self-control should increase with age. Second, and perhaps more controversially, these authors argue that once established, self-control is resilient to social interventions, especially to the "relatively weak forces of the criminal justice system."

Our findings indicate that self-control was stable in neither absolute nor relative terms during a short time period (6 months) in our sample. Analyses of the absolute level of self-control found that self-control decreased while imprisoned. Similarly, analyses of the relative stability of self-control also indicated self-control was instable between time periods. Correlations revealed modest positive associations between the dimensions of self-control measured at different time periods. Analyses of isolated offenders in the lowest quartile on the measure of self-control at baseline revealed that half of these offenders were also in the lowest quartile just prior to release.

Given the design of the present research, we are unable to assess whether the effect of imprisonment on self-control persists after release. Yet if this effect does persist, our findings suggest that imprisonment may increase one's propensity toward crime. Although this suggestion is inconsistent with public sentiment regarding the effects of imprisonment, it comports with the findings of a recent comprehensive synthesis of the effect of prison sentences on recidivism.

The current research found more support for Gottfredson and Hirschi's resiliency proposition. In fact, self-control was completely resilient to the intervention investigated in this research. In particular, individuals in both the boot-camp facility and the control facility reported decreased levels of self-control between baseline and exit. Boot-camp participants reported smaller decreases in self-control than nonparticipants; these differences were not statistically significant.

Future research assessing the resiliency hypothesis should examine a more intensive and less punitive intervention that targets dynamic risk factors using a behavioral approach. In spite of these limitations, the findings of this research call into question the stability of self-control.

QUESTIONS FOR DISCUSSION AND WRITING

1. According to Gottfredson and Hirschi's theory, when is self-control acquired? What plays a primary role in instilling self-control?

2. What did the findings show when the baseline and exit means were compared? What did the further examination reveal? What did the authors find when they simultaneously assessed resiliency and stability of self-control?

3. What were the authors unable to assess, and what do they argue the findings suggest regarding imprisonment?

TOWARD AN AGE-GRADED THEORY OF INFORMAL SOCIAL CONTROL

ROBERT J. SAMPSON

JOHN H. LAUB

INFORMAL SOCIAL CONTROL AND SOCIAL CAPITAL

Our theory emphasizes the importance of informal social ties and bonds to society at all ages across the life course. Hence, the effects of informal social control in childhood, adolescence, and adulthood are central to our theoretical model. Virtually all previous studies of social control in criminology have focused either on adolescents or on official (i.e., formal) social control mechanisms such as arrest and imprisonment. As a result, most criminological studies have failed to examine the processes of informal social control from childhood through adulthood.

Following Elder, we differentiate the life course of individuals on the basis of age and argue that the important institutions of informal and formal social control vary across the life span. For example, the dominant institutions of social control in childhood and adolescence are the family, school, peer groups, and the juvenile justice system. In the phase of young adulthood, the institutions of higher education or vocational training, work, and marriage become salient. The juvenile justice system is also replaced by the adult criminal justice system. Finally, in middle adulthood, the dominant institutions of social

control are work, marriage, parenthood, investment in the community, and the criminal justice system.

Within this framework, our organizing principle derives from the central idea of social control theory: Crime and deviance result when an individual's bond to society is weak or broken. As Janowitz has cogently argued, many sociologists mistakenly think of social control solely in terms of social repression and state sanctions (e.g., surveillance, enforced conformity, incarceration). By contrast, we adopt a more general conceptualization of social control as the capacity of a social group to regulate itself according to desired principles and values, and hence to make norms and rules effective. We further emphasize the role of *informal* social controls that emerge from the role "reciprocities and structure of interpersonal bonds linking members of society to one another and to wider social institutions such as work, family, and school."

In applying these concepts to the longitudinal study of crime, we examine the extent to which social bonds inhibit crime and deviance early in the life course, and the consequences this has for later development. Moreover, we examine social ties to both institutions and other individuals in the adult life course, and identify the transitions within individual trajectories that relate to changes in informal social control. In this context, we contend that pathways to crime and conformity are mediated by social bonds to key institutions of social control. Our theoretical model focuses on the transition to adulthood and, in turn, the new role demands from higher education, full-time employment, military service, and marriage. Hence, we explore the interrelationships among crime and informal social control at all ages, with particular attention devoted to the assessment of within-individual change.

We also examine social relations between individuals (for example, parent-child, teacher-student, and employer-employee) at each stage of the life course as a form of social investment or social capital. Specifically, we posit that the social capital derived from strong social relations (or strong social bonds), whether as a child in a family, as an adolescent in school, or as an adult in a job, dictates the salience of these relations at the individual level. If these relations are characterized by interdependence, they represent social and psychological resources that individuals can draw on as they move through life transitions that traverse larger trajectories. Thus, we see both social capital and informal social control as linked to social structure, and we distinguish both concepts as important in understanding changes in behavior over time.

Recognizing the importance of both stability and change in the life course, we develop three sets of thematic ideas regarding age-graded social control. The first concerns the structural and intervening sources of juvenile delinquency; the second centers on the consequences of delinquency and antisocial behavior for adult life chances; and the third focuses on the explanation of adult crime and deviance in relation to adult informal social control and social capital. Although this model was developed in the ongoing context of our analysis of the Gluecks' data and represents the best fit between our conceptual framework and available measures, we believe that our theoretical notions have wider appeal and are not solely bound by these data.

Structure and Process in Adolescent Delinquency

In explaining the origins of delinquency, criminologists have embraced either structural factors (such as poverty, broken homes) or process variables (such as attachment to parents or teachers). We believe such a separation is a mistake. We join structural and process variables together into a single theoretical model. In brief, we argue that informal social controls derived from the family (e.g., consistent use of discipline, monitoring, and attachment) and school (e.g., attachment to school) mediate the effects of both individual and structural background variables. For instance, previous research on families and delinquency often fails to account for social structural disadvantage and how it influences family life. As Rutter and Giller have argued, socioeconomic disadvantage has potentially adverse effects on parents, such that parental difficulties are more likely to develop and good parenting is impeded. If this is true, we would then expect poverty and disadvantage to have their effects on delinquency transmitted through parenting.

The effects of family process are hypothesized to mediate structural context in other domains as well. We argue that key factors such as family disruption, parental criminality, household crowding, large family size, residential mobility, and mother's employment have either direct or indirect effects on delinquency. All of these structural background factors have traditionally been associated with delinquency. It is our major contention, however, that these structural factors will strongly affect family and school social control mechanisms, thereby playing a largely indirect (but not unimportant) role in the explanation of early delinquency. The intervening processes of primary interest are family socialization (discipline, supervision, and attachment), school attachment, and the influence of delinquent siblings and friends.

The Importance of Continuity Between Childhood and Adulthood

Our second theme concerns childhood antisocial behavior (such as juvenile delinquency, conduct disorder, or violent temper tantrums) and its link to troublesome adult behaviors. The theoretical importance of homotypic continuity has been largely ignored among sociological criminologists. Criminologists still focus primarily on the teenage years in their studies of offending, apparently disregarding the connections between childhood delinquency and adult crime. Reversing this tide, our main contention is that antisocial and delinquent behavior in childhood—measured by both official and unofficial sources—is linked to later adult deviance and criminality in a variety of settings (e.g., family violence, military offenses, "street crime," and alcohol abuse). Moreover, we argue that these outcomes occur independent of traditional sociological and psychological variables such as class background, ethnicity, and IQ.

Although some criminologists have explored the connections among conduct disorder, juvenile delinquency, and adult crime, we argue that the negative consequences of childhood misbehavior extend to a much broader spectrum of adult life, including economic dependence, educational failure, employment instability, and marital discord. It is important to explore the adult worlds of work, educational attainment, and marriage as well as involvement in deviant behavior generally. As Hagan and Palloni argue, delinquent and criminal events "are linked into life trajectories of broader significance, whether those trajectories are criminal or noncriminal in form." Because most research by criminologists has focused either on the teenage years or on adult behavior limited to crime, this basic idea has not been well integrated into the criminological literature.

The Significance of Change in the Life Course

Our third focus, drawing on a developmental perspective and a steppingstone approach, is concerned with changes in deviance and offending as individuals age. Our thesis concerns adult behavior and how it is influenced not just by early life experiences but also by social ties to the adult institutions of informal social control (such as family, school, and work). We argue that trajectories of both crime and conformity are significantly influenced over the life course by these adult social bonds, regardless of prior individual differences in self-control or criminal propensity.

The third major theme of our research, then, is that changes that strengthen social bonds to society in adulthood will lead to less crime and deviance. Conversely, changes in adulthood that weaken social bonds will lead to more crime

and deviance. This premise allows us to explain desistance from crime as well as late onset. In addition, unlike most researchers, we emphasize the quality, strength, and interdependence of social ties more than the occurrence or timing of discrete life events. In our view, interdependent social bonds increase social capital and investment in social relations and institutions. Our theoretical model rests on social ties to jobs and family as the key inhibitors to adult crime and deviance.

Integrating Criminology and the Life Course

Our theoretical framework represents a challenge to several assumptions and ideas found in contemporary criminological thought. We believe that the field of criminology has been dominated by narrow sociological and psychological perspectives, coupled with a strong tradition of research using cross-sectional data on adolescents. As a result, scientific knowledge in the field has been hindered by a focus on a limited age range, a limited range of variation in crime and state sanctions, an examination of either structural or process variables, and by serious limitations found in previous research designs and analytic strategies. The overall consequence is that major gaps appear in the existing body of criminological literature.

We confront several of these knowledge gaps and, we hope, expand and enrich the focus of criminological theory and research. We do so by merging a life-course perspective on age and informal social control with the existing criminological literature on crime and delinquency. With this strategy, we believe that key issues of current debate in the field, such as the age-crime relationship and longitudinal versus cross-sectional data needs, can be resolved. Rather than pitting one view against the other in an either/or fashion, our theory of social bonding integrates what is conceptually sound and empirically correct from each perspective.

Take, for example, the issue of stability versus change. We posit that life-event transitions and adult social bonds can modify quite different childhood trajectories. Thus, our conception of change is that adult factors explain systematic variations in adult behavior independent of childhood background. This does not deny the significance of childhood. Our theory thus incorporates the juvenile period with the adult life course to provide a more unified picture of human development. The unique advantage of a sociological perspective on the life course is that it brings the formative period of childhood back into the picture yet recognizes that individual behavior is mediated over time through interaction with age-graded social institutions.

SOURCE: Reprinted by permission of the publisher from *Crime in the Making: Pathways and Turning Points Through Life* (pp. 17–23) by Robert J. Sampson and John H. Laub, 1993, Cambridge, MA.: Harvard University Press. Copyright © 1993 by the President and Fellows of Harvard College.

QUESTIONS FOR DISCUSSION AND WRITING

1. What have most studies of crime failed to examine?

2. How do the "important institutions of informal and formal social control" vary across the life span? On which "transition" does the authors' model focus?

3. What do the authors argue is linked to troublesome adult behaviors?

DOES MARRIAGE REDUCE CRIME?

A Counterfactual Approach to Within-Individual Causal Effects

ROBERT J. SAMPSON

JOHN H. LAUB

CHRISTOPHER WIMER

Your friends or me.

—Spouse of an adult offender who desisted from crime

The association of marriage with a wide range of adult outcomes is well accepted but controversial. Whether crime, mortality, binge drinking, drug use, depression, employment status, or wages, the literature is replete with findings suggesting that marriage is linked to well-being. The meaning of these associations is another matter altogether. Questions of selection and confounding are paramount. For example, we may observe that married men are less likely to commit crime or be unemployed than unmarried men, but problems with differential selection into marriage hamper causal conclusions. Yet unlike in some social experiments with housing vouchers or job training, we cannot randomly assign marriage partners. Research must thus rely on observational data that yield ambiguous results subject to alternative interpretations.

This [article] addresses the challenge of causality in a long-term study of marriage and crime over the life course. Our approach is to extend "counterfactual" methods for time-varying covariates to a within-individual analysis of the role of marriage in the lives of 500 men who entered the transition to adulthood at high risk for continued involvement in crime. Committed to reform schools in Massachusetts during their adolescence in the 1940s, these men were the original subjects of a classic study of juvenile delinquency and its aftermath. Followed to age 32 by the Gluecks, the early and young adult lives of these men were later investigated by Sampson and Laub. The analysis in this [article] is based on three sets of additional data. As described below, we first launched a 35-year follow-up study to age 70, in which we conducted state and national searches of both crime and death records for the original 500 delinquent men. Second, we tracked and conducted in-depth interviews with a targeted subsample of 52 of the men who varied in patterns of criminality in adulthood. During these interviews, we administered a life-history calendar to assess yearly changes in key life events (for example, marriage, crime, and incarceration). Finally, we coded yearly data on key time-varying covariates for the full sample of 500 over the ages 17 to 32 from the original study's data archives.

Unlike research that contrasts the outcomes of married with unmarried individuals, our strategy is to capitalize on variations within individuals over time, separating the effects of stable characteristics from change. We specifically capitalize on recent advances in counterfactual analysis for longitudinal data, proposing the basic idea of comparing the average causal effect of being married to being unmarried for the same person. By weighting for time-varying propensities to marriage over each year of the life course, our counterfactual strategy "thinks" like an experiment and provides an alternative to the static between-individual comparisons that dominate the marriage and adult outcome literature. Of course, one can never definitively identify the causal influence of social arrangements on behavior, even in an experiment. Yet by modeling within-individual changes in the propensity to be married, we can at least come closer to the goal of explaining consequences for crime by bringing what is typically viewed as a nuisance—selection into and out of marriage—explicitly into the investigation.

MARRIAGE MECHANISMS AND DESISTANCE FROM CRIME

It is not how many beers you have, it's who you drink with that matters.

—Wife of a man who desisted from crime after she insisted he switch drinking venues

The association of marriage with lower crime among men has been widely reported in both quantitative and qualitative studies. The idea of marriage as an inhibitor of male crime was illustrated by a former delinquent who had been married for 49 years when we interviewed him at age 70: "If I hadn't met my wife at the time I did, I'd probably be dead. It just changed my whole life . . . that's my turning point." What is it about marriage that fosters desistance from crime? Consistent with themes articulated by offenders themselves, we highlight four processes.

First, a change in criminal behavior may occur in response to the attachment or social bond that forms as a result of marriage. This notion reflects a classical social control or "social bonding" perspective, wherein the social tie of marriage is important because it creates interdependent systems of obligation, mutual support, and restraint that impose significant costs for translating criminal propensities into action.

A second reason marriage might influence desistance is because it leads to significant changes in everyday routines and patterns of association with others. It is well established that lifestyles and routine activities are a major source of variation in exposure to crime and victimization. Consistent with this theme, Osgood and colleagues showed that unstructured socializing activities with peers increased the frequency of deviant behaviors among those ages 18 to 26. Marriage has the potential to change such routine activities, especially with regard to deviant peer groups. As Osgood and Lee argued, marriage entails numerous obligations that tend to reduce leisure activities outside of the family. Importantly, we do not assume a miraculous transformation, only that it is reasonable to assume that the same person, when married, will spend less time with same-sex peers than when not married (or before marriage). There is supporting empirical evidence for this hypothesis in the finding that the transition to marriage is followed by a decline in time spent with friends and exposure to delinquent peer groups, controlling for age. Parenting responsibilities can also lead to changes in routine activities because more time is spent in family-centered activities than in unstructured time with peers.

Third, and perhaps more intriguing theoretically, marriage may lead to gendered desistance because of the direct social control exerted by female spouses. This seems particularly true of marriages in the 1950s and 1960s, when it was common for wives to limit the number of nights men could "hang with the guys," thus affecting their associations with peers. Along with providing a base of social support, many wives in this era also took control of the planning and management of household activities and acted as informal guardians of their husbands' social lives. Implicit was an obligation to family by the male partner, especially concerning economic support. Spouses provided additional support by exercising direct supervision. Umberson, for example, hypothesizes that marriage is beneficial to health because spouses monitor and attempt to control their spouse's behavior. She finds that women "nag" about health more than men and that men engage in more risky behaviors than women. In a similar vein, Waite and Gallagher argue, "Marriage makes people better off in part because it constrains them from certain kinds of behavior, which, while perhaps immediately attractive (i.e., staying up all night drinking beer, or cheating on your partner) do not pay off in the long run." From this viewpoint, marriage has the capacity to generate direct social controls, mainly in the form of supervision.

Fourth, marriage comes in a stylized "package" typically involving a number of identities, some of which can change one's sense of self through cognitive transformation. For some, getting married connotes getting "serious," in other words, becoming an adult. Although it may now seem a bit retrograde, the men we study came of age when getting married meant "taking responsibility," at least in theory. Patriarchal marriages meant having someone to care for and having someone to take care of you. This traditional view became even more evident once children entered the family. Cognitive mechanisms, then, have been hypothesized to account for the effect of getting married on desistance from crime.

An unanswered question is whether the hypothesized crime suppression benefits of marriage extend to those involved in cohabitation or other arrangements. Waite makes the case that married couples exhibit a greater sense of long-term responsibility and commitment toward each other than is evident in cohabitation. Another key difference involves legal obligations that extend over longer time horizons than typically seen in cohabitations. The data are conflicting on whether marriage yields different empirical results than cohabitation with respect to crime and deviance.

Horney, Osgood, and Marshall showed that monthly within-individual variations in crime for a sample of high-rate convicted felons were negatively associated with marriage but positively associated with cohabitation, though the pattern varied by crime type. It also appears that women are at greater risk for physical abuse from men when they are in shifting cohabitating relationships as opposed to marital relationships.

Yet, examining a wider range of licit and illicit activities using National Longitudinal Survey of Youth data, Duncan, Wilkerson, and England found that both marriage and cohabitation were associated with decreases in binge drinking and marijuana use. The reductions, however, were greater in marriage compared with cohabitation for men and women. They conclude that "the social control provided by 'social integration' of marriage apparently works mostly through the normative expectations about how married persons behave."

In short, our review provides theoretical motivation to suggest that marriage influences criminal behavior among men, especially those with damaged or high-risk backgrounds. We set aside the identification of what specific mechanism (for example, monitoring, social support, or norms) is at work, and focus instead on what we consider a prior, first-order issue: Is the effect of marriage causal? If it is not, the question of mechanisms becomes moot. Moreover, our perspective extends Sampson and Laub by conceiving of marriage in dynamic terms rather than as a single turning point. The reality is that people enter and exit (and often re-enter) marriage through time, leading us to conceptualize the potential causal effect on crime of being married (which hypothetically could be randomly or exogenously induced) compared with being unmarried for the same person. Furthermore, we test the hypothesis that marriage has an effect even if marital attachment is low and men tend to partner with criminally inclined wives. Our focus is on the straightforward but powerful question of whether being married is linked to lower crime by men compared to periods of being unmarried. Whether among married men attachment is associated with crime is a separate question; indeed, Sampson and Laub restricted their analysis of attachment to the sample of married men.

By applying causal reasoning to the case of within-individual variations in crime by men, we necessarily set aside the question of whether marriage has an analogous effect on crime by women. Because males commit by far the lion's share of crime, on average men marry "up" and women "down" when it comes to exposure to crime and violence by a spouse in heterosexual unions. It thus follows that marriage may reduce women's well-being even as at the same time it benefits their male partners. Feminist critics of marriage are justified in questioning generic arguments about "good marriage" effects. Good for whom? one must ask. We look to other scholars to uncover the causal role of marriage, if any, in criminal offending by women.

STUDY DESIGN

Our main source of data comes from a long-term follow-up of the original subjects studied by Glueck and Glueck in *Unraveling Juvenile Delinquency* (1950). The Gluecks' study of juvenile and adult criminal behavior involved a sample of 500 male delinquents ages 10 to 17 and 500 male nondelinquents ages 10 to 17 matched on age, ethnicity, IQ, and low-income residence. Over a 25-year period from 1940 to 1965, a wealth of information was collected in childhood, adolescence, and adulthood. Subjects were originally interviewed at an average of age 14, at age 15, and again at age 32 with only 8 percent attrition. Data reconstruction and an analysis of continuity and change in crime for Glueck men up to age 32 were described in *Crime in the Making: Pathways and Turning Points Through Life.*

The men were born between 1924 and 1932 and grew up in central Boston. When we launched a follow-up study in 1994, the oldest subject was nearing 70 and the youngest was 61. We collected three sets of data on the men: criminal records, both at the state and national levels; death records, also at the state and national levels; and interviews with a targeted subset of original delinquent subjects. We briefly describe each in turn; additional details on all aspects of the research design and data collection can be found in Laub and Sampson.

Criminal records were manually searched at the Massachusetts Office of the Commissioner of Probation for 475 of the original 500 delinquents. Operating since 1926, the Office of the Commissioner of Probation is the central repository of criminal record data for the state of Massachusetts. These data allowed us to update the official criminal history for the delinquents in the Glueck study after age 32, but do not provide information for those subjects who moved out of state or for those who reside in the state, but may have committed crimes out of state. We thus collected criminal histories from the FBI and coded all arrests after age 32 that did not appear in the Massachusetts criminal histories, consisting mostly of arrests that occurred out of state. Because of the rarity of crime at older ages, we focus on total crime counts from these combined state and national records.

By definition, official criminal records pertain only to offenses that came to the attention of the criminal justice system. Although limited in this way, official data capture serious offenses (such as robbery) fairly well. In Massachusetts, criminal histories contain a surprising amount of "nonserious" crime as well. The wide range of offenses captured is important given the lack of specialization in criminal careers. Our strategy is to analyze within-individual trajectories of propensity to crime and not the comparison of different groups or cohorts of men with different characteristics often thought to influence official processing (for example, race-ethnicity and social class). For example, it is hard to imagine why a 45-year-old man, compared to the same man at age 40, would be any more or less likely to be arrested given an offense. The criminal records from the Massachusetts Office of the Commissioner of Probation have also been validated in prior research and FBI rap sheets have for a long time been considered the gold standard in criminological research on criminal careers. Perhaps most important, age-specific self-reports of crime recalling back over 35 years are no less limited.

We searched the Massachusetts Registry of Vital Records and Statistics for all 475 subjects from their 32nd birthday onwards, unless an arrest date showed that a later search date was appropriate. (We already knew the dates and the cause of death for the 25 subjects who died during the Gluecks' study.) Once a record of death was found, we purchased the death certificate from the Registry. Next, we conducted a search for the remaining living men using the National Death Index (NDI) maintained by the National Center for Health. We searched this index and uncovered additional deaths, both in Massachusetts and out of state. From these sources we coded all dates of death and integrated them into the longitudinal data on criminal histories.

TRACING AND FINDING SUBJECTS

A key part of our follow-up study involved tracking and conducting detailed interviews with a targeted subset of the original delinquent subjects. After setting aside those men who had died (N = 245), phone books (paper and electronic), Web-based search engines like www .switchboard.com, criminal records, death records, motor vehicle records, and voter lists were used to locate the vast majority of men. In addition, records from the Massachusetts Department of Corrections and the Massachusetts Parole Board were used in our search. The Cold Case Squad of the Boston Police Department helped us find the most difficult to locate cases. Of the 230 members of the study who were alive and thus eligible for an interview at the time of the follow-up study, we located reliable information on 181 men, yielding a location rate of 79 percent.

We sought to yield maximum variability in trajectories of adult crime and so using the criminal history records we classified eligible men into strata that reflected persistence in crime, desistance, and "zigzag" offending patterns, including late onset and late desistance of violence. Our initial goal was to complete about 40 in-person interviews, but with the 35-year gap we anticipated less than a 50 percent completion rate. Given limited resources, 40 of the located men were reserved as possible replicates for future study if funds permitted—but no attempt was ever made on our part to contact them. Of the pool of 141 men selected, we interviewed 52. Twenty-seven refused (this included those who did not respond to messages left on answering machines); nine were willing but seriously ill and therefore declined; 53 had an unlisted phone number and never responded to our mailings. Because IRB restrictions prevented us from contacting these men in person, their ultimate eligibility status remains unknown.

Therefore, of those men we contacted about the study (N = 88), 52 (59 percent) were interviewed and 36 (41 percent) refused or were unable for health reasons to be interviewed. Eliminating refusals due to illness, our rate of interview participation was 66 percent of known eligibles. Both participation figures were beyond what we expected and compare favorably with other long-term follow-up studies with high risk samples.

CONCLUSIONS

I keep a close watch on this heart of mine
I keep my eyes wide open all the time
I keep the ends out for the tie that binds
Because you're mine, I walk the line

—Johnny Cash, 1956

The United States has witnessed extensive normative debates about the role of marriage in modern society. Indeed, the 2004 presidential campaign saw its energy boosted by groups as varied as Christian evangelicals and gay activists concerned about competing visions of the future of marriage. As noted at the outset, there is considerable disagreement in the broader social science literature as well, especially whether a causal effect of marriage exists on a wide range of adult behaviors, from wages to sex to health to crime.

Given this backdrop, we believe it is important to assess what is known about marriage in as non-ideological and rigorous a manner as possible. We attempted to do so by estimating the causal effects of marriage on crime using a unique compilation of data—arguably the longest longitudinal study to date on crime and adult development. We found that being married is associated with a significant reduction in the probability of crime, averaging approximately 35 percent across key models in both the full sample of nearly 500 men examined from ages 17 to 32 and the targeted subsample of 52 men assessed from ages 17 to 70. These basic findings were robust, and thus consistent with the notion that marriage causally inhibits crime over the life course.

Why is marriage important in the process of desistance from crime? Supported by a mix of theory and consistent narrative materials derived from in-depth interviews with the same men studied here, we have argued that marriage has the potential to "knife-off" the past from the present in the lives of disadvantaged men and lead to one or more of the following: opportunities for investment in new relationships that offer social support, growth, and new social networks; structured routines that center more on family life and less on unstructured time with peers; forms of direct and indirect supervision and monitoring of behavior; or situations that provide an opportunity for identity transformation and that allow for the emergence of a new self or script, what Hill described as the "movement from a hell raiser to a family man."

We wish to be clear that the results in this [article] do not confirm the existence of these or any other specific mechanisms. Yet even in true experimental designs, it is usually unclear what the exact mechanism is that produces a given result. In any randomized trial, the causal inference is about the specific treatment—for example, even if marriage could be randomly assigned, any crime outcome differences could still not be apportioned among hypothesized mediating mechanisms. To take another example, housing voucher experiments cannot tell us *why* individuals randomly assigned to low poverty neighborhoods do better (if they do). Or take job training experiments—is the mechanism specific skills one is taught? Personal counseling? Social solidarity and encouragement? Treatments are a package and the relative contributions of the components can't easily be disentangled. The problem of mechanisms is therefore not unique to our study. In terms of causality, we take the position that one must first demonstrate the effect of a treatment before tackling the question of mechanisms.

Because of data constraints, we also could not model yearly changes in the quality of marital attachment or in the criminal or deviant character of the man's spouse. We could and did, however, examine between-individual differences in marital attachment at age 25 and criminal involvement of spouses at age 25 among the subset of approximately 225 men who were married at that age. Controlling for these differences, our data reveal that within-individual variations in crime were still negatively and strongly associated with being married versus being unmarried. This implies that there is something about being married, at least during the young adult years, that inhibits crime regardless of the quality of the marriage and even the criminal involvement of the spouse. Perhaps the latter is not so surprising—because on average men are much more involved in crime than women, it is almost invariably the case that men marry "up" and women "down" when it comes to exposure to crime and violence. For these men in these times, any marriage may have worked as something like a "civilizing" effect.

Probably the biggest limitation of our study is that the Inverse Probability of Treatment Weighting (IPTW) modeling approach we

adopted assumes no unmeasured covariates linked to both treatment and outcome. In practice, the criterion of having no unobserved confounding is impossible to verify—the data in any observational study provide no definitive information. As discussed above, however, we tried to counteract this limitation by exploiting what we believe are rich individual baseline data and time-varying covariates over the full life course in order to model the propensity to marriage. It is hard to imagine what the missing time-stable or time-invariant covariates are that would overcome the magnitude and robustness of results. From IQ to the cumulative history of both the outcome and the treatment, we accounted for 20 baseline covariates and approximately a dozen time-varying confounders measured from widely varying sources—many of which predict the course of marriage as theoretically expected.

We thus argue that omitted confounders would have to be implausibly large to overturn the basic results obtained under a number of different model specifications and assumptions. It is also not clear what alternative methods are both better and practical. At the very least, a major advantage of the IPTW approach (and counterfactual logic more generally) is that it forces conceptual clarity and transparency in the assumptions and causal claims that are made, unlike much literature that continues to use causal language in informal or disguised terms.

IMPLICATIONS

More broadly, we see our work as informing debates about how social behavior changes over time as individuals connect or disconnect across a variety of institutional domains (for example, marriage, work, education, and the military). Even among high-risk offenders, as in the general population, most men marry and most that divorce get married again, underscoring the potential role of marriage as a time-varying source of variations in crime. We would note that though cohabitation is rare in our cohort of men, the results for the subsample of 52 men followed to age 70 are intriguing—there are hints in the data that desistance effects may not be limited to marriage or marital relationships as traditionally defined. This is an important area for future research using younger cohorts among which cohabitation is more normative, as is the casual effect of partnership on female crime, which is apparently growing. Is marriage a protective factor for female offending as it appears to be for female victimization? Note also that our theoretical approach is logically applicable to gay marriage—for example, we would predict that a gay man in a marital situation is less likely to be criminal or engage in high-risk sexual behavior than when the same gay man is otherwise unattached.

Our results bear on policies for ex-offenders as well. The state cannot (nor should it even if imaginable) force individuals to marry, especially given that ex-offenders do not make the most attractive marriage mates. At the same time, marriage is a potentially transformative institution that may assist in promoting desistance from criminal behavior. It is also the case that some women consciously choose to marry ex-cons, often with the foresight to recognize the heavy burdens that await them. Thus our results suggest more rigorous evaluation of recent policy initiatives that support marriage and stable relationships among ex-offenders. "Re-entry" is a growing concern as hundreds of thousands of ex-convicts, many with backgrounds like our

Glueck men, are being released each year, a trend projected to continue for the next decade. It may even be possible to design policy experiments where supports for marriage (for example, tax benefits) are randomly assigned to prisoners upon release as a way to more rigorously assess causal effects on recidivism.

In the meanwhile, we believe that counterfactual methods and IPTW models offer a promising approach to the inherent problem of making causal inferences, whether in criminology, demography and life-course dynamics, or the social sciences at large. Although certainly no panacea, we see the benefit in extending counterfactual life-course models to other hypothesized sources of desistance from crime at the within-individual level for young adult offenders, such as work, schooling, and military service. One can extend the logic of counterfactual models to other time-varying adult outcomes in the general population that have been associated with marriage such as wages, mental health, and physical well-being. Given secular declines in marriage, it would seem especially wise to further assess the effects of cohabitation on criminal behavior and other adaptations to life.

SOURCE: From *Criminology*, Vol. 44, No. 3, 2006: 465–508. Reprinted by permission of the American Society of Criminology.

QUESTIONS FOR DISCUSSION AND WRITING

1. What four "processes" did the authors highlight regarding how marriage fosters desistance from crime?

2. What did the authors find when they looked at the effects of being married on the probability of crime? What did they find when they examined between-individual differences in marital attachment at age 25 and criminal involvement of spouses at age 25?

3. What do the authors say about how their findings bear on policies for ex-offenders?

SOCIAL CHANGE AND CRIME RATE TRENDS

A Routine Activity Approach

LAWRENCE E. COHEN

MARCUS FELSON

I n its summary report, the National Commission on the Causes and Prevention of Violence presents an important sociological paradox:

> Why, we must ask, have urban violent crime rates increased substantially during the past decade when the conditions that are supposed to cause violent crime have not worsened—have, indeed, generally improved?

The Bureau of the Census, in its latest report on trends in social and economic conditions in metropolitan areas, states that most "indicators of well-being point toward progress in the cities since 1960." Thus, for example, the proportion of blacks in cities who completed high school rose from 43 percent in 1960 to 61 percent in 1968; unemployment rates dropped significantly between 1959 and 1967 and the median family income of blacks in cities increased from 61 percent to 68 percent of the median white family income during the same period. Also during the same period, the number of persons living below the legally defined poverty level in cities declined from 11.3 million to 8.3 million.

Despite the general continuation of these trends in social and economic conditions in the United States, the Uniform Crime Reports indicate that between 1960 and 1975 reported rates of robbery, aggravated assault, forcible rape, and homicide increased by 263 percent, 164 percent, 174 percent, and 188 percent, respectively. Similar property crime rate increases reported during this same period (e.g., 200 percent for burglary rate) suggest that the paradox noted by the Violence Commission applies to nonviolent offenses as well.

In the present [article], we consider these paradoxical trends in crime rates in terms of changes in the "routine activities" of everyday life. We believe the structure of such activities influences criminal opportunity and therefore affects trends in a class of crimes we refer to as *direct-contact predatory violations*. Predatory violations are defined here as illegal acts in which "someone definitely and intentionally takes or damages the person or property of another." Further, this analysis is confined to those predatory violations involving direct physical contact between at least one offender and at least one person or object which that offender attempts to take or damage.

We argue that structural changes in routine activity patterns can influence crime rates by affecting the convergence in space and time of the three minimal elements of direct-contact predatory violations: (1) motivated offenders, (2) suitable targets, and (3) the absence of capable guardians against a violation. We further argue that the lack of any one of these elements is sufficient to prevent the successful completion of a direct-contact predatory crime and that the convergence in time and space of suitable targets and the absence of capable guardians may even lead to large increases in crime rates without necessarily requiring any increase in the structural conditions that motivate individuals to engage in crime. That is, if the proportion of motivated offenders or even suitable targets were to remain stable in a community, changes in routine activities could nonetheless alter the likelihood of their convergence in space and time, thereby creating more opportunities for crimes to occur. Control therefore becomes critical. If controls through routine activities were to decrease, illegal predatory activities could then be likely to increase. In the process of developing this explanation and evaluating its consistency with existing data, we relate our approach to classical human ecological concepts and to several earlier studies.

The Structure of Criminal Activity

Sociological knowledge of how community structure generates illegal acts has made little progress since Shaw and McKay and their colleagues published their pathbreaking work, *Delinquency Areas*. Variations in crime rates over space long have been recognized, and current evidence indicates that the pattern of these relationships within metropolitan communities has persisted. Although most spatial research is quite useful for describing crime rate patterns and providing post hoc explanations, these works seldom consider—conceptually or empirically—the fundamental human ecological character of illegal acts as *events* which occur at specific locations in *space* and *time*, involving specific persons and/or objects. These and related concepts can help us to develop an extension of the human ecological analysis to the problem of explaining changes in crime rates over time. Unlike many criminological inquiries, we do not examine why individuals or groups are inclined criminally, but rather we take criminal inclination as given and examine the manner in which the spatio-temporal organization of social activities helps people to translate their criminal inclinations into action. Criminal violations are treated here as routine activities which share many attributes of, and are interdependent with, other routine activities. This interdependence between the structure of illegal activities and the organization of everyday sustenance activities leads us to consider certain concepts from human ecological literature.

Selected Concepts From Hawley's Human Ecological Theory

While criminologists traditionally have concentrated on the *spatial* analysis of crime rates within metropolitan communities, they seldom have considered the *temporal* interdependence of these acts. In his classic theory of human ecology, Amos Hawley treats the community not simply as a unit of territory but rather as an organization of symbiotic and commensalistic relationships as human activities are performed over both space and time.

Hawley identified three important temporal components of community structure: (1) *rhythm*, the regular periodicity with which events occur, as with the rhythm of travel activity; (2) *tempo*, the number of events per unit of time, such as the number of criminal violations per day on a given street; and (3) *timing*, the coordination among different activities which are more or less interdependent, such as coordination of an offender's rhythms with those of a victim. These components of temporal organization, often neglected in criminological research, prove usual in analyzing how illegal tasks are performed—a utility which becomes more apparent after noting the spatio-temporal requirements of illegal activities.

The Minimal Elements of Direct-Contact Predatory Violations

As we previously stated, despite their great diversity, direct-contact predatory violations share some important requirements which facilitate analysis of their structure. Each successfully completed violation minimally requires an *offender* with both criminal inclinations and the ability to carry out those inclinations, a person or object providing a *suitable target* for the offender, and *absence of guardians* capable of preventing violations. We emphasize that the lack of any of these elements normally is sufficient to prevent such violations from occurring. Although guardianship is implicit in everyday life, it usually is marked by the absence of violations; hence, it is easy to overlook. While police action is analyzed widely, guardianship by ordinary citizens of one another and of property as they go about routine activities may be one of the most neglected elements in sociological research on crime, especially since it links seemingly unrelated social roles and relationships to the occurrence or absence of illegal acts.

The conjunction of these minimal elements can be used to assess how structure may affect the tempo of each type of violation. That is, the probability that a violation will occur at any specific time and place might be taken as a function of the convergence of likely offenders and suitable targets in the absence of capable guardians. Through consideration of how trends and fluctuations in social conditions affect the frequency of this convergence of criminogenic circumstances, an explanation of temporal trends in crime rates can be constructed.

The Ecological Nature of Illegal Acts

This ecological analysis of direct-contact predatory violations is intended to be more than metaphorical. In the context of such violations, people, gaining and losing sustenance, struggle among themselves for property, safety, territorial hegemony, sexual outlet, physical control, and sometimes for survival itself. The interdependence between offenders and victims can be viewed as a predatory relationship between functionally dissimilar individuals or groups. Since predatory violations fail to yield any net gain in sustenance for the larger community, they can only be sustained by feeding upon other activities. As offenders cooperate to increase their efficiency at predatory violations and as potential victims organize their resistance to these violations, both groups apply the symbiotic principle to improve their sustenance position. On the other hand, potential victims of predatory crime

may take evasive actions, which encourage offenders to pursue targets other than their own. Since illegal activities must feed upon other activities, the spatial and temporal structure of routine legal activities should play an important role in determining the location, type, and quantity of illegal acts occurring in a given community or society. Moreover, one can analyze how the structure of community organization as well as the level of technology in a society provide the circumstances under which crime can thrive. For example, technology and organization affect the capacity of persons with criminal inclinations to overcome their targets, as well as affecting the ability of guardians to contend with potential offenders by using whatever protective tools, weapons, and skills they have at their disposal. Many technological advances designed for legitimate purposes—including the automobile, small power tools, hunting weapons, highways, telephones, and so on—may enable offenders to carry out their own work more effectively or may assist people in protecting their own or someone else's person or property.

Not only do routine legitimate activities often provide the wherewithal to commit offenses or to guard against others who do so, but they also provide offenders with suitable targets. Target suitability is likely to reflect such things as value (e.g., the material or symbolic desirability of a personal or property target for offenders), physical visibility, access, and the inertia of a target against illegal treatment by offenders (including the weight, size, and attached or locked features of property inhibiting its illegal removal and the physical capacity of personal victims to resist attackers with or without weapons). Routine production activities probably affect the suitability of consumer goods for illegal removal by determining their value and weight. Daily activities may affect the location of property and personal targets in visible and accessible places at particular times. These activities also may cause people to have on hand objects that can be used as weapons for criminal acts or self-protection or to be preoccupied with tasks which reduce their capacity to discourage or resist offenders.

While little is known about conditions that affect the convergence of potential offenders, targets, and guardians, this is a potentially rich source of propositions about crime rates. For example, daily work activities separate many people from those they trust and the property they value. Routine activities also bring together at various times of day or night persons of different backgrounds, sometimes in the presence of facilities, tools, or weapons which influence the commission or avoidance of illegal acts. Hence, the timing of work, schooling, and leisure may be of central importance for explaining crime rates.

The ideas presented so far are not new, but they frequently are overlooked in the theoretical literature on crime. Although an investigation of the literature uncovers significant examples of descriptive and practical data related to the routine activities upon which illegal behavior feeds, these data seldom are treated within an analytical framework. The next section reviews some of this literature.

RELATION OF THE ROUTINE ACTIVITY APPROACH TO EXTANT STUDIES

A major advantage of the routine activity approach presented here is that it helps assemble some diverse and previously unconnected criminological analyses into a single substantive framework. This framework also serves to link illegal and legal activities, as illustrated by a few examples of descriptive accounts of criminal activity.

Descriptive Analyses

There are several descriptive analyses of criminal acts in criminological literature. For example, Thomas Reppetto's study, *Residential Crime,* considers how residents supervise their neighborhoods and streets and limit access of possible offenders. He also considers how distance of households from the central city reduces risks of criminal victimization. Reppetto's evidence—consisting of criminal justice records, observations of comparative features of geographic areas, victimization survey data, and offender interviews—indicates that offenders are very likely to use burglary tools and to have at least minimal technical skills, that physical characteristics of dwellings affect their victimization rates, that the rhythms of residential crime rate patterns are marked (often related to travel and work patterns of residents), and that visibility of potential sites of crime affects the risk that crimes

will occur there. Similar findings are reported by Pope's study of burglary in California and by Scarr's study of burglary in and around the District of Columbia. In addition, many studies report that architectural and environmental design as well as community crime programs serve to decrease target suitability and increase capable guardianship, while many biographical or autobiographical descriptions of illegal activities note that lawbreakers take into account the nature of property and/or the structure of human activities as they go about their illegal work.

Evidence that the spatio-temporal organization of society affects patterns of crime can be found in several sources. Strong variations in specific predatory crime rates from hour to hour, day to day, and month to month are reported often, and these variations appear to correspond to the various tempos of the related legitimate activities upon which they feed. Also, at a microsociological level, Short and Strodtbeck describe opportunities for violent confrontations of gang boys and other community residents which arise in the context of community leisure patterns, such as "quarter parties" in black communities, and the importance, in the calculus of decision making employed by participants in such episodes, of low probabilities of legal intervention. In addition, a wealth of empirical evidence indicates strong spatial variations over community areas in crime and delinquency rates. Recently, Albert Reiss has argued convincingly that these spatial variations (despite claims to the contrary) have been supported consistently by both official and unofficial sources of data. Reiss further cites victimization studies which indicate that offenders are very likely to select targets not far from their own residence.

Macrolevel Analyses of Crime Trends and Cycles

Although details about how crime occurs are intrinsically interesting, the important analytical task is to learn from these details how illegal activities carve their niche within the larger system of activities. This task is not an easy one. For example, attempts by Bonger, Durkheim, Henry and Short, and Fleisher to link the rate of illegal activities to the economic condition of a society have not been completely successful. Empirical tests of the relationships postulated in the above studies have produced inconsistent results, which some observers view as an indication that the level of crime is not related systematically to the economic conditions of a society.

It is possible that the wrong economic and social factors have been employed in these macrostudies of crime. Other researchers have provided stimulating alternative descriptions of how social change affects the criminal opportunity structure, thereby influencing crime rates in particular societies. For example, at the beginning of the nineteenth century, Pat Colquhoun presented a detailed, lucid description and analysis of crime in the London metropolitan area and suggestions for its control. He assembled substantial evidence that London was experiencing a massive crime wave attributable to a great increment in the assemblage and movement of valuable goods through its ports and terminals.

A similar examination of crime in the period of the English industrial expansion was carried out by a modern historian, J. J. Tobias, whose work on the history of crime in nineteenth-century England is perhaps the most comprehensive effort to isolate those elements of social change affecting crime in an expanding industrial nation. Tobias details how far-reaching changes in transportation, currency, technology, commerce, merchandising, poverty, housing, and the like had tremendous repercussions on the amount and type of illegal activities committed in the nineteenth century. His thesis is that structural transformations either facilitated or impeded the opportunities to engage in illegal activities. In one of the few empirical studies of how recent social change affects the opportunity structure for crime in the United States, Leroy Gould demonstrated that the increase in the circulation of money and the availability of automobiles between 1921 and 1965 apparently led to an increase in the rate of bank robberies and auto thefts, respectively. Gould's data suggest that these relationships are due more to the abundance of opportunities to perpetrate the crimes than to short-term fluctuations in economic activities.

Although the sociological and historical studies cited in this section have provided some useful *empirical* generalizations and important insights into the incidence of crime, it is fair to say that they have not articulated systematically the *theoretical* linkages between routine legal activities and illegal endeavors. Thus, these studies cannot explain how changes in the larger social structure generate changes in the opportunity

to engage in predatory crime and hence account for crime rate trends. To do so requires a conceptual framework such as that sketched in the preceding section. Before attempting to demonstrate the feasibility of this approach with macrolevel data, we examine available microlevel data for its consistency with the major assumptions of this approach.

Microlevel Assumptions of the Routine Activity Approach

The theoretical approach taken here specifies that crime rate trends in the post-World War II United States are related to patterns of what we have called routine activities. We define these as any recurrent and prevalent activities which provide for basic population and individual needs, whatever their biological or cultural origins. Thus, routine activities would include formalized work, as well as the provision of standard food, shelter, sexual outlet, leisure, social interaction, learning, and child rearing. These activities may go well beyond the minimal levels needed to prevent a population's extinction, so long as their prevalence and recurrence makes them a part of everyday life.

Routine activities may occur (1) at home, (2) in jobs away from home, and (3) in other activities away from home. The latter may involve primarily household members or others. We shall argue that, since World War II, the United States has experienced a major shift of routine activities away from the first category into the remaining ones, especially those nonhousehold activities involving nonhousehold members. In particular, we shall argue that this shift in the structure of routine activities increases the probability that motivated offenders will converge in space and time with suitable targets in the absence of capable guardians, hence contributing to significant increases in the direct-contact predatory crime rates over these years.

If the routine activity approach is valid, then we should expect to find evidence for a number of empirical relationships regarding the nature and distribution of predatory violations. For example, we would expect routine activities performed within or near the home and among family or other primary groups to entail lower risk of criminal victimization because they enhance guardianship capabilities. We should also expect that routine daily activities affect the location of property and personal targets in visible and accessible places at particular times, thereby influencing their risk of victimization. Furthermore, by determining their size and weight, and in some cases their value, routine production activities should affect the suitability of consumer goods for illegal removal. Finally, if the routine activity approach is useful for explaining the paradox presented earlier, we should find that the circulation of people and property, the size and weight of consumer items, and so on will parallel changes in crime rate trends for the post-World War II United States.

The veracity of the routine activity approach can be assessed by analyses of both microlevel and macrolevel interdependencies of human activities. While consistency at the former level may appear noncontroversial, or even obvious, one nonetheless needs to show that the approach does not contradict existing data before proceeding to investigate the latter level.

Discussion

In our judgment, many conventional theories of crime (the adequacy of which usually is evaluated by cross-sectional data, or no data at all) have difficulty accounting for the annual changes in crime rate trends in the post-World War II United States. These theories may prove useful in explaining crime trends during other periods, within specific communities, or in particular subgroups of the population. Longitudinal aggregate data for the United States, however, indicate that the trends for many of the presumed causal variables in these theoretical structures are in a direction opposite to those hypothesized to be the causes of crime. For example, during the decade 1960–1970, the percentage of the population below the low-income level declined 44 percent and the unemployment rate declined 186 percent. Central-city population as a share of the whole population declined slightly, while the percentage of foreign stock declined 0.1 percent, and so on.

On the other hand, the convergence in time and space of three elements (motivated offenders, suitable targets, absence of capable guardians) appears useful for understanding crime rate trends. The lack of any of these is sufficient to prevent the occurrence of a successful direct-contact predatory crime. The convergence in

time and suitable targets and the absence of capable guardians can lead to a large increase in crime rates without any increase or change in the structural conditions that motivate individuals to engage in crime. Presumably, had the social indicators of the variables hypothesized to be the causes of crime in conventional theories changed in the direction of favoring increased crime in the post-World II United States, the increases in crime rates likely would have been even more staggering than those which were observed. In any event, it is our belief that criminologists have underemphasized the importance of the convergence of suitable targets and the absence of capable guardians in explaining recent increases in the crime rate. Furthermore, the effects of the convergence in time and space of these elements may be multiplicative rather than additive. That is, their convergence by a fixed percentage may produce increases in crime rates far greater than the fixed percentage, demonstrating how some relatively modest social trends can contribute to some relatively large changes in crime rate trends. The fact that logged variables improved our equations (moving Durbin-Watson values closer to "ideal" levels) lends support to the argument that such an interaction occurs.

Those few investigations of cross-sectional data which include house indicators produce results similar to ours. For example, Roncek and Choldin and Roncek report on block-level data for San Diego, Cleveland, and Peoria and indicate that the proportion of a block's households which are primary individual households consistently offers the best or nearly the best predictor of a block's crime rate. This relationship persisted after they controlled for numerous social variables, including race, density, age, and poverty. Thus, the association between household structure and risk of criminal victimization has been observed in individual-level and block-level cross-sectional data, as well as aggregate national time-series data.

Without denying the importance of factors motivating offenders to engage in crime, we have focused specific attention upon violations themselves and the prerequisites for their occurrence. However, the routine activity approach might in the future be applied to the analysis of offenders and their inclinations as well. For example, the structure of primary group activity may affect the likelihood that cultural transmission or social control of criminal inclinations will occur, while the structure of the community may affect the tempo of criminogenic peer group activity. We also may expect that circumstances favorable for carrying out violations contribute to criminal inclinations in the long run by rewarding these inclinations.

We further suggest that the routine activity framework may prove useful in explaining why the criminal justice system, the community, and the family have appeared so ineffective in exerting social control since 1960. Substantial increases in the opportunity to carry out predatory violations may have undermined society's mechanisms for social control. For example, it may be difficult for institutions seeking to increase the certainty, celerity, and severity of punishment to compete with structural changes resulting in vast increases in the certainty, celerity, and value of rewards to be gained from illegal predatory acts.

It is ironic that the very factors which increase the opportunity to enjoy the benefits of life also may increase the opportunity for predatory violations. For example, automobiles provide freedom of movement to offenders as well as average citizens and offer vulnerable targets for theft. College enrollment, female labor force participation, urbanization, suburbanization, vacations, and new electronic durables provide various opportunities to escape the confines of the household while they increase the risk of predatory victimization. Indeed, the opportunity for predatory crime appears to be enmeshed in the opportunity structure for legitimate activities to such an extent that it might be very difficult to root out substantial amounts of crime without modifying much of our way of life. Rather than assuming that predatory crime is simply an indicator of social breakdown, one might take it as a by-product of freedom and prosperity as they manifest themselves in the routine activities of everyday life.

SOURCE: From *American Sociological Review* 44:588–608. Copyright © 1979 by Lawrence E. Cohen and Marcus Felson. Reprinted by permission of The American Sociological Association.

QUESTIONS FOR DISCUSSION AND WRITING

1. How do structural changes in routine activity patterns influence crime rates? What role do capable guardians play in crime?

2. What is "one of the most neglected" elements in sociological research on crime?

3. What role does technology play in crime? What do "daily work activities" do?

4. What are routine activities? What happened to routine activities after World War II?

TRAVELING TO VIOLENCE

The Case for a Mobility-Based Spatial Typology of Homicide

GEORGE TITA

ELIZABETH GRIFFITHS

Routine activities theory is built upon a simple, but profoundly influential, supposition: that the occurrence of crime is the result of the spatial and temporal intersection of motivated offenders and suitable targets in the absence of agents of control. Traditionally, studies employing this framework have examined how changes in the social and economic landscape of post-World War II society resulted in changes in the organization of daily routine life. These alterations in individuals' routine activities modified the social organization of crime, primarily through shifting the distribution of opportunities for crimes against persons, but also by redefining the mobility patterns of individuals in pursuit of daily activities. Therefore, the crux of routine activities theory is that the demographic characteristics of *both* victims and offenders involved in interpersonal crimes influence the extent to which they *each* are mobile and, thus, their likelihood of meeting in time and space.

Research in the tradition of routine activities theory, however, is primarily focused on the daily routines of *victims* and their attendant victimization risk as a result of such routines. By contrast, environmental criminologists using related but distinct ecological theories of crime have concentrated on the well-traveled routes of *offenders* as the key to identifying why crimes happen where they do. According to this perspective, "criminal commutes" of varying distance to and from the offender's home residence are the result of an interaction between offender motivation and criminal opportunity. Although both theoretical traditions see mobility as an important feature influencing the distribution of crime and violence, neither is faithful to the complexity of ecological perspectives in that only one of the participants to the event is studied.

Using homicide incidents, we develop a spatial typology that conveys a clear sense of participant mobility in relation to the location of the event. We then determine if the demographic attributes of victims and offenders, such as race, sex, and age, along with the motive, weapon, and other characteristics of the event differ depending upon whether one, all, or none of the participants are local to the area in which the crime occurs.

Our spatial typology of homicide has its antecedents in the "mobility triangle" literature, which analyzes crime in terms of the joint distribution of the following:

Victim's Place of Residence

Offender's Place of Residence

Location of Incident

We use census tract assignment as a means of identifying local and nonlocal participants to the homicide incident. Tracts are conceptualized as a proxy measure for neighborhoods. Combinations of these locations in space produce five mutually exclusive categories, or spatial types, that we label as follows:

1. Internal: [V, O, I]
   all three share the same census tract

2. Predatory: O [V, I]
   victim/incident share same census tract, offender lives outside

3. Intrusion: V [O, I]
   offender/incident share same census tract, victim lives outside

4. Offense Mobility: I [V, O]
   offender/victim share same census tract, but incident takes place elsewhere

5. Total Mobility: V, O, I [ ]
   victim and offender live in different census tracts, incident occurs in third unique census tract

Using detailed data on homicide collected in Pittsburgh, Pennsylvania, we examine how the characteristics of the participants and the characteristics of the event culminate in the various joint mobility patterns of the spatial typology.

Literature Review

Routine Activities and Demography

In their classic conceptualization of routine activities theory, Cohen and Felson describe how grand global forces in the organization of North American society had implications for the frequency, prevalence, and type of crimes committed. These authors demonstrated that with the increase in labor force participation by women, more homes were left unoccupied during the day and thus offered inviting targets for motivated burglars. As a result, the temporal pattern of home burglary changed. Similarly, greater family/household income resulted in more people spending time away from their homes in pursuit of leisure activities, chiefly on weekends. Consequently, crimes increased during Friday and Saturday evenings with proportionately more criminal activity occurring in the public domain.

Although routine activities theory emphasizes how the routine activities of victims makes them targets of offenders, research has demonstrated that the demographic characteristics of both victims *and* offenders influence the types of routine activities that govern daily life. For example, young, single adults, particularly males, are more likely to spend time away from their homes during the evening and are more likely to frequent leisure establishments at night than are young married couples. The implications of these varying patterns of routine activities are twofold: first there is an increased *exposure* to personal crime among potential victims, and, second, there are increased *opportunities* for personal crime among potential offenders in public venues. According to routine activities theory, then, characteristics such as gender, age, race, and marital status of both victims and offenders influence their routine activities, and consequently their risk of victimization or opportunity for offending, respectively.

Our central argument is that it is the *joint mobility pattern of* victims and offenders that serves as the primary mechanism by which routine activities theory accounts for how demographic characteristics influence participation in crime.

Mobility Triangles and Violence

Our spatial typology is based on the mobility triangle literature. The term *mobility triangle* refers to a particular configuration of this spatial distribution in which the victim and offender live in the same community but the deviant act (promiscuity) occurs outside of the participants' community. However, researchers later adopted the term *mobility triangle* to generalize to all possible combinations of the distribution of the victim-offender-incident relationship across a variety of crime types.

An analysis of homicide incidents has been largely missing from this research. Instead, most of what we know about mobility and homicide comes from the journey-to-crime literature, which consistently finds that the distances traveled by murderers is shorter than that traveled by other criminals.

PARTICIPANT AND EVENT CHARACTERISTICS

We expect that two key factors will influence joint mobility patterns. First, participant characteristics (age, gender, and race) of both victims and offenders are expected to shape mobility. For instance, youth may be more likely to kill closer to home (internal/intrusion) because of constraints on their social ties outside of the area. Similarly, female victims are more often attacked near their home compared to males, in part because women's daily activities are historically more likely to involve domestic responsibilities in the household. We would anticipate, then, that homicides involving female victims would be distributed more heavily in the internal and predatory categories of the spatial typology. By contrast, race has not been found to affect the mobility patterns of victims or offenders in any consistent way in previous studies.

Second, we explore how event-specific characteristics such as motive, event location, weapon type, the presence of multiple offenders, and the nature of the victim-offender relationship differ across the typology. With respect to motive, previous research indicates that familial/intimate homicides are likely to involve limited mobility on behalf of the victim and/or offender, whereas felony events, often committed within commercial areas of the city, involve much greater mobility by the actors. Whereas these findings are intuitive, little empirical evidence exists related to the mobility patterns of participants involved in other types of events. We might expect gang-related, drive-by killings where one gang initiates (or retaliates for) an attack on a rival gang to characterize a predatory mobility pattern. Gang violence could alternatively (or additionally) be more common among intrusion type events because gangs traditionally provide mutual protection against rivals and defense of place. Similarly, homicides motivated by the distribution of illicit drugs are expected to be overrepresented among predatory and intrusion homicides. Open-air drug markets attract buyers from other communities to purchase drugs in cash-based transactions, making them attractive targets (intrusion), but possessing cash and product also make sellers attractive targets (predatory). The escalation of arguments into acts of lethal violence can occur under a host of circumstances/situations and are likely to be distributed fairly equally among the spatial typology.

The relationship between the victim and the offender will likely affect the spatial organization of the event as well. We would expect victims and offenders to be more familiar with one another the closer that they live to one another. As such, stranger relationships may dominate those events involving a high degree of mobility on the part of both the victim and offender (i.e., total mobility types).

Weapon type is also likely to differ across the spatial typology. We know that expressive forms of lethal violence often involve spur-of-the-moment attacks where weapon choice is limited to immediate availability. When homicides are premeditated, however, we might anticipate greater use of firearms in the assaults as they provide a more efficient means of conducting the murder. Therefore, we expect that the use of guns will differentiate predatory and total mobility types of events from others to the extent that the latter events involve a higher proportion of premeditated felonies.

The relationship between the typology and whether the event occurs on the street or indoors is likely to be a function of several factors, including motive and the social distance between the victim and offender. For example, domestic/familial homicides are hypothesized to occur more often not only within the same community, but also within the shared home of the victim and offender (i.e., internal types). Likewise, based upon the assumptions made about the motives (domestic, familial) and related social relationship among participants, we expect the presence of multiple offenders to be nonrandomly distributed across the spatial types. For instance, gang homicide should be overrepresented among predatory and intrusion-type homicides; thus, these categories should include a disproportionate number of homicides committed by two or more offenders.

The spatial typology provides a useful device in advancing the "dangerous places" versus "dangerous persons" debate. For instance, although involvement in either street gangs or drug markets is known to facilitate violent behavior, it has never been demonstrated where the participants in such violence reside. Research that focuses on neighborhood concentrations of violent incidents, generally from a routine activities framework, has debated whether disadvantaged neighborhoods tend to have high rates of violence due to the quantity of motivated offenders residing in the area, or to the intensity of "suitable targets" or opportunities available in the form of mixed residential and business/commercial establishments. The spatial typology helps to differentiate among places that are violent because offenders live there and places that are violent because offenders congregate there.

DATA AND MEASURES

The analysis uses data on homicides known to the police ($n = 420$) in the city of Pittsburgh during the period 1987 to 1995. Street addresses were collected for the location of the event, the residence of the victim, and the residence of all known offenders/suspects.

Demographic variables pertaining to the participants, such as age, sex, and race (White or Black), are included in the analyses along with event characteristics like gun usage, location (indoor/outdoor), and presence of multiple offenders. We created four variables measuring the victim-offender relationship: intimate partners (including estranged), other family members, friends (including acquaintances), and strangers.

Five variables were created to capture the primary motive of the homicide (gang, drug, familial/domestic, argument, and felony).

METHOD

The goal of our analysis is to determine if certain variables or sets of variables are able to distinguish statistically significant differences among, and between, the various types of homicide.

RESULTS

Internal Type

We find that the motive and social relationship between the parties play more prominent roles in distinguishing internal homicides from all other types. The routine activities that give rise to events involving local participants are likely to occur not only around the homes of the participants, but are more likely to occur indoors.

With the exception of the sex of the offender, individual-specific characteristics fail to distinguish internal homicides from other types. Instead, mobility for internal homicide is influenced primarily by the circumstances/motive surrounding the event.

We find that when compared to all other types of homicide, internal homicides are also much less likely to involve gangs, drugs, arguments or felonious acts.

Among participant characteristics, only sex of the offender is statistically significant. Although the offenders involved in internal homicides are overwhelmingly male, a higher proportion of internal events involve female offenders than do all the other types combined. We were somewhat surprised that age did not play a more significant role in distinguishing internal events from the other types, especially among victims.

To better illustrate these findings, we used the results to identify an example of a "modal" internal homicide in our data set.

> May, 1987: Police are called to the residence of both the victim and the offender at 5:30 P.M. An argument had broken out between siblings instigated by the brother's disapproval of his sister's choice of male companions. The fight escalated to the point where the sister (a 19-year-old, Black female) grabbed a 5-inch kitchen knife and stabbed her brother (21-year-old, Black male) once in the midsection.

Again, note that the offender in this case is a female, the relationship between victim and offender is familial, and that not only did the event take place within the same neighborhood, it took place inside of the participants' household. The mobility, or lack thereof, leading up to the event was predicated on the social relationship between the participants and not the individual-level characteristics of either participant.

Predatory Type

Predatory homicides can be distinguished from homicides involving all other mobility configurations in that victims are more likely to be female. Whereas the remaining victim and offender characteristics (race, age, gender) do not differ between predatory homicides and all other spatial types, there are some important differences between pairs of spatial types that warrant further examination. Although females are overrepresented as victims in predatory events in comparison to all other types, this relationship is especially strong when compared to total mobility homicides. The results also indicate that victims of predatory homicide are older than are victims of either offense-mobility or total-mobility homicide types, and the offender in predatory homicides is significantly more likely to be male than in internal events.

These incidents are more likely to take place indoors relative to the remaining categories of the spatial typology, but in particular when predatory homicides are compared to intrusion and total-mobility events. Other event characteristics including gun use and the presence of multiple offenders do not distinguish predatory homicides from the residual mobility configurations.

Predatory homicides are most clearly distinguished by their motives. These events are drug-related, gang-related, and/or felony-related more often than are all other spatial homicide types. The victim-offender relationship is not able to distinguish predatory homicides from other spatial types in general, but the results indicate that these homicides involve intimate partners to a greater extent than do total mobility events.

Taken together, these results suggest that homicides involving mobility only on the part of the offender are characterized by an aggressive foray into the victim's space for illegal purposes. Gang-related "drive-by" shootings, violence-laden drug transactions, and rape or robbery attempts in victims' homes typify predatory lethal violence. Furthermore, the results imply that it is not so much the individual characteristics of offenders that encourage their mobility to events, but rather, it is their motive for the offense. By contrast, the typical characteristics of victims of predatory homicides (i.e., victims are older and female) arguably limit victim mobility outside of the victim's home or census tract. We again present an incident from the case files of a modal predatory event:

> May, 1989: At approximately 7:00 P.M., the victim (an 81-year-old White female) was killed in her home. The offender (a 22-year-old Black male) worked as the victim's handyman doing odd jobs around the house for pay. The offender had been hanging around his neighborhood, drinking with friends, when he ran out of alcohol. Wanting to buy more, but having no money, the offender decided to travel to the victim's house and confront her for money. When the victim refused, the offender became enraged and attacked the victim: the victim died from manual strangulation and blunt force trauma to the head.

It once again appears that the mobility pattern in this example is better explained by motive than by personal traits. That is, the offender approached the victim because he learned through the shared-routine activity of work (albeit casual labor) that the victim often had money on her person. That she was older and offered a less mobile, more vulnerable target probably played some role in choice of target, but the offender targeted a specific, known individual. It should also be noted as well that the racial differences between victim and offender failed to limit the mobility of the offender. He clearly felt comfortable both working in the victim's predominantly White community and later traveling there to ask for money. This once again highlights the lack of a statistically significant finding regarding the race of either victim or offender among any of the typology types.

Intrusion Type

Only the relationship variables distinguish intrusion homicides from all other categories of homicide. These results suggest that strangers comprise the largest category of victims and offenders within intrusion-type homicides.

Looking across the pair-wise comparisons, we find little to distinguish between intrusion homicides and predatory-type events. Both are similar in terms of the characteristics of events, participants, and the victim-offender relationship. This finding is not totally unexpected because both spatial types rely on only one actor being mobile. The only difference between the two is that intrusion homicides are more likely to occur outside than are predatory acts. This finding suggests that the mobility of the offender in predatory acts is more purposeful and calculated as the event takes place within the home of the victim or inside another establishment, whereas the offender in the intrusion homicide appears to be more opportunistic. The intrusion offender does not seek out the victim, but rather, waits until the victim presents either a suitable target or a credible threat to the offender, as illustrated in the incident below.

> September, 1994: At approximately 5:00 P.M., several gang members (offenders) observed a car cruising through their territory. The car was occupied by at least four individuals, several of which were positively recognized as being members of a rival gang from another neighborhood. Five hours later, the offenders were still hanging out on the street and observed the car once again slowly rolling up the block. Thinking that their rivals were about to commit a drive-by shooting, the gang members launched a pre-emptive strike. What they failed to realize is that the car was driven by the victim, a 54-year-old Black male, who used his personal car as a "jitney" (unlicensed taxi cab). Though earlier in the day he had indeed been ferrying the rival gang members about, at the time of the shooting, he was the lone occupant of the car.

The above example illustrates the stranger relationship between victim and offender that distinguishes intrusion homicides, but it also highlights the extent to which the social dynamics of urban street gangs influence the way in which gang members interpret mobility of unknown persons as provocative forays (i.e., intrusion) into the social/geographic space of the gang. It also demonstrates how the presence of gangs changes the dangerousness of place. Local residents are likely to be known to the members who hang out in a particular area, thereby insulating them from cases of mistaken identity or misperceived threats. Nonlocal residents may be aware that a gang occupies an area, but if they are not recognizable to the members, then they may be at increased risk of victimization by the gang.

Total Mobility Type

Several interesting findings emerge from our analysis of total mobility homicides. When compared to all other types, these homicides tend to involve victims that are both younger and more likely to be male. The events are also less likely to involve guns but much more likely to occur outdoors. Given prior research on the mobility patterns of victims and offenders within the routine-activities framework, it is not surprising that when the victim and offender interact in a setting away from each of their home neighborhoods, they are likely to be strangers to one another.

Total mobility homicides are not distinguished from other types by the motivating factors associated with the event. This is surprising because we expected felony homicides to be significantly overrepresented among this spatial type. However, both drug-involved and felony motives are more common in total-mobility homicides than in internal events. The finding that total mobility homicides involve a much higher proportion of drug involvement than do internal homicides suggests that drug market areas may be more likely to involve sellers who do not even live in the vicinity. Otherwise, we find that activities that bring mobile victims and offenders together do not set this type apart from the other types.

The case narrative presented below highlights some of the distinguishing characteristics of total mobility homicides.

> July, 1987: On the evening of July 7, 1987, the victim, a 25-year-old White male who lived far outside the city limits, met up with the offender, also a 25-year-old White male, at a known gay bar. Patrons reported that the victim and offender left the bar together later that evening. None of the patrons witnessed any sort of behavior to suggest that the victim

and offender's exit was anything but consensual and mutual. Upon leaving the bar, the offender lured the victim to a riverside park under the pretences of having sexual relations. The offender told police that he was not a homosexual, but that he used this as ploy to lure the victim to the crime site. He claimed that the sexual advances of the victim incensed him; he lost control of his actions, and set about fatally punching and kicking the victim.

This homicide underscores some important elements of the findings, namely, that total mobility homicides tend to involve younger male victims, occur outside, and less frequently involve the use of guns than do the other types. It demonstrates that victims and offenders are likely to be strangers prior to their social interaction. But most important, it highlights how the routine activities of place influence mobility. The victim traveled from a small town to a larger city in hopes of meeting a same-sex partner. The offender, who lived within the city but not near the bar, was attracted to the bar (if he is to be believed) only by his desire to find a suitable robbery target that he felt he could lure to an area void of guardianship.

Offense-Mobility Type

Last, the configuration of the offense-mobility type is peculiar in that both the victim and offender reside in the same neighborhood, yet the offense takes place elsewhere. In fact, it seems plausible that these events are actually special cases of either internal or total-mobility homicides. In the first case, these events involve an offender and a victim who are known to one another, and the offender lures the victim to a location outside of their joint community in order to commit the murder. In the latter case, the victim and the offender happen to live in the same neighborhood, are unknown to one another, meet in a third neighborhood, and become involved in a lethally violent altercation. One could imagine that when the victim and offender are neighbors, there would be a higher probability that any type of social interaction would occur in their shared community. Thus, we might expect offense-mobility homicides to be differentiated among all other types by the same characteristics that identified the uniqueness

of the internal homicides. Alternatively, geographic proximity does not necessarily lead to social interaction, thus making the offense mobility more akin to total-mobility homicides. In comparing these events to all other types, our findings suggest that offense-mobility homicides, though rare, are distinct from all other types in ways that are not similar to either internal or total-mobility events. Instead, we find that these are more likely to involve female victims, that the victims are younger, and that when compared to all other types, offense-mobility homicides are likely to involve multiple offenders.

However, we also see that there are some similarities between offense-mobility events and internal homicides, especially in terms of the victim-offender relationship. As is the case with internal homicides, offense-mobility homicides also involve parties known to one another more often than do the other types. The following example underscores our findings:

September, 1990: At approximately 5:00 A.M., the body of a 21-year-old African American female was found in an alley. According to acquaintances of the victim, she was known to "give it away for crack" (exchange sex for drugs). Further, she also supported her own addiction by sometimes selling "soap" (fake or inferior drugs). Witnesses stated that earlier that night the victim was seen getting into the car with two young black males in their early 20s (the charged offenders). The offenders lived on the same street as the victim and were members of a notoriously violent gang. The victim often sold drugs or solicited sex partners in the gang's turf. For reasons that appear to be drug-related, the offenders lured the victim out of their neighborhood, drove to an alley in an industrial section of town, and fatally shot the victim twice at point blank range.

This case suggests that the mobility of the participants is dictated by the frequent social interactions (drug dealing, illicit sexual activity) that occur within the social and geographical space shared by the actors. The decision to conduct the killing outside of the area is likely predicated on the desire of offenders to escape detection and not guided by a chance meeting as a result of their normal mobility patterns/routine activities. In fact, one could easily imagine a homicide with the exact same precipitating factors that ended up being categorized as internal.

CONCLUSION

Our findings suggest that the characteristics of the participants are generally not the most important feature in distinguishing among the various mobility patterns. The race of the victim and the offender had no bearing on the mobility patterns of participants. Neither was age a strong distinguishing feature predicting the joint-mobility patterns of victims and offenders. If anything, our findings suggest that youth is not a factor limiting mobility, as victims involved in both offense-mobility and total-mobility events tended to be younger. The mobility patterns of male and female homicide participants differed in a way that would be expected by routine activities theory. Women who kill are more likely to kill in close proximity to both their residence and the victim's residence (i.e., internal). We also found that women represent a larger proportion of victims of predatory homicides compared to the other categories. By contrast, total-mobility homicides appear to be male-dominated events.

The event characteristics, such as presence of multiple offenders, choice of weapon, and whether the event occurred inside versus outside, also align with our expectations. Internal events, where victim and offender mobility is low, are much more frequently committed indoors than all other types, with the exception of predatory acts. Predatory and internal share in common limited victim mobility to the homicide. This finding suggests that events occurring outside are predicated primarily on the mobility of the victim. Guns, though less common among total mobility events, do not display a strong pattern of being utilized more frequently among any of the spatial types. Finally, with the exception of offense-mobility homicides, multiple-offender events are equally likely among the remaining types.

The social ties that link victim and offender do matter. Consistent with our expectations, close social relationships involve less mobility on the part of either the victim or the offender or both. Also, when mobility is limited, the events are much more likely to take place indoors. This

is not surprising in light of previous findings; when routine activities centered around the home turn violent, the incidents are less frequently going to involve strangers as either the victim or the offender. Also in support of routine activities theory, stranger homicides are more common when the offender and the victim venture into an area foreign to the both of them.

The motivating factors of events provide some of the best insight into how the circumstances and activities surrounding a homicide influence the mobility of victim and offender alike. The mobility pattern of the offenders in gang-motivated, drug-involved, and felony homicides is suggestive of a purposive behavior in that they distinguish predatory homicides from all other types. We were surprised to find that total-mobility homicides are not distinguished from other types by motive. This "non-finding" is quite intriguing as it suggests that the motive and activity that bring individuals together in a seemingly more purposeful manner for predatory killings, or acts of intrusion, are similar to the motives and circumstances that lead to the "chance meetings" one might associate with total-mobility homicide. Though this makes sense for felony homicides, as routine activity theory suggests that motivated offenders seek out suitable targets, be it in the homes of generally less mobile groups (the very young, elderly, and women) or in the busy central cities with ample targets and low guardianship, it contradicts our notion of gang and drug homicide. Given that both of these activities are location/turf based, one would think that at least one of the participants would be a member of local community.

Our results inform the debate over "dangerous people" versus "dangerous places." By summing the two types of homicides that involve mobility on the part of the offender (predatory and total mobility types), we find that just over 60 percent of all homicides involve nonlocal offenders. In more than 46 percent of incidents, victimization took place outside of the victim's census tract (intrusion and total mobility). Although prior research suggests that homicide is often characterized by limited mobility on the parts of the victim and offender, we find that only one quarter (26.9 percent) of all incidents were local to both participants (i.e., internal). Furthermore, as reported above, the majority of all internal homicides involved either intimate partners or family members.

By employing this spatial typology, we find also that it is as important to examine offender mobility as it is to examine victim mobility. We contend that the demographic characteristics of offenders are equally important for determining mobility to events as are the characteristics of victims. In fact, features of the event as well as the social relationship between victims and violence are often more important in producing violence than are the characteristics of either actor.

In sum, by disaggregating homicide incidents by the joint-mobility patterns of victims and offenders, this spatial typology of homicide clarifies how participants in lethally violent events come together in space, and under what circumstances.

SOURCE: From *Journal of Research in Crime and Delinquency,* Vol. 42, No. 3, 275–308, August 2005. Copyright © 2005 Sage Publications. Reprinted by permission of Sage Publications, Inc.

QUESTIONS FOR DISCUSSION AND WRITING

1. What are the five categories in the authors' spatial typology?

2. Where were internal homicides more likely to occur? When compared to all other types of homicide, what are internal homicides much less likely to involve? What is true about sex in internal homicides?

3. In predatory homicides, what is true about victim sex, victim age, and offender sex? Where do such homicides typically take place? What most clearly distinguishes predatory homicides? Taken together, what do these results suggest?

4. What is the largest category of victims and offenders in intrusion homicides? What is the only difference between predatory type and intrusion homicides?

5. What interesting findings emerged from the authors' analysis of total mobility homicides? Why were the authors surprised by the findings regarding motive in total-mobility homicides? What is peculiar about offense-mobility homicides? How are offense-mobility homicides different from internal or total-mobility homicides? How are offense-mobility homicides similar to internal homicides?

FOUNDATION FOR A GENERAL STRAIN THEORY OF CRIME AND DELINQUENCY

ROBERT AGNEW

After dominating deviance research in the 1960s, strain theory came under heavy attack in the 1970s, with several prominent researchers suggesting that the theory be abandoned. Strain theory has survived those attacks, but its influence is much diminished. In particular, variables derived from strain theory now play a very limited role in explanations of crime/delinquency. Several recent causal models of delinquency, in fact, either entirely exclude strain variables or assign them a small role. Causal models of crime/delinquency are dominated, instead, by variables derived from differential association/social learning theory and social control theory.

This [article] argues that strain theory has a central role to play in explanations of crime/delinquency, but that the theory has to be substantially revised to play this role. Most empirical studies of strain theory continue to rely on the strain models developed by Merton, A. Cohen, and Cloward and Ohlin. In recent years, however, a wealth of research in several fields has questioned certain of the assumptions underlying those theories and pointed to new directions for the development of strain theory. Most notable in this area is the research on stress

in medical sociology and psychology, on equity/justice in social psychology, and on aggression in psychology—particularly recent versions of frustration-aggression and social learning theory. Also important is recent research in such areas as the legitimization of stratification, the sociology of emotions, and the urban underclass. Certain researchers have drawn on segments of the above research to suggest new directions for strain theory, but the revisions suggested have not taken full advantage of this research and, at best, provide only incomplete models of strain and delinquency. (Note that most of the theoretical and empirical work on strain theory has focused on delinquency.) This [article] draws on the above literatures, as well as the recent revisions in strain theory, to present the outlines of a general strain theory of crime/delinquency.

The theory is written at the social-psychological level: It focuses on the individual and his or her immediate social environment—although the macroimplications of theory are explored at various points. The theory is also written with the empirical researcher in mind, and guidelines for testing the theory in adolescent populations are provided. The focus is on adolescents

339

because most currently available data sets capable of testing the theory involve surveys of adolescents. This general theory, it will be argued, is capable of overcoming the theoretical and empirical criticisms of previous strain theories and of complementing the crime/delinquency theories that currently dominate the field.

Strain Theory as Distinguished From Control and Differential Association/Social Learning Theory

Strain, social control, and differential association theory are all sociological theories: They explain delinquency in terms of the individual's social relationships. Strain theory is distinguished from social control and social learning theory in its specification of (1) the type of social relationship that leads to delinquency and (2) the motivation for delinquency. First, strain theory focuses explicitly on *negative relationships with others*: relationships in which the individual is not treated as he or she wants to be treated. Strain theory has typically focused on relationships in which others prevent the individual from achieving positively valued goals. Agnew, in 1985, however, broadened the focus of strain theory to include relationships in which others present the individual with noxious or negative stimuli.

Second, strain theory argues that adolescents *are pressured into delinquency by the negative affective states—most notably anger and related emotions*—that often result from negative relationships. This negative affect creates pressure for corrective action and may lead adolescents to (1) make use of illegitimate channels of goal achievement, (2) attack or escape from the source of their adversity, and/or (3) manage their negative affect through the use of illicit drugs.

Strain theory, then, is distinguished by its focus on negative relationships with others and its insistence that such relationships lead to delinquency through the negative affect—especially anger—they sometimes engender. Both dimensions are necessary to differentiate strain theory from control and differential association/social learning theory. In particular, social control and social learning theory sometimes examine negative relationships—although such relationships are not an explicit focus of these theories. Control theory, however, would argue that negative relationships lead to delinquency not because they cause negative affect but because they lead to a reduction in social control. A control theorist, for example, would argue that physical abuse by parents leads to delinquency because it reduces attachment to parents and the effectiveness of parents as socializing agents. Likewise, differential association/social learning theorists sometimes examine negative relationships—even though theorists in this tradition emphasize that imitation, reinforcement, and the internalization of values are less likely in negative relationships. Social learning theorists, however, would argue that negative relationships—such as those involving physically abusive parents—lead to delinquency by providing models for imitation and implicitly teaching the child that violence and other forms of deviance are acceptable behavior.

Phrased in the above manner, it is easy to see that strain theory complements the other major theories of delinquency in a fundamental way. While these other theories focus on the absence of relationships or on positive relationships, strain theory is the only theory to focus explicitly on negative relationships. And while these other theories view delinquency as the result of drift or of desire, strain theory views it as the result of pressure.

The Major Types of Strain

Negative relationships with others are, quite simply, relationships in which others are not treating the individual as he or she would like to be treated. The classic strain theories of Merton, A. Cohen, and Cloward and Ohlin focus on only one type of negative relationship: relationships in which others prevent the individual from achieving positively valued goals. In particular, they focus on the goal blockage experienced by lower-class individuals trying to achieve monetary success or middle-class status. More recent versions of strain theory have argued that adolescents are not only concerned about the future goals of monetary success/middle-class status but are also concerned about the achievement of more immediate goals—such as good grades, popularity with the opposite sex, and doing well in athletics. The focus, however, is still on the achievement of positively valued goals. Most recently, Agnew has argued that strain may result not only from the failure to achieve positively valued goals but also from the inability to escape legally from a painful situation. If one draws on the above theories—as well as the stress, equity/justice, and aggression literatures—one can begin to develop a more complete classification of the types of strain.

Three major types of strain are: other individuals may (1) prevent one from achieving positively valued goals, (2) remove or threaten to remove positively valued stimuli that one possesses, or (3) present or threaten to present one with noxious or negatively valued stimuli. These categories of strain are presented as ideal types.

Strain as the Failure to Achieve Positively Valued Goals

Three types of strain in this category have been listed: strain as the junction between (1) aspirations and expectations/actual achievement, (2) expectations and actual achievements, and (3) just/fair outcomes and actual outcomes. Strain theory in criminology has focused on the first type of strain, arguing that it is most responsible for the delinquency in our society. Major research traditions in the justice/equity field, however, argue that anger and frustration derive primarily from the second two types of strain. To complicate matters further, one can list still additional types of strain in this category. Certain of the literature, for example, has talked of the disjunction between "satisfying outcomes" and reality, between "deserved" outcomes and reality, and between "tolerance levels" or minimally acceptable outcomes and reality. No study has examined all of these types of goals, but taken as a whole the data do suggest that there are often differences among aspirations (ideal outcomes), expectations (expected outcomes), "satisfying" outcomes, "deserved" outcomes, fair or just outcomes, and tolerance levels. This [article] has focused on the three types of strain listed above largely because they dominate the current literature.

Given these multiple sources of strain, one might ask which is the most relevant to the explanation of delinquency. This is a difficult question to answer given current research. The most fruitful strategy at the present time may be to assume that all of the above sources are relevant—that there are several sources of frustration. Alwin, Austin, Crosby and Gonzalez-Intal, Hegtvedt, Messick and Sentis, and Tornblum all argue or imply that people often employ a variety of standards to evaluate their situation. Strain theorists, then, might be best advised to employ measures that tap all of the above types of strain. One might, for example, focus on a broad range of positively valued goals and, for each goal, ask adolescents whether they are achieving their ideal outcomes (aspirations), expected outcomes, and just/fair outcomes. One would expect strain to be greatest when several standards were not being met, with perhaps greatest weight being given to expectations and just/fair outcomes.

Strain as the Removal of Positively Valued Stimuli From the Individual

The psychological literature on aggression and the stress literature suggest that strain may involve more than the pursuit of positively valued goals. Certain of the aggression literature, in fact, has come to de-emphasize the pursuit of positively valued goals, pointing out that the blockage of goal-seeking behavior is a relatively weak predictor of aggression, particularly when the goal has never been experienced before. The stress literature has largely neglected the pursuit of positively valued goals as a source of stress. Rather, if one looks at the stressful life events examined in this literature, one finds a focus on (1) events involving the loss of positively valued stimuli and (2) events involving the presentation of noxious or negative stimuli. So, for example, one recent study of adolescent stress employs a life-events list that focuses on such items as the loss of a boyfriend/girlfriend, the death or serious illness of a friend, moving to a new school district, the divorce/separation of one's parents, suspension from school, and the presence of a variety of adverse conditions at work.

Drawing on the stress literature, then, one may state that a second type of strain or negative relationship involves the actual or anticipated removal (loss) of positively valued stimuli from the individual. As indicated above, numerous examples of such loss can be found in the inventories of stressful life events. The actual or anticipated loss of positively valued stimuli may lead to delinquency as the individual tries to prevent the loss of the positive stimuli, retrieve the lost stimuli or obtain substitute stimuli, seek revenge against those responsible for the loss, or manage the negative affect caused by the loss by taking illicit drugs. While there are no data bearing directly on this type of strain, experimental data indicate that aggression often occurs when positive reinforcement previously administered to an individual is withheld or reduced. And as discussed below, inventories of stressful life events, which include the loss of positive stimuli, are related to delinquency.

Strain as the Presentation of Negative Stimuli

The literature on stress and the recent psychological literature on aggression also focus on the actual or anticipated presentation of negative or noxious stimuli. Except for the work of Agnew, however, this category of strain has been neglected in criminology. And even Agnew does not focus on the presentation of noxious stimuli per se, but on the inability of adolescents to escape legally from noxious stimuli. Much data, however, suggest that the presentation of noxious stimuli may lead to aggression and other negative outcomes in certain conditions, even when legal escape from such stimuli is possible. Noxious stimuli may lead to delinquency as the adolescent tries to (1) escape from or avoid the negative stimuli; (2) terminate or alleviate the negative stimuli; or (3) seek revenge against the source of the negative stimuli or related targets, although the evidence on displaced aggression is somewhat mixed.

A wide range of noxious stimuli has been examined in the literature, and experimental, survey, and participant observation studies have linked such stimuli to both general and specific measures of delinquency—with the experimental studies focusing on aggression. Delinquency/ aggression, in particular, has been linked to such noxious stimuli as child abuse and neglect, criminal victimization, physical punishment, negative relations with parents, negative relations with peers, adverse or negative school experiences, a wide range of stressful life events, verbal threats and insults, physical pain, unpleasant odors, disgusting scenes, noise, heat, air pollution, personal space violations, and high density. In one

of the few studies in criminology to focus specifically on the presentation of negative stimuli, Agnew found that delinquency was related to three scales measuring negative relations at home and school. The effect of the scales on delinquency was partially mediated through a measure of anger, and the effect held when measures of social control and deviant beliefs were controlled. And in a recent study employing longitudinal data, Agnew found evidence suggesting that the relationship between negative stimuli and delinquency was due to the *causal* effect of the negative stimuli on delinquency (rather than the effect of delinquency on the negative stimuli). Much evidence, then, suggests that the presentation of negative or noxious stimuli constitutes a third major source of strain.

Certain of the negative stimuli listed above, such as physical pain, heat, noise, and pollution, may be experienced as noxious largely for biological reasons (i.e., they may be unconditioned negative stimuli). Others may be conditioned negative stimuli, experienced as noxious largely because of their association with unconditioned negative stimuli. Whatever the case, it is assumed that such stimuli are experienced as noxious regardless of the goals that the individual is pursuing.

THE LINKS BETWEEN STRAIN AND DELINQUENCY

Three sources of strain have been presented: strain as the actual or anticipated failure to achieve positively valued goals, strain as the actual or anticipated removal of positively valued stimuli, and strain as the actual or anticipated presentation of negative stimuli. While these types are theoretically distinct from one another, they may sometimes overlap in practice. So, for example, the insults of a teacher may be experienced as adverse because they (1) interfere with the adolescent's aspirations for academic success, (2) result in the violation of a distributive justice rule such as equity, and (3) are conditioned negative stimuli and so are experienced as noxious in and of themselves. Other examples of overlap can be given, and it may sometimes be difficult to disentangle the different types of strain in practice. Once again, however, these categories are ideal types and are presented only to ensure that all events with the potential for creating strain are considered in empirical research.

Each type of strain increases the likelihood that individuals will experience one or more of a range of negative emotions. Those emotions include disappointment, depression, and fear. Anger, however, is the most critical emotional reaction for the purposes of the general strain theory. Anger results when individuals blame their adversity on others, and anger is a key emotion because it increases the individual's level of felt injury, creates a retaliation/revenge, energizes the individual for action, and lowers inhibitions, in part because individuals believe that others will feel their aggression is justified. Anger, then, affects the individual in several ways that are conducive to delinquency. Anger is distinct from many of the other types of negative affect in this respect, and this is the reason that anger occupies a special place in the general strain theory. It is important to note, however, that delinquency may still occur in response to other types of negative affect—such as despair. Although delinquency is less likely in such cases, the experience of negative affect, especially anger, typically creates a desire to take corrective steps, with delinquency being one possible response. Delinquency may be a method for alleviating strain, that is, for achieving positively valued goals, for protecting or retrieving positive stimuli, or for terminating or escaping from negative stimuli. Delinquency may be used to seek revenge; data suggest that vengeful behavior often occurs even when there is no possibility of eliminating the adversity that stimulated it. And delinquency may occur as adolescents try to manage their negative affect through illicit drug use. The general strain theory, then, has the potential to explain a broad range of delinquency, including theft, aggression, and drug use.

Each type of strain may create a *predisposition* for delinquency or function as a *situational event* that instigates a particular delinquent act. In the words of Hirschi and Gottfredson, then, the strain theory presented on paper is a theory of both "criminality" and "crime" (or to use the words of Clarke and Cornish, it is a theory of both "criminal involvement" and "criminal events"). Strain creates a predisposition for delinquency in those cases in which it is chronic or repetitive. Examples include a continuing gap between expectations and achievements and a continuing pattern of ridicule and insults from

teachers. Adolescents subject to such strain are predisposed to delinquency because (1) nondelinquent strategies for coping with strain are likely to be taxed; (2) the threshold for adversity may be lowered by chronic strains; (3) repeated or chronic strain may lead to a hostile attitude—a general dislike and suspicion of others and an associated tendency to respond in an aggressive manner; and (4) chronic strains increase the likelihood that individuals will be high in negative affect/arousal at any given time. A particular instance of strain may also function as the situational event that ignites a delinquent act, especially among adolescents predisposed to delinquency. Qualitative and survey data, in particular, suggest that particular instances of delinquency are often instigated by one of the three types of strain listed above.

ADAPTATIONS TO (COPING STRATEGIES FOR) STRAIN

The discussion thus far has focused on the types of strain that might promote delinquency. Virtually all strain theories, however, acknowledge that only *some* strained individuals turn to delinquency. Some effort has been made to identify those factors that determine whether one adapts to strain through delinquency. The most attention has been focused on the adolescent's commitment to legitimate means and association with other strained/delinquent individuals.

There are many ways to cope with strain, only some of which involve delinquency. And data from the stress literature suggest that individuals vary in the extent to which they use the different strategies. These facts go a long way toward explaining the weak support for strain theory. With certain limited exceptions, the strategies are not taken into account in tests of strain theory.

The existence of the above coping strategies poses a serious problem for strain theory. If strain theory is to have any value, it must be able to explain the selection of delinquent versus nondelinquent adaptations. This issue has, of course, been raised before. Critics contend that Merton and other strain theorists fail to explain adequately why only *some* strained individuals turn to delinquency. This issue, however, is all the more pressing when one considers the full range of nondelinquent adaptations to strain listed above. It is therefore important to specify those factors that influence the choice of delinquent versus nondelinquent coping strategies.

The following discussion of influencing factors draws on the aggression, equity, and stress literatures; the aggression literature in psychology is especially useful. Adversity is said to produce a general state of arousal, which can facilitate a variety of behaviors. Whether this arousal results in aggression is said to be determined by a number of factors, many of which are noted below.

Those factors affect the choice of coping strategies by affecting (1) the constraints to nondelinquent and delinquent coping and (2) the disposition to engage in nondelinquent versus delinquent coping.

Constraints to Nondelinquent and Delinquent Coping

While there are many adaptations to objective strain, those adaptations are not equally available to everyone. Individuals are constrained in their choice of adaptation(s) by a variety of internal and external factors. The following is a partial list of such factors.

Initial Goals/Values/Identities of the Individual. If the objective strain affects goals/values/identities that are high in absolute and relative importance, and if the individual has few alternative goals/values/identities in which to seek refuge, it will be more difficult to relegate strain to an unimportant area of one's life. This is especially the case if the goals/values/identities receive strong social and cultural support (see below). As a result, strain will be more likely to lead to delinquency in such cases.

Individual Coping Resources. A wide range of traits can be listed in this area, including temperament, intelligence, creativity, problem-solving skills, interpersonal skills, self-efficacy, and self-esteem. These traits affect the selection of coping strategies by influencing the individual's sensitivity to objective strains and ability to engage in cognitive, emotional, and behavioral coping. Data, for example, suggest that individuals with high self-esteem are more resistant to stress. Such individuals, therefore, should be less likely to respond to a given objective strain with delinquency. Individuals high in self-efficacy are more likely to feel that their strain can be alleviated by behavioral coping of a nondelinquent

nature, and so they, too, should be less likely to respond to strain with delinquency.

Conventional Social Support. In 1988, Vaux provided an extended discussion of the different types of social support, their measurement, and their effect on outcome variables. Thoits argues that social support is important because it facilitates the major types of coping. The major types of social support, in fact, correspond to the major types of coping listed above. Thus, there is informational support, instrumental support, and emotional support. Adolescents with conventional social supports, then, should be better able to respond to objective strains in a nondelinquent manner.

Constraints to Delinquent Coping. The crime/delinquency literature has focused on certain variables that constrain delinquent coping. They include (1) the costs and benefits of engaging in delinquency in a particular situation, (2) the individual's level of social control, and (3) the possession of those "illegitimate means" necessary for many delinquent acts.

Macrolevel Variables. The larger social environment may affect the probability of delinquent versus nondelinquent coping by affecting all of the above factors. First, the social environment may affect coping by influencing the importance attached to selected goals/values/identities. For example, certain ethnographic accounts suggest that there is a strong social and cultural emphasis on the goals of money/status among certain segments of the urban poor. Many poor individuals, in particular, are in a situation in which (1) they face strong economic/status demands, (2) people around them stress the importance of money/status on a regular basis, and (3) few alternative goals are given cultural support. As such, these individuals should face more difficulty in cognitively minimizing the importance of money and status.

Second, the larger social environment may affect the individual's sensitivity to particular strains by influencing the individual's beliefs regarding what is and is not adverse. The subculture of violence thesis, for example, is predicated on the assumption that young black males in urban slums are taught that a wide range of provocations and insults are highly adverse.

Third, the social environment may influence the individual's ability to minimize cognitively the severity of objective strain. Individuals in some environments are regularly provided with external information about their accomplishments and failings, and their attempts at cognitively distorting such information are quickly challenged. Such a situation may exist among many adolescents and among those who inhabit the "street-corner world" of the urban poor. Adolescents and those on the street corner live in a very "public world"; one's accomplishments and failings typically occur before a large audience or they quickly become known to such an audience. Further, accounts suggest that this audience regularly reminds individuals of their accomplishments and failings and challenges attempts at cognitive distortion.

Fourth, certain social environments may make it difficult to engage in behavioral coping of a nondelinquent nature. Agnew has argued that adolescents often find it difficult to escape legally from negative stimuli, especially negative stimuli encountered in the school, family, and neighborhood. Also, adolescents often lack the resources to negotiate successfully with adults, such as parents and teachers. Similar arguments might be made for the urban underclass. They often lack the resources to negotiate successfully with many others, and they often find it difficult to escape legally from adverse environments—by, for example, quitting their job (if they have a job) or moving to another neighborhood.

The larger social environment, then, may affect individual coping in a variety of ways, and certain groups, such as adolescents and the urban underclass, may face special constraints that make nondelinquent coping more difficult. This may explain the higher rate of deviance among these groups.

Factors Affecting the Disposition to Delinquency

The selection of delinquent versus nondelinquent coping strategies is not only dependent on the constraints to coping but also on the adolescent's disposition to engage in delinquent versus nondelinquent coping. This disposition is a function of (1) certain temperamental variables; (2) the prior learning history of the adolescent, particularly the extent to which delinquency was reinforced in the past; (3) the adolescent's beliefs, particularly the rules defining the appropriate response to provocations; and (4) the adolescent's

attributions regarding the causes of his or her adversity. Adolescents who attribute their adversity to others are much more likely to become angry, and as argued earlier, that anger creates a strong predisposition to delinquency. Data and theory from several areas, in fact, suggest that the experience of adversity is most likely to result in deviance when the adversity is blamed on another. The attributions one makes are influenced by a variety of factors, as discussed in recent reviews by Averill, Berwin, R. Cohen, Crittenden, Kluegel and Smith, and Utne and Kidd. The possibility that there may be demographic and subgroup differences in the rules for assigning blame is of special interest.

A key variable affecting several of the above factors is association with delinquent peers. It has been argued that adolescents who associate with delinquent peers are more likely to be exposed to delinquent models and beliefs and to receive reinforcement for delinquency. It may also be the case that delinquent peers increase the likelihood that adolescents will attribute their adversity to others.

The individual's disposition to delinquency, then, may condition the impact of adversity on delinquency. At the same time, it is important to note that continued experience with adversity may create a disposition for delinquency. This argument has been made by Bernard, Cloward and Ohlin, A. Cohen, Elliott and his colleagues, and others. In particular, it has been argued that under certain conditions the experience of adversity may lead to beliefs favorable to delinquency, lead adolescents to join or form delinquent peer groups, and lead adolescents to blame others for their misfortune.

Virtually all empirical research on strain theory in criminology has neglected the constraints to coping and the adolescent's disposition to delinquency. Researchers, in particular, have failed to examine whether the effect of adversity delinquency is conditioned by factors such as self-efficacy and association with delinquent peers. This is likely a major reason for the weak empirical support for strain theory.

CONCLUSION

Much of the recent theoretical work in criminology has focused on the integration of different delinquency theories. This [article] has taken an alternative track and, following Hirschi's advice, has focused on the refinement of a single theory. The general strain theory builds upon traditional strain theory in criminology in several ways. First, the general strain theory points to several new sources of strain. In particular, it focuses on three categories of strain or negative relationships with others: (1) the actual or anticipated failure to achieve positively valued goals, (2) the actual or anticipated removal of positively valued stimuli, and (3) the actual or anticipated presentation of negative stimuli. Most current strain theories in criminology only focus on strain as the failure to achieve positively valued goals, and even then the focus is only on the disjunction between aspirations and expectations/actual achievements. The disjunctions between expectations and achievements and just/fair outcomes and achievements are ignored. The general strain theory, then, significantly expands the focus of strain theory to include all types of negative relations between the individual and others.

Second, the general strain theory more precisely specifies the relationship between strain and delinquency, pointing out that strain is likely to have a cumulative effect on delinquency after a certain threshold level is reached. The theory also points to certain relevant dimensions of strain that should be considered in empirical research, including the magnitude, recency, duration, and clustering of strainful events.

Third, the general strain theory provides a more comprehensive account of the cognitive, behavioral, and emotional adaptations to strain. This account sheds additional light on the reasons why many strained individuals do *not* turn to delinquency, and it may prove useful in devising strategies to prevent and control delinquency. Individuals, in particular, may be taught those nondelinquent coping strategies found to be most effective in preventing delinquency.

Fourth, the general strain theory more fully describes those factors affecting the choice of delinquent versus nondelinquent adaptations. The failure to consider such factors is a fundamental reason for the weak empirical support for strain theory.

Most of the above modifications in strain theory were suggested by research in several areas outside of traditional criminology, most notably the stress research in medical sociology and psychology, the equity/justice research in social

psychology, and the aggression research in psychology. With certain exceptions, researchers in criminology have tended to cling to the early strain models of Merton, A. Cohen, and Cloward and Ohlin and to ignore the developments in related fields. And while these early strain models contain much of value and have had a major influence on the general strain theory in this [article], they do not fully exploit the potential of strain theory.

At the same time, it is important to note that the general strain theory is not presented here as a fully developed alternative to earlier theories. First, the macroimplications of the theory were only briefly discussed. It would not be difficult to extend the general strain theory to the macro level, however; researchers could focus on (1) the social determinants of adversity (for an example, see Bernard on the urban underclass) and (2) the social determinants of those factors that condition the effect of adversity on delinquency. Second, the theory did not concern itself with the nonsocial determinants of strain, such as illness. It seems doubtful that adversity caused by nonsocial sources is a major source of delinquency because, among other things, it is unlikely to generate anger. Nevertheless, nonsocial sources of adversity should be investigated. Third, the relationship between the general strain theory and other major theories of delinquency must be more fully explored. As hinted earlier, the relationship is rather complex. While the general strain theory is clearly distinct from control and differential association theory, strain may lead to low social control and association with delinquent others. Further, variables from the three theories may interact with one another in producing delinquency. Individuals with delinquent friends, for example, should be more likely to respond to strain with delinquency. The general strain theory, then, is presented as a foundation on which to build.

It is not possible to test the general strain theory fully with currently available data sets, but it is possible to test core sections of the theory. Most data sets dealing with delinquency contain at least some measures of adversity and at least some measures of those factors said to condition the effect of adversity on delinquency. Given this fact, researchers could focus on the following core hypotheses derived from the theory.

First, adverse relations with others will have a positive effect on both general and specific measures of delinquency, with measures of social control and differential association held constant. This is especially true of adverse relations that are severe and that provide limited opportunities for nondelinquent coping. Prime examples, as discussed earlier, are adverse relations involving family, school, and neighborhood. It is hoped research will point to several measures of strain that are especially relevant to delinquency. Such measures can then be made a routine part of delinquency research, just as the elements of the social bond and measures of differential association are now routinely included in empirical studies.

Second, adverse relations will have a cumulative impact on delinquency after a certain threshold level is reached. Further, this cumulative impact will likely be interactive in nature; each additional increment in strain will have a greater impact than the one before.

Third, the impact of strain or adverse relations on delinquency will be conditioned by several variables, as listed above. Strain theory is the only major theory to focus explicitly on negative relations with others and to argue that delinquency results from the negative affect caused by such relations. As such, it complements social control and differential association/social learning theory in a fundamental way. It is hoped that the general strain theory will revive interest in negative relations and cause criminologists to "bring the bad back in."

SOURCE: From *Criminology*, Vol. 30, 1992:47–87. Reprinted by permission of the American Society of Criminology.

QUESTIONS FOR DISCUSSION AND WRITING

1. How is strain theory distinguished from social control and social learning theory?

2. What are three major types of strain? How can the actual or anticipated loss of positively valued stimuli lead to delinquency? How can noxious stimuli lead to delinquency?

3. What is the most "critical" emotional reaction? Which factors should lower adolescents' likelihoods of delinquency (i.e., constrain them in their choice of adaptation)?

A TEST OF GENERAL STRAIN THEORY

LISA M. BROIDY

Strain theory has enjoyed a resurgence in recent years, primarily because of Robert Agnew's introduction of a revised general strain theory. In this revised version of strain theory, Agnew attempts to overcome the inconsistencies that have plagued traditional strain theories, while remaining true to the underlying argument that strain lies at the root of delinquent/criminal behavior.

This [article] offers a test of general strain theory that focuses primarily on the aspects of the theory that distinguish it from earlier versions of strain theory proposed by Merton, Cohen, and Cloward and Ohlin. Specifically, this [article] tests general strain theory by examining relations among strain, anger and other types of negative affect, legitimate coping, and illegitimate outcomes (crime/deviance), while controlling for various demographic and personality variables thought to condition the relationship between strain and criminal outcomes.

OVERVIEW OF THE LITERATURE

Early strain theories have been criticized for their limited scope—these theories evolved to focus almost exclusively on the delinquent behavior of lower-class boys in urban environments. Early strain theories also rest on a number of questionable assumptions. For one, they assume an inverse relationship between class and crime. This assumption remains controversial. These theories also assume that strain is a direct cause of crime and delinquency. However, not all individuals who experience strain respond in criminal or delinquent ways. Still, strain does appear to have some impact on offending. The implication is that, although a relationship appears to exist between strain and crime/delinquency, certain conditioning influences exist that traditional strain theories have failed to establish.

Agnew's general strain theory represents a significant departure from earlier versions of strain theory. General strain theory centers on strain as a social psychological variable, as opposed to a social structural one. In this way, the theory is able to overcome the tendency of traditional strain theory to focus on lower-class criminality. Further, general strain theory allows for an individualized conceptualization of strain that does not rely on the identification of certain universal goals, allowing the theory to take gender, racial, class-based, and other personal differences in goals and strains into account. Finally, the theory offers a more detailed account of the factors that condition the relation between strain and criminal/deviant outcomes. As such, it helps to make sense of the fact that only *some* strained individuals turn to delinquency. General strain theory asserts that responses to strain are shaped by various factors, including the nature, intensity, and duration of the strain, the emotions that the strain engenders in the individual, the repertoire of coping mechanisms at an individual's disposal, and the social context within which the strain develops and the negative emotions take root.

According to general strain theory, strain triggers negative emotions, which in turn necessitate coping. If legitimate coping strategies are either ineffective or unavailable, an individual is likely to adopt illegitimate coping strategies. General strain theory identifies three types of strain—the failure to achieve positively valued goals, the removal of positively valued stimuli, and the presentation of negative stimuli. Although the theory does not explicitly rule out a direct relation among these various forms of strain and crime, it also proposes an indirect relation in which strain is linked to crime through its relation to negative emotions (especially anger) in conjunction with the effectiveness and availability of legitimate coping strategies. When strain invokes high levels of anger that individuals cannot alleviate using legitimate coping strategies because they are either unavailable or ineffective, criminal/deviant outcomes become likely. This helps to explain why crime is not inevitable given strain. For some individuals, anger may be an uncommon emotional response. Agnew argues that anger is distinctively linked to illegitimate outcomes, and he implies that individuals who experience negative emotional responses other than anger are comparatively less likely to respond with illegitimate coping strategies. Moreover, even among individuals who get angry in response to strain, legitimate coping strategies may mediate the impact of this anger, making an illegitimate/criminal response unlikely.

Agnew suggests that specific internal and external factors also affect the emotional impact of strain and shape individuals' coping repertoires. These factors include individual/personal resources such as self-esteem, mastery, temperament, and intelligence, along with social resources available through one's interpersonal network. Also important are more macrolevel constraints to criminal coping, such as a lack of illegitimate opportunity or high levels of social control, as well as factors that increase criminal opportunities, such as deviant peers and disorganized neighborhoods. Thus, one's larger personal and social environment can also affect the likelihood that an individual will adopt illegitimate coping strategies, but it is not the only, nor even the primary, influence.

Hence, according to general strain theory, the path to delinquency is more complex than traditional strain theories purport. Consistent with earlier strain theories, Agnew argues that strain can be criminogenic. However, the relation between strain and crime is not inevitable. Agnew argues that strain is most likely to trigger criminal responses in the company of negative affect (especially anger) and absent effective legitimate coping strategies. Moreover, this relation is further enhanced in the context of microlevel and macrolevel social environments conducive to illegitimate outcomes.

EMPIRICAL ASSESSMENTS OF GENERAL STRAIN THEORY

General strain theory is relatively new, and it has not been widely tested. However, the tests that have been done offer tentative support for the theory. Most of this research tests the relationship between delinquency and the various types of strain identified in the theory. Using cross-sectional data, the studies by Agnew and White and by Paternoster and Mazerolle find a positive association between strain and both delinquency and drug use. This association remains after the introduction of indicators of social control and differential association variables as controls. Results from Paternoster and Mazerolle's longitudinal analyses mirror their cross-sectional findings. Agnew and White find less support for the theory in their longitudinal analyses. However, as they point out, these null findings are likely because of the three-year time lag between data points. Because general strain theory hypothesizes that the effect of strain on delinquency will be fairly proximate, Paternoster and Mazerolle's one-year time lag seems more appropriate.

Mazerolle and Hoffman and Su extend the analysis of the relationship between strain and delinquency by considering possible variations in the strain/delinquency relationship across sex. Mazerolle reports evidence that shows a relationship between certain types of strain and delinquent outcomes for males and females both cross-sectionally and longitudinally. Although differences exist in the degree to which measures of strain correlate with delinquency, with one exception, these differences are not statistically significant. Findings reported by Hoffman and Su also suggest that the effects of general strain theory variables on delinquent outcomes are similar across sex. Their research focuses on the relationship among negative life events, attachment, and delinquent behavior and drug use. Estimating a series of structural equations representing both cross-sectional and longitudinal effects, they find some support for the general strain theory model cross-sectionally but not longitudinally. Specifically, negative life events are positively correlated with delinquency and drug use, and both negative life events and delinquency/drug use reduce levels of attachment. These findings do not hold longitudinally, but they appear to be invariant across sex. Agnew and Brezina also examine gender differences in the strain/delinquency relationship, focusing on interpersonal strain. They find interpersonal strain to be correlated with both male and female delinquency, but they find this correlation to be stronger among males than among females. Together, these findings suggest that general strain theory offers some insight into both male and female delinquency and further reinforce previous findings that suggest that the broad range of strains identified in general strain theory appear to be related to criminal outcomes, at least cross-sectionally.

Although these tests offer some support for the theory, they are limited. General strain theory does not propose a direct relationship between strain and delinquency; instead, it proposes one that is mediated by negative affective states and available coping strategies. Despite controls for various conditioning influences, such as gender and attachment, none of the above-mentioned tests include measures of these two central intervening variables, and, as such, do not permit assessment of the entire causal model.

Brezina reports a more complete test of the theory that includes measures of negative emotions and focuses on delinquency as a coping strategy. Brezina's analysis suggests that delinquency can have the short-term effect of reducing strain and the negative emotions associated with it. Although this analysis indicates that delinquency may help one cope with strains, it does not examine the influence of legitimate coping strategies on the likelihood that an individual will turn to delinquency as an alternative. A more recent article by Brezina indicates that anger in particular plays an intervening role in the relationship between strain (in the form of adolescent maltreatment) and delinquency. This is consistent with earlier work by Agnew and more recent work by Mazerolle and Piquero which also highlights

the intervening role of anger. Agnew finds that anger significantly increases the likelihood of delinquency, controlling for measures reflecting social control and social learning processes. Similarly, Mazerolle and Piquero report that anger remains a significant predictor of delinquency even after the introduction of controls for deviant peers and moral constraints against delinquency. Again, however, the possible intervening role of legitimate coping strategies is overlooked, as is the influence of negative emotions other than anger on the strain/crime relationship.

To date, no test of general strain theory has examined the mediating role of both varied emotional responses to strain and attendant coping strategies in the strain/crime relationship. Early tests focus only on the relationship between various forms of strain and criminal/delinquent outcomes. These tests suggest that the social psychological forms of strain identified in the theory appear to be related to criminal/deviant outcomes, but they do not explore the mechanisms through which this relationship is hypothesized to work. Further, although recent empirical tests suggest that anger intervenes in the relationship between strain and delinquency to date, no tests have assessed the possible mediating role of a wider range of negative emotions and legitimate coping strategies.

THE CURRENT RESEARCH

This research offers a unique test of general strain theory, focusing on the relationship among strain, negative emotions, legitimate coping, and criminal/deviant outcomes.

Hypotheses

In testing general strain theory, I examine three hypotheses that assess the proposed relationships among strain, negative emotions, legitimate coping strategies, and illegitimate outcomes.

General strain theory contends that various types of strain trigger negative emotions. In particular, the theory identifies three primary types of strain—the failure to achieve positively valued goals, the loss of positively valued stimuli, and the presentation of negative stimuli—each of which are hypothesized to be associated with negative emotions in general and anger in particular.

Hypothesis 1: Each of three types of strain is associated with anger and other negative emotions.

Individuals need to cope with the negative emotions they experience in response to strain. General strain theory identifies three primary coping strategies that individuals are hypothesized to invoke in response to negative emotions—cognitive, behavioral, and emotional—each of which may be adopted in response to strain-induced negative emotions.

Hypothesis 2: Anger and other negative emotional responses to strain are each associated with the use of legitimate coping strategies.

Agnew suggests that legitimate coping strategies are likely in response to both anger and other forms of negative affect. However, he also notes that anger is distinct from other negative emotions in that it "increases the individual's level of felt injury, creates a desire for retaliation/revenge, energizes the individual for action, and lowers inhibitions." In this way, anger, compared with other negative emotions, is uniquely conducive to delinquency. Hence, although initial coping strategies will likely be legitimate ones along the lines of those described above, in the case of anger, illegitimate coping strategies are also likely. Therefore, delinquency is more likely in response to anger than are other negative emotions.

Hypothesis 3: Controlling for the use of legitimate coping, strain-induced anger will increase the likelihood of illegitimate outcomes, whereas other negative emotional responses will not.

Data and Methods

Data come from a nonrandom, convenience sample of undergraduate students at a Northwestern University surveyed during the 1995 fall semester. Analyses use cross-sectional data collected in 18 undergraduate classes from 7 different departments (7 sociology, 3 human development, 3 political science, 2 biological science, 1 anthropology, 1 computer science, and 1 decision science class) In all, 896 students completed the survey.

Self-report data from a sample of college students are especially useful for the purpose at hand. General strain theory is a social-psychological theory that links criminal and deviant outcomes to individual-level characteristics, behaviors, and circumstances. Because

official sources do not include such variables, nor do they contain data about noncriminal deviance, self-report data are essential. Because most of the central variables in the theory are not measured in existing self-report data sets, an adequate test of general strain theory requires original data that capture the various types of strain, negative emotions, and coping strategies that general strain theory identifies. These data provide those measures.

Although this nonrandom sample of college students is not ideal, being neither representative of all college students nor generalizable to the population as a whole, it has numerous strengths for the purpose at hand. Generalizability is less important in the initial stages of theory evaluation than later, after the explanatory capability of a theory has been established. Early tests, like this one, have as their main goal ascertaining the empirical plausibility of a theory. This is best accomplished with a relatively homogeneous sample that minimizes variability across demographic variables. The less variation in extraneous variables, the more certain we can be that results bear on the theoretical process being tested, instead of being a function of diversity in the sample. Hence, testing general strain theory with a mostly white, middle-class college sample helps to assure that results are not spurious. If this and other tests with limited samples support the theory, an important next step will be to see how well the results generalize to more diverse samples.

Measurement of Variables

The variables used to test general strain theory fall into five categories: strain, negative emotions, legitimate coping strategies, illegitimate/deviant outcomes, and control variables. Tables 1 and 2 provide descriptive statistics for all of the variables in this study.

Strain

Failure to Achieve Positively Valued Goals. According to general strain theory, the failure to achieve positively valued goals may result from goal blockage or from unfair goal outcomes. Indicators of both of these types of strain are available in the data. The survey asked respondents to reflect on the success and fairness of their goal outcomes in five broad areas—academic/career goals, social/family life goals, athletic goals/financial goals, and health/appearance goals—"over the past five years." The specific goals each respondent associated with each area were not elicited in the survey and likely varied across respondents. In order to assess goal blockage, respondents were asked to report how successful they had been at reaching their goals in each of the above-listed areas over the past five years. Responses concerning blocked goals are coded very successful = 1, successful = 2, somewhat successful = 3, and not at all successful = 4. Similarly, for unfair outcomes, respondents were asked how fair outcomes concerning their goals in each area had been over the past five years. Responses are coded very fair = 1, fair = 2, somewhat fair = 3, and not at all fair = 4. In both instances, respondents who reported having no goals in a particular arena were given a score of 0 on that particular indicator. Indexes representing blocked goals and unfair outcomes represent the summed average of factor-weighted scores for each item (i.e., the level of goal. Blockage and unfair outcomes for each general category of goals). The resulting "blocked goals" scale has a reliability coefficient (Cronbach's alpha) of .73, and the "unfair outcomes" scale has a reliability coefficient of .76. For both measures, high scores represent higher levels of strain (see Table 1 for descriptive statistics).

As measured here, blocked goals and unfair outcomes represent respondents' perceptions of goal outcomes. General strain theory defines strain in social psychological terms and suggests that strain results when individuals perceive that they cannot reach their goals or that their goal outcomes are unfair. Further, the five-year time span is important because it reflects a history of strain. Although general strain theory hypothesizes that the relationship between strain and deviant outcomes is proximate, it also indicates that strain is most likely to lead to delinquency when it is recurring. Asking respondents to reflect on their experiences over the past five years (up to and including the present) helps to ensure that they are reflecting on a pattern of experiences with strain as opposed to an isolated incident that, if anomalous, is not likely to trigger a delinquent outcome.

Loss of Positively Valued Stimuli and Presentation of Negative Stimuli. Although traditional strain theories focus exclusively on strain derived from the failure to achieve ideal goals, general strain theory recognizes two other sources of strain rooted in stressful life events. These are the loss of positively valued stimuli and the presentation of negative stimuli. I derived a measure reflecting these two types of strain using a list of 21 stressful life events particularly relevant for a sample of young adults. Respondents reported how often they had experienced each of the events on the list (never = 0, once = 1, two to three times = 2, four or more times = 3). The "stress" scale represents the summed average of factor-weighted scores for each item

TABLE 1   Descriptive Statistics for Strain, Negative Emotion, Legitimate Coping, and Illegitimate Outcome Measures

Variable	Mean (S.D.)	Minimum Value	Maximum Value
Blocked goals	1.30 (.60)	−0.33	3.02
Unfair outcomes	1.07 (.63)	−0.27	3.30
Stress	0.91 (.37)	0.10	2.21
Anger	1.88. (.69)	0.03	4.00
Other negative emotions	2.55 (.51)	0.97	4.00
Legitimate coping	0.74 (.28)	−0.16	1.79
Crime	1.25 (.63)	0.82	5.11

(Cronbach's alpha = .76) (see Table 1 for descriptive statistics).

Negative Emotions

I created measures of anger and other negative emotions using questions that ask individuals how they "feel" when they cannot reach their goals, and in response to negative life events. Respondents were asked how often they feel each of the 16 emotions listed (4 = always, 3 = sometimes, 2 = rarely, 1 = never) in response to blocked goals (When I am unable to reach my goals, I feel . . .) and to negative life events (When bad things happen to me, I feel . . .). These emotions include feeling alone, angry, cheated, cranky, depressed, disappointed, frustrated, guilty, insecure, overwhelmed, resentful, scared, stressed, upset, worried, and worthless. Factor analysis indicated that the 32 items that reflect emotional responses to blocked goals and stressful events reflect one underlying factor. The largest decrease in eigenvalues (8.94) occurs between the first and second factor, with the difference of only .45 between the second and third factor. However, given the unique role of anger in general strain theory, the two items reflecting anger are removed from the overall measure of negative emotions and used to form a separate anger scale. The anger scale represents the summed average of factor-weighted scores for the two items that reflect the amount of anger respondents feel in response to blocked goals and in response to stressful life events (Cronbach's alpha = .89.). The negative emotions scale is the summed average of factor-weighted scores for all other negative emotion items (Cronbach's alpha = .94) (see Table 1 for descriptive statistics). It is important to note that these measures reflect the likelihood that an individual responds to strains with anger or other negative emotions, not an individual's current level of negative affect. In other words, it taps the types of negative affect strain engenders in individuals.

Legitimate Coping Strategies

I derived measures of legitimate coping strategies from responses to a checklist of ways respondents behave when faced with blocked goals and stressful life events. The items included in the checklist were developed to reflect the three coping strategies identified in general strain theory—cognitive, behavioral, and emotional. Respondents report how often (0 = never, 1 = rarely, 2 = sometimes, 3 = always) they rely on each coping strategy when they experience blocked goals (When I am unable to reach a certain goal . . .) and when they experience negative life events (When bad things happen to me . . .). Factor analysis reveals six factors with eigenvalues greater than one, but it also indicates that a single underlying legitimate coping factor may exist. The difference between eigenvalues for factors one and two is .80, whereas the difference in eigenvalues between the second and third factors is .29. Because the six factors identified as having eigenvalues greater than one do not reflect the three types of coping strategies identified in the theory, I created a single legitimate coping scale that combines all three coping styles. This coping scale is the summed average of the factor-weighted scores for all items that reflect legitimate coping responses to blocked goals and to negative life events (Cronbach's alpha = .71), with high scores indicating high levels of legitimate coping in response to strain.

This measure reflects the use of legitimate strategies to cope with strain, not the availability nor the effectiveness of these strategies. Hence, the data do not allow for a test of general strain theory propositions regarding the intervening role of available/effective legitimate coping strategies, only those concerning the use of such strategies in response to strain-induced negative affect.

Illegitimate/Criminal Outcomes

Measures of illegitimate/criminal outcomes are derived from questions that ask respondents about their involvement in a variety of deviant behaviors over the past five years (1 = never, 2 = once, 3 = twice, 4 = three times, 5 = four or more times). Exploratory factor analysis identified an illegitimate/criminal behavior scale that includes eight items: stealing something worth $10 or less, stealing something worth more than $50, selling marijuana or other illegal drugs, hitting or threatening to hit another person, purposely destroying property that did not belong to you, using force or a weapon to get money or things from another person, distorting the truth or falsely representing something to get something you could not otherwise obtain, and being picked up by the police. The scale represents the summed average of factor-weighted scores on each item (Cronbach's alpha = .81).

Control Variables

In order to help infer causal connections among central variables in the general strain theory model, analyses control for various demographic, personality, and social influences that may have an effect on the general strain theory process. Multiple regression analyses incorporate controls for sex, race, employment status, family class background, presence of a mother during childhood, presence of a father during childhood, friends in the area, membership in academic clubs, membership in social clubs, religious participation, self-esteem, the emotional and disciplinary environment of the respondent's family during childhood, peer involvement in delinquency, and deviant opportunities (see Table 2 for descriptive statistics). I also experimented with other control variables, such as age, marital status, involvement in sports and in politics, parental expectations, and feeling of mastery, but these variables are significantly correlated with one or more of the control variables included in the analyses and, as such, add nothing to the analyses. Additionally, little variation occurs across age or marital status in this college sample, which makes controls for these variables unnecessary.

Much empirical research shows strong correlations between criminal deviant outcomes and demographic characteristics (sex, race, employment status, and family structure), which makes it important to control for such influences. Other control variables tap into respondents' social networks because access to and involvement in conventional social networks and activities may reduce an individual's involvement in delinquency. Rosenberg's self-esteem scale (reflecting judgments individuals make about their self-worth) is included because self-esteem presumably makes individuals more resistant to strain and reduces the likelihood of deviant responses. This scale has a reliability of .85. Family background, assessed using responses to 12 questions designed to tap into the emotional and disciplinary atmosphere of respondents'

families while they were growing up, is controlled because it may affect strain, coping mechanisms, and deviant behavior. Six items are included in each family background. The family emotional and disciplinary atmosphere scales reflect the average of standardized scores for each item in the scale (Cronbach's alpha = .82 and .70, respectively), with high scores indicating affirmative responses to the included items.

Analyses using deviant outcomes as the dependent variable also include controls for deviant friends and deviant opportunities, because much research has established that a significant relationship exists between these variables and deviant outcomes. The deviant peers indicator is a scale representing the average of standardized scores to items that ask respondents how many of their friends had engaged in each of eight behaviors represented in the criminal/illegitimate outcome measures over the past five years. Responses ranged from 1 (none of them) to 4 (all of them). This scale has a reliability of .85. The deviant opportunities scale is the average of standardized scores that reflect how often the respondent perceived having the opportunity to engage in each of seven deviant activities over the past five years (being picked up by the police was not included as an item reflecting deviant opportunities). Responses to the question of "In the past five years, how often have you had the opportunity to . . ." ranged from 1 (never) to 4 (10 or more times). This scale has a reliability of .88.

Results

Hypothesis 1: Each of three types of strain are associated with anger and other negative emotions.

I test Hypothesis 1 with two separate ordinary least-squares (OLS) regression models. The first model regresses anger on strain measures, controlling for demographic and social influences. The second model regresses negative emotions on strain measures, controlling for various demographic and social influences. General strain theory suggests that the relationship between strain and negative emotions is fairly proximate, but it also suggests that negative emotions will be more common among those who experience repeated strains. Using variables that reflect strain over the past five years allows for an examination of the concurrent effects of strain

TABLE 2   Summary of Control Variables

Variable	Mean (S.D.)	Minimum Value	Maximum Value
Sex	1.43 (.49)	1	2
1 = female; 2 = male			
Race	1.13 (.34)	1	2
1 = white; 2 = other			
Employment status	1.36 (.48)	1	2
1 = unemployed; 2 = employed			
Family class background	2.39 (.73)	1	5
1 = working class to 5 = upper class			
Presence of mother	1.99 (.10)	1	2
1 = no; 2 = yes			
Presence of father	1.94 (.24)	1	2
1 = no; 2 = yes			
Number of friends in area	2.68 (1.08)	1	5
1 = none to 5 = all			
Membership in academic clubs	1.38 (.48)	1	2
1 = no; 2 = yes			
Membership in social clubs	1.49 (.50)	1	2
1 = no; 2 = yes			
Religious service/church attendance	2.27 (1.00)	1	4
1 = never to 4 = more than once a week			
Self-esteem scale	0.00 (.66)	−2.79	1.12
Family dynamics-emotions scale	0.00 (.72)	−3.17	0.83
Family dynamics-discipline scale	0.00 (.63)	−1.71	1.55
Deviant peers	0.00 (.69)	−0.84	4.38
Deviant opportunity	0.00 (.64)	−0.77	2.48

on the likelihood of related negative emotional responses, while taking into account the importance of repeated experiences with strain. Although this introduces the question of proper time ordering, the wording of the questions helps to ensure that the negative emotions are a response to strain. The survey specifically taps strain-induced negative affect by asking individuals to report how they feel when they experience strain (i.e., when they cannot reach their goals, and when bad things happen to them) as opposed to their current level of negative affect.

Support for the hypothesis would be reflected in significant, positive relationships between measures of strain and measures of anger and other negative emotions. Results are mixed (see Table 3). the effects of strain on negative emotions (other than anger) appear to be constrained to the positive effect of stress (the presentation of negative stimuli and removal of positive stimuli) on negative emotions. The measures of strain that reflect blocked goals and unfair outcomes are not significantly associated with the negative emotions measure. On the other hand, all three measures of strain (blocked goals, unfair outcomes, and stressful life events) are significantly related to strain-induced anger, but not all in the expected direction. In this model, strain as a reflection of stressful life events and unfair goal outcomes positively increases the likelihood that individuals report responding to strains with anger. However, the measure that reflects the failure to reach one's goals has a negative effect on strain-induced anger. So, a lack of success at reaching one's goals appears to reduce the likelihood that individuals respond to strain with anger, whereas stressful life events and lack of fairness in goal outcomes appears to increase strain-induced anger. It may

be that individuals realize that some of their goals are unrealistic, thus making those who experience this type of strain unlikely to report responding to strain with anger. On the other hand, if individuals perceive their goal outcomes to be unfair, the implication is that they were unfairly kept from reaching what they perceived to be realistic goals, which is more likely to trigger anger. This interpretation, although speculative, is consistent with the procedural justice literature, which suggests that individuals are more concerned with outcome fairness than with actual outcomes.

It appears, then, that although a relationship exists between strain and negative emotions, the exact nature of the relationship depends on the nature of the strain and the type of emotional response considered. Stressful life events are related to both anger and other negative

TABLE 3   Unstandardized and Standardized (in Parentheses) OLS Regression Coefficients Representing Coefficients Representing the Effect of Strain on Negative Emotions, With Relevant Controls

Independent Variables	Anger			Other Negative Emotions		
	Coeff.	(beta)	S.E.	Coeff.	(beta)	S.E.
Unfair outcomes	.21*	(.19)	.05	.05	(.06)	.03
Blocked goals	.22*	(−.19)	.06	−.03	(−.04)	.04
Stress	.25	(−.13)	.07	.20*	(.19)	.04
Sex	−.00	(−.00)	.05	−.20*	(−.20)	.03
Race	−.07	(−.03)	.05	−.07	(−.05)	.04
Respondent employed	−.10*	(−.07)	.05	−.02	(−.01)	.03
Class	.06	(−.06)	.03	.02	(.02)	.02
Childhood presence of mother	.02	(.00)	.23	−.10	(−.02)	.14
Childhood presence of father	.07	(.03)	.10	.10	(.06)	.06
Friends in area	.01	(.01)	.02	.01	(.02)	.01
Membership in academic club	−.04	(−.03)	.05	−.01	(−.01)	.03
Membership in social clubs	−.04	(−.03)	.05	.01	(.01)	.03
Religious participation	−.05*	(−.07)	.02	.00	(.01)	.01
Self esteem	−.21*	(−.20)	.04	−.33*	(−.42)	.03
Family emotion	.07*	(.08)	.04	−.01	(−.02)	.02
Family discipline	.09*	(.08)	.04	.00	(−.02)	.02
R-square			.09			.33

* $p < .05$

emotions. However, the inability to reach one's goals, if perceived as unfair, is related to anger, but not other negative emotions, whereas goal blockage reduces the likelihood of angry responses to strain and is unrelated to other negative emotional responses. Also notable is the influence of sex in these models. No sex differences exist in anger, but a significant positive correlation exists between sex and other negative emotions. This suggests that, controlling for strain, strain-induced anger is equally likely among males and females, but other negative emotional responses to strain are more likely among females. Hence, the type of negative emotion individuals exhibit in response to strain may be shaped by both the type of strain they experience and by sex.

Hypothesis 2: Anger and other negative emotional responses to strain are associated with the use of legitimate coping strategies.

I again use OLS regression to test Hypothesis 2. Here, the dependent variable is legitimate coping. Support for the hypothesis would be reflected in significant, positive coefficients that represent the effect of negative emotions and of anger on legitimate coping. In this analysis, the time ordering of the variables is more questionable than in tests of Hypothesis 1. This issue is partly mitigated by the fact that items comprising both the negative emotions and the legitimate coping scales reflect how individuals report responding to strain. The analysis controls for strain, thereby ensuring that any correlation between negative emotions measures and legitimate coping cannot be interpreted as a function of the influence of strain on these measures. Still, any relationship between negative emotions and legitimate coping that remains after controlling for the influence of strain could be interpreted as representing the influence of legitimate coping on negative emotions, and not the reverse. Unfortunately, no way exists to predict the direction of this relationship with cross-sectional data. However, given that general strain theory defines the relationship between emotions and coping as proximate, longitudinal data, with any significant lag between waves, could fail to capture the relationship entirely. Hence, following theoretical expectations, I will interpret any correlation between negative emotions and legitimate coping as reflecting the effect of emotions on coping. However, such an interpretation is admittedly speculative.

The model used to test Hypothesis 2 regresses legitimate coping on anger and other negative emotions, controlling for strain and for demographic and social influences. Results indicate that only non-angry negative emotions are significantly associated with legitimate coping. A significant positive relationship exists between strain-induced negative emotions and legitimate coping, supporting the hypothesis that negative emotional responses to strain trigger legitimate coping strategies. However, contrary to the hypothesis, the relationship between strain-induced anger and legitimate coping is insignificant. Although general strain theory suggests that anger will have a stronger effect on illegitimate than on legitimate coping, the theory still predicts a significant relationship between anger and legitimate coping. It may be that the individuals in the sample have learned, through experience, that legitimate coping strategies do not alleviate anger, and thus, those who report responding to strain with anger are unlikely to adopt legitimate coping strategies. These results also indicate that stressful events are directly related to legitimate coping and that females more commonly invoke legitimate coping strategies than do males.

Hypothesis 3: Controlling for the use of legitimate coping, strain-induced anger will increase the likelihood of illegitimate outcomes, whereas other negative emotional responses will not.

Hypothesis 3 is assessed by regressing illegitimate outcomes on anger and negative emotions, controlling for strain and legitimate coping along with various social and demographic controls. Again, the analyses must be interpreted with caution because of the time-ordering of the central variables. Although negative emotions and legitimate coping measures are derived from questions ensuring that these measures reflect responses to strain, the criminal/illegitimate outcome measures reflect deviant behavior "in the past five years," instead of after the occurrence of reported strains. Hence, no way exists to establish with certainty that these behaviors follow strain. However, because the relationship between general strain theory variables is thought to be relatively proximate, measures that reflect strain and deviant behavior within the same time frame may be preferable to measures with any significant time lag between the two. In other words, as with the model testing Hypothesis 2, the variables in this analysis should be thought of as concurrent because they reflect strain and illegitimate outcomes over the same five-year period. It is important to emphasize here that this is not a longitudinal analysis because no time lag exists between dependent and independent variables. However, concurrent measures are consistent with theoretical expectations that the relation among central general strain theory variables is fairly proximate and with findings from previous studies that show stronger concurrent effects compared with longitudinal effects among general train theory variables.

Additional analysis that is not shown here supports the general strain theory contention that strain-induced anger increases the likelihood of illegitimate outcomes, irrespective of legitimate

coping. However, inconsistent with expectations is the significant negative relation between other negative emotions and illegitimate coping. Results suggest that individuals who tend to respond to strain with negative emotions other than anger are significantly less likely to adopt illegitimate coping. Although general strain theory suggests that, other than anger, negative emotional responses to strain are unlikely to trigger illegitimate outcomes, the theory does not suggest that such emotions actually decrease the likelihood of illegitimate outcomes.

Notably, results also suggest that no significant relation exists between legitimate and illegitimate coping. This is inconsistent with general strain theory, which suggests that illegitimate

TABLE 4   Unstandardized and Standardized (in Parentheses) OLS Regression Coefficient Representing the Effect of Anger and Other Negative Emotions on Legitimate Coping, Controlling for Strain, and Other Relevant Variables

	Legitimate Coping		
Independent Variables	Coeff.	(beta)	S.E.
Anger	−.01	(−.03)	.01
Other negative emotions	.26*	(.48)	.02
Unfair outcomes	.01	(.03)	.02
Blocked goals	−.00	(−.01)	.02
Stress	.07*	(.09)	.02
Sex	−.05*	(−.10)	.02
Race	−.01	(−.01)	.02
Respondent employed	−.04*	(−.06)	.02
Class	−.02	(−.04)	.01
Childhood presence of mother	.08	(.03)	.07
Childhood presence of father	−.03	(−.02)	.03
Friends in area	.02*	(.08)	.01
Membership in academic clubs	−.01	(−.01)	.02
Membership in social clubs	.02	(.03)	.02
Religious participation	.01	(.04)	.01
Self-esteem	−.05*	(−.11)	.01
Family emotion	−.02	(−.06)	.01
Family discipline	.02	(.04)	.01
R-square		.38	

* $p < .05$.

coping follows or is concurrent with legitimate coping (implying a correlation between the two). Here, the use of illegitimate coping strategies is unrelated to the use of legitimate coping strategies. However, this may reflect the fact that the measure of legitimate coping used in these analyses reflects the adoption of legitimate strategies as opposed to their success. General strain theory suggests that the use of illegitimate coping is contingent on the success or availability of legitimate coping, not on the use of legitimate strategies per se. Unfortunately, the data do not allow for an examination of whether illegitimate coping is more likely when legitimate coping is unsuccessful because no measures tap the success or failure of these coping strategies.

The findings indicate, then, that individuals who report responding to strain with anger have an increased likelihood of adopting illegitimate/criminal outcomes, whereas those who respond to strain with other negative emotions have a reduced risk of adopting illegitimate coping strategies. This is in sharp contrast to the finding that legitimate coping is unrelated to anger but increases among those who report responding to strain with other negative emotions. Although anger and other negative emotions are positively correlated $(r = .52)$, they appear to stem from unique stressors (recall results from Hypothesis 1) and to trigger unique coping strategies. Angry responses to strain are more common among those who experience both unfair goal outcomes and stressful life events, and this tendency to respond to strain with anger increases the likelihood of illegitimate coping. Other negative emotional responses to strain are associated solely with stressful life events and are linked to an increased likelihood of legitimate coping and a reduced likelihood of illegitimate coping. It appears, then, that individuals cope with different strain-induced emotions in distinct ways, with anger that triggers criminal/illegitimate coping and other negative emotions that trigger legitimate coping strategies. This finding confirms the general strain theory contention that anger is especially central to the strain/crime relationship, but calls into question the contention that the availability of legitimate coping strategies intervenes in this relationship. Instead, results suggest that anger is unrelated to the use of legitimate coping strategies.

A further indication that the strain/crime relationship may be more complex than general

strain theory suggests is evidenced by the significance of sex in the final model. That sex remains a significant predictor of criminal outcomes, controlling for central general strain theory variables, indicates that the theory does not adequately account for sex differences in criminal outcomes. Broidy and Agnew argue that in the context of general strain theory, gender shapes criminal/illegitimate outcomes not through its effects on levels of strain, negative emotions, and coping, but through qualitative differences in the types of strain and negative emotions males and females experience, the resultant emotions, and the coping strategies they opt for. Consistent with this suggestion, t tests examining sex differences on strain, negative affect, and coping (legitimate and illegitimate) indicate that males and females do not report different levels of strain and are similarly likely to respond to strain with anger. However, females are significantly more likely to respond to strain with non-angry negative affect $(t = 8.23)$ and are significantly more likely to employ legitimate coping strategies $(t = 7.81)$, whereas males are significantly more likely to engage in illegitimate coping strategies $(t = 8.66)$. This suggests that males and females experience similar levels of strain, but respond with distinct constellations of emotions (males with anger, females with anger and other negative emotions) and distinct coping strategies (females with legitimate coping, males with illegitimate coping). Although examinations of potential sex differences across general strain theory processes have noted more similarities than differences, neither of these examinations has included measures of legitimate coping or negative affect, the two areas where these results suggest sex differences may be more acute. Future studies should explore, in more detail, the influence of sex differences in types of strain and negative affect on the use of legitimate versus illegitimate outcomes.

SUMMARY AND CONCLUSIONS

The results reported here offer some support for general strain theory, but also indicate that the theory does not adequately account for the complexity of the strain/crime relationship (see summary of results in Table 5). In keeping with general strain theory, results suggest that strains are associated with anger and other negative emotions. However, results differ by type of strain and by type of negative emotion. Lack of fairness in goal outcomes and stressful life events increase the likelihood that individuals respond to strain with anger, whereas blocked goals reduces the likelihood of anger in response to strain. Stressful life events are also associated with increases in non-angry negative emotional responses to strain, but neither blocked goals nor unfair outcomes influence these non-angry emotional responses. Hence, although evidence of a relationship exists between strain and negative emotions, the nature of this relationship depends on the specific type of strain and negative emotions considered, a caveat not suggested by the theory.

TABLE 5   Summary of Results

Central Results	Other Notable Results
Hypothesis One	*Hypothesis One*
• Unfair outcomes (+) → Anger	• Sex → (NS) Anger
• Blocked goals (−) → Anger	• Sex → (−) Negative emotions
• Stress (+) → Anger	
• Unfair outcomes (NS) → Negative emotions	
• Blocked goals (NS) → Negative emotions	
• Stress (+) → Negative emotions	
Hypothesis Two	*Hypothesis Two*
• Negative emotions (+) → Legitimate coping	• Sex (−) → Legitimate coping
• Anger (NS) → Legitimate coping	
Hypothesis Three	*Hypothesis Three*
• Negative emotions (−) → Crime	• Sex (+) → Crime
• Anger (+) → Crime	

In keeping with general strain theory, strain-induced anger significantly increases the likelihood of illegitimate/criminal outcomes. However, anger is unrelated to the likelihood of legitimate coping, a finding not anticipated by general strain theory. Conversely, negative emotional responses to strain other than anger are associated with a significant increase in legitimate coping and a significant decrease in illegitimate/criminal outcomes. Although these results support theoretical hypotheses concerning the primacy of anger in the strain/crime relationship, they also speak to the complexity of the relationship among negative emotions, legitimate coping, and illegitimate outcomes. Results indicate that individuals experience anger and other negative emotions concurrently, yet these emotions trigger distinct coping responses. In contrast to theoretical expectations, then, legitimate coping does not appear to intervene in the relationship between negative emotions and illegitimate outcomes. Instead, legitimate and illegitimate coping strategies appear to be adopted in response to distinct negative emotions, which result from distinct experiences with strain.

Another indication of the complexity of the strain/crime relationship is evidenced by the role of sex in the models. Controlling for levels of strain, emotional responses to strain appear to be conditioned by sex. Although mean levels of anger are similar across sex, other negative emotions are more likely among females than among males (Table 3). This, along with the finding that anger increases the likelihood of criminal outcomes, while other negative emotions are associated with a significant decrease in criminal outcomes, supports recent suggestions that more attention needs to be paid to the role of gender in the general strain theory process. Moreover, that sex remains a significant predictor of criminal outcomes controlling for anger and other negative emotions (Table 5) reinforces Broidy and Agnew's claim that sex differences in levels of strain and negative emotions are not enough to account for sex differences in outcomes. Instead, future work should pay attention to qualitative sex differences in types of strain, negative emotions, and coping.

The present analysis, then, offers some support for general strain theory. Central general strain theory variables—strain, negative emotions, and legitimate coping—all appear to be important in explaining the likelihood of criminal/illegitimate outcomes. However, the nature of the relationship among these variables appears to be more complex than the theory suggests. The findings reported here suggest that distinct pathways may exist to legitimate and illegitimate coping. Unfair goal outcomes appear to be related to angry responses to strain, which in turn increase the likelihood of illegitimate outcomes. Stressful life events are related to both angry and non-angry emotional responses to strain, with the non-angry responses triggering legitimate coping mechanisms and angry responses triggering illegitimate coping. Moreover, these pathways may be further influenced by sex differences in emotional responses to strain and resultant coping strategies. Future work should explore how both general and sex-specific differences in types of strain and negative emotions shape coping strategies and, ultimately, the likelihood of delinquent/criminal outcomes.

There are some important limitations to note regarding the present analysis. General strain theory indicates that the relationship between legitimate and illegitimate coping strategies is a function of the success and availability of legitimate coping strategies. However, the data only provide measures of the level of legitimate coping, not the success or the availability of legitimate coping. Future work should explore how the success or availability of these legitimate coping strategies shape the likelihood of legitimate coping.

It is also important to keep in mind that results reported here are based on cross-sectional analyses with a homogeneous college sample. The cross-sectional nature of these analyses does not allow for firm conclusions regarding causal relationships among the variables examined. However, general strain theory does suggest that the relationship among strain, negative emotions, and coping is fairly proximate, which makes longitudinal analyses problematic. Although results reported here are based on cross-sectional data, such data may be preferable to longitudinal data with a significant lag between waves. A diary type of approach to data collection in which respondents are asked to record stressful events and their emotional and behavioral responses to these events might provide a better test of general strain theory than do those that rely on available cross-sectional and longitudinal data. Future work should explore this or other alternative data collection techniques that could capture the proximate nature of the relationship among central general strain theory variables while avoiding problems of time ordering inherent in cross-sectional survey data. Further, future work should expand on the current analysis using more heterogeneous samples and exploring the influence of sex, race/ethnicity, class, and other axes of social stratification on the general strain theory process.

QUESTIONS FOR DISCUSSION AND WRITING

1. According to general strain theory, what does strain do? What are the three types of strain? What happens when individuals cannot alleviate strain using legitimate coping strategies? What specific internal and external factors can affect the emotional impact of strain and shape individuals' coping repertoires?

2. What do the findings for the third hypothesis (regarding the affect of responding to strain with anger versus with other negative emotions) indicate?

3. What, then, does the present analysis offer? How is the relationship among the variables more complex than the theory suggests? Moreover, what further influences these pathways?

PART IX

HOW DO WE EXPLAIN CRIME?

Contemporary Theories and Research II

Students will find that criminological theories in Part IX are very different. They are not, as has been the case in earlier sections, drawn from different perspectives within sociological criminology. Here, students will learn how truly interdisciplinary modern criminology is. We cannot explain crime by just relying on social structural (e.g., disorganization or anomie) or social psychological (differential association or control) theories. Here, students have the opportunity to read examples of cultural, critical (both are very much sociological approaches, but different from those examined thus far), biological, and psychological perspectives. Some of the ideas presented here can be seen as complementary, yet it will be obvious to students that some of the writers included in this section are in wholehearted spirited disagreement with one another and with other criminologists.

In Part VII students read about Wolfgang and Ferracuti's subculture of violence. Anderson's "The Code of the Streets" is at the same time similar to and very different from that earlier work. Wolfgang and Ferracuti argued that people who are carriers of pro-violence norms and values would resort to violent behavior. Anderson, studying the streets of Philadelphia, the same city in which the subculture of violence was conceptualized, describes how a code that demands that people fight for respect is produced when victims of racial and economic inequality are forced to live in close proximity to each other, and in isolation from the rest of society. This situation leads to the use of street justice because people come to believe that they cannot count on the criminal justice system to provide respect and justice. Anderson theorizes that the code of the street is a product of social structural inequalities. Stewart and Simons test Anderson's argument.

Two important versions of "critical theory"—so named because proponents critique both the social system and mainstream academic explanations of society—are critical race theory and feminist theory. Here we have included two pieces that represent the intersection of these two critiques. In "Beyond White Man's Justice: Race, Gender, and Justice in Late Modernity," Hudson presents a critique of criminal justice as it is practiced today. Potter demonstrates the importance of adding an important voice, that of black feminists, to the study of African American women's victimization by intimate partners. Critical criminologists are building on the tradition represented by conflict theorists. Students should take the opportunity to critically consider the criminal justice system, policy makers, the perspectives that we have described earlier, and, importantly, their own beliefs and assumptions about crime, crime control, and society.

A change from the earlier editions of this reader is the inclusion of both biological and psychological perspectives. As in the past, we have included a segment from Wilson and

Herrnstein's *Crime and Human Nature*. Important additional work is presented, but this by no means can give students a sense of the range of what biologists and psychologists are able to teach us about human behavior and consequently about crime. They can whet their appetites, however, and come to understand how interdisciplinary modern criminology is.

Wilson and Herrnstein's piece, "A Bio-Psychological Theory of Choice," briefly describes their bio-psychological theory of crime and delinquency. Their treatment is very behaviorist—they argue that some people are born with particular characteristics (e.g., they like threats, thrills, and adrenalin rushes) that when reinforced make it more likely that they will engage in dangerous behaviors, including crime. Choice is also an important component of their explanation: People engage in crime because they consider the cost (e.g., sanctions, danger) and benefits (e.g., money, thrills, excitement) and elect to break the law. After reading this article, students may find it interesting to read the piece by James Q. Wilson and George Kelling in Part X of this book.

The article by Savage and Vila is *not* a test of Wilson and Herrnstein, but it is an example of what we can learn by considering biology in the study of crime. Students should recognize that some people try to use biology to study crime in ways that we believe are best described as racist and sexist. Frequently these arguments are criticized by biologists as overly simple and naïve. Savage and Vila illustrate how ecological factors, which include social structure and culture, interact with individual characteristics to influence criminality. They argue that biological features should not be seen as having a direct relationship with crime, but as complexly linked to the human environment as a cause of law-violating behavior.

The article by psychologist Terrie Moffitt and her colleagues, "Males on the Life-Course-Persistent and Adolescence-Limited Antisocial Pathways," presents and assesses evidence on a very important criminological theory that she developed. She argues that adolescents are fundamentally different, some behaviorally developing in such a way that they are likely to be heavily involved in crime throughout their lives—life-course persistent—while others likely will age out of crime (remember Hirschi and Gottfredson's description of age and crime in Part V). This article is an example of how developmental psychologists are contributing to contemporary criminological discourse.

As was the case with biology, we are not presenting a test of the psychological theory presented (Moffitt et al. review the relevant research literature). "The Relationships Among Self-Blame, Psychological Distress, and Sexual Victimization" by Breitenbecher is a psychological study of a very important issue: how victims of intimate crime in particular can, under some circumstances, continue to suffer after the event. One of the reasons that societies treat sexual victimization differently from other crimes (and many argue that we have not done nearly enough in this regard) is because of the nature of these events. Victims not only frequently blame themselves in a way that they don't with other crimes, but too often people around them insinuate that they had some responsibility for their own victimization. This continues the victimization.

Modern criminology's strength is that it is an interdisciplinary enterprise. From the combined efforts of sociologists, psychologists, biologists, economists, and historians, along with scholars trained in interdisciplinary criminal justice programs, we are building richer, better understandings of the causes and consequences of crime.

 For a data analysis exercise that accompanies the material in this section, go to www.sagepub.com/crimereadings3study.

THE CODE OF THE STREETS

ELIJAH ANDERSON

Of all the problems besetting the poor inner-city black community, none is more pressing than that of interpersonal violence and aggression. It wreaks havoc daily with the lives of community residents and increasingly spills over into downtown and residential middle-class areas. Muggings, burglaries, carjackings, and drug-related shootings, all of which may leave their victims or innocent bystanders dead, are now common enough to concern all urban and many suburban residents. The inclination to violence springs from the circumstances of life among the ghetto poor—the lack of jobs that pay a living wage, the stigma of race, the fallout from rampant drug use and drug trafficking, and the resulting alienation and lack of hope for the future.

Simply living in such an environment places young people at special risk of falling victim to aggressive behavior. Although there are often forces in the community which can counteract the negative influences, by far the most powerful being a strong, loving, "decent" (as inner-city residents put it) family committed to middle-class values, the despair is pervasive enough to have spawned an oppositional culture, that of "the streets," whose norms are often consciously opposed to those of mainstream society. These two orientations—decent and street—socially organize the community, and their coexistence has important consequences for residents, particularly children growing up in the inner city. Above all, this environment means that even youngsters whose home lives reflect mainstream values—and the majority of homes in

the community do—must be able to handle themselves in a street-oriented environment.

This is because the street culture has evolved what may be called a code of the streets, which amounts to a set of informal rules governing interpersonal public behavior, including violence. The rules prescribe both a proper comportment and a proper way to respond if challenged. They regulate the use of violence and so allow those who are inclined to aggression to precipitate violent encounters in an approved way. The rules have been established and are enforced mainly by the street-oriented, but on the streets the distinction between street and decent is often irrelevant; everybody knows that if the rules are violated, there are penalties. Knowledge of the code is thus largely defensive; it is literally necessary for operating in public. Therefore, even though families with a decency orientation are usually opposed to the values of the code, they often reluctantly encourage their children's familiarity with it to enable them to negotiate the inner-city environment.

At the heart of the code is the issue of respect—loosely defined as being treated "right," or granted the deference one deserves. However, in the troublesome public environment of the inner city, as people increasingly feel buffeted by forces beyond their control, what one deserves in the way of respect becomes more and more problematic and uncertain. This in turn further opens the issue of respect to sometimes intense interpersonal negotiation. In the street culture, especially among young people, respect is viewed as almost an external entity that is hard-won but easily lost, and so must constantly be guarded. The rules of the code in fact provide a framework for negotiating respect. The person whose very appearance—including his clothing, demeanor, and way of moving—deters transgressions feels that he possesses, and may be considered by others to possess, a measure of respect. With the right amount of respect, for instance, he can avoid "being bothered" in public. If he is bothered, not only may he be in physical danger but he has been disgraced or "dissed" (disrespected). Many of the forms that dissing can take might seem petty to middle-class people (maintaining eye contact for too long, for example), but to those invested in the street code, these actions become serious indications of the other person's intentions. Consequently, such people become very sensitive to advances and slights, which could well serve as warnings of imminent physical confrontation.

This hard reality can be traced to the profound sense of alienation from mainstream society and its institutions felt by many poor inner-city black people, particularly the young. The code of the streets is actually a cultural adaptation to a profound lack of faith in the police and the judicial system. The police are most often seen as representing the dominant white society and not caring to protect inner-city residents. When called, they may not respond, which is one reason many residents feel they must be prepared to take extraordinary measures to defend themselves and their loved ones against those who are inclined to aggression. Lack of police accountability has in fact been incorporated into the status system: the person who is believed capable of "taking care of himself" is accorded a certain deference, which translates into a sense of physical and psychological control. Thus the street code emerges where the influence of the police ends and personal responsibility for one's safety is felt to begin. Exacerbated by the proliferation of drugs and easy access to guns, this volatile situation results in the ability of the street-oriented minority (or those who effectively "go for bad") to dominate the public spaces.

Decent and Street Families

Although almost everyone in poor inner-city neighborhoods is struggling financially and

therefore feels a certain distance from the rest of America, the decent and the street family in a real sense represent two poles of value orientation, two contrasting conceptual categories. The labels "decent" and "street," which the residents themselves use, amount to evaluative judgments that confer status on local residents. The labeling is often the result of a social contest among individuals and families of the neighborhood. Individuals of the two orientations often coexist in the same extended family. Decent residents judge themselves to be so while judging others to be of the street, and street individuals often present themselves as decent, drawing distinctions between themselves and other people. In addition, there is quite a bit of circumstantial behavior—that is, one person may at different times exhibit both decent and street orientations, depending on the circumstances. Although these designations result from so much social jockeying, there do exist concrete features that define each conceptual category.

Generally, so-called decent families tend to accept mainstream values more fully and attempt to instill them in their children. Whether married couples with children or single-parent (usually female) households, they are generally "working poor" and so tend to be better off financially than their street-oriented neighbors. They value hard work and self-reliance and are willing to sacrifice for their children. Because they have a certain amount of faith in mainstream society, they harbor hopes for a better future for their children, if not for themselves. Many of them go to church and take a strong interest in their children's schooling. Rather than dwelling on the real hardships and inequities facing them, many such decent people, particularly the increasing number of grandmothers raising grandchildren, see their difficult situation as a test from God and derive great support from their faith and from the church community.

Extremely aware of the problematic and often dangerous environment in which they reside, decent parents tend to be strict in their child-rearing practices, encouraging children to respect authority and walk a straight moral line. They have an almost obsessive concern about trouble of any kind and remind their children to be on the lookout for people and situations that might lead to it. At the same time, they are themselves polite and considerate of others, and teach their children to be the same way. At home, at work, and in church, they strive hard to maintain a positive mental attitude and a spirit of cooperation.

So-called street parents, in contrast, often show a lack of consideration for other people and have a rather superficial sense of family and community. Though they may love their children, many of them are unable to cope with the physical and emotional demands of parenthood, and find it difficult to reconcile their needs with those of their children. These families, who are more fully invested in the code of the streets than the decent people are, may aggressively socialize their children into it in a normative way. They believe in the code and judge themselves and others according to its values.

In fact the overwhelming majority of families in the inner-city community try to approximate the decent-family model, but there are many others who clearly represent the worst fears of the decent family. Not only are their financial resources extremely limited, but what little they have may easily be misused. The lives of the street-oriented are often marked by disorganization. In the most desperate circumstances people frequently have a limited understanding of priorities and consequences, and so frustrations mount over bills, food, and, at times, drink, cigarettes, and drugs. Some tend toward self-destructive behavior; many street-oriented women are crack-addicted ("on the pipe"), alcoholic, or involved in complicated relationships with men who abuse them. In addition, the seeming intractability of their situation, caused in large part by the lack of well-paying jobs and the persistence of racial discrimination, has engendered deep-seated bitterness and anger in many of the most desperate and poorest blacks, especially young people. The need both to exercise a measure of control and to lash out at somebody is often reflected in the adults' relations with their children. At the least, the frustrations of persistent poverty shorten the fuse in such people—contributing to a lack of patience with anyone, child or adult, who irritates them.

In these circumstances a woman—or a man, although men are less consistently present in children's lives—can be quite aggressive with children, yelling at and striking them for the least little infraction of the rules she has set down. Often little if any serious explanation follows the verbal and physical punishment. This response teaches children a particular lesson.

They learn that to solve any kind of interpersonal problem one must quickly resort to hitting or other violent behavior. Actual peace and quiet, and also the appearance of calm, respectful children conveyed to her neighbors and friends, are often what the young mother most desires, but at times she will be very aggressive in trying to get them. Thus she may be quick to beat her children, especially if they defy her law, not because she hates them but because this is the way she knows to control them. In fact, many street-oriented women love their children dearly. Many mothers in the community subscribe to the notion that there is a "devil in the boy" that must be beaten out of him or that socially "fast girls need to be whupped." Thus, much of what borders on child abuse in the view of social authorities is acceptable parental punishment in the view of these mothers.

Many street-oriented women are sporadic mothers whose children learn to fend for themselves when necessary, foraging for food and money any way they can get it. The children are sometimes employed by drug dealers or become addicted themselves. These children of the street, growing up with little supervision, are said to "come up hard." They often learn to fight at an early age, sometimes using short-tempered adults around them as role models. The street-oriented home may be fraught with anger, verbal disputes, physical aggression, and even mayhem. The children observe these goings-on, learning the lesson that might makes right. They quickly learn to hit those who cross them, and the dog-eat-dog mentality prevails. In order to survive, to protect oneself, it is necessary to marshal inner resources and be ready to deal with adversity in a hands-on way. In these circumstances physical prowess takes on great significance.

In some of the most desperate cases, a street-oriented mother may simply leave her young children alone and unattended while she goes out. The most irresponsible women can be found at local bars and crack houses, getting high and socializing with other adults. Sometimes a troubled woman will leave very young children alone for days at a time. Reports of crack addicts abandoning their children have become common in drug-infested inner-city communities. Neighbors or relatives discover the abandoned children, often hungry and distraught over the absence of their mother. After repeated absences, a friend or relative, particularly a grandmother, will often step in to care for the young children, sometimes petitioning the authorities to send her, as guardian of the children, the mother's welfare check, if the mother gets one. By this time, however, the children may well have learned the first lesson of the streets: survival itself, let alone respect, cannot be taken for granted; you have to fight for your place in the world.

Campaigning for Respect

These realities of inner-city life are largely absorbed on the streets. At an early age, often even before they start school, children from street-oriented homes gravitate to the streets, where they "hang"—socialize with their peers. Children from these generally permissive homes have a great deal of latitude and are allowed to "rip and run" up and down the street. They often come home from school, put their books down, and go right back out the door. On school nights eight- and nine-year-olds remain out until nine or ten o'clock (and teenagers typically come in whenever they want to). On the streets they play in groups that often become the source of their primary social bonds. Children from decent homes tend to be more carefully supervised and are thus likely to have curfews and to be taught how to stay out of trouble.

When decent and street kids come together, a kind of social shuffle occurs in which children have a chance to go either way. Tension builds as a child comes to realize that he must choose an orientation. The kind of home he comes from influences but does not determine the way he will ultimately turn out—although it is unlikely that a child from a thoroughly street-oriented family will easily absorb decent values on the streets. Youths who emerge from street-oriented families but develop a decency orientation almost always learn those values in another setting—in school, in a youth group, in church. Often it is the result of their involvement with a caring "old head" (adult role model).

In the street, through their play, children pour their individual life experiences into a common knowledge pool, affirming, confirming, and elaborating on what they have observed in the home and matching their skills against those of others. And they learn to fight. Even small children test one another, pushing and shoving, and are ready to hit other children over

circumstances not to their liking. In turn, they are readily hit by other children, and the child who is toughest prevails. Thus the violent resolution of disputes, the hitting and cursing, gains social reinforcement. The child in effect is initiated into a system that is really a way of campaigning for respect.

In addition, younger children witness the disputes of older children, which are often resolved through cursing and abusive talk, if not aggression or outright violence. They see that one child succumbs to the greater physical and mental abilities of the other. They are also alert and attentive witnesses to the verbal and physical fights of adults, after which they compare notes and share their interpretations of the event. In almost every case the victor is the person who physically won the altercation, and this person often enjoys the esteem and respect of onlookers. These experiences reinforce the lessons the children have learned at home: might makes right, and toughness is a virtue, while humility is not. In effect they learn the social meaning of fighting. When it is left virtually unchallenged, this understanding becomes an ever more important part of the child's working conception of the world. Over time the code of the streets becomes refined.

Those street-oriented adults with whom children come in contact—including mothers, fathers, brothers, sisters, boyfriends, cousins, neighbors, and friends—help them along in forming this understanding by verbalizing the messages they are getting through experience: "Watch your back." "Protect yourself." "Don't punk out." "If somebody messes with you, you got to pay them back." "If someone disses you, you got to straighten them out." Many parents actually impose sanctions if a child is not sufficiently aggressive. For example, if a child loses a fight and comes home upset, the parent might respond, "Don't you come in here crying that somebody beat you up; you better get back out there and whup his ass. I didn't raise no punks! Get back out there and whup his ass. If you don't whup his ass, I'll whup your ass when you come home." Thus, the child obtains reinforcement for being tough and showing nerve.

While fighting, some children cry as though they are doing something they are ambivalent about. The fight may be against their wishes, yet they may feel constrained to fight or face the consequences—not just from peers but also from caretakers or parents, who may administer another beating if they back down. Some adults recall receiving such lessons from their own parents and justify repeating them to their children as a way to toughen them up. Looking capable of taking care of oneself as a form of self defense is a dominant theme among both street-oriented and decent adults who worry about the safety of their children. There is thus at times a convergence in their child-rearing practices, although the rationales behind them may differ.

SELF-IMAGE BASED ON "JUICE"

By the time they are teenagers, most youths have either internalized the code of the streets or at least learned the need to comport themselves in accordance with its rules, which chiefly have to do with interpersonal communication. The code revolves around the presentation of self. Its basic requirement is the display of a certain predisposition to violence. Accordingly, one's bearing must send the unmistakable, if sometimes subtle, message to "the next person" in public that one is capable of violence and mayhem when the situation requires it, that one can take care of oneself. The nature of this communication is largely determined by the demands of the circumstances but can include facial expressions, gait, and verbal expressions—all of which are geared mainly to deterring aggression. Physical appearance, including clothes, jewelry, and grooming, also plays an important part in how a person is viewed; to be respected, it is important to have the right look.

Even so, there are no guarantees against challenges, because there are always people around looking for a fight to increase their share of respect—or "juice," as it is sometimes called on the street. Moreover, if a person is assaulted, it is important, not only in the eyes of his opponent but also in the eyes of his "running buddies," for him to avenge himself. Otherwise he risks being "tried" (challenged) or "moved on" by any number of others. To maintain his honor he must show he is not someone to be "messed with" or "dissed." In general, the person must "keep himself straight" by managing his position of respect among others; this involves in part his self-image, which is shaped by what he thinks others are thinking of him in relation to his peers.

Objects play an important and complicated role in establishing self-image. Jackets, sneakers, gold jewelry reflect not just a person's taste, which tends to be tightly regulated among adolescents of all social classes, but also a willingness to possess things that may require defending. A boy wearing a fashionable, expensive jacket, for example, is vulnerable to attack by another who covets the jacket and either cannot afford to buy one or wants the added satisfaction of depriving someone else of his. However, if they boy forgoes the desirable jacket and wears one that isn't "hip," he runs the risk of being teased and possibly even assaulted as an unworthy person. To be allowed to hang with certain prestigious crowds, a boy must wear a different set of expensive clothes—sneakers and athletic suit—every day. Not to be able to do so might make him appear socially deficient. The youth comes to covet such items—especially when he sees easy prey wearing them.

In acquiring valued things, therefore, a person shores up his identity—but since it is an identity based on having things, it is highly precarious. This very precariousness gives a heightened sense of urgency to staying even with peers, with whom the person is actually competing. Young men and women who are able to command respect through their presentation of self—by allowing their possessions and their body language to speak for them—may not have to campaign for regard but may, rather, gain it by the force of their manner. Those who are unable to command respect in this way must actively campaign for it—and are thus particularly alive to slights.

One way of campaigning for status is by taking the possessions of others. In this context, seemingly ordinary objects can become trophies imbued with symbolic value that far exceeds their monetary worth. Possession of the trophy can symbolize the ability to violate somebody—to "get in his face," to take something of value from him, to "dis" him, and thus to enhance one's own worth by stealing someone else's. The trophy does not have to be something material. It can be another person's sense of honor, snatched away with a derogatory remark. It can be the outcome of a fight. It can be the imposition of a certain standard, such as a girl's getting herself recognized as the most beautiful. Material things, however, fit easily into the pattern. Sneakers, a pistol, even somebody else's girlfriend, can become a trophy. When a person can take something from another and then flaunt it, he gains a certain regard by being the owner, or the controller, of that thing. But this display of ownership can then provoke other people to challenge him. This game of who controls what is thus constantly being played out on inner-city streets, and the trophy—extrinsic or intrinsic, tangible or intangible—identifies the current winner.

An important aspect of this often violent give-and-take is its zero-sum quality. That is, the extent to which one person can raise himself up depends on his ability to put another person down. This underscores the alienation that permeates the inner-city ghetto community. There is a generalized sense that very little respect is to be had, and therefore everyone competes to get what affirmation he can of the little that is available. The craving for respect that results gives people thin skins. Shows of deference by others can be highly soothing, contributing to a sense of security, comfort, self-confidence, and self-respect. Transgressions by others which go unanswered diminish these feelings and are believed to encourage further transgressions. Hence one must be ever vigilant against the transgressions of others or even *appearing* as if transgressions will be tolerated. Among young people, whose sense of self-esteem is particularly vulnerable, there is an especially heightened concern with being disrespected. Many inner-city young men in particular crave respect to such a degree that they will risk their lives to attain and maintain it.

The issue of respect is thus closely tied to whether a person has an inclination to be violent, even as a victim. In the wider society people may not feel required to retaliate physically after an attack, even though they are aware that they have been degraded or taken advantage of. They may feel a great need to defend themselves *during* an attack, or to behave in such a way as to deter aggression (middle-class people certainly can and do become victims of street-oriented youths), but they are much more likely than street-oriented people to feel that they can walk away from a possible altercation with their self-esteem intact. Some people may even have the strength of character to flee, without any thought that their self-respect or esteem will be diminished.

In impoverished inner-city black communities, however, particularly among young males and perhaps increasingly among females, such flight would be extremely difficult. To run away would likely leave one's self-esteem in tatters.

Hence people often feel constrained not only to stand up and at least attempt to resist during an assault but also to "pay back"—to seek revenge—after a successful assault on their person. This may include going to get a weapon or even getting relatives involved. Their very identity and self-respect, their honor, is often intricately tied up with the way they perform on the streets during and after such encounters. This outlook reflects the circumscribed opportunities of the inner-city poor. Generally people outside the ghetto have other ways of gaining status and regard, and thus do not feel so dependent on such physical displays.

BY TRIAL OF MANHOOD

On the street, among males these concerns about things and identity have come to be expressed in the concept of "manhood." Manhood in the inner city means taking the prerogatives of men with respect to strangers, other men, and women—being distinguished as a man. It implies physicality and a certain ruthlessness. Regard and respect are associated with this concept in large part because of its practical application: if others have little or no regard for a person's manhood, his very life and those of this loved ones could be in jeopardy. But there is a chicken-and-egg aspect to this situation: one's physical safety is more likely to be jeopardized in public *because* manhood is associated with respect. In other words, an existential link has been created between the idea of manhood and one's self-esteem, so that it has become hard to say which is primary. For many inner-city youths, manhood and respect are flip sides of the same coin; physical and psychological well-being are inseparable, and both require a sense of control, of being in charge.

The operating assumption is that a man, especially a real man, knows what other men know—the code of the streets. And if one is not a real man, one is somehow diminished as a person, and there are certain valued things one simply does not deserve. There is thus believed to be a certain justice to the code, since it is considered that everyone has the opportunity to know it. Implicit in this is that everybody is held responsible for being familiar with the code. If the victim of a mugging, for example, does not know the code and so responds "wrong," the perpetrator may feel justified even in killing him and may feel no remorse. He may think, "Too bad, but it's his fault. He should have known better."

So when a person ventures outside, he must adopt the code—a kind of shield, really—to prevent others from "messing with" him. In these circumstances it is easy for people to think they are being tried or tested by others even when this is not the case. For it is sensed that something extremely valuable is at stake in every interaction, and people are encouraged to rise to the occasion, particularly with strangers. For people who are unfamiliar with the code—generally people who live outside the inner city—the concern with respect in the most ordinary interactions can be frightening and incomprehensible. But for those who are invested in the code, the clear object of their demeanor is to discourage strangers from even thinking about testing their manhood. And the sense of power that attends the ability to deter others can be alluring even to those who know the code without being heavily invested in it—the decent inner-city youths. Thus a boy who has been leading a basically decent life can, in trying circumstances, suddenly resort to deadly force.

Central to the issue of manhood is the widespread belief that one of the most effective ways of gaining respect is to manifest "nerve." Nerve is shown when one takes another person's possessions (the more valuable the better), "messes with" someone's woman, throws the first punch, "gets in someone's face," or pulls a trigger. Its proper display helps on the spot to check others who would violate one's person and also helps to build a reputation that works to prevent future challenges. But since such a show of nerve is a forceful expression of disrespect toward the person on the receiving end, the victim may be greatly offended and seek to retaliate with equal or greater force. A display of nerve, therefore, can easily provoke a life-threatening response, and the background knowledge of that possibility has often been incorporated into the concept of nerve.

True nerve exposes a lack of fear of dying. Many feel that it is acceptable to risk dying over the principle of respect. In fact, among the hardcore street-oriented, the clear risk of violent death may be preferable to being "dissed" by another. The youths who have internalized this attitude and convincingly display it in their public bearing are among the most threatening people of all, for it is commonly assumed that they fear no man. As the people of the community say, "They are the baddest dudes on the street." They often lead an existential life that may acquire meaning only when they are faced with the possibility of imminent death. Not to be afraid to die is by implication to have few compunctions about taking another's life. Not to be afraid to die is the quid pro quo of being able to take somebody else's life—for the right reasons, if the situation demands it. When others believe this is one's position, it gives one a real sense of power on the streets. Such credibility is what many inner-city youths strive to achieve, whether they are decent or street-oriented, both because of its practical defensive value and because of the positive way it makes them feel about themselves. The difference between the decent and the street-oriented youth is often that the decent youth makes a conscious decision to appear tough and manly; in another setting—with teachers, say, or at his part-time job—he can be polite and deferential. The street-oriented youth, on the other hand, has made the concept of manhood a part of his very identity; he has difficulty manipulating it—it often controls him.

GIRLS AND BOYS

Increasingly, teenage girls are mimicking the boys and trying to have their own version of "manhood." Their goal is the same—to get respect, to be recognized as capable of setting or maintaining a certain standard. They try to achieve this end in the ways that have been established by the boys, including posturing, abusive language, and the use of violence to resolve disputes, but the issues for the girls are different. Although conflicts over turf and status exist among the girls, the majority of disputes seem rooted in assessments of beauty (which girl in a group is "the cutest"), competition over boyfriends, and attempts to regulate other people's knowledge of and opinions about a girl's behavior or that of someone close to her, especially her mother.

A major cause of conflicts among girls is "he say, she say." This practice begins in the early school years and continues through high school. It occurs when "people," particularly girls, talk about others, thus putting their "business in the streets." Usually one girl will say something negative about another in the group, most often behind the person's back. The remark will then get back to the person talked about. She may retaliate or her friends may feel required to "take up for" her. In essence this is a form of group gossiping in which individuals are negatively assessed and evaluated. As with much gossip, the things said may or may not be true, but the point is that such imputations can cast aspersions on a person's good name. The accused is required to defend herself against the slander, which can result in arguments and fights, often over little of real substance. Here again is the problem of low self-esteem, which encourages youngsters to be highly sensitive to slights and to be vulnerable to feeling easily "dissed." To avenge the dissing, a fight is usually necessary.

Because boys are believed to control violence, girls tend to defer to them in situations of conflict. Often if a girl is attacked or feels slighted, she will get a brother, uncle, or cousin to do her fighting for her. Increasingly, however, girls are doing their own fighting and are even asking their male relatives to teach them how to fight. Some girls form groups that attack other girls or take things from them. A hard-core segment of inner-city girls inclined toward violence seems to be developing. As one thirteen-year-old girl in a detention center for youths who have committed violent acts told me, "To get people to leave you alone, you gotta fight. Talking don't always get you out of stuff." One major difference between girls and boys: girls rarely use guns. Their fights are therefore not life-or-death struggles. Girls are not often willing to put their lives on the line for "manhood." The ultimate form of respect on the male-dominated inner-city street is thus reserved for men.

"GOING FOR BAD"

In the most fearsome youths, such a cavalier attitude toward death grows out of a very limited view of life. Many are uncertain about how long they are going to live and believe they could die violently at any time. They accept this fate; they live on the edge. Their manner conveys the message that nothing intimidates them; whatever turn the encounter takes, they maintain their attack—rather like a pit bull, whose spirit many such boys admire. The demonstration of such tenacity "shows heart" and earns their respect.

This fearlessness has implications for law enforcement. Many street-oriented boys are much more concerned about the threat of "justice" at the hands of a peer than at the hands of the police. Moreover, many feel not only that they have little to lose by going to prison but that they have something to gain. The toughening-up one experiences in prison can actually enhance one's reputation on the streets. Hence the system loses influence over the hard core who are without jobs, with little perceptible stake in the system. If mainstream society has done nothing *for* them, they counter by making sure it can do nothing *to* them.

At the same time, however, a competing view maintains that true nerve consists in backing down, walking away from a fight, and going on with one's business. One fights only in self-defense. This view emerges from the decent philosophy that life is precious, and it is an important part of the socialization process common in decent homes. It discourages violence as the primary means of resolving disputes and encourages youngsters to accept nonviolence and talk as confrontational strategies. But "if the deal goes down," self-defense is greatly encouraged. When there is enough positive support for this orientation, either in the home or among one's peers, then nonviolence has a chance to prevail. But it prevails at the cost of relinquishing a claim to being bad and tough, and therefore sets a young person up as, at the very least, alienated from street-oriented peers and quite possibly a target of derision or even violence.

Although the nonviolent orientation rarely overcomes the impulse to strike back in an encounter, it does introduce a certain confusion, and so can prompt a measure of soul-searching, or even profound ambivalence. Did the person back down with his respect intact or did he back down only to be judged a "punk"—a person lacking manhood? Should he or she have acted? Should he or she have hit the other person in the mouth? These questions beset many young men and women during public confrontations. What is the "right" thing to do? In the quest for honor, respect, and local status—which few young people are uninterested in—common sense most often prevails, which leads many to opt for the tough approach, enacting their own particular versions of the display of nerve. The presentation of oneself as rough and tough is very often quite acceptable until one is tested. And then that presentation may help the person pass the test, because it will cause fewer questions to be asked about what he did and why. It is hard for a person to explain why he lost the fight or why he backed down. Hence many will strive to appear to "go for bad," while hoping they will never be tested. But when they are tested, the outcome of the situation may quickly be out of their hands, as they become wrapped up in the circumstances of the moment.

AN OPPOSITIONAL CULTURE

The attitudes of the wider society are deeply implicated in the code of the streets. Most people in inner-city communities are not totally invested in the code, but the significant minority of hard-core street youths who are have to maintain the code in order to establish reputations, because they have—or feel they have—few other ways to assert themselves. For these young people the standards of the street code are the only game in town. The extent to which some children—particularly those who through upbringing have become most alienated and those lacking in strong and conventional social support—experience, feel, and internalize racist rejection and contempt from mainstream society may strongly encourage them to express contempt for the more conventional society in turn. In dealing with this contempt and rejection, some youngsters will consciously invest themselves and their considerable mental resources in what amounts to an oppositional culture to preserve themselves

and their self-respect. Once they do, any respect they might be able to garner in the wider system pales in comparison with the respect available in the local system; thus they often lose interest in even attempting to negotiate the mainstream system.

At the same time, many less alienated young blacks have assumed a street-oriented demeanor as a way of expressing their blackness while really embracing a much more moderate way of life; they, too, want a nonviolent setting in which to live and raise a family. These decent people are trying hard to be part of the mainstream culture, but the racism, real and perceived, that they encounter helps to legitimate the oppositional culture. And so on occasion they adopt street behavior. In fact, depending on the demands of the situation, many people in the community slip back and forth between decent and street behavior.

A vicious cycle has thus been formed. The hopelessness and alienation many young inner-city black men and women feel, largely as a result of endemic joblessness and persistent racism, fuels the violence they engage in. This violence serves to confirm the negative feelings many whites and some middle-class blacks harbor toward the ghetto poor, further legitimating the oppositional culture and the code of the streets in the eyes of many poor young blacks. Unless this cycle is broken, attitudes on both sides will become increasingly entrenched, and the violence, which claims victims, black and white, poor and affluent, will only escalate.

QUESTIONS FOR DISCUSSION AND WRITING

1. What are the circumstances of life among the ghetto poor? What is a "decent" family, according to inner city residents? What do decent families "often reluctantly" do?

2. What is true about many of the forms that "dissing" can take?

3. How do the childrearing practices of "decent" and "street" parents differ? Why are street parents quick to beat their children?

STRUCTURE AND CULTURE IN AFRICAN AMERICAN ADOLESCENT VIOLENCE

A Partial Test of the "Code of the Street" Thesis

ERIC A. STEWART

RONALD L. SIMONS

One of the most consistent findings in the criminological literature indicates that violence is concentrated disproportionately among African American youth, particularly those individuals residing in disadvantaged neighborhoods. However, reasons for the high rates of violence among young African Americans are not well understood and continue to baffle researchers.

Elijah Anderson's "code of the street" thesis details how neighborhood structural characteristics, as well as family characteristics and discrimination, influence cultural adaptations that influence violence. In particular, Anderson argues that the macro-structural patterns of disadvantage, social dislocation, and discrimination encountered by some African American adolescents residing in "street" families foster a street code that is conducive to violence. As Anderson points out, some residents are committed to conventional values, while others embrace a street culture. Individuals who adopt the street culture usually lack prosocial opportunities and their perceived self-worth is dependent on respect commanded in public via the street code. Adopting the street code preserves self-respect and status by showing that one is tough despite desperate neighborhood structural conditions.

Although Anderson presents an interesting and compelling explanation for the high rates of violence among African American adolescents, the major claims of his code of the street thesis have not been extensively tested beyond his ethnographic work in Philadelphia. In the current study, we attempt to fill this void by evaluating several hypotheses derived from the code of the street thesis with a longitudinal sample of 720 African American families from 259 neighborhoods. Specifically, we assess how neighborhood structural characteristics (i.e., neighborhood disadvantage and neighborhood violence), family characteristics (i.e., decent and street), and experiences with racial discrimination combine to influence adoption of the street code. Further, we assess whether adopting the street code mediates the combined effects of neighborhood context, family characteristics, and racial discrimination on violent delinquency.

THEORETICAL FOUNDATION

According to Anderson, the code of the street is a powerful informal system that governs the use of violence, especially among young African American males. The code of the street emphasizes maintaining the respect of others through a violent identity, toughness, and exacting retribution when someone disrespects (or "disses") you. Thus, the code regulates the use of violence and supplies a rationale allowing those who are inclined toward aggression to precipitate violent encounters in approved ways. The street-oriented individuals enforce the rules of the street code. Although most families who reside in these disadvantaged neighborhoods are decent, everyone in the neighborhood knows (or learns) that if the rules of the street code are violated there are penalties. Thus, knowledge of the code is necessary for operating in these environments, and the conditions that encourage its development are pronounced in disadvantaged African American communities.

Furthermore, in distressed areas where violence is common, some residents' mistrust and lack of faith in the criminal justice system and political officials lead them to take personal responsibility for their safety. Several studies have found that residents in disadvantaged neighborhoods often complain of dissatisfaction with the police, inadequate police protection, and police abuse, with the consequence being strained relationships between residents and legal authorities. As a result, disputes are frequently settled informally and violently because some residents believe they cannot depend upon, or trust, legal authorities. In an effort to shield against victimization, individuals adapt to the dangers in disadvantaged neighborhoods by developing a range of social identities to manage the threats and demands of a context that creates codes maintained by violence. In other words, residents must use or appear ready to use violence to defend their lives, property, and honor.

Simply living in such an environment places young people at risk for falling victim to violence. As Prothrow-Stith argues, youngsters residing in inner-city ghetto neighborhoods plagued by problems of social disorganization are likely to see violence as a way of life. They are likely to be taught violence, to witness violent acts, and to have role models who display high levels of aggression and violence. As a consequence, these youngsters take pride in being tough (which usually involves owning a firearm), presenting a violent self-image, and protecting themselves and their "boys" (a close peer group), which can often end with deadly consequences. Further, the street code and the respect it demands is so entrenched among the hard-core, street-oriented individuals that they are willing to risk dying violently rather than being "dissed" or victimized by another.

Decent/Street Families and the Street Code

Another aspect of Anderson's thesis focuses on the distinction between "decent" and "street" families who live in disadvantaged African American neighborhoods. Anderson notes that two opposing family orientations—decent and street—often coexist in the same disadvantaged African American neighborhoods. He contends, however, that most families in disadvantaged African American neighborhoods are decent. Decent families tend to accept mainstream values and try to instill these values in their children. These families value hard work and self-reliance and encourage their children to be hard working and to avoid trouble. Because of the dangers of the environment, decent families tend to be very authoritative and vigilant in their parenting styles, and recognize problem behaviors and peers that need to be avoided. Although they are stern, they also show high levels of warmth and support and spend quality time with their children. Furthermore, decent families discourage violence. At the same time, they recognize that it is important for their children to understand the street code without necessarily buying into it.

In contrast, street families do not embrace mainstream values and often show a lack of consideration for others. Anderson indicates that street families have home lives that are disorganized and filled with anger, hostility, physical altercations, and antisocial behavior that children often observe. Although street families love their children, many are unable to provide the emotional and physical support their children need. They frequently engage in ineffective parenting strategies, such as yelling, poor supervision, verbal insults, and inconsistent and harsh discipline. There is often little explanation given for harsh, explosive punishments, and children learn to solve problems through violence. Anderson suggests that street families are so immersed in the code of the street that they may aggressively socialize their children into it as a normative process. They encourage their children to follow the street code and use violence if they are disrespected to gain or maintain respect. In some street families, parents may reprimand their children if they are not aggressive enough. Street families are committed to the street code and want their children to be as well.

Summary of Hypotheses

We test several hypotheses derived from Anderson's code of the street thesis. First, we hypothesize that growing up in a street family will increase an adolescent's probability of adopting the street code, whereas growing up in a decent family will reduce a youth's chances of adopting the street code. Second, we hypothesize that adolescents who experience racial discrimination are more likely to adopt the street code. Third, we hypothesize that both neighborhood disadvantage and neighborhood violence increase the likelihood that adolescents will adopt the street code.

Finally, we explore whether the effects of neighborhood structural context, family type, and racial discrimination on violent delinquency are mediated by the code of the street. Anderson argues that the code of the street has a distinctive origin in the social ills that come from living in a disadvantaged neighborhood and is reinforced by street-oriented families. Importantly, those who embrace the code are more likely to use violence. This suggests that neighborhood context, family characteristics, and racial discrimination influence violence indirectly by increasing adoption of the street code. We test each of these hypotheses in our analyses.

METHODS

This study is based on the first two waves of data from the Family and Community Health Study (FACHS), a multi-site investigation of neighborhood and family effects on health and development. Two waves of data were collected in Georgia and Iowa. The first wave was collected in 1997 and the second in 1999. Complete data for the variables used in [this article] were available for 720 families.

Participants took part in a series of videotaped interactions in their home that lasted a total of 2 hours and 20 minutes. The tasks involved the primary caregiver and the target child. Interviewers provided instructions, set up and started video equipment, gave participants a set of cards containing discussion questions, and then left the room so they could not hear the video-recorded discussion.

In coding the videotapes, observational coders rated over 60 behavioral interactions. The scales have been used extensively to identify family interactions, such as parenting practices, parental warmth, parental involvement, relationship quality, marital stability, oppositional/defiant behavior, antisocial behaviors, and prosocial behaviors. In this analysis, the observer-coded data were used to form decent and street family constructs.

To take advantage of the longitudinal nature of the data and increase confidence in temporal ordering, we predict both street code$_{T2}$ and violent delinquency$_{T2}$ measured at wave 2, while controlling for previous measures of both variables at wave 1. We also estimated all of the independent variables at wave 1.

Adopting the Street Code$_{T2}$. A 7-item, self-report scale measured this construct at waves 1 and 2. Adolescents were asked to indicate the extent to which it was justifiable or advantageous to use violence *(1 = strongly disagree* to *4 = strongly agree).* The questions included "When someone disrespects you, it is important that you use physical force or aggression to teach him or her not to disrespect you; If someone uses violence against you, it is important that you use violence against him or her to get even; People will take advantage of you if you don't let them know how tough you are; People do not respect a person who is afraid to fight physically for his/her rights; Sometimes you need to threaten people in order to get them to treat you fairly; It is important to show others that you cannot be intimidated; People tend to respect a person who is tough and aggressive." The responses were summed to obtain a total score concerning the extent to which the respondent held beliefs that were consistent with adopting a street code.

Violent Delinquency$_{T2}$. The delinquency construct was measured at both wave 1 and wave 2 using eight questions that assessed violent offending. Respondents answered a series of questions regarding how often during the preceding year they had engaged in various violent acts such as physical assault, threatening others, bullying people, using a weapon, robbing others, and other aggressive behaviors. The response format was *1 = engaged in behavior* and *0 = did not engage in behavior*. About 28 percent of the sample reported engaging in violent delinquency$_{T2}$.

Neighborhood Violence. Respondents completed a seven-item neighborhood violence scale at wave 1. The items asked the extent to which various violent acts (e.g., fights, gang violence, drug violence, robbery, homicide, aggravated assaults, etc.) were a problem within the neighborhood. The response format ranged from *1 = not at all a problem* to *3 = a big problem*. The seven items were summed to form a construct of neighborhood violence.

Neighborhood Disadvantage. Five census variables were used to form this construct at wave 1: proportion of households that were female headed, proportion of persons on public assistance, proportion of households below the poverty level, proportion of persons unemployed, and proportion of persons who are African American.

"Decent" Family. This construct was measured at wave 1 using seven observational scales. The scales included consistent discipline, child monitoring, positive reinforcement, quality time, warmth/support, inductive reasoning, and prosocial behavior. Each dimension was rated using a 5-point scale ranging from *1 = no evidence of the behavior* to *5 = extreme evidence of the behavior*. These items were summed and combined to form a measure of "decent" family.

"Street" Family. This construct was measured at wave 1 using seven observational scales. The scales included inconsistent and harsh discipline, hostility, physical attacks, parental violence, verbal abuse, antisocial behavior, and child neglect. Each dimension was rated using a 5-point scale ranging from *1 = no evidence of the behavior* to *5 = extreme evidence of the behavior*. These items were summed and combined to form a measure of "street" family.

Racial Discrimination. This construct was measured at wave 1 using 13 items from the Schedule of Racist Events that adolescents answered. The items assess the frequency *(1 = never* to *4 = several times)* with which various discriminatory events were experienced over the past year. For example, the scale asks, How often has someone yelled a racial slur or racial insult at you just because you are African American? How often have the police hassled you just because you are African American? How often has someone threatened you physically just because you are African American? Other items focused on disrespectful treatment by sales clerks, false accusations by authority figures, and exclusion from social activities because of being African American.

Controls

Consistent with prior research, we controlled for a number of factors at wave 1 that have been linked with the outcomes considered in our research. The items we controlled for included family SES, family structure, target gender, number of children per household, associating with violent peers, school attachment, and experiencing strain.

DISCUSSION

Our results suggested that family characteristics, racial discrimination, and neighborhood context are significant predictors of the street code. In particular, adolescents reared in a family characterized as street appeared to embrace the street code. This finding is consistent with Anderson's contention that street families engage in a style of parenting in which they socialize their children to embrace the code of the street as a normative process. This finding is also consistent with past research showing that children are at risk for developing an antisocial pattern of beliefs and behaviors when they are exposed to antisocial parents and ineffective parenting practices.

Evidence is also found in support of the racial discrimination/street code hypothesis. The results suggest that adolescents who were victims of discrimination were more likely to adopt the street code. This finding is consistent with Anderson's assertion about the harmful effects of racial discrimination. Experiencing discrimination is apt to be especially troubling because there is usually little recourse one can take, thereby generating the perception that the system is unfair and unjust and thus illegitimate. If this is the case, one might expect that being a victim of racial discrimination might foster the belief that aggression and violence is a necessary coping mechanism for solving grievances and injustices.

Furthermore, neighborhood violence and neighborhood disadvantage are also predictors of the street code. These findings suggest that the code of the street may be a response to neighborhood disadvantage and social problems, as Anderson suggests. For example, adolescents who view their neighborhood as having many social problems may develop a social identity that is conducive to toughness and violence, as a way of negotiating and maintaining the respect necessary to avoid being victimized or "dissed."

One hypothesis that was not supported in our analysis was the relationship between decent family and street code. The non-significant finding indicates that decent families have little impact on adopting the code of the street. It is possible that decent families recognize the dangers in disadvantaged neighborhoods and encourage their children to understand the street code, but not to embrace the demeanor that accompanies it. Another explanation is that decent families are more vigilant over their adolescents' friends and behaviors. As a result, decent families exercise high levels of control to protect their children, reprimand inappropriate behaviors, and restrict access to problem friends.

We also assessed whether the street code mediated the effects of family characteristics, racial discrimination, and neighborhood context on violent delinquency. The results provided partial support for the mediation argument. Once street code was entered into the model, it slightly mediated the effects of family characteristics and partially mediated discrimination experiences and neighborhood effects on violent delinquency. In particular, the decent family variable was slightly mediated by the street code, but remained a significant predictor of violence. This finding suggests that while decent families may have little impact on influencing the street code, they serve as an important social control mechanism for reducing violence. It appears that decent families do not see violence as a viable option for their children.

Also, the street code mediated the effect of racial discrimination on violent delinquency. The effect of discrimination became marginally significant when street code was added to the model. This suggests that racial discrimination is related primarily to violent offending through the code of the street. It is possible that discrimination leads to "angry aggression." Discrimination produces inequality and anger because it involves intentionally harming, threatening, or insulting individuals, as well as blocking their goal-directed activities, with frustration and aggression being two of many detrimental consequences. As a result, African American adolescents may endorse the street code as a necessary and effective interpersonal strategy for coping with negative events. It is also possible that adopting the street code in the face of discrimination allows adolescents to maintain (or regain) status and self-respect among peers in the presence of the demoralizing influence of discrimination.

Moreover, our data suggest that neighborhood structural conditions influence violent delinquency primarily through the street code. Neighborhood violence and neighborhood disadvantage became marginally significant predictors of adolescent violence when street code was entered into the equation. One interpretation of this pattern of findings is that the code of the street may indeed be a response to neighborhood conditions. It is possible that the stress and strain of living in a chronically disadvantaged and violent neighborhood leads to adopting the code of the street. Because such neighborhoods provide residents with few avenues for gaining status and prestige, these neighborhoods lead to the formation of alternative normative codes for some residents that legitimate violence as a means of enhancing one's street reputation. Very disadvantaged, high-crime neighborhoods reduce conventional opportunities for status attainment and generate alternative routes to gaining respect, such as adopting the code of the street.

In sum, researchers interested in studying the disproportionate prevalence of violence among African American adolescents should move beyond purely macro-structural analyses or purely cultural-level analyses. Following Anderson's code of the street thesis, we have presented a model that bridges the macro-structural and cultural divide inherent in many violence studies. We hope that our findings will encourage continued interest in how neighborhood structural conditions, family characteristics, and racial discrimination combine to shape the formation of street codes that are associated with violence.

QUESTIONS FOR DISCUSSION AND WRITING

1. Who enforces the rules of the street code, and what does everyone know (or learn) about it? Why is knowledge of the code important?

2. Why are disputes settled informally and violently? How did the authors measure whether a family was "decent"? How did the authors measure whether a family was a "street family"? What control variables did the authors include in their study?

3. What did the authors' results suggest? What did the authors find with respect to the racial discrimination/street code hypothesis? What did they find with respect to neighborhood violence and neighborhood disadvantage? Which hypothesis was not supported?

BEYOND WHITE MAN'S JUSTICE

Race, Gender, and Justice in Late Modernity

BARBARA HUDSON

INTRODUCTION: BEYOND WHITE MAN'S JUSTICE

My purpose in this article is to discuss principles that would characterize a justice that has the potential to escape being sexist and racist. I find that the principles which I think justice must incorporate if it is to move beyond white man's justice are approached more closely in restorative justice than in formal criminal justice as it exists in Western criminal justice systems at the moment, but I would argue that all justice processes should embrace my three principles of *discursiveness*, *relationalism* and *reflectiveness*.

It has long been argued that law in modern Western societies reflects the subjectivity of the dominant white, affluent, adult, male. This dominant subjectivity is both subject and object of law: it is object in that it is he whose behavior law has in mind when it constructs its proscriptions and remedies; and it is this subject who constructs the law. Through its discourse and its practices, criminal justice continually invokes and reproduces the male, white subjectivity of law.

Suffice it to say here that the general charges against conventional Western criminal justice systems in regard to race and gender are that they fail to protect women and members of minority racial or ethnic groups from harms that they suffer by virtue of their gender and/or

race/ethnicity and that they discriminate by over-penalizing offenders to the degree that they are removed from the characteristics of white masculinity.

Critics point out that law treats women in the same way that dominant society treats them: law cannot be expected to remedy injustices legally before they are recognized as injustices socially. The same is true for racial injustices. We can see this in the length of time it has taken for racialized as well as sexualized harms to be taken seriously by law. MacKinnon's and Smart's argument is that since law's thinking is that of the dominant white male, its innovations will be in redressing harms recognized as such by the dominant white male. While legislators may sometimes take the progressive side (in relation to race discrimination, for example), MacKinnon's and Smart's argument is that law will not itself be formative of the progressive argument because its reasoning is that of the dominant male.

Moving from documenting injustices to looking at the roots of these injustices in the constructions of law, and the liberal philosophies on which Western law is based, reveals the closures of law and therefore the limits of justice that can be expected. As MacKinnon has argued, liberal justice can only provide redress for women who can demonstrate that they are "the same" as men. Women who are "like men" will be treated equally with men by law in redressing harms or claiming rights related to those aspects in which they have established themselves as the same. Professional women doing the same work as male colleagues have reasonable chances of success in bringing complaints against unequal pay; female house-holders or car-owners who are burgled or whose cars are stolen will be responded to in the same way as male victims. On the other hand, aspects of their lives and personalities in which they are not "the same" as men will not receive equal treat-ment or redress for harms. It has been much more difficult for women to gain rights relating to the body rather than to property or to life in the public sphere. Abortion rights, fertility rights, maternity rights, redress for rape in many forms and in many circumstances remain contested and only patchily available.

The legal treatment of racial and ethnic minori-ties parallels the treatment of (white) women in this regard: in order to gain rights and remedies they have to demonstrate that they are "the same" as white men. Again, professionals or property owners who suffer harms and injustices in relation to these attributes (discrimination in the work-place, burglary and robbery) will find themselves (at least in principle, if not always effectively) sup-ported by law. But when their demands for justice concern acts or omissions directly related to their race/ethnicity, these demands will be contested or remain unrecognized. Demands for cultural recog-nition or protection of religious expression are still contested. Justice is confined to respects in which claimants are like white men in their mode of being in the world as well as their basic character-istics. For women, this has meant that justice has not extended to the private sphere of home and family, since this is designated "woman's world" in contrast to the male world of work and political life. For racial and ethnic minorities, this of course means that there were no rights extended to slav-ery: the conditions of slavery were unlike the con-ditions of white male free citizens.

Ironically, as Western societies have become more responsive to women's and minorities' demands for justice, attempts to remedy these have demonstrated the white-maleness of law, and they have shown the limits to the justice that can be offered to subordinated social identities. Criminal justice responses to rape, and to partner violence, for example, reveal the dependence of law on stereotypes of male and female sexual roles (rape); and dependence on the idea of the behavior of "the reasonable man" (provocation and self-defense) further illustrates the maleness of criminal law. Taking these harms more seriously has not resulted in more prosecutions and convictions. At the same time that more women are reporting rape, and police are improving the way in which they deal with women complainants (having special "rape suites" for example, with less intimidating offices, specially trained officers, access to showers and other amenities), this has not been reflected in a corresponding rise in convictions. In fact the con-viction rate has not risen in most Western jurisdic-tions, and in the UK, at least, it has actually fallen.

Dithering over definitions of "racial" crimes, lack of protection of religions other than Chris-tianity and (to some extent) Judaism and differ-ences in sentencing attributable to the race/ethnicity of victims show the entrenched white-ness of criminal law. Critical race theorists have demonstrated that law is structurally racist: the racialization of crime and the criminalization of race, and the discriminatory sentencing and lack of serious legal response to attacks on the persons and property of minority citizens, are structural rather than the product of individual jurists' racist beliefs.

Feminist and critical race critiques of liberal-ism point out that the exclusions are not acciden-tal oversights, but are inevitable because of the structures of liberal political philosophy. The construction of the liberal subject—the post-Enlightenment, modern man of reason—depends on the existence of an Other, constituted from the opposites of the qualities of the liberal self. Said and Gilroy point out that liberalism needs the irrational, uncivilized, Black and oriental "Others" who are defined by their lack of everything that distinguishes the citizen of the West. They are defined by their lack of democratic governance, their religious rather than formal legal systems, their lack of human rights and their lack of scien-tific achievements. The narratives which consti-tute this Otherness of "lesser breeds without the law" are necessary not only to justify colonialism and slavery; they are necessary also to constitute the Western subject's idea of (his) self-identity.

This imperative of the negative Other means that liberal societies must constantly reproduce divisions and constitute new divisions between the rational and the irrational, the civilized and the barbaric. As we move towards more equal citizenship in broad racial/ethnic terms, new distinctions open up within groups. Immigrants who accept the British, American, Australian or

European "way of life" are distinguished from those who do not; followers of non-Christian religions are divided into the moderate and the fanatical; foreign nations are divided into the democratic and the anti-democratic. The rights and privileges of national and global citizenship are distributed according to these endlessly multiplied distinctions.

MOVING FORWARD: SOME NEW PRINCIPLES OF JUSTICE

To move beyond white man's justice, new models must be able to dissolve the *logic of identity*, the logic by which justice will only be available if claims are based on being the same as the white, male, "reasonable person" of law. I derive some principles of justice from the overlapping critiques and proposals of feminist, post-structuralist and communitarian perspectives. Three principles are discursiveness, relationalism and reflectiveness.

Justice Must Be Discursive

If the logic of identity means that justice is seen as something that obtains between persons who share certain characteristics (being capable of reasoning; sharing commitment to principles of justice), and feminist and race critical analyses reveal that these shared characteristics assumed by liberal theories of justice are revealed as not universal but as the idealized characteristics of white Western man, then it follows that certain identities are outside the constituency of justice. A major theme of feminist and post-structural, post-colonial critiques, then, is that established liberal justice suppresses the voice of the outsider. The first principle, and the principle that is common to most post-liberal or reconstructed liberal theories of justice is, therefore, that those who are presently outside the discursive circle of justice must be brought inside.

As well as placing certain identities outside the discursive circle, the logic of identity means that claims to justice can only be acknowledged if they are voiced in the terms of the dominant group. Harms have to be described in terms of legally recognized offence categories; denial of rights can only be contested if those rights can be accommodated to definitions of the rights already acknowledged. The further demand is

therefore that the outsider must be able to put her claims in her own terms, not have to accommodate to the dominant modes of legal/political discourse.

Discursiveness is, of course, a key feature of restorative justice. One of the advantages claimed by almost all restorative justice models is that all parties are allowed to tell their stories in their own words: the point is to establish a story of "what happened" and of the responsibilities and culpabilities involved.

Discursiveness, as a principle, means much more than allowing a space in proceedings for various participants to speak. It means openness to challenges to the identity of law, and openness to identity claims that are not based on similarity. Discursiveness as a principle also means that any topic can be raised by any participant, and for feminist critics of liberal justice, this has meant in particular that behavior in the private sphere must not be off-limits: for women, this means acknowledgement that harm suffered in the domestic environment and within other intimate relationships are "crimes," which must be dealt with by robust, effective process of justice.

Justice Must Be Relational

The second principle of a reformulated model of justice is relationalism. While the term "relational justice" has several connotations in current criminal justice writing, in this context it refers primarily to two key elements of justice: identities and rights.

Feminist, post-colonial and post-structuralist writers emphasize the contingent, relational nature of identity. We are not, it is argued, possessors of a fixed, stable identity that, once developed, remains dependably, unchangingly and essentially "myself." This is to say, we develop our identities in interactions with others; we are conscious of identity in relation to others; different elements of identity are salient in some situations and relationships; and other elements are salient in different situations and relationships.

Blackness, for example, has a different implication for identity according to whether the Black person is in a country or neighborhood where blackness is a majority or minority trait; it has different significance according to the race/ethnicity structures and fissures of the society of which a Black person is a member. In a Black neighborhood, gender, age, lifestyle and reputation become more significant than blackness; in a white-dominated location or grouping, blackness may well be the first (and possibly the only) quality that the white person sees.

Rights are also relational. Liberal theories of justice have posited rights as possessions of individuals ("the freeborn Englishman/American/Australian," for example). Iris Young criticizes the liberal paradigm of rights as possessions to be distributed, arguing instead that rights are rules that limit behavior: they are, she says, rules of conduct that protect freedom and dignity. Young's argument is that justice must go beyond the liberal "distributive paradigm," conceptualizing justice instead as the removal of oppression. On her account, rights are regulatory safeguards against oppression. Martha Minow also proposes understanding rights as relationships, as constructions to demarcate reciprocal rights and duties, freedoms and limits in relationships of difference. For feminist and post-colonial theorists, rights are, above all, to do with conditions of discourse: denial of rights means silencing of the Other; denying her pain (and exclusion); refusing her membership, her freedom and her identity.

The relationalism that I am advocating here is not the same as the emphasis on a *particular relationship*—victim/offender, abused/abuser— which is the target of some of the critics of restorative justice, and I would be concerned if restorative justice is too closely identified with mediation or reparation. Relationalism in the sense proposed here recognizes individuals as embodied in a network of relationships, which include relationships with community and with the state. So the relationalism I am proposing has two aspects: that elements of identity and rights are relational concepts, as proposed by the feminist theorists mentioned earlier, and also that responsibility and culpability are relational.

Justice Must Be Reflective

Criminal law in Western liberal societies delineates a series of proscribed act; schedules of penalties for perpetrators of these acts; defences, mitigating and aggravating circumstances, all of which are derived from white, male idealized characteristics and modes of life. This means that criminal justice processes must decide what class of proscribed act the deed in a case is, and it means that legal rules define what circumstances, biographical details and experiences are relevant or irrelevant in coming to judgment. The courts, rather than those coming before the courts, victims, offenders and their supporters, decide what is relevant or irrelevant.

This lack of opportunity to decide what is relevant or irrelevant, admissible or inadmissible, obviously goes against the discursive principle that any topic can be raised by any participant. As well as demonstrating the whiteness and maleness of law, however, this closure also illustrates the abstract generality of law: actual individual acts have to be fitted into general categories. This generality, this abstraction, means that justice can never be done for the individual case because some of its aspects are bound to be lost in rejecting all those unique circumstances which are not present in the paradigm case. Liberal justice thus expels difference in two senses: it expels differences in subjectivity, so that claimants to justice have to suppress those facets of identity which do not conform to the generalized white, male, subjectivity in law; it expels difference in cases because individual biographical and situational circumstances will be overlooked. Race, gender, being in an abusive relationship and economic coercion are some of the features of cases which are generally ruled "out of court" in formal Western criminal justice processes.

New models of justice propose replacing orientation to the general with orientation to the particular. Benhabib and Young take issue with the concept of the *generalized Other*, which is the counterpart to the self in liberal theories of justice. This Other is not a flesh-and-blood unique individual, but an abstract identity, whom I should treat justly because she is like me. The generalized Other, they argue, is thus no Other at all, but an identical self who is presumed to be like me, rather than a genuine Other who is given the opportunity to establish her own identity, to state her needs and make her demands. This generalized Other must be replaced by a concrete Other as protagonist in justice processes, if justice is to be available for actual persons.

Acts and the circumstances that surround them should be considered in their uniqueness, according to the theory of *reflective justice*. This means that individual cases should not be subsumed into a restricted range of legal categories; rather, they should be considered in the totality of their features and weighed against broader horizons of justice. Concretely, reflective justice means that each case should be considered in terms of all its subjectivities, harms, wrongs and context, and then measured against concepts such as oppression, freedom, dignity and equality. Looking at unique circumstances in reflective justice does not mean abstracting circumstances from wider social structures and social inequalities; on the contrary, it means situating particular circumstances in their wider social context rather than only considering the restricted range of legal categories of crime aggravations and mitigations which act precisely to abstract individuals from wider inequalities and oppressions.

Reflective justice, which is individualized, open to the full accounts of those concerned, considers circumstances and biographies and transcends fixed categories and rules of admissibility of law—all of this features as an ideal within restorative justice processes. However, this ideal has to be constrained if it is to satisfy the claims and expectations of participants, especially of victims. The first demand of victims of sexualized and racialized offences is that the crimes should be *named* and clearly pronounced to be wrongs as well as harms. Rape and racial assaults are the prime examples here; across the world, whether certain sexual encounters are "really" rape or whether certain inter-racial violent assaults are "really" racially motivated remain contested issues. Naming, which is a demand that the authoritative tiers of society censure these behaviours as serious wrongs, usually means attaching the strong condemnatory label of a legally recognized crime category.

Concluding Comments: Some Unresolved Dilemma

Restorative justice incorporates the principles proposed here to a greater degree than other forms of criminal justice process, but their application poses problems with regard to meeting needs and expectations of participants, satisfying claims to justice, performing the symbolic function of law in conveying wrongness and censure, protecting participants from intimidation by others and deflecting responsibility from communities and states. Some of these problems are generally well understood by restorative justice theorists, practitioners and evaluators, so that most meetings and conferences are carefully structured and managed to avoid intimidation of victims, pressures on offenders to admit to offences which they have not committed or dominance by one participant or group of participants.

Restorative justice (or indeed any form of criminal justice) cannot, of course, solve problems of social inequalities and oppressions in wider societies. This is not what I am demanding. Rather, I am saying that thinking in terms of oppression, inequality and domination can guide practical implementation of justice policies and processes. For example, how can we decide whether to support minority/Indigenous communities in wanting to deal with gendered violence within their own communities following their own processes or whether to support including them in generalized procedures (whether formal criminal justice or restorative justice) unless we have some inkling of the relationships of oppression and domination within those communities, and between the communities and the wider societies? These are pressing questions for those involved with, for example, Indigenous women in Australia, New Zealand and Canada, and for minorities such as Pakistani Muslim women in the UK. By adopting oppression and domination as the horizons against which to consider these questions and to make decisions in individual cases, we can bring our practice/political encounters with the multiple identities of "north" and "south" women together with our theoretical understandings of the distribution and operation of power in late modernity. While questions of relativism and the grounding of universal principles of justice may not be settled philosophically, adoption of the principles of discursiveness, relationalism and reflectiveness, implemented in the context of systems and patterns of oppression, domination and inequalities in late modern societies, could provide a model of justice helpful to principled continuing development of restorative justice.

SOURCE: From *Theoretical Criminology*, Vol. 10, No. 1, 29–47, 2006. Copyright © 2006 Sage Publications. Reprinted by permission of Sage Publications, Ltd.

QUESTIONS FOR DISCUSSION AND WRITING

1. Under what circumstances can women and racial minorities gain rights and remedies under law?

2. What do feminist and critical race critiques of liberalism point out?

3. What three principles of justice does the author feel must be incorporated into the justice system? How is discursiveness related to restorative justice? To what does relationism refer? What does reflective justice mean for individual cases?

AN ARGUMENT FOR BLACK FEMINIST CRIMINOLOGY

Understanding African American Women's Experiences With Intimate Partner Abuse Using an Integrated Approach

HILLARY POTTER

Just as there are many types of feminisms and feminists, it undoubtedly follows that there are adaptations on feminist criminology and no single feminist criminology can exist. The impetus for proposing a Black feminist criminology (BFC) is supported by Britton's argument that traditional feminist criminology still has much work to accomplish in theorizing from intersecting identities as opposed to placing emphasis on a solitary component—such as considering gender but not race—at the forefront of an analysis. Although feminist criminology has its roots in mainstream feminist theories, the approach presented in this article, BFC, is grounded in Black feminist theory and critical race feminist theory (CRFT). To begin to understand and fully conceptualize BFC, this article considers intimate partner abuse against African American women as an illustration of its ability to explain this transgression.

Feminist criminology has aided in a notably improved understanding of gender variations in criminal activity and victimization and of the crime-processing system's dealings with female and male victims and offenders. Feminist criminology has significantly expanded the foci within the field of criminology beyond simply exploring female criminal offending and female offenders to also examining violent acts against girls and women. Although gender is certainly important and crucial to considering women's (and men's) involvement in crime either as victims or as offenders, for Black women, and arguably for all women, other inequities must be considered principal, not peripheral, to the analysis of women. This includes incorporating key factors, such as race and/or ethnicity, sexuality, and economic status into any examination. Daly argued that considering how gender, race, and class distinctions intersect is absolutely unnecessary in criminology. Because traditional feminist criminology is built on mainstream feminism, which historically placed issues of race as secondary to gender, it is reasoned here that starting at Black feminist theory and CRFT to investigate and explain the source of and reactions to crime among African Americans will be sure to explicitly take into account Black women's positions in society, in their communities, and in their familial and intimate relationships.

At the outset, this article presents an historical overview of the attention given to the issue of intimate partner abuse by feminist activists and the problems with examining African American women's encounters with domestic abuse using theory based on White women's experiences. A comprehensive description of BFC is then provided and followed by the Black feminist and critical race feminist concepts on which it is constructed. Support for a BFC is demonstrated by evaluating African American women's experiences with and responses to intimate partner abuse and the crime-processing system's intervention in domestic violence incidents involving Black women under this model.

HISTORICAL DEVELOPMENT OF FEMINIST ADVOCACY AGAINST INTIMATE PARTNER ABUSE

An increased awareness of the problem of intimate partner abuse against women has occurred only during the past few decades. Until the 1970s, concern, advocacy, and protection for battered women by the general public and officials of the crime-processing system were tremendously lacking. During the 1970s, there was an accelerating trend toward the criminalization of domestic violence perpetrators and an increase in the assistance afforded battered women. Feminist organizations began to highlight intimate partner violence against women as a social problem needing to be remedied, and books written by battered women and their advocates began to appear with fervor. In 1973, the United States saw one of its first shelters to assist wives battered by their alcoholic husbands at the Rainbow Retreat in Phoenix, Arizona, and since this time, shelters have rapidly appeared across the country. In addition, law enforcement and court intervention agents began to address woman battering more seriously with the enactment and increased enforcement of laws and sanctions relating to intimate abuse. In 1994, President Bill Clinton signed into law the landmark Violence Against Women Act to combat violence against women by providing assistance to criminal processing agents (e.g., training), support for battered women's shelters and a national telephone "hotline," and funding for research on violence against women.

Although intimate partner violence has experienced increased attention, abuse among intimate partners as a social problem is still not receiving the level of attention it deserves from criminal processing agents and health professionals. For instance, there is fairly recent evidence that police officers still respond leniently to male batterers. In addition, battered women's shelters continue to suffer from poor financial support and the inability to house every woman and child in need of and requesting sanctuary from their abusers. As indicated by a survey conducted by the Center for the Advancement of Women, a sizeable number of women deem that intimate partner violence warrants continued attention. In fact, the report indicates that 92% of the women surveyed believed that domestic violence and sexual assault should be the top priority for the women's movement.

It is unmistakable that with the identification of domestic violence as a social problem approximately three decades ago came an unprecedented amount of research and activism surrounding the plight of battered women. In both the research and responses to intimate partner abuse, however, cultural, racial, and ethnic distinctions among women victims of intimate partner abuse have not been afforded equal levels of consideration. Much of the extant research and policies regard all battered women as victims with similar life experiences, yet African American women and other women of color typically have life-experiences distinct from White women. The research in the 1970s was conducted with predominately White samples and a failure to take into account how the surveys and findings might be problematic in reference to victims and offenders of color.

BFC AND ITS ORIGINS

The Tenets of BFC

BFC incorporates the tenets of interconnected identities, interconnected social forces, and distinct circumstances to better theorize, conduct research, and inform policy regarding criminal behavior and victimization among African Americans. The interconnected identities to be considered among African American individuals include race and/or ethnicity, gender, sexuality, class status, national origin, and religion.

These interconnected identities are greatly shaped by larger social forces. That is, groups of individuals and society at large produce and perpetuate conflict, competition, and differences in merit between the members of society. It is not battered Black women's identities that exclusively form their perceptions and reactions but the treatment of these identities filtered down from (a) the impact of the social structure through (b) the community or culture and to (c) familial and intimate exchanges. Nevertheless, this does not necessitate a linear association in every case; instead, it serves to demonstrate that a patriarchal, paternalistic, and racialized social structure affects all other institutions and interactions in society. Black women's reactions to abuse are affected by their "place" in society because of their intersecting identities. Being at the least valued end of the spectrum for both race and gender places these women in a peculiar position not faced by Black men or White women. In a similar manner, other women of color, such as Latinas, Native American women, Asian American women, and immigrant women of color, can easily be placed alongside Black women in this analysis.

BLACK FEMINIST AND CRITICAL RACE FEMINIST ORIGINS OF BFC

BFC addresses concerns in the lives of Black women that are categorized into four themes: (a) social structural oppression, (b) the Black community and culture, (e) intimate and familial relations, and (d) the Black woman as an individual. The first three themes are components of interconnected social forces, whereas the fourth considers the interconnected identities of the Black woman as affected by the societal influences. The tenets of BFC are cultivated from Black feminist theory and CRFT. Black feminist theory is the theoretical perspective that places the lived experiences of Black women, including any forms of resistance to their situations, at the focal point of the analysis. It considers Black women as individuals encompassing numerous and interwoven identities. The standpoint is that Black women are frequently oppressed within both the Black community (by Black men) and society at large based on their subordinated statuses within each of these spheres and that research on Black women should be conducted

based on this perspective. Although the sexist oppression in the Black community may not appear as obvious as that in larger society, and presents itself in a different form, it undeniably exists. CRFT is similar to Black feminist theory in that it also considers women of color as individuals with multiple intersecting identities where one does not eclipse another.

Mainstream feminist theory places gender as the primary consideration in women's liberation efforts. Black women have expressed difficulty in identifying with mainstream feminist theory because of its focus on this single aspect of womanhood and because the lives and concerns of White middle-class women were placed at the forefront of the liberation efforts. Black women regularly convey that they deal not only with issues of gender inequality but with racial inequality as well. It is this status, Crenshaw argued, that relegates women of color to an invisible class and pulls these women's loyalties in two directions, that is, feeling the need to either choose between being loyal to feminist ideas or being loyal to their racial or ethnic community.

This collective, yet individualized, aspect of Black women's lives is an important aspect in Black feminism and when considering Black women.

In summation, numerous Black feminist and critical race feminist scholars have addressed the "intersecting oppressions" of Black women. In the classic article "Double Jeopardy: To Be Black and Female," Frances Beale, journalist and civil rights activist, wrote of the burden of the Black woman's disadvantaged status based on gender, race, and class. Gordon's analysis identified these three conditions as Black women's "trilogy of oppression" and stated that Black women are often confronted with determining which form of oppression is most important. King advocated for the term *multiple jeopardy* to describe Black women's oppression, given that Black women often undergo even more forms of subjugation and that these categories of oppression affect Black women simultaneously. Wing, who used the term *multiplicative identity* to capture the identity of women of color, argued that "women of color are not merely White women *plus* color or men of color *plus* gender. Instead, their identities must be multiplied together to create a holistic One when analyzing the nature of the discrimination against them." Intimate partner abuse has been considered by many Black feminist scholars and although still in its youthful stage, CRFT has been specifically applied to domestic violence in the lives of women of color. Using Black feminist theory and CRFT as foundations in considering the issues with intimate partner abuse against African American women, as well as considering their involvement in criminal behavior, will assist in addressing this limitation and contribute to the development of BFC.

Understanding Intimate Partner Abuse in the Lives of Black Women Using BFC

As established above, the four themes considered within BFC include social structural oppression, interactions within the Black community, intimate and familial relations, and the Black woman as an individual, all operating under the premise that these segments are interconnected. Use of this framework allows the connection between woman battering and structural, cultural, and familial restraints to be made.

Social Structural Oppression

Under the theme of social structural oppression, matters of institutional racism, damaging stereotypical images, sexism, and classism are routinely addressed by Black feminists and critical race feminists. Included in the examination is the limited access to adequate education and employment as consequences of racism, sexism, and classism. As education and employment deficiencies have been found to be common among battered women, this area of focus by BFC considers the impact of these shortcomings on battered Black women's lives.

Concerns external to remaining in abusive relationships because of poor financial status must be considered with all battered Black women, particularly women belonging to higher socioeconomic statuses. Stigmatizing constraints forcing battered Black women to remain in abusive settings could include their resistance to engendering the controlling stereotypical image of the single, Black matriarch. Based on socially constructed perceptions of Black women, BFC scrutinizes how stereotypical image of these women affect the ways in which others respond to them. Poor responses by social services

professionals and crime-processing agents to Black women's interpersonal victimization crises can be considered under the auspices of this framework. Social services used by domestic violence victims in their process of leaving abusive relationships include medical assistance, battered women's shelters, and therapeutic agents. The barriers to using these sources may be in relation to not only the short supply of battered women's shelters and therapeutic resources in Black communities but also the ability of and lack of trust in those working in the helping professions who are not able to deliver adequate culturally competent services to women who have suffered abuse.

The criminal processing system also has not been swift to aid battered Black women, and battered women of color report distrust in using the formal criminal processing system to assist with their exodus from abusive relationships. A history of poor relations between criminal processing agencies and communities of color can account for these misgivings. Reservations about using the crime-processing system are also said to transpire because speaking out about intimate partner violence can involve the risk of generating racial shame, and Black women may be viewed as traitors to their race for adding more African American men to the system's offender population.

A focus by BFC on this documented history of poor systemic responses allows for an examination of the way in which professionals working with battered Black women may rely on stereotypical assumptions of Black women when making decisions about how to respond to them. An example of the harm of cultural insensitivity and typecasting is found in this author's in-depth interviews with a diverse sample of battered Black women. For many of the participants, assuming the role of the Strong Black Woman, as well as being perceived as a Strong Black Woman, had policy implications for battered women's shelter and counseling services. The women who capitalized on using shelters and therapy to assist them with terminating the abusive relationships were often singled out because of their distinguishing experiences with abuse and as Black women. When the participants' experiences with intimate partner abuse were pointed out by the other clients, it tended to be done for the purposes of placing battering and abuse in a hierarchical sequence and served as a perverse source of competition for the other battered women. When the participants were singled out by counselors, it was for the seemingly innocuous purposes of benefiting the battered Black women, to highlight how they are stronger than the other women (i.e., the White women) and strong enough to get out of the relationships. Even if these assertions by other battered women and service providers were true, they often served as a detriment to battered Black women's inclination to leave abusive relationships.

Black Community and Black Culture

The second theme addressed by BFC is based on the cultural distinctions of African Americans. The nature of relationships among Blacks is a topic scrupulously discussed by critical race and Black feminists. These discussions often include the impact of historical experiences of African Americans in the United States. Some specific subjects addressed include issues of women's and men's roles in the Black community, the occurrence of violence within the Black community, and the role of spirituality and the Black church as a staple. Such a concentration allows for each of these features to be considered in how it affects Black women's encounters with domestic abuse. For instance, if indeed Black women's role in the Black community is one of an egalitarian and independent nature, how are issues of a batterer's power and control behaviors (i.e., typical qualities among batterers) displayed in relationships among Black couples? By scrutinizing the characteristics of batterers' abusive behaviors and the motivations for battered women to remain in abusive relationships, a sufficient explanation can be formed to demonstrate the method in which these men are still able to assert some level of power and control over the women. Again, recent qualitative research determines that battered Black women remain in abusive relationships more so out of fear of being without companionship, being without a father or father figure for minor children, and being stigmatized as yet another single Black mother than fear of further and more perilous battering incidents or of financial independence.

The role of religion and spirituality must be strongly regarded when considering African American women's experiences with abuse. Although battered Black women rely heavily on religion and/or spirituality, a number of clergy members have not always demonstrated the support that is expected of them by battered Black women parishioners.

Familial and Intimate Relations

The intimate and familial relationships theme is the third area on which BFC concentrates. The family of origin and generational characteristics of the Black family is one of the foci here, including the embeddedness in other mothers and family members outside of the immediate family unit (i.e., extended family). By considering family embeddedness as a major focal point, a more thorough assessment of their dependency on this custom as a resource, as opposed to relying on systemic resources, can be made. This same embeddedness can demonstrate how abuse in the family of origin and among other close family members can be a detrimental and compounding factor on the victims.

Intimate relationships of Black women and their roles within these relationships, including interracial and/or lesbian couples, are essential elements of BFC, particularly as they function in and are affected by the larger societal composition. Research on interracial battering relationships is particularly lacking, but this cross-cultural dynamic would be well served by study under the auspices of BFC in determining how the various lived experiences of the members of interracial couples may affect the relationship circumstances differently. Lesbian battering relationships among Black women can be examined from the compounding element of sexuality, especially in how this component of Black lesbians' identity is viewed by others and how the quality of the relationship is consequently affected. The implications for Black women who identify as both lesbian and battered clearly require future research and would prosper under BFC investigation that considers intersectionality.

Black Woman as Individual

Last, the theme of Black women as individuals is afforded considerable examination in BFC. Although examined as an individual, the life of the Black woman is strongly connected to her location, status, and role in the social structure, the community, and interpersonal relationships. Within this category, issues such as mental health, sexual health, and sexuality are addressed. Inclusion of this precept allows a personal yet comprehensive view of battered Black women.

Consequently, battered Black women's personal strategies for dealing with the abuse can be analyzed under this notion. These strategies include how a battered Black woman may frame the effects of the abuse. Black women face many forms of oppression, and this subjugation will undoubtedly affect a woman's mental fitness. It is clear that being abused by an intimate partner serves only to deteriorate a woman's mental health beyond the injury of the bias bestowed on countless African American women on a daily basis.

Another strategy exercised by battered women includes the use of physical force against batterers. The propensity of Black women to physically strike back against their intimate abusers has been determined to be at greater rates than battered White women's retaliation. Although it is seen as a personal tactic among many battered Black women, considering their self-defense strategies through BFC would allow for the introduction of structural and cultural influences to be considered to begin to explain this phenomenon.

Conclusion

This article provides an analysis of how approaching intimate partner abuse against African American women from this position may offer a more comprehensive appraisal of their experiences

with and responses to their victimization. Considering the historical experiences of Black women in the United States, which have been couched in multiple forms of domination, the approach advanced in this article is based on a fresh standpoint that regards how African American women's lives may position them to encounter intimate partner abuse differently than women of other races and ethnicities (especially in comparison to White women).

The argument expounded here by no intention undervalues the important and noble work done by original feminist criminology and its adherents. Indeed, mainstream feminist theory and feminist criminology allow for a more suitable assessment of women and criminal victimization than traditional male-centered criminology, but BFC necessarily provides for Black women's multiple and interconnected identity and their position in U.S. society to be considered as a central element of any analysis. Black feminist theory stresses that the Black woman encompasses many components that frame her identity. These elements include the general categories of race, ethnicity, gender, class, nationality, and sexuality. Moreover, the Black woman is not one or the other at different times and places in her life but all components at all times. BFC deems that being oppressed and discriminated against based on any or all of these parts of the Black woman's identity can occur at the structural societal level, within the Black community, and within interpersonal relationships.

SOURCE: From *Feminist Criminology*, Vol. 1, No. 2, 106–124, April 2006. Copyright © 2006 Sage Publications. Reprinted by permission of Sage Publications, Inc.

QUESTIONS FOR DISCUSSION AND WRITING

1. Why does traditional feminist theory place issues of race as secondary to gender, and what do BFC and CRFT take into account?

2. What four concern themes in the lives of black women does BFC address? From where are the tenets of BFC cultivated?

3. What analysis does this article provide? On which "fresh standpoint" is the approach advanced in this article based?

A BIO-PSYCHOLOGICAL THEORY OF CHOICE

JAMES Q. WILSON

RICHARD HERRNSTEIN

CRIME AS CHOICE: THE THEORY IN BRIEF

Our theory rests on the assumption that people, when faced with a choice, choose the preferred course of action. This assumption is quite weak; it says nothing more than that whatever people choose to do, they choose it because they prefer it. In fact, it is more than weak; without further clarification, it is a tautology. When we say people "choose," we do not necessarily mean that they consciously deliberate about what to do. All we mean is that their behavior is determined by its consequences. A person will do that thing the consequences of which are perceived by him or her to be preferable to the consequences of doing something else. What can save such a statement from being a tautology is how plausibly we describe the gains and losses associated with alternative courses of action and the standards by which a person evaluates those gains and losses.

These assumptions are commonplace in philosophy and social science. Philosophers speak of hedonism or utilitarianism, economists of value or utility, and psychologists of reinforcement or reward. We will use the language of psychology, but it should not be hard to translate our terminology into that of other disciplines. Although social scientists differ as to how much behavior can reasonably be described as the result of a choice, all agree that at least some

behavior is guided, or even precisely controlled, by things variously termed pleasure, pain, happiness, sorrow, desirability, or the like. Our object is to show how this simple and widely used idea can be used to explain behavior.

At any given moment, a person can choose between committing a crime and not committing it (all these alternatives to crime we lump together as "noncrime"). The consequences of committing the crime consist of rewards (what psychologists call "reinforcers") and punishments; the consequences of not committing the crime (i.e., engaging in noncrime) also entail gains and losses.

The larger the ratio of the net rewards of crime to the net rewards of noncrime, the greater the tendency to commit the crime. The net rewards of crime include, obviously, the likely material gains from the crime, but they also include intangible benefits, such as obtaining emotional or sexual gratification, receiving the approval of peers, satisfying an old score against an enemy, or enhancing one's sense of justice. One must deduct from these rewards of crime any losses that accrue immediately—that are, so to speak, contemporaneous with the crime. They include the pangs of conscience, the disapproval of onlookers, and the retaliation of the victim.

The value of noncrime lies all in the future. It includes the benefits to the individual of avoiding the risk of being caught and punished and, in addition, the benefits of avoiding penalties not controlled by the criminal justice system, such as the loss of reputation or the sense of shame afflicting a person later discovered to have broken the law and the possibility that, being known as a criminal, one cannot get or keep a job.

The value of any reward or punishment associated with either crime or noncrime is, to some degree, uncertain. A would-be burglar rarely knows exactly how much loot he will take away or what its cash value will prove to be. The assaulter or rapist may exaggerate the satisfaction he thinks will follow the assault or the rape. Many people do not know how sharp the bite of conscience will be until they have done something that makes them feel the bite. The anticipated approval of one's buddies may or may not be forthcoming. Similarly, the benefits of noncrime are uncertain. One cannot know with confidence whether one will be caught, convicted, and punished, or whether one's friends will learn about the crime and as a result withhold valued esteem, or whether one will be able to find or hold a job.

Compounding these uncertainties is time. The opportunity to commit a crime may be ready at hand (an open, unattended cash register in a store) or well in the future (a bank that, with planning and preparation, can be robbed). And the rewards associated with noncrime are almost invariably more distant than those connected with crime, perhaps many weeks or months distant. The strength of reinforcers tends to decay over time at rates that differ among individuals. As a result, the extent to which people take into account distant possibilities—a crime that can be committed only tomorrow, or punishment that will be inflicted only in a year—will affect whether they choose crime or noncrime.

THE THEORY AS A WHOLE

We assert that the chief value of a comprehensive theory of crime is that it will bring to our attention all the factors that explain individual differences in criminality and thus prevent us from offering partial explanations or making incomplete interpretations of research findings. The larger the ratio of the rewards (material and nonmaterial) of noncrime to the rewards (material and nonmaterial) of crime, the weaker the tendency to commit crimes. The bite of conscience, the approval of peers, and any sense of

inequity will increase or decrease the total value of crime; the opinions of family, friends, and employers are important benefits of noncrime, as is the desire to avoid the penalties that can be imposed by the criminal justice system. The strength of any reward declines with time, but people differ in the rate at which they discount the future. The strength of a given reward is also affected by the total supply of reinforcers.

Some implications of the theory are obvious: Other things being equal, a reduction in the delay and uncertainty attached to the rewards of noncrime will reduce the probability of crime. But other implications are not so obvious. For instance, increasing the value of the rewards of noncrime (by increasing the severity of punishment) may not reduce a given individual's tendency to commit crime if he believes that these rewards are not commensurate with what he deserves. In this case, punishing him for preferring crime to noncrime may trigger hostility toward society in retaliation for the shortfall. The increased rewards for noncrime may be offset by an increased sense of inequity and hence an increased incentive for committing a crime. Or again: It may be easier to reduce crime by making penalties swifter or more certain, rather than more severe, if the persons committing crime are highly present-oriented (so that they discount even large rewards very sharply) or if they are likely to have their sense of inequity heightened by increases in the severity of punishment. Or yet again: An individual with an extroverted personality is more likely than one with an introverted one to externalize his feelings of inequity and act directly to correct them.

In laboratory settings involving both human and animal subjects, each element of the theory has received at least some confirmation and the major elements have been confirmed extensively. Extrapolating these findings outside the laboratory, into real-world settings, is a matter on which opinions differ. We propose to bring together evidence from a variety of disciplines bearing on the connection between elements of the theory and the observed characteristics of crime and criminals.

The connection between crime and impulsiveness has been demonstrated, as has the link between (low) intelligence and crime. Those features of family life that produce stronger or weaker internalized inhibitions will be seen to have a connection to the presence or absence of aggressiveness and criminality. Certain subcultures, such as street-corner gangs, appear to affect the value members attach to both crime and noncrime. The mass media, and in particular television, may affect both aggressiveness directly and a viewer's sense of inequity that can affect crime indirectly. Schooling may affect crime rates by bringing certain persons together into groups that reinforce either crime or noncrime and by determining the extent to which children believe that their skills will give them access to legitimate rewards. The condition of the economy will have a complex effect on crime depending on whether the (possibly) restraint-weakening impact of affluence dominates the restraint-strengthening influence of employment opportunities.

The theory is applicable to the most common crimes, but is also quite consistent with the more bizarre and unusual forms of crime. Psychopathic personalities lack to an unusual degree internalized inhibitions on crime. Persons possessed by some obsessive interest— for example, pyromania—attach an inordinately high value to the rewards of certain crimes. If everyone loved fire too much, society would try hard to teach the moral evil of fire, as well as its practical danger. As it is, what society does teach is sufficient to overcome whatever slight tendency toward pyromania every average person may have, but it is insufficient to inhibit the rare pyromaniac. One reason society punishes arsonists is not only to make it more costly for persons to use fire for material gain but also to provide extra moral education to the occasional person who loves fire for its own sake.

In addition to pathological drives, there are ordinary ones that can, under certain conditions, become so strong as to lead to crime. History and literature abound with normal men and women in the grip of a too-powerful reinforcement. Many people have broken the law for love, honor, family, and country, as well as for money, sex, vengeance, or delusion. Such criminals may be psychologically unremarkable; they transgressed because as they perceived the situation the reward for crime exceeded that for noncrime, and an opportunity presented itself. The legal system often tries to minimize the punishment inflicted on such people.

SOURCE: Reprinted with the permission of Simon & Schuster Adult Publishing Group from *Crime and Human Nature: The Definitive Study of the Causes of Crime* by James Q. Wilson and Richard Herrnstein. Copyright © 1985 by James Q. Wilson and Richard J. Herrnstein.

QUESTIONS FOR DISCUSSION AND WRITING

1. On what assumption does the authors' theory rest?

2. What is associated with "greater tendency" to commit crime?

3. Where does the "value" of noncrime lie? Can individuals calculate the value of any given reward or punishment? Which two "connections" have been demonstrated, according to the authors?

HUMAN ECOLOGY, CRIME, AND CRIME CONTROL

Linking Individual Behavior and Aggregate Crime

JOANNE SAVAGE

BRYAN VILA

This [article] addresses two fundamental questions from the literature on human ecology and crime. The first is why some individuals commit a great deal more crime than others. Although Cohen and Machalek (alluding to Durkheim) stress that crime can be " 'normal' behavior performed by 'normal' individuals in unexceptional social systems," it is evident from research that roughly half of all crimes are committed by "chronic offenders"— the 5 to 7 percent of the population who commit five or more crimes. The second concern is about the disjuncture between understanding crime at the individual level and crime at the aggregate. This is the question that Cohen and Machalek suggest has "both intrigued and frustrated social scientists since Durkheim: What is the relation between the behavior of individual human beings and the organized aggregates in which they live?" The [article] addresses these questions using the ecological lens and incorporating recent research on chronic offending by revisiting Vila's general paradigm for understanding criminal behavior and focusing on biological, developmental, and ecological factors thought to be associated with the development of criminal strategic styles. This [article] then applies principles of evolutionary ecology and cultural evolution to the problem of crime prevention, emphasizing the need to address chronic offending.

EVOLUTIONARY-ECOLOGICAL THEORY: THE NEW SYNTHESIS

Although Vila explicitly adds the idea of "criminality" to the evolutionary-ecological framework, some criticize this addition because it implies a value-laden view of behavior inconsistent with the ecological paradigm, which sees behavior as normal. This raises an age-old debate on the "normalcy" and pathology of crime. The data suggest that crime rates at aggregate levels are due to both situational factors that open the door for behavioral innovation *and* to the prevalence of individuals whose behavioral repertoires favor dishonest, expropriative, and/or violent strategies. Unlike most models of crime, Vila's model allows for both criminal strategies that are "normal" given a particular situation *and* chronic criminality (that is seen by many as aberrant). Studies cited earlier suggest that some individuals are chronically

395

criminal in their behavior, and many psychological studies suggest that there are pathological elements to the development of chronic offending. Even some evolutionary analyses and genetic studies suggest an element of genetic transmission of "deviant" behavior. And, of course, a large volume of studies suggests that situations, community factors, and structural factors affect crime rates. A *general* paradigm, then, appropriately incorporates both "normal" crime (likely due to situation) and pathologically chronic criminality (likely due to individual biology and development).

As Cohen and Machalek noted, the probability that an individual will adopt one strategy over another in any given situation depends in part upon the value he assigns to the goal and his ability to achieve the goal using that strategy. Early life experiences may shape both the goals and the behaviors used to achieve those goals, and appear to have an especially strong influence on the development of strategic styles. Criminal strategies are likely to be of low prevalence in a population because formal and informal sanctions will act to minimize them. It follows that the development of criminal strategic styles is likely to be somewhat rare in a population. Then what causes the development of chronic offending? Moffitt has forwarded the view that "the juxtaposition of a vulnerable and difficult infant with an adverse rearing context initiates risk for the life-course-persistent pattern of antisocial behavior." This has largely been interpreted to suggest that a combination of one or more "biological" risk markers and several environmental risk factors will lead to heightened likelihood of chronicity. Translating Moffitt's view into an ecological one would change "adverse rearing" to a physical and social environment that does not provide the resources or teach non-criminal values or provide the individual with culturally legitimated opportunities to obtain what he desires. Such an environment would tend to favor the use of criminal strategies rather than productive and cooperative strategies.

In the following sections we will first discuss biological factors associated with chronic criminality and the role of child development in the acquisition of criminal strategic styles. It will be clear from this discussion that a general paradigm of criminal behavior must include these components and that the current research on chronic offending suggests it is best explained by biology and development. We will then discuss the unique features of the human ecological environment that affect criminal behavior and behavioral style development.

Etiology of Chronic Offending vs. "Normal" Criminal Behavior

Biological Factors. It is beyond the scope of this [article] to review the extensive evidence on the links between biology and criminality and criminal behavior. (Fishbein provides an excellent review of this voluminous literature.) Here we will limit ourselves to some recent research on chronic offending and early onset. Before we do it is important to note that contemporary researchers do not often suggest direct effects of biology on offending. Rather, the effects of genetic factors, intellectual or attention or learning deficits, exposure to toxins, and the like are believed to affect criminal behavior only indirectly. Walters provides an example of the dynamic: "Certain temperaments have a higher likelihood of eliciting negative parental feedback than other temperaments. Consequently, irregular children given to frequent negative moods, suggestive of a difficult temperament, more typically evoke hostility and criticism from their parents than children with more positive moods and greater regularity." Lytton points out that having a biological disposition for conduct disorder may *elicit* negative interactions with parents and others, thus preventing the formation of social bonds that might prevent further conduct problems. Moffitt provides a very thorough description of these processes. Although these factors set the physical boundaries of human behavior and influence affective state, they do not *determine* which of the myriad possible behaviors we perform.

Further, most biologists disparage the idea that biological factors are distinguishable from environmental factors—since both appear to affect each other in a reciprocal manner. For example, Tremblay, Schaal, Boulerice, Arseneault, Soussignan, and Perusse found that testosterone level had a dynamic relationship with social adjustment.

Although predictors of *chronic* offending (as compared to *any* offending) are slow in coming in the published research, numerous published studies have reported that early onset of offending is associated with chronicity. Thus, several authors have turned their attention to the prediction of early onset. Because Moffitt had earlier proposed a theory to guide research distinguishing offenders by offending chronicity, her proposal of a biological component has been a chief source of empirical testing in this area. Several studies do support a biological component in early onset and/or chronic offending. For example, Tibbetts and Piquero found an effect of low birth weight on early onset of offending (among low-SES subjects only). Gibson, Piquero, and Tibbetts found that maternal cigarette smoking was predictive of age at first police contact (early onset) among African American males in their sample. Moffitt reports in her study of New Zealand boys that neuropsychological deficits are linked to "the kind of antisocial behavior that begins in childhood and is sustained for lengthy periods." Findings by Gibson, Piquero, and Tibbetts directly support Moffitt's interactional hypothesis—the chances of early onset of offending in their sample was significantly increased by the combined effect of low verbal IQ scores and family adversity. Taylor, Iacono, and McGue suggest that early-onset delinquency has an underlying genetic link, whereas later-onset delinquency is likely to be environmentally mediated.

In summary, the current thinking in this line of research suggests that biological factors play an important role in the development of chronic offending.

Development. As part of the reexamination of Vila's general paradigm undertaken here, we also would like to discuss the difference between "developmental criminology" and the field of child development from psychology. Though criminologists frequently write about "developmental" factors, they typically are referring to factors that *affect* the development of children, not the developmental stages known to occur across humans. Here we suggest that integrating the view of development from developmental psychology—and what is known about developmental stages in learning, language, cognitive development, morality, etc.—could guide our understanding of the impact of those other "developmental" factors on criminality.

From this point of view, development is the process of physical, intellectual, and emotional growth that begins with conception and ends with death. Contrary to a "blank slate" view,

developmental psychologists agree that development of the physical self and cognitive and emotional competencies proceeds in an orderly manner, some believe in sequential stages, and is consistent across humans—suggesting innate, gene-driven processes. Because of this, the stages at which humans face the biological and sociocultural intrusions we have been discussing may determine whether or not those factors encourage the development of criminal strategic styles. In other words, rather than having an independent effect, as in Vila's model, it might be more useful to see developmental status as an intervening factor that mediates the effect of biology and environment on the development of criminal strategic styles (motivation in the model).

During early childhood, for example, needs and desires are different from those later in life, and cognitive and emotional skills are less developed. Young children are particularly vulnerable to the parenting practices of their parents, physical or emotional abuse, certain neurotoxins, school problems, and criminal role models, and their behavioral development is deeply affected by these factors. Growing up in a disrupted family is strongly associated with child antisocial behavior—of which crime is one type. During adolescence and adulthood, these factors are likely to have a weaker effect on strategic styles because these experiences are set against a lifetime of past experiences and behavioral consequences. By adolescence, behavioral styles and psychological character are thought to be largely established. Further, highly developed cognitive skills and emotional maturity may buffer adolescents against the effects of adverse stimuli. Nevertheless, "adolescence-limited" delinquent behavior is very common, suggesting that special characteristics of human development around the age of puberty encourage or facilitate delinquent behavior. During adolescence, too, changes in needs and desires and the demands of life may change the factors that affect immediate motivation for crime. For example, situational factors such as school attachment, peer deviance, and neighborhood environment may play a significant role in the manifestation of criminal behavior. Some variability in criminal activity among adults will be expected based on needs and goals, motivations, and opportunities that arise among that age group. For example, previously unavailable opportunities to steal from the workplace may arise. Research on criminal careers and the life course also suggests that changes in social bonds (such as marriage or employment) can alter trajectories of criminal behavior.

We will discuss some of the data that bear on the development of criminality. With respect to moral valuations, it has been found that by age three children have developed the cognitive ability to reflect on intentionality and evaluate responsibility. By kindergarten, they start to apply criteria to the assessment of blame and impose a hierarchy on criteria for blameworthiness (e.g., harm should not occur, one should not cause harm, one should not mean to cause harm, and one should not mean to cause harm with malevolent motives). This suggests that children are able to learn prohibitions against aggression at a very young age and it is possible that there is a critical window for this type of social learning, which underscores the importance of socializing children against aggression early in life if we wish to minimize the use of this strategy in the population. Dodge's work suggests that the link between child abuse and later violence is the development of cognitive styles—such as hostile attribution bias—that favor interpretations of the world as hostile and aggressive, and thus favor an aggressive response to that world. The effects of child abuse, then, are probably going to vary depending on the age of the child and be at their most extreme when children are developing these cognitive processes.

In summary, the interaction between biology, experience, and developmental stage is likely to be highly relevant in the prediction of chronic offending—and chronic offending, as we know, is an important component of aggregate crime levels. The most important developmental factors include not only age, generally, but certain cognitive and physical abilities. The development of criminality requires an interaction of certain environmental or biological influences occurring at the right time. Further, if it is true that aggression is learned (and unlearned) at an early age, environmental features that are likely to promote aggressive behavioral strategies will do their best work among small children. Periods during which children are learning cognitive styles are probably very important. Data that suggest that early onset of offending is associated with later chronicity, and that biological factors are associated with early onset, provide an important indication that it is early development that creates most chronic offenders and that finding the biological and experiential correlates of early onset should be a research priority.

Unique Character of the Human Ecological Environment. Vila's model refers to "socio-cultural factors" that influence criminal behavior. Because of the ecological emphasis of this article, these factors may be seen as "ecological factors" and treated as part of the human ecological environment that affects strategy choice. In order to understand the role of ecological factors on strategy choice and style development, it is first useful to discuss what the landscape of "human ecology" looks like and the unique features of "human" ecology compared to the ecologies of other species.

Although Hawley and colleagues were sure in their definition of what constitutes an ecological factor, the literature on crime and human behavior is far more ambiguous on this point. In this discussion we see biological factors as those that inhere in the individual—including genetic factors, physiological factors, even psychological factors because they inhere in brain chemistry (even if these are caused by the environment). Like McKenzie, we refer to those factors in the physical environment that affect human behavior as being ecological. In our view this includes a wealth of factors, including those that are reminiscent of ecological studies of other species—topography, weather, and food availability, for example. We recognize that many ecological factors affect behavior by affecting brain function. For example, overcrowding may increase hostility or affect the immediate fear or well-being that individuals feel from moment to moment in different physical surroundings. Hot weather has been found to be related to deadly assault and there is some evidence for seasonality in offending, although this could be mediated by routine activities—which, in turn, often are affected by weather. People respond quite differently in hot, crowded subways or gridlocked freeways than they do in dark, lonely parking lots or serene parks.

The human physical environment has unique features. For example, the extent of man-made buildings with a variety of materials rivals that of even the most industrious animal species including ants and bees. The effects of these large-scale structures—which affect our ability to acquire food and other resources, to find mating opportunities, to rear our offspring—on our behavioral repertoire are enormous.

The human ecological environment also includes factors that affect us because of our advanced intellectual abilities and euculture. For example, indicators of "social disorganization" and signs of "social control" such as the presence of graffiti, trash, incivilities, or "broken windows," affect our behavior. Political factors, identified by Bursik, such as the presence of racial covenants, prevalence of unemployment or owner-occupied dwellings, the location of public housing, and the like, may limit our mobility or living arrangements and funnel the strategies chosen by individuals in neighborhoods.

Finally, social and cultural characteristics—beliefs, morals, behaviors, and social situations—present in the environment can be seen as part of human ecology. These are factors in the environment that affect our behavior. Though these usually manifest themselves in communications (as do bird calls or scent markings in other species), they exist as factors in the ecological landscape that shape behavior. In fact, these often overlooked features of our "ecological" environment exert an enormous effect on behavior. The human ability to learn complex language allows us to develop ideas, form concepts, and has fostered a "euculture" characterized by our unique ability to reify information. The human mind absorbs information, most of which lacks immediate relevance, and "constructs an internal reality." Although we are not the only organisms that teach and learn, humans are the only eucultural species. And the extent of behavior learned through verbal communications is exceptional among animals. Such a euculture allows factors such as political structure, zoning laws, and the like to affect behavior.

Research on environmental factors and crime center on factors that are easiest to measure. There is research that suggests that factors such as family environment (parenting practices, conflicts, and role modeling), school environment (which interacts with the characteristics of the individual to produce achievement, attachment, and attainment), neighborhood environment (social disorganization and signs of disorder and urban design), poverty, and social isolation are all correlates of criminality.

Linking Micro-Level Behavior With Macro-Level Evolution

In this discussion we have proposed that an ecological view of crime can incorporate both (a) the view that crime is "normal," and (b) the evidence that certain individuals develop criminal habits and therefore are responsible for an inordinate amount of crime. We have suggested, like Moffitt and Taylor et al., that "normative" criminal behavior strategies probably are most affected by features of the environment, including, as Cohen and Machalek suggest, their frequency-dependent payoffs. "Pathological" criminal behavior—committed by those who develop chronic offending patterns in spite of the fact that frequency-dependent payoffs tend to be low—is likely due to factors that influence the development of criminal behavioral styles in children. Now we turn to the matter of counter-strategies and the implications of what we have been discussing for the control of crime.

The biologically-rooted ecological theorists at some level assume that human motivations to behave *at all* are consistent with those of other species—and that we have evolved unconscious psychological mechanisms that enhance our ability to survive, mate, and promote our offspring. First it is useful to discuss two distinct processes from evolutionary theory that are important here. The first is that humans are likely to be equipped with psychological mechanisms designed to recognize promising behavioral strategies when they see them, to learn them easily, and to devise their own in the face of circumstances making it difficult to obtain resources in the ways they have already learned. The field of evolutionary psychology has proposed a host of related psychological mechanisms including those related to mate selection, resource acquisition (especially among males), sociability, etc. This point of view suggests that we can never eliminate criminal activity because humans are competitive, selfish, and malleable in behavior. And as long as there are resource asymmetries, or resource shortages, some humans will be motivated to use novel strategies to get what they need. From this point of view we can never hope to eliminate crime, only to minimize it. The good news for those of us living in high-crime societies like the United States, as opposed to much lower-crime societies like Canada, is that this minimum appears to be a long way off.

A second important lesson from evolutionary theory is that culture evolves in much the same way as genes do. Culture—learned behaviors, attitudes, and beliefs—is an informational medium. Culturally transmitted behavioral strategies that are successful proliferate over time. As a consequence, the relative frequency of more successful variants in a population tends to increase over time while less successful variants tend to become more rare.

Which strategies are successful tends to vary over time due to new opportunities and threats. The relative frequency with which a behavioral variant is applied in a population also affects its success, either positively or negatively (e.g., everyone driving on the same side of the road improves coordination and safety but too many people making a living as litigators can reduce average legal salaries). The implication of this is that humans learn and invent criminal behavioral strategies readily. Consequently, crime control efforts must either be very flexible and capable of countering newly devised criminal behaviors (i.e., highly adaptable) *or* they must try to prevent individuals from attempting criminal behavior strategies by making the frequency-dependent payoffs of production high when compared with crime. The former tends to result in an arms race; the latter underlines the importance of strategies that promote the distribution of resources and strong cultural prohibitions against criminal behavior.

Evolutionary theory suggests that the "ends" of *any* human behavior (including crime) are going to be consistent with the human tendency to do those things that enable us to survive, mate, and promote our offspring. For example, all else equal, humans will try to avoid physical danger, a loss of freedom, and—as inherently social beings—conflict with others because of the risks it entails and the anxiety it causes us.

From this point of view, we might expect that concerns about relationships with other human beings would have a strong influence on behavior for most people and that, to the extent that society abhors criminal behavior, most people would learn alternative strategies for getting what they need and desire. These observations suggest several courses of action in preventing "normal" criminal behavior by "normal" people, most of which have been exploited already (protection/avoidance, deterrence). But chronic offenders appear to have aberrant socialization, do not appear to respond to punishment in the same way that most people do, and confront the criminal justice system with a real conundrum. We suggest that the most efficacious way to address chronic offending is through the least-exploited of crime control strategies: nurturance

(also referred to as "developmental prevention"). In the following sections we will spend some time on each of these crime control strategies.

Protection/Avoidance Strategies. Protection/avoidance strategies attempt to reduce criminal opportunities by changing people's routine activities, increasing guardianship, or incapacitating convicted offenders. These strategies are always necessary because of the need to limit the desirability of crime and opportunities for it—and probably are most useful in preventing crime among "normal" individuals who want to avoid getting in trouble. Individuals who have other behaviors and resources at hand can easily pass up criminal opportunities where protection/avoidance is in place, choose another strategy, and crime can thus be prevented. Unfortunately, for individuals who are very criminal in their behavioral habits, the effects of new protection/avoidance counterstrategies almost invariably tend to be transitory because of arms race dynamics. Motivated offenders will respond to each counterstrategy with efforts to come up with some new expropriative or violent strategy in an endless coevolutionary cycle.

Incapacitation through incarceration, although very expensive, can be expected to have some effect on crime if chronic offenders are targeted. Other incapacitation strategies such as electronic monitoring and/or tracking bracelets that help enforce "home detention" programs also show promise. The trick is to incapacitate only the right people, and the current "three strikes and you're out" laws that proliferated in the 1980s have been criticized for definitions of "chronic offender" that include non-dangerous offenders, mostly drug addicts and dealers.

Deterrence Strategies. Deterrence strategies attempt to diminish motivation for crime by increasing the perceived certainty, severity, or celerity of punishment. A properly functioning deterrence strategy causes people who otherwise would commit a crime not to do so. Chronic offenders are particularly difficult to deter through conventional means because they already have developed criminal habits and any new experience is simply weighed against their vast past experience with offending. Since most of the time offenders do not get caught or punished for their offenses, the more crimes someone commits, the lower his estimate of his chances of being caught. Empirically, chronic offenders are more likely to be reckless, impulsive, and present-oriented than most people, suggesting that in order to affect their behavior, we need consistent and immediate sanctions.

Instead of relying on punishment alone, "neo-deterrence" theories recommend that we also increase the stake individuals have in conventional activities. These approaches seek to change individuals' cost/benefit calculations by increasing risk and opportunity costs associated with crime. Thus, they may be particularly useful for correcting the "life trajectories" of people who are spiraling toward chronic offending—or even those who have had an extended involvement in serious offending. This approach blends with the nurturant approach discussed next.

The threat of punitive sanctions will always be needed to deter more rational calculators from crime because crime often is an attractive alternative for obtaining desired resources. However, the effectiveness of punitive deterrence appears quite limited for controlling many crimes in a free society. For one thing, punitive deterrence only can work on those who have developed the skills necessary for rational calculation and the propensity to use them. It has little effect on those who are highly impulsive or who cannot calculate risks and benefits logically because, for example, they are impaired developmentally, intellectually, or perhaps, by drugs. Much crime is impulsive in nature, and the certainty of punishment for any particular criminal act generally is very low.

Nurturant Strategies. Nurturant strategies focus on prevention of the development of criminal strategic styles rather than on remediation of crime. These strategies also are referred to as "developmental prevention" because they intervene during the period when we believe criminal strategies are emerging in the developing child. These strategies are particularly important because their greatest effect will probably be in limiting the production of chronic offenders who commit a substantial proportion of crime.

There are two main types of nurturant strategies: those that improve early life experiences to forestall the development of strategic styles based on criminality, and those that channel child and adolescent development in an effort to improve the match between individuals and their environment. Social programs that attempt to address early life-course problems and channel people in productive directions are not new. But they seldom are identified explicitly as crime control strategies in public discussions, and their importance for the control of crime often is neglected. This increases the vulnerability of child development programs by making it easier for their funding to be diverted to traditional crime control strategies involving the police, courts, or prison systems.

It is well established that nurturant strategies can be effective at the individual level. Tremblay and Craig's exhaustive review of experimental research assessing the effectiveness of developmental crime prevention strategies on later delinquency and antisociality among preschool and school-age children found statistically significant treatment effects, especially when "the interventions are aimed at more than one risk factor [e.g., socially disruptive behavior, cognitive deficits, and poor parenting], last for a relatively long period of time, and are implemented before adolescence." Similar effects have been shown for earlier interventions such as pre- and perinatal health care and nutrition.

Lagged Effects. One major drawback of nurturant approaches to crime control is the long time between the institution of a nurturant program and a subsequent reduction in crime. Since few young people commit serious crimes before they enter middle adolescence, nurturant interventions tend to require a decade or more to have an impact on crime. Furthermore, even though nurturant strategies work on individuals, their impact on macro-level crime rates has not been tested extensively. Early cross-national tests of this "lagged nurturance" hypothesis yielded mixed results. However, recent evidence supports the hypothesis, suggesting that changes in national measures of early childhood health and education are negatively associated with later shifts in national crime rates and positively associated with academic achievement—which has a well-established negative relationship with crime.

DISCUSSION

The present [article] extends Vila's general paradigm of criminal behavior. Here we have presented the case that using an evolutionary-ecological paradigm, crime can both be "normal" and "pathological." Normal human beings respond to situations, act in their own self-interest, and are willing learners of any behavioral strategies that help them achieve their goals. Some human beings, who are biologically or socially disadvantaged, are repeatedly exposed to conditions that lead them to develop an inordinate dependence on criminal strategies—inordinate because the payoff for using these strategies is low.

In this [article] we have also attempted to show how this model can bridge the gap between understanding crime at the individual level and crime at the aggregate. *Individuals* develop behavioral styles; environmental factors affect the development of behavioral styles in those persons exposed to them and affect immediate situations and opportunities that affect individual criminal behavior in the moment. If environmental factors in a large society are very favorable toward criminality—pervasive poverty in a city, for example—we believe that large cohorts of individuals may develop a dependence on criminal strategies and that this can affect crime rates when those individuals reach the age of peak offending. Environmental factors may also cause cohorts of individuals who are not especially "criminal" to turn to criminal behavioral strategies when more desirable strategies do not work or their payoffs are comparatively low, for example, in times of high unemployment or civil unrest or unusually profitable criminal opportunity (like alcohol prohibition or the crack epidemic).

A unique feature of an evolutionary ecological approach to crime is that it clearly prescribes a balanced mix of protection/avoidance, deterrence, and nurturant strategies for the control of crime. An evolutionary ecological approach to understanding criminal behavior and crime control provides a flexible and useful framework for integrating information from a variety of fields and unifies our understanding of individual-level and aggregate-level crime. It also provides a format for testing hypotheses about crime causation and control at both individual and aggregate levels. The ecological model helps us understand rapidly changing dynamics of crime in urban centers. For example, in the 1980s and 1990s significant numbers of inner-city youths became involved in drug trafficking when the introduction of crack

cocaine created an opportunity for monetary gain that required little economic or social capital. The ease with which resources could be acquired by selling crack cocaine probably was weighed against the relative difficulty of working long hours for minimum wages. Those who were poor and unemployed were most vulnerable to the temptation, and many persons with borderline levels of criminality probably were lured into the drug business. Few extant theories or crime would have predicted this dramatic phenomenon.

This perspective also is able to bridge micro and macro views of criminality. It suggests that in addition to situational factors, aggregate crime rates may be affected by the size of the cohort of chronic offenders. Research already has uncovered discernible "cohort" effects but has not examined the characteristics of the cohorts that make them so criminal. It is proposed here, and remains to be empirically tested, that cohorts which are exposed to more criminogenic biological or sociocultural factors at important stages in their development—namely, early childhood—will tend to be more criminal as a group than other age cohorts.

Evolutionary ecological theory provides a natural utilitarian framework for organizing what we already know with reasonable confidence about the causes of criminal behavior. The general paradigm developed from this approach holistically describes how ecological, micro-level, and macro-level factors associated with criminal behavior interact and evolve over time, and how they influence individual development over the life course and across generations.

Applying the same well-established techniques and concepts that have unified our understanding of complex organic systems in the biological sciences—while giving special consideration to the unique properties of culture—provides a truly general perspective on human behavior. It allows us to view crime as a cultural trait whose frequency and type evolve over time as a result of dynamic interactions between individual and group behavior in a physical environment. Moreover, an appreciation of the indeterminability of these processes encourages us to consider ways to guide the evolution of culture in desirable directions.

SOURCE: From *Social Biology*, Spring 2003. Reprinted by permission of *Social Biology*.

QUESTIONS FOR DISCUSSION AND WRITING

1. What have numerous published studies reported regarding early onset of offending and chronicity?

2. What two important lessons can we learn from evolutionary theory?

3. What is a unique feature of an evolutionary ecological approach to crime? What does an evolutionary ecological approach to understanding criminal behavior and crime control provide? How can the ecological model help us understand rapidly changing dynamics of crime in urban centers? What else is this perspective able to do?

MALES ON THE LIFE-COURSE-PERSISTENT AND ADOLESCENCE-LIMITED ANTISOCIAL PATHWAYS

TERRIE E. MOFFITT

AVSHALOM CASPI

HONALEE HARRINGTON

BARRY J. MILNE

This article tests and refines a developmental taxonomy of antisocial behavior, which proposed two primary hypothetical prototypes: life-course-persistent (LCP) offenders, whose antisocial behavior begins in childhood and continues worsening thereafter, versus adolescence-limited (AL) offenders, whose antisocial behavior begins in adolescence and desists in young adulthood. If proven accurate, the taxonomic theory could usefully improve classification of subject groups for research, focus research into antisocial personality and violence toward the most promising causal variables, and guide the timing and strategies of interventions for delinquent types.

Two previous reports have described clinically defined groups of childhood-onset and adolescence-onset antisocial youths in the Dunedin birth cohort. We reported that the boys and their families could be distinguished during their childhoods on risk factors specified by the theory. We also reported each group's course of problem behavior from age 3 years to age 18 years and their distinguishing psychosocial characteristics at age 18 years. Recently we followed up the cohort at age 26 years, and here we describe how the two groups of males fared in adulthood. In so doing, we test an hypothesis *critical to the theory:* that childhood-onset, but not adolescent-onset, antisocial behavior is associated in adulthood with antisocial personality, violence, and continued serious antisocial behavior that expands into maladjustment in work life and victimization of partners and children.

THE TWO PROTOTYPES AND THEIR PREDICTED ADULT OUTCOMES

According to the theory, LCP antisocials are few, persistent, and pathological. AL antisocials are common, relatively temporary, and near normative. The developmental typology hypothesized that childhood-onset versus adolescent-onset conduct problems have different etiologies. In addition, the typology differed from other developmental crime theories by predicting different outcome pathways for the two types across the adult life course. In a nutshell, we suggested that "life-course-persistent" antisocial behavior originates early in life, when the difficult behavior of a high-risk young child is exacerbated by a high-risk social environment. According to the theory, the child's risk emerges from inherited or acquired neuropsychological variation, initially manifested as subtle cognitive deficits, difficult temperament, or hyperactivity. The environment's risk comprises factors such as inadequate parenting, disrupted family bonds, and poverty. The environmental risk domain expands beyond the family as the child ages, to include poor relations with people such as peers and teachers, then later with partners and employers. Over the first 2 decades of development, transactions between individual and environment gradually construct a disordered personality with hallmark features of physical aggression and antisocial behavior persisting to midlife. The theory invokes the developmental principle of cumulative continuity to predict that antisocial behavior will infiltrate multiple adult life domains: illegal activities, problems with employment, and victimization of intimate partners and children

In contrast, we suggested that "adolescence-limited" antisocial behavior emerges alongside puberty, when otherwise healthy youngsters experience dysphoria during the relatively roleless years between their biological maturation and their access to mature privileges and responsibilities, a period we called the maturity gap. While adolescents are in this gap it is virtually normative for them to find the LCP youths' delinquent style appealing and mimic it as a way to demonstrate autonomy from parents, win affiliation with peers, and hasten social maturation. However, because their predelinquent development was normal and healthy, most young people who become AL delinquents are able to desist from crime when they age into real adult roles, turning gradually to a more conventional lifestyle. This recovery may be delayed if the antisocial activities of AL delinquents attract factors we called snares, such as a criminal record, incarceration, addiction, truncated education without credentials, becoming a teen parent, sexually transmitted disease, or injury. Such snares can compromise the ability to make a successful transition to adulthood, impair health, and lead to social disadvantage.

DIFFERENTIAL CHILD AND ADOLESCENT RISK FACTORS FOR MALES ON THE LCP VERSUS AL PATHS IN THE DUNEDIN STUDY

Our studies of males in the Dunedin cohort have operationalized the two prototypes of antisocial behavior using both categorical and continuous statistical models, and have examined both childhood predictors and adolescent outcomes. Our studies of childhood predictors measured between ages 3 and 13 years have shown that the LCP path is differentially predicted by difficult temperament, neurological abnormalities, low intellectual ability, reading difficulties, hyperactivity, poor scores on neuropsychological tests, and slow heart rate. In contrast, study members on the AL path, despite being involved in delinquency to the same extent as their counterparts on the LCP path, tended to have backgrounds that were normative or sometimes better than the average Dunedin child's.

Our studies of adolescent outcomes measured at ages 15 and 18 years have shown that the LCP path is differentially associated in males with weak bonds to family, early school leaving, and psychopathic personality traits of alienation, impulsivity, and callousness, and with conviction for violent crimes. In contrast, the AL path is differentially associated with delinquent peers, a tendency to endorse unconventional values and a personality trait called social potency, and with nonviolent delinquent offenses.

Our findings about differential childhood risk for childhood-onset versus adolescent-onset offenders are generally in keeping with findings reported from several samples in six countries. Other studies, although not necessarily presented as a test of the two types, have reported findings consonant with predictions from the taxonomy. For example, children's hyperactivity interacts with poor parenting skill to predict early-onset antisocial behavior escalating to delinquency, a finding fitting the hypothesized origins of the LCP path. Despite this body of research, to date no study has followed the two types from preschool to adulthood to test the theory's predictions about differential adult adjustment, as does the present report.

Are Two Groups Enough? Following up "Recoveries" and "Abstainers"

The original theoretical taxonomy asserted that two prototypes, LCP and AL offenders, account for the preponderance of the population's antisocial behavior and thus warrant the preponderance of attention by theory and research. Researchers testing for the presence of the two types have since uncovered a third type that replicates across longitudinal studies. These offenders have been labeled "low-level chronics" because they offend persistently, but at a low rate, from childhood to adolescence or from adolescence to adulthood. We previously reported a small group of Dunedin study males who had exhibited extreme, pervasive, and persistent antisocial behavior problems during childhood but who, surprisingly, engaged in only low to moderate delinquency during adolescence, thus failing to meet our criterion for LCP group membership. In that report, we optimistically labeled this group "recoveries." However, persuaded by the findings about low-level chronics in other samples, we follow up the "recovery" group at age 26 years to uncover whether they indeed had recovered or instead had become low-level chronic offenders. We also examined the group's characteristics to determine what might have protected these high-risk children from becoming high-level offenders.

A final group followed up here are the rare males who manage to avoid virtually all antisocial behavior during childhood and adolescence. We earlier labeled this small group "abstainers." The taxonomic theory argued that delinquency is such a nonnative peer-group activity in adolescence that complete abstainers from delinquency must be "protected" from it by undesirable characteristics causing other teens to exclude them from social relationships. Consistent with this prediction, Dunedin abstainers described themselves at age 18 years on personality measures as extremely overcontrolled, fearful, interpersonally timid, and socially inept, and they also remained virgin. Nonetheless, they were staying the course to pursue higher education at 18 years, and thus, we follow them here to uncover whether they developed into healthy or problematic adults.

Method

The Birth Cohort

Participants are male members of the Dunedin Multidisciplinary Health and Development Study, a longitudinal investigation of health and behavior. The cohort of 1,037 children (52% male, 48% female) was constituted at age 3 years, when the investigators enrolled 91% of the consecutive births between April 1972 and March 1973 in Dunedin, New Zealand. Cohort families represent the full range of socioeconomic status in the general population of New Zealand's South Island, and they are primarily White; fewer than 7% self-identified at age 18 years as Maori or Pacific Islanders. Assessments have been conducted at ages 3 ($n = 1{,}037$), 5 ($n = 991$), 7 ($n = 954$), 9 ($n = 955$), 11 ($n = 925$), 13 ($n = 850$), 15 ($n = 976$), 18 ($n = 993$), 21 ($n = 961$), and, most recently, at age 26 years ($n = 980$; 499 males, 96% of living cohort members). Rates of diagnosed conduct disorder, self-reported delinquency, and crime victimization in New Zealand are similar to those in the United States.

Measures of Adult Outcomes

We present data for 79 measures taken at age 26 years, selected to represent five domains of adult outcome implicated by the theory: criminal offending (property crimes, rule violations, drug crimes, and violence; 24 measures), personality (8 measures), psychopathology (substance abuse and mental disorders; 19 measures), personal life (relationships with women and children; 12 measures), and economic life (education, occupation, income, unemployment and work problems; 16 measures). Each of the five domains was measured via at least two sources of data: personal interviews, official records, or questionnaires completed by informants who knew the study member well.

The Comparison Groups of the Taxonomy

This article compares groups of males already defined and described in earlier reports. To operationalize the theory of two types, comparison groups were designated on the basis of individual life histories from ages 5 to 18 years. The scales measuring antisocial behavior that were used to define the groups came from the Rutter Child Scales, completed by parents and teachers when the children were ages 5, 7, 9, and 11 years, and from the Self-Reported Delinquency interview, administered to study members at ages 15 and 18 years. The first step of the computerized algorithm divided the sample into study members who had childhood histories of antisocial behavior problems versus those who did not. Study members were considered to be antisocial children if they had evidence of extreme childhood antisocial behavior problems that were both stable across time (at least three of the assessment occasions at ages 5, 7, 9, and 11 years) and pervasive across situations (reported by parents at home and corroborated by teachers at school). The second step divided the sample into study members who participated in many antisocial acts during mid-adolescence versus those who did not. Study members were considered to be antisocial adolescents if they self-reported extreme delinquency at the age 15 interview or at the age 18 interview. On the third step, the childhood and adolescent categories were combined to yield developmental profiles.

Table 1 presents the study groups. Study members who met criteria for extreme antisocial behavior across both childhood and adolescence were designated on the *LCP path* (47 males, 10%). Study members who met criteria for extreme antisocial behavior as adolescents, but who had not been extremely antisocial as

children, were designated on the *AL path* (122 males, 26%). The LCP- and AL-path males were indistinguishable on offending, showing virtually identical and statistically indistinguishable scores at their 18th birthdays on self-reported delinquency, parent-reported conduct problems, police arrests, and court convictions.

Three additional groups were defined. Study members who met criteria for extreme antisocial behavior in childhood but whose delinquency was not extreme enough in adolescence to warrant assignment to the LCP path were designated on the *recovery* path (40 males, 8%). The few study members who had not engaged in antisocial behavior from age 5 to 18 years according to parent, teacher, or self-reports were designated as *abstainers* (25 males, 5%). Males not meeting criteria for any of the four clinical comparison groups were designated as *unclassified;* as a group their antisocial behavior was approximately normative, never differing significantly from the cohort's mean score on any of the antisocial measures from age 5 to 18 years (243 males, 51%).

Missing Follow-Up Data

All 10 measures required for classifying behavioral histories were present for 477 males (90% of cohort members alive when the groups were defined). Elsewhere we have shown that the 477 study members assigned to groups closely

TABLE 1   Follow-Up: Comparisons of Male Group Percentages With Complete Data at Age 26 Years From Self-Reported Measures, Court Conviction Records, and Informants' Reports

	Group					X2 Test of Diffs Among Groups
	Unclassified	Abstainer	Recovery	LCP Path	AL Path	
Percentage of 477 cohort males	51	5	8	10	26	
N	243	25	40	47	122	
Present data at age 26 years (%)						
Interviewed	96	100	98	89	98	ns
Court record searched[a]	98	100	100	97	97	ns
Informant questionnaire received	93	96	87	87	93	ns

NOTES:

a. Some study members who were not interviewed gave consent for records searches.

match the original representative cohort on the study's measures of antisocial behavior. Table 1 shows that at age 26 years the percentage who were successfully followed up via interviews, record searches, and informant questionnaires did not differ significantly among the five taxonomy groups.

Cumulative Index of Adjustment Problems

Figure 1 compares the groups on a composite index of 10 problems in adult adjustment (1 point each was summed for a violent conviction record, a nonviolent conviction record, a substance-dependence diagnosis, a psychiatric diagnosis, partner abuse, child abuse, no high school qualification, out-of-wedlock fatherhood, government welfare benefits, and long-term unemployment of more than 6 months). The clear majority of unclassified men had 2 or fewer of these problems. Most abstainers were problem free or had only 1 problem. Only 15% of the recovery group was free from adjustment problems, emphasizing that our earlier "recovery" label was a misnomer. Likewise, only 15% of LCP men were free of problems; moreover, two thirds of the LCP men had 3 or more problems. In contrast, two thirds of AL men had 2 or fewer problems. Four times more LCP than AL men scored at the extreme by suffering 7–10 life problems, and 70% of the cohort men with these extreme problems were LCP men. An analysis of variance test of mean group differences on this index, $F (4, 444) = 23.4, p < .001$, with planned contrasts revealed that the LCP, AL, and recovery groups had significantly more problems than the unclassified and abstainer groups, but the LCP group had significantly more problems than each of the other four groups (all $p < .01$). The AL and recovery groups did not differ significantly from each other.

DISCUSSION

This look at 79 outcome variables attests that antisocial disorders have a very wide nomothetic net, and reinforces the usefulness of heterotypic continuity as a developmental concept. This section will discuss each of the four groups in turn, summarize how each group fared at age 26 years, observe whether the group's outcomes fit the theory's predictions, note how outcomes

may follow from the group's childhood or adolescent characteristics, speculate about how group members will fare in the future as they age, and discuss implications for intervention.

The Abstainer Group: Now Successful Young Adults

Abstainers were originally defined as males with no more than one antisocial problem at any assessment age from 5 to 18 years, according to all reporters. Abstainers so defined comprised 5% of cohort males. The theory anticipated that abstainers would be this rare because it argued that some delinquency is virtually normative for contemporary adolescents. According to the theory, if adolescence-limited delinquency is normative, adaptational social behavior, then the existence of teens who abstain from delinquency requires explanation. The theory speculated that teens committing no antisocial behavior must have either structural barriers that prevent them learning about delinquency, no experience of the maturity gap because of early access to adult roles, or personal characteristics that exclude them from peer networks. Our study of the Dunedin abstainers as teens suggested that the latter might be true; as 18-year-olds they were overcontrolled, timid, and socially awkward, unusually good students, and latecomers to heterosexual relationships. Dunedin abstainers fit the profile Shedler and Block reported for youth abstaining from drug experimentation at a time when it was normative, who were described as overcontrolled, not curious, not active, not open to experience, socially isolated, and lacking social skills. Dunedin abstainers also fit the profile of the compliant good student who during adolescence becomes unpopular with peers.

In our 1996 paper we speculated that Dunedin abstainers might as adults be late bloomers. Data at age 26 years show that they have bloomed. From adolescence they retained their personality profile of unusually strong self-constraint, but in adulthood this style seems to have become successful. As adults the abstainer men had virtually no crime or diagnosable mental disorders, and a count of 10 possible adjustment problems showed they were virtually free of these. According to their informants they had the least problem behaviors of all men in the cohort. As a group they were the most likely to

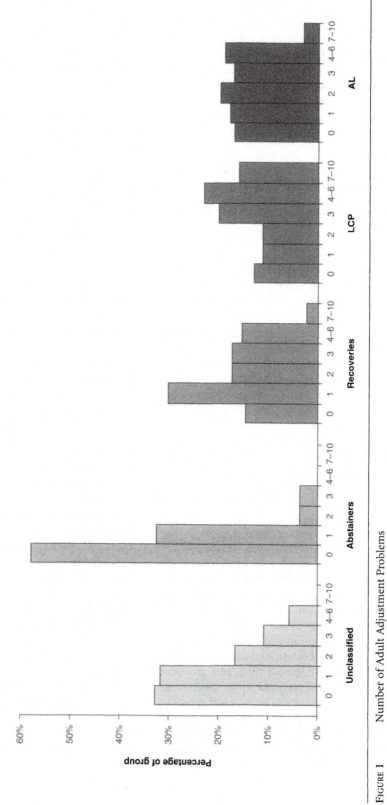

FIGURE 1   Number of Adult Adjustment Problems

have settled into marriage and to have a happy relationship, and they were delaying children (a desirable strategy for a generation needing prolonged education to succeed). They held the highest status jobs in the cohort, though their incomes were not the highest, probably because they pursued postgraduate studies or held entry-level white-collar jobs. They were the most likely to be college educated and financially responsible, the least likely to have problems in their work lives, and they expressed optimism about their own futures. We share that optimism.

The Recovery Group: Misnamed Earlier, Now Suffering "Internalizing" Problems

The so-called recovery group was originally defined as males with stable, pervasive, and extreme antisocial problems in childhood but whose participation in delinquency during adolescence was only moderate and not extreme enough to meet criteria for membership in the LCP group. Recoveries so defined comprised 8% of cohort males. This group was something of a surprise to the theory, because it argued that early onset antisocial behavior initiates a chain of cumulative disadvantage that perpetuates disordered behavior, and on that basis it predicted that "false positive subjects, who meet criteria for a stable and pervasive antisocial childhood history and yet recover (eschew delinquency) after puberty, should be extremely rare." The data at age 26 years suggest that, as predicted, true recoveries are extremely rare. Recovery was clearly a misnomer prematurely assigned to some group members, as more than one quarter subsequently engaged in illegal behavior as adults. Their offending pattern may fit an oft-observed pattern referred to as "intermittency" or "suspension," in which some offenders are not convicted for a period but then reappear in the courts. The group's self-reported offending at age 26 years is at the cohort norm, 28% had been convicted of crimes as adults (10% for violent crimes), and the group accounted for approximately its share of offenses and convictions of all types. Regarding illegal activities, this group of antisocial children participated as adolescents and as adults, albeit at low levels. Over time, the Dunedin recovery group's offending pattern closely resembles that of the "low-level chronic offenders," first identified in trajectory analyses of a British cohort.

Researchers have been curious about this group since it was described in our 1996 paper, speculating optimistically that recoveries might be children who experienced some strong protective factor(s). Anticipating true recoveries to be extremely rare, the theory had proffered no specific explanation for what sort of people they would be. However, the theory had broadly argued that teens who engage in less delinquency than expected might have off-putting personal characteristics that excluded them from the peer groups in which most delinquency happens. Thus, to keep faith with the theory, we were obliged to consider whether boys in the recovery group might be social isolates. Our earlier study of the recoveries revealed no protective factors; they had extremely undercontrolled temperaments as 3-year-olds, and as teens they had unremarkable scores on most measures. (Unpublished analyses showed that they shared with the LCP males low IQ and family adversity in childhood.)

This in-depth age 26 years follow-up reveals more, suggesting that this group is unique from the other males in suffering from internalizing forms of psychopathology. As many as one-third of this group had diagnosed depression or anxiety disorders, their personality profile showed elevated neuroticism, and their informants rated them as the most depressed and anxious men in the cohort. Members of this group, unlike other cohort men, were often social isolates; their informants reported that they had difficulty making friends, none had married, and many had diagnoses of agoraphobia or social phobia. Almost all adults with social phobia meet criteria for co-morbid avoidant, dependent, or schizotypal personality disorders. Thus, although these personality disorders have not been diagnosed in the Dunedin study, we speculate that men in this group may suffer from them. This pattern in which formerly antisocial boys develop into depressed, anxious, and socially isolated men resembles closely a finding from a British longitudinal study of males followed from ages 8 to 32 years. In that study, boys at high risk who were as adults "false positives" (committing less crime than predicted) were found to have few or no friends, had low-paying jobs, lived in dirty home conditions, and had been described in case records as withdrawn, highly strung, obsessional, nervous, or timid. If we look to this Dunedin group of high-risk boys to reveal what protective factors prevented them from involvement in serious crime, our findings and Farrington's are not uplifting. To the extent that much delinquency is a group activity, the members of the recovery group may have been "protected" by their social isolation. Consistent with this hypothesis, they were at age 26 years quite unlikely to be involved with drugs or alcohol (also a finding in the British study), perhaps the most social among the problem behaviors we measured.

There was good evidence that the men in the recovery group suffered life impairment. One-third had experienced treatment for mental health problems in the past year. As a group they had completed less education than average and few had attended college. They had low-status occupations, many financial difficulties, and expressed the least hope for their futures. Robins is often quoted as having said that one half of conduct-problem boys do not grow up to have antisocial personalities. Such quotations imply that early conduct problems are fully malleable and need not be a cause for pessimism. However, less often quoted is Robins' observation that conduct-problem boys who do not develop antisocial personalities generally suffer other forms of maladjustment as adults. Our count of 10 adjustment problems showed that only 15% of Dunedin's 87 young boys with childhood-onset conduct problems (i.e., 47 LCP and 40 recoveries) truly "recovered," escaping all adjustment problems. Farrington et al. noted that, "there seemed to be no real success stories." This finding is consistent with our theory's emphasis on the importance of childhood adjustment for adult adjustment. It also suggests that prevention programs targeting antisocial children will not be wasted on the half who are not on course to become LCP offenders.

The LCP Group: Most Violent and Least Likely to Reform

The LCP group comprised males with stable, pervasive, and extreme antisocial behavior in childhood plus extreme delinquent involvement in adolescence. The males so defined comprised 10% of cohort males. The theory predicted that these males would still be antisocial when they reached adulthood, and would have worse outcomes than their AL counterparts. In the year prior to age 26 years, Dunedin LCP men compared to AL men were significantly more involved as a group in serious criminal offending, according to self-reports. They were 2–3 times more likely than AL men to have been convicted as adults, which attests to the relatively greater seriousness of their offenses. A comparison of specific offenses suggested that LCP men tended to specialize in serious offenses (carrying a hidden weapon, assault, robbery, violating court orders), whereas AL men specialized in nonserious offenses (theft less than $5, public drunkenness, giving false information on application forms, pirating computer software). According to their informants' reports, LCP men had significantly more symptoms of antisocial personality disorder than AL men. As predicted by the theory, LCP men as a group particularly differed from AL men in the realm of violence, including violence against women and children. LCP men accounted for 5 times their share of the cohort's violent offenses. This violence difference was corroborated by all three data sources (self-reports, informant reports, official records) with large effect sizes. In addition, compared to AL men, LCP men had a more psychopathic personality profile (present since 18 years) and the informants who knew them well viewed them as having more serious psychiatric and behavior problems. Our count of 10 possible adjustment problems showed that most of the LCP men were heavily burdened by problems in multiple life domains.

The theory predicted that LCP offenders would have difficulty desisting from crime at turning point opportunities such as marriage or employment, because unlike AL delinquents, LCP delinquents would selectively get undesirable jobs and partners, and their limited behavioral repertoire would lead them to express antisocial behavior at work and at home. This article did not examine within-individual change in response to turning point opportunities, but several findings suggest that the LCP men are unlikely to benefit in the near future from the reforming effects of a good job. At age 26 years, relative to their peers, they had poor work histories in low status unskilled jobs, lacked the minimum education qualifications needed to get a good job, made a poor interpersonal impression in an interview-type situation, and had official records for serious crimes that may deter employers. LCP men's substance-dependence problems and tendency to get into conflicts at work are likely to prevent advancement in the low-skill jobs they are able to get. They are also unlikely to benefit in the near future from the reforming effects of a good woman and family, in view of their extreme personality traits of negative emotionality and callousness, their tendency to use abuse to control women, and their inclination to father unusual numbers of children but not stay to help rear them.

At first, our assertion that opportunities for change will often be turned by LCP men into opportunities for continuity seems at odds with the work of Sampson and Laub's turning point theory. These sociologists have generated the compelling theory, and lots of empirical evidence, that desistence from crime is due to salient life events at key points in the life course (e.g., a good marriage, a stable job, new opportunities in the military). The events engender social bonds which exert informal social controls on criminals and help them to reform. However, our theory and our findings here question whether LCP men develop such bonds. In related research in the Dunedin study, we found that only about one quarter of the study members with a preexisting antisocial propensity had elevated scores on social bonds that might deter crime in young adulthood, compared to about three quarters of the other study members. Elsewhere, we reported that young men with an antisocial history are very likely to pair off with an antisocial woman, and that when they do, this promotes further continuity of offending. These studies suggest that although new social bonds *can* generate turning points in the life course, they do not *do* so for the majority of LCP-type men because these men are unlikely to encounter salubrious turning point opportunities. We think our findings fit turning point theory, as it emphasizes that jobs or relationships must be of *good quality* to reform an offender, and would see little reforming potential in the jobs and relationships of the Dunedin LCP men at age 26 years.

Although Sampson and Laub have shown the power of turning points while controlling for prior delinquency during adolescence (official delinquent status, yearly arrest rate, unofficial delinquency), we have found that such adolescent measures do not differentiate AL from LCP trajectories. Turning point theory may thus apply best to that majority of offenders who are AL, not LCP. Research on criminal reform has not yet isolated the longitudinal LCP trajectory to test whether LCP offenders benefit from

turning points. Sampson and Laub note that turning points can occur well into midlife, and their generative theory will be a focus of our longitudinal research as members of the Dunedin study age into midlife. Indeed, we expect Dunedin LCP men to encounter more turning point opportunities after age 26 years, as we explain in the next section. However, at age 26 years, we see mainly evidence of transactions between LCP men's undesirable behavior and negative reactions to it from courts, employers, women, and informants who know them well. Such person-environment transactional processes have been shown to promote persistence of antisocial behavior.

The AL Group: Problems Not Limited to Adolescence

Males on the AL trajectory were originally defined as males with unremarkable antisocial behavior in childhood but extreme delinquent involvement in adolescence. The males so defined comprised 26% of cohort males. The theory predicted that these males would have better outcomes when compared to their LCP counterparts. This particular prediction was supported for 68 of the 79 outcome measures, albeit only 33 with statistical significance (the previous section summarized the significant differences between AL and LCP men).

The theory also predicted that "before taking up delinquency adolescence-limited offenders have ample years to develop a repertoire of prosocial behaviors and basic academic skills that make them eligible for post-secondary education, good marriages, and desirable jobs." This prediction also found support. At age 26 years, AL men as a group stand a better chance than LCP men of benefiting from a good job; they had better work histories and skilled occupations, 80% of them had the high school qualifications needed to get a good job, they made a reasonable if not salutary impression in an interview-type situation, and fewer of them had conviction records to deter employers. As a result, at age 26 years they held higher status jobs than LCP men. This is not surprising because, as children and adolescents, AL men had average or better scores on factors known to predict labor-market success, they had normal IQ scores and were good readers, and they had elevated scores on a personality trait called social potency.

AL men also stand a better chance than LCP men of benefiting from the reforming effects of a good woman. They described themselves as being about as agreeable (not callous) and extraverted as the average male; they had engaged in some physical conflict with partners but were not inclined to be unusually controlling of them. As children and adolescents, AL men had average or better scores on factors that predict relationship success; they had average family relationships, average temperaments, and were not rejected by peers, and they had close attachments to their parents and elevated scores on a personality trait called social closeness. The findings at age 26 years are consistent with the theory's note that "adolescence-limited delinquents can profit from opportunities for desistence, because they retain the option of resuming a conventional lifestyle."

Despite all this promise, the AL men at 26 years were still in trouble. Although AL men fared better overall than the LCP men, they fared poorly relative to the "unclassified" men (who represented males with no remarkable delinquency history). AL men accounted for twice their share of the property and drug convictions accumulated by the cohort during adulthood, and they also self-reported an impressive number of past-year property and drug-related offenses at age 26 years. Though their informants said they had fewer mental health problems than LCP men, as many AL men as LCP men self-reported symptoms sufficient to earn a psychiatric diagnosis. Our count of 10 possible adjustment outcomes revealed that it was normative for AL men to suffer 1–3 of those.

Why are so many AL men still in trouble past the transition to adulthood? The very name "adolescence-limited" reveals that this much offending by AL men at age 26 years was not anticipated by our theory. One possible explanation for the AL men's poor outcomes at 26 years is that the theory is fundamentally incorrect in its assertion that the characteristics and experiences distinguishing LCP from AL men in childhood also have consequences for adulthood. It is possible that once a person becomes delinquent he has the same chance as any other delinquent to persist, no matter what his life was like prior to offending. However, we retain the theory's view that this is unlikely, because this follow-up at age 26 years has revealed distinctions between the LCP and AL men that auger greater reform potential for AL men. Consider personality, for

example. The LCP men rated significantly worse than the AL men on negative emotionality and callousness, traits in the psychopathic cluster associated with long-term persistence of antisocial behavior even in the face of strong treatment. In contrast, the AL group's personality profile at age 26 years was remarkable mainly for impulsivity. Impulsivity may contribute to the AL men's problems at 26 years but is also known to be the trait most susceptible to change with adult experience, so it should not preclude crime desistence in the future. Others have shown that delinquents with intellectual and emotional resources like the Dunedin AL men's are unlikely to offend as adults. We speculate that Dunedin AL men have the capacity to reform, and will do so in future, but for historical reasons they have not yet had the opportunity.

Our expectation that desistence from crime would be well underway by age 26 years was based on age-crime curves for cohorts born in the 1930s to 1950s, but these curves may no longer apply. The Dunedin cohort, like other young people born in developed nations after 1970, is experiencing a prolonged and unprecedented maturity gap. This shift has prompted the contemporary view that true adulthood now begins after age 25 years, whereas a new developmental stage called "emerging adulthood" prolongs the crime-promoting conditions of adolescence. This stage is characterized by roleless floundering, in which young people neither perceive themselves to be adults nor choose to occupy any of the adult roles historically favored by people in their 20s (e.g., parenthood, marriage). In New Zealand at the turn of the millennium the mean age of men's first marriage is 29 years, the mean age men first become the identified father of a child is 31 years, and jobs are remote because the unemployment rate is 18% for workers under age 24 years and 50% for workers lacking high school graduation. This suggests that up to the time they were interviewed at their 26th birthdays, Dunedin men were still inside the "maturity gap" that (according to the theory) promotes AL offending. Our theory predicted that AL offenders would reform, because "when aging delinquents attain the adult privileges they coveted as teens the consequences of illegal behavior shift from rewarding to punishing." Sampson and Laub similarly predict that offenders reform because they form bonds to jobs and spouses. Whether privileges or bonds, adulthood's turning points are yet in the future for most of the men in our study. The account of AL crime participation at age 26 years advanced in this paragraph is consistent with our theory's argument that AL delinquency is "a byproduct of modernization" and its prediction that the strongest predictors of offending by AL individuals should be "attitudes toward adulthood and autonomy, and cultural and historical context."

Prolonged adolescence may delay the helpful turning point experiences that prompt ALs to reform, but prolonged adolescence may also increase the period of exposure to "snares," which are harmful turning point experiences. The theory predicted that "variability in age at desistance from crime should be accounted for by the cumulative number and type of ensnaring life events that entangle persons in a deviant lifestyle." Many AL men at 26 years appeared to suffer such snares that might retard desistance from crime. Though most AL men earned a high school certification, most lost out on higher education. Though the AL men have better jobs than LCP men, many AL men relied on crime for a significant portion of their incomes, echoing ethnographic findings that crime can be too profitable to give up. Though the AL men's conviction records were not as extensive as those of LCP men, many AL men believed that their criminal record harms their employment chances, reinforcing legal scholars' plea to the courts to give AL offenders "room to reform." Ominously, many of the AL men had substance-dependence problems.

Is the label "adolescence-limited" still appropriate? We think so, because the theory as written can account for the poor outcomes of Dunedin AL men at age 26 years. The theory specified adolescence as the developmental period for AL offending, and the crime-promoting conditions of adolescence now extend to the mid-20s. The theory acknowledged that some AL delinquents would desist later than others because they encountered snares, and this appears to be happening. At 26 years, the AL men may be poised to desist crime in their late 20s (if the theory is right) or they may be on a trajectory toward equifinality with the LCP men's very poor outcomes in a few years (proving the theory wrong). Whether Dunedin AL men are in trouble at 26 years because their cohort's maturity gap is prolonged (and the

theory is right), or because adult adjustment is not influenced by childhood experience (and the theory is wrong), awaits further follow-up.

Limitations and Implications

This study has clear limitations. First, we did not examine females, but we were hampered in our capacity to do this because the 1% population base rate of LCP women is too low to study their outcomes with statistical power in a cohort the size of ours. Second, the comparison groups we studied were defined several years ago using cutoff methods that have recently been superseded by trajectory-detection methods less susceptible to misclassification error. Our future studies will adopt trajectory methods to determine if similar groups emerge from a nonparametric theory-free search of the Dunedin data set, and if their prevalence rates, predictors, and correlates fit the theory. Third, the analyses here compared the groups' outcomes at a cross section in their lives but did not examine within-individual change in variables such as delinquency or substance-dependence symptoms during the transition from adolescence (age 18 years) to adulthood (age 26 years). Our future studies will adopt growth modeling approaches to examine whether change in antisocial participation is responsive to individual differences in the timing of jobs and relationships and whether such responsiveness is a function of childhood history and snares. These methods will help to determine whether our taxonomic prototypes can be justified in place of the more parsimonious theories linking delinquency as a dimension to its correlates. The findings from this follow-up must be confirmed by other researchers and extended in our studies using trajectory and growth models (and future follow-ups), before there is a solid evidence base to support detailed recommendations for intervention. For now, our findings from comparisons of the groups in childhood, adolescence, and young adulthood make three suggestions. First, the antisocial trajectory defined by persistent disregard of the rights of others from ages 3 to 26 years (and associated with a host of neurodevelopmental, family, school, and peer problems) warrants early, sustained, and assiduous intervention to prevent economic failure, mental illness, street violence, and family violence. Second, the antisocial trajectory defined by conduct problems in childhood but only low-level antisocial involvement thereafter also warrants early intervention, mainly to prevent poor economic outcomes. When treating this group, we must keep in mind that, whereas their depression, anxiety, and social isolation are undesirable, they may protect against the delinquency and drug use that is otherwise expected. Third, the trajectory defined by post-pubertal onset of delinquency clearly warrants intervention, mainly to prevent future acquisitive crimes and, in particular, drug- and alcohol-related problems. In other words, effective intervention is needed for antisocial behavior exhibited early, or late.

SOURCE: From *Development and Psychopathology*, Vol. 14, 179–207. Copyright © 2002 Cambridge University Press. Reprinted with the permission of Cambridge University Press.

QUESTIONS FOR DISCUSSION AND WRITING

1. In a nutshell, what is life-course-persistent pathways antisocial behavior? In contrast, what is adolescence-limited antisocial behavior?

2. Who were abstainers and what did data at age 26 show for them? Who were the recovery group and what did data at age 26 show for them?

3. Who were the LCP group and what did data at age 26 show for them? Who were the AL group and what did data at age 26 show for them?

THE RELATIONSHIPS AMONG SELF-BLAME, PSYCHOLOGICAL DISTRESS, AND SEXUAL VICTIMIZATION

KIMBERLY HANSON BREITENBECHER

The primary purpose of this investigation was to examine the factor structure of survivors' attributions for previously experienced assaults and implications of these attributions for psychological adjustment. Previous research on this issue has yielded mixed findings. Some studies have found that behavioral self-blame and characterological self-blame are related to poor psychological adjustment. One study found that, although both types of self-blame are associated with poor adjustment, the relationship between characterological self-blame and poor adjustment is stronger than that between behavioral self-blame and adjustment. One study found that, although characterological self-blame is associated with poor outcomes, behavioral self-blame is somewhat protective against distress.

Our ability to interpret these findings is limited by several factors, including possible problems with the content validity of the scales that researchers have used to measure behavioral self-blame. For example, the scales by Frazier and Meyer and Taylor include items such as "I am too trusting" and "I am too impulsive." One could argue that these items might be more accurately described as assessing personality variables. In addition, inspection of these items suggests that they may not adequately sample

the theoretical construct of behavioral self-blame among survivors of acquaintance rape. This problem is particularly important because research suggests that the majority of victims of sexual assault have been assaulted by someone they know. One primary purpose of the current investigation was to develop a more comprehensive measure of self-blame, a measure that more adequately samples self-blaming statements relevant to survivors of acquaintance rape. Based on previous research in this area, it was hypothesized that factor analysis of this measure would yield at least two factors, one reflecting characterological self-blame and one reflecting behavioral self-blame.

A second purpose of the current investigation was to assess the relationship between self-blame and frequency of past victimizations. Although previous researchers hypothesized that behavioral self-blame would be associated with perceived future avoidability of assault, no researchers have directly assessed whether behavioral self-blame is associated with actual avoidance of assault. Based on intuitive notions about behavioral self-blame, one could posit two competing hypotheses. For example, self-blame of any type might lead to a sense of demoralization and low self-efficacy, which could in turn limit a woman's ability to defend herself in a rape-threatening situation. Thus, behavioral self-blame might be associated with increased frequency of sexual victimization. On the other hand, research shows that certain situational variables, such as alcohol consumption and isolation of incident site, are associated with sexual victimization. A woman who blames her own behaviors for her assault might change her behavior in such a way as to minimize her exposure to such situational variables. For example, she might reduce her tendency to drink alcohol while on dates. Thus, behavioral self-blame could also be associated with decreased frequency of victimization. Given the plausibility of these two competing hypotheses, no specific hypotheses regarding the relationship between behavioral self-blame and frequency of sexual victimization were made in the current study.

METHOD

Participants

Participants in this investigation included 416 women recruited from undergraduate psychology classes at a small, Midwestern university. Recruitment sheets described a study of "sexual experiences among college women." Preliminary screening (described below) indicated that 224 (54%) of these women had experienced sexual victimization. Analysis of demographic data indicated that these survivors of sexual assault were primarily heterosexual (97%), White (90%) women in their first (65%) or second (17%) year of college. Eighty percent of the women were single; 16% were married. The women ranged in age from 17 to 53 years, and the mean age was 21.7. Most women reported that they were involved in long-term monogamous relationships with men (44%) or dated men casually (25%).

Procedures

Participants read and signed a consent form that described the study and compensation for participation. Participants then responded to the survey instruments described below. After completing the survey instruments, participants were provided with a debriefing form and awarded partial course credit.

Measures

Demographic Survey. All participants responded to a brief demographic survey assessing such variables as age, race, sexual orientation, and socioeconomic status.

Modified Sexual Experiences Survey. To assess sexual victimization history, participants responded to a modified version of the Sexual Experiences Survey (SES). Originally developed by Koss et al., the SES reflects various degrees of sexual victimization and does not include the word *rape*. Research suggests that women respond to the SES in an accurate and truthful manner, and that the SES has good internal consistency reliability. The original version of the SES was modified to expand the definition of *intercourse* to include anal intercourse and oral intercourse (as well as vaginal intercourse). The modified version of the SES used in the current investigation contains nine items written in yes/no format. To create a summary score reflective of history of victimization, participants' responses to the nine items of the modified SES were summed. Thus, scores could range from zero to nine, with higher scores being reflective of increased frequency of past victimizations.

Situational Factors Survey. The Situational Factors Survey (SFS) includes 13 items that have been used by previous researchers to assess assault characteristics such as the nature of the relationship between the victim and the perpetrator, the forcefulness of the assault, the nature of the victim's resistance, and whether victim and/or perpetrator were using drugs or alcohol.

Sexual Victimization Attributions Measure. As previously described, one important goal of the current investigation was to develop a measure that more thoroughly samples the construct of self-blame, particularly among survivors of acquaintance assault. The Sexual Victimization Attributions Measure (SVAM) contains 55 statements reflecting factors that a survivor may perceive as having contributed to her assault. Typical of such items are the following: "I am a poor judge of character" and "There is too much violence on TV." In addition, the SVAM contains multiple newly developed items intended to assess self-blame such as "I am naïve," "I made out with him," and "I didn't run away." To minimize a possible victim-blaming message, the SVAM also includes multiple newly developed items to assess perpetrator blame. Typical items include the following: "He gave me alcohol or drugs," "He is cruel or mean," and "He used physical force or threatened to physically force me." Participants were instructed to indicate the extent to which they perceived that each item explained why they were assaulted by responding on a Likert-type scale ranging from 1 (not at all true) to 5 (completely true). Participants who had experienced more than one victimization were asked to consider their first, most severe experience (i.e., the highest numbered item on the modified SES to which they responded "yes") as they responded to items on the SVAM.

Perceptions of Future Avoidability. The current investigation included one item assessing participants' perceptions of future avoidability. This item was "Do you feel that the experience could be avoided in the future?" Participants responded on a Likert-type scale, ranging from 1 (not at all) to 5 (completely).

Psychological Distress. To assess psychological distress, participants responded to the Symptom Checklist-90-Revised (SCL-90-R). the SCL-90-R includes scales measuring somatization, obsessive-compulsive symptoms, interpersonal sensitivity, depression, anxiety, hostility, phobic anxiety, paranoid ideation, psychoticism. The SCl-90-R also includes a Global Severity Index.

Results

Preliminary Screening for Sexual Victimization History

Participants' responses to the modified SES were analyzed to screen for sexual victimization history. Results indicated that 224 (54%) participants had experienced sexual victimization prior to their participation in the current study. These data are consistent with national survey data on the prevalence of sexual assault among college women. Summary modified SES scores among this group of survivors ranged from 1 to 9, with a mean of 2.5 and a standard deviation of 1.7. Analysis of participants' responses to the SFS indicated that 194

(88%) of victimized women had been assaulted by someone they knew.

Discussion

The primary purpose of the current investigation was to assess the survivors' attributions for previously experienced assaults. Inherent in this task was the development of a new measure called the Sexual Victimization Attributions Measure (SVAM). Results indicated that survivors' attributions for their assaults were composed of five factors: perpetrator blame, characterological self-blame, situational and/or chance blame, behavioral self-blame, and societal blame. The emergence of two separate factors for characterological self-blame and behavioral self-blame supports the first hypothesis regarding the existence of these two constructs. It should be noted, however, that although these constructs are separable, they are also related. The bivariate correlation between the characterological self-blame factor and the behavioral self-blame factor was significant, $r = .43$, $p < .05$. This finding is consistent with previous research. The emergence of the factor representing societal blame is consistent with the findings of Frazier and Meyer and Taylor, who documented similar survivor attributions. The situational and/or chance factors are new to the current investigation.

Unlike most previous research, the results of the current study indicate that behavioral self-blame and characterological self-blame are differentially related to psychological distress. Characterological self-blame, but not behavioral self-blame, was positively correlated with psychological distress. These results are consistent with that of Hill and Zautra and Koss et al., who documented stronger relationships between characterological self-blame and distress than behavioral self-blame and distress. In the current investigation, the analysis indicated that characterological self-blame was the only significant predictor of psychological distress. It is interesting to note that characterological self-blame was a more important predictor of distress than frequency of past victimization and perceived avoidability of future assaults.

A second goal of the current study was to investigate the relationship between behavioral self-blame and frequency of past sexual victimization. Although behavioral self-blame was significantly correlated with perceptions of future avoidability, it was not significantly correlated with frequency of past sexual victimization. The results of the current study indicated that the best predictor of frequency of past victimization was perpetrator blame. Given the retrospective nature of these data, it is unclear whether higher levels of perpetrator blame for the index victimization led to greater risk for future victimization, whether histories of more frequent victimization led to greater levels of perpetrator blame for the index victimization, or whether some third variable (not measured in the current study) was responsible for the association between these two constructs. Characterological self-blame, although positively correlated with frequency of victimization, did not emerge as a significant predictor in the multiple regression analysis.

Limitations of the current study include the fact that the results are generalizable only to college women, and that the data are retrospective in nature. Thus, definitive causal interpretations about the relationships among characterological self-blame, perpetrator blame, and negative outcomes (greater levels of distress and victimization, respectively) cannot be made. The results of a recent longitudinal investigation indicate that decreases in behavioral self-blame over time are associated with decreases in distress. In contrast, the results of a recent cross-sectional study suggest that characterological self-blame is distressing and harmful to health, whereas behavioral self-blame is somewhat protective against distress. Thus, the available data are conflicting, and future prospective studies are needed to clarify this issue.

SOURCE: From *Journal of Interpersonal Violence*, Vol. 21, No. 5, 597–611, May, 2006. Copyright © 2006 Sage Publications. Reprinted by permission of Sage Publications, Inc.

QUESTIONS FOR DISCUSSION AND WRITING

1. What was one primary purpose of the current investigation?

2. What was the second purpose of the current investigation? Which two competing hypotheses did the author note for the relationship between self-blame and avoidance of assault?

3. What do the results of the current study indicate regarding the relationship of behavioral self-blame and characterological self-blame to psychological distress?

PART X

How Do We Control Crime?

Crime and Social Control

This section ends the volume, but it also represents a beginning. After one learns about the nature and explanations of crime, one is better prepared to consider what society should do to control crime.

We have seen that many social structures and forces, such as families, schools, and communities, are implicated in the control of crime. These institutions and structures, although not created to control crime, are nonetheless effective regulators of behavior. In fact, many criminologists believe that the informal structures of social control are more important than the formal mechanisms of the criminal justice system. Informal controls, together with the norms and values they reinforce, are a more effective means of social control because they are always with us. Police and other control agents cannot possibly keep us under surveillance at all times, nor do we want them to. Yet although informal systems of control are more effective than the formal criminal justice system, complex modern societies need police, courts, and means of punishing and reforming those who violate the law.

Unfortunately, there is a tendency for some people with a public voice, by virtue of their political position, media platform, or "expert" status, to shoot from the hip when making pronouncements about crime and how we should reform the criminal justice system. This is unfortunate because such statements are often made by speakers with a superficial understanding of the crime problem and what is likely to improve crime control. That is why we say that these concluding chapters are, in some sense, a beginning. Having studied a sample of criminology, the reader is now prepared to learn more about crime. This volume provides only a foundation, not everything there is to know about criminology

In this section, we present six articles that represent important dimensions of informed debates on crime control. We say "informed" because the articles reflect an understanding of crime and its causes that, unlike many ideas and arguments that students will have read and heard, is based on study and considered thinking. Nevertheless, the articles reflect radically different positions and have significant disagreements. Students should examine each of these articles with at least three issues in mind:

1. What are the authors' recommendations for controlling crime?

2. What are the authors' underlying assumptions about the causes of crime (or factors related to trends in crime)?

3. Are the authors' assumptions about crime, its causes, and its control consistent with what we have learned from readings in the previous chapters?

The first selection is by Steven Messner and Richard Rosenfeld, "Strengthening Institutions and Rethinking the American Dream." Messner and Rosenfeld call into question crime control reforms over the past four decades, arguing that none have yielded major reductions in criminal behavior. In reviewing these reforms, they assert that none have achieved the fundamental social and cultural changes needed to reduce crime. Reducing crime requires that we significantly strengthen our schools and families and also promote a culture that accords importance to individual restraint and collective interest.

James Q. Wilson and George Kelling's "Broken Windows," originally published in the *Atlantic Monthly,* sparked national debate over the role of police in crime control in the 1980s. Wilson and Kelling draw an analogy between petty crimes in communities and broken windows in abandoned buildings. They argue that petty crimes will lead to more crimes if there is no community or societal response, just as one broken window in an abandoned building will lead to more, if left unrepaired. Their essay stimulated a new approach to policing that shifted the emphasis of police work from simply enforcing laws to maintaining public order in communities.

It does not matter whether readers agree with Wilson and Kelling or Messner and Rosenfeld, but we would like to convince those who part these pages to see the wisdom in raising the level of public discourse about crime and criminal justice. Unfortunately, many people, some in positions of power and influence, have, as a former mayor of Seattle put it, slipped into speaking in bumper sticker slogans about what we should do about crime. When we reduce criminal justice reform to changes that are intuitively appealing yet inconsistent with what we know of crime and criminals (e.g., "three strikes and you're out"), we fail to consider fully the wisdom, or folly, of such a policy in light of our knowledge about crime. To confront crime more effectively, we need fewer bumper stickers and more reasoned debate. Wilson and Kelling and Messner and Rosenfeld provide models of how this discussion should proceed.

The authors of the next three chapters take on specific issues and reforms in criminal justice. Radelet and Borg examine 25 years of debate about the death penalty in the U.S. They were especially interested in the influence of social science research on public opinion about the most severe sanction. Their review leads them to conclude that what we have been learning is influencing a move toward less use of execution, and they predict that with time, the U.S. will abolish the death penalty.

"Abolish the Juvenile Court" by Barry Feld will seem like a radical idea to many students. If they recognize that Feld is a real champion of child offenders they may be even more confused. Those students should recognize that the juvenile court has changed a great deal since its inception in 1899. Feld argues that the contemporary court provides neither the solicitous care that founders envisioned, nor justice. In fact, recent decades have seen a number of changes where state legislatures have required the juvenile court to be more punitive, yet in most instances young offenders are not afforded protections that adults routinely enjoy. If this is the case, Feld reasons, the juvenile court should be abolished, age should be a factor taken into account by the criminal justice system, and young citizens should be guaranteed the same justice that adults receive.

Mara Schiff's paper about restorative justice will give students the opportunity to learn about a very different form of justice system, one not focusing on punishing the offenders, but on striving to repair the damage to the offended (both the victim and the community), while setting the wrongdoer on a better behavioral path. This approach is drawn from traditional non-industrial societies; the modernized version of it has been used in small groups with some success, but the jury remains out on how reforms based on restorative justice ideas will work in contemporary juvenile and adult courts. Schiff concludes that when implemented correctly, restorative justice is a promising path to reform for juvenile courts.

We end with a piece by Western and Pettit that looks at consequences of changes in criminal justice, specifically, corrections policies in the U.S. in recent decades. What they show us is how these policies have caused hardship on a segment of the population that is already disadvantaged. Some may be inclined to respond, "So what? They're criminals." Those whose knee jerk reaction runs in this direction should realize that our policies have set the stage for even more inequality, increased disadvantage that will imperil the guilty and innocent alike.

We hope that students recognize that these and other dire consequences are products of reforms that are not based on sound social science. Criminologists have a lot to offer that could keep us from continuing to make policy mistakes. We hope students, as they finish this excursion into criminology, will better understand how society might best respond when some among us violate the laws, when others argue for changes in those laws, and when still others challenge those ideas. We also hope that some among you will be intrigued enough by the work of criminologists to join us in the study of crime and criminal justice.

 For a data analysis exercise that accompanies the material in this section, go to www.sagepub.com/crimereadings3study.

STRENGTHENING INSTITUTIONS AND RETHINKING THE AMERICAN DREAM

STEVEN F. MESSNER

RICHARD ROSENFELD

It is needless to waste words in painting the situation in our country today. The headlines of any metropolitan newspaper any day do so only too clearly. Crime of the most desperate sort is so rampant that unless a robbery runs into six figures or a murder is outstandingly brutal or intriguing, we no longer even read below the headings.

—James Truslow Adams, 1929

There is a hollowness at the core of a society if its members share no common purpose, no mutual goals, no joint vision—nothing to believe in except self-aggrandizement.

—Marian Wright Edelman, 1992

James Truslow Adams, historian of the American Dream, never pursued a rigorous analysis of the influence of the American Dream on crime. Nonetheless, he believed that the task of reducing crime in America was urgent and that it would require alterations in basic social and cultural patterns. He also recognized the role of human agency in social change and the importance of leadership at the highest levels in mobilizing the resources necessary to reform the "very foundations" of American life. In his view, nothing less than American democracy itself was at stake. "We must rule or be ruled," he wrote, because unless the crime problem is brought under control, social order will sooner or later give way to chaos, opening the way for "the dictator who inevitably 'saves society' when social insubordination and disintegration have become intolerable."

Adams directed his message for change, published originally in a 1929 essay on law observance, to Herbert Hoover. It is easy in retrospect to dismiss as futile his effort to educate President Hoover on the nature of the crime problem. However, Adams was well aware of the President's public policy limitations. Hoover may not have understood the "magnitude and the causes of the danger which we face," but at least he acknowledged that there was a crime problem. By contrast, his predecessor, Calvin Coolidge, never troubled himself over the rising tide of crime and lawlessness, beyond seeing to it that Mrs. Coolidge was accompanied on her shopping by an armed protector.

Several important lessons remain in Adams' attempts to educate the President and the public about crime. If Adams exaggerated the specter of social collapse and dictatorship, he recognized the genuine vulnerability of democratic rights and freedoms to demagogic appeals for "law and order." He also understood the importance of establishing a supportive intellectual climate for effective political leadership and public action. Hoover's moral appeals to citizens to do their "duty" by obeying the Eighteenth Amendment's prohibition against the manufacture, sale, or transportation of intoxicating liquors were ineffective, in Adams' view, because they reflected a shallow appreciation of the American crime problem:

> The American problem, though complicated by Prohibition, lies far deeper; and it is the lack of understanding as to what the problem is that so greatly diminishes the force of Mr. Hoover's appeal to us as citizens anxious to do our duty toward society.

Adams also contributes very important insights regarding the causes of crime and prospects for crime policy in America. His message is organized around two themes that are central to our arguments. First, the roots of the American crime problem lie deep within our cultural and institutional history. "Lawlessness," by which Adams meant a generalized disrespect for law as such, is part of the American heritage. Prohibition may have contributed to the problem, he wrote in a 1928 article published in the *Atlantic* entitled "Our Lawless Heritage,"

> but it is operating upon a population already the most lawless in spirit of any in the great modern civilized countries. Lawlessness has been and is one of the most distinctive American traits. . . . It is needless to say that we are not going to be able to shed this heritage quickly or easily.

Second, because high rates of crime are neither recent nor ephemeral characteristics of American society, responses to crime must be equally fundamental if they are to be effective. According to Adams, the "spirit" of lawlessness, which is very similar to what we have termed the "ethic" of anomie, will give way only when the preconditions for respect for law have been established. These include knowledge of the nature and limits of law on the part of law makers and the public, and the impartial application of legal sanctions against "millionaires" and "highly placed officials in Washington," as well as against the "ordinary criminal." Most important, the American spirit of lawlessness will not abate "until the ideal of quickly accumulated wealth, by any means whatever, is made subordinate to the ideal of private and public virtue."

Adams does not describe in detail how these changes are to come about, in particular how virtue would overcome the goal of material accumulation, except to propose that the President has, if he would only seize it, an opportunity to exercise essential moral leadership. Although directed at Herbert Hoover in 1929, Adams' call for moral "regeneration" continues to be relevant to present-day political and cultural conditions, as the quotation from Marian Wright Edelman at the beginning of this [article] suggests. If the President

> will undertake to show the people what underlies their problem, and assume the leadership in a crusade to reform the very foundations of their life, . . . then he will prove the leader for whom America waits, and patriotism and nobility may again rise above efficiency and wealth. By that path only can America regain respect for law and for herself. . . . America can be saved, but it must be by regeneration, not by efficiency.

We share Adams' belief that significant reductions in crime in the United States will require fundamental changes in the social and cultural order. If our diagnosis of the problem is correct—if high levels of crime derive from the very organization of American society—the logical solution is social reorganization. This will entail, in our view, both institutional reform and cultural regeneration. Before sketching the kinds of institutional and cultural changes that might reduce crime rates, however, it is important first to consider conventional approaches to crime control and their limitations.

CONVENTIONAL STRATEGIES FOR CRIME CONTROL

The point of departure for this discussion is current policy, and proposals for alternative policies, championed by what we will call the "conservative" and "liberal" political camps. Current policy, informed largely by conservative views, has not stemmed the tide of high levels of serious crime in the United States. However, proposals from the liberal camp to complement conservative "get tough" strategies with social reforms to expand opportunities for those "locked out" of the American Dream have not been any more successful in reducing levels of serious crime. The reason for these failures, we suggest, is that both conservative and liberal strategies reinforce the very qualities of American culture that lead to high rates of crime in the first place.

The Conservative Camp: The War on Crime

Conservative crime control policies are draped explicitly in the metaphors of war. We have declared war on crime, and on drugs, which are presumed to promote crime. Criminals, according to this view, have taken the streets, blocks, and sometimes entire neighborhoods from law-abiding citizens. The function of crime control policy is to recapture the streets from criminals to make them safe for the rest of us. This is accomplished by a range of initiatives encompassing law enforcement, criminal prosecution, court decisions, and sanctions policy.

Let us summarize briefly the conservative scenario. The police will act swiftly to remove criminals from the streets; prosecutors will vigorously bring their cases to court without plea-bargaining them to charges carrying lesser penalties; judges and juries will have less discretion in determining the penalties imposed; and more criminals will serve longer sentences for their crimes. Corrections officials will thus keep offenders in prison for longer periods of time, both because offenders are serving longer sentences and because officials will have less discretion in granting parole to offenders. The cumulative effects of these "get tough" actions will be lower crime rates brought about by increases both in the deterrent effects of punishment and in what criminologists term the incapacitation effects of imprisonment.

With respect to deterrence, stiffer penalties will raise the costs of crime, thereby dissuading potential offenders from committing their first crimes and convincing previous offenders that it is too costly to repeat their misdeeds. The simple logic of incapacitation is that offenders who are in prison will be unable to commit crimes against the innocent public.

Conservatives have been successful in influencing crime control policies over the course of recent decades. For the twenty-four-year period between 1968 and 1992, the White House was occupied for all but four years by Republican Presidents who proudly proclaimed their credentials as "law and order" advocates. Republican control over the Presidency resulted in the nomination of conservative justices to the Supreme Court and conservative judges to the federal judiciary, and facilitated legislative changes consistent with the conservative agenda on crime control. Among the most important of these changes was the widespread adoption during the 1980s of mandatory-minimum sentencing laws.

Sentencing in the Drug War. Mandatory-minimum laws specify the minimum sentence for crimes and in principle prohibit court and correctional agencies from modifying them. The intent of such sentencing policy is to increase both the certainty and the severity of punishment for persons convicted of the most serious crimes. Mandatory-minimum sentencing has been applied with special force to drug trafficking, resulting in extraordinary increases in the incarceration rates of drug offenders. Data from the National Corrections Reporting Program (NCRP) indicate that over half (52 percent) of the increase in prison admissions during the 1980s were for drug offenses. According to a leading criminal justice policy analyst, the use of mandatory-minimum sentencing in the war on drugs has "elevated the severity of punishment for drug sales to a level comparable to that for homicide."

By any reasonable standard, the policies associated with the war on crime and drugs have been a dismal failure. There have been no appreciable changes in rates of serious crime in America that can be unambiguously attributed to conservative policies. Moreover, Americans do not perceive themselves to be safer than in the past. If anything, fear of crime and preoccupation with personal safety have intensified over the past twenty-five years.

The Expansion of Punitive Social Control. The war on crime has achieved one noteworthy victory, suggested in our discussion of mandatory-minimum sentencing, although it is surely a pyrrhic one: Incarceration levels have soared. The number of persons sentenced to more than one year in state and federal prisons increased to 823,414 in 1991 (a rate of 310 persons per 100,000 population) from 315,974 (139 per 100,000 population) in 1980. The rapid escalation of incarceration has produced a costly and potentially very dangerous "capacity crisis" in the correctional system. As incarceration rates increased throughout the 1970s and 1980s, national attention began to focus on the problem of overcrowding in prisons and jails. By the end of 1991, state prisons were operating with inmate populations that averaged 116 percent of their "highest" capacity, which is the capacity level required to maintain basic custody, security, and custodial operations, limited programming, and little else. The federal system operated at 146 percent of inmate capacity. The American Correctional Association, meanwhile, recommends that a prison never run at greater than 90 percent of capacity, to allow for administrative flexibility and response to emergencies. Only six states met this "industry standard" in 1991, and thirty-six states operated above 100 percent of "highest" capacity. The situation in local jails is no better, in part because thousands of state prisoners are held in local jails due to crowding in state facilities.

The extraordinary increase in the population of prisons and jails is only part of a larger expansion of formal, punitive social control in the United States. As of the end of 1989, over 4 million Americans, 2.2 percent of all adults, were under some form of correctional sanction. Roughly 1 million were in prison or jail, and the remaining 3 million were under supervision in the community (roughly 2.5 million on probation and 0.5 million on parole). Between 1984 and 1988 alone, the number of adults under some form of correctional sanction in the United States increased by 39 percent. At present rates of growth, 6 percent of the adult population will be subject to some form of correctional supervision by the year 2000, and 10 percent of American adults will be under correctional control by 2006. . . . African Americans currently are subject to levels of punitive social control that are much higher than these projected estimates for the population as a whole. African Americans have been hit hard by the war against crime—and especially by the war against drugs. In his 1992 presidential address to the American Society of Criminology, Alfred Blumstein characterized rising levels of arrest and incarceration of black Americans as nothing less than

> a major assault on the black community. One can be reasonably confident that if a similar assault was affecting the white community, there would be a strong and effective effort to change either the laws or the enforcement policy.

Whether or not black Americans have been targeted explicitly, there are disturbing parallels between the massive expansion in formal social control during the 1980s and the infamous "black codes" of the post-Civil War South. Most of the southern states passed such vagrancy laws, allowing for the arrest of unemployed and "idle" blacks. However, the aggressive sanctions policies of recent years have not resulted in declines in offending among blacks. On the contrary, rates of violent crime and drug offending among young blacks increased sharply during the last half of the 1980s.

Unintended Consequences of Expanded Control. Not only has the extension of the reach of the criminal justice system failed to reduce crime, it tends to undermine the capacity of the system to realize an equally important objective: justice. Excessive case loads put pressure on the major participants in the adjudication process—district attorneys, defense lawyers (especially public defenders), and judges—to dispense with cases quickly. The result is a preoccupation with efficiency rather than with the rights of criminal defendants. A concern with the simple management of large numbers of cases also pervades the correctional system. Indeed, criminologists Malcolm Feeley and Jonathan Simon have recently argued that a new way of perceiving the very functions of criminal sanctions has become dominant in criminology and criminal justice. According to this "new penology," the focus of corrections has shifted away from a concern with administering levels of punishment that individuals deserve, or a concern with rehabilitating these offenders, to a preoccupation with more efficient "risk management" of dangerous populations.

The unfortunate and unintended consequences of the war on crime, however, extend far beyond the criminal justice system itself. Crackdowns on crime are directed at those populations considered to be most dangerous to society. This implies that minority groups will be affected disproportionately by these efforts. As we have seen, this has been precisely the case for black Americans, many of whom quite understandably resent the differential treatment imposed on them by vigorous law enforcement efforts. It should come as little surprise, therefore, that police-citizen confrontations involving minority group members are likely to be filled with tension and hostility, and can ignite episodes of collective disorder.

In addition, given the greater criminal involvement of males in comparison. with females, and of young males in particular, extremely high levels of incarceration can have devastating implications for the sex ratio of a community and, in turn, for family relations. The large-scale removal of young males from the general population depletes the supply of potential marriage partners for young females. In so doing, expansive incarceration policies impede the formation of traditional families and thereby encourage, indirectly, higher rates of female-headed households and illegitimacy—precisely the types of family conditions that have been linked with high rates of crime. Thus the war on crime has not only failed to realize the goal of significant crime reduction; it has exacerbated the very problem that it is supposed to solve.

The failure of conservative crime control policies reflects the warfare mentality that provides their justification. This is why it is so politically dangerous to call for an end to current policy, even for those who are willing to acknowledge its limitations. It appears defeatist to advocate limits on the costs of criminal sanctions, or on the proportion of the population it is reasonable or desirable to place under correctional control, when crime control is imbued with the metaphors of war. A former official in the current drug war is said to have compared the drug problem with Humpty Dumpty:

> When all the King's horses and all the King's men couldn't put Humpty together again, the response was merely to double the number of horses and men, rather than to recognize at some point the futility of the effort.

However, reports of violent conflict from the "battle zones" of American cities suggest that the war on crime is more than just a rhetorical device: It is a classic instance of the sociological self-fulfilling prophesy. It begins with a definition of the situation that likens the crime problem to war. The war on crime, in turn, reinforces the cultural and social arrangements that produce warlike conditions in the society. The response is to intensify the war on crime. An alternative response would be to change the initial definition of crime as war and criminals as "enemies." This is the approach to crime control taken by the liberal camp, although it too ends up reproducing social and cultural conditions conducive to crime.

The Liberal Camp: The War on Poverty and on Inequality of Opportunity

In contrast to conservative crackdowns on criminals, the liberal approach to crime control emphasizes correctional policies and broader social reforms intended to expand opportunities for those "locked out" of the American Dream. This approach is based on the premise that the poor and disadvantaged want to conform to the law and that they commit crimes only when doing so is necessary to achieve goals that cannot be achieved through conformity. The temptations for crime can thus be lessened by providing access to the legitimate means of success for those who lack opportunities. For those who have already become enmeshed in the criminal justice system, liberals call for rehabilitation and reform, with a heavy emphasis on training and skill development to allow offenders to compete more effectively for jobs upon reentry into society.

Liberals, like conservatives, have enjoyed some notable successes in getting their policies implemented. A good example of liberal strategies for general social reform is provided by the War on Poverty during the 1960s. Many of the programs associated with this initiative were justified with explicit reference to crime reduction. Perhaps the most famous of these was the Mobilization for Youth program, which sought to reduce crime and delinquency in a depressed area of Manhattan by expanding educational and employment opportunities. This program was organized in part by Richard Cloward, one of the leading figures associated with the anomie perspective on crime and delinquency.

Effects of Liberal Policies on Crime Rates. There is little evidence to suggest that the liberal strategies, including the Mobilization for Youth program, have been any more effective than the conservative approaches in reducing levels of crime. Crime rates increased markedly during the height of liberal social reform in the 1960s and early 1970s. Some liberal advocates have argued that their approach was never really tried, that the War on Poverty was underfunded, that it was more image than reality, or that it was quickly overwhelmed by other issues, such as the Vietnam War. Typical of this view is Ruth Sidel's comment:

> The War on Poverty was woefully inadequate
> to reverse the damage that was done,
> particularly to blacks, in our society; and no
> sooner did it get started than Vietnam,
> inflation, and the Nixon administration had
> begun to subvert it.

However, the fact is that poverty rates in the United States did decline during the 1960s and most of the 1970s. Unless official poverty rates are rejected as grossly invalid indicators of impediments to economic opportunity, then, based on the liberal view, some relief from serious crime should have coincided with the realization of genuine social reform.

There are additional reasons to question the liberal approach to crime control. First, it is difficult to see how the liberal explanation of crime and the policies based on it would apply to the crimes committed by persons at the top of the opportunity structure, crimes that are far from rare and that are very costly to society. Second, although certain forms of serious crime are disproportionately committed by the poor, crime rates do not rise and fall in a direct way with poverty rates, unemployment rates, or other indicators of economic deprivation. In fact, the opposite is the case for certain historical periods.

Crime rates fell during the Great Depression of the 1930s and rose dramatically during the prosperous 1960s. Crime rates declined during the mid-1970s and then again during the early 1980s, but in both instances the reductions coincided with periods of economic recession. A full assessment of changes in levels of serious crime must, of course, encompass a wide range of causal factors in addition to economic opportunities, such as changes in the age composition of the population and in the routine activities that make people and property more or less vulnerable or attractive targets for crime. Even so, the evidence fails to support the proposition that reductions in crime follow directly from an expansion of economic opportunities.

The failure of the liberal approach to crime control is not surprising given our thesis that widespread crime is a product of cultural pressures for the unrestrained pursuit of monetary success and weak social control deriving from an imbalanced institutional structure. Greater equality of opportunity will not alter in any appreciable way either of these cultural and structural conditions. Genuine equality of opportunity would undoubtedly redistribute the economic winners and losers, but it would not by itself diminish either the importance of winning and losing or the concomitant pressures to try to win by any means necessary.

Unintended Consequences of Liberal Reform. Not only do liberal crime control strategies fail to target the underlying cultural and structural causes of high crime rates in the United States, but like conservative strategies, they are self-defeating when enacted in the absence of more fundamental social change. Policies that reduce discriminatory barriers to occupational achievement and broaden access to education, to the extent that they are successful, promote social mobility and extend the reach of the American Dream to persons and groups who have historically been excluded from its benefits. This is, of course, the very point of much liberal social policy. But in so doing, these policies reinforce the commitment to the American Dream itself and hence sustain its criminogenic consequences. A population would not long remain wedded to the idea that everyone should struggle relentlessly to get ahead if hardly anyone actually ever did get ahead.

In addition, the social mobility fostered by liberal social reform may aggravate the crime problem in another way, as suggested by the sociologist William Julius Wilson. Wilson describes the process through which poverty, crime, and other social problems become concentrated in urban neighborhoods. When better-off residents depart for other areas of the city or for the suburbs, they take with them skills, resources, and models of conventional behavior that contribute to community stability. They leave behind, all else equal, a community that is less able to exercise informal social control over its members, less able to protect itself from outsiders, and therefore more vulnerable to crime. As crime rates rise, more residents depart, again those with the best "prospects" being the first to go. The concentration of economic and social disadvantage increases, and crime rates continue to climb.

Wilson's analysis of neighborhood transition draws heavily on the social disorganization tradition associated with the Chicago school in urban sociology; in fact, he illustrates his argument with data from Chicago community areas. Writing in the 1980s, however, Wilson supplements his analysis with an account of the growth in mobility opportunities for middle- and working-class blacks that accompanied declines in discriminatory barriers in education and work and, to a more limited degree, in housing during the previous two decades. The opening of the opportunity structure enabled many, though far from all, blacks to join the urban exodus of the previous thirty years. Even blacks who did not leave the central city because of continuing residential discrimination in suburban areas were able in greater numbers than ever before to move away from "declining" neighborhoods. As whites had been able to do for decades, blacks could now abandon old and declining neighborhoods for new, more stable ones. They could participate in the American tradition of linking geographic and social mobility. Now, like other Americans, when they moved up, they could move out. As a result, unintentional to be sure, expansions in opportunities for some black Americans led to expansions in crime rates for others.

We do not mean to exaggerate either the effects on neighborhood crime rates of the outmigration of better-off residents or, for that matter, the number of black Americans who have benefited from equal-opportunity policies. Nor do we condone in any way the racial discrimination that "kept blacks in their place" in earlier periods. Further, it would be absurd to blame those who flee crime-ridden communities in search of greater personal security. Their decisions and actions are understandable and, from an individual point of view, entirely justifiable.

We also do not mean to belittle the achievements of liberal social reform. The expansion of opportunities produces a broad range of benefits regardless of any impact on crime rates; there is more to improving the quality of life in a society than reducing the risks of criminal victimization. Finally, we personally believe that providing everyone with the maximum feasible degree of opportunity for the realization of human potential is a worthy cultural goal as a matter of simple justice. Our point is simply that a war on poverty or on inequality of opportunity is not likely to be an effective strategy for *crime control* in the absence of other cultural and structural changes.

Beyond Liberalism and Conservatism

The failure of both liberals and conservatives to offer effective solutions to the crime problem ultimately reflects the inability, or unwillingness, of advocates of either approach to question the fundamental features of American society. In a sense, both are prisoners of the dominant culture. Conservatives and liberals alike embrace the American Dream without reservation and search for an external "enemy" with which to engage in a war. Conservatives direct the war against the "wicked" persons who are held to represent a danger to society. The enemies for liberals are not bad persons but bad social conditions, imperfections of the social structure that make it difficult or impossible for some people to conform to dominant norms. These social imperfections, including poverty, racial discrimination, and lack of education, are typically viewed by liberals as a "betrayal" of the American Dream. Neither group entertains the possibility that the enemy comes from within, that the causes of crime lie within the dominant culture itself.

As a consequence of this intellectual blind spot, the policies of both conservatives and liberals are severely constrained by the logic of the existing culture and, in ironic ways, reflect this logic. The conservative approach promotes crime control policies without limits and at any cost. This expansive and expensive strategy for controlling crime embodies the anomic quality of American culture: the cultural imperative to pursue goals by any means necessary. Liberal policies, in contrast, strengthen the other element of American culture that is criminogenic: the excessive emphasis on the competitive struggle for monetary success. Liberals propose, in effect, that strengthening the American Dream will solve the problems caused by the American Dream. In short, both liberal and conservative policies for crime control are ultimately self-defeating because they reproduce the very cultural and social conditions that generate the distinctively high levels of crime for which the United States is known throughout the world.

Any significant reduction in crime will require moving beyond the failed ideas and policies associated with both ends of the conventional political spectrum. However, the policies that we suggest are also not likely to bring about substantial reductions in crime in the short run. We are not aware of any policy solutions for the crime problem that could have this effect. This is not simply because past and present policies have been hamstrung by the liberal and conservative alternatives; it is also because the conditions that lead to crime cannot be ameliorated by "policy" as such, or at least by policy that is politically feasible. In the United States, substantial crime reductions require *social change*, and not simply new social policy. Policy, on the other hand, is most often concerned with making existing arrangements more "efficient." The function of policy is to improve existing means of achieving collective goals; rarely does policy seek to alter the goals themselves. As one analyst suggests, addressing the "basic causes" of a problem may be of little interest to policymakers, because they are under strong political pressures to define problems in terms of available solutions, and they typically lack the material or political resources to alter basic causes.

Genuine crime control requires transformation from within, a reorganization of social institutions and a regeneration of cultural commitments. This is certainly a formidable task, given the powerful influence of existing cultural beliefs and structural arrangements. The task is not, however, an impossible one. Culture and social structure inevitably place constraints on human action, but these constraints are of a unique type. Unlike the limits imposed by the natural world, the social world is ultimately created and recreated by the participants themselves.

Sociologist Peter Berger uses the metaphor of a puppet to describe the paradox of constraint and potentiality in human action. He compares the expectations and requirements of social roles to the strings that regulate the movements of a puppet. The puppet's movements are, of course, constrained by the strings. At the same time, Berger cautions that the puppet metaphor should not be stretched too far. Human beings are not mindless puppets. Each of us individually is able to look up and examine the mechanism

from which the strings hang, and, collectively, we can redesign the mechanism. Human actors, in other words, have the capacity to become aware of the social constraints on action and to change these constraints. In the section that follows, we sketch the kinds of changes in the institutional and cultural "mechanism" of American society that offer some promise of meaningful reductions in levels of serious crime.

CRIME REDUCTION THROUGH SOCIAL REORGANIZATION

Our prescriptions for crime reduction follow logically from our analysis of the causes of high levels of crime. To recapitulate very briefly: We contend that criminal activity is stimulated by strong cultural pressures for monetary success combined with anomie, a normative order with weak restraints on the selection of the means to pursue success. This anomic cultural condition is accompanied by an institutional balance of power in which the economy assumes dominance over other social institutions. Economic dominance diminishes the attractiveness of alternatives to the goal of monetary success and impedes the capacity of other institutions to perform their distinctive functions, including social control. High levels of crime thus reflect intrinsic elements of American culture and the corrosive impact of these cultural elements on social structure.

It follows from this analysis, moving back up the causal chain from high levels of crime through social structure and culture, that crime reductions would result from policies that strengthen social structure and weaken the criminogenic qualities of American culture. More specifically, crime reductions would follow from policies and social changes that vitalize families, schools, and the political system, thereby enhancing the "drawing power" of the distinctive goals associated with these institutions and strengthening their capacity to exercise social control. This institutional vitalization would, in turn, temper the anomic qualities and the intense pressures for monetary success associated with the American Dream. Finally, cultural regeneration—modifications in the American Dream itself—would promote and sustain institutional change, and would reduce cultural pressures for crime. We begin our discussion of social reorganization with a consideration of the structural dimension: institutional reform.

Institutional Reform

The Family and Schools. Initiatives such as the provision of family leave, job sharing for husbands and wives, flexible work schedules, employer-provided child care, and a host of other "pro-family" economic policies should help to alter the balance between the economic demands faced by parents and their obligations and opportunities to devote more time and energy to exclusively "family" concerns. In many families, parents and children spend very little time with each other. In a 1990 survey of American students in the sixth through the twelfth grades, half of the high school students reported that they did not share evening meals with their parents on a daily basis, and nearly half of the sixth-graders reported that they spent two or more hours a day at home without an adult present.

Policies that enable parents to spend more time with their children should not only strengthen family controls over children's behavior but should also enable the schools to carry out their control functions more effectively. School teachers and educational researchers alike maintain that the absence of parental support for education handicaps the schools in their efforts to motivate learning and keep children engaged in the educational process. Yet only about half of the ninth- and twelfth-graders in the survey cited above reported that their parents "talk with me about school." Only one-third reported that their parents attended school meetings or events.

These examples illustrate the interdependent nature of social institutions: The capacity of any institution to fulfill its distinctive function is dependent on the effective functioning of the others. Not surprisingly, then, the lack of articulation between the family and the schools has unfortunate consequences for society at large. As one educational researcher observes, the poor articulation between the home and the school reflects and reinforces a "serious erosion of social capital" in American communities. If children do not see adults often, if their relationships with adults are "fleeting," adults cannot serve as effective deterrents and as positive influences on children's behavior. The social bonds necessary for discipline, emanating from both the family and the schools, are weakened as a result.

Policies aimed at strengthening the schools, then, must proceed in concert with those designed to improve family functioning. These policies must confront two interrelated problems: (1) strengthening external controls; and (2) strengthening the engagement of people—parents and teachers, as well as children and students—in the distinctive goals and "logics" of these institutions. It is worth pondering the mixed messages that our society currently sends regarding the best way to repair and strengthen families and schools.

The message regarding families is to avoid having one as long as possible. It is difficult to think of a single source of cultural encouragement in the United States today for young people to get married and to have children—in either order. In the current obsession with out-of-wedlock births, it is scarcely noticed that birth rates among young women have declined sharply since 1960. The proportion of births to unmarried women has risen, but this is because marriage rates have fallen even faster than birth rates. Over 75 percent of males and more than 60 percent of females between the ages of twenty and twenty-four were single (i.e., never married) in 1989, compared with 55 percent of males and 36 percent of females in this age group in 1970. Over the same period, the percentage of males in their late twenties who were single grew from 19 percent to 46 percent. Over 25 percent of males in their early thirties were single in 1989, compared with less than 10 percent two decades earlier. Although in each age group females were more likely than males to be married, the fraction remaining single grew just as rapidly.

Yet the loud message to young people is to stop having children rather than to start having families. Whatever the salutary effects of this message, it serves to reinforce the view of families as "burdens" to be shouldered only after a long period of economic preparation. We do not necessarily advocate early marriage as a form of crime control, but it seems that a society with a professed commitment to "family values" should provide more cultural and social support for family formation. As a practical matter, this support will require lessening the dependence of marital and family decision-making on purely economic considerations.

With respect to schools, a popular message of the 1990s sounds the market-oriented theme of "choice": Bad schools will be driven out of business by good ones if obstacles blocking open markets in schooling are eliminated. This will occur if people are given the options of purchasing their educations in either public or private schools and of enrolling in schools outside of specific attendance areas or districts. Again, although such proposals may have particular merits, their general effect is to reinforce the market mentality of American education. One can scarcely blame students for asking whether this or that aspect of their education "pays" when this is exactly the question that dominates current educational policy discussion.

A rather different type of policy for schools is suggested by our argument. Schools should be enabled to devote themselves to their distinctive goal of formal learning. This requires, as we have suggested, stronger parental support for the educational function. However, it also requires that children's economic prospects become tied less closely to their performance in school.

Those who look back fondly to the "good old days" of strict discipline and respect for learning that are supposed to have once characterized the American public school system often forget that one reason the schools could educate more effectively in the past is because they did not have to educate as universally. In a world where labor markets offered jobs that did not require a high school education, the public schools operated much more selectively than they do now. Students who flunked out or who were expelled for disciplinary reasons, or who left because they simply did not like school, did not as a rule end up in the streets; they went to work, they formed families, or they joined the military.

Not long ago, Americans depended less on schools for economic rewards. In 1940, 39 percent of whites and 11 percent of blacks between the ages of twenty-five and thirty-four had completed four or more years of high school. By 1970, 75 percent of whites and 52 percent of blacks in this age group had completed high school. In a society where "good jobs" require a college degree or some other form of training beyond high school, and where military service requires a high school diploma, schools will daily confront students who, at best, calculate their "investment" in education according to future earnings. At worst, they will find themselves in chronic conflicts with students made hopeless by the knowledge that education is a necessary—but far from sufficient—condition for economic success.

The Polity. Turning to the institution of the polity, our analysis points to two types of policy shifts: (1) reform of the formal system of crime control, particularly the correctional system; and (2) the creation of broader patterns of social participation and social control beyond the criminal justice system.

Correctional policy that is consistent with our analysis of the crime problem begins with a fundamental question that neither the liberal nor the conservative camp addresses: What is the optimum proportion of the population that should be under the jurisdiction of correctional agencies? One may be tempted to answer zero to this question, but unless we are willing to assume a crime rate of zero or are willing to let all convicted offenders go unpunished, some proportion of the population must be under some form of correctional control at all times. So, again, what is the optimum proportion?

This is not a "policy question," narrowly defined; it is a question designed to stimulate a different way of thinking about crime control policy. It is a political question, and it most certainly is a moral question, because it requires judgments about the goals of crime control and not simply choices among more efficient or less efficient means to achieve a predefined goal or, as in current policy, among several ill-defined and conflicting goals. A central goal of any approach to crime control that is based on our analysis is to reduce cultural support for crime. A prerequisite for accomplishing this objective is to end the war on crime. We are not proposing, of course, to end efforts at crime control. On the contrary, we believe that effective crime control can begin only when control is gained over current crime policy. Achieving control of crime policy requires placing limits on the costs of crime control, especially the costs of corrections. Although cost containment will not be easy, it is essential if the anomic and perverse consequences of the war on crime are to be halted.

The idea of *intermediate sanctions,* which are community-based punishments situated between ordinary probation and prison, has been promoted by correctional reformers as a way to reduce the costs and crowding of correctional supervision while maintaining a high level of public safety. Sentencing policy based on the principle of intermediate sanctions would impose the kinds of limits on crime control that are consistent with our analysis. We question, however, whether the intensified supervision associated with most intermediate sanctions will produce the cost savings claimed by some advocates.

A key issue is whether the flow of offenders into the new community programs consists primarily of those who would have gone to prison or those who would have been placed on ordinary probation. If intermediate sanctions programs draw primarily from the pool of prison-bound offenders, they can help to lower correctional costs and to relieve overcrowding in correctional facilities. However, the great majority of persons serving time in prison have been convicted of violent crimes, have committed violent crimes in the past, or are repeat felony offenders. These offenders are not likely to be deemed suitable candidates for community-based programs, no matter how intensive the supervision. If, on the other hand, offenders who would otherwise have received ordinary probation are the main recipients of intermediate sanctions, then the cost savings of these intermediate punishments are greatly reduced in order to pay for heightened supervision of offenders in the community.

The net impact of intermediate sanctions is, then, difficult to discern. Interestingly, however, this is one of their great advantages over current policy. Reconciling tough choices regarding cost, safety, and justice presupposes some agreement over the priorities of the criminal justice system. Current policy is politically pleasing because it does not require consensus building or difficult tradeoffs among competing values and interests; there are no limits in a war on crime. The system we prefer does not have this spurious benefit because, by introducing a measure of restraint into crime control policy, it would make explicit both the scope and the purposes of punishment.

Reforms that are limited to the criminal justice system, however, will not by themselves produce appreciable reductions in crime. Broader changes within the polity are necessary to nurture the sense of collective obligation and individual duty essential for the effective functioning of formal social controls. One proposal that appears especially promising in this respect is the creation of a national service corps. If it is to contribute to crime control, such a system must be universalistic and involve an array of opportunities and obligations to serve local communities and the society as a whole. It can perform a particularly important integrative function by providing education, training in needed skills, and meaningful social controls for adolescents and young adults who have graduated from or dropped out of school, have not found work that will lead to a career, and who have outgrown the reach of their parents but have not yet formed families of their own. In short, by offering an institutional mooring for young people during the transition to adulthood, national service promises to bolster social control and to facilitate "maturational reform," i.e., the process through which young people involved in common forms of delinquency turn away from illegal behavior as they mature and assume adult obligations.

A specific form of national service with direct relevance to crime control policy is a Police Corps of young people trained as police officers who would serve on local forces for periods of two to four years. The concept was endorsed by President Bill Clinton as part of his proposal to provide college assistance in return for community service. One commentator suggested that the Police Corps might serve as the basis for President Clinton's efforts to build support for his broader philosophy of national service:

> It's the logical place to start now, as the new President embarks on his most ambitious goal—to rebuild a national sense of community, responsibility, and public altruism.

Social Stratification and the Economy. Finally, our analysis has important implications for the system of social stratification and the interrelations between this system and the economy. The relationship between stratification and crime has been the focus of extensive research and theorizing in modern criminology. Conventional approaches to the stratification-crime relationship, however, direct attention almost exclusively to a single feature of the stratification system: the distribution of opportunities for economic rewards. These explanations typically attribute crime to inequality in economic opportunities. We have maintained that greater equality of opportunity is not likely to eliminate, and in fact may aggravate, pressures to turn to illegitimate means to realize the goal of economic success. The mere existence of unequal *outcomes* is likely to generate such pressures, regardless of the openness of the stratification system, if monetary success reigns supreme as a cultural goal and the economy dominates the institutional structure of society.

It might seem on the surface that the solution to the crime problem lies in greater equality of results. However, it is not merely the shape of the distribution of material and symbolic rewards in America that contributes to crime but rather the mechanism by which rewards are distributed. In this respect, our analysis is informed by Marx's insight that the distribution of the means of consumption is ultimately dependent on the "conditions of production themselves." The conditions of production in American society dictate that the distribution of rewards be tied to economic functions: either the performance of economic roles or the possession of capital. In other words, the wealth that is produced within the economy is also distributed almost exclusively in accordance with economic criteria by labor and capital markets. To shore up such other institutions as the family, schools, and the polity relative to the economy, a greater share of the national wealth will have to be allocated on the basis of noneconomic criteria.

We are not endorsing the nationalization of the means of production to rebalance institutions. The political and economic failures of state socialist societies have been made glaringly apparent by recent history. Rather, the model that appears promising is that of the mixed economies in Europe and Japan. These nations have implemented a wide range of social policies and programs to ensure that material well-being is not strictly tied to economic functions and to guarantee that noneconomic roles receive meaningful financial support from collective resources.

To summarize: The structural changes that could lead to significant reductions in crime are those that promote a rebalancing of social institutions. These changes would involve reducing the subordination to the economy of the family, schools, the polity, and the general system of social stratification. Most of the specific proposals for institutional change that we have put forth are not particularly novel. They have been advanced by others in different contexts and with different agendas. These proposals, however, typically are considered in isolation from one another. For example, conservatives who bemoan the demise of the family and call for its rejuvenation rarely pursue the logical implications of their analyses and proposals. They fail to recognize or acknowledge that the vitalization of the family requires changes in the economy that are likely to be very distasteful to conservatives on ideological grounds.

The distinctive and powerful feature of the sociological paradigm is that it directs attention to the interconnections among social institutions. Because of these interconnections, piecemeal reforms are likely to be ineffective. Moreover, our analytical framework implies that institutional reforms must go hand in hand with cultural change, because culture and institutional structure are themselves inextricably bound. It is to the matter of cultural change that we now turn.

The Task of Cultural Regeneration

A basic premise of this [article] is that the beliefs, values, and goals associated with the American Dream are firmly entrenched in the American historical experience and consciousness. If this premise is correct, it would be fanciful to entertain the possibility of any wholesale rejection of the American Dream. Such a radical cultural transformation is not required, however, to vitalize noneconomic institutions. Instead, by moderating the excesses of the dominant cultural ethos, and emphasizing its useful features, institutional reform can be stimulated and significant reductions in crime can be realized.

We have characterized the American Dream as the commitment to the goal of monetary success, to be pursued by all members of society under conditions of open, individual competition. The most important and valuable theme running through this cultural ethos is that of a universal entitlement to strive for a better life, which can be attained as a consequence of one's own achievements. In other words, the American Dream empowers everyone to dream about a brighter future and about participating in the creation of that future. This vision of possibilities, of hope, is liberating, and it serves the interests of both individuals and the larger society by inspiring people to develop their talents and abilities.

The criminogenic tendencies of the American Dream derive from its *exaggerated* emphasis on monetary success and its resistance to limits on the means for the pursuit of success. Any significant lessening of the criminogenic consequences of the dominant culture thus requires the taming of its strong materialistic pressures and the creation of a greater receptivity to socially imposed restraints. To dampen the materialistic pressures, goals other than the accumulation of wealth will have to be elevated to a position of prominence in the cultural hierarchy. This implies greater recognition of and appreciation for the institutional realms that are currently subservient to the economy. More specifically, social roles such as parenting, "spousing," teaching, learning, and serving the community will have to become, as ends in themselves, meaningful alternatives to material acquisition. Furthermore, enhancing the respect for these noneconomic roles implies that money will no longer serve as the principal gauge of social achievement and personal worth. Money will not be, in the words of Marian Wright Edelman, the preeminent "measure of our success."

The other, complementary task of cultural regeneration will involve fostering a cultural receptivity to restraints. The dominant cultural ethos glorifies the individual pursuit of material well-being. People are encouraged to maximize personal utility, to be guided by self-interest, and to regard others as potential competitors in the race for economic rewards. However, many of the institutional reforms to which we point entail the subordination of individual interests to larger collectivities, such as the family and the community. In short, it seems unlikely that social change conducive to lower levels of crime will occur in the absence of a cultural reorientation that encompasses an enhanced emphasis on the importance of mutual support and collective obligations and a decreased emphasis on individual rights, interests, and privileges.

An Intellectual Foundation for Change

An important intellectual component accompanies the task of balancing social obligations with individual interests. The extreme individualism of American culture impedes a full understanding of the interdependencies between the individual and society. Human beings are inherently social beings. As a consequence, their individual development and maturation presuppose social relationships that are necessarily constraining. To borrow from Marx once again:

> Only in association with others has each individual the means of cultivating his [or her] talents in all directions.

The idea that individual growth requires social motivation, support, and regulation forms part of the distinctive corpus of classical sociological thought. It figures significantly not only in Marx's analysis of capitalist society but also in George Herbert Mead's theory of the social formation of the self and in Emile Durkheim's conception of the collective conscience. It is one of the few ideas in the history of sociological thought that is not readily identified as belonging to one or another intellectual or ideological camp. It links the micro and the macro levels of analysis, and informs conflict theories of social change as well as consensus theories of social order. As a defining element in the common heritage of the discipline, it prepares the conceptual ground for a sociological reappraisal of the American Dream.

This reappraisal suggests that different parts of the American Dream work at cross-purposes. Its universalism and achievement orientation inspire ambition and in so doing stimulate the motivational dynamic necessary for the realization of human potential. However, its exaggerated materialism and extreme individualism narrow the range of human capacities that receive cultural respect and social support and discourage people from assuming obligations that in principle could be liberating. By helping to clarify this internal contradiction, a sociological understanding of the American Dream can perhaps lay the intellectual groundwork for the cultural and institutional changes necessary for reducing crime in our society.

Toward a Mature Society

In closing, we return to James Truslow Adams for a final observation of the legacy and the future of the American Dream. Adams traces the possibilities of the Dream to the American Revolution. The cultural significance of the revolt lay in "the breaking down of all spiritual barriers to the complete development of whatever might prove to be fertile, true, and lasting in the American dream." However, Adams lamented the fact that this developmental potential was inhibited by the "debilitating doctrine" that, two centuries after its birth, the United States is still a "young" nation. He asked:

Is it not time to proclaim that we are not children but men [and women] who must put away childish things; that we have overlooked that fact too long; that we have busied ourselves overmuch with fixing up the new place we moved into 300 years ago, with making money in the new neighborhood; and that we should begin to live a sane, maturely civilized life?

The promise of a mature America is the cultural encouragement for all persons to develop their full range of talents and capacities on the basis of mutual support and collective obligations. James Truslow Adams' American Dream, and ours, must be reinvented so that its destructive consequences can be curbed, and so that its fertile, true, and lasting promise of human development can be fulfilled.

QUESTIONS FOR DISCUSSION AND WRITING

1. Which belief of Adams' do the authors "share"?

2. How do both the conservative and liberal policies reflect the fact that American culture is the cause of crime?

3. What "follows from this analysis"?

BROKEN WINDOWS

The Police and Neighborhood Safety

JAMES Q. WILSON

GEORGE L. KELLING

In the mid-1970s, the State of New Jersey announced a "Safe and Clean Neighborhoods Program," designed to improve the quality of community life in twenty-eight cities. As part of that program, the state provided money to help cities take police officers out of their patrol cars and assign them to walking beats. The governor and other state officials were enthusiastic about using foot patrol as a way of cutting crime, but many police chiefs were skeptical. Foot patrol, in their eyes, had been pretty much discredited. It reduced the mobility of the police, who thus had difficulty responding to citizen calls for service, and it weakened headquarters control over patrol officers.

Many police officers also disliked foot patrol, but for different reasons: it was hard work; it kept them outside on cold, rainy nights; and it reduced their chances for making a "good pinch." In some departments, assigning officers to foot patrol had been used as a form of punishment. And academic experts on policing doubted that foot patrol would have any impact on crime rates: it was, in the opinion of most, little more than a sop to public opinion. But since the state was paying for it, the local authorities were willing to go along.

Five years after the program started, the Police Foundation in Washington, D.C., published an evaluation of the foot-patrol project. Based on its analysis of a carefully controlled experiment carried out chiefly in Newark, the foundation concluded, to the surprise of hardly anyone, that foot patrol had not reduced crime rates. But residents of the foot-patrolled neighborhoods seemed to feel more secure than persons in other areas, tended to believe that crime had been reduced, and seemed to take fewer steps to protect themselves from crime (staying at home with the doors locked, for example). Moreover, citizens in the foot-patrol areas had a more favorable opinion of the police than did those living elsewhere. And officers walking beats had higher morale, greater job satisfaction, and a more favorable attitude toward citizens in their neighborhoods than did officers assigned to patrol cars.

These findings may be taken as evidence that the skeptics were right—foot patrol has no effect on crime; it merely fools the citizens into thinking that they are safer. But in our view, and in the view of the authors of the Police Foundation study (of whom Kelling was one), the citizens of Newark were not fooled at all. They knew what the foot-patrol officers were doing, they knew it was different from what motorized officers do, and they knew that having officers walk beats did in fact make their neighborhoods safer.

But how can a neighborhood be "safer" when the crime rate has not gone down—in fact, may have gone up? Finding the answer requires first that we understand what most often frightens people in public places. Many citizens, of course, are primarily frightened by crime, especially crime involving a sudden, violent attack by a stranger. This risk is very real, in Newark as in many large cities. But we tend to overlook or forget another source of fear—the fear of being bothered by disorderly people. Not violent people, nor, necessarily, criminals, but disreputable or obstreperous or unpredictable people: panhandlers, drunks, addicts, rowdy teenagers, prostitutes, loiterers, the mentally disturbed.

What foot-patrol officers did was to elevate, to the extent they could, the level of public order in these neighborhoods. Though the neighborhoods were predominantly black and the foot patrolmen were mostly white, this "order-maintenance" function of the police was performed to the general satisfaction of both parties.

One of us (Kelling) spent many hours walking with Newark foot-patrol officers to see how they defined "order" and what they did to maintain it. One beat was typical: a busy but dilapidated area in the heart of Newark, with many abandoned buildings, marginal shops (several of which prominently displayed knives and straight-edged razors in their windows), one large department store, and, most important, a train station and several major bus stops. Though the area was run-down, its streets were filled with people, because it was a major transportation center. The good order of this area was important not only to those who lived and worked there but also to many others, who had to move through it on their way home, to supermarkets, or to factories.

The people on the street were primarily black; the officer who walked the street was white. The people were made up of "regulars" and "strangers." Regulars included both "decent folk" and some drunks and derelicts who were always there but who "knew their place." Strangers were, well, strangers, and viewed suspiciously, sometimes apprehensively. The officer—call him Kelly—knew who the regulars were, and they knew him. As he saw his job, he was to keep an eye on strangers, and make certain that the disreputable regulars observed some informal but widely understood rules.

Drunks and addicts could sit on the stoops, but could not lie down. People could drink on side streets, but not at the main intersection. Bottles had to be in paper bags. Talking to, bothering, or begging from people waiting at the bus stop was strictly forbidden. If a dispute erupted between a businessman and a customer, the businessman was assumed to be right, especially if the customer was a stranger. If a stranger loitered, Kelly would ask him if he had any means of support and what his business was; if he gave unsatisfactory answers, he was sent on his way. Persons who broke the informal rules, especially those who bothered people waiting at bus stops, were arrested for vagrancy. Noisy teenagers were told to keep quiet.

These rules were defined and enforced in collaboration with the "regulars" on the street. Another neighborhood might have different rules, but these, everybody understood, were the rules for this neighborhood. If someone violated them, the regulars not only turned to Kelly for help but also ridiculed the violator. Sometimes what Kelly did could be described as "enforcing the law," but just as often it involved taking informal or extralegal steps to help protect what the neighborhood had decided was the appropriate level of public order. Some of the things he did probably would not withstand a legal challenge.

A determined skeptic might acknowledge that a skilled foot-patrol officer can maintain order but still insist that this sort of "order" has little to do with the real sources of community fear—that is, with violent crime. To a degree, that is true. But two things must be borne in mind. First, outside observers should not assume that they know how much of the anxiety now endemic in many big-city neighborhoods stems from a fear of "real" crime and how much from a sense that the street is disorderly, a source of distasteful, worrisome encounters. The people of Newark, to judge from their behavior and their remarks to interviewers, apparently assign a high value to public order, and feel relieved and measured when the police help them maintain that order.

Second, at the community level, disorder and crime are usually inextricably linked, in a kind of developmental sequence. Social psychologists and police officers tend to agree that if a window in a building is broken *and is left unrepaired,* all the rest of the windows will soon be broken. This is as true in nice neighborhoods as in run-down ones. Window-breaking does not necessarily occur on a large scale because some areas are inhabited by determined window-breakers whereas others are populated by window-lovers; rather, one unrepaired broken window is a signal that no one cares, and so breaking more windows costs nothing. It has always been fun.

Philip Zimbardo, a Stanford psychologist, reported in 1969 on some experiments testing the broken-window theory. He arranged to have an automobile without license plates parked with its hood up on a street in the Bronx and a comparable automobile on a street in Palo Alto, California. The car in the Bronx was attacked by "vandals" within ten minutes of its "abandonment." The first to arrive were a family—father, mother, and young son—who removed the radiator and battery. Within twenty-four hours, virtually everything of value had been removed. Then random destruction began—windows were smashed, parts torn off, upholstery ripped. Children began to use the car as a playground. Most of the adult "vandals" were well-dressed, apparently clean-cut whites. The car in Palo Alto sat untouched for more than a week. Then Zimbardo smashed part of it with a sledgehammer. Soon, passersby were joining in. Within a few hours, the car had been turned upside down and utterly destroyed. Again, the "vandals" appeared to be primarily respectable whites.

Untended property becomes fair game for people out for fun or plunder, and even for people who ordinarily would not dream of doing such things and who probably consider themselves law-abiding. Because of the nature of community life in the Bronx—its anonymity, the frequency with which cars are abandoned and things are stolen or broken, the past experience of "no one caring"—vandalism begins much more quickly than it does in staid Palo Alto, where people have come to believe that private possessions are cared for, and that mischievous behavior is costly. But vandalism can occur anywhere once communal barriers—the sense of mutual regard and the obligations of civility—are lowered by actions that seem to signal that "no one cares."

We suggest that "untended" behavior also leads to the breakdown of community controls. A stable neighborhood of families who care for their homes, mind each other's children, and confidently frown on unwanted intruders can change, in a few years or even a few months, to an inhospitable and frightening jungle. A piece of property is abandoned, weeds grow up, a window is smashed. Adults stop scolding rowdy children; the children, emboldened, become more rowdy. Families move out, unattached adults move in. Teenagers gather in front of the corner store. The merchant asks them to move; they refuse. Fights occur. Litter accumulates. People start drinking in front of the grocery; in time, an inebriate slumps to the sidewalk and is allowed to sleep it off. Pedestrians are approached by panhandlers.

At this point it is not inevitable that serious crime will flourish or violent attacks on strangers will occur. But many residents will think that crime, especially violent crime, is on the rise, and they will modify their behavior accordingly. They will use the streets less often, and when on the streets will stay apart from their fellows moving with averted eyes, silent lips, and hurried steps. "Don't get involved." For some residents, this growing atomization will matter little, because the neighborhood is not their "home" but "the place where they live." Their interests are elsewhere; they are cosmopolitans. But it will matter greatly to other people, whose lives derived meaning and satisfaction from local attachments rather than worldly involvement; for them, the neighborhood will cease to exist except for a few reliable friends whom they arrange to meet.

Such an area is vulnerable to criminal invasion. Though it is not inevitable, it is more likely that here, rather than in places where people are confident they can regulate public behavior by informal controls, drugs will change hands, prostitutes will solicit, and cars will be stripped. That the drunks will be robbed by boys who do it as a lark and the prostitutes' customers will be robbed by men who do it purposefully and perhaps violently. That muggings will occur.

Among those who often find it difficult to move away from this are the elderly. Surveys of citizens suggest that the elderly are much less likely to be the victims of crime than younger persons, and some have inferred from this that the well-known fear of crime voiced by the elderly is an exaggeration: perhaps we ought not to design special programs to protect older persons; perhaps we should even try to talk them out of their mistaken fears. This argument misses the point. The prospect of a confrontation with an obstreperous teenager or a drunken panhandler can be as fear-inducing for defenseless persons as the prospect of meeting an actual robber; indeed, to a defenseless person, the two kinds of confrontation are often indistinguishable. Moreover, the lower rate at which the elderly are victimized is a measure of the steps they have already taken—chiefly, staying behind locked doors to minimize the risks they face. Young men are more frequently attacked than older women, not because they are easier or more lucrative targets but because they are on the streets more.

Nor is the connection between disorderliness and fear made only by the elderly. Susan Estrich, of the Harvard Law School, has recently gathered together a number of surveys on the sources of public fear. One, done in Portland, Oregon, indicated that three fourths of the adults interviewed cross to the other side of a street when they see a gang of teenagers; another survey, in Baltimore, discovered that nearly half would cross the street to avoid even a single strange youth. When an interviewer asked people in a housing project where the most dangerous spot was, they mentioned a place where young persons gathered to drink and play music, despite the fact that not a single crime had occurred there. In Boston public housing projects, the greatest fear was expressed by persons living in the buildings where disorderliness and incivility, not crime, were the greatest. Knowing this helps one understand the significance of such otherwise harmless displays as subway graffiti. As Nathan Glazer has written, the proliferation of graffiti, even when not obscene, confronts the subway rider with the "inescapable knowledge that the environment he must endure for an hour or more a day is uncontrolled and uncontrollable, and that anyone can invade it to do whatever damage and mischief the mind suggests."

In response to fear, people avoid one another, weakening controls. Sometimes they call the police. Patrol cars arrive, an occasional arrest occurs, but crime continues and disorder is not abated. Citizens complain to the police chief, but he explains that his department is low on personnel and that the courts do not punish petty or first-time offenders. To the residents, the police who arrive in squad cars are either ineffective or uncaring; to the police, the residents are animals who deserve each other. The citizens may soon stop calling the police because "they can't do anything."

The process we call urban decay has occurred for centuries in every city. But what is happening today is different in at least two important respects. First, in the period before, say, World War II, city dwellers—because of money costs, transportation difficulties, familial and church connections—could rarely move away from neighborhood problems. When movement did occur, it tended to be along public-transit routes. Now mobility has become exceptionally easy for all but the poorest or those who are blocked by racial prejudice. Earlier crime waves had a kind of built-in self-correcting mechanism: the determination of a neighborhood or community to reassert control over its turf. Areas in Chicago, New York, and Boston would experience crime and gang wars, and then normalcy would return, as the families for whom no alternative residences were possible reclaimed their authority over the streets.

Second, the police in this earlier period assisted in that reassertion of authority by acting, sometimes violently, on behalf of the community. Young toughs were roughed up, people were arrested "on suspicion" or for vagrancy, and prostitutes and petty thieves were routed. "Rights" were something enjoyed by decent folk, and perhaps also by the serious professional criminal, who avoided violence and could afford a lawyer.

This pattern of policing was not an aberration or the result of occasional excess. From the earliest days of the nation, the police function was seen primarily as that of a night watchman: to maintain order against the chief threats to order—fire, wild animals, and disreputable behavior. Solving crimes was viewed not as a police responsibility but as a private one. In the March, 1969, *Atlantic,* one of us (Wilson) wrote a brief account of how the police role had slowly changed from maintaining order to fighting crimes. The change began with the creation of private detectives (often ex-criminals), who worked on a contingency-fee basis for individuals who had suffered losses. In time, the detectives were absorbed into municipal police agencies and paid a regular salary; simultaneously, the responsibility for prosecuting thieves was shifted from the aggrieved private citizen to the professional prosecutor. This process was not complete in most places until the twentieth century.

In the 1960s, when urban riots were a major problem, social scientists began to explore carefully the order-maintenance function of the police, and to suggest ways of improving it—not to make streets safer (its original function) but to reduce the incidence of mass violence. Order-maintenance became, to a degree, coterminous with "community relations." But, as the crime wave that began in the early 1960s continued without abatement throughout the decade and into the 1970s, attention shifted to the role of the police as crime-fighters. Studies of police behavior ceased, by and large, to be accounts of the order-maintenance function and became, instead, efforts to propose and test ways whereby the police could solve more crimes, make more arrests, and gather better evidence. If these things could be done, social scientist assumed, citizens would be less fearful.

A great deal was accomplished during this transition, as both police chiefs and outside experts emphasized the crime-fighting function in their plans, in the allocation of resources, and in deployment of personnel. The police may well have become better crime-fighters as a result. And doubtless they remained aware of their responsibility for order. But the link between order-maintenance and crime-prevention, so obvious to earlier generations, was forgotten.

That link is similar to the process whereby one broken window becomes many. The citizen who fears the ill-smelling drunk, the rowdy teenager, or the importuning beggar is not merely expressing his distaste for unseemly behavior, he is also giving voice to a bit of folk wisdom that happens to be a correct generalization—namely, that serious street crime flourishes in areas in which disorderly behavior goes unchecked. The unchecked panhandler is, in effect, the first broken window. Muggers and robbers, whether opportunistic or professional, believe they reduce their chances of being caught or even identified if they operate on streets where potential victims are already intimidated by prevailing conditions. If the neighborhood cannot keep a bothersome panhandler from annoying passersby, the thief may reason, it is even less likely to call the police to identify a potential mugger or to interfere if the mugging actually takes place.

Some police administrators concede that this process occurs, but argue that motorized-patrol officers can deal with it as effectively as foot-patrol officers. We are not so sure. In theory, an officer in a squad car can observe as much as an officer on foot; in theory, the former can talk to as many people as the latter. But the reality of police-citizen encounters is powerfully altered by the automobile. An officer on foot cannot separate himself from the street people; if he is approached, only his uniform and his personality can help him manage whatever is about to happen. And he can never be certain what that will be—a request for directions, a plea for help, an angry denunciation, a teasing remark, a confused babble, a threatening gesture.

In a car, an officer is more likely to deal with street people by rolling down the window and looking at them. The door and the window exclude the approaching citizen; they are a barrier. Some officers take advantage of this barrier, perhaps unconsciously, by acting differently if in the car than they would on foot. We have seen this countless times. The police car pulls up to a corner where teenagers are gathered. The window is rolled down. the officer stares at the youths. They stare back. The officer says to one, "C'mere." He saunters over, conveying to his friends by his elaborately casual style the idea that he is not intimidated by authority. "What's your name?" "Chuck." "Chuck who?" "Chuck Jones." "What'ya doing, Chuck?" "Nothing." "Got a P.O. [parole officer]?" "Nah." "Sure?" "Yeah." "Stay out of trouble, Chuckie." Meanwhile, the other boys laugh and exchange comments among themselves, probably at the officer's expense. The officer stares harder. He cannot be certain what is being said, nor can he join in and, by displaying his own skill at street banter, prove that he cannot be "put down." In the process, the officer has learned almost nothing, and the boys have decided the officer is an alien force who can safely be disregarded, even mocked.

Our experience is that most citizens like to talk to a police officer. Such exchanges give them a sense of importance, provide them with the basis for gossip, and allow them to explain to the authorities what is worrying them (whereby they gain a modest but significant sense of having "done something" about the problem). You approach a person on foot more easily, and talk to him more readily, than you do a person in a car. Moreover, you can more easily retain some anonymity if you draw an officer aside for a private chat. Suppose you want to pass on a tip about who is stealing handbags, or who offered to sell you a stolen TV. In the inner city, the culprit, in all likelihood, lives nearby. To walk up to a marked patrol car and lean in the window is to convey a visible signal that you are a "fink."

The essence of the police role in maintaining order is to reinforce the informal control mechanisms of the community itself. The police cannot, without committing extraordinary resources, provide a substitute for that informal control. On the other hand, to reinforce those natural forces the police must accommodate them. And therein lies the problem.

Should police activity on the street be shaped, in important ways, by the standards of the neighborhood rather than by the rules of the state? Over the past two decades, the shift of police from order-maintenance to law-enforcement has brought them increasingly under the influence of legal restrictions, provoked by media complaints and enforced by court decisions and departmental orders. As a consequence, the order-maintenance functions of the police are now governed by rules developed to control police relations with suspected criminals. This is, we think, an entirely new development. For centuries, the role of the police as watchmen was judged primarily not in terms of its compliance with appropriate procedures but rather in terms of its attaining a desired objective. The objective was order, an inherently ambiguous term but a condition that people in a given community recognized when they saw it. The means were the same as those the community itself would employ, if its members were sufficiently determined, courageous, and authoritative. Detecting and apprehending criminals, by contrast, was a means to an end, not an end in itself; a judicial determination of guilt or innocence was the hoped-for result of the law-enforcement mode. From the first, the police were expected to follow rules defining that process, though states differed in how stringent the rules should be. The criminal apprehension process was always understood to involve individual rights, the violation of which was unacceptable because it meant that the violating officer would be acting as a judge and jury—and that was not his job. Guilt or innocence was to be determined by universal standards under special procedures.

Ordinarily, no judge or jury ever sees the persons caught up in a dispute over the appropriate level of neighborhood order. That is true not only because most cases are handled informally on the street but also because no universal standards are available to settle arguments over disorder, and thus a judge may not be any wiser or more effective than a police officer. Until quite recently in many states, and even today in some places, the police make arrests on such charges as "suspicious person" or "vagrancy" or "public drunkenness"—charges with scarcely any legal meaning. These charges exist not because society wants judges to punish vagrants or drunks but because it wants an officer to have the legal tools to remove undesirable persons from a neighborhood when informal efforts to preserve order in the streets have failed.

Once we begin to think of all aspects of police work as involving the application of universal rules under special procedures, we inevitably ask what constitutes an "undesirable person" and why we should "criminalize" vagrancy or drunkenness. A strong and commendable desire to see that people are treated fairly makes us worry about allowing the police to rout persons who are undesirable by some vague or parochial standard. A growing and not-so-commendable utilitarianism leads us to doubt that any behavior that does not "hurt" another person should be made illegal. And thus many of us who watch over the police are reluctant to allow them to perform, in the only way they can, a function that every neighborhood desperately wants them to perform.

This wish to "decriminalize" disreputable behavior that "harms no one"—and thus remove the ultimate sanction the police can employ to maintain neighborhood order—is, we think, a mistake. Arresting a single drunk or a single vagrant who has harmed no identifiable person seems unjust, and in a sense it is. But failing to do anything about a score of drunks or a hundred vagrants may destroy an entire community. A particular rule that seems to make sense in the individual case makes no sense when it is made a universal rule and applied to all cases. It makes no sense because it fails to take into account the connection between one broken window left untended and a thousand broken windows. Of course, agencies rather than the police could attend to the problems posed by drunks or the mentally ill, but in most communities—especially where the "deinstitutionalization" movement has been strong—they do not.

The concern about equity is more serious. We might agree that certain behavior makes one person more undesirable than another, but how do we ensure that age or skin color or national origin or harmless mannerisms will not also become the basis for distinguishing the undesirable from the desirable? How do we ensure, in short, that the police do not become the agents of neighborhood bigotry?

We can offer no wholly satisfactory answer to this important question. We are not confident that there is a satisfactory answer, except to hope that by their selection, training, and supervision, the police will be inculcated with a clear sense of the outer limit of their discretionary authority. That limit, roughly, is this—the police exist to help regulate behavior, not to maintain the racial or ethnic purity of a neighborhood.

Consider the case of the Robert Taylor Homes in Chicago, one of the largest public-housing projects in the country. It is home for nearly 20,000 people, all black, and extends over ninety-two acres along South State Street. It was named after a distinguished black who had been, during the 1940s, chairman of the Chicago Housing Authority. Not long after it opened, in 1962, relations between project residents and the police deteriorated badly. The citizens felt that the police were insensitive or brutal; the police, in turn, complained of unprovoked attacks on them. Some Chicago officers tell of times when they were afraid to enter the Homes. Crime rates soared.

Today, the atmosphere has changed. Police-citizen relations have improved—apparently, both sides learned something from the earlier experience. Recently, a boy stole a purse and ran off. Several young persons who saw the theft voluntarily passed along to the police information of the identity and residence of the thief, and they did this publicly, with friends and neighbors looking on. But problems persist, chief among them the presence of youth gangs that terrorize residents and recruit members in the project. The people expect the police to "do something" about this, and the police are determined to do just that.

But do what? Though the police can obviously make arrests whenever a gang member breaks the law, a gang can form, recruit, and congregate without breaking the law. And only a tiny fraction of gang-related crimes can be solved by an arrest; thus, if an arrest is the only recourse for the police, the residents' fears will go unassuaged. The police will soon feel helpless, and the residents will again believe that the police "do nothing." What the police in fact do is to chase known gang members out of the project. In the words of one officer, "We kick ass." Project residents both know and approve of this. The tacit police-citizen alliance in the project is reinforced by the police view that the cops and the gangs are the two rival sources of power in the area, and that the gangs are not going to win.

None of this is easily reconciled with any conception of due process or fair treatment. Since both residents and gang members are black, race is not a factor. But it could be. Suppose a white project confronted a black gang, or vice versa. We would be apprehensive about the police taking sides. But the substantive problem remains the same: how can the police strengthen the informal social-control mechanisms of natural communities in order to minimize fear in public places? Law enforcement, per se, is no answer. A gang can weaken or destroy a community by standing about in a menacing fashion and speaking rudely to passersby without breaking the law.

We have difficulty thinking about such matters, not simply because the ethical and legal issues are so complex but because we have become accustomed to thinking of the law in essentially individualistic terms. The law defines *my* rights, punishes *his* behavior, and is applied by *that* officer because of *this* harm. We assume, in thinking this way, that what is good for the individual will be good for the community, and what doesn't matter when it happens to one person won't matter if it happens to many. Ordinarily, those are plausible assumptions. But in cases where behavior that is tolerable to one person is intolerable to many others, the reactions of the others—fear, withdrawal, flight—may ultimately make matters worse for everyone, including the individual who first professed his indifference.

It may be their greater sensitivity to communal as opposed to individual needs that helps explain why the residents of small communities are more satisfied with their police than are the residents of similar neighborhoods in big cities. Elinor Ostrom and her coworkers at Indiana University compared the perception of police services in two poor, all-black Illinois towns—Phoenix and

East Chicago Heights—with those of three comparable all-black neighborhoods in Chicago. The level of criminal victimization and the quality of police-community relations appeared to be about the same in the towns and the Chicago neighborhoods. But the citizens living in their own villages were much more likely than those living in the Chicago neighborhoods to say that they do not stay at home for fear of crime, to agree that the local police have "the right to take any action necessary" to deal with problems, and to agree that the police "look out for the needs of the average citizen." It is possible that the residents and the police of the small towns saw themselves as engaged in a collaborative effort to maintain a certain standard of communal life, whereas those of the big city felt themselves to be simply requesting and supplying particular services on an individual basis.

If this is true, how should a wise police chief deploy his meager forces? The first answer is that nobody knows for certain, and the most prudent course of action would be to try further variations on the Newark experiment, to see more precisely what works in what kinds of neighborhoods. The second answer is also a hedge—many aspects of order-maintenance in neighborhoods can probably best be handled in ways that involve the police minimally, if at all. A busy, bustling shopping center and a quiet, well-tended suburb may need almost no visible police presence. In both cases, the ratio of respectable to disreputable people is ordinarily so high as to make informal social control effective.

Even in areas that are in jeopardy from disorderly elements, citizen action without substantial police involvement may be sufficient. Meetings between teenagers who like to hang out on a particular corner and adults who want to use that corner might well lead to an amicable agreement on a set of rules about how many people can be allowed to congregate, where, and when.

Where no understanding is possible—or if possible, not observed—citizen patrols may be a sufficient response. There are two traditions of communal involvement in maintaining order. One, that of the "community watchmen," is as old as the first settlement of the New World. Until well into the nineteenth century, volunteer watchmen, not policemen, patrolled their communities to keep order. They did so, by and large, without taking the law into their own hands—without, that is, punishing persons or using force. Their presence deterred disorder or alerted the community to disorder that could not be deterred. There are hundreds of such efforts today in communities all across the nation. Perhaps the best known is that of the Guardian Angels, a group of unarmed young persons in distinctive berets and T-shirts, who first came to public attention when they began patrolling the New York City subways but who claim now to have chapters in more than thirty American cities. Unfortunately, we have little information about the effect of these groups on crime. It is possible, however, that whatever their effect on crime, citizens find their presence reassuring, and that they thus contribute to maintaining a sense of order and civility.

The second tradition is that of the "vigilante." Rarely a feature of the settled communities of the East, it was primarily to be found in those frontier towns that grew up in advance of the reach of government. More than 350 vigilante groups are known to have existed; their distinctive feature was that their members did take the law into their own hands, by acting as judge, jury, and often executioner as well as policeman. Today, the vigilante movement is conspicuous by its rarity, despite the great fear expressed by citizens that the older cities are becoming "urban frontiers." But some community-watchmen groups have skirted the line, and others may cross it in the future. An ambiguous case, reported in the *Wall Street Journal*, involved a citizens' patrol in the Silver Lake area of Belleville, New Jersey. A leader told the reporter, "We look for outsiders." If a few teenagers from outside the neighborhood enter it, "we ask them their business," he said. "If they say they're going down the street to see Mrs. Jones, fine, we let them pass. But then we follow them down the block to make sure they're really going to see Mrs. Jones."

Though citizens can do a great deal, the police are plainly the key to order-maintenance. For one thing, many communities, such as the Robert Taylor Homes, cannot do the job by themselves. For another, no citizen in a neighborhood, even an organized one, is likely to feel the sense of responsibility that wearing a badge confers. Psychologists have done many studies on why people fail to go to the aid of persons being attacked or seeking help, and they have learned that the cause is not "apathy" or "selfishness" but the absence of some plausible grounds for feeling that one must personally accept responsibility. Ironically, avoiding responsibility is easier when a lot of people are standing about. On streets and in public places, where order is so important, many people are likely to be "around," a fact that reduces the chance of any one person acting as the agent of the community. The police officer's uniform singles him out as a person who must accept responsibility if asked. In addition, officers, more easily than their fellow citizens, can be expected to distinguish between what is necessary to protect the safety of the street and what merely protects its ethnic purity.

But the police forces of America are losing, not gaining, members. Some cities have suffered substantial cuts in the number of officers available for duty. These cuts are not likely to be reversed in the near future. Therefore, each department must assign its existing officers with great care. Some neighborhoods are so demoralized and crime-ridden as to make foot patrol useless; the best the police can do with limited resources is respond to the enormous number of calls for service. Other neighborhoods are so stable and serene as to make foot patrol unnecessary. The key is to identify neighborhoods at the tipping point—where the public order is deteriorating but not unreclaimable, where the streets are used frequently but by apprehensive people, where a window is likely to be broken at any time, and must quickly be fixed if all are not to be shattered.

Most police departments do not have ways of systematically identifying such areas and assigning officers to them. Officers are assigned on the basis of crime rates (meaning that marginally threatened areas are often stripped so that police can investigate crimes in areas where the situation is hopeless) or on the basis of calls for service (despite the fact that most citizens do not call the police when they are merely frightened or annoyed). To allocate patrol wisely, the department must look at the neighborhoods and decide, from first-hand evidence, where an additional officer will make the greatest difference in promoting a sense of safety.

One way to stretch limited police resources is being tried in some public-housing projects. Tenant organizations hire off-duty police officers for patrol work in their buildings. The costs are not high (at least not per resident), the officer likes the additional income, and the residents feel safer. Such arrangements are probably more successful than hiring private watchmen, and the Newark experiment helps us understand why. A private security guard may deter crime or misconduct by his presence, and he may go to the aid of persons needing help, but he may well not intervene—that is, control or drive away—someone challenging community standards. Being a sworn officer—a "real cop"—seems to give one the confidence, the sense of duty, and the aura of authority necessary to perform this difficult task.

Patrol officers might be encouraged to go to and from duty stations on public transportation and, while on the bus or subway car, enforce rules about smoking, drinking, disorderly conduct, and the like. The enforcement need involve nothing more than ejecting the offender (the offense, after all, is not one with which a booking officer or a judge wishes to be bothered). Perhaps the random but relentless maintenance of standards on buses would lead to conditions on buses that approximate the level of civility we now take for granted on airplanes.

But the most important requirement is to think that to maintain order in precarious situations is a vital job. The police know this is one of their functions, and they also believe, correctly, that it cannot be done to the exclusion of criminal investigation and responding to calls. We may have encouraged them to suppose, however, on the basis of our oft-repeated concerns about serious, violent crime, that they will be judged exclusively on their capacity as crime-fighters. To the extent that this is the case, police administrators will continue to concentrate police personnel in the highest-crime areas (though not necessarily in the areas most vulnerable to criminal invasion), emphasize their training in the law and criminal apprehension (and not their training in managing street life), and join too quickly in campaigns to decriminalize "harmless" behavior (though public drunkenness, street prostitution, and pornographic displays can destroy a community more quickly than any team of professional burglars).

Above all, we must return to our long-abandoned view that the police ought to protect communities as well as individuals. Our crime statistics and victimization surveys measure individual losses, but they do not measure communal losses. Just as physicians now recognize the importance of fostering health rather than simply treating illness, so the police—and the rest of us—ought to recognize the importance of maintaining, intact, communities without broken windows.

SOURCE: From *The Atlantic Monthly* (March, 1982):29–83. Reprinted by permission of The Atlantic Monthly Company.

QUESTIONS FOR DISCUSSION AND WRITING

1. How can a neighborhood be "safer" when the crime rate does not go down?

2. What happens when a broken window is left unrepaired, and why does this happen?

3. What do the authors call a "mistake," and why do they feel this way?

THE CHANGING NATURE OF DEATH PENALTY DEBATES

MICHAEL L. RADELET

MARIAN J. BORG

In a monumental 1972 decision by the U.S. Supreme Court, all but a few death penalty statutes in the United States were declared unconstitutional. Consequentially, each of the 630 or so inmates then on America's death rows was resentenced to life imprisonment. The nine opinions in the case, decided by a 5–4 vote, remain the longest ever written by the Supreme Court. Four years later, defying predictions that the United States would never again witness executions, the Supreme Court reversed its course toward abolition by approving several newly enacted capital statutes. By mid-1999 there were some 3,500 men and 50 women (including 65 juveniles whose capital offenses predated their eighteenth birthdays) on death rows in 38 states and two federal jurisdictions. Another 550 death row inmates had been executed in the two preceding decades.

The goal of this [article] is to review recent social science research that has examined various dimensions of capital punishment. We organize this review by examining how the public debate on the death penalty in the United States has changed over the past quarter century. We attempt to show that arguments supporting the death penalty today, compared to 25 years ago, rely less on such issues as deterrence, cost, and religious principles, and more on grounds of retribution. In addition, those who support the death penalty are more likely today than in years past to acknowledge the inevitability of racial and class bias in death sentencing, as well as the inevitability of executing the innocent. We suggest that many of these arguments have changed because of social science research and that the changing nature of the death penalty debate in this country is part of a worldwide historical trend toward abolition of capital punishment.

DETERRENCE

In the early 1970s, the top argument in favor of the death penalty was general deterrence. This argument suggests that we must punish offenders to discourage others from committing similar offenses; we punish past offenders to send a message to potential offenders. In a broad sense, the deterrent effect of punishment is thought to be a function of three main elements: certainty, celerity, and severity. First, people do not violate laws if they are certain that they will be caught and punished. Second, celerity refers to the elapsed time between the commission of an offense and the administration of punishment. In theory, the more quickly a punishment is carried out, the greater its deterrent effect. Third, the deterrent effect of a punishment is a function of its severity. However, over the last two decades more and more scholars and citizens have realized that the deterrent effect of a punishment is not a consistent direct effect of its severity—after a while, increases in the severity of a punishment no longer add to its deterrent benefits. In fact, increases in a punishment's severity have decreasing incremental deterrent effect, so that eventually any increase in severity will no longer matter. If one wishes to deter another from leaning on a stove, medium heat works just as well as high heat.

Scores of researchers have examined the possibility that the death penalty has a greater deterrent effect on homicide rates than long-term imprisonment. Overall, the vast majority of deterrence studies have failed to support the hypothesis that the death penalty is a more effective deterrent to criminal homicides than long imprisonment.

There is widespread agreement among both criminologists and law enforcement officials that capital punishment has little curbing effect on homicide rates that is superior to long-term imprisonment. In a recent survey of 70 current and former presidents of three professional associations of criminologists, 85% of the experts agreed that the empirical research on deterrence has shown that the death penalty never has been, is not, and never could be superior to long prison sentences as a deterrent to criminal violence. Similarly, a 1995 survey of nearly 400 randomly selected police chiefs and county sheriffs from throughout the United States found that two-thirds did not believe that the death penalty significantly lowered the number of murders.

Opinion polls show that the general public is gradually learning the results of this body of research. According to a 1991 Gallup Poll, only 51% of Americans believed the death penalty had deterrent effects, a drop of 11% from 1985. By 1997 this had fallen to 45%. In short, a remarkable change in the way the death penalty is justified is occurring. What was once the public's most widely cited justification for the death penalty is today rapidly losing its appeal.

INCAPACITATION

A second change in death penalty arguments involves the incapacitation hypothesis, which suggests that we need to execute the most heinous killers in order to prevent them from killing again. According to this view, we need the death penalty to protect the public from recidivist murders. On its face it is a simple and attractive position: No executed prisoner has ever killed again, and some convicted murderers will undoubtedly kill again if, instead of being executed, they are sentenced to prison terms.

Research addressing this issue has focused on calculating precise risks of prison homicides and recidivist murder. This work has found that the odds of repeat murder are low, and that people convicted of homicide tend to make better adjustments to prison (and, if released, exhibit lower rates of recidivism) than do other convicted felons. The best research on this issue has been done by James Marquart and Jonathan Sorensen, sociologists at Sam Houston State University, who tracked down 558 of the 630 people on death row when all death sentences in the United States were invalidated by the Supreme Court in 1972. Contrary to the predictions of those who advocate the death penalty on the grounds of incapacitation, Marquart and Sorensen found that among those whose death sentences were commuted in 1972, only about 1% went on to kill again. This figure is almost identical with the number of death row prisoners later found to be innocent. Interpreted another way, these figures suggest that 100 prisoners would have to be executed to incapacitate the one person who statistically might be expected to repeat. Arguably, today's more sophisticated prisons and the virtual elimination of parole have reduced the risks of repeat homicide even further.

While the incapacitation argument might have made sense in an era when there were no prisons available for long-term confinement, the empirical evidence suggests that today's prisons and the widespread availability of long prison terms are just as effective as capital punishment in preventing murderers from repeating their crimes. Still, Gross concludes that next to retribution, incapacitation is the second most popular reason for favoring the death penalty. But in the last two decades it has become clear that if citizens are convinced that convicted murderers will never be released from prison, support for the death penalty drops dramatically.

A key factor that has changed in sentencing for capital crimes since the *Furman* decision in 1972 has been the increased availability of "life without parole" as an alternative to the death penalty. Today, at least 32 states offer this option, although it is clear that most citizens and jurors do not realize this and vastly underestimate the amount of time that those convicted of capital murders will spend in prison. Another segment of the population realizes that life without parole is an alternative to the death penalty, but in spite of this, believe that future political leaders or judges will find ways to release life-sentenced inmates. It is a paradoxical position: Such citizens support giving the government the ultimate power to take the lives of its citizens but do so because of distrust of these same governments and/or the perception of governmental incompetency.

CAPRICE AND BIAS

As new death penalty laws were being passed in the 1970s to replace those invalidated by the *Furman* decision, many thought that the death penalty could be applied in a way that would avoid the arbitrariness and racial and class bias that had been condemned in *Furman*. However, research conducted in the years since has all but unanimously concluded that the new laws have failed to achieve this goal.

Most of these analyses conclude that for crimes that are comparable, the death penalty is between three and four times more likely to be imposed in cases in which the victim is white rather than black.

In the most recent overview of the problem of racial bias in the administration of the death penalty, Amnesty International concluded that it was "undeniable" that the death penalty in the United States "is applied disproportionately on the basis of race, ethnicity, and social status."

By any measure, the most comprehensive research ever produced on sentencing disparities in American criminal courts is the work of David Baldus and his colleagues conducted in Georgia in the 1970s and 1980s. After statistically controlling for some 230 variables, these researchers concluded that the odds of a death sentence for those who kill whites in Georgia are 4.3 times higher than the odds of a death sentence for those who kill blacks. Attorneys representing Georgia death row inmate Warren McCleskey took these data to the Supreme

Court in 1987, claiming unfair racial bias in the administration of the death penalty in Georgia. But the Court rejected the argument, as well as the idea that a statistical pattern of bias could prove any bias in McCleskey's individual case.

The vote in the McCleskey case was 5 to 4. Interestingly, the decision was written and the deciding vote cast by Justice Lewis Powell, who was then serving his last year on the Court. Four years later, Powell's biographer asked the retired justice if he wished he could change his vote in any single case. Powell replied, "Yes, *McCleskey v. Kemp*." Powell, who voted in dissent in *Furman* and in his years on the Court remained among the justices who regularly voted to sustain death sentences, had changed his mind. "I have come to think that capital punishment should be abolished . . . [because] it serves no useful purpose."

Public opinion on the death penalty shows that while most Americans recognize the problems of race and class bias, they do not view such discrimination as a reason to oppose the death penalty. In the 1999 Gallup Poll, for example, 65% of the respondents agreed that a poor person is more likely than a person of average to above-average income to receive the death penalty for the same crime. Half the respondents believed that black defendants are more likely than whites to receive a death sentence for the same crime. Despite recognizing these inequities, 71% of those polled favored the death penalty.

COST

A fourth way in which death penalty arguments have changed in the past 25 years involves the issue of its fiscal costs. Two decades ago, some citizens and political leaders supported the death penalty as a way of avoiding the financial burdens of housing inmates for life or long prison terms. A 1985 Gallup Poll found that 11% of those supporting the death penalty cited the high fiscal costs of imprisonment as a reason for their positions.

Since then, however, research has firmly established that a modern death penalty system costs several times more than an alternative system in which the maximum criminal punishment is life imprisonment without parole. This research has been conducted in different states with different data sets by newspapers, courts and legislatures, and academics. Estimates by the *Miami Herald* are typical: $3.2 million for every electrocution versus $600,000 for life imprisonment. These cost figures for capital punishment include expenses for not only those cases that end in execution, but also the many more cases in which the death penalty is sought that never end with a death sentence, and cases in which a death sentence is pronounced but never carried out. They also include the costs both for trials and for the lengthy appeals that are necessary before an execution can be authorized. Consequently, the cost issue today has become an anti-death penalty argument, albeit of debatable strength.

MISCARRIAGES OF JUSTICE

Death penalty arguments are changing in a fifth way: Death penalty retentionists now admit that as long as we use the death penalty, innocent defendants will occasionally be executed. Until a decade ago, the pro-death penalty literature took the position that such blunders were historical oddities and could never be committed in modern times. Today the argument is not over the existence or even the inevitability of such errors, but whether the alleged benefits of the death penalty outweigh these uncontested liabilities. Several studies conducted over the last two decades have documented the problem of erroneous convictions in homicide cases. Since 1970 there have been 80 people released from death rows in the United States because of innocence.

Citing research by social scientists on racial disparities in death sentencing and on the inevitability of wrongful convictions, Supreme Court Justice Harry Blackmun, who until then counted himself as a supporter of the death penalty, wrote in 1994:

> From this day forward, I no longer shall tinker with the machinery of death. For more than 20 years I have endeavored . . . along with the majority of this Court, to develop procedural and substantive rules that would lend more than the mere appearance of fairness to the death penalty endeavor. Rather than continue to coddle the Court's delusion that the desired level of fairness has been achieved . . . I feel

morally and intellectually obligated to concede that the death penalty experiment has failed.

THE GROWING FOCUS ON RETRIBUTION

Thus far we have argued that in the last two dozen years, debates over deterrence, incapacitation, cost, fairness, and the inevitability of executing the innocent have all been either neutralized or won by those who stand opposed to the death penalty. But while death penalty advocates increasingly acknowledge that these traditional justifications are growing less persuasive, in their place we have witnessed the ascendancy of what has become the most important contemporary pro-death penalty argument: retribution. Here one argues that justice requires the death penalty. Those who commit the most premeditated or heinous murders should be executed simply on the grounds that they deserve it.

Retributive arguments are often made in the name of families of homicide victims, who are depicted as "needing" or otherwise benefiting from the retributive satisfaction that the death penalty promises. Perhaps the question most frequently posed to death penalty opponents during debates is "How would you feel if your closest loved one was brutally murdered?"

Those who oppose capital punishment can reasonably respond by pointing out that the death penalty offers much less to families of homicide victims than it first appears. For example, by diverting vast resources into death penalty cases—a small proportion of all homicide cases—the state has fewer resources for families of noncapital homicide victims and for more effective assistance for families of homicide victims. Or, one could argue that the death penalty hurts families of homicide victims in cases in which the killer is *not* sentenced to death, since the prison sentence risks making them feel as if their loved one's death was not "worth" the life of the killer. Or, one could argue that the death penalty serves to keep the case open for many years before the execution actually occurs, often through resentences or retrials, continuously preventing the wounds of the family of the victim from healing.

Unlike the arguments reviewed above, retribution is a non-empirical justification and thus all but impossible to test with empirical data. After all, there are no mathematical formulae available or on the horizon that can tell us precisely (or even roughly) how much of a given punishment a murderer—or any other offender—"deserves." In the end, the calculation of how much punishment a criminal "deserves" becomes more a moral and less a criminological issue.

To the extent that the death penalty is justified on moral (retributive) grounds, it is paradoxical that much of what can be called the "moral leadership" in the United States is already opposed to the death penalty. Leaders of Catholic, most Protestant, and Jewish denominations are strongly opposed to the death penalty, and most formal religious organizations in the United States have endorsed statements in favor of abolition.

There is also evidence that the general public recognizes some limits to retributive punishments. In 1991, the Gallup Poll asked respondents which method of execution they preferred. After all, if one were *really* retributive, and if people like Oklahoma City bomber Timothy McVeigh *really* got what they "deserved," the preferred method might be slow boiling or public crucifixion. Yet, 66% of the respondents favored lethal injection, an increase of ten points from six years earlier. This preference likely reflects, at least in part, the belief that inmates might suffer too much in electric chairs and gas chambers. In contrast, lethal injection offers an ostensibly less painful death.

The concern to reduce the prisoner's suffering is inconsistent with the idea that we need the death penalty on the grounds of retributive justice.

Trends Toward Abolition

The above changes in death penalty debates come at a time when there is a relatively rapid worldwide movement away from the death penalty. In 1998, five countries combined for over 80% of the world's executions—China, the Democratic Republic of the Congo, Iran, Iraq, and the United States. These first four are countries with whom, normally, the United States does not share domestic policies.

A century ago, only 3 countries had abolished the death penalty for all crimes; by the time of *Furman* in 1972 the number had risen to 19. But since then the number of abolitionist countries has tripled. By the end of 1998, 67 countries had abolished the death penalty for all offenses, 14 more retained it only for "exceptional" crimes (i.e., during wartime), and 24 others had not had an execution in at least 10 years. All 15 members of the European Union have abolished the death penalty, and the Council of Europe, with 41 members, has made the abolition of the death penalty a condition of membership. In the first decision ever made by the newly constituted South African Constitutional Court in 1995—that country's Supreme Court—the death penalty was abolished as "cruel, inhuman and degrading." Russia, a country that was among the world's leaders in executions in the early 1990s, announced in 1999 that it, too, was abolishing the death penalty. In June, 1999, President Boris Yeltsin commuted over 700 death sentences to terms of imprisonment. Clearly, in a comparatively short historical time span, more than half of the countries in the world have abolished the death penalty, and the momentum is unquestionably in the direction of total worldwide abolition.

The above is not meant to suggest the absence of countries that continue to swim against the tide of worldwide abolition. Internationally, the death penalty is slowly expanding in a few countries, such as the Philippines, Taiwan, Yemen, and the English-speaking Caribbean. In the United States, both Congress and the Supreme Court are increasingly restricting access to federal courts by inmates contesting their death sentences. Few would disagree with the prediction that the next few years will be busy ones for America's executioners.

On the other hand, as the 1990s draw to a close, more and more countries are signing international treaties that abolish or restrict the death penalty. For the third year, in 1999, the UN Commission on Human Rights, headquartered in Geneva, passed a resolution calling for a moratorium on death sentencing. The resolution was cosponsored by 72 states (compared to 47 in 1997). Toward this end, the 1999 resolution reaffirms an international ban on executions of those under 18, those who are pregnant, and those who are suffering from mental illness. The resolution also calls for non-death penalty nations to refuse to extradite suspects to countries that continue to use executions as a form of punishment.

Other calls for moratoriums on death sentencing are also being made. In May, 1999, the Nebraska legislature passed a resolution calling for a two-year moratorium on executions because of questions of equity in the administration of its state's death penalty. In March, 1999, the Illinois House of Representatives passed a similar resolution calling for a moratorium on executions; authorities in that state have acknowledged that 12 prisoners have been sent to death row in the past two decades who turned out to be innocent. Finally, in February, 1997, on behalf of its 400,000 members, the normally conservative House of Delegates of the American Bar Association called for a moratorium on the death penalty. The House of Delegates cited four principal reasons: the lack of adequate defense counsel, the erosion of state post-conviction and federal habeas corpus review, the continuing problem of racial bias in the administration of the death penalty, and the refusal of states and the courts to take action to prevent the execution of juveniles and the mentally retarded.

CONCLUSION

The goal of this [article] has been to present a brief overview of recent scholarship on the death penalty. We conclude with three observations derived from the foregoing discussion.

First, the past two dozen years have witnessed significant changes in the nature of death penalty debates. Those who support the death penalty are less likely, and indeed less able, to claim that the death penalty has a deterrent effect greater than that of long imprisonment, or that the death penalty is cheaper than long imprisonment, or that it gives significant incapacitative benefits not offered by long imprisonment. Fewer and fewer religious leaders adopt a pro-death penalty position, and advocates of capital punishment have been forced to admit that the death penalty continues to be applied with unacceptable arbitrariness, as well as racial

and class bias. A fair assessment of the data also leads to the conclusion that as long as the executioner is in the state's employ, innocent people will occasionally be executed. Increasingly, the best (and arguably the sole) justification for the death penalty rests on retributive grounds.

Second, at the same time as American discourse on the death penalty is changing, there is an accelerating worldwide decline in the acceptance of capital punishment. Indeed, the trend toward the worldwide abolition of the death penalty is inexorable. To be sure, the immediate future will continue to bring high numbers of executions in American jurisdictions. In all probability, these will increase over the numbers witnessed today. Nonetheless, taking a long-term historical view, the trend toward the abolition of the death penalty, which has now lasted for more than two centuries, will continue. Things could change quickly; the final thrust might come from conservative politicians who turn against the death penalty in the name of fiscal austerity, religious principles (e.g., a consistent "pro-life" stand), responsible crime-fighting, or genuine concern for a "smaller" government. Public support for the death penalty might also drop if there emerged absolute incontrovertible proof that an innocent prisoner had been executed. For those who oppose the death penalty, the long-term forecast should fuel optimism.

Finally, our review sends a positive message to criminologists and other social scientists who often feel as if their research is ignored by the public and by policy makers. As our review suggests, changes in the nature of death penalty debates are a direct consequence of social scientists' close and careful examination of the various dimensions of these arguments. Scholars have examined questions of deterrence, race, cost, methods of execution, innocence, juror decision-making, and the political and social environments in which death penalty legislation has emerged. Clearly, this is one area of public policy where social science research is making a slow but perceptible impact.

QUESTIONS FOR DISCUSSION AND WRITING

1. What is the goal of this article, and what do the supporting arguments show? To what do the authors attribute the change?

2. What significant changes in the nature of death penalty debates have occurred in the past two dozen years?

3. What has happened at the same time as American discourse on the death penalty is changing?

ABOLISH THE JUVENILE COURT

Youthfulness, Criminal Responsibility, and Sentencing Policy

BARRY C. FELD

I. INTRODUCTION

Within the past three decades, judicial decisions, legislative amendments, and administrative changes have transformed the juvenile court from a nominally rehabilitative social welfare agency into a scaled-down, second-class criminal court for young people. These reforms have converted the historical ideal of the juvenile court as a social welfare institution into a penal system that provides young offenders with neither therapy nor justice. The substantive and procedural convergence between juvenile and criminal courts eliminates virtually all of the conceptual and operational differences in strategies of criminal social control for youths and adults. No compelling reasons exist to maintain, separate from an adult criminal court, a punitive juvenile court whose only remaining distinctions are its persisting procedural deficiencies. Rather, states should abolish juvenile courts' delinquency jurisdiction and formally recognize youthfulness as a mitigating factor in the sentencing of younger criminal offenders. Such a policy would provide younger offenders with substantive protections comparable to those afforded by juvenile courts, assure greater procedural regularity in the determination of guilt, and avoid the disjunctions in social control caused by maintaining two duplicative and inconsistent criminal justice systems.

II. TRANSFORMED BUT UNREFORMED: THE RECENT HISTORY OF THE JUVENILE COURT

A. The Juvenile Court

Ideological changes in cultural conceptions of children and in strategies of social control during the nineteenth century led to the creation of the juvenile court in 1899. The juvenile court reform movement removed children from the adult criminal justice and corrections systems, provided them with individualized treatment in a separate system, and substituted a scientific and preventative alternative to the criminal law's punitive policies. By separating children from adults and providing a rehabilitative alternative to punishment, juvenile courts rejected both the criminal law's jurisprudence and its procedural safeguards such as juries and lawyers. Judges conducted confidential and private hearings, limited public access to court proceedings and court records, employed a euphemistic vocabulary to minimize stigma, and adjudicated youths to be delinquent rather than convicted them of crimes. Under the guise of *parens patriae*, the juvenile court emphasized treatment, supervision, and control rather than punishment. The juvenile court's "rehabilitative ideal" envisioned a specialized judge trained in social science and child development whose empathic qualities and insight would enable her to make individualized therapeutic dispositions in the "best interests" of the child. Reformers pursued benevolent goals, individualized their solicitude, and maximized discretion to provide flexibility in diagnosis and treatment of the "whole child." They regarded a child's crimes primarily as a symptom of her "real needs," and consequently the nature of the offense affected neither the degree nor the duration of intervention. Rather, juvenile court judges imposed indeterminate and non-proportional sentences that potentially continued for the duration of minority.

B. The Constitutional Domestication of the Juvenile Court

In *In re Gault* the Supreme Court began to transform the juvenile court into a very different institution than the Progressives contemplated. The Supreme Court engrafted some formal procedures at trial onto the juvenile court's individualized treatment sentencing scheme. Although the Court did not intend its decisions to alter juvenile courts' therapeutic mission, in the aftermath of *Gault*, judicial, legislative, and administrative changes have fostered a procedural and substantive convergence with adult criminal courts. Several subsequent Supreme Court decisions furthered the "criminalizing" of the juvenile court. In *In re Winship*, the Court required states to prove juvenile delinquency by the criminal law's standard of proof "beyond a reasonable doubt."

Gault and *Winship* unintentionally, but inevitably, transformed the juvenile court system from its original Progressive conception as a social welfare agency into a wholly-owned subsidiary of the criminal justice system. By emphasizing criminal procedural regularity in the determination of delinquency, the Court shifted the focus of juvenile courts from paternalistic assessments of a youth's "real needs" to proof of commission of a crime. And, ironically, *Gault* and *Winship's* insistence on greater criminal procedural safeguards in juvenile courts may have legitimated more punitive dispositions for young offenders.

In *McKeiver v. Pennsylvania,* however, the Court denied to juveniles the constitutional right to jury trials in delinquency proceedings and halted the extension of full procedural parity with adult criminal prosecutions. Without elaborating upon or analyzing the distinctions, *McKeiver* relied upon the rhetorical differences between juvenile courts' *treatment* rationale and criminal courts' *punitive* purpose to justify the procedural disparities between the two settings. Because *McKeiver* endorsed a *treatment* justification for its decision, the right to a jury trial provides the crucial legal condition precedent to *punish* youths explicitly in juvenile courts. Several recent juvenile justice legislative reforms provide some youths with a statutory right to a jury in order to expand the punitive sentencing options available to juvenile court judges.

C. The Transformation of the Juvenile Court

In the decades since *Gault*, legislative, judicial, and administrative changes have modified juvenile courts' jurisdiction, purpose, and procedures and fostered their convergence with criminal courts. These interrelated developments—increased procedural formality, removal of status offenders from juvenile court jurisdiction, waiver of serious offenders to the adult system, and an increased emphasis on punishment in sentencing delinquents—constitute a form of criminological "triage," crucial components of the criminalizing of the juvenile court, and elements of the erosion of the theoretical and practical differences between the two systems. This "triage" strategy removes many middle-class, white, and female non-criminal status offenders from the juvenile court; simultaneously transfers persistent, violent, and disproportionally minority youths to criminal court for prosecution as adults; and imposes increasingly punitive sanctions on those middle-range delinquent criminal offenders who remain under the jurisdiction of the juvenile court. As a result of these implicit triage policies, juvenile courts increasingly function similarly to adult criminal courts.

1. Status Offenses

Legislative recognition that juvenile courts often failed to realize their benevolent purposes has led to a strategic retrenchment of juvenile courts' jurisdiction over non-criminal misconduct such as truancy or incorrigibility, behavior that would not be a crime if committed by an adult. In the 1970s, critics objected that juvenile courts' status jurisdiction treated non-criminal offenders indiscriminately like criminal delinquents, disabled families and other sources of referral through one-sided intervention, and posed insuperable legal issues for the court. Judicial and legislative disillusionment with juvenile courts' responses to noncriminal youths led to diversion, deinstitutionalization, and decriminalization reforms that have removed much of the "soft" end of juvenile court clientele. These legislative and judicial reforms represent a strategic withdrawal from "child saving," an acknowledgment of the limited utility of coercive intervention to provide for child welfare, a reduced role in enforcing normative concepts of childhood, and a diminished prevention mission.

2. Waiver of Juvenile Offenders to Adult Criminal Court

A second jurisdictional change entails the criminalizing of serious juvenile offenders as courts and legislatures increasingly transfer chronic and violent youths from juvenile to criminal courts for prosecution as adults. Transfer laws simultaneously attempt to resolve both fundamental crime control issues and the ambivalence embedded in our cultural construction of youth. The jurisprudential conflicts reflect many of the current sentencing policy debates: the tensions between rehabilitation or incapacitation and retribution, between basing decisions on characteristics of the individual offender or the seriousness of the offense, between discretion and rules, and between indeterminacy and determinacy. Waiver laws attempt to reconcile the contradictions posed when the child is a criminal and the criminal is a child.

In most states, judges decide whether a youth is a criminal or a delinquent in a waiver hearing and base their discretionary assessments on a juvenile's "amenability to treatment" or "dangerousness." The inherent subjectivity of waiver criteria permits a variety of racial inequalities and geographic disparities to occur when judges attempt to interpret and apply these vague laws. A "lack of fit" between judicial waiver decisions and criminal court sentencing practices often produces a "punishment gap" that allows many chronic and active young criminals to fall

between the cracks of the two systems. By contrast, when judicial waiver decisions, legislatively excluded offenses, or prosecutorial charging decisions focus on violent young offenders, these youths often receive substantially longer sentences as criminals than do their delinquent counterparts who remain in juvenile court simply because of their new-found "adult" status.

In response to the rise in youth homicide and gun violence in the late 1980s, almost every state has amended its waiver statutes and other provisions of its juvenile codes in a frantic effort to "get tough" and to stem the tide. These recent changes signal a fundamental inversion in juvenile court jurisprudence from treatment to punishment, from rehabilitation to retribution, from immature child to responsible criminal. Legislatures increasingly use age and offense criteria to redefine the boundaries of adulthood, coordinate juvenile transfer and adult sentencing practices, and reduce the "punishment gap." The common over-arching legislative strategy reflects a jurisprudential shift from the *principle of individualized justice* to the *principle of offense*, from rehabilitation to retribution, and an emphasis on the seriousness of the offense rather than judges' clinical assessments of offenders' "amenability to treatment."

Regardless of the details of these legislative strategies, the efforts to "crack down" and to "get tough" repudiate rehabilitation and judicial discretion, narrow juvenile courts' jurisdiction, base youths' "adult" status increasingly on the offense charged, and reflect a shift toward more retributive sentencing policies. Finally, the legal shift to punish more young offenders as adults exposes at least some youths to the possibility of capital punishment for the crimes they committed as juveniles.

Although legislatures and courts transfer youths to criminal court so that they may receive longer sentences as adults than they could in the juvenile system, chronic property offenders constitute the bulk of juveniles judicially waived in most states, and they often receive shorter sentences as adults than do property offenders retained in juvenile court. By contrast, youths convicted of violent offenses in criminal courts appear to receive substantially longer sentences than do their retained juvenile counterparts. For youths and adults convicted of comparable crimes, both types of disparities raise issues of sentencing policy fairness and justice. No coherent policy rationales justify either type of disparities. Rather, some youths experience dramatically different consequences than do other offenders simply because of the disjunction between two separate criminal justice systems. The transition to adulthood also occurs during the peak of youths' criminal careers. Thus, jurisdictional bifurcation undermines the ability of the adult justice system to respond adequately to either persistent or violent young offenders. Without an integrated record system that merges juvenile with adult criminal histories, some chronic offenders may "slip through the cracks" and receive inappropriately lenient sentences as adults.

3. Sentencing Delinquent Offenders

The same public impetus and political pressures to waive the most serious young offenders to criminal courts also impel juvenile courts to "get tough" and punish more severely the remaining criminal delinquents, the residual "less bad of the worst." Several indicators reveal whether a juvenile court judge's disposition punishes a youth for his past offense or treats him for his future welfare. Increasingly, juvenile court legislative purpose clauses and court opinions explicitly endorse punishment as an appropriate component of juvenile sanctions. Currently, nearly half of the states use determinate or mandatory minimum sentencing provisions that base a youth's disposition on the offense she committed rather than her "real needs" to regulate at least some aspects of sentence duration, institutional commitment, or release. Empirical evaluations of juvenile courts' sentencing practices indicate that the present offense and prior record account for most of the explained variance in judges' dispositions of delinquents, and reinforce the criminal orientation of juvenile courts. Despite their penal focus, however, the individualized discretion inherent in juvenile courts' treatment ideology is often synonymous with racial discrimination. Finally, evaluations of conditions of confinement and treatment effectiveness belie any therapeutic "alternative purpose" to juvenile incarceration. In short, all of these indicators consistently reveal that *treating* juveniles closely resembles *punishing* adults. A strong, nationwide policy shift both in theory and in practice away from therapeutic dispositions toward punishment or incapacitation

of young offenders characterizes sentencing practice in the contemporary juvenile court.

4. Procedural Justice in Juvenile Courts

Procedure and substance intertwine inextricably in juvenile courts. The increased procedural formality since *Gault* coincides with the changes in legal theory and administrative practice from therapeutic, individualized dispositions toward more punitive, offense-based sentences. Indeed, *Gault's* procedural reforms may have encouraged these changes by legitimating punishment. These changes contradict *McKeiver's* premise that therapeutic juvenile dispositions require fewer procedural safeguards than do adult criminal prosecutions and raise questions about the quality of procedural justice in juvenile courts.

Although the formal procedures of juvenile and criminal courts have converged under *Gault's* impetus, a substantial gulf remains between theory and reality, between the "law on the books" and the "law in action." Theoretically, the Constitution and state juvenile statutes entitle delinquents to formal trials and assistance of counsel. But, the actual quality of procedural justice differs considerably from theory. Despite the criminalizing of juvenile courts, most states provide neither special procedures to protect youths from their own immaturity nor the full panoply of adult procedural safeguards. Instead, states treat juveniles just like adult criminal defendants when treating them equally places youths at a practical disadvantage, and use less effective juvenile court safeguards when those deficient procedures provide an advantage to the state.

A. Jury. Although the right to a jury trial is a crucial procedural safeguard when states punish offenders, the vast majority of jurisdictions uncritically follow *McKeiver's* lead and deny juveniles access to juries. Because judges and juries decide cases and apply *Winship's* "reasonable doubt" standard differently, it is easier to convict youths in juvenile court than in criminal court with comparable evidence. Moreover, *McKeiver* simply ignored the reality that juries protect against a weak or biased judge, inject the community's values into the law, and increase the visibility and accountability of justice administration. These protective functions acquire even greater importance in juvenile courts, which typically labor behind closed doors immune from public scrutiny.

On the other hand, several states have recently enacted legislation to increase the sentencing authority and punishment capacities of juvenile courts. These "blended" sentences begin with a youth's trial in juvenile court and then authorize the judge to impose enhanced sentences beyond those used for ordinary delinquents. New Mexico, Minnesota, and Texas provide examples of three different versions of these enhanced juvenile sentences for youths whom judges have not transferred to criminal court for prosecution as adults. Although these statutes differ in many details, all of the variants of "blended jurisdiction" provide these "intermediate" youths with adult criminal procedural safeguards, including the right to a jury trial. Once a state provides a youth with the right to a jury trial and other criminal procedural safeguards, it preserves the option to punish explicitly, as well as to extend jurisdiction for a period of several years or more beyond that available for ordinary delinquents. Thereby the state also gains greater flexibility to treat a youth. Finally, these statutes recognize the futility of trying to rationalize social control in two separate systems. These "blended" jurisdictional provisions represent a significant procedural and substantive convergence with an erosion of the differences between juvenile and criminal courts. They provide a conceptual alternative to binary waiver statutes by recognizing that adolescence comprises a developmental continuum that requires an increasing array of graduated sanctions for youths and procedural equality with adults to reflect the reality of punishment.

B. Counsel. Procedural justice hinges on access to and the assistance of counsel. Despite *Gault's* formal legal changes, the promise of quality legal representation remains unrealized for many juveniles. In several states, half or less of all juveniles receive the assistance of counsel to which the Constitution and state statutes entitle them. Moreover, rates of representation vary substantially within states and suggest that differences in rates of appointment of counsel reflect judicial policies to discourage representation. The most common explanation for why so many juveniles are unrepresented is that judges find that they waived their right to counsel. Courts typically use the adult legal standard of "knowing, intelligent, and voluntary" under the "totality of the circumstances" to gauge the validity of juveniles' waivers of rights. Because juveniles possess less ability than adults to deal effectively with the legal system, formal equality results in practical procedural inequality.

III. The Inherent Contradiction of the Juvenile Court

In this section, I contend that juvenile courts' social welfare mission cannot and should not be rehabilitated. In the next section, I advocate abolishing the juvenile court and trying all offenders in one integrated criminal court with modifications for the youthfulness of some defendants.

A. Social Welfare Versus Penal Social Control

The juvenile court treatment model constitutes an inappropriate policy response to young offenders. If we formulated a child welfare policy *ab initio,* would we choose a juvenile court as the most appropriate agency through which to deliver social services, and make criminality a condition precedent to the receipt of services? If we would not create a court to deliver social services, then does the fact of a youth's criminality confer upon a court any special competency as a welfare agency? Many young people who do not commit crimes desperately need social services, and many youths who commit crimes do not require or will not respond to social services. In short, criminality represents an inaccurate and haphazard criterion upon which to allocate social services. Because our society denies adequate help and assistance to meet the social welfare needs of all young people, the juvenile court's treatment ideology serves primarily to legitimate the exercise of judicial coercion of some *because of their criminality.*

Quite apart from its unsuitability as a social welfare agency, the individualized justice of a rehabilitative juvenile court fosters lawlessness and thus detracts from its utility as a court of law as well. Despite statutes and rules, juvenile court judges make discretionary decisions effectively unconstrained by the rule of law. If judges intervene to meet each child's "real needs," then every case is unique and decisional rules or objective criteria cannot constrain clinical intuitions. The *idea* of treatment necessarily entails individual differentiation, indeterminacy, a rejection of proportionality, and a disregard of normative valuations of the seriousness of behavior. But, if judges possess neither practical scientific bases by which to classify youths for treatment nor demonstrably effective programs to prescribe for them, then the exercise of "sound discretion" simply constitutes a euphemism for idiosyncratic judicial subjectivity. Racial, gender, geographic, and socioeconomic disparities constitute almost inevitable corollaries of a treatment ideology that lacks a scientific foundation. At the least, judges will sentence youths differently based on extraneous personal characteristics for which they bear no responsibility. At the worst, judges will impose haphazard, unequal, and discriminatory punishment on similarly situated offenders without effective procedural or appellate checks.

Is the discretion that judges exercise to classify for treatment warranted? Do the successes of rehabilitation justify its concomitant lawlessness? Do the incremental benefits of juvenile court intervention outweigh the inevitable inequalities and racial disparities that result from the exercise of individualized discretion? These questions require more sophisticated cost-benefit policy analyses than Progressives' claims that "if we save even one child, then it is worth it." Evaluations of the effectiveness of juvenile court intervention on recidivism rates counsel skepticism about the availability of programs that consistently or systematically rehabilitate juvenile offenders. Moreover, even if some model programs do "work" for some offenders under some conditions, fiscal constraints, budget deficits, and competition from other interest groups make it unlikely that states will provide universally such treatment services for ordinary delinquents. In the face of unproven efficacy and inadequate resources, the possibility of an effective rehabilitation program constitutes an insufficient justification to confine young offenders "for their own good" while providing them with fewer procedural safeguards than those afforded adults charged, convicted, and confined for crimes.

The juvenile court predicates its procedural informality on the assumptions that it provides benign and effective treatment. The continuing absence or co-optation of defense counsel in many jurisdictions reduces the likelihood that juvenile courts will adhere to existing legal mandates. The closed, informal, and confidential nature of delinquency proceedings reduces the visibility and accountability of the justice process and precludes external checks on coercive interventions. So long as the mythology prevails that juvenile court intervention constitutes only benign coercion and that, in any event, children should not expect more, youths will continue to receive the "worst of both worlds."

B. Failure of Implementation Versus Conception

The fundamental shortcoming of the juvenile court's welfare *idea* reflects a failure of conception rather than *simply* a failure of implementation. The juvenile court's creators envisioned a social service agency in a judicial setting, and attempted to fuse its welfare mission with the power of state coercion. The juvenile court *idea* that judicial clinicians successfully can combine social welfare and penal social control in one agency represents an inherent conceptual flaw and an innate contradiction. Combining social welfare and penal social control functions in one agency assures that the court does both badly. Providing for child welfare is a societal responsibility rather than a judicial one. Juvenile courts lack control over the resources necessary to meet child welfare needs exactly because of the social class and racial characteristics of their clients. In practice, juvenile courts subordinate welfare concerns to crime control considerations.

The juvenile court inevitably subordinates social welfare to criminal social control because of its built-in penal focus. Legislatures do not define juvenile courts' social welfare jurisdiction on the basis of characteristics of children for which they are not responsible and for which effective intervention could improve their lives. For example, juvenile court law does not define eligibility for services or create an enforceable right or entitlement based upon young peoples' lack of access to decent education, lack of adequate housing or nutrition, unmet health needs, or impoverished families—*none of which are their fault.* In all of these instances, children bear the social burdens of their parents' circumstances literally as innocent bystanders. If states defined juvenile courts' jurisdiction on the basis of young people's needs for social welfare, then they would declare a broad category of at-risk children who are eligible for public assistance.

Such a policy would require a substantial commitment of social resources and public will to children's welfare.

Instead, states' juvenile codes define juvenile courts' jurisdiction based on a youth committing a crime, a prerequisite that detracts from a compassionate response. Unlike disadvantaged social conditions that are not their fault, criminal behavior represents the one characteristic for which adolescent offenders do bear at least partial responsibility. As long as juvenile courts define eligibility for "services" on the basis of criminality, they highlight that aspect of youths which rationally elicits the least sympathy, and ignore personal circumstances or social conditions that evoke a desire to help.

IV. YOUTHFULNESS, CRIMINAL RESPONSIBILITY, AND SENTENCING POLICY: YOUNG OFFENDERS IN CRIMINAL COURTS

Once we uncouple social welfare from penal social control, then no need remains for a separate juvenile court for young offenders. We can try all offenders in criminal court with certain modifications of substantive and procedural criminal law to accommodate younger defendants. In this article, I do not propose simultaneously to completely reform the criminal justice system, but rather only to identify the sentencing policy issues raised when the criminal is a child. Because legislatures, prosecutors, and juvenile court judges already transfer increasing numbers and younger offenders to criminal courts for prosecution as adults, formulating a youth sentencing policy has considerable contemporary salience whether or not states abolish juvenile courts in their entirety.

If the child is a criminal and the "real" reason for formal intervention is criminal social control, then states should abolish juvenile courts' delinquency jurisdiction and try young offenders in criminal courts alongside their adult counterparts. But, if the criminal is a child, then states must modify their criminal justice system to accommodate the youthfulness of some defendants. Before prosecuting a child as a criminal in an integrated court, a legislature must address issues of substance and procedure. Substantive justice requires a rationale to sentence younger offenders differently, and more

leniently, than older defendants, a formal recognition of *youthfulness as a mitigating factor in sentencing*. Procedural justice requires providing youths with full procedural parity with adult defendants and additional safeguards to account for the disadvantages of youth in the justice system. Taken in combination, these substantive and procedural modifications can avoid the "worst of both worlds," provide youths with protections functionally equivalent to those accorded adults, and do justice in sentencing.

Formulating a youth sentencing policy entails two tasks. First, I will develop a rationale to sentence younger offenders differently, and *more leniently*, than older defendants. Explicitly punishing young offenders rests on the premise that adolescents possess sufficient moral reasoning, cognitive capacity, and volitional controls to hold them responsible and accountable for their behavior, albeit not necessarily to the same degree as adults. Secondly, I will propose a "youth discount" as a practical administrative mechanism to implement youthfulness in sentencing.

A. Substantive Justice: Juveniles' Criminal Responsibility

Questions about youths' accountability or criminal responsibility arise at two different stages in the justice system, either when deciding guilt or when imposing a sentence. In the former instance, questions of responsibility focus on the minimum age at which the state may find a person guilty of an offense. In making judgments about criminal responsibility, the criminal law's *mens rea* construct focuses narrowly on cognitive ability and capacity to make choices and excludes from consideration the goals, values, emotions, and psychological development that motivate a person's choices. In the absence of insanity, compulsion, or some cognizable legal excuse, any actor who has the capacity to choose to act otherwise than the way she did possesses criminal responsibility. For questions of criminal responsibility and guilt, the common law's insanity and infancy *mens rea* defenses provide most of the answers. These doctrines excuse from criminal liability only those who lack the requisite criminal intent, the *mens rea*, because of mental illness or immaturity. Knowledge of "right from wrong" entails only minimally rational understanding, and infancy *mens rea* does not provide an especially useful analytical prism through which to view youthfulness as a "special circumstance." Even very young children may act purposefully and with knowledge of the wrongfulness of their conduct.

Quite apart from decisions about guilt or innocence, individual accountability and criminal responsibility also relate to questions of disposition or sentence. Even if a court finds a youth criminally responsible for causing a particular harm, should the criminal law treat a fourteen-year-old as the moral equivalent of a twenty-four-year-old and impose an identical sentence, or should youthfulness mitigate the severity of the consequences? "Old enough to do the crime, old enough to do the time" provides an overly simple answer to a complex, normative, moral, and legal question.

Contemporary juvenile courts typically impose shorter sentences on serious young offenders than adult offenders convicted of comparable crimes receive. These shorter sentences enable young offenders to survive the mistakes of adolescence with a semblance of life chances intact. The juvenile court reifies the idea that young people bear less criminal responsibility and deserve less punishment than adults. Shorter sentences recognize that young people *do differ somewhat* from adults. These differences stem from physical, psychological, or developmental characteristics of young people, and as by-products of the legal and social construction of youth. Adolescents differ from adults physically and psychologically, and their immaturity affects their judgment. Youthfulness provides a rationale to mitigate sentences to some degree without excusing criminal conduct. But, shorter sentences for young people do not require a separate justice system in which to try them. Both juvenile and adult courts separate adjudication of guilt or innocence from sentencing, confine consideration of individual circumstances largely to the latter phase, and criminal courts may impose lenient sentences on young offenders when appropriate.

Responsibility for choices hinges on cognitive and volitional competence. Do young offenders make criminal choices that constitute the moral equivalents of those made by more mature actors?

1. Developmental Psychology

Developmental psychology posits that young people move through a sequence of psychological stages and their operational processes, legal reasoning, internalization of social and legal expectations, and ethical decision making change as they pass through these stages. Children's moral reasoning at different developmental stages differs from that which they use at other stages, and differs qualitatively from that which adults use. The descriptions of the developmental sequence and changes in cognitive processes parallel strikingly the imputations of responsibility associated with the common law infancy defense and suggest that by mid-adolescence youths acquire most of the cognitive and moral reasoning capacity that will guide their behavior through later life. Somewhere between about eleven and fourteen years of age, children achieve the highest stage of cognitive development, the "formal operational" stage, in which they can think abstractly and hypothetically, weigh and compare consequences, and consider alternative solutions to problems.

Many developmental psychologists question the appropriateness of advocating for presumptive legal equality based on adolescents' cognitive parity with adults to make informed medical decisions. Cognitive capacity alone does not comprise the only relevant dimension on which policymakers can distinguish between young people and adults. More recent research indicates that child development occurs more continuously and gradually, rather than as an all-or-nothing invariant stage and sequence, and that young people use different reasoning processes simultaneously in different task domains. Youths' developmental skills and knowledge may accrue unevenly in different task areas rather than as a uniform increase in overall capacity. Moreover, differences in language ability, knowledge, experience, and culture affect the ages at which different individuals' various competencies emerge. A comprehensive analytical review of developmental psychological research concludes that while those findings undermine support for the treatment of adolescents as incompetent and categorically different from adults, they do not support the converse proposition that young people and adults therefore function equally and that no legally significant differences exist between them.

Even a youth fourteen years of age or older who abstractly knows "right from wrong," who understands intentionality, and who possesses the requisite criminal *mens rea* for a finding of guilt still deserves neither the blame nor the comparable punishment of an adult offender. Juveniles possess less ability than adults to make sound judgments or moral distinctions, or to act with the same culpability as adults. Because youths possess less ability than adults to control their impulses or to appreciate the consequences of their acts, they *deserve* less punishment even when they commit the same criminal harm. Three developmentally unique attributes of youth—temporal perspective, attitudes toward and acceptance of risk, and susceptibility to peer influences—may affect young peoples' qualities of judgment in ways that distinguish them from adults and bear on their criminal responsibility.

2. Risk-Taking

Risk entails a chance of loss; risk-taking behavior entails conduct that exposes the actor to those potential adverse consequences. Young people are more impulsive, exercise less self-control, fail adequately to calculate long-term consequences, and engage in more risky behavior than do adults. Adolescents may estimate the magnitude or probability of risks, may use a shorter time-frame, or focus on opportunities for gains rather than possibilities of losses differently than adults. The greater prevalence of accidents, suicides, and homicides as the primary causes of death of the young reflect greater "risk-taking" behavior. Teenagers' greater proclivity to engage in unprotected sex, to speed and drive recklessly, and to engage in criminal behavior reflect their taking risks with respect to health and safety.

Criminal behavior constitutes a specific form of highly risky behavior, and every theory of crime attempts to account for the age-specific nature of offending. The differences between adolescent and adult decision-making with regard to risk are relevant in assessing criminal responsibility for the quality of their choices. A decision-making calculus requires the actor to identify possible outcomes, identify possible consequences that may follow from each option, evaluate the positive or negative desirability of those consequences, estimate the likelihood of those various consequences occurring, and develop a decisional rule to optimize outcomes. Experimental and developmental psychological literatures suggest that adolescents may approach these various decision-making steps differently from adults. Youths may engage in a riskier behavior than adults because they differ both in the extent of knowledge they possess and the amount of information they actually use when they make decisions.

Rational choice theory also helps to account for adolescents' greater propensity for risk-taking. People make utility-maximizing choices within a context of constraints, and people at different stages of their lives will make different valuations of uncertain future events. Knowledge about one's self, social environment, and life-course trajectory increase with age and affect a person's short-term versus long-term calculus. Because young people have much less clarity about their futures than do adults, "a focus on the immediate rather than the long-term consequences of a decision is a rational response to uncertainty about the future." As a result, young people may discount the negative value of future consequences because they have more difficulty than adults in integrating a future consequence into their more limited experiential baseline. Thus, adolescents may discount the cost of longer-term future consequences and weigh shorter-term benefits more heavily than adults.

Another developmental perspective for assessing adolescent risk-taking emphasizes *temperance* or the ability to limit impulsivity and evaluate a situation thoroughly. Developmental psychological studies examine ways in which adolescents' judgments may differ from adults' because of their disposition toward sensation-seeking, impulsivity related to hormonal or physiological changes and mood volatility. For example, hormonal and physiological changes, mood volatility, and predisposition toward sensation-seeking affect the quality of decision making and maturity of judgments, and cause adolescents to experience more difficulty controlling their impulses than adults. Because adolescents' predisposition to risk-taking reflects generic developmental processes rather than malevolent personal choices, it provides one sentencing policy rationale to protect the adult that the youth eventually will become from the detrimental consequences of immature decisions.

3. Peer Group Influences

Adolescents respond to peer group influences more readily than adults because of the crucial role peer relationship play in identity formation. Youths' greater desire for acceptance and approval renders them more susceptible to peer influences as they adjust their behavior and attitudes to conform to those of their contemporaries. Significantly, young people "commit crimes, as they live their lives, in groups." Police arrest a larger proportion of two or more juveniles for involvement in a single criminal event than they do adults. Young peoples' developmentally greater susceptibility to peer group influences and group process dynamics than their older counterparts lessens, but does not excuse, their criminal responsibility. It takes time, experience, and opportunities for young people to develop the capacity for autonomous judgments and resistance to the influences of peers. Because the group nature of youth crime renders all equally as criminally liable, it poses a challenge to formulate a youth sentencing policy that recognizes differential participation and culpability of different adolescent members of a group.

4. Reduced Culpability

In *Thompson v. Oklahoma*, the Supreme Court analyzed the criminal responsibility of young offenders and provided additional support for shorter sentences for reduced culpability even for youths older than the common law infancy threshold of age fourteen. *Thompson* presented the issue whether executing an offender for a heinous murder committed when he was fifteen years old violated the Eighth Amendment prohibition on "cruel and unusual punishments." In vacating Thompson's capital sentence, the plurality concluded that "a young person is not capable of acting with the degree of culpability that can justify the ultimate penalty."

Although the Court provided several rationales for its decision, it explicitly concluded that juveniles are less culpable for their crimes than are their adult counterparts. Significantly, even though the Court found Thompson responsible for his crime, it concluded that he could not be punished as severely as an adult, simply because of his age.

The *Thompson* Court emphasized that even though youths may inflict blameworthy harms, the culpability of their choice is less than that of adults. The Court cited numerous other areas of life (e.g., serving on a jury, voting, marrying, driving, and drinking) as instances in which the legal system treated adolescents differently from adults because of juveniles' lack of experience

and judgment. In all of those cases, the Court noted, the state acts paternalistically and imposes legal disabilities because of youths' presumptive incapacity to "exercise choice freely and rationally." The Court emphasized that it would be both inconsistent and ironic suddenly to find juveniles the equals of adults for purposes of capital punishment.

5. Subjective Time

Quite apart from differences in culpability, because of differences in their "time perspective," juveniles deserve less severe punishment than do adults for comparable criminal harms. Although we measure penalties in units of time—days, months, or years—youths and adults subjectively and objectively conceive of and experience similar lengths of time differently. The developmental progression in thinking about and experiencing time—future time perspective and present duration—follows a developmental sequence that affects the evolution of judgment and criminal responsibility. The ability to project events and consequences into the future evolves gradually during adolescence into early adulthood. Without a mature appreciation of future time, juveniles less fully understand or appreciate the consequences of their acts, may give excess weight to immediate goals, and, as a result, engage in riskier behavior. Because youths do not perceive present time duration equivalently with adults, a policy of "adult crime, adult time," which imposes equal sentences on adults and juveniles, would be disproportionately more severe for the latter. Because of developmental differences, time seems to pass more slowly when we are younger. Consequently, youths experience objectively equal punishment subjectively as more severe. While a three-month sentence may seem lenient for an adult offender, for a child it represents the equivalent of an entire summer vacation—a long period of time. Because young people depend upon their families, sentences of home removal or confinement are more developmentally disruptive than they would be for more formed and independent adults.

B. Administering Youthfulness as a Mitigating Factor at Sentencing: The "Youth Discount"

Implementing a youth sentencing policy entails legal, moral, and social judgments.

Because of developmental differences and the social construction of adolescence, younger offenders are less criminally responsible than more mature violators. But, they are not so essentially different and inherently incompetent as the current legal dichotomy between juvenile and criminal court suggests. The binary distinction between infant and adult that provides the bases for states' legal age of majority and the jurisprudential foundation of the juvenile court ignores the reality that adolescents develop along a continuum and creates an unfortunate either-or choice in sentencing. In view of the developmental psychological research that suggests several ways in which youths systematically differ from adults, should the criminal law adopt a "youth-blind" stance and treat fourteen-year-olds as the moral equivalent of adults for purposes of sentencing, or should it devise a youth sentencing policy that reflects more appropriately the developmental continuum?

Shorter sentences for reduced responsibility represents a more modest and attainable reason to treat young offenders differently than adults than the rehabilitative justifications advanced by Progressive child savers. In this context, adolescent criminal responsibility represents a global judgment about the degree of youths' deserved punishment, rather than a technical legal judgment about whether or not a particular youth possessed the requisite *mens rea* or mental state defined in the criminal statute. If adolescents as a class characteristically exercise poorer judgment than do adults, then sentencing policies can reduce the long-term harm that they cause to themselves. Protecting young people from the full penal consequences of their poor decisions reflects a policy to preserve their life chances for the future when they presumably will make more mature and responsible choices. Such a policy simultaneously holds young offenders accountable for their acts because they possess sufficient culpability, and yet mitigates the severity of consequences because their choices entail less blameworthiness than those of adults.

A statutory sentencing policy that integrates youthfulness, reduced culpability, and restricted opportunities to learn self-control with principles of proportionality would provide younger offenders with categorical fractional reductions of adult sentences. Because "youthfulness" constitutes a universal form of "reduced responsibility," states should treat it unequivocally as a mitigating factor without regard to nuances of individual developmental differences. Treating youthfulness as a formal mitigating sentencing factor represents a social, moral, and criminal policy judgment rather than a clinical or psychiatric evaluation. Such an approach avoids the risks of discretionary clinical subjectivity inherent in individualized adolescent culpability determinations.

This categorical approach would take the form of an explicit "youth discount" at sentencing. A fourteen-year-old offender might receive, for example, 25–33% of the adult penalty, a sixteen-year-old defendant, 50–60%, and an eighteen-year-old adult the full penalty, as presently occurs. The "deeper discounts" for younger offenders correspond to the developmental continuum and their more limited opportunities to learn and exercise responsibility. A youth discount based on reduced culpability functions as a sliding scale of diminished responsibility. Just as adolescents possess less criminal responsibility than do adults, fourteen-year-old youths should enjoy a greater mitigation of blameworthiness than would seventeen-year-olds. Because the rationale for youthful mitigation rests upon reduced culpability and limited opportunities to learn to make responsible choices, younger adolescents bear less responsibility and deserve proportionally shorter sentences than older youths. The capacity to learn to be responsible improves with time and experience.

The rationale for a "youth discount" also supports requiring a higher in/out threshold of offense seriousness as a prerequisite for imprisonment. Because juveniles depend upon their families more than do adults, removal from home constitutes a more severe punishment. Because of differences in "subjective time," youths experience the duration of imprisonment more acutely than do adults. Because of the rapidity of developmental change, sentences of incarceration are more disruptive for youths than for adults. Thus, states should require a higher threshold of offense seriousness and a greater need for social defense before confining a youth than might be warranted for an older offender.

The specific discount value—the amount of fractional reduction and the in/out threshold—reflects several empirical and normative considerations. It requires an empirically-informed sentencing policy judgment about adolescent development and criminal responsibility. To what extent do specific physical, social, and psychological characteristics of youth—depreciation of future consequences, risk-taking, peer influences, lack of self-control, hormonal changes, and lack of opportunities to learn to make responsible choices—induce them to engage in behavior simply because they are young? How much developmental difference should a state require to produce what degree of moral and legal mitigation in its sentencing policy?

1. Individualization vs. Categorization

Youthful development is highly variable. Young people of the same age may differ dramatically in their criminal sophistication, appreciation of risk, or learned responsibility. Chronological age provides, at best, a crude and imprecise indicator of maturity and the opportunity to develop a capacity for self-control. However, a categorical "youth discount" that uses age as a conclusive proxy for reduced culpability and a shorter sentence remains preferable to an "individualized" inquiry into the criminal responsibility of each young offender. The criminal law represents an objective standard. Attempts to integrate subjective psychological explanations of adolescent behavior and personal responsibility into a youth sentencing policy cannot be done in a way that can be administered fairly without undermining the objectivity of the law. Developmental psychology does not possess reliable clinical indicators of moral development or criminal sophistication that equate readily with criminal responsibility or accountability. For young criminal actors who possess at least some degree of criminal responsibility, relying upon inherently inconclusive or contradictory psychiatric or clinical testimony to precisely tailor sanctions hardly seems worth the judicial burden and diversion of resources that the effort would entail. Thus, for ease of administration, age alone provides the most useful criterion upon which to allocate mitigation.

2. Youth and Group Crime

While the law treats all participants in a crime as equally responsible and may sentence them alike, young people's susceptibility to peer group influences requires a more nuanced assessment of their degree of participation, personal responsibility, and culpability. The group nature of youth crime affects sentencing policy in several ways. The presence of a social audience of peers may induce youths to participate in criminal behavior that they would not engage in if alone. Even though the criminal law treats all accomplices as equally guilty as a matter of law, they may not all bear equal responsibility for the actual harm inflicted and may *deserve* different sentences. To some extent, state criminal sentencing laws already recognize an offender's differential participation in a crime as a "mitigating" factor. Similarly, some states' juvenile court waiver laws and juvenile sentencing provisions also focus on "the culpability of the child in committing the alleged offense, including the level of the child's participation in planning and carrying out the offense." Thus, the group nature of adolescent criminality requires some formal mechanism to distinguish between active participants and passive accomplices, with even greater "discounts" for the latter.

The juvenile court's "rehabilitative ideal" elevated determinism over free will, characterized delinquent offenders as victims rather than perpetrators, and envisioned a therapeutic institution that resembled more closely a preventive, forward-looking civil commitment process rather than a criminal court. By denying youths' personal responsibility, juvenile courts' treatment ideology reduces offenders' duty to exercise self-control, erodes their obligation to change, and sustains a self-fulfilling prophecy that delinquency occurs inevitably for youths from certain backgrounds.

Affirming responsibility encourages people to learn the virtues of moderation, self-discipline, and personal accountability.

Because a criminal conviction represents an official condemnation, the idea of "blame" reinforces for the public and provides for the individual the incentive to develop responsibility. A culture that values autonomous individuals must emphasize both freedom and responsibility.

While the paternalistic stance of the traditional juvenile courts rests on the humane desire to protect young people from the adverse consequences of their bad decisions, protectionism simultaneously disables young people from the opportunity to make choices and to learn responsibility for their natural consequences. Even marginally competent adolescents can only learn self-control by exercising their capacity for autonomy. Accountability for criminal behavior may facilitate legal socialization and moral development in ways that juvenile courts' rejection of criminal responsibility cannot.

4. Integrated Criminal Justice System

A graduated age-culpability sentencing scheme in an integrated criminal justice system avoids the inconsistencies and injustices associated with the binary either-juvenile-or-adult drama currently played out in judicial waiver proceedings and in prosecutorial charging decisions. It also avoids the "punishment gap," when youths make the transition from the one justice system to the other. Depending upon whether or not a judge or prosecutor transfers a case, the sentences that violent youths receive may differ by orders of magnitude. Moreover, appellate courts eschew proportionality analyses and allow criminal court judges to sentence waived youths to the same terms applied to adults without requiring them to consider or recognize any differences in their degree of criminal responsibility.

An integrated criminal justice system eliminates the need for transfer hearings, saves the considerable resources that juvenile courts currently expend ultimately to no purpose, reduces the "punishment gap" that presently occurs when youths make the passage from the juvenile system, and assures similar consequences for similarly situated offenders. Adolescence and criminal careers develop along a continuum. But the radical bifurcation between the two justice systems confounds efforts to respond consistently and systematically to young career offenders.

5. Integrated Record Keeping

The absence of an integrated record keeping system that enables criminal court judges to identify and respond to career offenders on the basis of their cumulative prior record constitutes one of the most pernicious consequences of jurisdictional bifurcation. Currently, persistent young offenders may "fall between the cracks" of the juvenile and criminals systems, often at the age at which career offenders approach their peak offending rates. A unified criminal court with a single record keeping system can maintain and retrieve more accurate criminal histories when a judge sentences an offender.

6. Decriminalize "Kids' Stuff"

Despite juvenile courts' overcrowded dockets and inadequate treatment resources, their procedural deficiencies and informality allow them to process delinquents too efficiently. Expedited procedures, fewer lawyers and legal challenges, and greater flexibility allows juvenile courts to handle a much larger number of cases per judge than do criminal courts and at lower unit cost. Merging the two systems would introduce an enormous volume of cases into an already overburdened criminal justice system that barely can cope with its current workload. Legislators and prosecutors forced to allocate scarce law enforcement resources would use the seriousness of the offense to rationalize charging decisions and "divert" or "decriminalize" most of the "kids' stuff" that provides the grist of the juvenile court mill until it became chronic or escalated in severity. Unlike a rehabilitative system inclined to extend its benevolent reach, an explicitly punitive process would opt to introduce fewer and more criminally "deserving" youths into the system.

7. Sentencing Expertise

Contemporary proponents of a specialized juvenile court contend that juvenile court judges require substantial time and commitment to become familiar with youth development, family dynamics, and community resources, and cite judges' dispositional expertise as a justification for a separate justice system. Whether juvenile court judges actually acquire such expertise remains unclear. In many jurisdictions, non-specialist judges handle juvenile matters as part of their general trial docket or rotate through a juvenile court on short-term assignments without developing any special expertise in sentencing juveniles. Even in specialized juvenile courts, the court services personnel, rather than the judge herself, typically possess the information necessary to recommend appropriate sentences.

8. Age-Segregated Dispositional Facilities and "Room to Reform"

Questions about young offenders' criminal responsibility and length of sentence differ from issues about appropriate places of confinement or the services or resources the state should provide to them. Even explicitly punitive sentences do not require judges or correctional authorities to confine young people with adults in jails and prisons, as is the current practice for waived youths, or to consign them to custodial warehouses or "punk prisons." States should maintain separate age-segregated youth correctional facilities to protect both younger offenders and older inmates. Even though youths may be somewhat responsible for their criminal conduct, they may not be the physical or psychological equals of adults in prison. While some youths may be vulnerable to victimization or exploitation by more physically developed adults, other youths may pose a threat to older inmates. Younger offenders have not learned to "do easy time," pose more management problems for correctional administrators, and commit more disciplinary infractions while they serve their sentences.

Virtually all young offenders return to society, and the state should provide them with resources for self-improvement on a voluntary basis because of its basic responsibility to its citizens and its own self-interest. If a state fails to provide opportunities for growth and further debilitates already disadvantaged youths, it guarantees greater long-term human, criminal, and correctional costs. A sentencing and correctional policy that offers young offenders "room to reform," opportunities, and resources does not covertly reinstate a treatment ideology, but facilitates young offenders' constructive use of their time. With maturity, most young offenders develop a capacity for self-control and desist from criminality.

V. Summary and Conclusions: Let's Be Honest About Youth Crime Control

The shortcomings of the "rehabilitative" juvenile court run far deeper than inadequate resources and rudimentary and unproven treatment techniques. Rather, the flaw lies in the very *idea* that the juvenile court can combine successfully criminal social control and social welfare in one system. Similarly, a separate "criminal" juvenile court cannot succeed or long survive because it lacks a coherent rationale to distinguish it from a "real" criminal court. A scaled-down separate criminal court for youths simply represents a temporary way-station on the road to substantive and procedural convergence with the criminal court. Only an integrated criminal justice that formally recognizes adolescence as a developmental continuum may effectively address many of the problems created by our binary conceptions of youth and social control.

SOURCE: From *The Journal of Criminal Law and Criminology,* Vol. 88, No. 1, 68–136, 1988. Copyright © 1988 by Northwestern University School of Law. Reprinted by special permission of Northwestern University School of Law.

QUESTIONS FOR DISCUSSION AND WRITING

1. What did the historical juvenile court's "rehabilitative ideal" envision, and how did reformers view crimes committed by children? What type of sentences resulted from those views?

2. In short, what do all the indicators discussed by the author consistently reveal? What strong, nationwide policy shift has occurred in the contemporary juvenile court?

3. Why should states maintain separate age-segregated youth correctional facilities?

4. How "deep" do the shortcomings of the "rehabilitative" juvenile court run? Where does the flaw lie?

THE IMPACT OF RESTORATIVE INTERVENTIONS ON JUVENILE OFFENDERS

Mara F. Schiff

INTRODUCTION

This [article] is about evaluating the effects of restorative justice interventions on juvenile offenders.

This [article] distinguishes between restorative justice processes and sanctions. Restorative justice processes deal with the means through which the offender and the victim agree to some form of compensation for the harm caused or damage done. Such processes may include victim-offender mediation, family group conferencing, circle sentencing, reparative probation, and possibly victim awareness or victim impact panels. *Sanctions*, on the other hand, refer to the actual agreements reached through such processes. These include strategies such as restitution, community service, and other responses to delinquency designed to repair harm to victims and communities.

This [article] examines the outcomes of restorative justice processes and sanctions for juvenile offenders, looking first at the results of *processes* and then at the impacts of the *sanctions* subsequently imposed through such processes. Significant gaps in the literature are examined, and recommendations are made for future research on restorative justice.

RESTORATIVE JUSTICE PROCESSES

The primary restorative justice processes on which research has been conducted include victim-offender mediation and family group conferencing. In addition, circle sentencing, reparative probation, and victim impact panels are increasingly gaining recognition in some jurisdictions. These strategies all aim to increase contact between victims and offenders as a means of "humanizing" the justice system as well as involving victims, offenders, and the community equally in the justice process.

Victim-Offender Mediation

Overview

Much VOM research has focused on victim impact rather than on offenders. Program goals, however, often include offender rehabilitation, reduced recidivism, diversion of cases from the courts and prevention of further "trouble." In fact, one survey found that most programs saw their primary goal as offender accountability, followed by restitution to victims, offender rehabilitation, victim reparation, reconciliation between victim and offender, and the avoidance of a custodial term. VOM is designed to allow victims and offenders an opportunity to reconcile and mutually agree on solutions. The object is to deal with crime as a conflict to be resolved between the persons directly affected, rather than as an opportunity for state intervention.

Though some programs have served a higher proportion of prior offenders, VOM cases typically deal with property crimes such as theft, burglary, criminal damage or vandalism, although a small but growing trend toward applying VOM in more serious, violent cases is apparent.

Reasons for Participation

When confronted with the prospect of facing their victims, some offenders have felt shame and embarrassment or humiliation; some have perceived double punishment and/or feared violent assault from the victims. The vast majority of offenders studied felt that VOM was a difficult and demanding experience. Those who participated often did so with the hope that it would help in court or to get a job, be an opportunity to demonstrate remorse, offer an apology, and/or repair a relationship.

In some cases, offenders felt more resentment toward the victim when he or she was a family member or a neighbor. Others felt that negotiating and paying restitution, discussing the event with the victim, and apologizing were important, and were concerned what the victim thought of them.

Marshall and Merry conducted one of the most comprehensive and methodologically sound evaluations on the effects of mediation in several U.K. Home Office-funded mediation and reparation projects. They found that mediation increased offenders' sense of responsibility. Marshall and Merry also found, however, that because the system inherently favors offender interests by focusing on "fairness" and due process, programs had trouble equally involving victim and offender, and "had difficulty maintaining their restorative focus in the face of a dominating criminal justice system." Moreover, some offenders were unclear about the purpose of VOM, and many juveniles in the police diversionary programs participated because they believed they would be prosecuted if they did not.

Marshall and Merry found that in the court-based programs, some offenders believed the program was primarily intended to assist them, but most saw advantages for both parties and regarded the meeting as a chance to achieve understanding with the victim. Reparation, however, was not necessarily seen as part of this process. The extent to which offenders thought participation might reduce their sentence varied across programs, and most offenders saw the incident as "opportunistic" and expressed regret. The most important impact felt by offenders was the opportunity to see the actual human and material consequences of their actions.

Satisfaction With the Process and the Outcomes Achieved

Most research indicates offender satisfaction with both the process and the outcome of VOM. However, not all offenders have been satisfied with their level of input. Juveniles who met their victim were more likely to perceive the process as fair and to experience mediation as "humanizing the justice system response." Most offenders surveyed who were unable to participate stated that they would have liked to if given the choice. Participants found the VOM process to be fair and no less demanding than the traditional court response.

Umbreit and Coates found that most offenders were happy with the contract achieved through VOM. Novak et al. found offenders to be most satisfied with the program when required to complete both financial and community service restitution, and that most offenders found restitution requirements to be fair. These findings highlight the difficulty in identifying if such satisfaction is a result of the actual mediation process or its outcome. It is possible that the process of mediation is less important than achieving the right mix of subsequent sanctions. Or, conversely, that the sanctions imposed are of less actual importance to the offender than the process through which they were realized.

Compliance With Agreements Achieved Through Mediation

Umbreit and Coates found that most VOM cases result in financial restitution, followed by community and personal service. They also found that completion rates have been significantly better following VOM participation than after other, more traditional, processes.

Compliance with agreements achieved through mediation varies from program to program, generally hovering around 80%. Some research found higher completion rates and increased involvement in the process when there was a relationship between the parties, while other studies found *less* compliance when the parties were acquainted. This suggests that while the relationship between the victim and the offender affects completion and compliance rates, the exact nature and direction of this relationship is unclear and may be important in determining successful outcomes.

Effects on Court Sentences

There is some evidence that VOM in Britain has resulted in decreased use of custody, conditional discharge, probation and community service orders. This same research indicates a higher use of compensation orders (the British term for court-ordered restitution) for offenders who participate in VOM than among the general court population. Offenders who participate in VOM may be treated more leniently by judges, perhaps because of the appearance of regret and willingness to "put things right." In addition, it is possible that taking material responsibility (through restitution) for the harm caused might decrease the judiciary's perception that a retributive punishment is required.

On the other hand, some research has found that a poor mediation outcome may negatively impact the subsequent sentence, and one study found that an antagonistic victim more than doubled the likelihood of a custodial sanction (which may also have been related to the severity of the offense and subsequent victim response); this may reflect how little control offenders (and victims) actually have over outcomes, and how much decision-making power continues to rest, finally, firmly within the traditional judicial process.

VOM may increase public and state awareness of the effect that minor offenses have on victims, resulting in net widening as the state's ensuing desire to control petty offenders intensifies. In restorative justice, net widening can be distinguished as either governmental or communitybased, and while expansion of "government nets" may have detrimental implications for juvenile offenders, strengthening "community nets" may be beneficial and serve to (re)integrate the offender into the community. Diverting first-time offenders to community

sanctioning processes such as mediation may reduce future offending, as community groups and citizens become more aware of the needs and risks presented by such offenders. This may, in turn, induce the community to take responsibility for preventative action at the neighborhood and institutional levels.

Recidivism

Although there is limited data on reoffending following VOM, available research has found decreased recidivism among VOM participants when compared with similar offenders going through the traditional juvenile justice system process. One study concluded that not only were recidivism rates lower among juveniles who participated in VOM, but those who did reoffend committed less serious offenses than a comparable control group.

A variety of structural and demographic factors have been found to influence recidivism rates following VOM. Nugent and Paddock identify family size, and particularly the number of siblings, as an important influence on rearrest rates among juveniles who went through a traditional juvenile justice process.

VOM Conclusion

Over all, research suggests that VOM has positive impacts on offenders. Offenders seem to benefit from and be satisfied with the process, to feel themselves to be held appropriately accountable and subject to fair and equitable outcomes, and to tend to commit fewer subsequent crimes. Moreover, compliance rates are generally good, suggesting that offenders tend to hold themselves accountable for accomplishing goals agreed upon through this process. Court sentences also tend to be reduced following participation in VOM. While the evidence is limited and may or may not be generalizable, the overwhelming sense is that there are more positive than negative impacts of VOM, and that, given a choice, juveniles prefer this approach to more traditional processes.

Family Group Conferencing

Family group conferencing (FGC) has been emerging as a promising restorative intervention. In both New Zealand and Australia, FGC has been institutionalized through legislative acts requiring that it be used either in place of, or in addition to, more traditional juvenile justice methods. There is, however, little research on the process itself, and even less on the effects of FGCs on participants.

Concerns About the Process

Important concerns have been cited about the potential for FGC to widen the net of social control, in addition to being coercive, inconsistent, and not proportional. While these specific concerns are untested, available research does suggest a decrease in the number of cases processed through the court system as well as placed in residential custody. In fact, some evidence has indicated that offenders *themselves* may argue for tougher penalties in an effort to demonstrate their willingness to earn respect. Some advocates caution that due process may be threatened when youths are not adequately apprised of their rights while other research highlights the fear that FGC may result in punitive, rather than restorative, sanctions and/or be insensitive to victims. There is no conclusive evidence either for or against these hypotheses.

Offender Satisfaction With the Process

Research in New Zealand has found high levels of participant satisfaction with the FGC process and its subsequent outcomes, although victims were somewhat less satisfied than offenders. Preliminary reports from the U.S. suggest similar findings.

One concern has been that only a limited number of the youths have reported feeling "involved," "partly involved," or "a party to the decision-making process." This may simply reflect traditional norms holding adults as primary decision makers, although while low, the figures are still considerably higher than the proportion of youths who exit the traditional juvenile court process feeling involved.

Current research in Canberra, Australia (RISE: the Reintegrative Shaming Experiments) has been randomly assigning separate groups of adult drunk drivers and youthful offenders to either FGC or court. This research is finding that offenders do not see FGC as a "soft" option, and youthful offenders spend an average of 71 minutes in a conference as compared with about 13 minutes in court.

Offenders in the Australian RISE experiments were more likely than those processed through the court to believe that the outcome of their case was fair (72% versus 54%); adult drunk drivers were over three times more likely to leave the process feeling "bitter and angry" following court than after a conference. Youthful offenders sent to conferences were more likely than court-processed offenders to believe that they would be caught for a reoffense, and that the prospect of being later sent to court represented a significant threat. Sherman and Strang offer that perhaps "once the offender has put family and friends to all the trouble of attending the conference," they generally become more committed to "helping [offender] avoid repeat offending." Youthful offenders also said they felt significantly more likely to obey the law following a conference than after court.

Recidivism Rates

It is impossible to draw any valid conclusions from the limited data on recidivism following participation in FGC. One study suggested a 42% reconviction rate, but the lack of a control group or pre-test sample makes it impossible to know whether this figure was lower or higher than expected. About one-quarter of the youths in this New Zealand study became "persistent offenders," but this seemed more related to the offender's prior criminal history and the imposition of a custodial placement than the FGC process itself. In general, however, New Zealand has reported a decrease in juvenile offending rates following the implementation of FGC that has not been observed among court-processed adults during the same period. It remains unclear how much of this can be attributed to the FGC process itself.

Family Group Conferencing Conclusion

Over all, FGC represents a promising restorative alternative to traditional justice system processes. There is, however, little comprehensive research from which to draw conclusions about its effectiveness. Concerns about net widening, the fairness of the process, and consistent outcome measures should dominate future research agendas, with particular attention to the results of the process and its effects on compliance rates and subsequent offending.

Other Restorative Processes

Circle sentencing has been in use in the Yukon and other parts of Canada since 1992 and is among the most recent restorative interventions to be applied outside its traditional native environment. It represents an innovative adaptation of traditional Native American sanctioning processes wherein members of the offended community collectively determine an appropriate response to the harm caused. Circle sentencing can be used as a diversion or an alternative to formal court proceedings, and depends on an admission of guilt by the offender and demonstration of a sincere willingness to change. There has been virtually no research documenting outcomes from this process.

Another model currently being tested in Vermont is reparative probation. This strategy is grounded in the traditional probation model and is directed primarily at non-violent probationers. It is implemented by a reparative coordinator on the staff of the department of probation, and carried out by a community reparative board that collectively determines appropriate restorative sanctions. While a study is under way to document the effects of this strategy, no data have yet been published.

A final, though also not well-documented, process is the victim awareness or victim impact panel. In these panels, meetings are arranged "between offenders and victims to educate the offender." There are no reliable data on this process from which to draw conclusions about its efficacy.

RESTORATIVE JUSTICE SANCTIONS

To date, restorative justice sanctions have been primarily limited to restitution and community service. Only restorative sanctions on which consistent and reliable research has been performed are presented here.

Restitution

Overview

Restitution aims to simultaneously hold an offender accountable for his or her actions, while also making amends to the victim for the harm and/or damage done. When properly implemented, restitution seeks to restore the victim (and/or the community) to the state of wholeness that existed prior to the offense. Ideally, restitution enables the offender to both make reparation and "put things right" with the victim.

Offender Attitudes and Satisfaction With Restitution

Schneider found that while incarcerated juveniles were more remorseful and felt their sanctions to be less fair than those subject to restitution, they also felt that incarceration was not as severe as restitution. The lower degree of remorse shown by youths under restitution orders may have resulted from restitution emphasis on accountability and making amends, as opposed to a more traditional focus on repentance; in other words, "feeling bad" may ultimately be a less meaningful component in restitution programs than accepting responsibility for one's actions.

Reports conflict on the degree of punitiveness experienced by offenders in restitution programs. Research has stressed that some offenders experience restitution as more punitive that restorative, especially when the experience is limited to just making payments rather that being involved in a more comprehensive support system. Schneider, on the other hand, found most restitution programs studied rated relatively low on a scale of punitiveness. The degree to which these findings reflect sentiments about the process through which the sanction was imposed, or the sanction itself, is ambiguous, but it appears that juveniles did not perceive restitution as "soft."

Compliance With Restitution Orders

In general, success rates in juvenile restitution programs studied have been over 75%, and often as high as 86%. Schneider and Schneider found that restitution was considerably more effective when delivered through a formal restitution program, rather than through *ad hoc* court-appended projects. Restitution completion rates in this study were about 40% higher that those achieved by the probation department, suggesting that the success of restoration may depend as much on program structure as on conditions of the order itself.

Smaller orders, in either monetary or community service terms, tend to increase compliance rates.

Closer offender monitoring has also been found to increase compliance rates, which may derive from better enforcement mechanisms in comprehensive restitution-only programs. Such monitoring and enforcement is unlikely in traditional probation departments facing large caseloads and multiple offenders with diverse sanction obligations.

Finally, some research has found higher compliance rates when the sanction is ordered through a restorative process, such as VOM, rather than through a more traditional criminal justice process. Offenders who negotiate directly with their victims are more likely to complete restitution than those so ordered through the court.

Recidivism Rates

In general, research has found lower recidivism rates resulting from restitution than from other, potentially more severe, justice system sanctions such as incarceration or probation. Again, this is particularly true when restitution was successfully completed as part of a comprehensive restitution-specific program, implying that direct accountability for repayment, with enforcement and follow-up mechanisms, may result in lower subsequent offending. Schneider stressed that while restitution programs may not always significantly decrease recidivism, they certainly do not increase it.

Finally, some research has not found decreased recidivism rates following restitution or has found that the effect of restitution on subsequent recidivism rates was not sufficiently isolated to enable drawing conclusions. That is, while much research suggests that youths sentenced to restitution programs may have lower recidivism rates, it is not clear that such results derive from the restitution program itself; it is possible that other factors—such as the type of defendants selected for participation, other services simultaneously offered, or the process through which the sanction was determined—may have been responsible for the outcome.

Restitution Conclusion

In sum, these findings imply that there are some clear benefits of restitution, but that these benefits may be related to other program elements such as academic or employment services, or the process through which the sanction is determined or delivered.

Over all, restitution has the potential to be a meaningful restorative sanction, from which both offenders and society in general can derive multiple benefits. The primary obstacle is the ease with which restitution can be imposed in the absence of a comprehensive restorative framework, facilitating the appearance—but not the actual development—of a restorative agenda. Moreover, distinguishing the effects of restitution as separate from other services provided, program structure, and the process through which it was imposed is important, and research must strive to isolate these separate effects.

Community Service

Overview

While a number of community service programs exist, very few have been implemented in a restorative context. In fact, many community service programs have been implemented in the absence of *any* theory relating program activities to desired objectives, limiting the degree to which restorative, or any other, effects can legitimately be claimed.

While community service for juveniles was originally designed to be rehabilitative, there are more recent case studies of restorative community service projects. However, research of the effects of such programs on offenders is still limited, and that lack of standards for such programs has led some to conclude that such services should not be included as a part of a reparative sanctioning system.

The best known study of community service in the U.S. was McDonald's examination of community service for adult offenders in New York City, a program developed and implemented under expressly retributive assumptions. Many of the original community service programs followed this model, predominantly focusing on diverting offenders from jails and prisons as a cost-saving device. As such, the effectiveness of community service has not typically been gauged in terms of offender, victim, or other social benefits. Programs typically offer a few restorative benefits, and offenders are often restricted to menial and sometimes humiliating tasks specifically designed to be punitive.

Offender Satisfaction and Completion Rates

Varah found that most offenders studied saw community service as a serious sanction, and that the vast majority felt they were given meaningful work to do. Most of these same offenders believed they learned useful skills, and among those who had previously been to prison, most felt that community service benefited others and enabled them to feel good about having done something for society. Thorvaldson found more favorable attitudes among offenders toward community service that toward fines and probation.

Completion rates have generally been between 70% and 90%. An important component of community service seems to be the extent to which the offender believed he or she was doing something useful.

Recidivism Rates

Some studies have found lower recidivism rates among offenders sentenced to community service than among comparable control groups, while others have not.

Community Service Conclusion

The lack of restorative intent in most community service programs has had some negative impact on offenders. When sentenced to perform only menial labor that has no clear benefit for the victim, the community, or the offender, offenders can be expected to derive little benefit from a community service sentence. However, when community service is imposed as a restorative sanction that meets real victim and community needs, and where input from the victim and the community is included in the sanctioning process, the possibility that community service will benefit offenders, victims, and the community is considerably increased.

GAPS IN EXISTING RESEARCH

While extant research clearly implies promising effects of restorative interventions on juvenile offenders, the lack of controlled studies, the absence of consistent effectiveness measures, and paucity of research on some of the more recent interventions tends to engender more questions than answers. In part, this reflects the newness of some of the restorative interventions in juvenile justice from which final evaluation results have yet to be published. Additionally, some innovative sanctions have simply not to date been subject to rigorous review and evaluation.

In part, this abundance of questions also arises from the tension of trying to distinguish the impact of restorative processes from those of restorative sanctions. Focusing developmental attention on processes over sanctions may often mean that existing retributive sanctions, such as restitution and community service, are simply relabeled as restorative with little substantive change. In other words, the importance of implementing restorative processes may be overshadowing the need to assure that associated sanctions are indeed restorative. Even when restoration is considered an explicit goal, there is a tendency to concentrate on program-specific rather than systemic interventions, leaving little changed in the overall structure, operation, or philosophy of the juvenile justice system.

A research agenda for the future must first develop a language that speaks directly to the concerns of skeptics who would dismiss restorative justice interventions as simply another fad in the long history of failed rehabilitative programs. Such a language must be grounded in methodologically sound empirical research that both demonstrates the benefits, and meaningfully addresses the deficits, of such interventions.

Broad Systemic Issues

Research on systemic issues must identify the extent to which a program is truly restorative in nature and not simply a transmogrified retributive approach. It must clarify precisely what characterizes restorative processes and sanctions, as well as present such findings in terms that are meaningful to advocates and skeptics alike. Two particularly important systemic concerns include the potential for discrimination in restorative processes, and the degree to which net widening and net strengthening result from such interventions.

First, some evidence suggests that more white, middle-class offenders are sent to VOM and thus receiving restitution, while minorities subject to traditional processes may end up in custody. If this is true, then programs must be made aware of such potential discrimination in order to correct it.

Second, if restorative programs are increasing the number of juveniles coming under official control, i.e., expanding government nets, then the extent to which program goals may have been co-opted to serve broader social control objectives must be explored. However, if it is community nets that are being expanded or strengthened, then the overall effect might be positive. Research must examine if official over-control occurs because restorative sanctions are imposed *in addition* to other, more traditional sanctions as well as what happens in cases of non-compliance and subsequent recidivism. In particular, there must be safeguards against subjecting offenders to significantly harsher sanctions upon resentence after either "failing" to complete, or reoffending during or after, a restorative program. This can significantly increase the number of juveniles subject to cus-todial terms, drastically altering the system's restorative intent.

Other systemic concerns worthy of research attention include:

- Identifying whether restorative processes or sanctions are having the greatest impacts on juvenile offenders. It is important to identify whether it is the process in which the offender participates, or completion of the sanction itself, that results in the most positive impact. Important indicators here include the type of process, the type of sanction, completion of the process, completion of the sanction, and time to completion.
- The extent to which offenders develop empathy for the victim, a sense of justice and fairness, and feelings of responsibility and accountability. It is not only important to identify whether such characteristics may result from participation in restorative process, but also if such attributes can be linked to increased program compliance, decreased recidivism rates, and other successful outcome measures. Indicators here should rely on criteria derived from offender interviews and questionnaires, with specific definitions to indicate the presence of such attributes. These must then be related to more concrete outcome indicators, such as completion and recidivism rates.
- The extent to which participation in restorative programs is voluntary or coerced and the impact this has for program "failure" and participants satisfaction. Research findings that restorative programs are less effective when participants feel coerced into a process must either be confirmed or rejected. Measures here must address offender perceptions of coercion, paying careful

attention to consistent measurement and unbiased interview questions.

- The extent to which interventions are restorative for the victim and the community, while also holding offenders accountable and helping them to develop valuable skills. Research has suggested that offenders benefit most when they are held accountable by a target, comprehensive program, can perform meaningful work and are directly accountable to the victim. These factors are not only important in increasing compliance and decreasing recidivism rates, but are also fundamental to the restorative model. Research must examine the extent to which these conditions are met, and identify what elements may prevent the achievement of such goals. Process evaluations would be particularly useful here, enabling mid-course corrections whenever possible.
- The extent to which programs are implemented in isolation or in the context of a comprehensive restorative framework. Research must identity the extent to which programs are developed and implemented comprehensively or in isolation from a restorative framework. Such research must clarify whether and how programs are operating outside of the restorative context, and the impact this has on the evolution of the restorative model.

Program-Specific Empirical Issues

Program-specific empirical issues are impor-tant insofar as they demonstrate actual impacts of restorative interventions on victims, communi-ties, and offenders. Such outcome measures are particularly important because they can commu-nicate the impacts of restorative interventions in terms that are meaningful to both supporters and opponents alike. Specific empirical indicators are suggested by the existing literature:

- *Recidivism rates.* Research must demonstrate that recidivism following a restorative intervention is, if not significantly reduced, at least no worse than what occurs following traditional juvenile justice methods. Policy makers and the public must both be convinced that they are no worse off, and potentially significantly better off, under a restorative juvenile justice system than a retributive one. Rearrest, reconviction, and reincarceration rates should all be examined, with particular controls for time at risk to assure comparable follow-up periods.

- *Compliance rates.* Studies should look to see if and how compliance rates may be related to recidivism. If higher completion rates result in lower recidivism, then programs should concentrate resources on increasing compliance as a means of reducing juvenile crime rates and increasing public perceptions of safety. Specific outcome measures here should include program and sanction completion rates, time to completion, and the relationship of program compliance to recidivism and offender satisfaction.

- *Victim and offender satisfaction rates.* If an important aspect of the restorative model includes satisfaction with the process and with the outcomes, consistent indicators that can be applied across different types of programs and jurisdictions must be developed. To date, "satisfaction" remains a somewhat ambiguous term subject to the definition of the evaluator. Satisfaction measures must distinguish between perceptions of the process and of the outcome. They must also precisely define the parameters of victim, offender, and community satisfaction.

- *More methodologically sound, controlled evaluations of some of the newer processes and sanctions.* These evaluations should focus on FGC, circle sentencing and victim impact panels, as well as on evaluations of some of the more traditional interventions undertaken in restorative contexts.

CONCLUSIONS AND DIRECTIONS FOR THE FUTURE

Restorative justice is a "holistic" approach to justice. In a holistic model, no part of the system nor actor in the process is presumed to function independent of the others, but rather the success of any individual component is contingent on that of the others. In terms of restorative justice, this means that the actions of each participant are directly related to those of the others, and only through shared interaction, communication, and commitment between the victim, the offender, and the community can "justice" in fact be served. To this end, is it important to develop a "language of restorative justice" that defines its own unique and precise terminology.

Holistic restorative models clearly show great promise for juvenile justice, and seem to offer some significant advantages over current retributive strategies for both offenders and victims. Considerably more research remains to be undertaken, however. Current limitations in the research make it difficult to unequivocally argue the benefits of restorative programs, suggesting that the time is ripe for developing a systematic research agenda dedicated to showing both the benefits and shortcomings of restorative interventions for juvenile offenders.

SOURCE: From *Restorative Juvenile Justice: Repairing the Harm of Youth Crime,* edited by Gordon Bazemore and Lode Walgrave. Copyright © 1999 by Criminal Justice Press. Reprinted by permission of Criminal Justice Press.

QUESTIONS FOR DISCUSSION AND WRITING

1. What are the differences between restorative justice processes and restorative justice sanctions? What are the goals of victim offender mediation (VOM) programs?

2. What has research on recidivism among VOM participants found? Overall, what kind of impacts does research suggest that VOM has?

3. What does the author say about FGC (family group conferencing) and recidivism? What does the author say about restitution and recidivism? What does the author say about community service and recidivism?

BEYOND CRIME AND PUNISHMENT

Prisons and Inequality

BRUCE WESTERN

BECKY PETTIT

THE EXPANSION OF THE PENAL SYSTEM

Between 1920 and 1970, about one-tenth of one percent of Americans were confined in prisons. The prison population increased sixfold in the three decades after 1970. By June, 2000, about 1.3 million people were held in state and federal prisons, and 620,000 inmates were in local jails. This translates into a total incarceration rate of seven-tenths of one percent of the U.S. population. The current incarceration rate is five times the historical average of the 1925–70 period and six to eight times the incarceration rates in Western Europe. With the important exception of homicide, however, American levels of crime are similar to those in Western Europe.

These numbers mask the concentration of imprisonment among young black men with little schooling. Although there are no official statistics, we've calculated the proportion of penal inmates among black and white men at different ages and levels of education by combining data from labor force and correctional surveys. Incarceration rates doubled among working-age men between 1980 and 1999 but increased threefold for high school dropouts in their 20s. By 1999, fewer than one percent of working-age white men were behind bars, compared to 7.5 percent of working-age black men.

Figures for young black unskilled men are especially striking: 41 percent of all black male high school dropouts aged 22–30 were in prison or jail at midyear in 1999.

Although 9 out of 10 inmates are male, women represent the fastest-growing segment of the inmate population. During the recent penal expansion, the female inmate population has grown more than 60 percent faster than the male inmate population. African-American women have experienced the greatest increase in criminal justice supervision.

Racial disparities in incarceration are even more stark when one counts the men who have ever been incarcerated rather than just those in prison on a given day. In 1989, about 2 percent of white men in their early thirties had ever been to prison compared to 13 percent of black men of the same age. Ten years later, these rates had increased by 50 percent. The risks of going to prison are about three times higher for high school dropouts. At the end of the 1990s, 14 percent of white and 59 percent of black male high school dropouts in their early 30s had prison records.

The high rate of imprisonment among black men is often explained by differences in patterns of arrest and criminal behavior. Blacks are eight times more likely to be incarcerated than whites.

478

With the important exception of drug offenses, blacks are overrepresented among prison inmates due to race differences in crime and arrest statistics. In 1991, for instance, black men accounted for 55 percent of all homicide arrests and 47 percent of homicide offenders in prison. Drug offenses aside, about three-quarters of the racial disparity in imprisonment can be linked to racial differences in arrests and in criminal offending as reported in surveys of crime victims. Although age and educational differences in incarceration have not been studied as closely as race, crime rates are also known to be high among young, poorly educated men. In short, young, black, male high school dropouts are overrepresented in prison mainly because they commit a disproportionate number of crimes (or, at least, street crimes) and are arrested for them. But that is not the whole story.

The explosion of the penal population after 1970 does not reflect increasing crime rates. The prison population has grown steadily every year since 1974, but crime rates have fluctuated up and down with no clear trend. For example, 13.4 million crimes were reported to the police in 1980. In that year 182,000 people were admitted to state and federal prisons. In 1998, 12.4 million crimes were reported, and 615,000 people were sent to prison. Crime had gone down but the number of people going to prison had tripled.

To explain the prison boom, we need to look beyond trends in crime. The exceptional pattern of incarceration among drug offenders provides an important clue. Drug offenders account for a rapidly increasing share of the prison population and the surge in drug-related imprisonment coincides with shifts in drug policy. Beginning in the 1970s, state and federal governments increased criminal penalties and intensified law enforcement in an attempt to reduce the supply, distribution and use of illegal narcotics. Drug arrests escalated sharply throughout the 1980s and 1990s, and drug offenders were widely sentenced to mandatory prison terms. While the total state prison population grew at about 8 percent annually between 1980 and 1996, the population of drug offenders in state prisons grew twice as quickly.

The war on drugs was just one part of a broad trend in criminal justice policy that also toughened punishment for violent and repeat offenders. For example, between 1980 and 1996,

the average time served in state prison for murder increased from 5 to more than 10 years. Habitual offender provisions, such as California's three-strikes law, mandated long sentences for second and third felony convictions. Rates of parole revocation have also increased, contributing to more than a third of all prison admissions by the late 1990s.

Why did the punitive turn in criminal justice policy affect young male dropouts so dramatically? Consider two explanations. First, socially marginal men are the most likely to commit crimes and be arrested for them, so simply lowering the threshold for imprisonment—jailing offenders who in an earlier era would have just been reprimanded—will have the biggest impact on this group. Second, some legal scholars claim that policy was redrawn in a way that disproportionately affected young minority males with little schooling. Michael Tonry makes this argument in a prominent indictment of recent anti-drug policy. Street sweeps of drug dealers, mass arrests in inner cities and harsh penalties for crack cocaine were all important elements of the war on drugs. These measures spotlighted drug use among disadvantaged minorities but neglected the trade and consumption of illicit drugs in the suburbs by middle-class whites. From this perspective the drug war did not simply lower the threshold for imprisonment, it also targeted poor minority men.

Although the relative merits of these two explanations have not yet been closely studied, it is clear that going to prison is now extremely common for young black men and pervasive among young black men who have dropped out of school. Imprisonment adds to the baggage carried by poorly educated and minority men, making it harder for them to catch up economically and further widening the economic gap between these men and the rest of society.

INCARCERATION CONCEALS INEQUALITY

Regardless of its precise causes, the effects of high incarceration rates on inequality are now substantial. Although the 1990s was a period of economic prosperity, improved job opportunities for many young black men were strongly outweighed by this factor. The stalled economic progress of black youth is invisible in conventional labor force statistics because prison and jail inmates are excluded from standard counts of joblessness.

Employment rates that count the penal population among the jobless paint a bleak picture of trends for unskilled black men in the 1990s. Standard labor force data show that nearly two-thirds of young black male high school dropouts had jobs in 1980 compared to just half in 1999. When inmates are counted in the population, however, the decline in employment is even more dramatic. In 1980, 55 percent of all young black dropouts had jobs. By the end of the 1990s fewer than 30 percent had jobs, despite historically low unemployment in the labor market as a whole. Incarceration now accounts for most of the joblessness among young black dropouts, and its rapid growth drove down employment rates during the 1990s economic boom.

Because black men are overrepresented in prison and jail, incarceration also affects estimates of racial inequality. A simple measure of inequality is the ratio of white to black employment rates. In 1999, standard labor force data (which do not count convicts) show that young white dropouts were about one and a half times more likely to hold a job than their black counterparts. Once prison and jail inmates are counted among the jobless, the employment rate for young white dropouts is about two and a half times larger than for blacks. If we relied just on the usual labor force surveys, we would underestimate employment inequality for this marginal group by 50 percent.

Isolating many of the disadvantaged in prisons and jails also masks inequality in wages. When low earners go to prison and are no longer counted in the wage statistics, it appears that the average wage of workers has increased. This seeming rise in average wages doesn't represent a real improvement in living standards, however. We estimate that the wage gap between young black and white men would be 20 percent wider if all those not working, including those in prison and jail, were counted.

INCARCERATION INCREASES INEQUALITY

The penal system not only conceals inequality, it confers stigma on ex-prisoners and reduces their readiness for the job market. Consequently, ex-convicts often live at the margins of the labor market, precariously employed in low-wage jobs. Ethnographic research paints a vivid picture. For example, in Mercer Sullivan's *Getting Paid*, delinquent youth in New York City cycled through many jobs, each held for just weeks or months at a time. One subject, after entering an ex-offender employment program at age 20, briefly held a factory job, but "he was fired for being absent and then went through three different jobs in the next four months: he tried delivering groceries, being a messenger, and doing maintenance in a nursing home." His experience was typical of Sullivan's subjects.

James Austin and John Irwin's interviews with current and former inmates in *It's About Time* reveal some of the difficulties ex-convicts have finding jobs. Released prisoners may have to disclose their criminal history or risk its discovery in a background check, or jobs may require special licenses or membership unavailable to most ex-convicts. Both may serve as substantial obstacles to employment. For example, a 38-year-old ex-convict living in the San Francisco Bay Area recalls, "I was supposed to get this light industrial job. They kept putting obstacles in front of me and I talked my way over them every time, till she brought up my being on parole and then she went sour on me. If they catch me lying on the application about being in prison or being on parole, they will [report a violation] and give me four months [in prison]." He also was unable to get a job in dry cleaning because he lacked certification: "I had dry-cleaning training a long time ago, but this time I wasn't in long enough to go through the program. It takes several years. You have to have the paper to get a job. I could jump in and clean anything—silks, wools—remove any spot, use all the chemicals, but I don't got any paper. They won't let you start without the paper."

Statistical studies have tried to estimate the toll incarceration takes on earnings after release. Ideally, to measure the effect of prison time, we would compare the pay of groups who were the same in all respects except for their prison records. However, criminal offenders are unusual in ways that are hard to observe. They may be more impulsive or aggressive, and these sorts of characteristics aren't consistently measured by our usual surveys. Thus different studies yield different estimates.

With these caveats in mind, statistical studies suggest that serving time in prison, by itself and with other characteristics of workers accounted for, reduces wages by between 10 and 30 percent. However, this is a simplified picture of how imprisonment affects job opportunities. Research also shows that incarceration affects the growth—and not just the level—of wages. While pay usually increases as men get older, this is not so true for ex-convicts. This suggests that men with prison records find it hard to get jobs with career ladders or seniority pay. Instead, they are more likely to work in day labor or other casual jobs.

Because young black men with little education are imprisoned in such large numbers, the economic effects of incarceration on individual ex-convicts can add up to large economic disadvantages for minority communities. Neighborhoods with many people going to prison develop bad reputations that smear even the law abiding. In *When Work Disappears,* William Julius Wilson reports on interviews with Chicago employers which show how the stigma of criminality can attach to entire minority communities. Considering job candidates from the West Side, one employer observed, "Our black management people [would] say No, stay away from that area. That's a bad area . . . And then it came out, too, that sooner or later we did terminate everybody from that area for stealing . . . [or] drinking." National statistics also show how imprisonment widens the inequality between groups. Estimates for 1998 show that the reduced earnings of ex-convicts contribute about 10 percent to the wage gap between black and white men. About 10 percent of the pay gap between all male college graduates and all high school dropouts is due to the reduced wages that inmates earn after they are released.

THE PRICE OF SAFETY

The inequalities produced by the penal system are new. The state and federal governments have never imprisoned so many people, and this increase is the result not of more crime but of new policies toward crime. This expansion of imprisonment represents a more massive intrusion of government into the lives of the poor than any employment or welfare program. Young black men's sustained contact with official authority now sets them apart from mainstream America in a novel way.

The inegalitarian effects of criminal justice policy may be justified by gains in public safety. We have in this article treated the penal population primarily as disadvantaged and not as dangerous people, but a large proportion of prisoners are violent offenders. Many commit crimes again and again. Criminals may be poor men, but they also perpetrate crime in poor neighborhoods. From this viewpoint, the proliferation of prisons represents a massive investment in the public safety of disadvantaged urban areas.

But can enduring public safety be achieved by policies that deepen social inequality? A great deal of research indicates that effective crime control depends on reducing economic divisions, not increasing them. There is a strong link between criminal behavior and economic disadvantage. To the extent that prison undermines economic opportunities, the penal boom may be doing little to discourage crime in communities where most men have prison records. If high incarceration rates add to the stigma of residence in high-crime neighborhoods, the economic penalties of imprisonment may affect ex-convicts and law-abiding citizens alike. The criminal justice system is now a newly significant part of a uniquely American system of social inequality. Under these conditions, the punitive trend in criminal justice policy may be even tougher on the poor than it is on crime.

QUESTIONS FOR DISCUSSION AND WRITING

1. Why did the punitive turn in criminal justice policy affect young male dropouts so dramatically?

2. What happened to employment of black male dropouts during the 1990s, a time period generally considered "a period of economic prosperity"?

3. How does incarceration affect estimates of racial inequality?

SUGGESTED READINGS

Part I: What Is Criminology? The History and Definitions of Crime and Criminology

Defining Crime: An Issue of Morality
John Hagan

- Chambliss, W., & Seidman, R. (1982). *Law, order, and power.* Reading, MA: Addison-Wesley.
- Morris, N., & Hawkins, G. (1970). *The honest politicians' guide to crime control.* Chicago: University of Chicago Press.
- Quinney, R. (1974). *Critique of legal order: Crime control in capitalist society.* Boston: Little, Brown.
- Schur, E. (1965). *Crimes without victims: Deviant behavior and public policy.* Englewood Cliffs, NJ: Prentice Hall.
- Turk, A. (1969). *Criminality and legal order.* Chicago: Rand McNally.

Historical Explanations of Crime: From Demons to Politics
C. Ronald Huff

- Beccaria, C. (1996). *Of crimes and punishments.* New York: Marsilio.
- Becker, H. (1963). *Outsiders: Studies in the sociology of deviance.* New York: Free Press.
- Bonger, W. (1916). *Criminality and economic conditions.* Boston: Little, Brown.
- Goring, C. (1972). *The English convict: A statistical study.* Montclair, NJ: Patterson Smith.
- Merton, R. (1957). *Social theory and social structure.* Glencoe, IL: Free Press.
- Quinney, R. (1974). *Critique of legal order: Crime control in capitalist society.* Boston: Little, Brown.

Part II: How Do We View Crime? Images of Crime, Criminality and Criminal Justice

A Youth Violence Epidemic: Myth or Reality?
Franklin E. Zimring

- Blumstein, A. (1995). Youth violence, guns, and the illicit drug industry. *Journal of Criminal Law and Criminology, 86,* 10.
- Cook, P. J. (1991). The technology of personal violence. In M. Tonry (Ed.), *Crime and justice: An annual review of research* (pp. 1–71). Chicago: University of Chicago Press.
- Cook, P. J., & Laub, J. (1998). The unprecedented epidemic in youth violence. In M. Tonry and M. Moore (Eds.), *Youth violence. Crime and justice: An annual review of research* (Vol. 24, pp. 27–64). Chicago: University of Chicago Press.
- Fox, J. A. (1996). *Trends in juvenile violence: A report to the United Sates Attorney General on current and future rates of juvenile offending.* Boson: Northeastern University Press.
- Zimring, F. (1979). American youth violence: Issues and trends. In N. Morris and M. Tonry (Eds.), *Crime and justice: An annual review of research* (pp. 67–107). Chicago: University of Chicago Press.

Realities and Images of Crack Mothers
Drew Humphries

- Chasnoff, I. J. (1989). Drug use and women: Establishing a standard of care. *Annals of the New York Academy of Science, 562,* 208–210.
- Chasnoff, I. J., Landress, H. J., & Barrett, M. E. (1990, April 26). The prevalence of illicit drug or alcohol use during pregnancy and discrepancies in mandatory reporting in Pinellas County, Florida. *New England Journal of Medicine, 322,* 1202–1206.
- Humphries, D. (1998). Crack mothers at 6. *Violence Against Women, 4,* 45–61.
- Mayes, L. C., Granger, R. H., Gornstein, M. H., & Zuckerman, B. (1992). The problem of perinatal cocaine exposure: A rush to judgment. *Journal of the American Medical Association, 267,* 406–408.
- National Institute on Drug Abuse (NIDA). (1992). *National household survey on drug abuse: Population estimates 1991* (Revised). (DHHS Publication No. (ADM) 92–1987). Rockville, MD: National Institutes of Health, U.S. Department of Health and Human Services.

Breaking News: How Local TV News and Real-World Conditions Affect Fear of Crime
Ronald Weitzer and Charis E. Kubrin

- Chermank, S. (1995). *Victims in the news: Crime and the American news media.* Boulder, CO: Westview.
- Chiricos, T., Eschholz, S., & Gertz, M. (1997). Crime, news, and fear of crime. *Social Problems, 44,* 342–357.
- Eschholz, S. (1997). The media and fear of crime: A survey of the research. *University of Florida Journal of Law and Public Policy, 9,* 37–59.
- Lipschultz, J., & Hilt, M. (2002). *Crime and local television news.* Mahwah, NJ: Lawrence Erlbaum.
- Surette, R. (1998). *Media, crime, and criminal justice.* Belmont, CA: Wadsworth.
- Warr, M. (2000). Fear of crime in the United States: Avenues for research and policy. In D. Duffee (Ed.), *Criminal justice 2000: Vol. 4. Measurement and analysis of crime and justice* (pp. 451–489). Washington, DC: National Institute.

The Politics of Crime
Katherine Beckett and Theodore Sasson

- Currie, E. (1985). *Confronting crime: An American challenge.* New York: Pantheon.
- Edelman, M. (1988). *Constructing the political spectacle.* Chicago: University of Chicago Press.
- Garland, D. (1990). *Punishment and modern society: A study in social theory.* Chicago: University of Chicago Press.
- Omi, M., & Winant, H. (1986). *Racial formation in the United States.* New York: Routledge and Kegan Paul.
- Piven, F., & Cloward, R. (1969). *Poor people's movements: Why they succeed, how they fail.* New York: Arlington House.

Part III: Enduring and Changing Patterns of Crime

Youth Gangs and Troublesome Youth Groups in the United States and the Netherlands:
A Cross-National Comparison
Finn-Aage Esbensen and Frank M. Weerman

- Battin, S. R., Hill, K. G., Abbott, R., Catalano, R. F., & Hawkins, J. D. (1998). The contribution of gang membership to delinquency beyond delinquent friends. *Criminology, 36,* 93–115.
- Campbell, A. (1991). *The girls in the gang* (2nd ed.). Cambridge, MA: Basil Blackwell.
- Curry, G. D., & Decker, S. H. (2003). *Confronting gangs: Crime and community* (2nd ed.). Los Angeles: Roxbury.

- Elliott, D. S., & Menard, S. (1996). Delinquent friends and delinquent behaviour: Temporal and developmental patterns. In J. D. Hawkins (Ed.), *Delinquency and crime: Current theories* (pp. 28–67). New York: Cambridge University Press.
- Fagan, J. (1990). Social processes of delinquency and drug use among urban gangs. In C. R. Huff (Ed.), *Gangs in America* (pp. 183–219). Newbury Park, CA: Sage.
- Klein, M. W. (2001). Gangs in the United States and Europe. In J. Miller, C. L. Maxson, & M. W. Klein (Eds,), *The modern gang reader* (2nd ed.). Los Angeles: Roxbury.

Specialization and Persistence in the Arrest Histories of Sex Offenders: A Comparative Analysis of Alternative Measures and Offense Types
Terance D. Miethe, Jodi Olson, and Ojmarrh Mitchell

- Blumstein, A., Cohen, J., Das, S., & Moitra, S. D. (1988). Specialization and seriousness during adult criminal careers. *Journal of Quantitative Criminology, 4*(4), 303–345.
- Groth, A. N., & Birnbaum, H. J. (1979). *Men who rape.* New York: Plenum.
- Hanson, R. K., Scott, H., & Steffy, R. A. (1995). A comparison of child molesters and nonsexual criminals: Risk predictors and long-term recidivism. *Journal of Research in Crime and Delinquency, 32,* 325–337.
- Prentky, R. A. (1996). Community notification and the constructive risk reduction. *Journal of Interpersonal Violence, 11,* 295–300.
- Zimring, F. E. (2004). *An American travesty: Legal responses to adolescent sexual offending.* Chicago: University of Chicago Press.

The Novelty of "Cybercrime": An Assessment in Light of Routine Activity Theory
Majid Yar

- Grabosky, P. (2001). Virtual criminality: Old wine in new bottles? *Social & Legal Studies, 10,* 243–249.
- Joseph, J. (2003). Cyberstalking: An international perspective. In Y. Jewkes (Ed.), *Dot.cons: Crime, deviance and identity on the Internet.* Cullompton, UK: Willan Press.
- Newman, G., & Clarke, R. (2003). *Superhighway robbery: Preventing ecommerce crime.* Cullompton, UK: Willan Press.
- Thomas, D., & Loader, B. (2000). Introduction—Cybercrime: Law enforcement, security and surveillance in the information age. In D. Thomas & B. Loader (Eds.), *Cybercrime: Law enforcement, security and surveillance in the information age.* London: Routledge.
- Wall, D. (2001). Cybercrimes and the Internet. In D. Wall (Ed.), *Crime and the Internet* (pp. 1–17). London: Routledge.

How Does Studying Terrorism Compare to Studying Crime?
Gary LaFree and Laura Dugan

- Crenshaw, M. (1983). *Terrorism, legitimacy and power.* Middleton, CT: Wesleyan University Press.
- Hoffman, B. (1998). *Recent trends and future prospects of terrorism in the United States.* Santa Monica, CA: Rand.
- McCauley, C. (1991). Terrorism research and public policy: An overview. In C. McCauley (Ed.), *Terrorism research and public policy* (pp. 126–144). London: Frank Cass.
- McCauley, C., & Segal, M. E. (1997). Social psychology of terrorist groups. In C. Hendrick (Ed.), *Group processes and intergroup relations* (pp. 231–256). Newbury Park, CA: Sage.
- Merari, A. (1991). Academic research and government policy on terrorism. *Terrorism and Political Violence, 3,* 88–102.
- Silke, A. (2001). The devil you know: Continuing problems with research on terrorism. *Terrorism and Political Violence, 13,* 1–14.
- Smith, B. L., & Orvis, G. P. (1993). America's response to terrorism: An empirical analysis of federal intervention strategies during the 1980s. *Justice Quarterly, 10,* 661–681.

- United States Department of State. (2001). *Introduction: Patterns of global terrorism, 2000.* Retrieved from http://www.state.gov/s/ct/rls/crt/2000/2419.htm

Part IV: How Is Crime Measured? The Observation and Measurement of Crime

Locating the Vanguard in Rising and Falling Homicide Rates Across U.S. Cities
Steven F. Messner, Glenn D. Deane, Luc Anselin, and Benjamin Pearson-Nelson

- Baumer, E. P., Lauritsen, J. L., Rosenfeld, R., & Wright, R. (1998). The influence of crack cocaine on robbery, burglary, and homicide rates: A cross-city, longitudinal analysis. *Journal of Research in Crime and Delinquency, 35,* 316–340.
- Blumstein, A. (1995). Youth violence, guns, and the illicit-drug industry. *Journal of Criminal Law and Criminology, 86,* 10–36.
- Cook, P. J., & Laub, J. H. (1999). Examining space-time interaction in city-level homicide data: Crack markets and the diffusion of guns among youth. *Journal of Quantitative Criminology, 15,* 379–406.
- Rosenfeld, R. (2002). Crime decline in context. *Contexts: Understanding People in Their Social Worlds, 1,* 25–34.
- Wintemute, G. (2000). Guns and gun violence. In A. Blumstein & J. Wallman (Eds.), *The crime drop in America.* New York: Cambridge University Press.

Reconciling Race and Class Differences in Self-Reported and Official Estimates of Delinquency
Delbert S. Elliott and Suzanne S. Ageton

- Farrington, D. (1973). Self-reports of deviant behavior: Predictive and stable? *Journal of Criminal Law and Criminology, 64,* 99–110.
- Gold, M. (1966). Undetected delinquent behavior. *Journal of Research in Crime and Delinquency, 3,* 27–46.
- Hardt, R., & Peterson-Hardt, S. (1977). On determining the quality of the delinquency self-report method. *Journal of Research in Crime and Delinquency, 14,* 247–261.
- Hindelang, M. (1978). Race and involvement in common law personal crimes. *American Sociological Review, 43,* 93–109.
- Short, J., & Nye, I. (1958). Extent of unrecorded juvenile delinquency: Tentative conclusions. *Journal of Criminal Law, Criminology, and Police Science, 49,* 296–302.
- Williams, J., & Gold, M. (1972). From delinquent behavior to official delinquency. *Social Problems, 20,* 209–229.

Gender and Adolescent Relationship Violence: A Contextual Examination
Jody Miller and Norman A. White

- Dobash, R. P., Dobash, R. E., Cavanagh, K., & Lewis, R. (1998). Separate and interesting realities: A comparison of men's and women's accounts of violence against women. *Violence Against Women, 4,* 382–414.
- Felson, R. B., & Messner, S. F. (2000). The control motive in intimate partner violence. *Social Psychology Quarterly, 63,* 86–94.
- Giordano, P. C., Millhollin, T. J., Cernkovich, S. A., Pugh, M. D., & Rudolph, J. L. (1999). Delinquency, identity, and women's involvement in relationship violence. *Criminology, 37,* 17–37.
- Hanley, M. J., & O'Neill, P. (1997). Violence and commitment: A study of dating couples. *Journal of Interpersonal Violence, 12,* 685–703.
- Kimmel, M. (2002). "Gender symmetry" in domestic violence: A substantive and methodological research review. *Violence Against Women, 8,* 1332–1363.
- Moffitt, T. E., Robins R. W., & Caspi, A. (2001). A couple's analysis of partner abuse with implications for abuse-prevention policy. *Criminology and Public Policy, 1,* 5–36.

- Morse, B. J. (1995). Beyond the conflict tactics scale: Assessing gender differences in partner violence. *Violence and Victims, 4,* 251–272.
- Orbuch, T. L. (1997). People's accounts count: The sociology of accounts. *Annual Review of Sociology, 23,* 455–478.

The Criminology of Genocide: The Death and Rape of Darfur
John Hagan, Wenona Rymond-Richmond, and Patricia Parker

- Branigan, A., & Hardwick, K. (2003). Genocide and general theory. In C. Britt & M. Gottfredson (Eds.), *Control theories of crime and delinquency: Advances in criminological theory* (Vol. 12). Piscataway, NJ: Transaction Books.
- Chalk, F., & Jonassohn, K. (1990). *The history and sociology of genocide: Analyses and case studies.* New Haven, CT: Yale University Press.
- Hagan, J., & Greer, S. (2002). Making war criminal. *Criminology, 40,* 231–264.
- Horowitz, I. L. (2002). *Taking lives: Genocide and state power.* New Brunswick, NJ: Transaction.
- Power, S. (2002). *A problem from hell: America and the age of genocide.* New York: Basic Books.

Part V: Who Are the Criminals? The Distribution and Correlates of Crime

Neighborhood Disadvantage and the Nature of Violence
Eric Baumer, Julie Horney, Richard Felson, and Janet L. Lauritsen

- Jencks, C., & Mayer, S. E. (1990). The social consequences of growing up in a poor neighborhood. In L. E. Lynn, Jr. & M. G. H. McGeary (Eds.), *Inner-city poverty in the United States.* Washington, DC: National Academy Press.
- Kornhauser, R. R. (1978). *Social sources of delinquency: An appraisal of analytic models.* Chicago: University of Chicago Press.
- Lauritsen, J. L. (2001). The social ecology of violent victimization: Individual and contextual effects in the NCVS. *Journal of Quantitative Criminology, 17,* 3–32.
- Sampson, R. J., Raudenbush, S. W., & Earls, F. (1997). Neighborhoods and violent crime: A multilevel study of collective efficacy. *Science, 277,* 918–924.

Explaining Racial and Ethnic Differences in Adolescent Violence: Structural Disadvantage, Family Well-Being, and Social Captial
Thomas L. McNulty and Paul E. Bellair

- Anderson, E. (1999). *Code of the street: Decency, violence, and the moral life of the inner city.* New York: W. W. Norton.
- Cernkovich, S. A., & Giordano, P. C. (1992). School bonding, race, and delinquency. *Criminology, 30,* 261–291.
- Krivo, L., & Peterson, R. D. (1996). Extremely disadvantaged neighborhoods and urban crime. *Social Forces, 75,* 619–648.
- LaFree, G. (1995). Race and crime trends in the United States, 1946–1990. In D. F. Hawkins (Ed.), *Ethnicity, race, and crime: Perspectives across time and place* (pp. 169–193). Albany NY: SUNY Press.
- McNulty, T., & Holloway, S. R. (2000). Race, crime, and public housing in Atlanta: Testing a conditional effect hypothesis. *Social Forces, 79,* 707–729.
- Sampson, R. J. (1987). Urban black violence: The effect of male joblessness and family disruption. *American Journal of Sociology, 93,* 348–382.
- Sampson, R. J., & Wilson, W. J. (1995). Toward a theory of race, crime, and urban inequality. In J. Hagan & R. D. Peterson (Eds.), *Crime and inequality* (pp. 37–54). Stanford, CA: Stanford University Press.
- Short, J. F., Jr. (1997). *Poverty, ethnicity, and violent crime.* Boulder, CO: Westview Press.

Age and the Explanation of Crime
Travis Hirschi and Michael Gottfredson

- Blumstein, A., & Cohen, J. (1979). Estimation of individual crime rates from arrest records. *Journal of Criminal Law and Criminology, 70,* 4.
- Elliott, D., Ageton, S., & Canter, R. (1979). An integrated theoretical perspective on delinquent behavior. *Journal of Research in Crime and Delinquency, 16,* 3–27.
- Empey, L. (1978). *American delinquency.* Homewood, IL: Dorsey.
- Greenberg, D. (1979). Delinquency and the age structure of society. In S. L. Messinger & E. Bittner (Eds.), *Criminology review yearbook* (pp. 586–620). Beverly Hills, CA: Sage.
- Petersilia, J. (1980). Criminal career research: A review of recent evidence. In N. Morris & M. Tonry (Eds.), *Crime and justice: An annual review of research* (Vol. 2). Chicago: University of Chicago Press.

Juvenile Delinquency and Gender
Josine Junger-Tas, Denis Ribeaud, and Maarten J. L. F. Cruyff

- Adler, F. (1975). *Sisters in crime.* New York: McGraw-Hill.
- Cernkovich, S. A., & Giordano, P. C. (1987). Family relationships and delinquency. *Criminology, 25,* 295–321.
- Chesney-Lind, M. (1989). Girls' crime and women's place: Towards a feminist model of female delinquency. *Crime and Delinquency, 35.*
- Glueck, S., & Glueck, E. (1950). *Unraveling juvenile delinquency.* Cambridge, MA: Harvard University Press.
- Heimer, K. (1995). Gender, race, and the pathways to delinquency: An interactionist analysis. In J. Hagan & R. D. Peterson (Eds.), *Crime and inequality.* Stanford, CA: Stanford University Press.
- Moffit, T. E., Caspi, A., Rutter, M., & Silva, P. A. (2001). *Sex differences in antisocial behaviour.* Cambridge: Cambridge University Press.
- Simon, R. J. (1975). *The contemporary woman and crime.* Washington, DC: National Institute of Mental Health.

Part VI: How Do We Explain Crime? Foundational Theories of Modern Criminology I

Juvenile Delinquency and Urban Areas
Clifford R. Shaw and Henry McKay

- Park, R., Burgess, E., & McKenzie, R. (1925). *The city.* Chicago: University of Chicago Press.
- Shaw, C. (1929). *Delinquency areas.* Chicago: University of Chicago Press.
- Wirth, L. (1928). *The ghetto.* Chicago: University of Chicago Press.

Neighborhood Inequality, Collective Efficacy, and the Spatial Dynamics of Urban Violence
Jeffrey D. Morenoff, Robert J. Sampson, and Stephen W. Raudenbush

- Bursik, R. J., Jr. (1988). Social disorganization and theories of crime and delinquency: Problems and prospects. *Criminology, 26,* 519–552.
- Sampson, R. J, & Groves, W. B. (1989). Community structure and crime: Testing social-disorganization theory. *American Journal of Sociology, 94,* 774–802.
- Sampson, R. J., Morenoff, J., & Earls, F. (1999). Beyond social capital: Spatial dynamics of collective efficacy for children. *American Sociological Review, 64,* 633–660.
- Sampson, R. J., & Wilson, W. J. (1995). Toward a theory of race, crime, and urban inequality. In J. Hagan & R. Peterson (Eds.), *Crime and inequality.* Stanford, CA: Stanford University Press.
- Shaw, C., & McKay, H. (1942). *Juvenile delinquency and urban areas.* Chicago: University of Chicago Press.

A Theory of Crime: Differential Association
Edwin H. Sutherland

- Bordua, D. (1962). Some comments on theories of group delinquency. *Sociological Inquiry, 32*, 245–260.
- Cressey, D. (1952). Application and verification of the differential association theory. *Journal of Criminal Law, Criminology, and Police Science, 43*, 43–52.
- Eynon, T., & Reckless, W. (1961). Companionship at delinquency onset. *British Journal of Criminology, 13*, 162–170.
- Glaser, D. (1956). Criminological theories and behavioral images. *American Journal of Sociology, 61*, 433–444.
- Reiss, A., Jr., & Rhodes, L. (1964). An empirical test of differential association theory. *Journal of Research in Crime and Delinquency, 1*, 5–18.
- Short, J., Jr. (1960). Differential association as a hypothesis: Problems of empirical testing. *Social Problems, 8*, 14–25.

Differential Association in Group and Solo Offending
Andy Hochstetler, Heith Copes, and Matt DeLisi

- Cloward, R. A., & Ohlin, L. E. (1960). *Delinquency and opportunity: A theory of delinquent gangs.* New York: Free Press.
- Costello, B. J., & Vowell, P. R. (1999). Testing control theory and differential association: A reanalysis of the Richmond Youth Project data. *Criminology, 37*, 815–842.
- Heimer, K., & Matsueda, R. L. (1994). Role-taking, role commitment, and delinquency: A theory of differential social control. *American Sociological Review, 59*, 365–390.
- Matsueda, R. L. (1992). Reflected appraisals, parental labeling, and delinquency: Specifying a symbolic interactionist theory. *American Journal of Sociology, 97*, 1577–1611.
- Warr, M. (1993). Age, peers and delinquency. *Criminology, 31*, 17–40.

Social Structure and Anomie
Robert K. Merton

- Durkheim, E. (1951). *Suicide: A study in sociology.* New York: Free Press.
- Horney, K. (1937). *The neurotic personality of our time.* New York: W.W. Norton.
- Mayo, E. (1933). *The human problems of an industrial civilization.* New York: The Macmillan Company.
- Plant, J. (1937). *Personality and the cultural pattern.* London: Oxford University Press.
- Siegfried, A. (1927). *America comes of age: A French analysis.* New York: Harcourt, Brace and Company.

Poverty, Socioeconomic Change, Institutional Anomie, and Homicide
Sang-Weon Kim and William Alex Pridemore

- Friedman, W. (1998). Volunteerism and the decline of violent crime. *Journal of Criminal Law and Criminology, 88*, 1453–1474.
- LaFree, G. (1998). *Losing legitimacy: Street crime and the decline of social institutions in America.* Boulder, CO: Westview Press.
- Messner, S. F., & Rosenfeld, R. (1997). Political restraint of the market and levels of criminal homicide: A cross-national application of institutional-anomie theory. *Social Forces, 75*, 1393–1416.
- Morenoff, J. D., & Sampson, R. J. (1997). Violent crime and the spatial dynamics of neighborhood transition: Chicago, 1970–1990. *Social Forces, 76*, 31–64.
- Osgood, D. W., & Chambers, J. M. (2000). Social disorganization outside the metropolis: An analysis of rural youth violence. *Criminology, 38*, 81–115.
- Piquero, A., & Piquero, N. L. (1998). On testing institutional anomie theory with varying specifications. *Studies on crime and crime prevention, 7*, 61–84.

Part VII: How Do We Explain Crime? Foundational Theories of Modern Criminology II

The Subculture of Violence
Marvin E. Wolfgang and Franco Ferracuti

- Bandura, A., & Walters, R. H. (1959). *Adolescent aggression.* New York: Ronald Press.
- Berkowitz, L. (1962). *Aggression.* New York: McGraw Hill.
- Lawson, R. (1965). *Frustration: The development of a scientific concept.* New York: MacMillan.
- Reckless, W. (1961). *The crime problem* (3rd ed.). New York: Appleton Century Crofts.
- Trasler, G. (1962). *The explanation of criminality.* London: Routledge and Kegan Paul.

Exposure to Community Violence and Childhood Delinquency
Justin W. Patchin, Beth M. Huebner, John D. McCluskey, Sean P. Varano, and Timothy S. Bynum

- Anderson, E. (1999). *Code of the street.* New York: Norton.
- Bernard, T. J. (1990). Angry aggression among the "truly disadvantaged." *Criminology, 28*(1), 73–96.
- Farrell, A. D., & Bruce, S. E. (1996). Impact of exposure to community violence on violent behavior and emotional distress among urban adolescents. *Journal of Clinical Child Psychology, 26,* 2–14.
- Wikström, P. H., & Loeber, R. (2000). Do disadvantaged neighborhoods cause well-adjusted children to become adolescent delinquents? A study of male juvenile serious offending, individual risk and protective factors, and neighborhood context. *Criminology, 38*(4), 1109–1142.
- Woflgang, M. E., Figlio, R. M., & Sellin, T. (1972). *Delinquency in a birth cohort.* Chicago: University of Chicago Press.

Causes and Prevention of Juvenile Delinquency
Travis Hirschi

- Hirschi, T. (1969). *Causes of delinquency.* Berkeley: University of California Press.
- Matza, D. (1964). *Delinquency and drift.* New York: Wiley.
- Thrasher, F. (1963). *The gang.* Chicago: University of Chicago Press.
- Toby, J. (1957). Social disorgaization and stake in conformity: Complementary factors in the predatory behavior of young hoodlums. *Journal of Criminal Law, Criminology and Police Science, 48,* 12–17.
- Wilson, J. (1975). *Thinking about crime.* New York: Vintage.

Exploring the Utility of Social Control Theory for Youth Development: Issues of Attachment, Involvement, and Gender
Angela J. Huebner and Sherry C. Betts

- Chesney-Lind, M. (1999). *What to do about girls? Thinking about programs for young women.* Paper presented at the International Community Corrections Annual Research Conference, Washington, DC, September, 1998.
- Esbensen, F., Deschenes, E., & Winfree, L. (1999). Differences between gang girls and gang boys: Results from a multi-site survey. *Youth & Society, 31*(1), 27–53.
- Gilligan, C., & Attanucci, J. (1988). Two moral orientations: Gender differences and similarities. *Merrill-Palmer Quarterly, 34*(3), 223–237.
- Kempf, K. (1993). The empirical status of Hirschi's control theory. In F. Adler & W. S. Laufer (Eds.), *New directions in criminological theory: Advances in criminological theory* (Vol. 4, pp. 143–185). New Brunswick, NJ: Transaction Books.
- Werner, E., & Smith, R. (1992). *Overcoming the odds: High risk children from birth to adulthood.* Ithaca, NY: Cornell University Press.

Labeling Criminals
Edwin M. Schur

- Becker, H. (1963). *Outsiders: Studies in the sociology of deviance.* New York: Free Press.
- Lemert, E. (1951). *Social pathology.* New York: McGraw-Hill.
- Merton, R. (1961). Social problems and sociological theory. In R. Merton & R. Nisbet (Eds.), *Contemporary social problems.* New York: Harcourt, Brace and World.
- Schur, E. (1963). Recent social problems texts: An essay-review. *Social Problems, 10,* 287–292.
- Tannenbaum, F. (1938). *Crime and the community.* New York: Ginn and Company.

Official Labeling, Criminal Embeddedness, and Subsequent Delinquency: A Longitudinal Test of Labeling Theory
Jón Gunnar Bernburg, Marvin D. Krohn, and Craig J. Rivera

- Becker, H. (1963). *Outsiders: Studies in the sociology of deviance.* New York: Free Press.
- Davies, S., & Tanner, J. (2003). The long arm of the law. *The Sociological Quarterly, 44,* 385–404.
- Hagan, J. (1993). The social embeddedness of crime and unemployment. *Criminology, 31,* 465–491.
- Klein, M. W. (1974). Labeling, deterrence and recidivism: A study of police dispositions of juvenile offenders. *Social Problems, 22,* 292–303.
- Paternoster, R., & Iovanni, L. (1989). The labelling perspective and delinquency: An elaboration of the theory and assessment of the evidence. *Justice Quarterly, 6,* 359–394.
- Ray, M. C., & Downes, W. (1986). An empirical test of labelling theory using longitudinal data. *Journal of Research in Crime and Delinquency, 23,* 169–194.
- Schur, E. M. (1971). *Labeling deviant behavior.* New York: Harper & Row.
- Triplett, R. A., & Jarjoura, G. R. (1994). Theoretical and empirical specification of a model of informal labeling. *Journal of Quantitative Criminology, 10,* 241–276.

Crime and Structural Contradictions
William J. Chambliss

- Chambliss, W. (1973). *Sociological readings in the conflict perspective.* Reading, MA: Addison-Wesley.
- Chambliss, W. (1974). The state, the law and the definition of behavior as criminal or delinquent. In D. Glaser (Ed.), *Handbook of criminology.* Chicago: Rand McNally.
- Duster, T. (1970). *The legislation of morality: Law, drugs and moral judgement.* New York: Free Press.
- Gusfield, J. (1963). *Symbolic crusade: Status politics and the American temperance movement.* Urbana: University of Illinois Press.
- Hall, J. (1952). *Theft, law and society.* Indianapolis, IN: Bobbs-Merrill and Co.

Vigilantism, Current Racial Threat, and Death Sentences
David Jacobs, Jason T. Carmichael, and Stephanie L. Kent

- Chiricos, T. G., & Crawford, C. (1995). Race and imprisonment: A contextual assessment of the evidence. In D. Hawkins (Ed.), *Ethnicity, race, and crime* (pp. 281–309). Albany, NY: SUNY Press.
- Garland, D. (1990). *Punishment and modern society.* Chicago: University of Chicago Press.
- Paternoster, R. (1991). *Capital punishment in America.* New York: Lexington Books.
- Phillips, C. D. (1987). Exploring relations among forms of social control: The lynching and execution of blacks in North Carolina. *Law and Society Review, 21,* 361–374.
- Zimring, F. E. (2003). *The contradictions of American capital punishment.* New York: Oxford University Press.

Part VIII: How Do We Explain Crime? Contemporary Theories and Research I

The Nature of Criminality: Low Self-Control
Michael Gottfredson and Travis Hirschi

- Bentham, J. (1970). *An introduction to the principles of morals and legislation.* London: The Athlone Press. (Original work published 1789)
- Glueck, S., & Glueck, E. (1950). *Unraveling juvenile delinquency.* Cambridge, MA: Harvard University Press.
- Gottfredson, M. (1984). *Victims of crime: The dimensions of risk.* London: HMSO.
- Robins, L. (1966). *Deviant children grown up.* Baltimore: Williams and Wilkins.
- West, D., & Farrington, D. (1973). *Who becomes delinquent?* London: Heinemann.

The Stability and Resiliency of Self-Control in a Sample of Incarcerated Offenders
Ojmarrh Mitchell and Doris Layton MacKenzie

- Arneklev, B. J., Cochran, J. K., & Gainey, R. R. (1998). Testing Gottfredson and Hirschi's "low self-control" stability hypothesis: An exploratory study. *American Journal of Criminal Justice, 23*(1), 107–127.
- Evans, T. D., Cullen, F. T., Burton, V. S., Jr., Dunaway, R. G., & Benson, M. L. (1997). The social consequence of self-control: Testing the general hypothesis of crime. *Criminology, 35,* 475–504.
- Gibbs, J. J., Giever, D., & Martin, J. S. (1998). Parental management and self-control: An empirical test of Gottfredson and Hirschi's general theory. *Journal of Research in Crime and Delinquency, 35*(1), 40–70.
- Grasmick, H. G., Tittle, C. R., Bursik, R. J., Jr., & Arneklev, B. J. (1993). Testing the core empirical implications of Gottfredson and Hirschi's general theory of crime. *Journal of Research in Crime and Delinquency, 30*(1), 5–29.
- Hay, C. (2001). Parenting, self-control, and delinquency: A test of self-control theory. *Criminology, 39,* 707–736.
- Perrone, D., Sullivan, C., Pratt, T. C., & Margaryan, S. (2004). Parental efficacy, self-control, and delinquency: A test of a general theory of crime on a nationally representative sample of youth. *International Journal of Offender Therapy and Comparative Criminology, 48,* 294–312.
- Pratt, T. C., & Cullen, F. T. (2000). The empirical status of Gottfredson and Hirschi's general theory of crime: A meta-analysis. *Criminology, 38,* 931–964.

Toward an Age-Graded Theory of Informal Social Control
Robert J. Sampson and John H. Laub

- Blumstein, A., Cohen, J., Roth, J., & Visher, C. (Eds.). (1986). *Criminal careers and career criminals.* Washingon, DC: National Academy Press.
- Coleman, J. (1988). Social capital in the creation of human capital. *American Journal of Sociology, 94,* S95–S120.
- Elder, G. (1975). Age differentiation and the life course. In A. Inkeles (Ed.), *Annual review of sociology* (Vol. 1, pp. 165–190). Palo Alto, CA: Annual Reviews.
- Kornhauser, R. (1978). *Social sources of delinquency.* Chicago: University of Chicago Press.
- Loeber, R., & LeBlanc, M. (1990). Toward a developmental criminology. In M. Tonry & N. Morris (Eds.), *Crime and justice* (Vol. 12, pp. 375–437). Chicago: University of Chicago Press.
- Rutter, M., Quinton, D., & Hill, J. (1990). Adult outcomes of institution-reared children: Males and females compared. In L. N. Robbins & M. Rutter (Eds.), *Straight and devious pathways from childhood to adulthood* (pp. 135–157). Cambridge, UK: Cambridge University Press.

Does Marriage Reduce Crime? A Counterfactual Approach to Within-Individual Causal Effects
Robert J. Sampson, John H. Laub, and Christopher Wimer

- Brown, S. L. (2000). The effect of union type on physiological well-being: Depression among cohabitors versus marrieds. *Journal of Health and Social Behavior, 41*, 241–255.
- Bushway, S., Piquero, A., Broidy, L., Cauffman, E., & Mazerolle, P. (2001). An empirical framework for studying desistance as a process. *Criminology, 39*, 491–515.
- Duncan, G. J., Wilkerson., B., & England, P. (2003). *Cleaning up their act: The impacts of marriage and cohabitation on licit and illicit drug use.* Unpublished manuscript, Northwestern University.
- Glueck, S., & Glueck, E. (1968). *Delinquents and nondelinquents in perspective.* Cambridge, MA: Harvard University Press.
- Hill, T. W. (1971). From hell-raiser to family man. In W. David (Ed.), *Conformity and conflict: Readings in cultural anthropology.* Boston: Little, Brown.
- Laub, J. H., & Sampson, R. J. (2003). *Shared beginnings, divergent lives: Delinquent boys to age 70.* Cambridge, MA: Harvard University Press.
- Sampson, R. J., & Laub, J. H. (1994). Urban poverty and the family context of delinquency: A new look at structure and process in a classic study. *Child Development, 65*, 523–540.

Social Change and Crime Rate Trends: A Routine Activity Approach
Lawrence E. Cohen and Marcus Felson

- Ferdinand, T. (1970). Demographic shifts and criminality. *British Journal of Criminology, 10*, 169–175.
- Gould, L. (1969). The changing structure of property crime in an affluent society. *Social Forces, 48*, 50–59.
- Hindelang, M. (1976). *Criminal victimization in eight American cities: A descriptive analysis of common theft and assault.* Cambridge, MA: Ballinger.
- Kobrin, F. (1976). The primary individual and the family: Changes in living arrangements in the U.S. since 1940. *Journal of Marriage and the Family, 38*, 233–239.
- Land, K., & Felson, M. (1976). A general framework for building dynamic macro social indicator models. *American Journal of Sociology, 85*, 565–604.

Traveling to Violence: The Case for a Mobility-Based Spatial Typology of Homicide
George Tita and Elizabeth Griffiths

- Brantingham, P. J., & Brantingham, P. L. (1981). *Environmental criminology.* Beverly Hills, CA: Sage.
- Caywood, T. (1998). Routine activities and urban homicides: A tale of two cities. *Homicide Studies, 2*(1), 64–82.
- Cohen, L. E., & Felson, M. (1979). Social change and crime rate trends: A routine activities approach. *American Sociological Review, 44*, 588–608.
- Felson, M. (1987). Routine activities and crime prevention in the developing metropolis. *Criminology, 25*, 911–931.
- Messner, S. F., & Tardiff, K. (1986). The social ecology of urban homicide: An application of the "routine activities" approach. *Criminology, 22*, 241–267.
- Stahura, J. M., & Sloan, J. J., III. (1988). Urban stratification of places, routine activities, and suburban crime rates. *Social Forces, 66*, 1102–1118.

Foundation for a General Strain Theory of Crime and Delinquency
Robert Agnew

- Agnew, R. S. (1983). Social class and success goals: An examination of relative and absolute aspirations. *Sociological Quarterly, 24*, 435–452.

- Akers, R. L. (1985). *Deviant behavior: A social learning approach* (3rd ed.). Belmont, CA: Wadsworth.
- Bandura, A. (1983). Psychological mechanisms of aggression. In R. G. Geen & E. I. Donnerstein (Eds.), *Aggression: Theoretical and empirical reviews*. New York: Academic Press.
- Elliott, D., Ageton, S. S., & Canter, R. J. (1979). An integrated theoretical perspective on delinquent behavior. *Journal of Research in Crime and Delinquency, 16*, 3–27.
- Kemper, T. D. (1978). *A social interactional theory of emotions*. New York: John Wiley & Sons.

A Test of General Strain Theory
Lisa M. Broidy

- Agnew R., & White, H. R. (1992). An empirical test of general strain theory. *Criminology, 30*, 457–499.
- Hoffman, J. P., & Su, S. S. (1997). The conditional effects of stress on delinquency and drug use: A strain theory assessment of sex differences. *Journal of Research in Crime and Delinquency, 34*, 46–78.
- Mazerolle, P. (1998). Gender, general strain, and delinquency: An empirical examination. *Justice Quarterly, 15*, 65–91.
- Tittle, C. R., & Meier, R. (1990). Specifying the SES/delinquency relationship. *Criminology, 28*, 271–299.
- Tyler, T. R. (1990). *Why people obey the law*. New Haven, CT: Yale University Press.

Part IX: How Do We Explain Crime? Contemporary Theories and Research II

The Code of the Streets
Elijah Anderson

- Anderson, E. (1978). *A place on the corner*. Chicago: University of Chicago Press.
- Anderson, E. (1989). Sex codes and family life among poor inner-city youths. In W. J. Wilson (Ed.), *The ghetto underclass: Social science perspectives. Special edition of The Annals of the American Academy of Political and Social Science, 501*, 59–78.
- Anderson, E. (1990). *Streetwise: Race, class and change in an urban community*. Chicago: University of Chicago Press.
- Drake, S. C., & Cayton, H. (1962). *Black metropolis*. New York: Harper and Row.
- Wolfgang, M., & Ferracuti, F. (1967). *The subculture of violence*. London: Tavistock.

Structure and Culture in African American Adolescent Violence: A Partial Test of the "Code of the Street" Thesis
Eric A. Stewart and Ronald L. Simons

- Anderson, E. (1999). *Code of the street: Decency, violence, and the moral life of the inner city*. New York: W. W. Norton.
- Bruce, M. A., Roscigno, V. J., & McCall, P. L. (1998). Structure, context, and agency in the reproduction of black-on-black violence. *Theoretical Criminology, 2*, 29–55.
- Horowitz, R. (1983). *Honor and the American dream: Culture and identity in a Chicano community*. New Brunswick, NJ: Rutgers University Press.
- Kubrin, C. E., & Weitzer, R. (2003). Retaliatory homicide: Concentrated disadvantage and neighborhood culture. *Social Problems, 50*, 157–180.
- Majors, R., & Billson, J. M. (1992). *Cool pose: The dilemmas of black manhood in America*. New York: Touchstone.
- McNulty, T. L., & Bellair, P. E. (2003). Explaining racial and ethnic differences in adolescent violence: Structural disadvantage, family well-being, and social capital. *Justice Quarterly, 20*, 1–31.
- Sampson, R. J., & Wilson, W. J. (1995). Toward a theory of race, crime, and urban inequality. In J. Hagan & R. D. Peterson (Eds.), *Crime and inequality*. Stanford, CA: Stanford University Press.

Beyond White Man's Justice: Race, Gender and Justice in Late Modernity
Barbara Hudson

- Daly, K., & Stubbs, J. (2006). Feminist engagement with restorative justice. *Theoretical Criminology, 10*(1), 9–28.
- Harris, A. P. (1990). Race and essentialism in feminist legal theory. *Stanford Law Review, 42*, 581–616.
- Hudson, B. (2003). *Justice in the risk society: Challenging and reaffirming justice in late modernity.* London: Sage.
- MacKinnon, C. A. (1991). Reflections on sex equality under the law. *Yale Law Journal, 100*(5), 1281–1328.
- Naffine, N. (1990). *Law and the sexes.* Sydney: Allen & Unwin.
- Smart, C. (1989). *Feminism and the power of law.* London: Routledge.

An Argument for Black Feminist Criminology: Understanding African American Women's Experiences With Intimate Partner Abuse Using an Integrated Approach
Hillary Potter

- Belknap, J. (2001). *The invisible woman: Gender, crime, and justice* (2nd ed.). Belmont, CA: Wadsworth.
- Collins, P. H. (2000). *Black feminist thought: Knowledge, consciousness, and the politics of empowerment* (2nd ed.). New York: Routledge.
- Crenshaw, K. W. (1994). Mapping the margins: Intersectionality, identity politics, and violence against women of color. In M. A. Fineman & R. Mykitiuk (Eds.), *The public nature of private violence: The discovery of domestic abuse* (pp. 93–118). New York: Routledge.
- Daly, K., & Chesney-Lind, M. (1988). Feminism and criminology. *Justice Quarterly, 5*(4), 499–535.
- Richie, B. E. (1996). *Compelled to crime: The gender entrapment of battered black women.* New York: Routledge.
- Weis, L. (2001). Race, gender, and critique: African-American women, white women, and domestic violence in the 1980s and 1990s. *Signs: Journal of Women in Culture and Society, 27*, 139–169.

A Bio-Psychological Theory of Choice
James Q. Wilson and Richard Herrnstein

- Beccaria, C. (1963). *On crimes and punishments* (H. Paolucci, Trans.). Indianapolis, IN: Library of Liberal Arts/Bobbs-Merrill. (Original work published 1764)
- Herrnstein, R. (1983). Some criminogenic traits of offenders. In J. Q. Wilson (Ed.), *Crime and public policy.* San Francisco: ICS Press.
- Wilson, J. Q. (1983). *Thinking about crime.* New York: Basic Books.

Human Ecology, Crime, and Crime Control: Linking Individual Behavior and Aggregate Crime
Joanne Savage and Bryan Vila

- Axelrod, R. (1986). An evolutionary approach to norms. *American Political Science Review, 80*, 1095–1111.
- Bottoms, A. (1994). Environmental criminology. In M. Maguire, R. Morgan, & R. Reiner (Eds.), *The Oxford handbook of criminology* (pp. 585–658). Oxford: Clarendon Press.
- Bursik, R. J., Jr. (1986). Ecological stability and the dynamics of delinquency. In A. J. Reiss, Jr. & M. Tonry (Eds.),. *Communities and crime: Vol. 8. Crime and justice: A review of research* (pp. 35–66). Chicago: University of Chicago Press.
- Dodge, K. A., Bates, J. E., & Pettit, G. S. (1990). Mechanisms in the cycle of violence. *Science, 250*, 1678–1683.
- Loeber, R. (1982). The stability of antisocial child behavior: A review. *Child Development, 53*, 1431–1446.

- Mealey, L. (1995). The sociobiology of sociopathy: An integrated evolutionary model. *Behavioral and Brain Sciences, 18,* 523–542.
- Patterson, G. R., Debaryshe, B. D., & Ramsey, E. (1989). A developmental perspective on antisocial behavior. *American Psychologist, 44,* 329–335.

Males on the Life-Course-Persistent and Adolescence-Limited Antisocial Pathways
Terrie E. Moffitt, Avshalom Caspi, Honalee Harrington, and Barry J. Milne

- Blumstein, A., Cohen, J., & Farrington, D. P. (1988). Criminal career research: Its value for criminology. *Criminology, 26,* 1–35.
- Fagan, J., & Freeman, R. B. (1999). Crime and work. *Crime and justice: A review of research, 25,* 225–290.
- Moffitt, T. E. (1993). "Life-course-persistent" and "adolescence-limited" antisocial behavior: A developmental taxonomy. *Psychological Review, 100,* 674–701.
- Patterson, G. R., Forgatch, M. S., Voerger, K. L., & Stoolmiller, M. (1998). Variables that initiate and maintain an early-onset trajectory of offending. *Development and Psychopathology, 10,* 531–547.
- Piquero, A. (2001). Testing Moffitt's neuropsychological variation hypothesis for the prediction of life-course persistent offending. *Psychology, Crime and Law, 7,* 193–216.

The Relationships Among Self-Blame, Psychological Distress, and Sexual Victimization
Kimberly Hanson Breitenbecher

- Abbey, A., Ross, L. T., McDuffie, D., & McAuslan, P. (1996). Alcohol and dating risk factors for sexual assault among college women. *Psychology of Women Quarterly, 20,* 147–169.
- Frazier, P. A. (1990). Victim attributions and post-trauma. *Journal of Personality and Social Psychology, 59,* 298–304.
- Hill, J. L., & Zautra, A. J. (1989). Self-blame attributions and unique vulnerability as predictors of post-rape demoralization. *Journal of Social and Clinical Psychology, 8,* 368–375.
- Koss, M. P., Gidycz, C. A., & Wisniewski, N. (1987). The scope of rape: Incidence and prevalence of sexual aggression and victimization in a national sample of higher education students. *Journal of Consulting and Clinical Psychology, 55,* 162–170.
- Ullman, S. E. (1997). Attributions, world assumptions, and recovery from sexual assault. *Journal of Child Sexual Abuse, 6,* 1–19.

Part X: How Do We Control Crime? Crime and Social Control

Strengthening Institutions and Rethinking the American Dream
Steven F. Messner and Richard Rosenfeld

- Adams, J. (1931). *Epic of America.* Boston: Little, Brown.
- Blumstein, A. (1993). Making rationality relevant—The American Society of Criminology 1992 presidential address. *Criminology, 31,* 1–16.
- Braithwaite, J. (1989). *Crime, shame and reintegration.* New York: Cambridge University Press.
- Feeley, M., & Simon, J. (1992). The new penology: Notes on the emerging strategy of corrections and its implications. *Criminology, 30,* 449–474.
- Rosenfeld, R., & Kempf, K. (1991). The scope and purposes of corrections: Exploring alternative responses to crowding. *Crime and Delinquency, 37,* 481–505.

Broken Windows: The Police and Neighborhood Safety
James Q. Wilson and George L. Kelling

- No suggested readings

The Changing Nature of Death Penalty Debates
Michael L. Radelet and Marian J. Borg

- Acker, J. R., Bohn, R. M., & Lanier, C. S. (Eds.). (1998). *America's experiment with capital punishment.* Durham, NC: Carolina Academic Press.
- Baldus, D. C., Woodworth, G., & Pulaski, C. A., Jr. (1990). *Equal justice and the death penalty: A legal and empirical analysis.* Boston: Northeastern University Press.
- Bedau, H. A. (1997). *The death penalty in America: Current controversies.* New York: Oxford University Press.
- Hood, R. (1996). *The death penalty: A world wide perspective* (Rev. ed.). New York: Oxford University Press.
- Paternoster, R. (1991). *Capital punishment in America.* New York: Lexington Books.
- Radelet, M. L., & Akers, R. L. (1996). Deterrence and the death penalty: The views of the experts. *Journal of Criminal Law and Criminology, 87,* 1–16.

Abolish the Juvenile Court: Youthfulness, Criminal Responsibility, and Sentencing Policy
Barry C. Feld

- Edwards, L. P. (1992). The juvenile court and the role of the juvenile court judge. *Juvenile & Family Court Journal, 43,* 1, 19.
- Feld, B. C. (1993). Criminalizing the American juvenile court. *Crime & Justice, 17,* 197.
- Feld, B. C. (1995). Violent youth and public policy: A case study of juvenile justice law reform. *Minnesota Law Review, 79,* 965.
- Garland, D. (1990). *Punishment and modern society: A study in social theory.* Chicago: University of Chicago Press.
- Rubin, H. T. (1979). Retain the juvenile court? Legislative developments, reform directions and the call for abolition. *Crime & Delinquency, 25,* 281, 289.

The Impact of Restorative Interventions on Juvenile Offenders
Mara F. Schiff

- Klein, A. R. (1990). Restitution and community work service: Promising core ingredients for effective supervision programming. In T. Armstrong (Ed.), *Intensive interventions with high risk youths.* Monsey, NY: Criminal Justice Press.
- Lawrence, R. (1990). Restitutions as a cost-effective alternative to incarceration. In B. Galaway & J. Hudson (Eds.), *Criminal justice, restitution and reconciliation.* Monsey, NY: Criminal Justice Press.
- Marshall, T., & Merry, S. (1990). *Crime and accountability: Victim offender mediation in practice.* London: Home Office.
- Morris, A., Maxwell, G., & Robertson, J. (1993). Giving victims a choice: A New Zealand experiment. *Howard Journal, 32*(4), 304–321.

Beyond Crime and Punishment: Prisons and Inequality
Bruce Western and Becky Pettit

- Tonry, M. (1996). *Malign neglect: Race, crime, and punishment in America.* New York: Oxford University Press.
- Western, B., Kling, J. R., & Weiman, D. F. (2001, July). The labor market consequences of incarceration. *Crime and Delinquency, 47,* 410–427.
- Wilson, W. J. (1996). *When work disappears: The world of the new urban poor.* New York: Knopf.

INDEX

ABOUT THE EDITORS

Robert D. Crutchfield is Professor and the Clarence and Elissa Schrag Fellow in the Department of Sociology at the University of Washington where he has been a winner of the university's Distinguished Teaching Award. He served on the Washington State Juvenile Sentencing Commission and is also a former juvenile probation officer, adult parole officer, and a deputy editor of *Criminology*. He is a past Vice President of the American Society of Criminology and currently serves on the National Academies' Committee on Law and Justice. His research focuses on labor markets and crime and on racial and ethnic disparities in the administration of justice.

Charis E. Kubrin is Associate Professor of Sociology at George Washington University. Her research examines neighborhood correlates of crime, with an emphasis on race and violent crime. She is co-author (with Gregory D. Squires) of *Privileged Places: Race, Residence and the Structure of Opportunity* (Lynne Rienner, 2006). Her work has been published in several academic journals including *Social Forces, Social Problems, Criminology, Journal of Research in Crime and Delinquency, Justice Quarterly, Sociological Quarterly, Sociological Perspectives, Urban Studies, Homicide Studies,*

and *Research in Community Sociology.* In 2005, Charis received the American Society of Criminology's Ruth Shonle Cavan Young Scholar Award and the Morris Rosenberg Award for Recent Achievement from the District of Columbia Sociological Society.

George S. Bridges is the President of Whitman College in Walla Walla, Washington. He has served as a staff member of the policy office of the Attorney General of the United States as well as deputy editor of *Criminology*. He has been a member of the Washington State Minority and Justice Commission. He has published many papers on racial biases in American law and is co-editor, with Martha Myers, of *Crime, Inequality, and Social Control.*

Joseph G. Weis is Professor of Sociology at the University of Washington. He served for a number of years as the Director of the National Center for the Assessment of Delinquent Behavior and Its Prevention, funded by the U.S. Department of Justice, and as a member of the Washington State Governor's Juvenile Justice Advisory Committee. He is a past editor of the journal *Criminology* and a co-author, with Michael J. Hindelang and Travis Hirschi, of *Measuring Delinquency.*